LONDON UNDERGROUND BY DESIGN

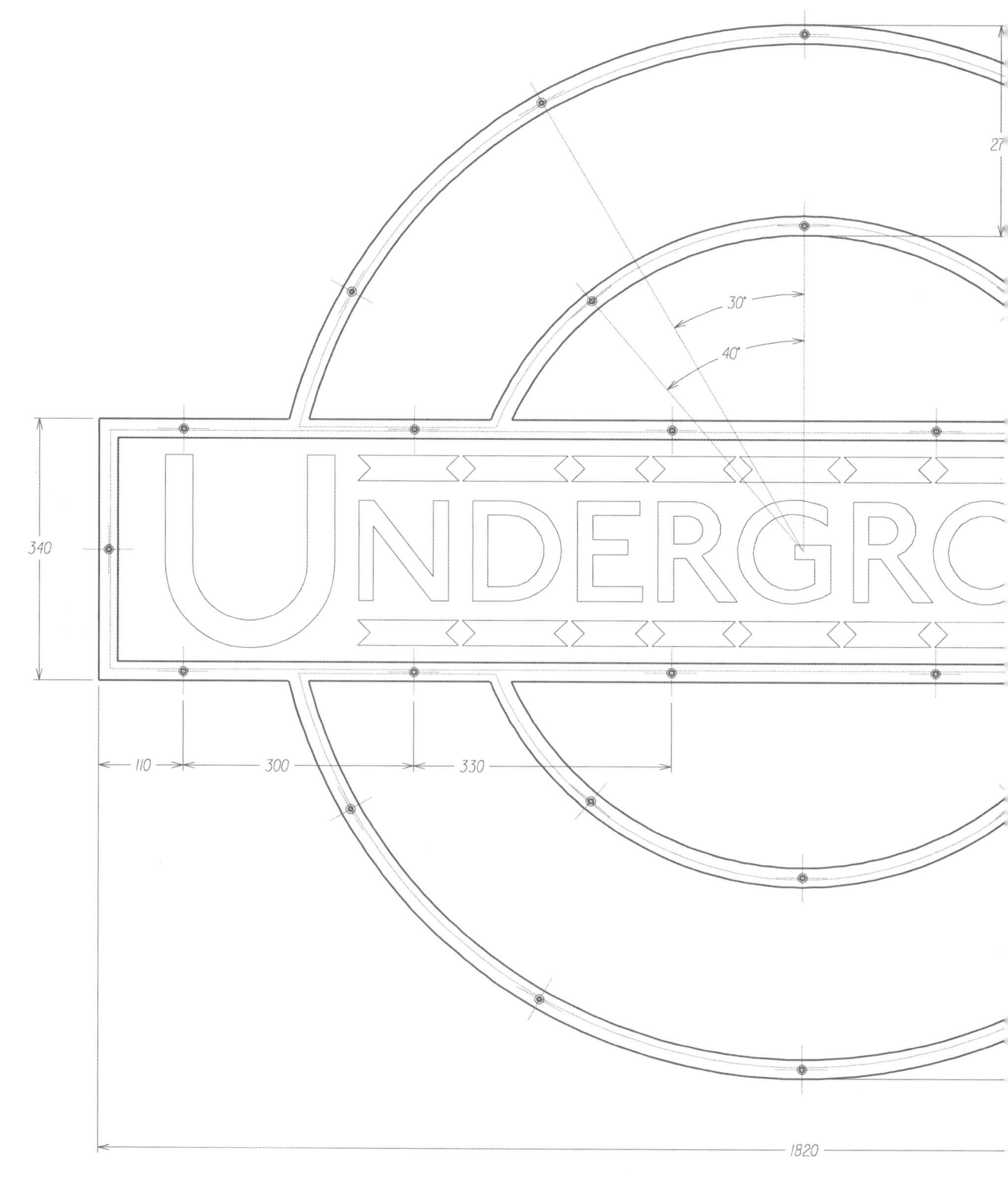

27
30°
40°
UNDERGRO
340
110
300
330
1820

Mark Ovenden

LONDON UNDERGROUND BY DESIGN

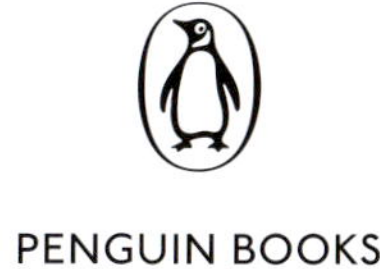

PENGUIN BOOKS

For Pat and Derek who picked Penguins for Tube travel

PENGUIN BOOKS

UK | USA | Canada | Ireland | Australia
India | New Zealand | South Africa

Penguin Books is part of the Penguin Random House group of companies
whose addresses can be found at global.penguinrandomhouse.com.

Penguin Random House UK,
One Embassy Gardens, 8 Viaduct Gardens, London SW11 7BW

penguin.co.uk

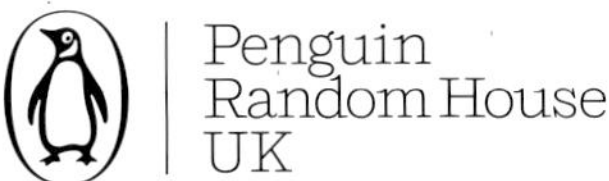

First published 2013
8

Set in New Johnston TfL Book by kind permission of Transport for London
Colour Reproduction by Altaimage Ltd.
Printed in Estonia by Print Best OÜ

The authorised representative in the EEA is Penguin Random House Ireland,
Morrison Chambers, 32 Nassau Street, Dublin D02 YH68

A CIP catalogue record for this book is available from the British Library

ISBN: 978-1-846-14417-2

Penguin Random House is committed to a sustainable future
for our business, our readers and our planet. This book is made from
Forest Stewardship Council® certified paper.

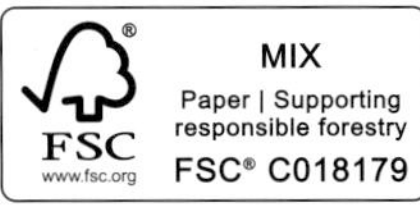

Picture Credits

The majority of the images in this book have been
sourced from and reproduced with kind permission
of the London Transport Museum, TfL Archives and
the extensive private collections of those such as
Mike Ashworth, Peter Lloyd, Derek Mayes and Max
Roberts, plus many images from the author's own
collection.

Additional images have been provided by courtesy
of and with much appreciation to: Acanthus LW
Architects (p. 277), Nick Agnew (p. 240), Stephen
Bone Estate (p. 118), Helen Cauldwell (p. 153),
Chicago Transit Authority (p. 126), Glenn Dearing
(p. 6), Tim Demuth (pp. 237, 251), Jennie Doble
(p. 223), Andrew Dow (p. 153), Andrew Emmerson
(p. 23), Edward Johnston Foundation (p. 112),
Essex Archives (p. 68), Innes Ferguson (p. 266),
Ken Garland (p. 154), David Harris (p. 229), Stephen
Jolly, (p. 240), Ronald Kluvers (p. 162), Eiichi Kono
(pp. 236, 250), David Lawrence Collection (p. 41,
from Vivien Castle and p. 134, from Adams, Holden
and Pearson/Martin Angus), David LeBoff (pp. 21,
30, 42, 56, 93), Chris Ludlow (p. 238), Jeff Mills
(pp. 239, 253), mishablackawards.com (p. 234),
Mark Moss (p. 239), Paul Moss (pp. 55, 188, 253,
256-7), Nederlands Architectuurinstituut (p. 150-1,
162, 182), Felix Ormerod (pp. 236, 254), Julian
Pepinster (pp. 44, 48-49, 54, 71, 80, 204, 255),
Pratheep (p. 191), Jane Rabagliati (p. 207), Kim
Rennie (pp. 22, 39, 188, 212, 253, 256-7, 272-3),
Doug Rose (pp. 61, 71, 238), Robert Schwandl
(pp. 133, 162), Rodney Seddon/McFall Estate
(p. 235), Siemens (p. 277), Peter Taylor (p. 229),
Maggie Turner (p. 22), Mike Walton (p. 241) and
Wikimedia Commons/ GNU (pp. 8, 14, 34, 37, 40,
150, 162, 277).

Images lent by various collectors above including
from periodicals: *Electric Review* (p. 48), *Illustrated
London News* (pp. 12, 18-20, 64), *Locomotive
Magazine* (p. 55), *Railway Gazette* (p. 43), *Vanity
Fair* (pp. 14, 15, 64), The copyright of all of the images
remains with the original owners.

Contents

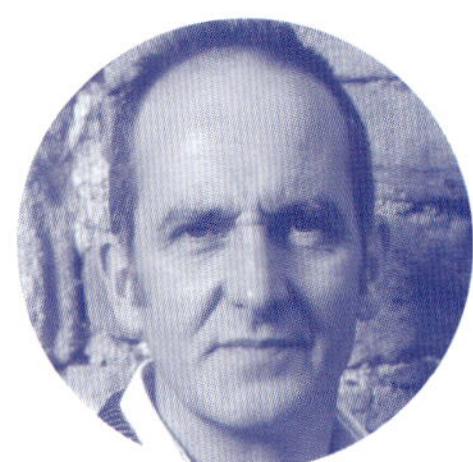

Introduction

Kevin McCloud, Channel 4's *Grand Designs* presenter and architect

To travel the underground is to travel through design time. One hundred and fifty years of it. From the crystalline concrete light wells of Heathrow Terminal 5 you can trundle six stops to the Art Deco triumphalism of Osterley, thence straight on to visit the glorious Arts and Crafts facade of Russell Square before changing at King's Cross to admire the original Victorian brickwork of the Metropolitan line, the first underground railway in the world, completed in 1863. This will lead you to the planetarium for a forty-five minute tour of Deep Time. Nothing, however, rivals the architectural and design experience of the Underground. It is encapsulating and immersive; a contrived world that you cannot confuse with a National Trust tour, thanks to the advertising, the smell of brakes and the purposefulness of it all. The Underground is no heritage site or fusty working museum. It is a complex, functioning piece of infrastructure, animated by the one billion people that use it every year, as much as by the trains.

Travelling within the confines of the Circle line, it would be tempting to think of the Underground as a principally twentieth-century invention. It was not. It was a twentieth-century reinvention — or integration — of a system that had grown with lightning speed between 1863 and the end of the nineteenth century, created by rival operating companies of different lines: the Met, the District, the City and South London Railway, the Central London Railway or 'Tube' and the Underground Electric Railway Company of London. Their separate identities are still clearly visible on the suburban lines. Was there a coherent style? No. There was a jumbled mass of architecture, typefaces and liveries, especially in those early years of steam. Simple wooden stations vied with ornate brickwork and the lunatic Ottoman extravagance and thirty-metre minarets of Blackfriars Underground station. Timetables and maps were printed with gothic tracery and vignettes of the corners of the Empire. Amidst all this mayhem, however, there were the inklings of clarity. For example, the original Metropolitan Railway had, almost from the start, adopted clear, sans-serif typography for its signage, redolent of the mainline railways, and a relatively consistent architectural language in the popular Italianate style.

With the passing of the decades and with electrification of the Underground came greater coherence. With electric lighting came white glazed tiling that was to influence the style of Underground stations from Budapest to Paris (which lifted London's emerging design ethos wholesale). And all the while, thanks to its decades-long head start, London's Underground was haphazardly forging, from the scramble of the vying companies' ambitions, a design code, architectural language and 'brand identity'. Not that any of these terms or concepts existed as such.

The overwhelmingly period — and coherent - feel of the Tube results in no small part from the co-ordinated work of Frank Pick, erstwhile publicity officer, commercial manager and finally managing director of the Underground Electric Railways Company of London. He steered its branding and identity out of the Edwardian period into the Modern age. Nikolaus Pevsner described him as 'the greatest patron of the arts whom this century has so far produced in England, and indeed the ideal patron of our age.' Pick adopted the famous topological map, designed by engineering draughtsman Harry Beck in 1931 in his spare time (not commissioned and not received with a great deal of enthusiasm from London Underground); he commissioned the typeface designed by Edward Johnston to Pick's brief in 1913 (surely it feels much later?); he coordinated signage and architecture across the entire network.

The Underground's latterday character has been as accretive and (almost) as clearly directed. It remains a glorious palimpsest of design, a repository of design work and design values of the last one hundred and fifty years, a sort of working reference that charts the history of taste and style. So this is not a book merely about the growth of London's Tube network. It records the birth of a new idea in the nineteenth century — the transport interchange — and unfolds the invention of branding in the twentieth. It plots the organization of commercial illustration, lettering design and printing into a new discipline called graphic design. It follows the adaptation of architecture into a commercial tool. It also roundly celebrates the Titans of engineering and design, individuals like Benjamin Baker, who built a transport system so coherent, it paved the way for London to grow into the international city it now is.

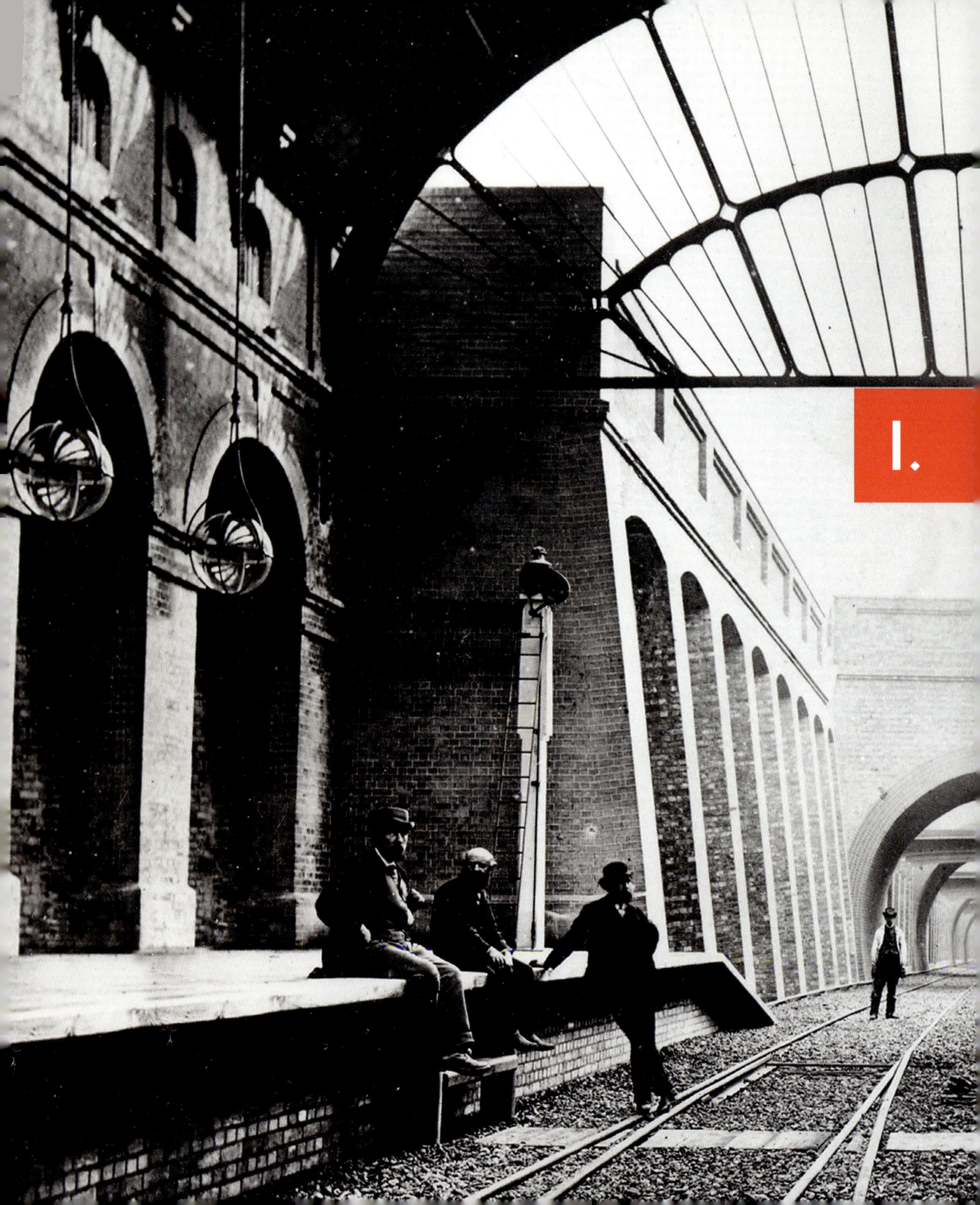
I.

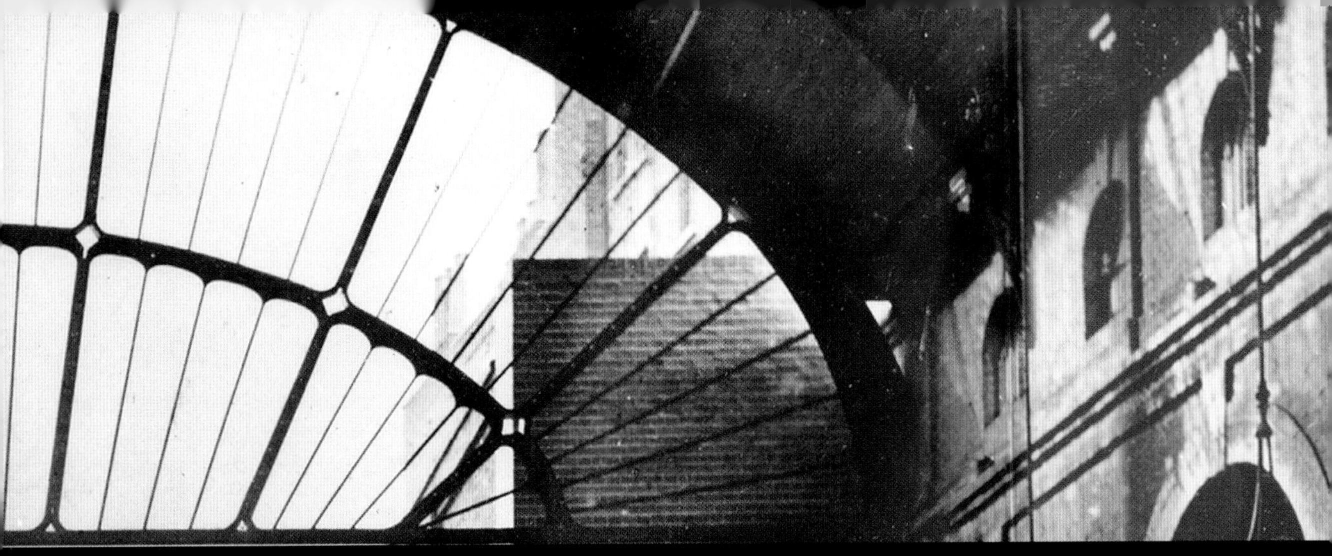

Establishing a New Style of Railway
1863–89

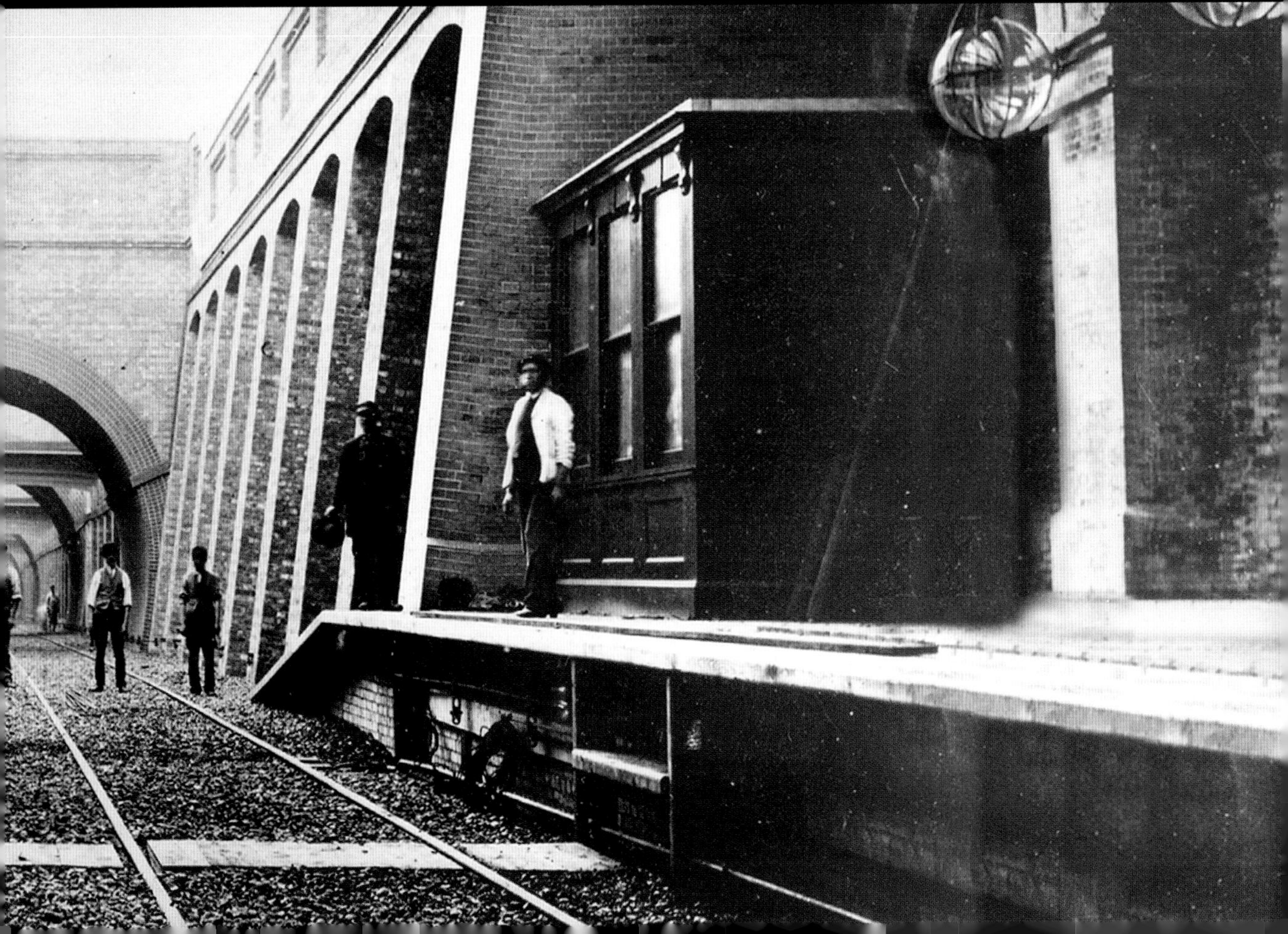

I. Establishing a New Style of Railway, 1863–89

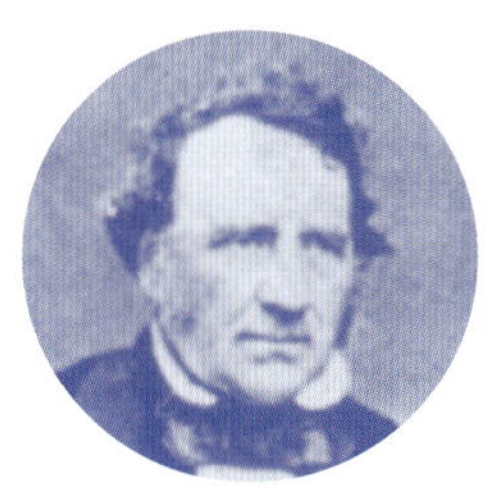

Charles Pearson (1793–1862), born in London, is the true visionary of the underground railway concept. His proposals date back to 1845 when he envisaged a Fleet Valley rail tunnel. In 1846 he proposed a huge central London rail terminal shared by all the operators and approached underground. He promoted the plan in 1854 for a 'Metropolitan Railway' between Praed Street and Farringdon which grew into the scheme that opened in 1863, just months after his death.

Underground trains began running beneath the streets of London in January 1863. It was the first service of its kind, anywhere in the world, a feat of engineering that embraced typically visionary Victorian values, but the design of the stations, vehicles, passenger information, maps and other printed ephemera was equally impressive for its day. Though much has been written about the Underground's later design initiatives, a study of this early period reveals a coherency (albeit possibly accidental) so far overlooked but which this chapter sets out to explore. Every detail was considered, from the station architecture to lighting, maps and even signage. What would become one of Britain's greatest achievements in the design of the public built environment had its beginnings in the 1860s; indeed, information graphics and concepts such as 'wayfinding' and corporate identity can all trace their roots to this period.

Such modern terms of reference would have been virtually incomprehensible in the 1860s,[1] but companies were nonetheless keen to promote themselves and employed people to perform similar tasks to the ones they might do today. It was only the technology or craft name that was different. Commercial artists of the Victorian era equate with today's graphic designers, for instance, gas-lighting mechanics with electricians and wagon painters with livery designers. Those tradesmen (with the exception of textile workers, they were invariably male) were inscribing the vehicles, buildings and printed material of the very first underground railway company, the Metropolitan (or 'Met'), with motifs and insignia that were as recognizably part of the collective iconography of a company then as they would be today.

The Met project was led by City of London solicitor Charles Pearson, engineer-in-chief John Fowler and resident engineer Thomas Marr Johnson. The architect of the first seven surface stations[2] was either Fowler or John Hargrave Stevens, but whoever drew up the plans was clearly at great pains to present a coherent look both above and below ground (p. 18), despite having some awkward spaces in which to insert them (a problem that was to afflict most urban rail builders) and some major engineering challenges for transporting people through dark tunnels.

There is relatively little in the archives specifying the style or decor of these first stations, but designing public buildings of a similar type in varying locations had a precedent during the 'railway-mania' age of the 1840s, in which a 'house style', as it might now be called, was clearly visible among major railway companies such as the Great Western Railway (GWR) or the Great Eastern (GER), which had just three models – a terminus, a town station and a more rural offering.[3]

How to make visible a hidden railway

The first design conundrum the Met faced was by what manner and to what extent to
broadcast at street level the existence of a railway below it, given that most of the
infrastructure, including the platforms and trackbed, was to be hidden, for the first time
in railway history, entirely below the surface. Mainline companies had been making bold
architectural statements for some time, throwing up gargantuan temples to train travel
across Britain.[4] Such extravagance was not considered necessary for the Met because
the very heart of the operation was so neatly tucked out of view. Pearson recognized that
all that was required above ground was the most basic protection of the stairway down
to the platforms below. Indeed, later on the decision was made by subterranean-railway
designers elsewhere (including those in Paris, New York, Berlin, Buenos Aires and Madrid)
to dispense entirely with surface buildings apart from some ornate ironwork around stairs
leading from the pavement. This was not, however, the solution favoured for London in
1863 (p. 19).

Dispelling the gloom

Below ground the greatest problem, of course, was the dark.[5] Victorians were terrified
of it.[6] The Met addressed the issue at the three stations with platforms entirely under
the ground by devising an innovative system of apertures to the street through which
light could penetrate (p. 18). These were observed by the magazine *Leisure Hour* in 1862:
'Although we were upwards of forty feet below the earth's surface, we found that it was
as light as day … daylight in fact being shed down upon us by ingenious contrivances
in the forecourts of the houses and the street pavements.' Where artificial illumination
was needed, it was provided by gas lighting from large suspended glass globes[7] (p. 26).
Aside from the cost benefit of buying identical items in bulk, their ubiquity suggests that
there must have been a conscious decision on aesthetic grounds to use the same lamp
style throughout. Though similar lighting was used elsewhere (and modern replicas exist
at Hyde Park and along the Embankment), the consistent approach gives validity to the
labelling of these as a signature design feature.

Careful consideration was given to lighting inside the carriages, described by the
Manchester Guardian the day after opening (11 January 1863) as 'commodious' – first class
even having leather seats. In the words of the paper: 'the novel introduction of gas into
the carriages is calculated to dispel any unpleasant feelings which passengers, especially
ladies, might entertain against riding for so long a distance through a tunnel.' The Met's
engines were originally painted green, with brass names – and eventually numbers – fixed
to the sides, until 1885 when it was changed to a muddy brown or 'chocolate'. The splash
of colour may have been deliberately chosen to add vibrancy in the gloom. Christian
Wolmar's history (2004, Bibliography) cites a Fred Jane of *English Illustrated Magazine*

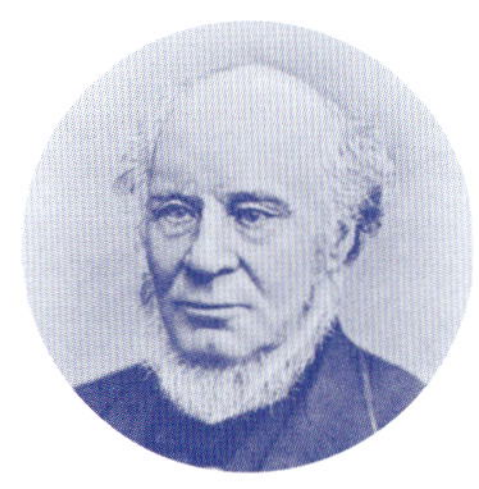

John Fowler (1817–98), born
in Yorkshire, was the railway
engineer and cartographer
tasked with designing the
complex engineering that
Charles Pearson needed to
put the Met tracks and platforms beneath the ground.
He later went on to design
London Victoria, Glasgow
St Enoch and Manchester
Central mainline stations
(among others) and became
chief engineer of the Forth
Railway Bridge. He was
created a baronet in 1890,
just after the bridge was
completed.

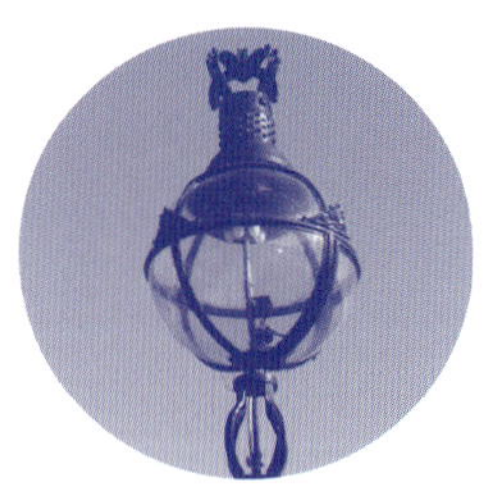

Although gas lighting had spread throughout Britain by the 1860s, large glass globes were rarely seen on anything other than public buildings. Suspended from platforms and outside stations, they became an early design feature of Met and District stations. Replicas are still in use in London's Royal Parks.

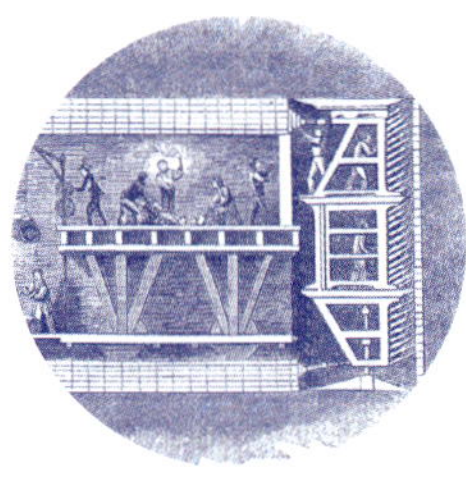

Much improved later by James Greathead and others, this early device used for building the Thames Tunnel (1825–43) was one of the key engineering designs which enabled the later construction of the deep-level tubes in London and elsewhere.

who reports entering Baker Street while riding in the driver's cab — itself 'a medley of crimson and gold' — from which he observed slivers of sunlight piercing through the sooty atmosphere: 'a harmony of blue and silver'.

Met signage and map design

As there are no known photographs of stations before 1868, the only way to glean an idea of the original signage is from contemporary illustrations: one nameboard was provided in the centre of each platform, as on mainline stations of the era (p. 22). On station frontages the words 'METROPOLITAN RAILWAY' were displayed below the parapet, mimicking another feature of the mainline railways, one that continues to this day.

There were many maps showing Met plans, although the company did not produce any for the public for the first few years. Other early printed ephemera are scarce but a timetable poster for the opening day (p. 21), despite using a variety of lettering, displays the words 'METROPOLITAN RAILWAY' in a remarkably similar form to the lettering used on the station frontages. This appears too big a coincidence for that style not to have been consciously selected.

Retaining the design and departing from it

The Met board's prediction of the line's popularity, and its vision of the railway as a subterranean extension for mainline trains, led it to seek Parliamentary approval[8] for an eastwards extension to Finsbury Circus (to be called Moorgate Street station). The line penetrating London's financial centre duly opened with an intermediate station — the first with three storeys — at Aldersgate Street (now Barbican) on 23 December 1865. A fine seasonal gift, as it was within spitting distance of the Bank of England. On the same day, the new surface building at Farringdon Street opened (p. 20). With its long frontage in Suffolk stone, Roman arches, decorative ornamental roof urns and fine finials, it improved upon the first stations and served as a model for future Met architecture.

The Met was never destined to be the only player in town, and despite predictions of death by 'noxious subterranean gases', proposals for new lines connecting to and competing with it were numerous.[9] The first to be completed — without any need for expensive tunnelling as it skirted the existing built-up area — was a joint venture between the GWR and the Met, the Hammersmith and City Railway (HCR), opening on 13 June 1864.[10] Architecturally all its stations were rudimentary in the extreme,[11] borrowing nothing from the Met's style and consisting of little more than traditional wooden canopies over somewhat exposed platforms. Such a pointless leap away from the already established Met style became a hallmark of much Underground design undertaken by different privately run operators until full integration under the London Passenger Transport Board in 1933 (p. 154).

Drawing a full circle

The Met's success brought it to the attention of an 1864 House of Lords Select Committee, which concluded that it would be desirable to join up the two ends of the existing tracks to form an inner circuit.[12] As the costs would be prohibitive for the Met alone, a new company was created in 1866 to construct the southern section, named, somewhat confusingly, the Metropolitan District Railway (or 'District'). The Met went along with this while pursuing bigger ideas of its own: in April 1868 it began by opening a single-track branch from new platforms at Baker Street to virtually unpopulated Swiss Cottage.[13] Despite the installation of intermediate stations at St John's Wood Road (later renamed Lords) and Marlborough Road, passenger numbers were low, but the aim was to veer eastwards towards more lucrative Hampstead. This gave rise in 1869 to the first underground 'interchange': passengers from St John's Wood were obliged to disembark at Baker Street and walk through 'communicating galleries' to continue their journey. The style of the new stations matched and improved upon the earlier Met architecture – a useful test for the next 'Inner Circle' tranche. Pressing slightly further west and then south from Paddington, this extension duly opened on 10 October 1868 as far as Brompton (Gloucester Road).[14] With John Fowler appointed to oversee them, both branches were quite similar in construction. Most were in deep cuttings with only a few tunnelled sections where necessary.[15]

Architecturally the nine new surface-level station buildings were also almost identical in their Italianate style (p. 20), which was highly popular at this time.[16] All except Brompton (Gloucester Road) were single-storey structures of white Halsey perforated brick with stone dressings. As at the Farringdon Street rebuild of 1865, each of the windows and doorways sat under a high Roman arch. The parapets featured a balustrade topped at intervals with decorative urns. Each station front had an attractive iron and glazed roof canopy over the entrance – a design concept which was to endure, albeit in varying form, right up to the present day. Attached to the station front just below the parapet were enamelled iron plates – the first such signage for which photographic evidence survives – giving the company and station name at the top and, fixed to the canopy, a smaller plate announcing 'booking office'. The white lettering was in capitals, on a dark background (p. 20),[17] while gas-lit globes were installed both outside and inside. Overall these were so close design-wise to the original seven stations that it must have been possible for passengers to discern a coherent style, even if only subconsciously and even if, again, they were only identical to save money.

The District borrows design features and introduces new ones

While the Met was making progress, work was beginning on the first section of the District from South Kensington eastwards towards the City to a temporary terminus at

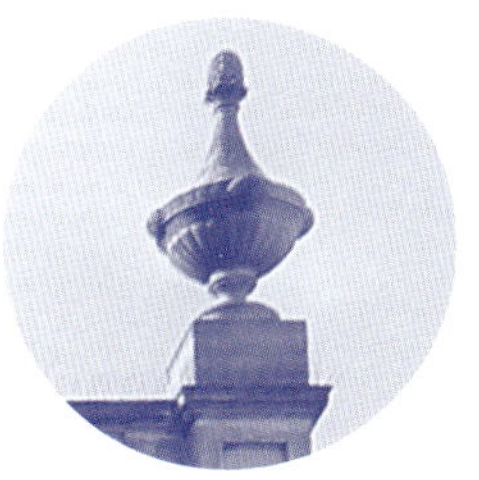

Decorative urns were features of the popular Italianate style and appeared on the roofs of most early Met and District stations, including Gloucester Road, pictured.

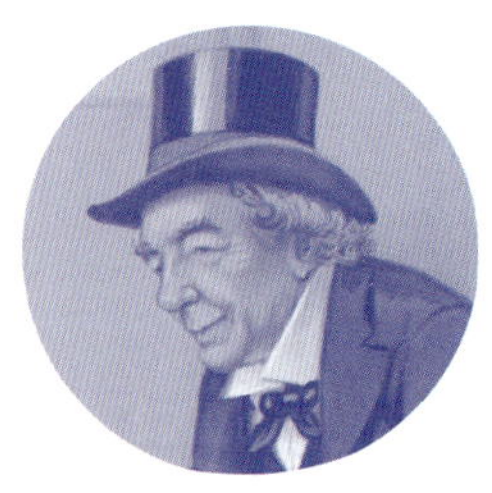

James Staats Forbes (1823–1904), born in Aberdeen, studied under Brunel and became general manager of a Dutch rail company before returning to the UK in 1861. He took over the District in 1871 and worked with the LSWR, among other rail companies, to extend links into the southern suburbs and beyond.

Westminster Bridge (now Westminster). Ruffling the Met's feathers right from the start, it poached John Fowler, who, alongside engineer Thomas Marr Johnston, was charged with the architectural and engineering work. The first section opened in December 1868, with three intermediate stations: Sloane Square, Victoria and St James's Park. In April 1869, the second stretch – a short westward branch from Brompton (Gloucester Road) to West Brompton – was opened.[18] Its stations were in a similar Italianate style to the Met's, but the locos were different, painted bright green. Almost all platforms were in deep cuttings, covered by arched glazed roofs (just like those at Notting Hill Gate), though at West Brompton a pitched roof over the platforms was tried.[19] There was no station at Earl's Court because it was just farmland, but as new housing arrived, wooden platforms were constructed and the station opened in 1871 – replaced in 1878 by the building that still stands (p. 26), though much altered over the years.

Initially, the District was more vigorous at self-promotion but the only maps of the first lines were made by private printing companies (p. 21) and unlikely to incorporate any of either company's style. When the District did produce its own maps (in 1874, p. 29), these were also included in the Met's timetable books.

Expanding the line and adapting the style

The District's 2 km extension from Westminster to Blackfriars was to be undertaken as part of Joseph Bazalgette's complete rebuild of the Thames embankment, and though expensive and challenging, even this was rapidly completed, on 30 May 1870, with intermediate stations at Charing Cross (now Embankment) and Temple. Both stations were single-storey buildings constructed in brick, with Renaissance detailing and balustraded parapets – though Charing Cross had a pavilion roof and Temple was required by neighbours to be flat – and both were reconstructed in 1914 by Harry Wharton Ford (p. 102). Blackfriars was a complete aberration (not completed until 1873, p. 27): architect Frederick J. Ward had a Moorish fascination and built extravagant minarets on two 30m towers. Three storeys high, the building was faced in blue and white tiles and dark red brick, and had balconies with iron railings. The station name, in bold capitals, occupied a large dark band across the entire width.[20] The impact was so different from that of any other station that only the presence of the globular gaslights announced it as a part of the District. Sadly this unique building was damaged in the Second World War and demolished when the area was redeveloped. It was rebuilt again in 2012.

The next short section took the District one more station along from Blackfriars to Mansion House. Opening on 3 July 1871, the platforms were in a deep cutting (long since built over), so glass canopies were installed overhead to protect passengers. It was to remain the end of the line (and of aspirations to complete the Inner Circle) until 1884. On the other side of town, the HCR had a bright idea that was to prove a trendsetter: it rebuilt and enlarged its station at Westbourne Park (opening on 1 November 1871) to provide direct access between the GWR and its own platforms from a long thin frontage on the railway overbridge. Interchanging seamlessly between different lines and modes has since become a cornerstone of integrated public transport.

Completing the Circle or going rural

It was not until February 1875 that the Met was at last able to go ahead with its contribution to the Inner Circle by first arriving at Bishopsgate (now called Liverpool Street) alongside the mainline terminal at Broad Street (now demolished) and the site of the new GER terminus. Just a year later, in 1876, the Met pushed through to Aldgate, where only a small facade was possible, erected between two existing street-level buildings.[21]

The District, meanwhile, instead of completing its remaining section of the Inner Circle, joined forces with the London and South Western Railway (LSWR) and expanded westwards. Opening on 1 June 1877, the new line went from Hammersmith via Shaftesbury Road (now Ravenscourt Park) to Turnham Green (serving the world's first 'garden suburb' – the Arts and Crafts-inspired Bedford Park), before turning south to stop at Gunnersbury, Kew Gardens and highly desirable Richmond. Stations along this section were executed in a new, more rural style, reminiscent of branch lines. Earl's Court was now becoming a pivotal junction, and following a fire at the old wooden station, a replacement was opened on 1 February 1878 (p. 26). Meanwhile, the District still pressed on, building further west from Turnham Green to a terminus at Ealing Broadway, where a grander, two-storey building was erected. On 1 March 1879, the District completed its trio of extensions with a push southwards from the short stub at West Brompton to Putney Bridge & Fulham (now simply Putney Bridge) (p. 26).

Not to be outdone by the District's piercing of London's hinterland, the short, underused Met branch from Baker Street to Swiss Cottage was gradually extended towards the north-west, reaching Harrow by 1880.[22] The District introduced some long-distance services, albeit short-lived,[23] and opened its next major extension (on 1 May 1883 – one that would give rise to an important development many decades later, p. 236) – an easterly line to Hounslow Town[24]. Built by a separate company, the Hounslow and Metropolitan Railway, it ran from Mill Hill Park (now Acton Town) via South Ealing, Boston Road (now Boston Manor, p. 94) to Osterley & Spring Grove (now just 'Osterley') and finally Hounslow Town. A year later, in 1884, a little branch was built to Hounslow Barracks (now Hounslow West). With the exception of the Town station (three storeys in height), most of the buildings on this route consisted of a two-storey stationmaster's house and a single-storey station entrance, usually on the overbridge and often – at South Ealing, Boston Manor and Osterley, for example – looking more like rural dwellings than railway buildings.

The Met and District bickered over design and running arrangements on shared track[25]

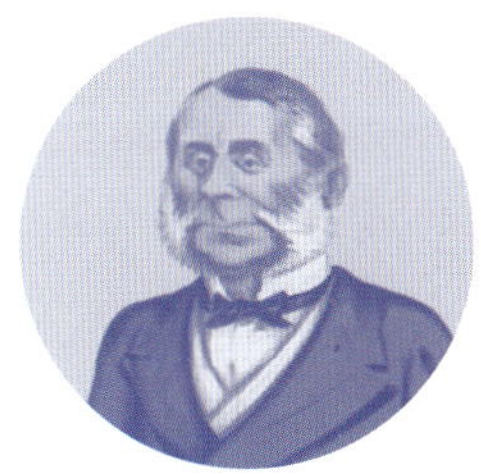

Edward Watkin (1819–1901), born in Salford, had interests in many northern English railways (as well as the GWR and GER and rail companies in Greece, USA and Canada) before he took over the Met in 1872. Passionate about joining England to France via a rail link under the Channel, he constructed the last main line into London (the Great Central) and started work on a tower to rival Eiffel's. He was knighted in 1868 and made a baronet in 1880.

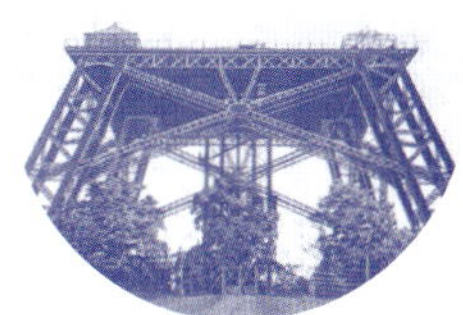

Dreams of linking Manchester to Paris via the Met and a Channel tunnel were not limited to railways. At Wembley, Edward Watkin began a tower echoing Eiffel's Parisian landmark, but it was never completed and had to be cleared in 1908 for the siting of the new stadium.

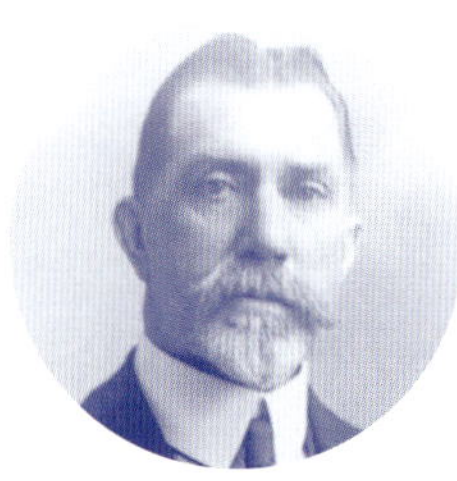

John Wolfe-Barry (1836–1918), one of Britain's leading civil engineers, was architect on much of the District (including completion of the Inner Circle). He went on to build Surrey Commercial Docks and his masterpiece Tower Bridge (which opened in 1894). He was knighted in 1886.

but agreed to join with four mainline companies for a new link between the eastern and south-eastern suburbs of the city. The East London Railway (ELR) opened on 7 December 1884 between New Cross Gate and Wapping by cleverly re-using a magnificent structure under the Thames that had never been employed for its original purpose.[26] The Thames Tunnel was an engineering triumph but no money was left to build the vehicular access at either end, so it was never used as intended by horse-drawn vehicles. It was therefore split into two 'carriage-ways' by elaborate arches and was so far upstream from the existing bridges that it attracted millions of pedestrians.[27] Though not connected then to the Met or District, the ELR which was destined to play a bigger role in their development (p. 100) converted the tunnel for rail use. Architecturally ELR stations were roughly in keeping with those of the Met and District, if far more rudimentary — Wapping being little more than a wooden frontage — although Rotherhithe consisted of several brick arches.

Completing the Circle

Amidst the flurry of expansion into Middlesex and Berkshire, work had finally begun on completing the Inner Circle. Both the Met and District had to pool resources for this last costly link beneath what was already the world's most expensive real estate. The first short part, which became operative on 25 September 1882, pushed south from Aldgate to a single-storey station, Tower of London (later Mark Lane).[28] This was then joined up on 6 October 1884 to Mansion House (via stations erected at the Monument (p. 78), and Canon Street by architects John Wolfe-Barry and John Hawkshaw). Following the long-dreamed-of completion of the Inner Circle, the running of the line was split between the companies, the 'outer' service clockwise being run by the Met, while the District ran 'inner' anti-clockwise trains.

The high costs incurred by the construction of this line focused the minds of railway engineers and investors; proposals for routes penetrating the loop had been circulating for years, but there could be no new services under the centre of the city unless an alternative method of tunnelling could be devised that did not necessitate major demolition or give rise to exorbitant compensation claims. Luckily for Londoners and the history of subterranean railways, that solution was close at hand. The key engineering problem of tunnel building is the risk of collapse,[29] but that issue had been addressed, very ingeniously, during the construction of the Thames Tunnel (by 1869 housing the ELR), which had been built using a special 'shield' to protect the workers from cave-ins (p. 12) and assist in the placement of tunnel linings. The idea was further developed for the creation of the Barlow Greathead shield used to build another tunnel under the Thames for what became known as the Tower Subway.[30] Such was the success of the shield that in 1870 a more ambitious scheme was considered for boring tunnels under parts of London to carry railway trains.[31] The idea was shelved but revisited in 1884 when Parliament authorized the City & Southwark Subway between Elephant & Castle and the City. Work began in 1886 (pp. 34–42, 44). Planned initially for cable haulage, the CSLR, as it became known, was upgraded to be run by electrically-powered engines – becoming the world's first major electric railway when it opened in 1890.

East peace and separate departures

Despite growing antagonism between the Met and District, they agreed to jointly take over the running of the ELR and each built separate spurs off the Circle on to it via shared stations from Aldgate East to Whitechapel (with an intermediate station at St Mary's featuring more of those signature balustrades on the roof).[32] Stations along the ELR all had single-storey facades with arches above every window and doorway, though some of the newer stations (Shadwell, Whitechapel) had elongated arches over entrances which, while practical, looked somewhat inelegant. When the joint running began, each station was equipped with a large enamelled iron nameplate on the exterior using condensed capitals in a style that was not dissimilar to that of the 1868 Met stations (p. 31).

The District paid for a quirky addition which opened in May 1885: this was a long foot tunnel beneath Exhibition Road running from South Kensington station to the growing cluster of museums (the Natural History, Science and Victoria & Albert).[33] Architecturally it was quite beautiful and has recently been restored. Just 2m below the surface, it benefited from light-wells which allowed sunshine to creep in and bounce off the beige brick and pale blue ironwork.[34]

The Met was now careering ahead on a north-westerly trajectory which opened in sections from Harrow to Chesham between 1885 and 1889 (p. 28). Given the District's Windsor service (achieved by running over GWR mainline tracks) had ceased operating four years earlier, this Met section became by far the longest tendril of the emerging 'underground' network. Watkin planned to push even further, setting Chesham's modest station building to one side so the tracks could continue into Buckinghamshire. Although plans to develop this route were dropped, even this was not to be the furthest outpost, as the next decades were about to reveal.[35]

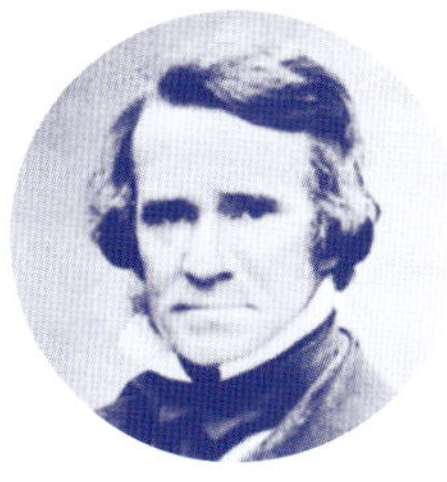

Leeds-born John Hawkshaw (1811–91) was knighted in 1873. A civil engineer, he worked on many rail projects before collaborating with Wolfe-Barry on the District stations.

Station design, 1860–63

Early designs for stations under Marylebone Road (2) were remarkably similar in the finished works. An 1860 illustration (3) exaggerates the amount of surface light but the concept was employed at Baker Street, Portland Road and Gower Street. 'Cut-and-cover' building was used for all early Met and District construction but digging up an entire road, lining it with bricks and then covering with replacement road surface was immensely disruptive. On Marylebone Road (1861, 4) the mayhem can be seen as workers prepare to reinstate the street over the newly created trench. Mainline railways and Italianate styling were the design inspiration for the seven Met stations (the only known contemporary graphic, from *Illustrated London News*, December 1862, 6). At Bishop's Road (named erroneously as 'Paddington Junction'), the single-storey terminal facade (just north of the GWR station at Paddington) had a tiled pitched roof. At Edgware Road an ornate iron and glass canopy was erected over the entrance – an idea that caught on elsewhere. Baker Street had a single-storey building on either side of Marylebone Road. Portland Road was capped with two dome-like structures (removed about 1870 to give better ventilation). Gower Street had two buildings facing each other across Euston Road. King's Cross's platforms were in an open cutting, allowing an enormous glazed arch roof. When complete, stations like Baker Street (1) were filled with passengers – and smoke; despite air holes and clever engines (5) designed to recycle exhaust.

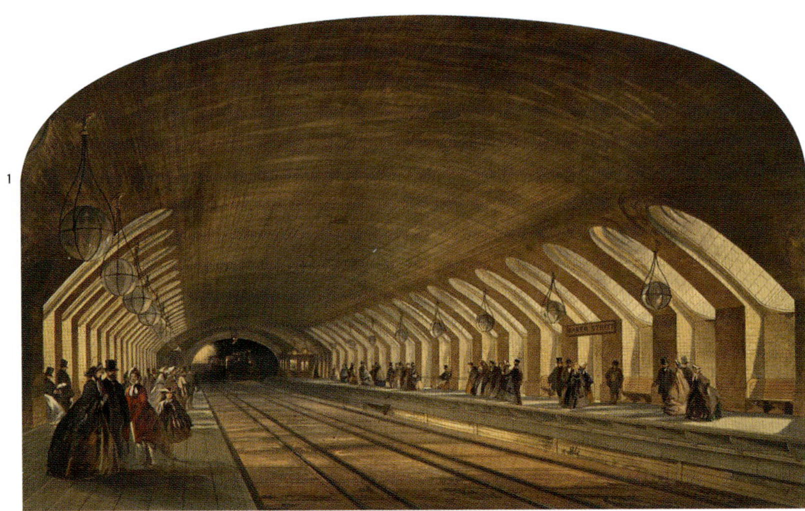

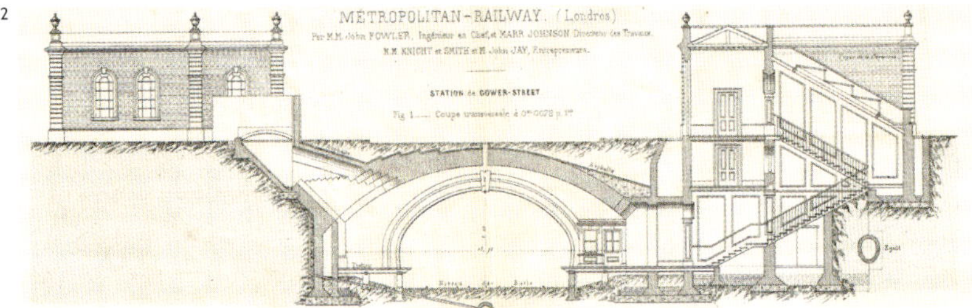

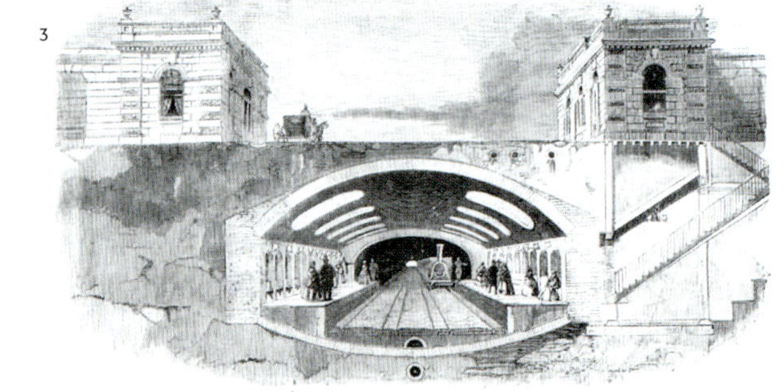

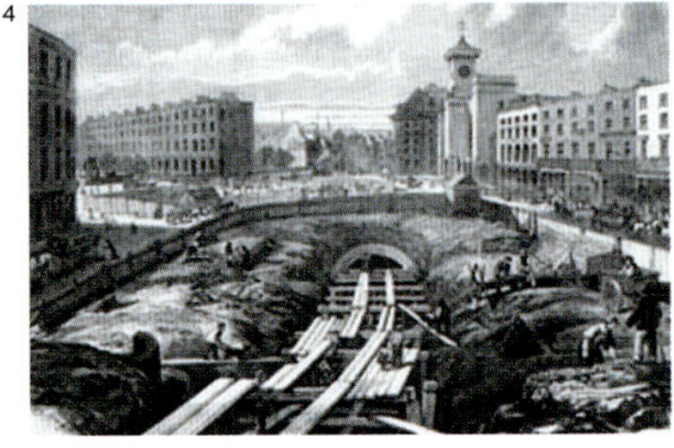

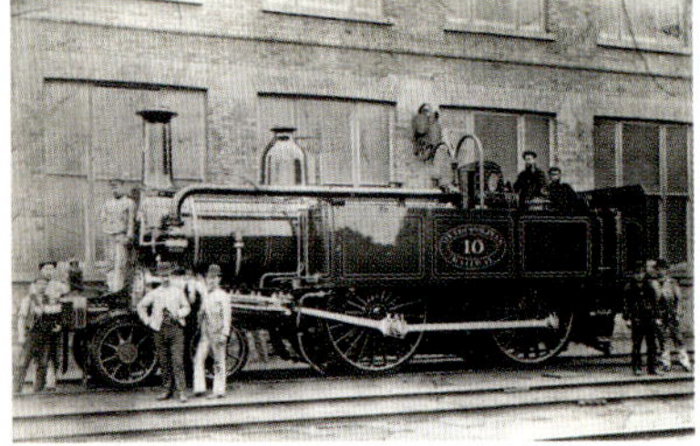

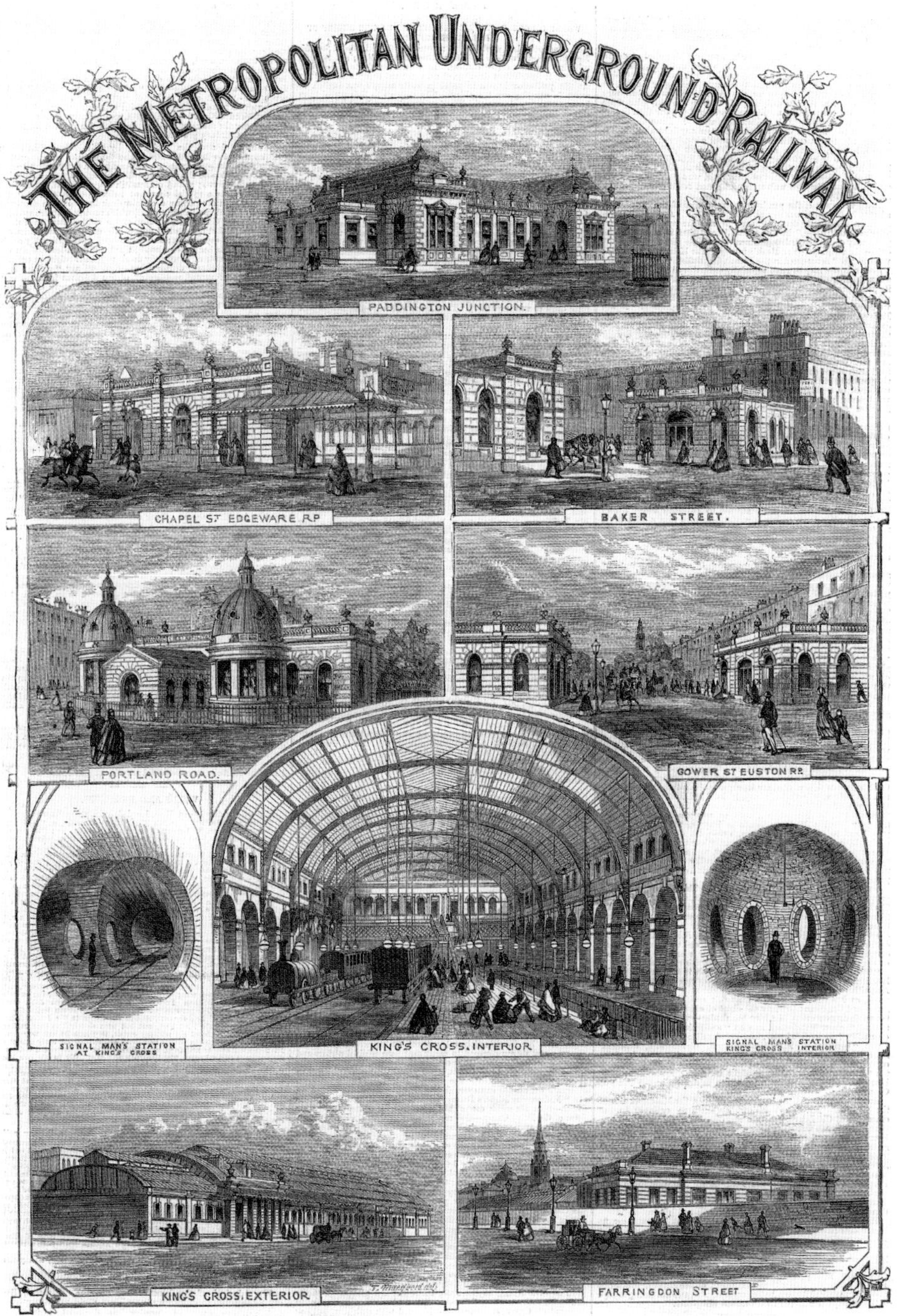

I. Establishing a New Style of Railway, 1863–89

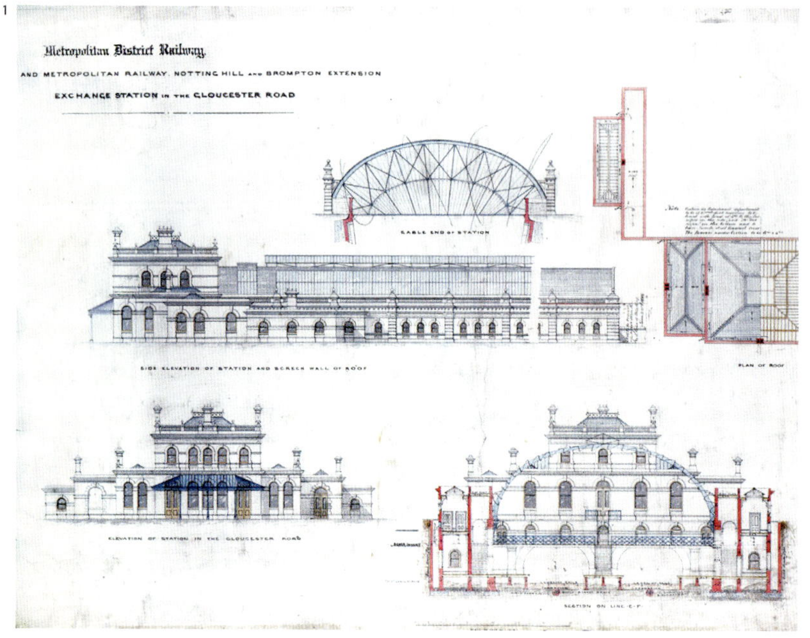

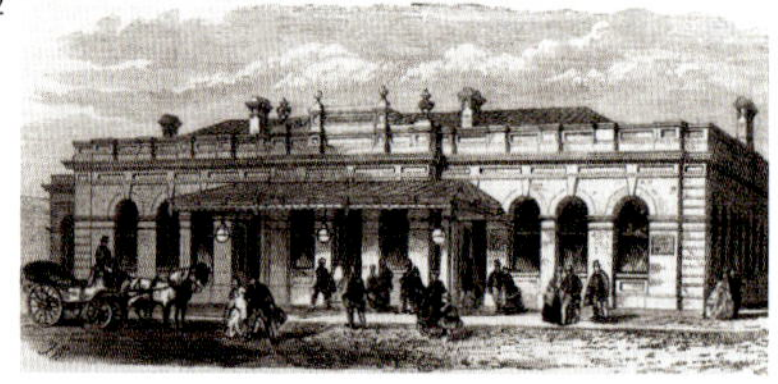

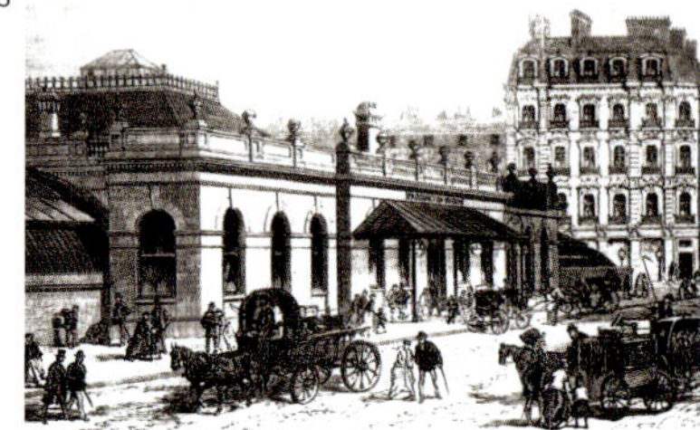

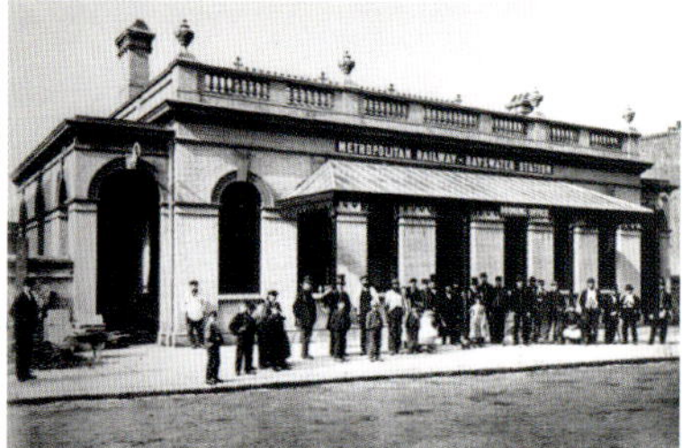

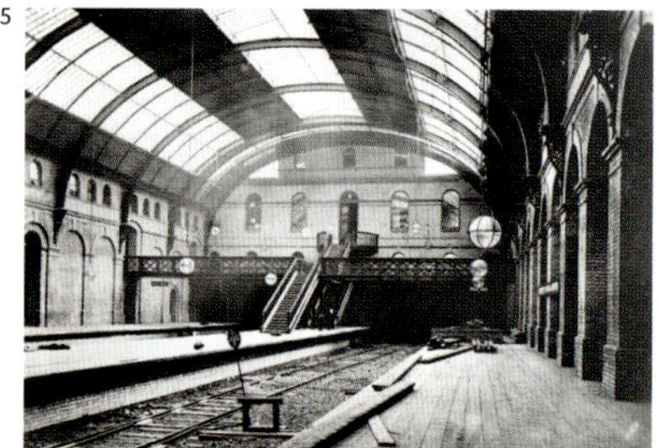

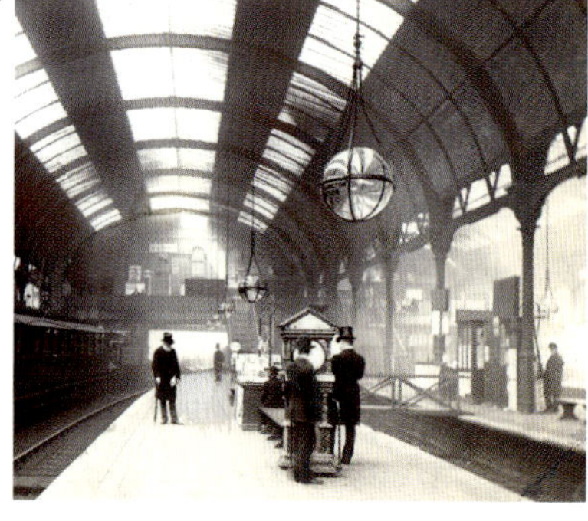

Grand extensions, 1868

Farringdon Street station being a terminus (albeit temporary) and built mainly in a cutting, began life as nothing more than a wooden structure, but by the time the extension to Moorgate Street was envisaged, a fine stone edifice was under way, making the 1865 rebuild (2) the grandest of all the early Met buildings and the model for future ones. Demonstrating increasing attention to architectural detail, almost all the stations built between 1863 and 1868 displayed remarkable similarities that would today be acknowledged as a 'house style' (as shown in the drawings of Gloucester Road, 1). Due to the sharp south-westerly angle that the line parted company from the original, a new station was required on the opposite side of the mainline Paddington station, which was called Praed Street (3). Like the others (Gloucester Road, 5, and Bayswater, 4), this came with a glass canopy, neo-classical arches framing doors and windows, balustraded parapets complete with decorative urns (first seen on the early Met stations), right down to matching signage and the 'signature' gas lighting of large glass globes. All the new stations were located in a cutting; at South Kensington (6), for example, this enabled vast 'windows' to be constructed over the tracks, creating light and airy platforms. The glass was supposed to give protection from the elements, but some sections were not even glazed.

London Underground by Design

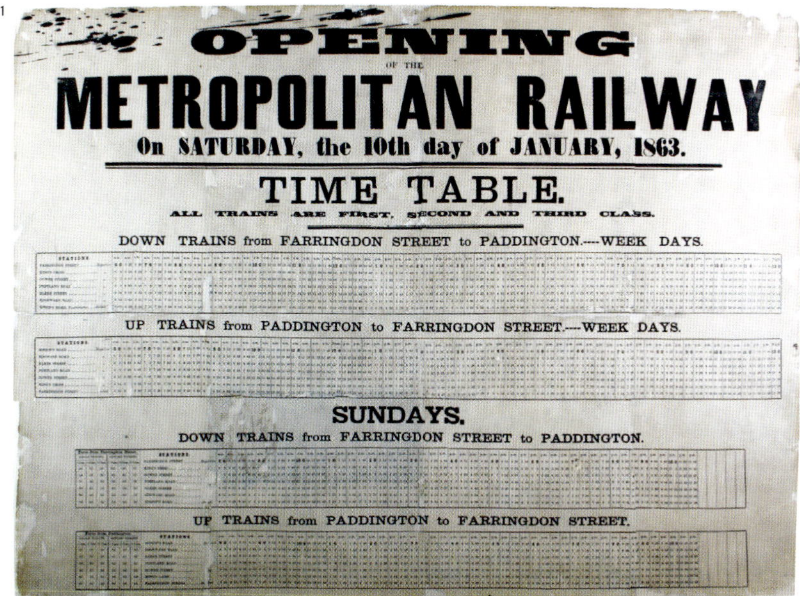

A poster giving the timetable for the Met's opening weekend (1863, 1) is a rare surviving example of printed ephemera from the period. It was laid out in a handful of jobbing type founts (common practice then) but 'METROPOLITAN RAILWAY' appears remarkably similar (bold, condensed sans serif caps) to the lettering on station buildings. This might just be a coincidence, but if intentional it could be regarded as an early example of house style or corporate branding. The Met did not produce its own maps until much later (p. 30), but one of the earliest examples from a commercial printers, Kell Brothers, dates to 1866 (2). The Met lines (and projected routes of the District, shown dotted) are overprinted in red on a pre-existing street plan showing the full extent of London's built-up area, perfectly illustrating the challenges faced during the construction of the new railways. The tracks between Bishops Road and Farringdon Street are all buried beneath wide roads, for instance. Here Hammersmith and Kensington in the west, to Moorgate Street in the east, are shown as in service. Additional tunnels linking mainline trains onto Met tracks from King's Cross and Paddington are also marked. Proposed extensions and anticipated routes of the District are all visible — only the right-hand swerve of the St John's Wood Railway towards Hampstead was never built. Overprinting rail lines onto existing engravings is a trick that dates back to 1830 maps of the Liverpool and Manchester Railway.

Sans-serifs, 1816–present

Sans-serif letterforms were used on posters, signage and handbills since their inception, as exemplified by William Caslon's 'Two Lines English Egyptian' (1), from 1816. British letter founder Vincent Figgins created an eponymous primer in 1830 which contained the first use of the expression 'sans-serif' ('Two Line Pearl', 2). Sans-serif type became the letterform of choice not just for many of Britain's early mainline rail companies, but for the Met, District, the Underground (p. 122) and, later, British Rail, with the Paris Métro and most American sub-surface rail companies following suit. Serifed letters are rarely used in mass transit, though London's Docklands flirted with them in the 1980s (p. 254). The GWR was groping towards a uniform look: its workshop, which produced the 'LYDNEY JUNCTION' sign, (photo taken circa 1875, 3) may have been responsible for all Met (and possibly some District) signage during the early period. Another example from Lancashire and Yorkshire Railway signage of the 1840s/50s shows how widespread this type of lettering was by this time ('HEBDEN BRIDGE', 4). It was also used in other public buildings, such as Waterloo's York Road hospital (5). Digitally enhanced from an 1868 photo of Notting Hill (6), the signage here and throughout the Met at the time appear to have been made from cut-out sans-serif wooden letters, painted white and mounted on black wooden boards. Occasionally the letters were pressed into wet concrete, such as the sign 'TO KENSINGTON' from sometime after 1868 (7).

Signage, 1863–89

At least four letterforms are evident on the 1860s signage: the most common was on nameboards and 'WAY OUT' signs on the 1868 extension from Paddington (Praed Street) to Gloucester Road, but may have been used on the first seven stations. It was invariably used for the 'BOOKING OFFICE' sign above the entrance. Nameboards on platforms were in the same style (1), virtually an identical letterform – a Grotesque block capital – to that seen on many mainline stations, particularly on the GWR with which the Met had strong links. This letter shape was a standard Grotesque similar to Figgins Sans Serif (opposite, 2). An 1883 drawing captures the look (2). The second most common letterform was a condensed bold sans-serif, frequently used for the operating company name – on both Met and District stations (4, p.20). A third type of sans-serif (slightly bolder than that seen elsewhere) was used for District station nameboards from the late 1860s onwards. The fourth variety of lettering, seen from the 1870s, had a serif and was used for both the operating company and station name – for example, outside Parsons Green, Whitechapel (p. 31) and Westminster Bridge. A variation was also used in some District printed ephemera. Though it may all be conjecture, and unlikely to have been enforced with anything like the rigour with which companies adhere to design guidelines today, modern historians suspect that some bright spark in the sign-making rooms of each rail company was at least attempting to maintain some kind of consistency in style. A few examples of stained-glass signs also survive (3).

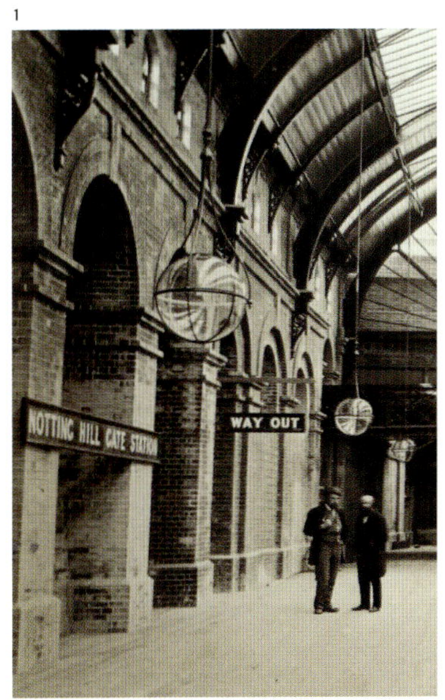

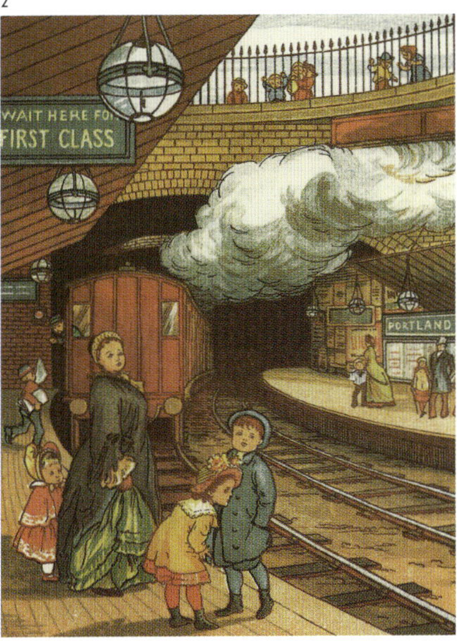

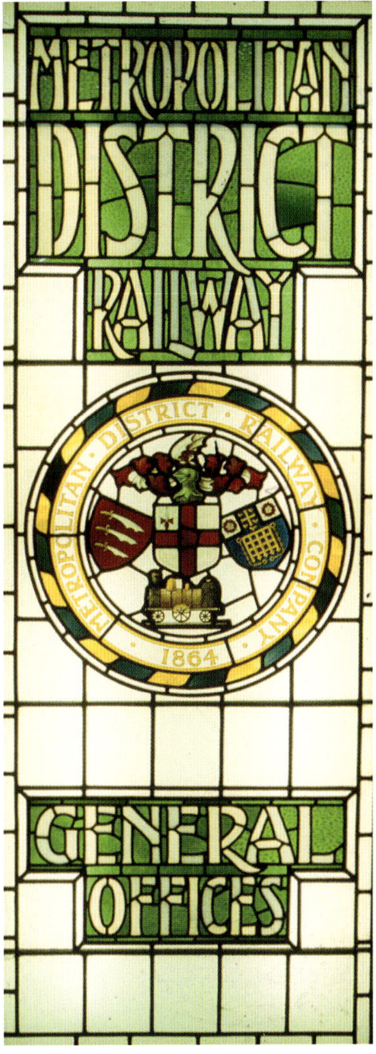

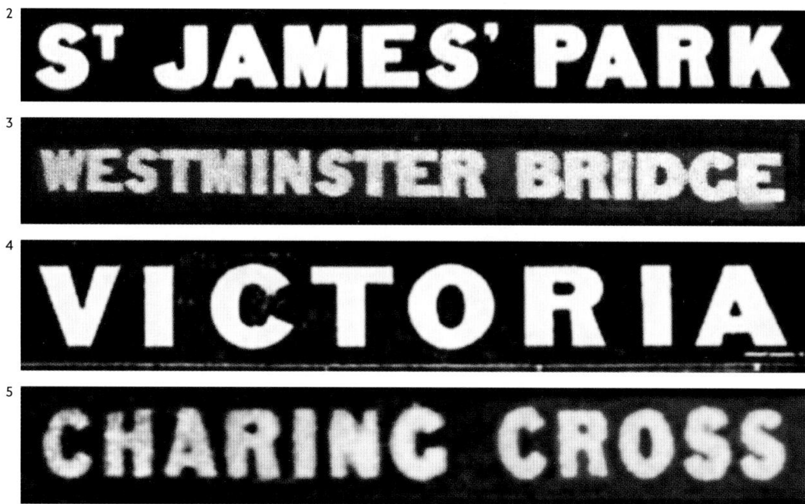

District differences, 1868–89

Whether the style of lettering used by the District on its nameboards was simply a 'bolder' form of that used on Met stations or an entirely different style, produced by a different manufacturer, it resembles bolder Grotesques of the period. Some digital recreations of either 'font' (as typefaces are now called) have been made (Johnathan Martins Old Railway Sans, 7), and modern URW Grotesque and Franklin Gothic (1) could be seen as close relatives of these early hand-cut Victorian letterforms. Platform nameboards followed mainline traits, being made from white painted wooden capitals on a black background (2, 3, 4, 5). At West Brompton (6), cut-out relief letters were individually mounted on the brickwork (a practice that was to be oft repeated in later years), and it is just possible to discern minor differences between the lettering used for 'DISTRICT RAILWAY' and that of the station name; look closely at the R, S, W and A in each line — the company name appears similar in style to that of the platform nameboards, while 'WEST BROMPTON' seems closer to the style predominating on the first Met stations.

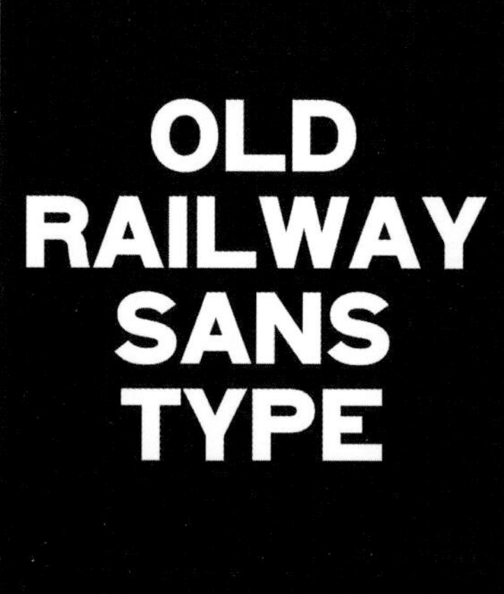

London Underground by Design

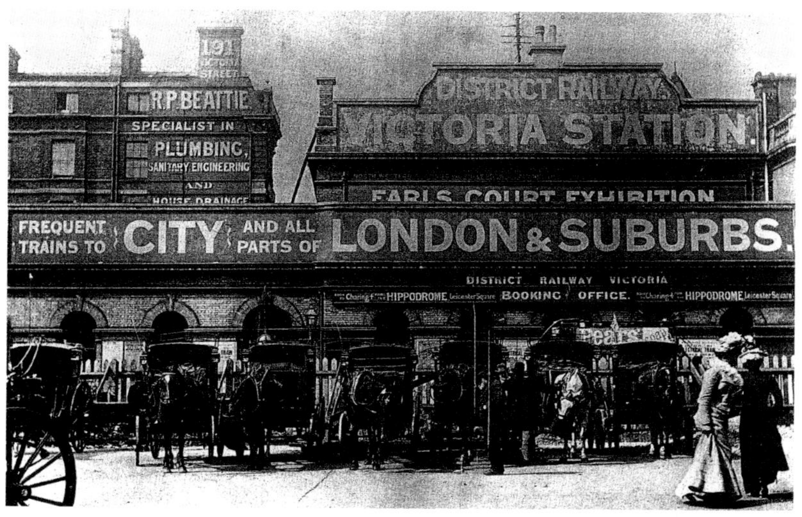

Hoarding on the ridiculous, 1870s–1890s

As the power of signage and advertising became recognized during the 1870s and 80s, new hoardings were erected on station frontages (especially along the District line as it was playing catch-up with the Met). Some of these quite heavily obscured the architectural features and were less than kind to the original elegant signage. At Victoria (1), for instance, the original station name is hard to spot. By late 1889/ early 1890, the graceful decor of Sloane Square (2) had all but disappeared beneath 'shouty' hoardings declaring the station's proximity to other parts of London. The same phenomenon was to be seen on the platforms of both the Met and District, such as at Notting Hill Gate (a later photo, no less beguiling, 4). Much of the exterior signage was untidy or downright misleading. At St James's Park (3), for instance, passengers must have wondered quite which direction they should take to find the station.

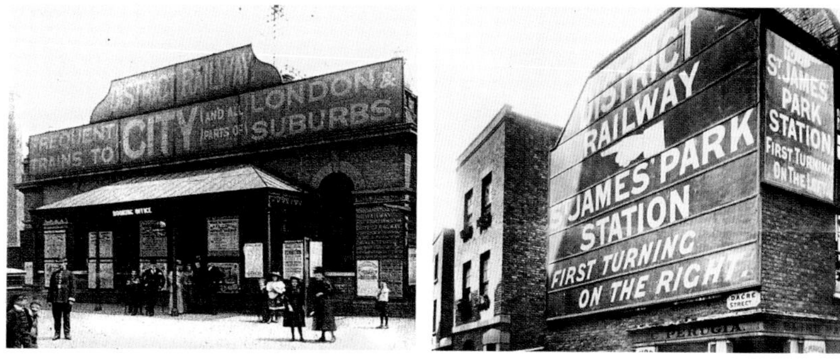

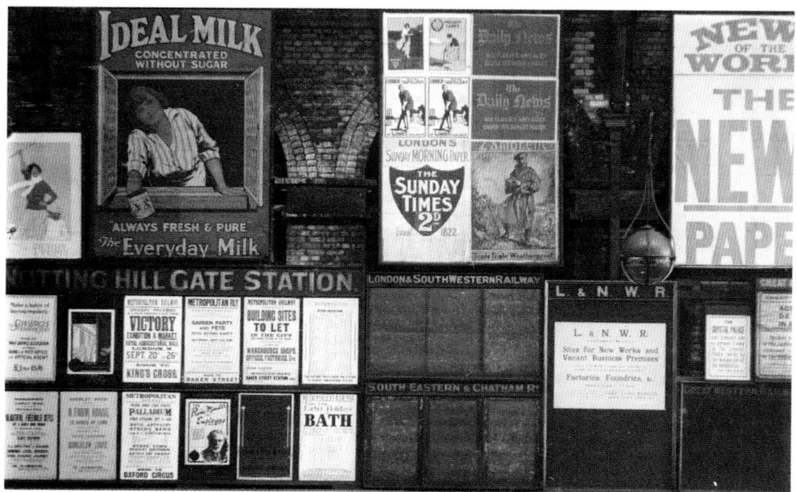

Station architecture, 1868–80

Lords, Marlborough Road and Swiss Cottage (1) were almost identical in design to stations on the Met's Gloucester Road branch. One of the earliest District buildings, at West Brompton (1869, 2), featured all the signature elements; architecture, lighting and signage bear striking similarities to that of the early Met stations. Blackfriars was so elaborate it was not completed until three years after the opening in 1870 (5). Between Earl's Court and Hammersmith (which opened on 9 September 1874), the District downgraded its design spec, either due to cost or to match the LSWR style. Earl's Court was rebuilt after a fire in 1878 (3); the first to be designed by District engineer John Wolfe-Barry (p. 16). It was less fancy and hence cheaper to construct; roof mouldings and parapets were lost but the glass gas globes were kept. Individually mounted sans-serif capitals spelled 'EARL'S COURT STATION' above the arches. The stations from Turnham Green to Ealing Broadway consisted of Acton Green (now Chiswick Park), Mill Hill Park (now Acton Town) and Ealing Common. Opening on 1 July 1879, they had a rustic look, which was fitting as much of the route was in open country. Several – including the Broadway terminus – had two or three storeys. On 1 March 1880, the District opened from West Brompton to Putney Bridge & Fulham (4) with intermediate stops at Walham Green (now Fulham Broadway) and Parsons Green. Wolfe-Barry oversaw both Ealing and Putney branches (architect John L. Clemmence is credited with their design). Putney branch buildings were simpler still in style, while station and company names were set in mounted capitals on brickwork as at Earls Court.

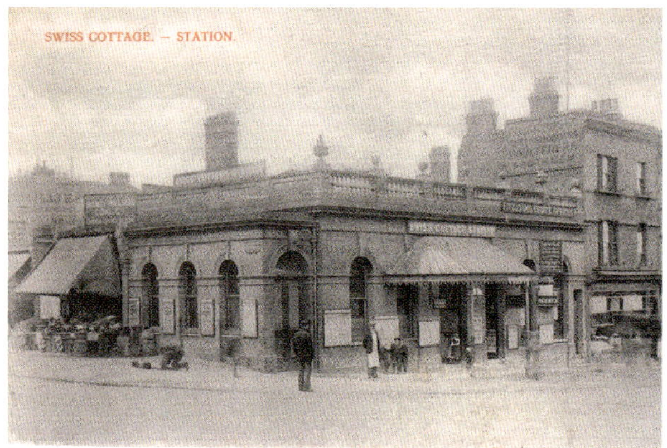

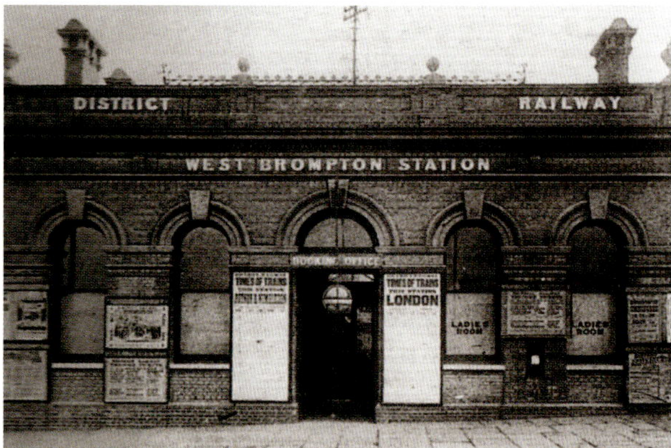

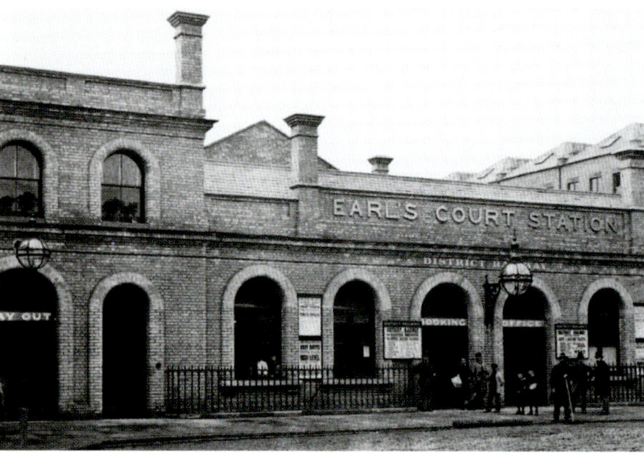

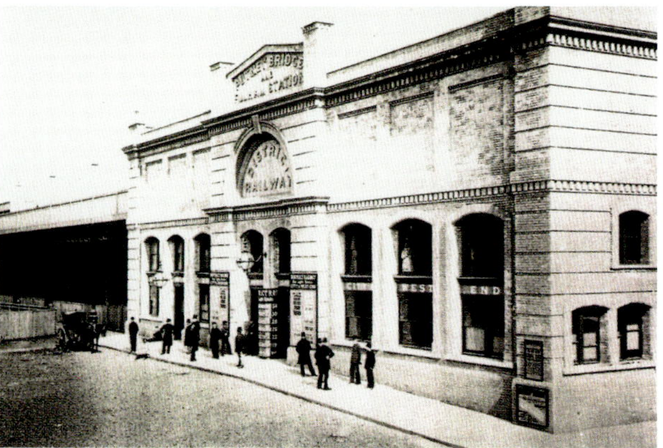

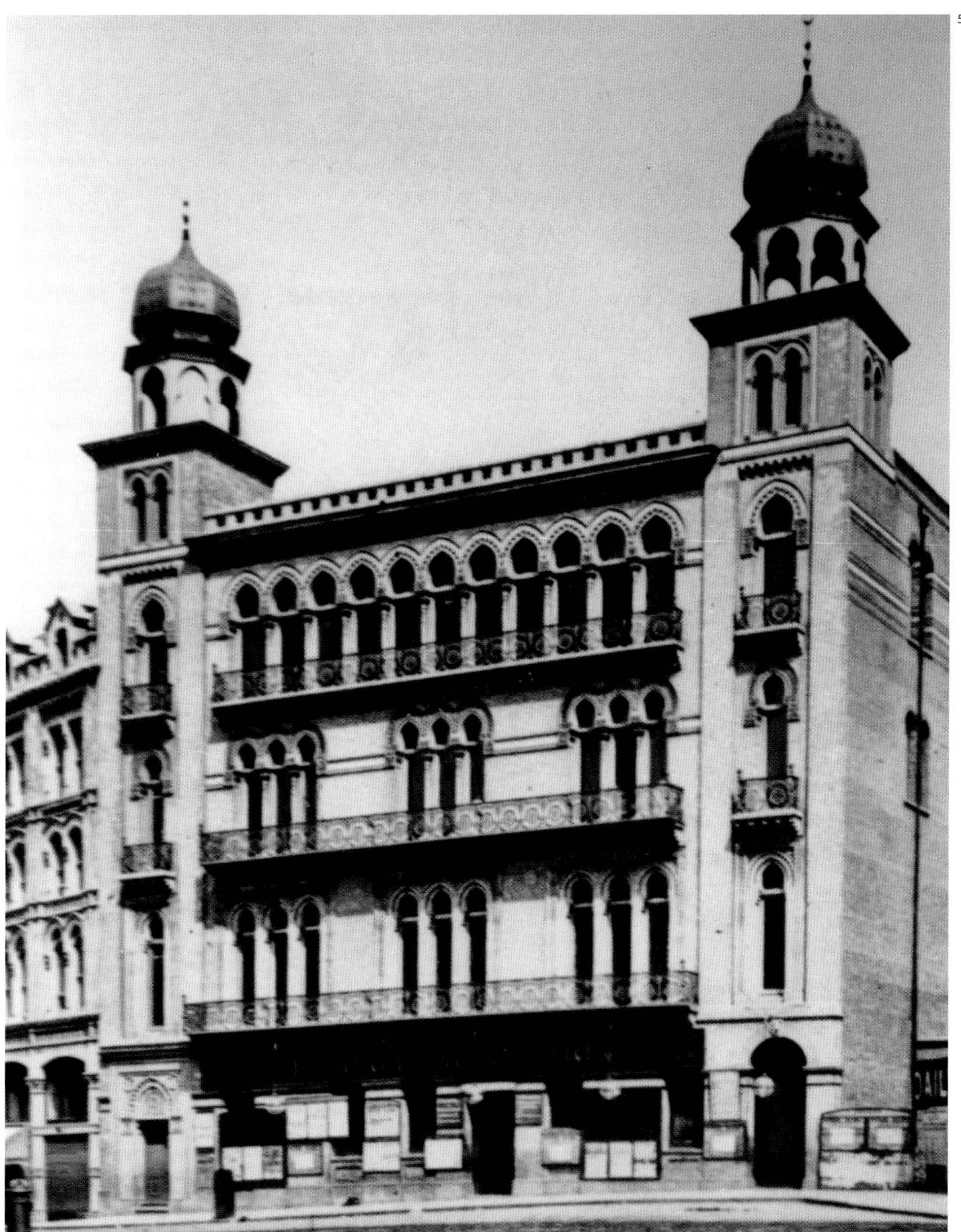

I. Establishing a New Style of Railway, 1863–89

Roots of 'Metro-land', 1873–89

A Met fares list (1873, 1) includes Camden Town, which was not directly served by the line. Unforeseen at the start of construction during the 1880s, the Met was laying the foundations for what became one of the key spokes of London's urban expansion (p. 68–9). This was a by-product of Watkin's north-westward thrust (p. 17), so the branch to Swiss Cottage duly gained a short extension to West Hampstead (with a single intermediate station at Finchley Road) in June 1879. Five months later, the next section of the line from West Hampstead to Willesden Green – with a stop at Kilburn & Brondesbury (now Kilburn) – was ready for passengers. By August 1880, the much longer route to a quiet and quaint Harrow was opened with an intermediate stop in the middle of what was then nowhere at Kingsbury & Neasden (4). The Met architects then busied themselves with the Harrow to Pinner section (shown as 'EXTENSION TO HARROW' on this 1881 map, (2), with Gothic cover, (3), and opened on 25 May 1885), then it was Pinner to Rickmansworth with a stop at Northwood (1 September 1887), followed by a long run to the village of Chesham via Chorley Wood and Chalfont Road (8 July 1889). Stations along this entire section of the Met were considerably more rudimentary than had been seen elsewhere, mostly consisting of a single storey with a tiled pitched roof and square windows – arches were obviously deemed too grand for stations sited in such rural outposts.

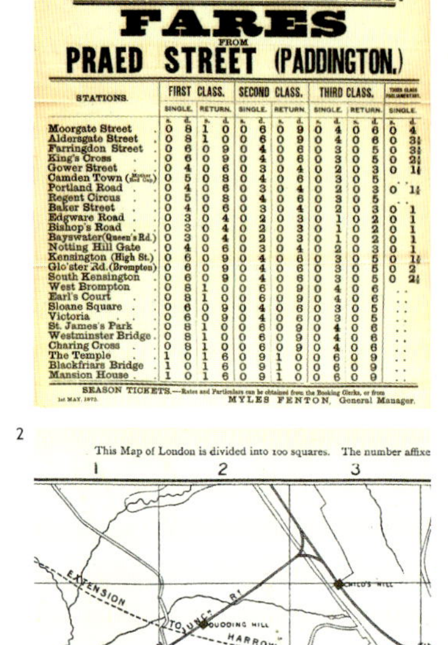

METROPOLITAN RAILWAY.
FARES
FROM
PRAED STREET (PADDINGTON.)

STATIONS.	FIRST CLASS. SINGLE.		FIRST CLASS. RETURN.		SECOND CLASS. SINGLE.		SECOND CLASS. RETURN.		THIRD CLASS. SINGLE.		THIRD CLASS. RETURN.		THIRD CLASS PARLIAMENTARY. SINGLE.	
	s.	d.	s.	d.	s.	d.	s.	d.	s.	d.	s.	d.	s.	d.
Moorgate Street	0	8	1	0	0	6	0	9	0	4	0	6	0	4
Aldersgate Street	0	8	1	0	0	6	0	9	0	4	0	6	0	3½
Farringdon Street	0	6	0	9	0	4	0	6	0	3	0	5	0	3½
King's Cross	0	6	0	9	0	4	0	6	0	3	0	5	0	2½
Gower Street	0	4	0	6	0	3	0	4	0	2	0	3	0	1½
Camden Town (Mother Cap.)	0	5	0	8	0	4	0	6	0	3	0	5		
Portland Road	0	4	0	6	0	3	0	4	0	2	0	3	0	1½
Regent Circus	0	5	0	8	0	4	0	6	0	3	0	5		
Baker Street	0	4	0	6	0	3	0	4	0	2	0	3	0	1
Edgware Road	0	3	0	4	0	2	0	3	0	1	0	2	0	1
Bishop's Road	0	3	0	4	0	2	0	3	0	1	0	2	0	1
Bayswater (Queen's Rd.)	0	3	0	4	0	2	0	3	0	1	0	2	0	1
Notting Hill Gate	0	4	0	6	0	3	0	4	0	2	0	3	0	1
Kensington (High St.)	0	6	0	9	0	4	0	6	0	3	0	5	0	1½
Glo'ster Rd. (Brompton)	0	6	0	9	0	4	0	6	0	3	0	5	0	2
South Kensington	0	6	0	9	0	4	0	6	0	3	0	5	0	2½
West Brompton	0	8	1	0	0	6	0	9	0	4	0	6	..	
Earl's Court	0	8	1	0	0	6	0	9	0	4	0	6	..	
Sloane Square	0	6	0	9	0	4	0	6	0	3	0	5	..	
Victoria	0	6	0	9	0	4	0	6	0	3	0	5	..	
St. James's Park	0	8	1	0	0	6	0	9	0	4	0	6	..	
Westminster Bridge	0	8	1	0	0	6	0	9	0	4	0	6	..	
Charing Cross	0	8	1	0	0	6	0	9	0	4	0	6	..	
The Temple	1	0	1	6	0	9	1	0	0	6	0	9	..	
Blackfriars Bridge	1	0	1	6	0	9	1	0	0	6	0	9	..	
Mansion House	1	0	1	6	0	9	1	0	0	6	0	9	..	

SEASON TICKETS.—Rates and Particulars can be obtained from the Booking Clerks, or from

1st MAY, 1873.   MYLES FENTON, General Manager.

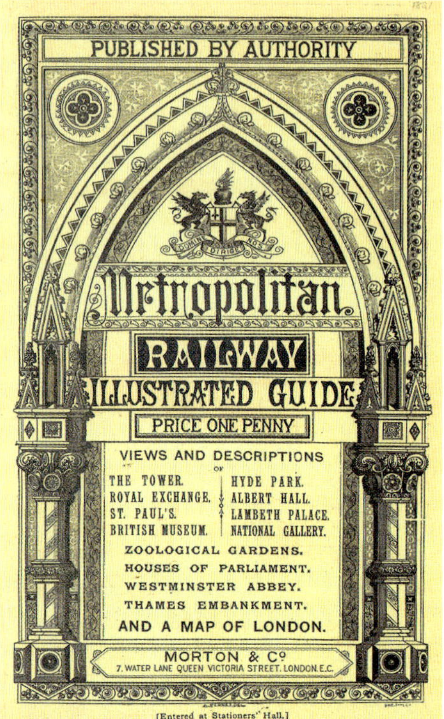

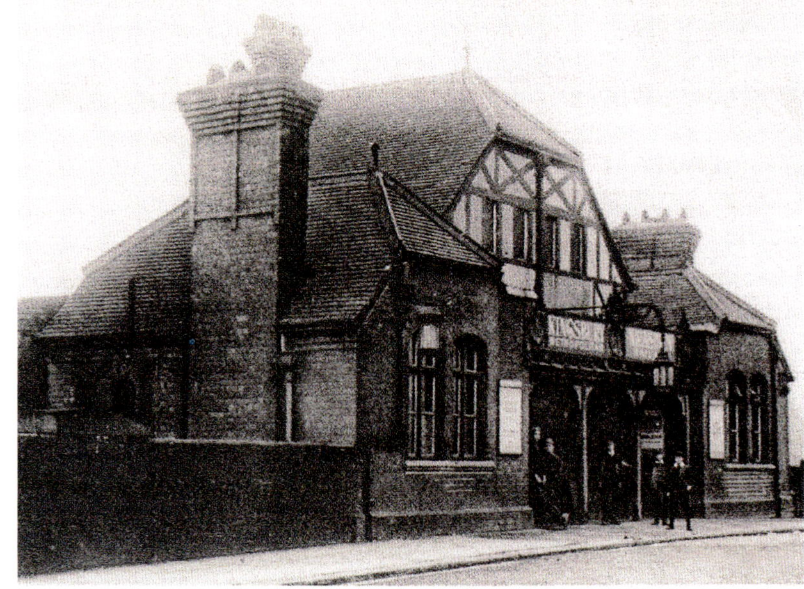

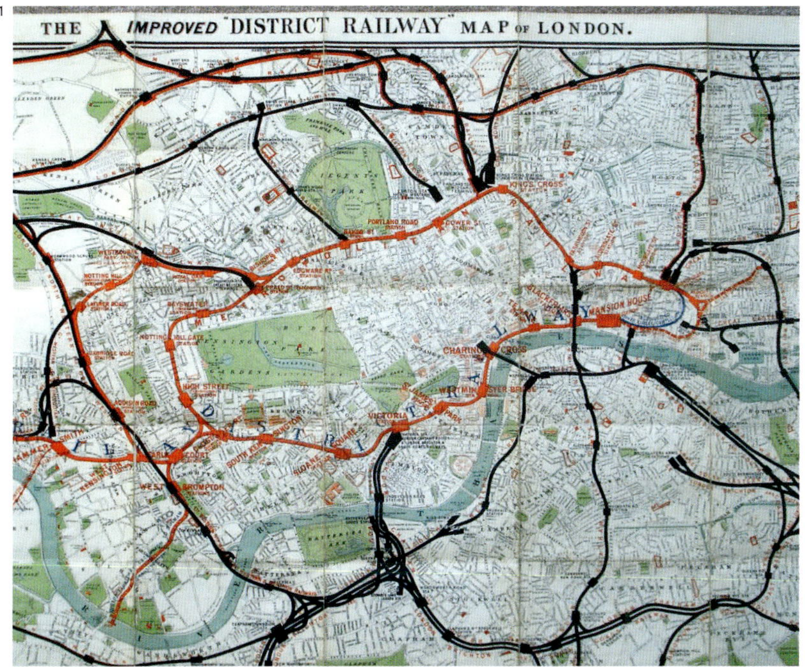

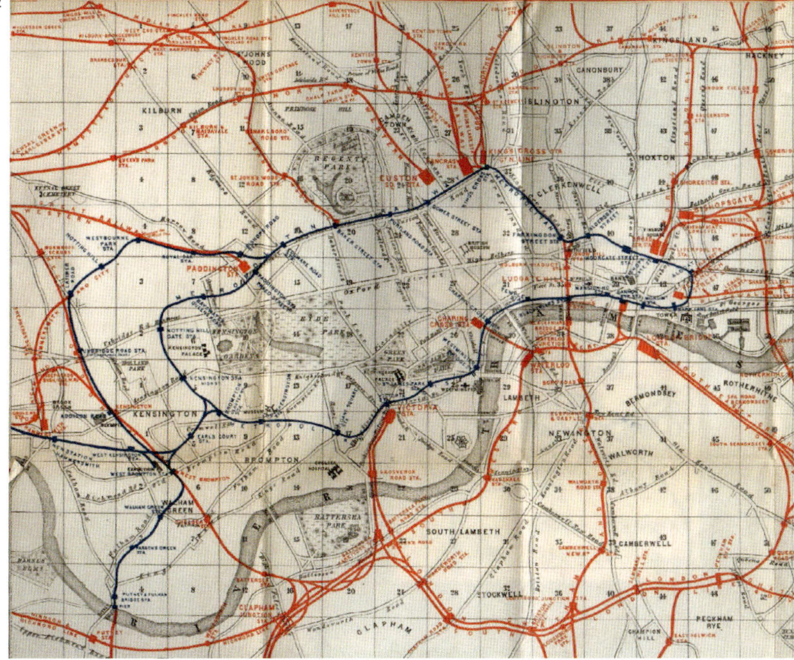

With cartography by Stanfords and printed by Waterlow's in 1879 (1), this is probably the first map published in the name of the District (p. 12). The last miles of the Inner Circle are still incomplete. The route under construction from Mansion House (opened September 1884) is shown dotted, but the other dotted extension, of the Met to Barnes, never materialized. The last extension of this period, the Thames crossing at Putney for a four-station overground run to Wimbledon (opened 3 June 1889), was a collaboration between the District and the LSWR (p. 15). It allowed architects to experiment. Wimbledon was expanded and replaced in the 1930s but Wimbledon Park, East Putney and Southfields survive with original features pretty much intact. In 1884 the Inner Circle was finally completed (p. 16), the line marked in blue on this 1889 map (2) from *London and its Environs: Handbook for Travellers* by Karl Baedeker. A better illustration of the issues facing the network cannot be found, for the transport planners' problem was that, without new technology, none of the existing railways that ran up to the edge of and around the city were able to take passengers all the way to their intended destinations in the West End. The only line traversing the City (the London Chatham & Dover Railway) was nowhere near London's shopping and theatre districts and did very little to bring passengers anywhere closer than the Met or District could, crossing at the narrowest part of the Circle via Ludgate Hill and Holborn Viaduct.

Met makes its map mark, 1882–3

Having published no maps since 1863, by the 1880s the Met had realized the sense in producing its own, such as this example from 1882 (1), which not surprisingly gives stronger emphasis to its own lines. Even the GWR and the GER appear in bold while the poor District is demoted to nothing more than a trifling nuisance. Such petty and entirely unhelpful cartographic exaggerations only increased animosity between the two operators. It is interesting to note, though, how closely the typeface used on the map for the company name matches the lettering on station frontages. Demonstrating the Met's early inclination to lure people along its north-westerly branch, the small village of Harrow, where a station had just opened (1880), is positively trumpeted with the largest name on the entire map. This exuberant self-promotion has echoes of what was to come four decades later with the expansion of 'Metro-land' (pp. 69, 109). A most bizarre map (2) with green, Pythonesque fish overprint, was produced by the District for the 1883 Fisheries Exhibition behind the Natural History Museum in South Kensington. Note the Regent's Canal, City and Docks Railway (parliamentary approval was granted in 1882), which would have run alongside or replaced the canal between Paddington and Limehouse in the heady days when railways could do no wrong. At least one bridge (at Lisson Green) was constructed to leave room, but the project never materialized and was dumped in 1902, along with a raft of other uncompleted schemes.

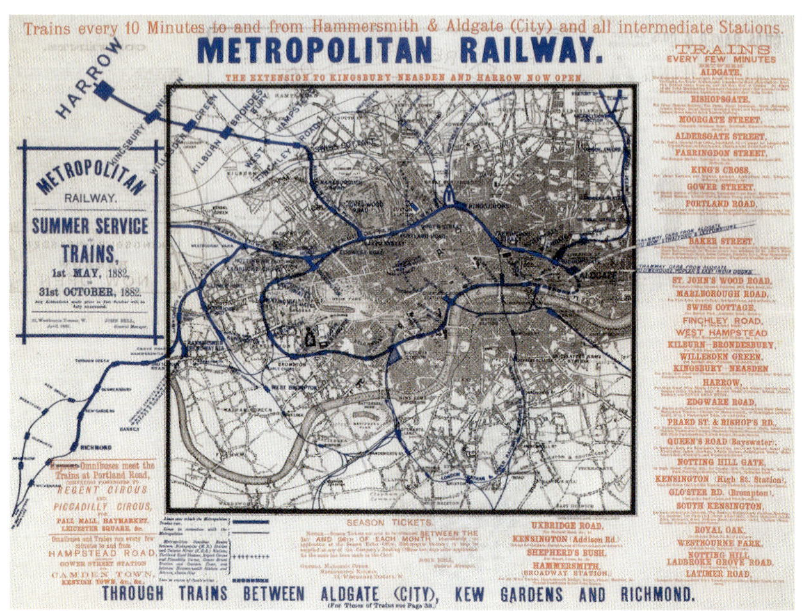

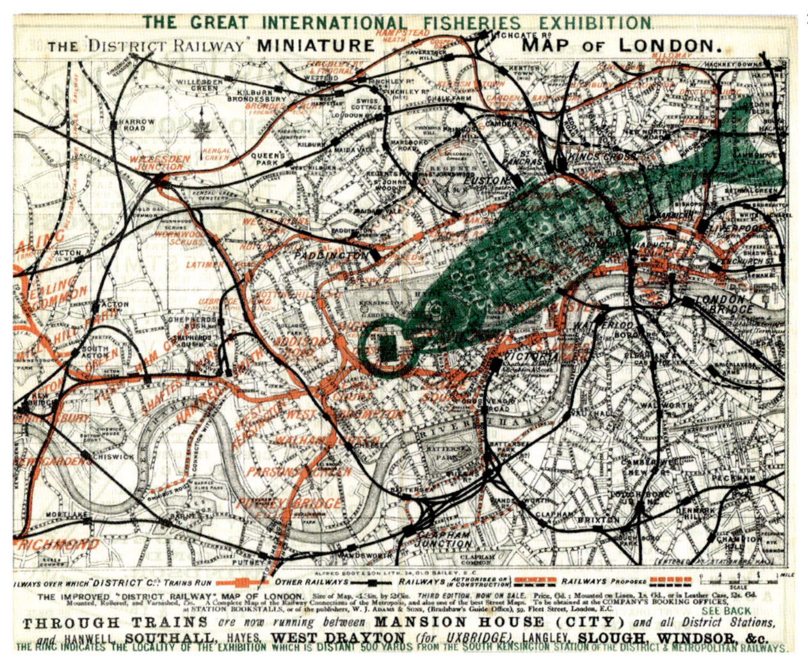

London Underground by Design

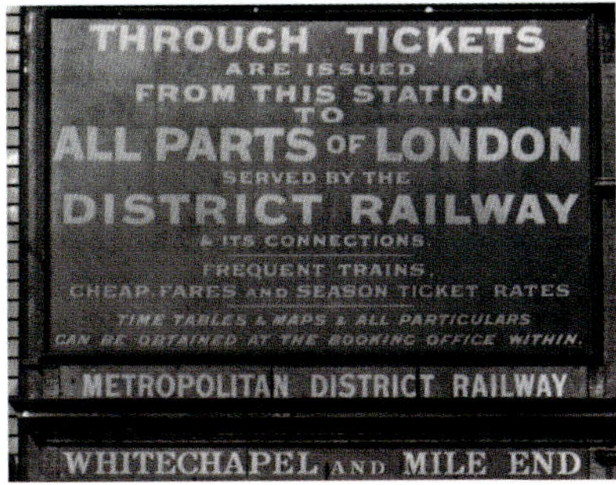

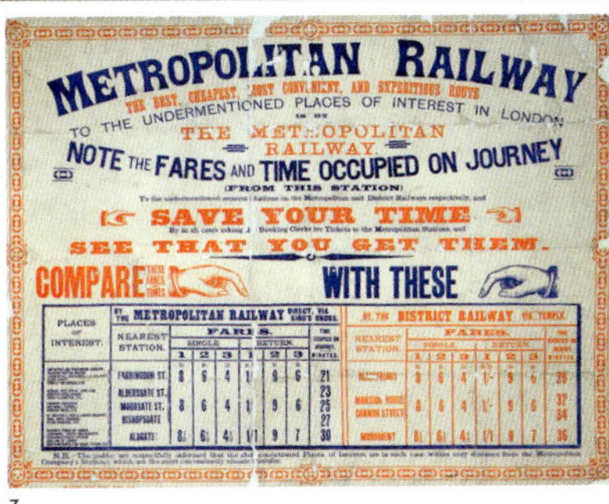

Rivalry spurs design improvements, 1884–7

By the time the District opened Whitechapel station in 1884, competition with the Met had reached fever pitch, some issues even thrashed out in court. Both companies were keen to advertise their own routes to 'ALL PARTS OF LONDON' (set in sans-serif caps on the new Whitechapel entrance, 2) and refused tickets issued by the other, even if that route was shorter. The more serifed lettering of the lines in smaller type were made using a form which had become standard for the District (also used on map covers, p. 28). The side elevation of Gloucester Road (opened 1868) was later used for self-promotion by the Met as competition heated up. The lettering (1) was rendered in tiles, one of the earliest examples of a material that would become ubiquitous in the decor and signage of the Underground network, appearing as early as 1890. With the Met now producing posters (like this one proclaiming time savings, 3) and maps marginalizing the District's services, the latter responded with big improvements to its printed material. The 1880s covers were exquisite, depicting both London landmarks and implausibly well-lit tunnels, but the 1887 edition (4) takes the biscuit for barefaced delusions of grandeur. Surrounding a long list of London and Home Counties stations, vignette illustrations of four continents seem to suggest that there is almost no corner of the planet that the District does not reach. Clever Victorian marketing or not, no Met service even merits a mention.

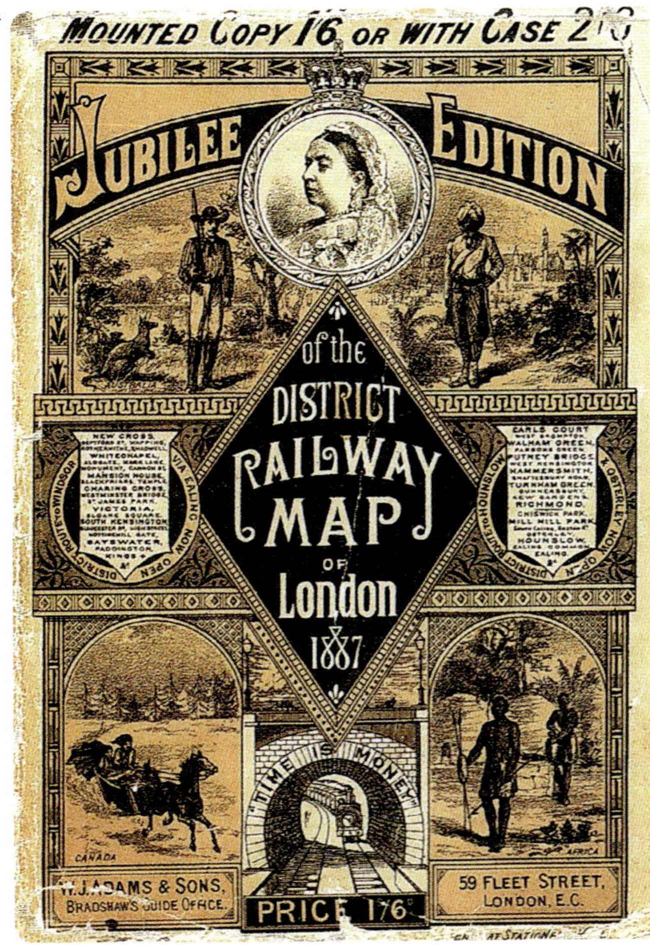

II.

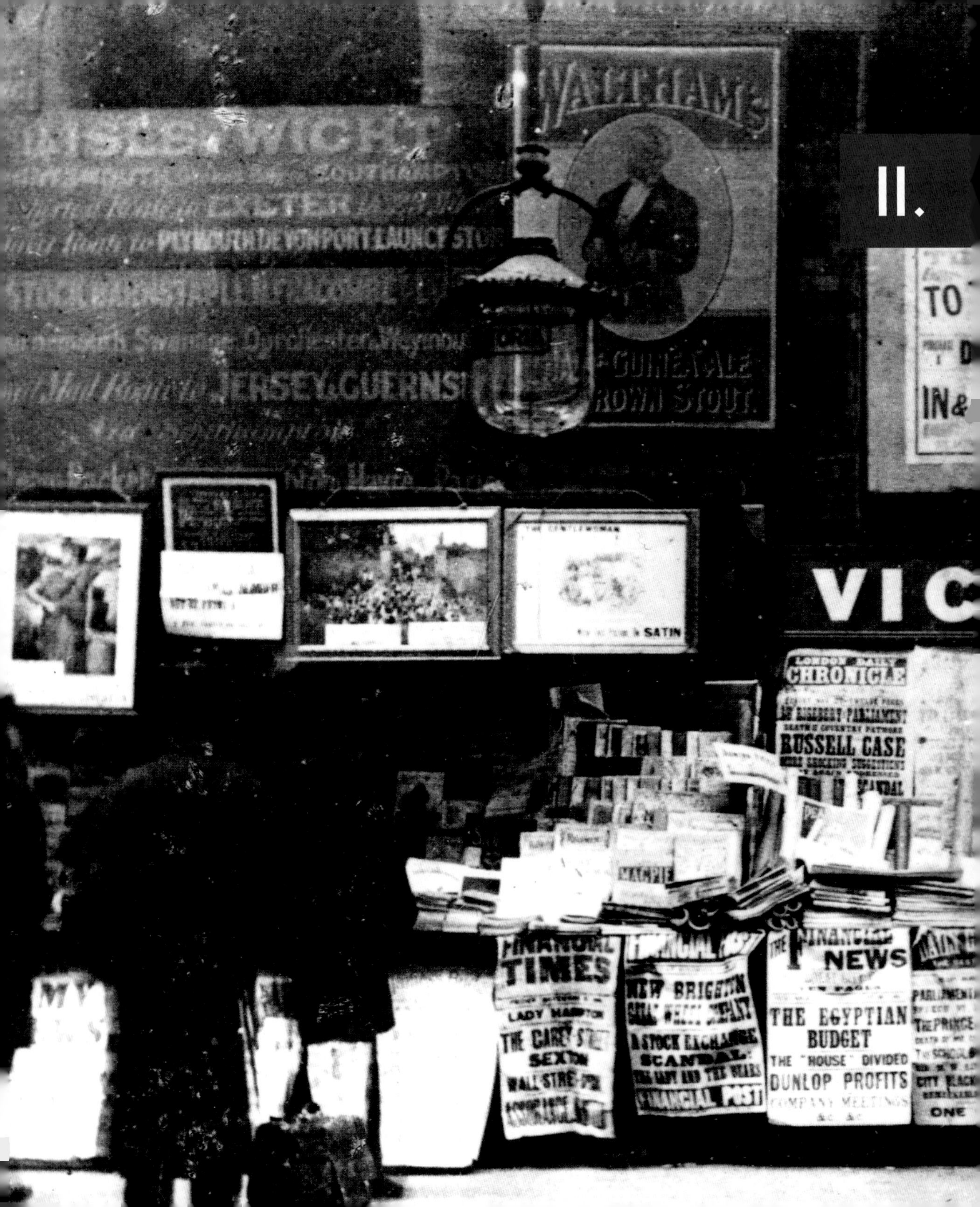

The Design of the First Tubes
1890–1905

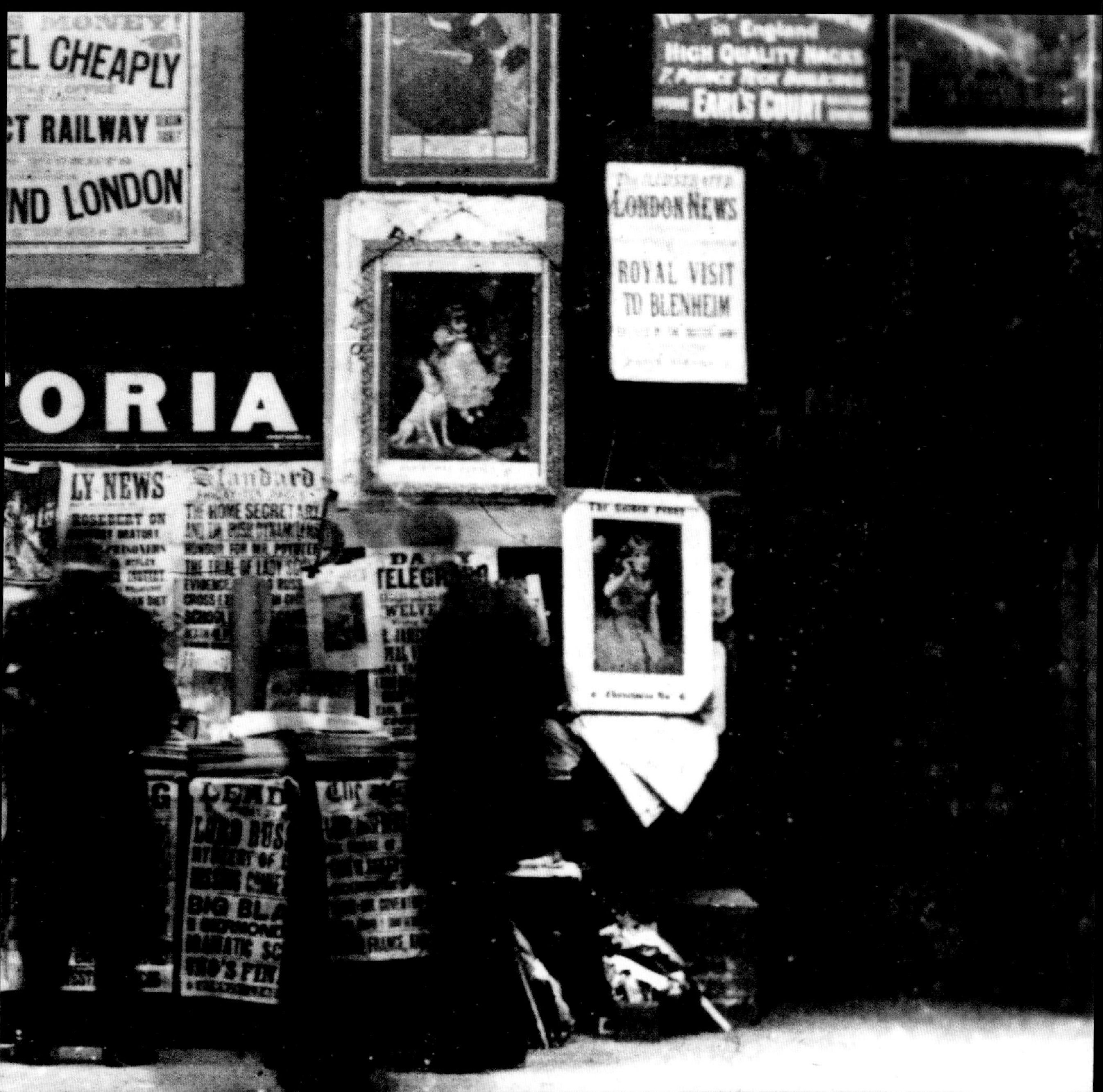

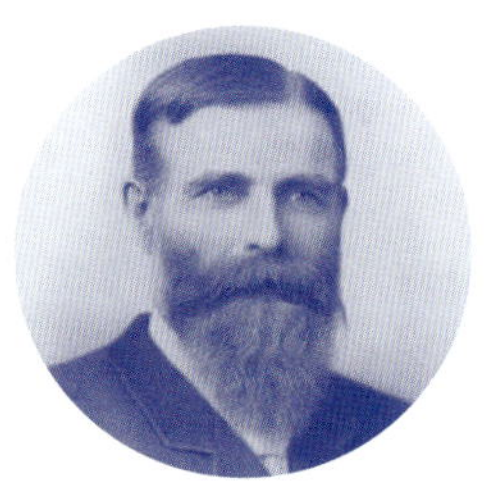

James Henry Greathead (1844–96), born in South Africa, experienced engineering success on the Tower Subway (p. 16), adapting the protective shield that he developed with Peter W. Barlow. After working on the Hammersmith extension and the District plus several other projects, he was engaged by the CSLR and later the CLR with Sir John Fowler and Benjamin Baker. His contribution to the Underground is commemorated in a 1994 statue outside Bank Tube station.

II. The Design of the First Tubes, 1890–1905

Constructing railways and stations that were only just below ground level had taxed the prowess of the most ingenious Victorian engineers, but to serve the very heart of London any new tunnels under the built-up city would have to be much deeper – and the design solutions required would be yet more challenging.

South London soars ahead of the pack

The Met and District had effectively formed a skeleton urban transport network around the edge of London on the north side of the Thames, but the technological and design innovations which became possible between 1890 and just after the turn of the century enabled underground railway lines to penetrate into the very heart of the capital. The City and South London Railway (CSLR) opened in 1890, providing the world's first service operating via deep-level, bored 'tubes' (as opposed to the 'cut-and-cover' tunnelling used up until then). It was pioneering in other respects too: the first underground line to be powered by electric traction,[1] it was also the first electric railway to be constructed under a major waterway, the first to install lifts at all stations and the first to line the walls of platforms and passageways with white ceramic tiles. Everything had to be designed from scratch, in every detail, including the lighting and signage. Given its influence on the development of urban transit, not just in London but around the world, it is surprising how little recognized the CSLR is for its innovation. Designers of most subsequent underground rail platforms copied the CSLR's use of white ceramic tiling, for instance, and both the Met and District lines would be using electric power by 1905, setting the stage for the biggest expansion of the system since its inception.

The CSLR[2] was initially envisaged as a cable-hauled line between Elephant & Castle and the City, but following plans in 1886 to extend it from Elephant to Stockwell, the chairman, Charles Grey Mott, and his fellow directors revised their ideas, making what was to prove a pivotal decision in engineering design.[3] Advances in new tunnelling methods pioneered by James Henry Greathead's Tower Subway of 1870 (p. 16) and in electric railway engines – exhibited at the 1879 Berlin Trades Fair – brought the possibility of crossing beneath the Thames by electrically operated railway into the realms of reality. Having confidence in the evolving technology of the day,[4] the CSLR took the bold step of switching traction power to electricity. Equally radical and trendsetting – though less well documented – was the station design. Realizing from the outset that there would be no way of allowing even a modicum of daylight into their stations, even with the Met's clever trick of using light-wells (p. 18), Mott decided that the walls of the deeper CSLR passageways and platforms should all be cloaked from floor to ceiling in brilliant white oblong tiles (an idea possibly borrowed from public conveniences of the era – typically

London Underground by Design

subterranean, white-porcelain-clad palaces).[5] A small but tasteful concession to decoration was permitted: a burnt-red border in the burgeoning Arts and Crafts style[6] ran the length of most walls at a height of approximately one metre from the ground (p. 44). This feature alone provided a sense that all the stations belonged to a collective whole: in essence, a very early demonstration of what now would be termed a 'house style'.

A new look emerges

At street level, the five CSLR stations designed by architect Thomas Phillips Figgis, with their single-storey, red-brick buildings and distinctive lead-covered domes, were very different from those of the Met and District. Not even the signature gas lamps were in evidence. This was clearly a deliberate attempt by the new company at individual branding (as it would be termed now).[7] At Stockwell, Kennington Oval (now Oval), Kennington New Street (now Kennington), Elephant & Castle and Great Dover Street (opened as 'Borough'), the domes (a neat way of hiding the lift mechanism) integrated functionality with elegance and simplicity. David Lawrence describes them in more detail, mentioning the 'cupola lantern and weathervane' at the top and side walls 'pierced by mullioned windows between brick pilasters' (1994, Bibliography). Company and station names appeared in relief on signs as individually mounted, gilded capitals, each approximately 30cm in height. Railings, where used, such as at Stockwell, contained nested Arts and Crafts motifs, echoing the tiled friezes below stairs. None of this detail was present in the entrances to King William Street, CSLR's northern terminus, as these were built into an existing property. Although almost everything from 1890 has been lost over time, Kennington station alone retains much of its original frontage and a restored leaded dome. Surviving examples of the original interior ceramics can be found only in a stairwell at Elephant & Castle.

The CSLR carriages were curious. As it was an underground railway in the full sense of the term,[8] the cars had incredibly narrow windows (57cm wide and only 23cm high), situated high above the longitudinal seats. These minuscule openings, combined with the copious red cushioning along the backrests, soon earned the carriages the nickname of 'padded cells'. Thankfully station names were announced at each stop by the guard as passengers could not see out of the windows without standing up.

Others get in on the act

Back on the Met, the push towards the Midlands and the north-west was taking shape;[9] the first direct service between the City and Verney Junction started on 1 September 1894. At a whopping 80km from Baker Street, this and Brill became the furthest 'underground' stations from the centre of London. Coincidentally, the terminus at Verney marked the end of Edward Watkin's dream to connect the Met all the way up to

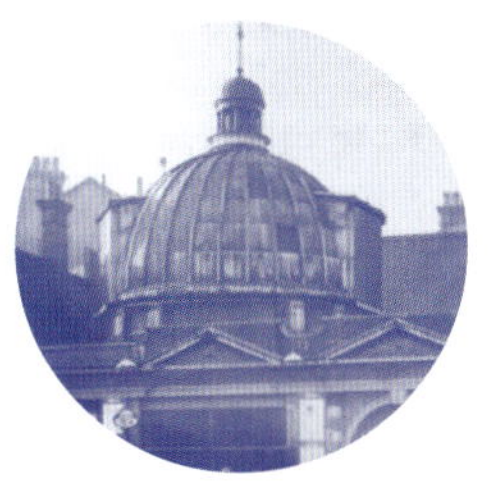

Thomas Phillips Figgis (aka 'T. P.', 1858–1948), born in Dublin, was architect for the original five surface buildings of the CSLR (Elephant & Castle pictured). Although he went on to design Clapham North and Moorgate, he was not employed on any other underground stations after that. His later work included four stations for the Meon Valley railway, and some churches.

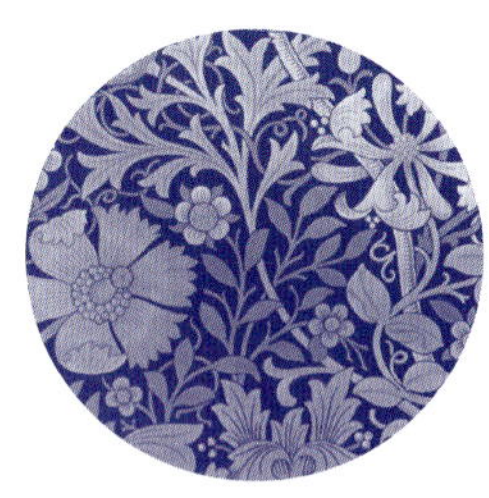

William Morris (1834–96) was a writer, textile designer and early socialist campaigner who was one of the leading instigators of the Arts and Crafts movement. Although not directly associated with the Underground, his work influenced the design of CSLR ceramics, was commemorated in a 1934 exhibition (detail from Underground poster, above) and also motivated Leslie Green (p. 61).

Manchester.[10] The stations looked much like those along other rural branches, but the signage did at least reflect the company style, sporting a single dark nameboard with white capitals in a sans-serif style (p. 45). Indeed, it's interesting to note that even this far out of the city the Met was attempting to retain a co-ordinated appearance. The District, by contrast, opened no new stations or sections during this period but consolidated its work on publicizing existing routes. Regularly updated maps improved with each new edition (pp. 50–51), and with rail lines printed over existing street plans, these also served as handy navigation guides at a time when London was expanding rapidly.

Now that the CSLR had proved that deep tube lines could be constructed and could operate viably, other cities were quick to copy. Glasgow built a 10.4km circle in 1896; tiling and glazed bricks were used sparingly in passageways and on some platform signal boxes.[11] Officials from the Austro-Hungarian capital visited London because they wanted to build an underground railway. Opening in 1896, Budapest's 'Földalatti' was cable-hauled and stations there were elaborately tiled.[12] In the United States, Boston, which already operated many miles of elevated urban transit lines, opened a short tunnel for trams (Tremont Street Subway) in 1897. Here station names were represented as tiled friezes[13] on the trackside wall, and these may have had an influence in turn on the later work of Leslie Green (p. 71). Chicago went heavily for electrified elevated lines – the system opening in 1892 – using painted wooden boards to show station names. New York, which had also had elevated rails since 1868, was looking into building an underground railway and in the event plumped for ceramics,[14] on view for the first time when the Subway opened in 1904. But it was Paris which went for the complete package – electrification and full tiling – beginning work on a six-line network in 1896.[15] The Métro opened in 1900 and blatantly emulated the white tiling of the deeper London stations for platforms and passageways, causing many to believe (erroneously) that it invented the style.

The digging of 'the Drain'

Thanks to the CSLR proving that electricity could be used to power railways, designs for deeper tunnels with electric trains could finally become a reality for piercing the Inner Circle, crossing central London and the West End. The first such line to be completed (though only just nipping under the District and pushing a little into Circle territory) became another curiosity of the system. This was a 2.4km tube line, built wholly under-ground,[16] which ran from beneath the vast Waterloo mainline station[17] to a terminus between the Bank and Mansion House (called 'City' until 1940, when it was renamed Bank). Built by the LSWR, it opened on 8 August 1898, rapidly proving popular at peak times and allowing the company to experiment with electric traction.[18] No surface station building was necessary at Waterloo, but to connect with the forthcoming Central London Railway (CLR, p. 48), which temporarily terminated at Bank, a long, gently sloping connecting foot tunnel (still in use) was created, giving passengers a direct link between the two new lines and an easier exit. A contemporary report in *Railway Magazine* refers to 'two entrances from the street level to the City station of the new railway. One of these is placed near the premises of the National Safe Deposit Company, and the other opposite the premises of Messrs. Mappin and Webb, at the corner of Cheapside and Queen Victoria Street.' These appear to have been removed when the CLR opened two years later. The cars were the prettiest so far seen beneath London, painted to match the existing LSWR livery in chocolate brown with salmon-pink stripes.[19]

The early termination of a terminus

Due to technical problems at King William Street,[20] the desire to extend north and the need to construct a new headquarters building, the CSLR abandoned its original terminus there, opening a northerly extension from Borough to Moorgate Street (where its new offices would be situated), with intermediate stops at London Bridge and Bank, on 25 February 1900.[21] Tunnelling engineer Benjamin Baker and others cleverly redesigned the route to give passengers from the London Bridge[22] mainline terminus easy access to the City, as well as creating new connections between three different lines: the Met (at Moorgate) and the Waterloo & City & CLR (at Bank). The idea of interchanging between lines was first introduced in London, which now had a handful of linked stations. Indeed, it is impossible to overestimate the value of this concept in transportation history: interchanges are at the heart of any good integrated mass-transit system.

At Moorgate, Figgis created the tallest station so far constructed: a five-storey headquarters for the CSLR (p. 46). The ground floor was faced in Portland stone and incorporated carved foliage in the Arts and Crafts style, somewhat reminiscent of the tiled friezes below ground. An extravagant company crest, complete with arcs of lightning, was set over the entrance to the building. The walls of the upper floors were red brick with stone bands. The corner housing the station entrance was a curved turret with lead-lined windows and topped with a domed 'hat', while the booking office was finished with polished teak and ceramic tiling. Much is still visible today, after sympathetic renovation in the 1990s.

Following its abandonment of the unsatisfactory King William Street station, the CSLR went on to construct a modest extension south from Stockwell to Clapham Common (p. 46), which opened on 3 June 1900. An intermediate station was built at Clapham Road (which became Clapham North). For the first time on the emerging network, island platforms were introduced, which necessitated the creation of wide tunnels (9.1m diameter) but, unlike in Paris, the ceramic work extended only about one metre up the wall from the trackbed.[23]

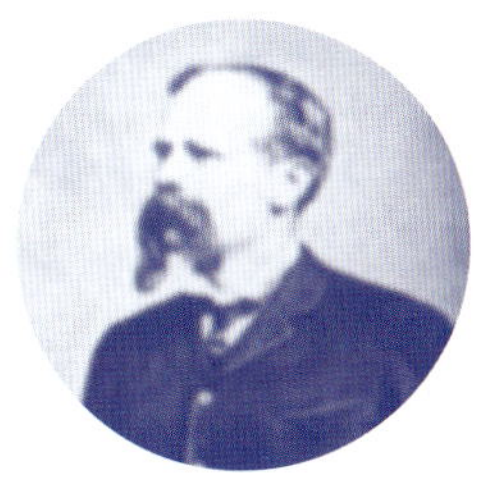

Benjamin Baker (1840–1907), born in Somerset, was a civil engineer who worked on 19km of elevated railways in New York and wrote a book in 1870 called *Long Railway Bridges*, about the merits of using steel in civil engineering. He joined the Met, worked on a failed north London tube project and then for the CLR in 1894. He went on to a distinguished career which included work on the old Aswan Dam, the Forth Bridge and the replacement Tay Bridge.

Central London hosts a design step change

The scheme which drew the most attention, however – not just due to its length or its handy West End route, but also because of its attention to architectural design – was the Central London Railway (CLR). Its roots go back to 1889 when an interchange was proposed with the CSLR at King William Street,[24] but it was not until March 1894 that architect Harry Bell Measures was appointed, along with other contractors and staff.[25] The whole thing should have been open by 1896,[26] and although the tunnels were completed by 1898, not all the stations were finished. The problem was the complexity of the underground ticket hall at Bank.[27] The other twelve stations were more or less ready, however.[28] Designed by Measures, these were all single-storey, steel-framed buildings clad in pinkish-brown unglazed terracotta. Many of them, in keeping with the commercial districts they served, had much larger entrances than the Met or CSLR stations, featuring big 'picture' windows – mini shopfronts, almost – with white porcelain letters glued to the glass, spelling out 'CENTRAL LONDON RAILWAY', 'STATION ENTRANCE' and the name of the station[29] (p. 49). The move to install wider entrances for unimpeded passenger flow was to become a regular design feature of almost all subsequent stations.

Their structure was deliberately made sufficiently sturdy to support more floors above, and the CLR cleverly sold the 'air rights' to build over most of them. This is one of the reasons why so many of the original buildings survive, even at busy Oxford Circus. David Lawrence describes how the frontages were 'based on a series of segmental arches, between which pilasters were carried up to an architrave'. These 'had superimposed corbels and narrow pediments above roof level; a small "grotesque" was set below each. The frieze itself was bellied out and decorated with swags of fruit' (1994, Bibliography). At selected stations a triangular pediment was topped by a sculpted cherub holding a lamp above its head (all of which have sadly disappeared over time). Booking offices had quaint ceramic-framed windows and two-toned tiled walls, each section (the lower one being darker) separated by a patterned band (p. 49) – another idea later copied by Green (p. 61).

Echoing the CSLR, the walls of all the platforms and inner passageways were lined with 'brilliant' white oblong tiles – chosen because they helped to reflect and amplify the (somewhat dimmer than hoped for) electric light. On platforms, station names were shown on enamelled iron plates surrounded by wooden frames. Historians believe the background of these plates was dark blue and the lettering in white sans-serif capitals. Almost nothing else was allowed on this side, although some space on the wall facing the platform (the trackside wall) was allocated for advertising posters (p. 48). 'WAY OUT' signs were in an identical style (p. 48) to the nameboards. Exterior lighting came from suspended globes of frosted glass – much smaller than those installed on the Met years before.

The CLR, dubbed a 'Tube' railway by the press, was finally opened on 27 June 1900 by the Prince of Wales.[30] With its dazzling white ceramic-lined walls, electric lamps and snazzy brown-, white- and purple-painted cars (p. 54), it aroused huge interest and was soon carrying 45 million passengers a year. This was partly due to its electric trains, trajectory right through the heart of central London and the flat 2d fare[31] for any length of journey, but also because the stations were so distinctive and easy to spot in the streetscape. Measures's conscious attempt to design a coherent, recognizable look may have separated them still further from those of the District, Met and CSLR, but it enabled the edifices to stand out clearly in already busy environments, and certainly influenced Green whose even larger batch of stations were soon to follow (p. 70).

Success sparks innovation by rival companies

The Met and District, which had both opposed the building of the CLR, were understandably ruffled by its popularity and innovative designs, so they stepped up their publicity campaigns (p. 52). Lessons were being learnt, however, and both companies began to explore how they might electrify their old steam systems and improve their signage. The CSLR already had plans to extend its line from Moorgate to Euston and on 17 November 1901 managed to open the section as far as Angel.[32] These stations also had island platforms and surface buildings in a similar style to those at Clapham. At Old Street, situated on a corner, there was a long side elevation of five arched window bays. At Angel the two side arches were larger still, reaching to the first storey; it remained a terminal for six years until Euston could be made ready. In 1902 the District pulled a neat trick by building the Whitechapel and Bow Railway – running through a short section of cut-and-cover tunnel[33] – but as there were already stations at both ends of the line, the only new surface buildings were at Mile End and Stepney Green. Both benefited from long station frontages, the former having the largest, and sported wide brick arches and tiled roofs – though only the latter survives.

UERL goes deeper and electrifies the District

Spurred on by the success of the CSLR and the CLR, yet more schemes for new deep-level tube lines were now emerging. Parliament refined them down to just three, all owned by the American financier Charles Tyson Yerkes (p. 40). The first of these, the Charing Cross, Euston and Hampstead Railway (CCEHR or 'Hampstead Tube'), was bought by Yerkes in 1900, a year before acquiring the District, which he planned to electrify using an engineering company he also owned. A proposed Great Northern and Strand Railway that had been acquired by Yerkes was combined with other schemes,[34] to form a second deep-level line, the Great Northern, Piccadilly and Brompton Railway (GNPBR or 'Piccadilly Tube'). The third line was the Baker Street and Waterloo Railway (BSWR or

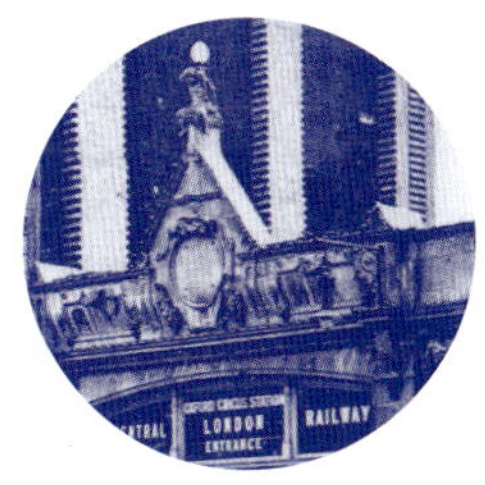

Harry Bell Measures (1862–1940) was an English architect who began his career by designing grand homes around London, although he also produced accommodation for poorer people, such as the Rownton Houses chain of hostels in London and Birmingham. In 1894 he was hired by the CLR as architect of all twelve of its surface stations (Oxford Circus pictured). He went on to design the massive Redford Cavalry Barracks in Edinburgh.

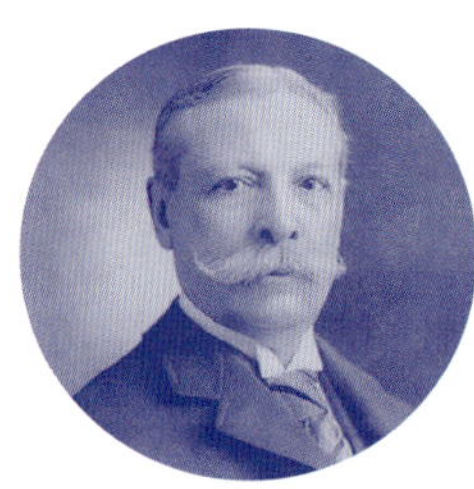

American Charles Tyson Yerkes (1837–1905), who had been involved with development of mass-transit systems in Chicago, was in many ways the saviour of London's under-ground projects. Though his financial affairs have been described as dodgy at best to downright illegal, without his intervention from 1900 onwards it is possible that many of the deep-level tubes which opened under his UERL umbrella from 1906 would never have materialized, due to lack of funding.

'Bakerloo Tube'), on which substantial construction work (half of the tunnelling between Elephant and Marylebone) had already been completed, but then faltered due to insuf-ficient funding.

In April 1902, a crucial development occurred which would affect all aspects of trans-port in the capital, particularly the design of the new deep-level tubes: Yerkes formed the Underground Electric Railway Company of London (UERL). With reliable funding in place, building recommenced on the Bakerloo and construction began on both the Piccadilly and the Hampstead lines under the charge of the newly appointed young UERL architect Leslie Green (p. 61). The District, meanwhile, had been in the process of completing a new section of line between Ealing and South Harrow and decided to use it as a testing ground for the forthcoming transfer from steam power. Electrified from the outset, and with new engines and carriages designed accordingly, the line opened on 23 June 1903. The stations (North Ealing, Park Royal & Twyford Abbey, Alperton, Sudbury Town and Sudbury Hill) were, by contrast, relatively modest timber structures – the one at Park Royal so awkwardly sited that it looked as though it might teeter off the embankment! The single exception was North Ealing, where a smart, two-storey brick-built station was erected.

A stylish orphan

While electrification was being tested and the three deep-level lines were under construc-tion, another odd line came into being, also adopting the white ceramic tile model for its interior decor. The Great Northern and City Railway (GNCR), opened in 1904, was planned as a direct branch of the Great Northern Railway (GNR), peeling off from the main line at Finsbury Park and diving underground near Drayton Park to run all the way to Moorgate (and one day, it was hoped, to head south of the river).[35] The tunnel size was wider, bored to a diameter of 4.9m to accommodate mainline trains. Platform signage was also unusual in that it had black lettering on a white background. The stations on this line also sported unique features: Essex Road had a 12m tower, Highbury a small dome and Drayton Park looked semi-rural (see p. 47 for all three), while each had moulded lettering in its signage that seemed to foreshadow Green's leaning towards Arts and Crafts motifs (p. 72).

The stage is set for further electrification

The Met was still pushing into open farmland; it had acquired the Harrow and Uxbridge Railway with the aim of running an electrified service from the first day, but because the power station had not been built (and the Met was still ruminating over its choice of supply), the 11km route opened with steam trains on 4 July 1904. With the exception of Ruislip (a long grand brick building with a set-back wing and tiled roofs), stations along this section were some of the most elementary yet seen. Only Ruislip opened on the day,

London Underground by Design

Ickenham following in 1905 and Eastcote a year later — the latter two existing for many years as little more than wooden-platformed halts in the middle of fields.

Although the Met and District had bickered with each other almost since the District's inception, they were both agreed on one thing: the success of electric traction on the CSLR and CLR had proved that the days of steam trains in underground tunnels were numbered. Despite more arguments (over whether to supply power from an overhead wire or fourth-rail system) the District's tracks (including the entire Inner Circle, shared with the Met) were finally electrified in February 1905 by one of the UERL's companies. The electricity was generated by an immense new power station at Lots Road on the edge of Chelsea Creek (decommissioned in 2002).

On 10 October 1905, the District opened a station between West Kensington and Hammersmith in an entirely new style for the company. Designed by Harry Wharton Ford, Barons Court appears to be an interesting hybrid of the old and new; appropriate, as it was to serve both the District and the new Piccadilly, which was about to arrive there. Ford, meanwhile, was destined to play a bigger role in the Underground's design history (p. 63).

The advances in architectural design and engineering made by London's emerging urban transport network were already a source of inspiration for the subterranean electric railways being set up in Paris, New York and Boston. But as companies expanded and competed with each other, and with the UERL Group's three major new lines now under construction, the stage was now set for an unprecedented boom in underground rail travel and a revolution in transport design.

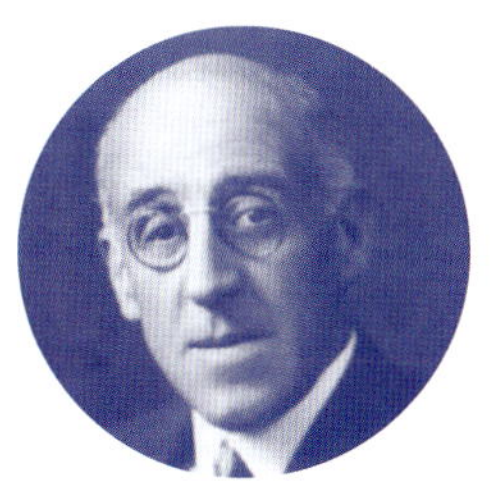

Harry Wharton Ford (1875–1947), born in London, was District Railway/UERL staff architect (1899–1901) before setting up his own practice in 1909. Involved in the design or reconstruction of at least seventeen stations, Ford's style varied from Arts and Crafts (Barons Court) to classical (Charing Cross (Embankment)). While he claimed to have designed not only the red discs around nameboards but also the enlarged 'U' and 'D' of the Underground wordmark (p. 63), other individuals may have had a hand in the discs and the jury is still out concerning the oversized first and last letters.

A southward spoke, 1890

Although drawn in 1886 for the CSLR's predecessor, the City of London and Southwark Subway, this beautifully executed map (1) shows very clearly how the proposed new tube (in red) would fit into the populated borough of Lambeth and link it directly to the City (when the line was built and opened in 1890 (p. 44),

it ran three stations further down to Stockwell). A fascinating monochrome map (opposite, 1) from the 1890 *Ward & Lock's Pictorial Guide to London* shows the full extent of the CSLR as opened from Stockwell to King William Street. Apart from containing an early, if not the first, example of 'open casing' (thin strokes outlining a thicker line – seen on later Tube maps, p. 91), the map is

curious in being oriented with the south at the top and the north at the bottom. It looks as if it was taken from an earlier engraving as the place names are upside down, while the names of CSLR stations and a couple of major roads have been set the right way up.

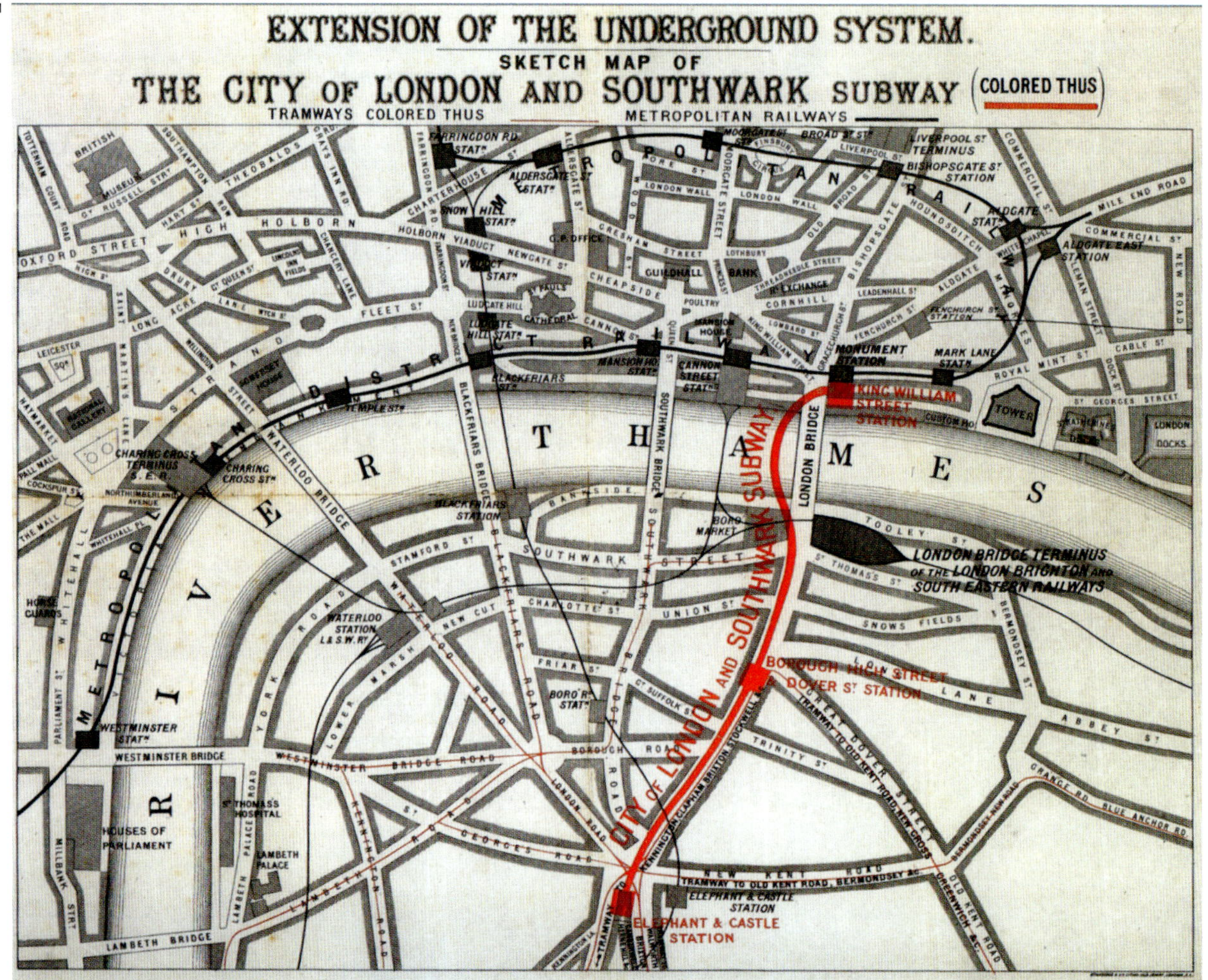

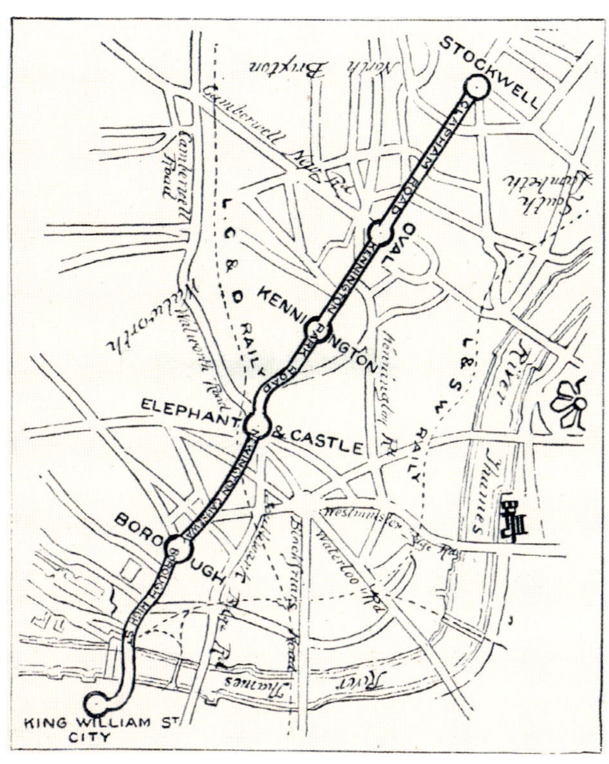

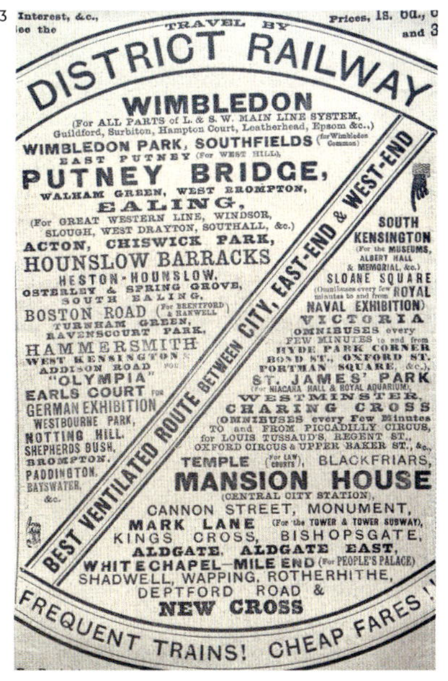

One of the best ways for the emerging underground lines to attract new passengers was to publicize the many and varied 'exhibitions' so popular at the time. At every opportunity a new map was produced (often simply an overprint of an existing map or cover) extolling the virtues of using one line over another in getting to the venue. One District map cover (2) proclaims how useful the line's services are for reaching the 1891 Royal Naval Exhibition – though the actual site was still a fair walk from Sloane Square station. The serifed letterform popular with the District has not been used for the company name in this instance but employed instead for the exhibition name and the word 'GUIDE'. Fliers and posters of the period were almost invariably a sea of different type styles, and this example from 1891 (3) is no exception. As it optimistically claims, the District offers the 'best ventilated' route across the city; probably true if the passenger enjoys their fresh air mixed with a good dose of sulphur and soot!

CSLR design firsts, 1890

Below the domed stations (such as
Stockwell, 1), CSLR passages and
platforms were covered in white
oblong 'glazed bricks' (2 and p. 35).
A stylized fern motif bordered by tiles
in burnt red (3) provided a distinctive
touch, and possibly influenced later
station designs. Given how grubby and
cluttered Met and District platform
walls had become (p. 25), passengers
must have felt the CSLR's white-tiled
walls with simple station names were
a breath of fresh air. This antiseptically
clean decor clearly influenced the CLR
(p. 48) and the Paris Métro — both of
which opened in 1900 with almost
identical white tiling. The station
name lettering was probably the same
at each location. The only recorded
1890 example is from the abandoned
King William Street terminus (p. 35) —
rediscovered during a 1930s press tour
of the derelict station (now sealed off).
Digitally restored for this book, this
photo (6) gives an idea of how well the
dark letters of the station name stood
out against an uncluttered white background. The 'WAY OUT' sign with pointing
fingers was positioned high above
the tiled frieze (4). Station name signs
may have been paper labels, possibly
integral to the design or possibly added
afterwards. It was undoubtedly seen by
Leslie Green (p. 71) and other designers
working on the sub-surface railway
lines. Tunnels needed to be wider for
the island platforms introduced at CSLR
stations (5), the white tiles helping to
reflect the gas lighting, which, compared
with modern illumination, was very dim
indeed.

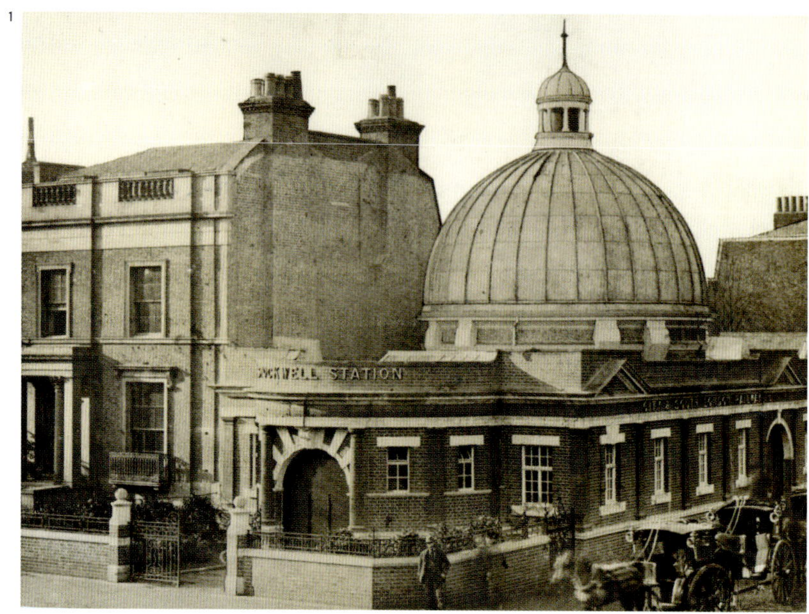

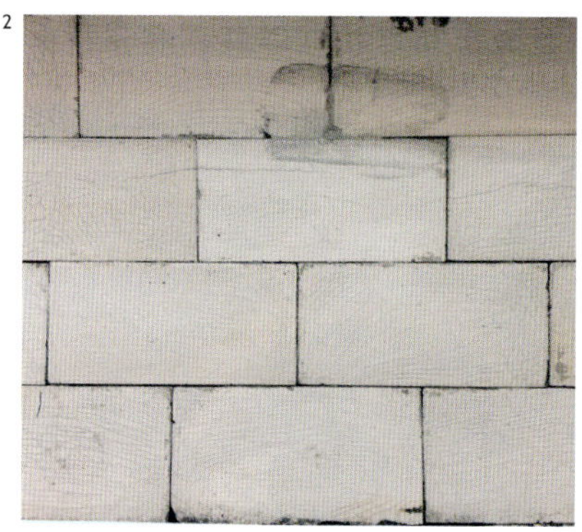

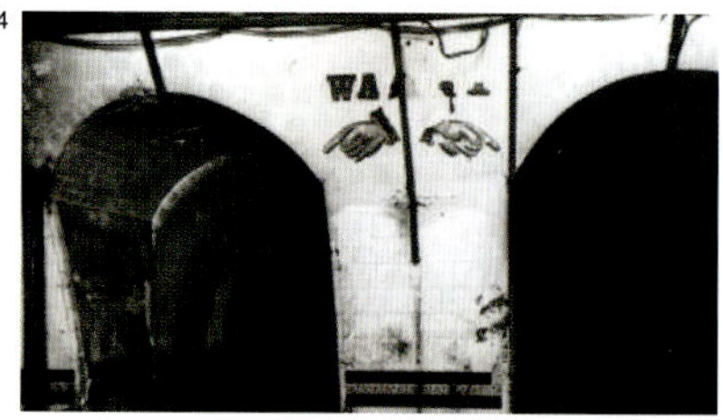

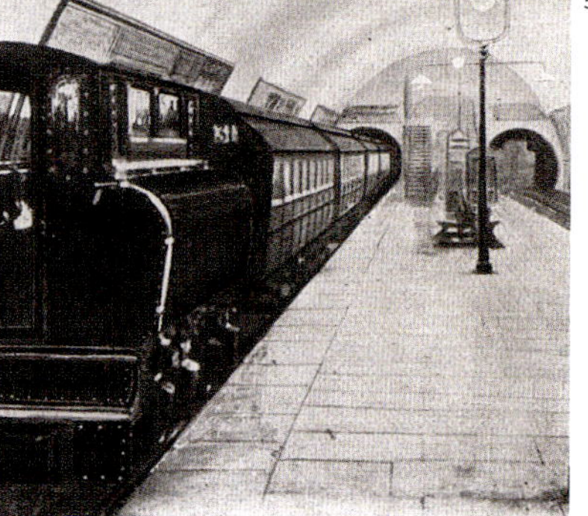

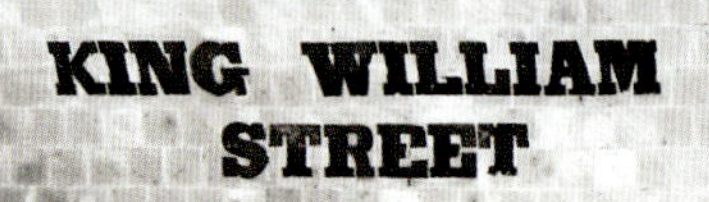

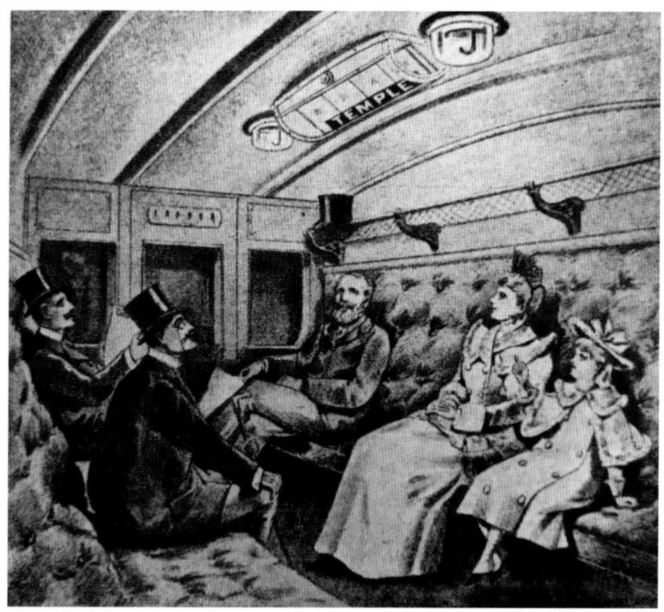

In the 1860s, only basic signage was provided — the station name and the exit — but by the 1890s other forms of passenger information were introduced. A *Railway Gazette* sketch (from around 1894, 1) shows a 'direction of travel indicator' inside a District carriage. Railway signage was always in shouty capital letters, yet standardization was already in evidence: company and station name appear in District serif lettering, while destinations were rendered in the 'platform' style of sans-serif capitals. High brick walls on Met and District platforms were festooned with advertisements, as at Victoria (pp. 32–3). The adverts generated income, but the sheer number of them caused nameboards to be lost in a morass of varying lettering. Further afield nameboards appeared on their own, however, such as these for Brill Tramway (2 and 3), owned by the Met and using the company style. The name sign shape proved key to the later evolution of the bullseye and corporate identity generally (pp. 67 and 84). Believed to be the earliest known photograph of a railway map *outside* a station, this 1892 shot of Parsons Green (4) shows a District map pasted either side of the entrance, raising the question why maps were not placed at these crucial entry points before. The practice would become standard at London Underground stations and rail systems worldwide.

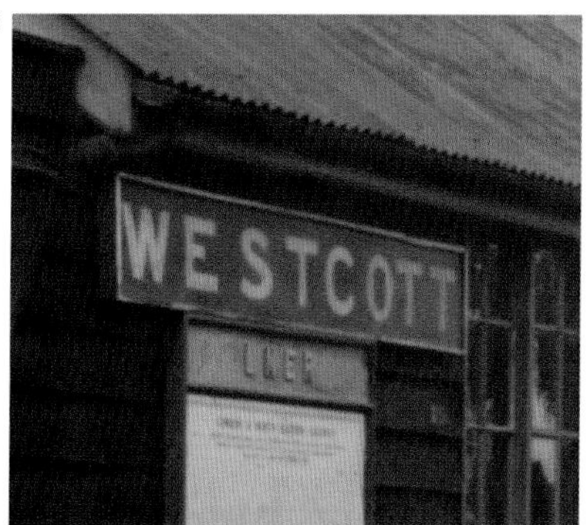

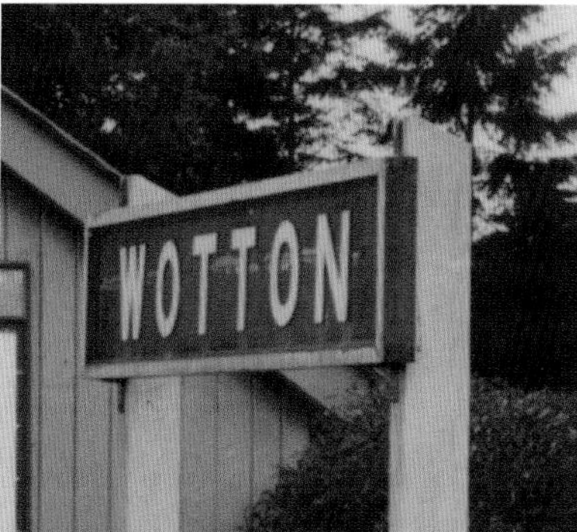

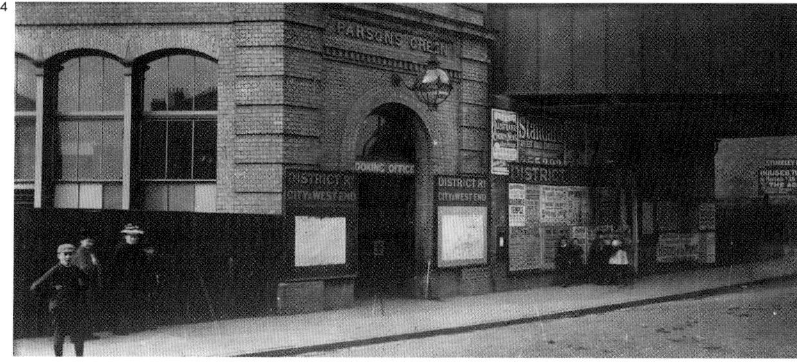

CSLR station architecture, 1900

Opened in 1900, the two new Clapham stations were both single-storey, brick-built affairs with wide-arched windows and entranceways topped by decorated pediments. Each had a stone-banded parapet approximately a metre high, but other details were different: the station at the Common (1) had a curved pediment, for instance, while the other, Clapham Road (now Clapham North) had a triangular one. Both buildings have since been replaced. The CSLR company headquarters was situated above Moorgate station in offices designed by Figgis (detail, 2). Though opened in 1900, it is pictured here (3) at a later date (1915), when the floors above were for rent – possibly after the CSLR had moved out following its takeover (p. 68). Much of the original building remains in use, though renovated several times.

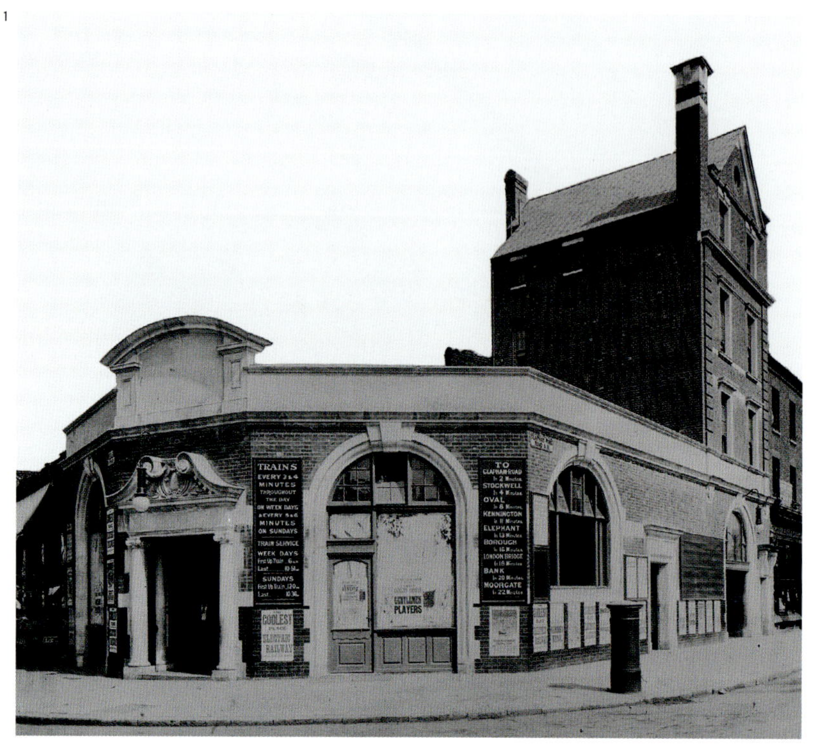

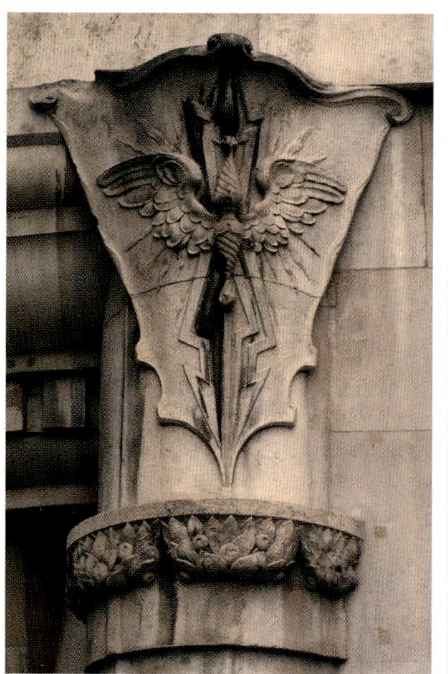

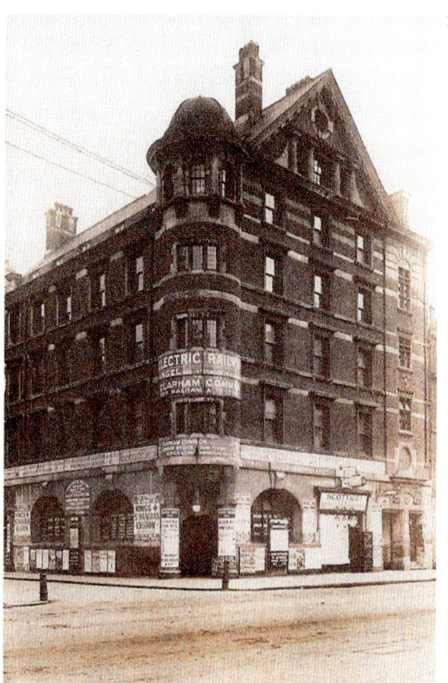

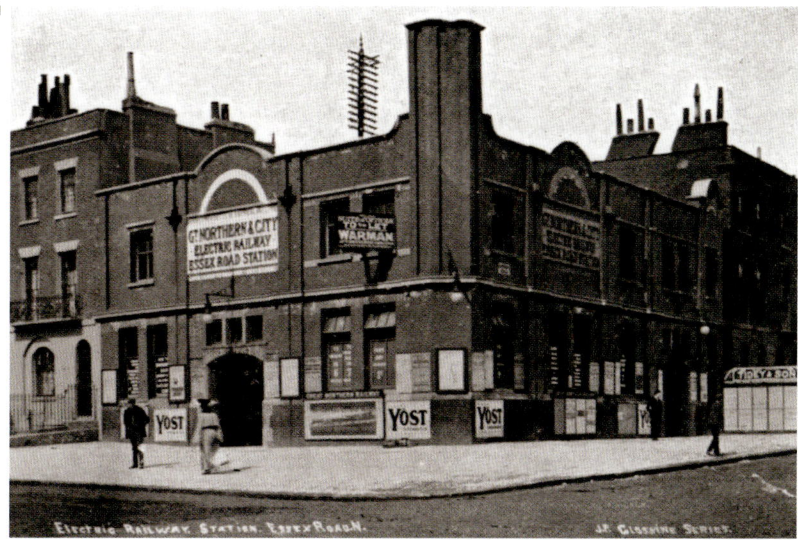

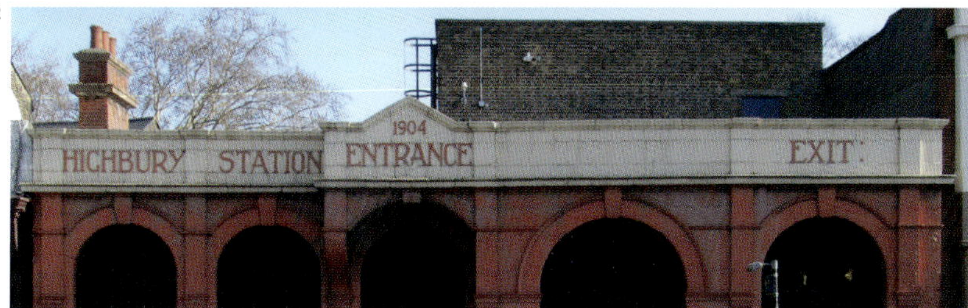

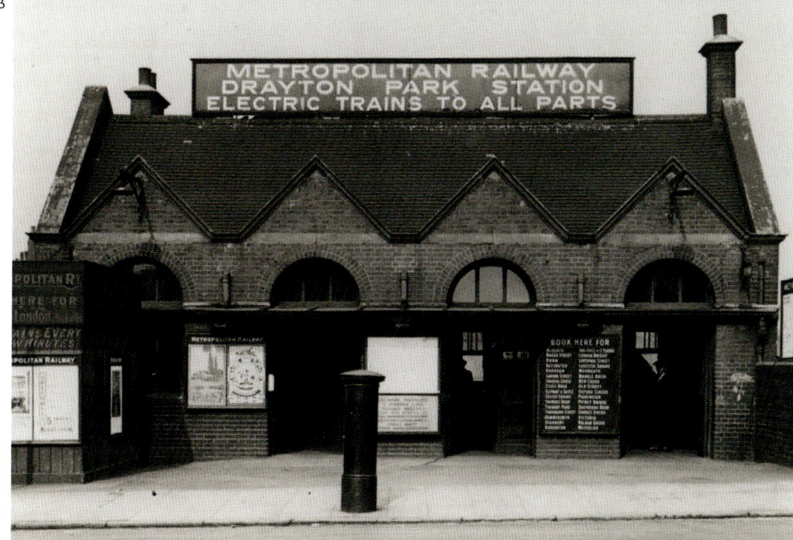

Architectural experiments, 1904

While the GNCR, which opened in 1904, was innovative with its wider running tunnels (p. 40), it also tried a new approach at the surface. Lettering was more serifed and station style unique to each site. At Essex Road station (1), a two-storey brick structure, the corner featured a small tower (12m high) and in the centre of each side elevation there was a large panel where the company name was mounted in serifed capitals below a semicircular parapet with a white stone band, the shape of it coincidentally in harmony with later signage. The building still stands today. At Highbury (later Highbury & Islington, 2) a single-storey building was constructed, consisting of five arched bays with a separate entrance and exit, and a small dome sitting over the left-hand end. Though later abandoned (in 1968), this building also still stands; its doors may now be boarded up but the station name on the parapet, in serifed relief lettering, remains proudly displayed. Drayton Park (shown after the line was taken over by the Met on 1 September 1913, 3), being a surface station, was another one-off design, more resembling rural railway buildings of the period with its pitched roof and gable ends echoed on the front elevation with triangular pediments above four arched bays. The station building remains relatively unchanged, including the pillar box!

CLR raises design standards, 1900

The CLR took its design cues from
the CSLR. For the opening of the CLR
in 1900, a set of 'way out' exit signs
(at least four for each station) were
ordered from the Chromographic
Enamel Company of Dudley Road,
Wolverhampton (established in 1885
and invariably abbreviated on the
bottom right corner of each sign as
'Chromo Wolverhampton'). Most had
the finger-pointing direction arrow (3).
They were about 120cm wide x 30cm
high, with white sans-serif capitals on a
dark (black or blue) background. Though
all now replaced, a few exceptional
signs survive, like this one with a white
background (4) at Holland Park. Queen's
Road (which became Queensway),
seen just before opening in 1900 (5),
is resplendent in its bright, white tiles,
electric lighting and large, clear nameboard. Similar decor and fittings, with
additional signage and platform-facing
advert spaces, can be seen in these
photos of Shepherd's Bush from the
early 1900s (1 and 2) – design features
that would not seem out of place on
an underground platform today. These
images were produced as souvenir
postcards for the line's opening.

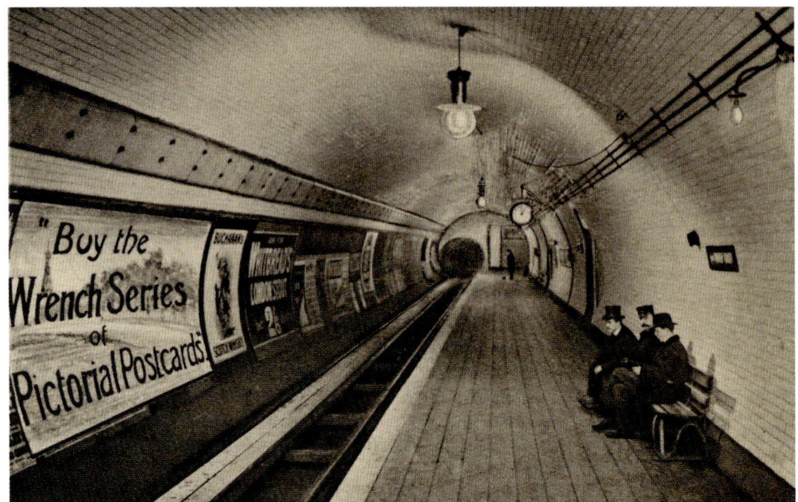

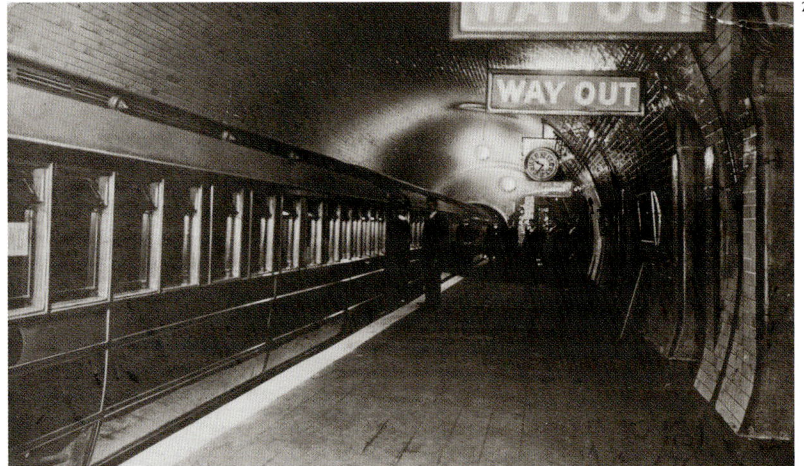

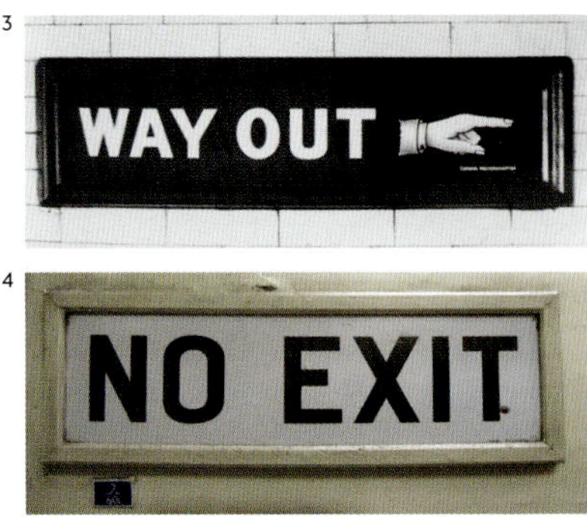

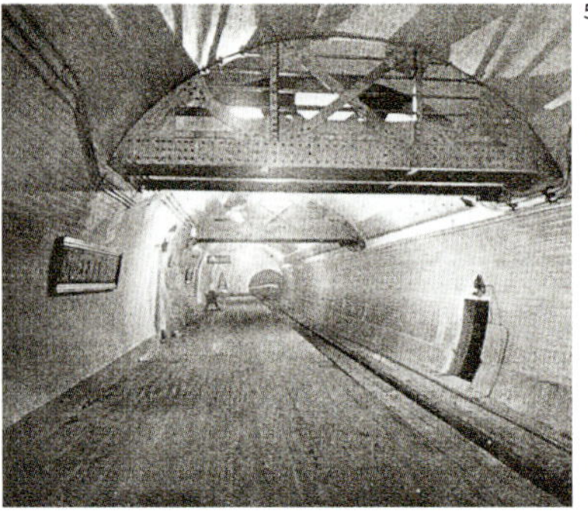

London Underground by Design

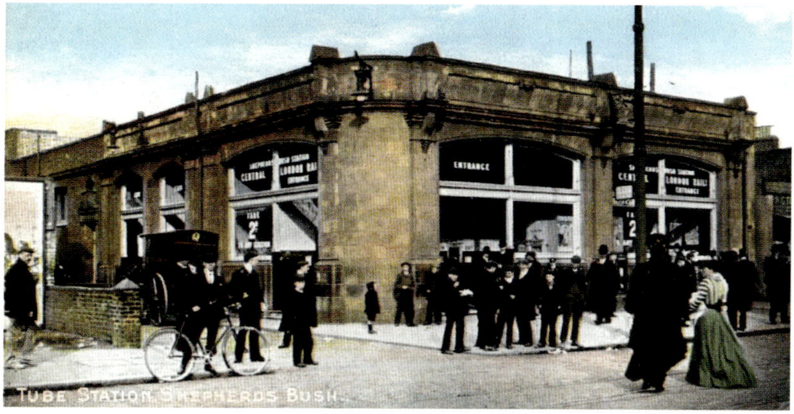

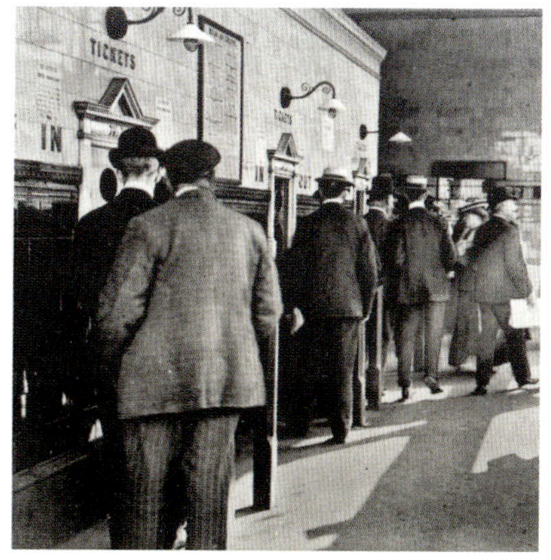

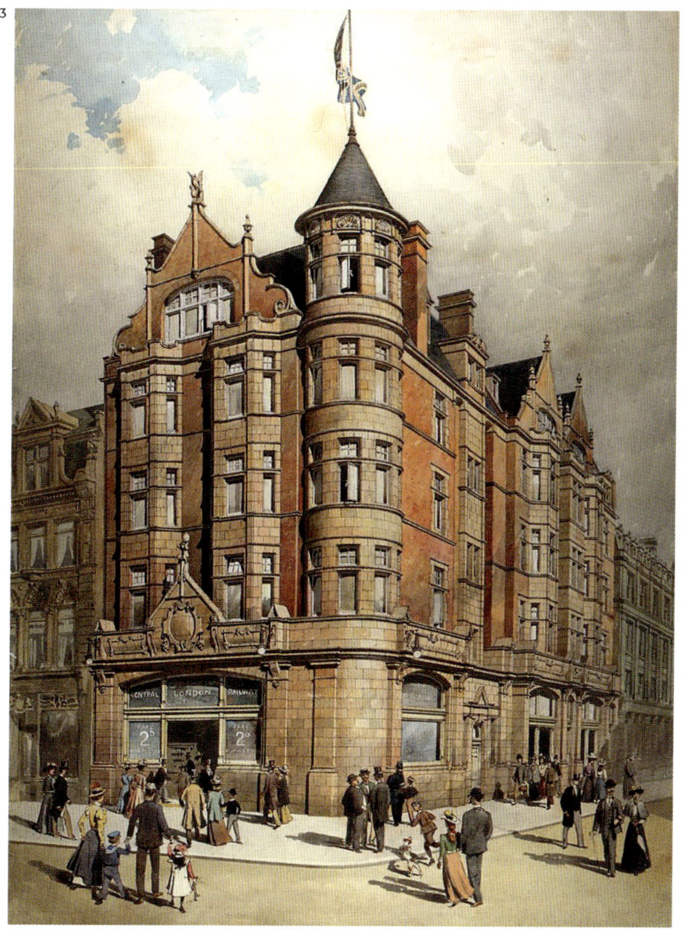

A hand-coloured postcard of Shepherd's Bush station just after its opening in 1900 (1), shows the pinkish terracotta of Harry Bell Measures's new design, looking bright and distinctive in the London streetscape. Here signs made using cut-out letters can be seen glued to the windows. In the booking office (2) signage is mounted in relief on the tiled wall above a window capped with a stylish pediment, behind which sat the ticket seller. Designed to be strong enough to have further storeys added (p. 38), almost all CLR stations were built on, enabling many to survive, even in the heart of London's expensive real estate — for example, at Oxford Circus where the booking hall soon proved too small and has long since been reconstructed (3). Holland Park is the only CLR building not to have had floors added above it. Notting Hill Gate was built on a separate site from the Met station of the same name, obliging passengers to rise to street level before making a connection between the two lines (until almost sixty years later, p. 228).

District leads the way in rail map design, 1892–7

The 1892 District map cover (1) was illustrated with London landmarks and the slogan 'time is money'. The company name is similar to much platform signage and 'MAP OF LONDON' rendered in an almost identical letterform to that on station fronts. If not deliberate, the similarity of lettering used on stations and in print is noteworthy. The map itself (2) shifts focus west to highlight the District's new hinterland. Other lines, including the Met and the new CSLR, are shown in a narrower stroke. A proposed line from Paddington around the northern edge of Regents Park to Stratford might have been a boon but was among many that never materialized.

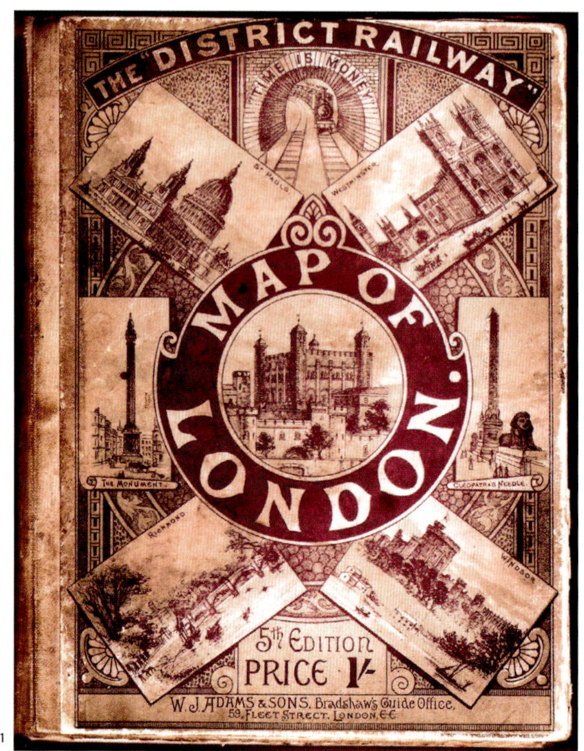

1

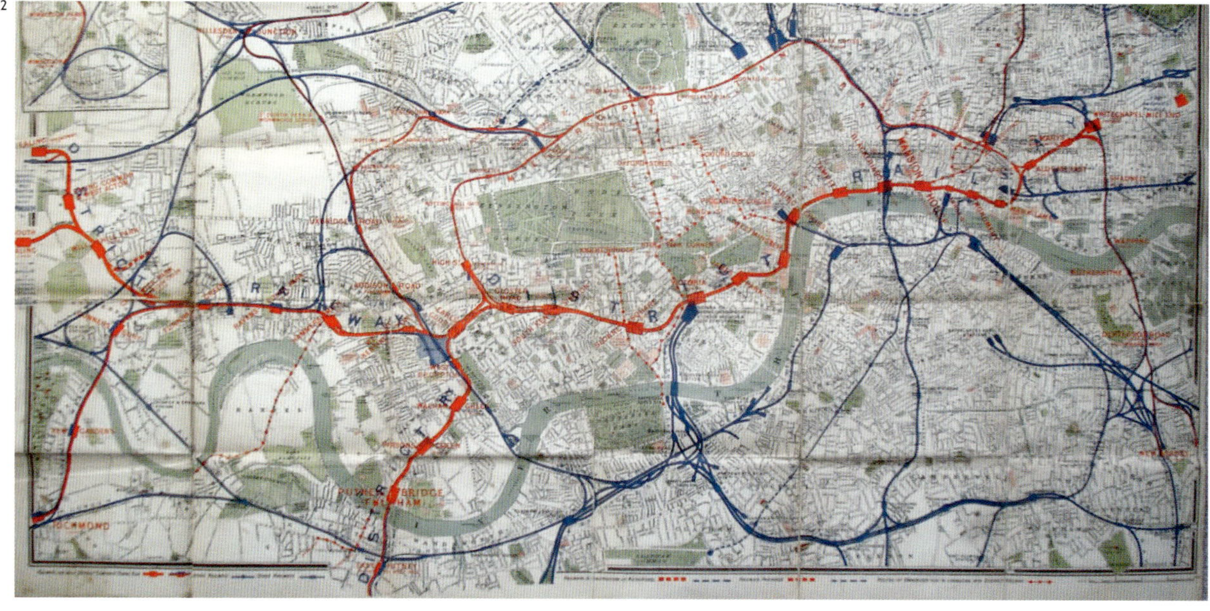

2

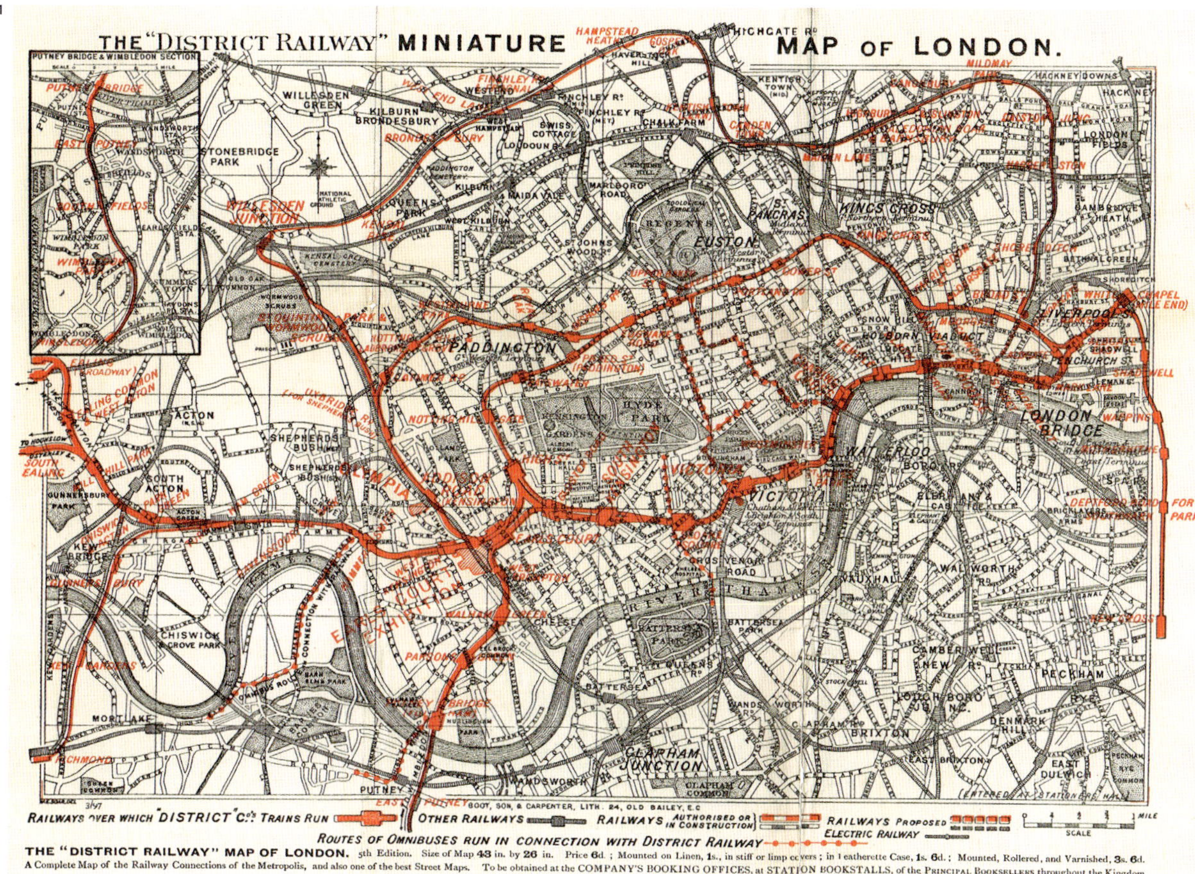

The 1897 District pocket map, at 28.5 x 22.5cm (1), was not the smallest and nor was it an entirely new concept – forerunners of this map had appeared 'tipped in' to guide books since at least 1883 – but this one was entirely self-standing, folding down neatly to 14.5 x 10cm. Perfect for portability, it was therefore arguably the first official pocket map ever produced. The cartographer's name, 'W. E. Soar', is printed on it – possibly for the first time – although the base engraving of London's streets is not so new, dating to at least the early 1880s. An inset panel for the Wimbledon branch is added top left and the ELR is squeezed in somewhat ungainly fashion on the right, begging for a new background to be drawn to include that part of the city.

Publicity hots up, 1901–5

Mainline railway companies had already adopted the poster as an effective marketing tool, and as competition stiffened in London, the District and Met both used the same strategy in their attempt to woo back passengers from the CLR. A 1901 quad royal-sized District poster (1) gives the names of nearby streets to its stations. In another poster (2), the Met advertises that its trains will run until 02.30 hours to allow revellers to join in the fun of King Edward VII's coronation in 1902. Despite its earlier success, the CLR was forced to hit back, and this 1905 example (3) certainly gives the impression that the route was light, bright and clean. The reality, with hot platforms (a problem even then) and metal dust from the brakes, was perhaps a little different. Of greater interest is the inclusion of a map — almost a route diagram, one of the first of its kind — and the well-thought-through design, combining key aspects of the CLR's look (the distinctive station architecture, interior decor and vehicle design) with clever catchphrases. It makes this poster the first to highlight the entire passenger journey through the system using a mixture of graphics/cartographic elements and memorable slogans. This pioneering piece of publicity can be seen as an early groping towards a coherent corporate identity on multiple levels, just pre-dating, and therefore possibly influencing, the work of those designing the new deep-level tubes.

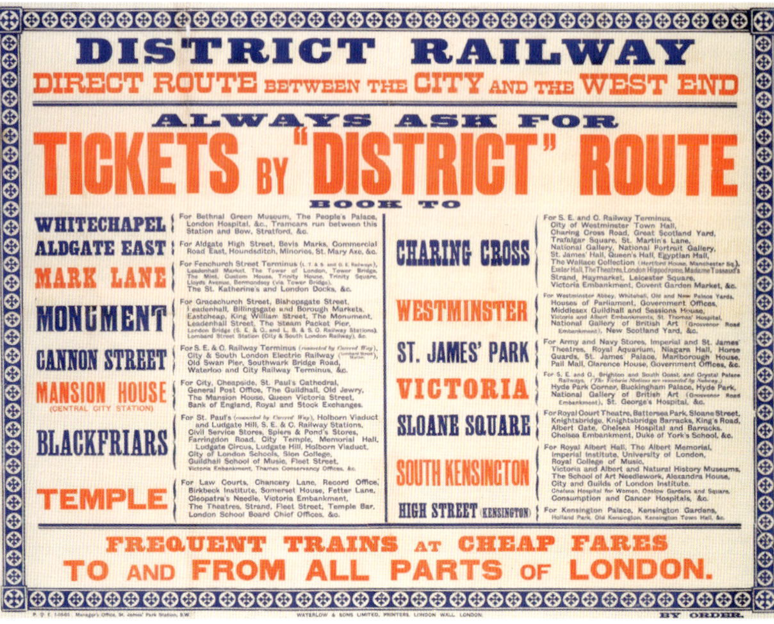

1

2

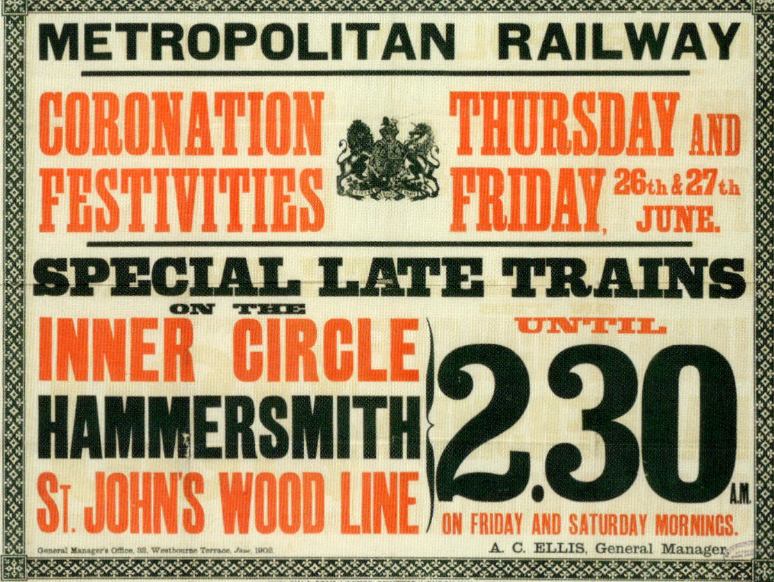

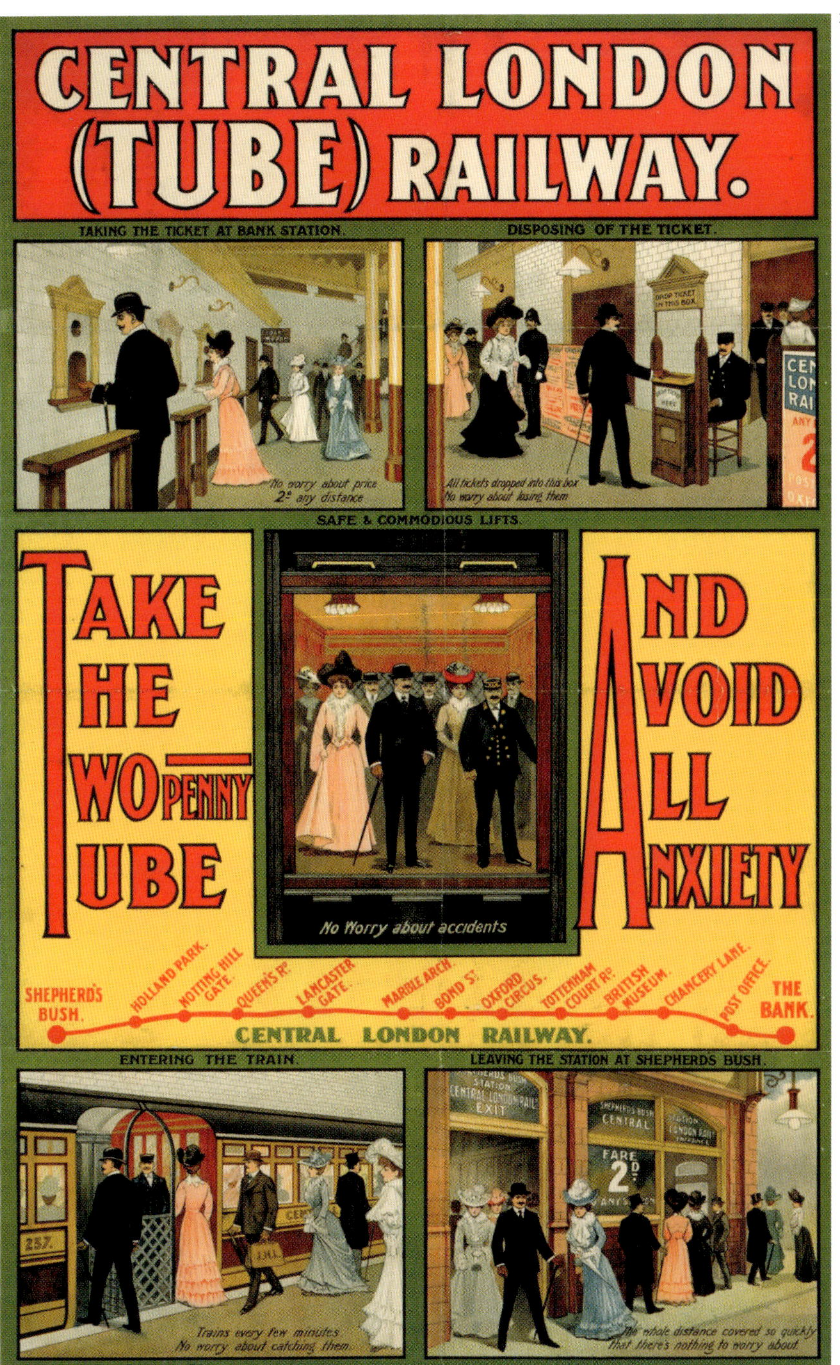
CENTRAL LONDON
(TUBE) RAILWAY.
TAKING THE TICKET AT BANK STATION.
DISPOSING OF THE TICKET.
DROP TICKET IN THIS BOX.
No worry about price
2ᵈ any distance
All tickets dropped into this box
No worry about losing them
SAFE & COMMODIOUS LIFTS.
TAKE
THE
TWO PENNY
TUBE
AND
AVOID
ALL
ANXIETY
No Worry about accidents
SHEPHERD'S BUSH.
HOLLAND PARK.
NOTTING HILL GATE.
QUEEN'S Rᴰ
LANCASTER GATE.
MARBLE ARCH.
BOND Sᵀ
OXFORD CIRCUS.
TOTTENHAM COURT Rᴰ
BRITISH MUSEUM.
CHANCERY LANE.
POST OFFICE
THE BANK.
CENTRAL LONDON RAILWAY.
ENTERING THE TRAIN.
LEAVING THE STATION AT SHEPHERD'S BUSH.
FARE 2ᵈ
Trains every few minutes
No worry about catching them.
The whole distance covered so quickly
that there's nothing to worry about.

Vehicle design, 1900–1905

The CSLR had led the world in electric railways running through petite circular tunnels (p. 34), but the larger-bore and much longer CLR tunnels gave vehicle manufacturers the chance to build more powerful and smarter cars. The CLR's first batch of 44-ton, American-built 'camel-backed' electric locomotives (1) were deemed to cause too much vibration (and were very noisy), so replacements were ordered from another US company, Sprague-Thomson-Houston (which also supplied the Paris Métro for many years). It pioneered a 'multiple-unit' system (in which each car powers its own wheels but all the motors are controlled from the driver's cab) initially tried in Chicago, 1898. The CLR vehicles became the first of their kind in the UK and the design went on to be used for all subsequent Tube train manufacture. Cars were plum-coloured at the front end and lower half, with a white stripe under the windows and 'CENTRAL LONDON' (the word 'RAILWAY' seemingly deemed unnecessary) in 30cm-high, gold sans-serif capitals (2). In the 1900 Stock (3), armrests were padded but the seating was not cushioned (by contrast with the CSLR), consisting of wooden panels with ventilation holes drilled in an aesthetically pleasing pattern. By 1903 the seating had been cushioned, sprung and upholstered in an attractive moquette. The front had a distinctive faceted roof and windows either side of a central door through which the driver accessed the cab: a feature to be repeated for many years on the London Tube.

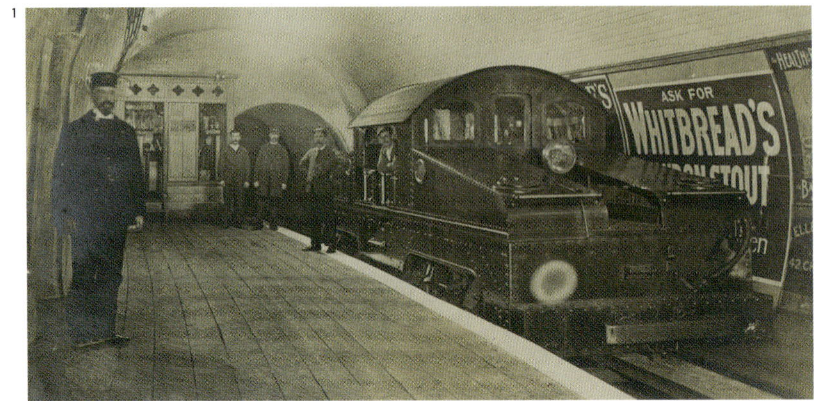

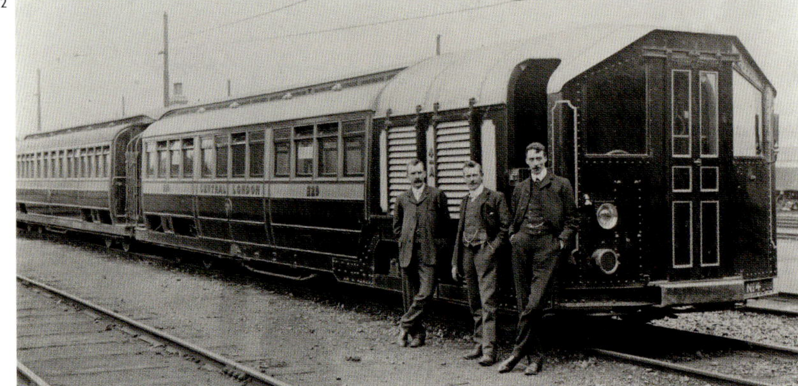

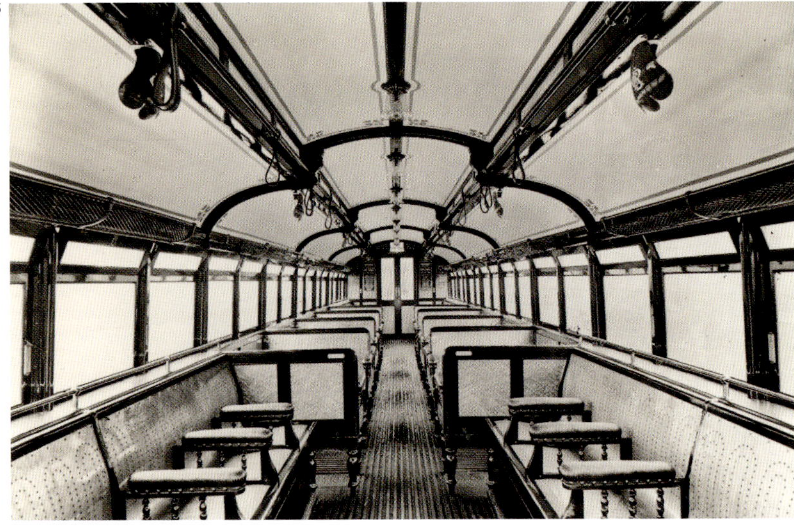

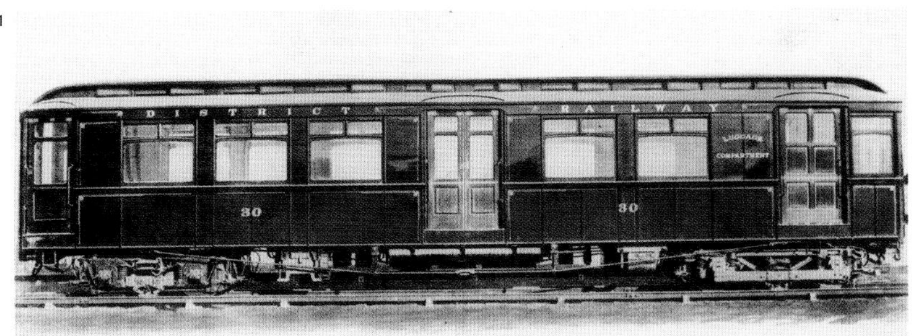

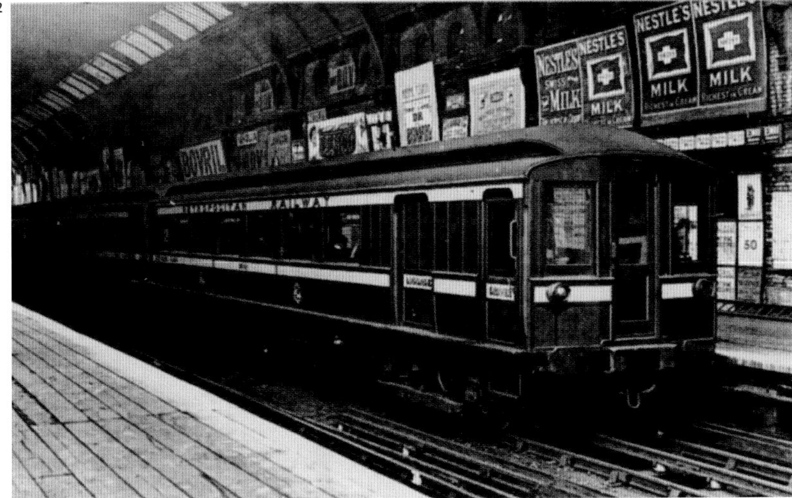

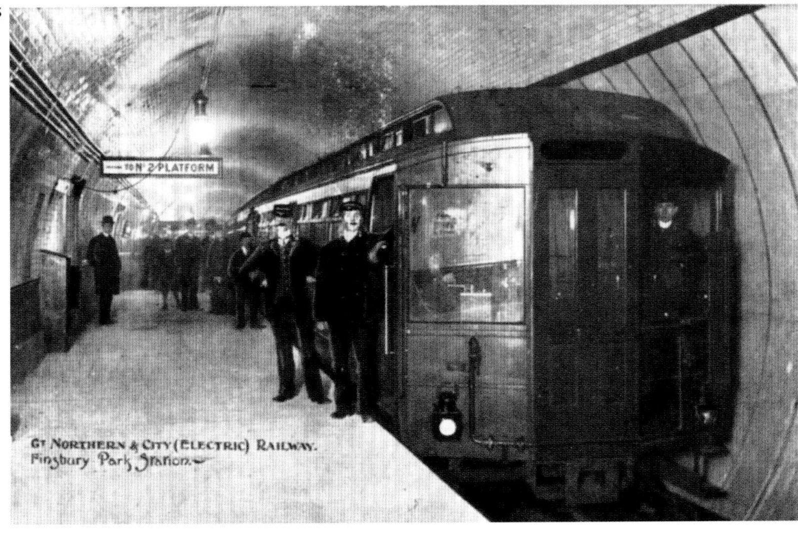

The sooty, grimy atmosphere on the District and Met was now in stark contrast to the clean, modern and smoke-free environment of the newer electric railways, so the evolution to electrification from steam power was inevitable. After several experiments (and many arguments) the main sections of both lines were converted to electric traction and new engines and trailer cars were ordered. The District's first electric rolling stock was brought into full passenger service in 1905 (1). Larger than the tube-railway cars, they were equally influenced by American designers (brought over specially from the US by Yerkes to work on the electrification project), though these were entirely built in the UK and France. The wooden bodies featured classic, American-style 'clerestory' roofs, for extra light at surface sections. The earliest ones were painted bright yellow with maroon detailing – a colour scheme that was quickly abandoned as, after nearly four decades of being caked in soot, there was still a lot of dirt in the tunnels. The next batch were maroon all over with varnished natural-wood doors. The words 'DISTRICT RAILWAY' were painted in serifed capitals above the windows. The Met had been preparing for its Uxbridge branch to be run by electric rolling stock from day one. Its cars were all built at Neasden and one is shown here at Bayswater station in 1905 (2). GNCR trains of 1904 were the same size as mainline ones (3), and now the line is linked to the national network, full-sized stock use the tunnels. The Waterloo & City line was so popular in the rush hour it had to buy extra cars by 1900.

Mapping the new tubes, 1900–1904

One of a number of postcards produced around the time of the CLR's opening is the Power House at Wood Lane (1904, 1), but of special interest is the line diagram underneath the photograph. This was the most simplified route map shown to date (line maps did not appear inside the trains until about 1908, p. 93). Although the CLR stations were fairly evenly spaced along the line, here they are shown as equidistant, introducing a degree of schematics — distorting the representation of a geographic space. The line is smoothed out into a pure horizontal and, significantly for what Beck achieved in the 1930s (p. 168), the two ends are both turned up at almost exactly 45 degrees. Other lines, including the as yet unopened Bakerloo and what became the Piccadilly, are shown thinner and also given somewhat unrealistic trajectories. In complete contrast to the CLR diagram, the GNCR used a purely geographic map (detail, also 1904, 2) to show the position and connections of its short line. Points of interest are the CSLR extension to Angel and the blue marking of the Waterloo & City line (not often shown), but once again the unhelpful rivalry between railway companies is evident in that other services, including the Met, District and ELR, are reduced to thin black lines, although the CLR, oddly, is shown slightly bolder. Such petty treatment of the other lines was one of the reasons why the entire system was ripe for melding together — a long overdue amalgamation that was about to happen (pp. 61–4).

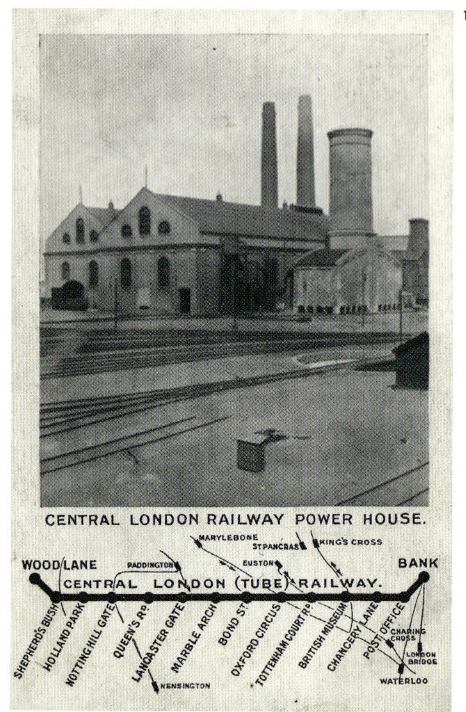

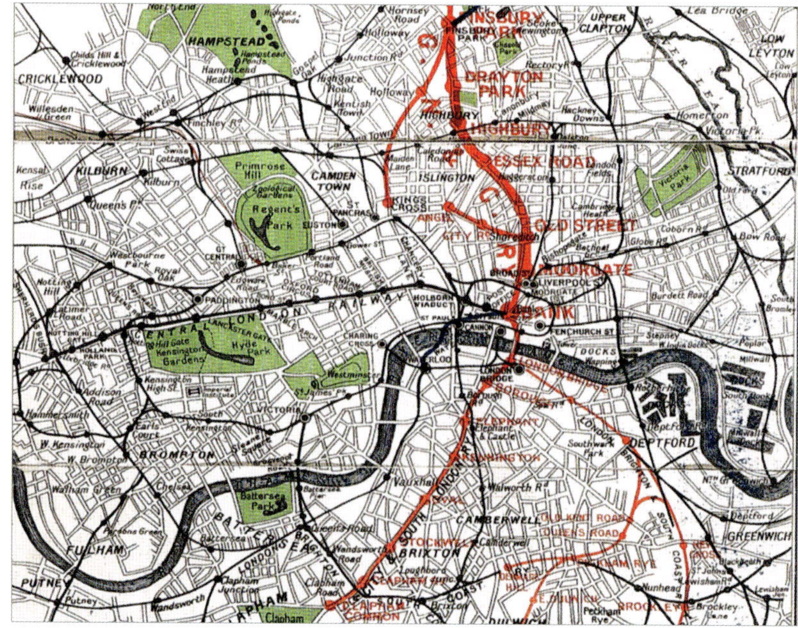

London Underground by Design

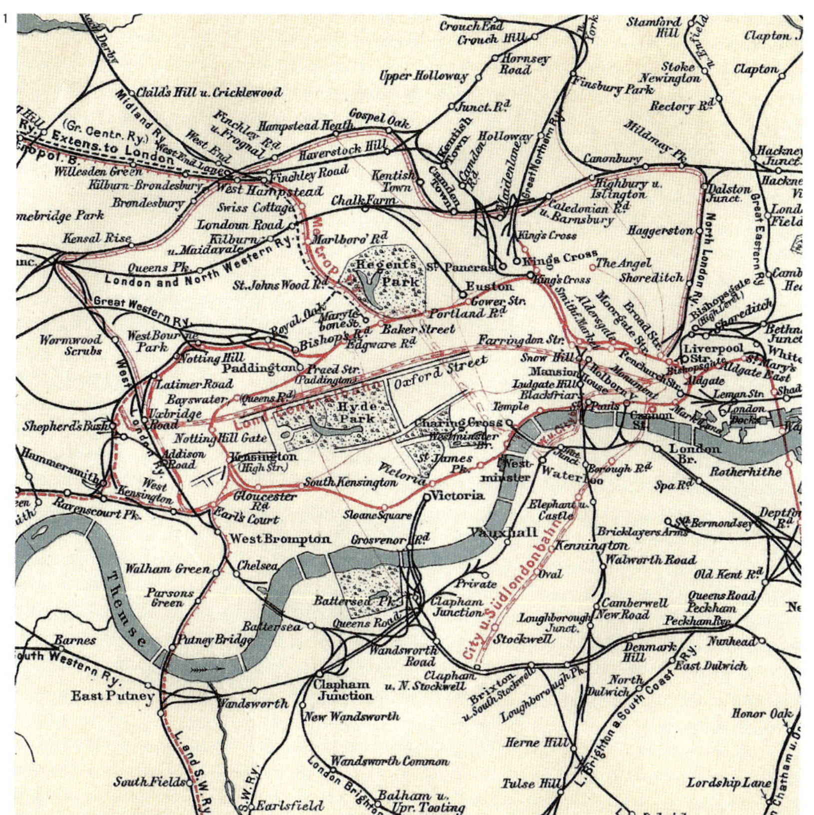

Baedeker's *London and its Environs 1900* had included a map of the capital's railways before the CLR was open (detail, 1). The trajectory of the new route beneath Oxford Street, London's longest and best-known thoroughfare, was easy to visualize, but the CLR understood the power of maps. One of its first (from 1902, 2) followed the trend of rivals by overprinting a red line on a pre-existing, highly detailed street plan. The density of the black ink makes it difficult to make out station names, but for any new line establishing itself, the marking of the route on a topographic map is undeniably sensible. Partial routes of the forthcoming deep-level tubes are shown as dotted black lines. The CLR took advantage of its almost straight line in subsequent publicity (p. 93) and a larger sized version of this map was pasted on walls inside stations.

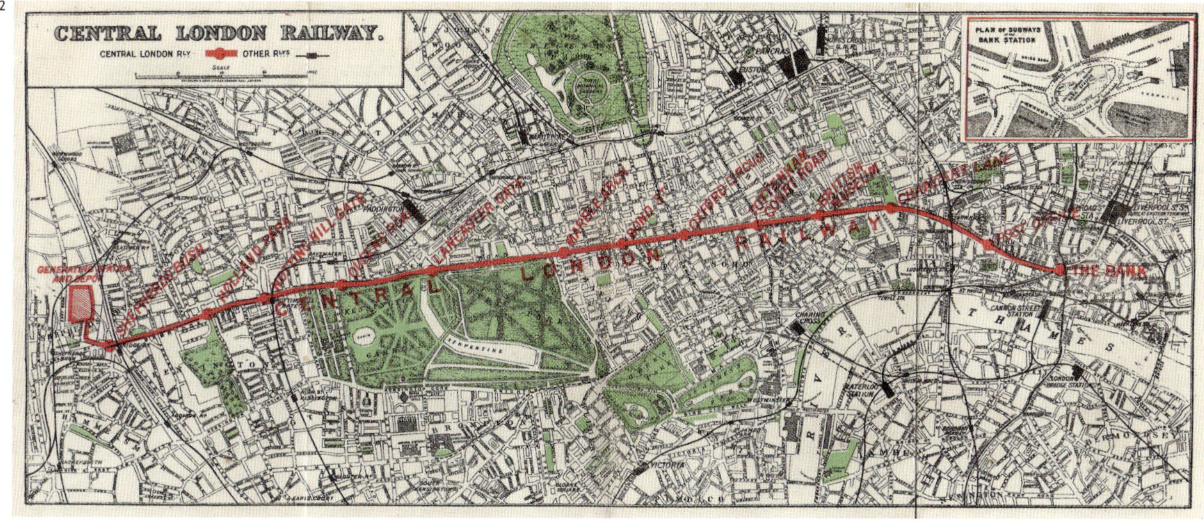

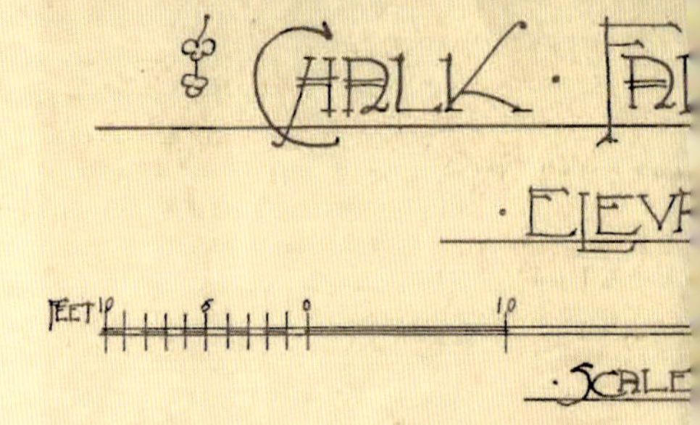
CHALK · FA
· ELEVA
SCALE

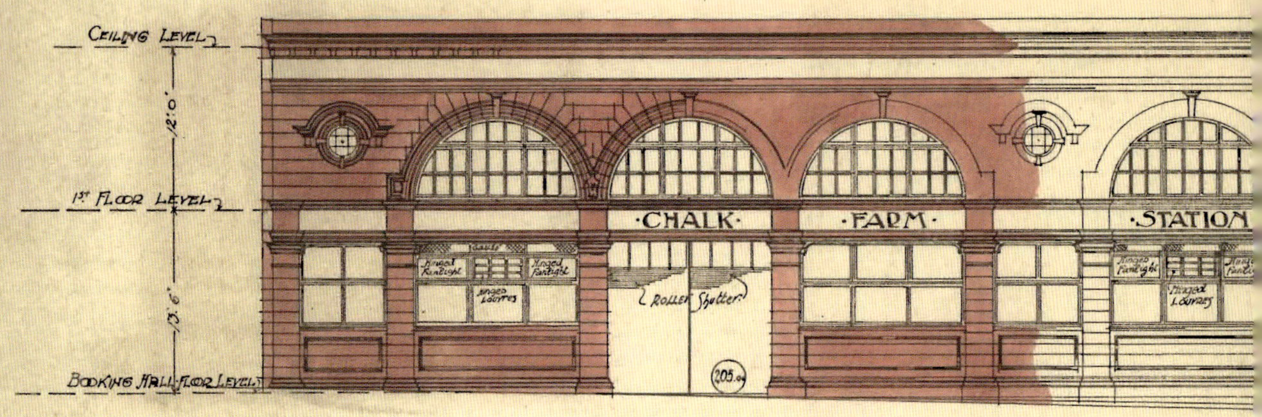
CEILING LEVEL
1ST FLOOR LEVEL
BOOKING HALL FLOOR LEVEL
12'0"
13'6"
·CHALK· ·FARM· ·STATION
Hinged Fanlight
Hinged Louvres
Hinged Fanlight
Roller Shutter
205.0
Hinged Fanlight
Hinged Louvres
Approx
ELEVATION · T

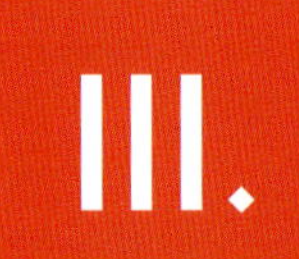
III.

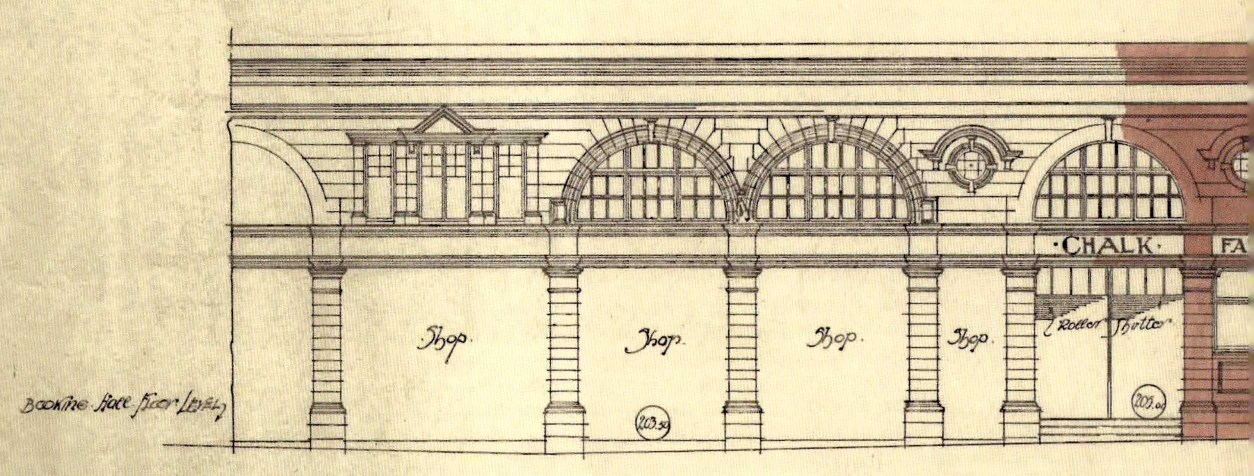
·CHALK· FA
Shop. Shop. Shop. Shop. Roller Shutter
205.0
BOOKING HALL FLOOR LEVEL
203.0

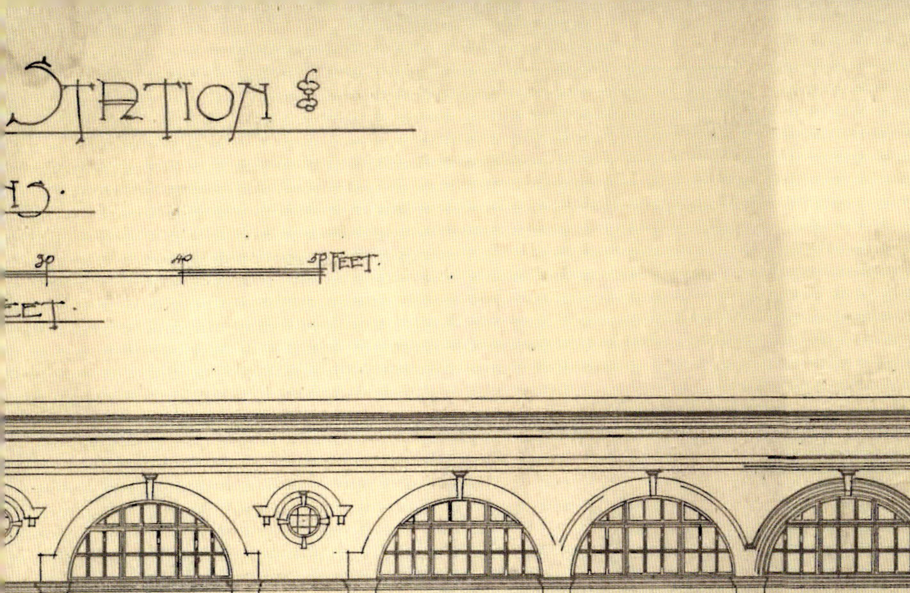

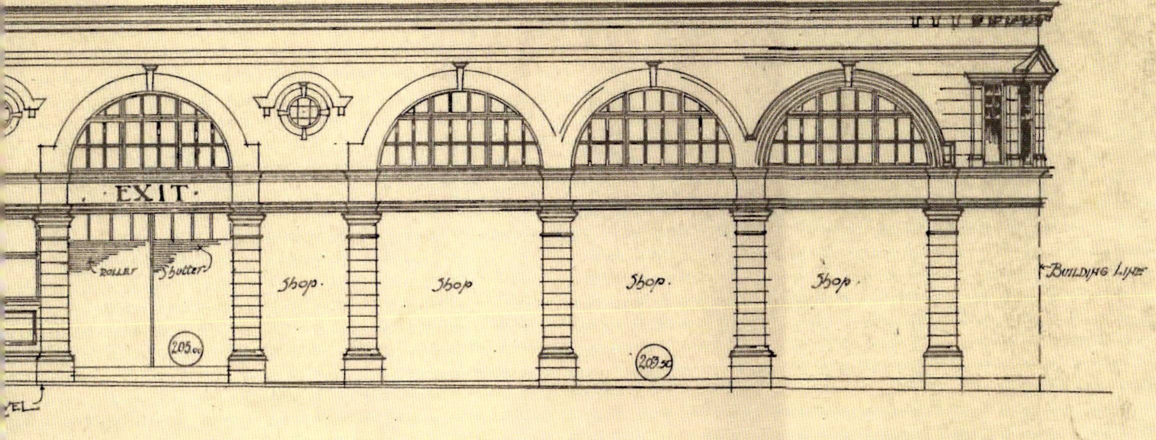

Deep-level Tubes and the Birth of a Logo
1906–15

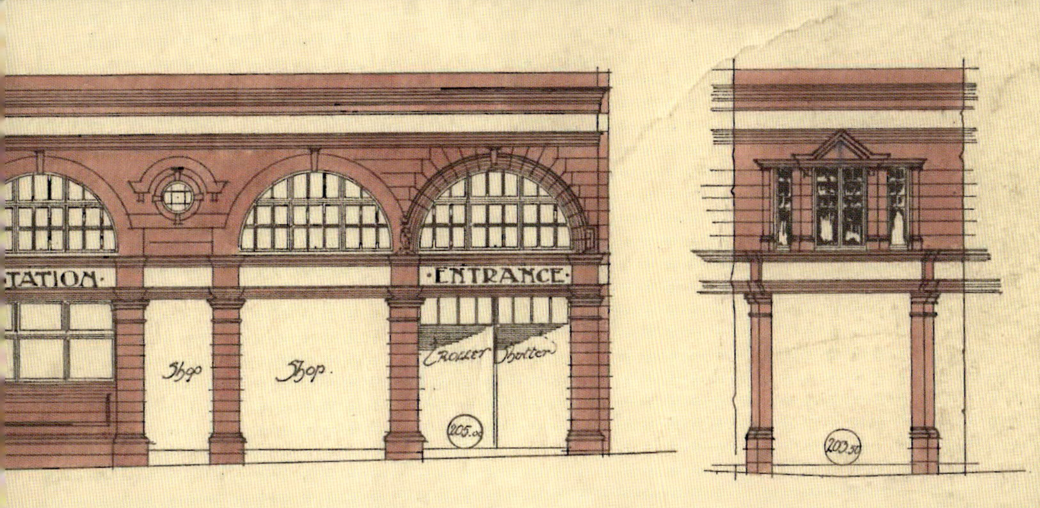

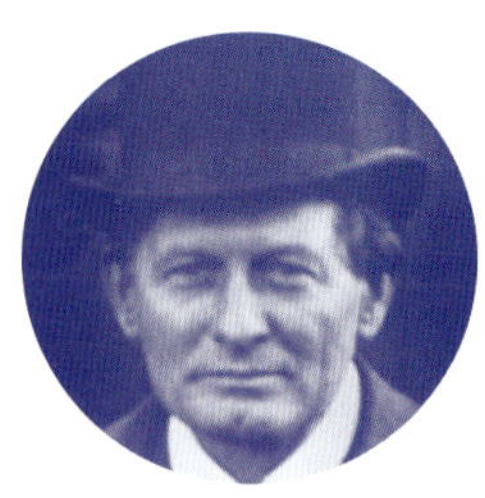

George Stegmann Gibb (1850–1925), born in Scotland, moved from the GWR to the North Eastern Railway (NER) in 1882 where he became general manager, improving services and increasing efficiency. In 1906, as UERL managing director, he recruited Frank Pick and Albert Stanley. Though he left the Underground in 1910 for a job improving highways, he returned to railways in 1919 and advised the NER about implementation of the 1921 Grouping Act. He was knighted in 1904.

PREVIOUS PAGES: Leslie Green's architectural drawing for Chalk Farm (opened 22 June 1907), the longest individual frontage of the surface buildings he designed. (These numbered thirty-eight in total, seven with double frontages and Piccadilly Circus with three. The six other stations he worked on were all entirely underground.)

III. Deep-level Tubes and the Birth of a Logo, 1906–15

The seeds of almost everything now regarded as the 'core' corporate identity of the London Underground (the 'roundel' logo, the Johnston typeface and the ruby-red glazed station fronts) were sown in the early years of the twentieth century. A number of key developments happened in the frenetic period between 1906 and 1912, one of the most far-reaching of which was the appointment in 1906 by UERL managing director George Gibb of a young solicitor called Frank Pick (p. 62) as his assistant. Construction was already under way on three lines that would give London more than forty new stations (pp. 70–74), this in turn providing an unparalleled opportunity for the UERL to introduce some uniformity of style.

New stations transform the London streetscape

The UERL had hired a young architect called Leslie Green[1] for the task in 1903. In the space of just three years, Green designed and oversaw the erection of around fifty surface buildings at forty-three sites. North–south and east–west communications became possible for the first time, taking travellers right through the heart of London's West End. The purpose of the station buildings was primarily functional – to house the ticket hall, lift machinery and staff facilities – but they needed to attract customers too, with a welcoming entrance. Yet keeping some uniformity of design was not easy when each building was so different, constrained by the varying nature and size of its site – some constructed on corners, many on odd-shaped 'footprints', some in key central locations, others in less prominent areas. Green rose to the challenge with a standard but adaptable design and, in the blink of an eye, created almost single-handedly an entirely new landmark for the streets of London.

Green's solution was brilliant: taking his cue from the CLR stations of Harry Bell Measures, he designed a standard load-bearing steel structure around which pre-moulded glazed terracotta brickwork could be positioned in a virtual kit form (quite advanced for the time). It was a solution only made possible by new technology, the steel frame freeing Green from the constraints of using brick or stone alone, enabling him to create much wider entrances (a process that would continue later, pp. 116, 150). Most stations now consisted of two storeys[2] (and thanks again to the steel-frame construction, each storey could be higher than previously) with several bays and semicircular windows set over the majority of them. Between the entranceways, shopfronts (or at least, window displays) were envisaged.[3] Instead of the unglazed bricks selected by Measures, Green chose a magnificently distinctive deep ruby-red or 'ox-blood' faience for the glazed bricks.[4] There's no record of the reasoning behind this, but the self-cleaning nature of the material and the bold colouring certainly helped the buildings stand out in London's (still

London Underground by Design

somewhat grimy) streets. Lewis Isaacs's 1873 Holborn Viaduct station, with its many-arched bays, possibly inspired Green. Others have postulated that he may have been influenced by the designer of the Paris Métro stations, Hector Guimard[5] (for example, at Knightsbridge, p. 70).

The name of the station and the line – 'Bakerloo Tube' (an amalgam of its main interchanges, Baker Street and Waterloo), 'Piccadilly Tube' or 'Hampstead Tube' (which eventually became part of the Northern line) – were to be placed above each bay or just beneath the top pediment.[6] The choice of lettering is especially relevant to design historians: it was the first time that a letterform was consciously chosen to match (if, occasionally, somewhat loosely) on station exteriors and interiors. Any similarity between letters used on earlier stations both inside and out may be regarded as coincidental rather than deliberate. The effect at street level, as each new building was revealed between 1905 and 1908, was astounding: the red brick was inviting, the gold serif lettering (where employed) striking. Having the names fired into the platform wall tiles in letters 30cm high was inspired to the point that even when stations were refurbished a hundred years later, many of the old signs were kept for their inherent beauty.[7]

Interior decor sets new standards

If Green's station exteriors were vivid, his concept for the interior design represented a step change too. Here it was not simply a case of throwing up white tiles with an occasional flourish (though white or cream did form the backdrop to much of Green's design) but a number of well-thought-through ideas were introduced which might nowadays be defined as 'wayfinding' aids. They included features that were seen and utilized by passengers from their first sight of the surface station building, right down to the platform and back out again (p. 70–73).

Despite the thoroughness and ingenuity of Green's designs, they were almost too successful, posing a conundrum for the UERL. Green's work was not flawed, far from it, but at a time when the company was groping towards a collective identity for the entire system (the three deep-level tubes and the District – and later the CSLR and CLR), it both kick-started the process and to an extent got in the way of developing a unified look.

The emergence of a co-ordinated appearance

It is now recognized that the rapid pace of development between 1906 and 1912 was the principal impetus behind the creation of almost all the cornerstones of the London Underground corporate identity. Several significant developments were happening simultaneously, each potentially prompted by the others. It was during 1906–8, for example, that the 'UNDERGROUND' name and presentation of the lettering was adopted

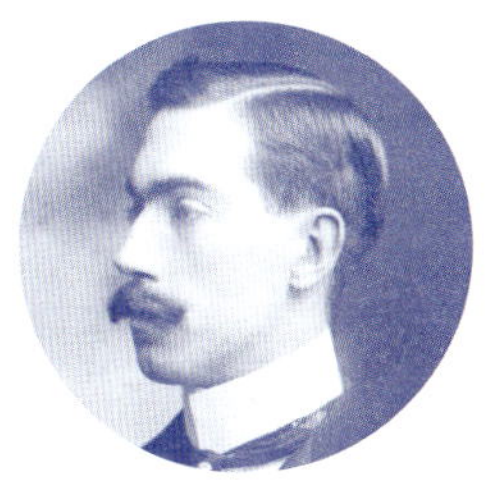

Leslie William Green (1875–1908) was born in London and studied in Paris, where he was influenced by the Art Nouveau style. He set up a practice in London but his first major commission in 1903 was for the UERL. Having to design and oversee the construction of so many stations in such a short time, and over-stretching himself with the station interiors as well, put a strain on his health; he contracted tuberculosis and died in 1908, aged just thirty-three.

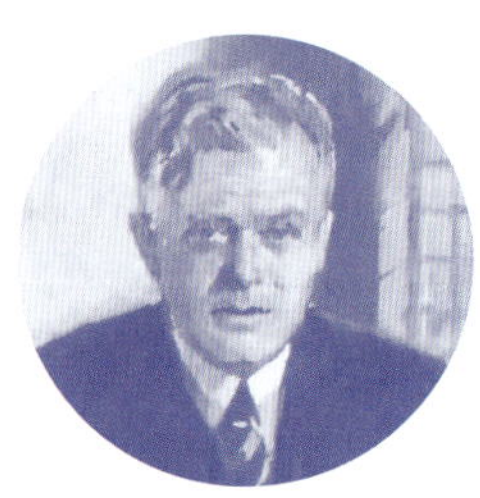

Frank Pick (1878–1941), born in Lincolnshire, played a pivotal role in London Transport. Having joined UERL as Gibb's assistant, he was quickly promoted to publicity officer (1908) and commercial manager (1912). In his efforts to increase off-peak usage of the Underground, he commissioned typographer Edward Johnston to create a new letterform (p. 112) and architect Charles Holden to design new station buildings from 1924 (p. 116), a collaboration that continued until Pick's retirement in 1940 due to ill-health. He declined knighthoods and peerages but did accept an award for his consulting role with the Moscow Metro. A founding member of the Design and Industries Association, his comment on best design practice echoes down the ages: 'the test of the goodness of a thing is its fitness for use. If it fails on this first test, no amount of ornamentation or finish will make it any better; it will only make it more expensive, more foolish.' A memorial to him was installed at Piccadilly Circus in 2016.

(pp. 78–83), in a distinctive form that nowadays would be called a 'logotype' or 'wordmark'. The streamlining of nameboards happened in unison with this (p. 84). Posters and publicity were co-ordinated, slogans introduced and by 1911/12 a combination of graphic elements came together to form the logo (p. 98) that remains little changed to this day. These were the factors that contributed to it:

- The UERL had agreed to work with London United Tramways; so early in 1907 the group's passenger agent, Walter Gott, was commissioned to devise a trademark incorporating both trams and trains (p. 79).
- Staff on the District (which had been gobbled up by the UERL in 1902) were grappling with how to improve the way their stations were signed at platform level, as early as 1906 (p. 84). This was undoubtedly inspired by the clarity of station naming shown by the CSLR/CLR and what had been glimpsed of Green's pioneering designs for platforms then being built.
- Green's signage was well received from the first openings in March 1906 and inspired others to use similar lettering.
- Despite the new routes, overall the UERL was not making the financial returns anticipated and its managers were motivated to increase revenue with a massive publicity drive for the Underground as a whole.

The re-siting of the 1908 Summer Olympics to London,[8] plus the impending Franco-British Exhibition (in May 1908), were both to be held at a vast west London location (which came to be known as White City). It had already been earmarked for the first extension to the CLR, and the UERL was mindful of the pivotal role the burgeoning Underground would need to play in moving millions of visitors to the area.

Booking 'through' tickets where an interchange was needed onto another company's line was a confusing business; in addition to varying fare structures, the disparate lines each had different monikers (both official names and nicknames).[9] It must have been quite a bewildering process for the passenger. The UERL bosses were evidently acutely aware of this.

As early as 1906, the secretary of the District, Joseph Carter, had been considering how to make station names more prominent on platform walls swathed in other companies' publicity. Carter had asked a junior buying clerk, William H. Hilton, to draw some sketches using shapes that might be placed around the station nameboards to help them stand out. After some research, Carter concluded that a disc, comprising semicircles placed either side of the name sign, might be the most effective, but took no further action at that point.

A brand name is chosen

At a joint committee of all London transport operators in late 1907 (which included the CSLR, CLR and surprisingly also the Met[10]), agreement was reached over a fare structure to make the system more competitive, and at a later meeting in early 1908 discussion of how to amalgamate the lines and multiple companies into one recognizable network centred around an operating term that would be generally accepted. 'Tube' was commonly used, at least on the CLR, from its opening in 1900, and it was being adopted by default for the new deep-level lines,[11] each with its own logo (p. 76) and publicity. But the word 'Underground' had also been in circulation since the opening of the very first line in 1863.[12] Albert Stanley, appointed by the UERL in 1907 to boost passenger numbers, made the wise decision of pushing for its adoption as the company name (or, as it might be termed nowadays, 'brand name') – it was already in the UERL title and was more accurate than the word 'Tube' (which the District was not built in[13]).

An early rebranding exercise

While the UERL's deep-level tubes were still under construction, and in response to the shaky financial situation, Stanley ordered the publicity office (then headed by Frank Pick) to make a photographic survey of every station (pp. 78–9) with a view to installing signage showing the new collective title.[14] In the meantime, he and Pick considered how the word was to be displayed. Stanley, who was becoming adept at public relations, also convinced a London newspaper to run a competition to find a good slogan (p. 94). A budget of £50,000 (worth about £4.5 million today) was allocated for a publicity drive but it would entail the creation of a brand new trademark. It was the District's architect Harry Wharton Ford who claimed to have come up with the idea of graphically balancing the rather cumbersome four-syllable word 'Underground' by enlarging the first and last letters, 'U' and 'D'. The word appeared from 1908 in white on a black (or sometimes dark blue) background, each letter being set in its own square (p. 80) like individual blocks of type or tiles laid together. Early manifestations of the wordmark were a little inelegant – but the idea stuck. It was a kind of visual shorthand[15] as only the first and last letters needed to be seen for immediate recognition of the word by members of the public. Alongside the enlarged U and D of 'UNDERGROUND', a key element of an earlier (1907) emblem was incorporated: a somewhat fanciful 'silhouette' of the London skyline (p. 83).

After having seen how the proposed wordmark might look from station photographs with signs painted on or inked in by hand (p. 78–9), the joint committee agreed to the purchase and erection of a huge batch of signs (electrically illuminated and both horizontal and vertical, p. 82) and poster frames, the building of glass-covered canopies over entrances (p. 95) and the manufacture of glass 'shields' with the Underground logo embedded in them for the so-called 'Tiffany' lampshades (p. 83). All these were to be

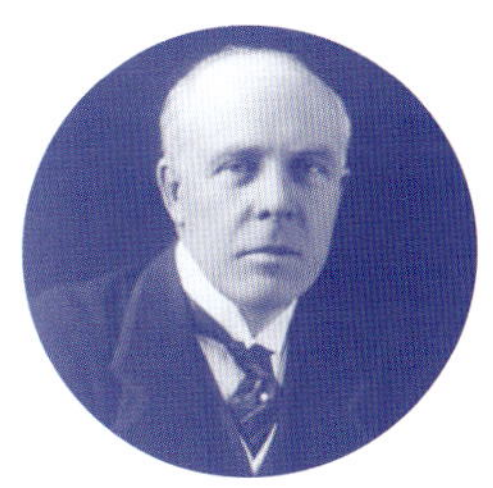

Albert Stanley (1874–1948), born in Derbyshire, spent his formative years in the USA improving street-cars (trams). He was approached by George Gibb in 1907 to run UERL. Under his leadership the 'combine' prospered. He became an MP in 1916 and was made a baron (Lord Ashfield) in 1920. Returning to the UERL in 1919, he took the group into public ownership and became chairman of the board (1933). He has a memorial at 55 Broadway.

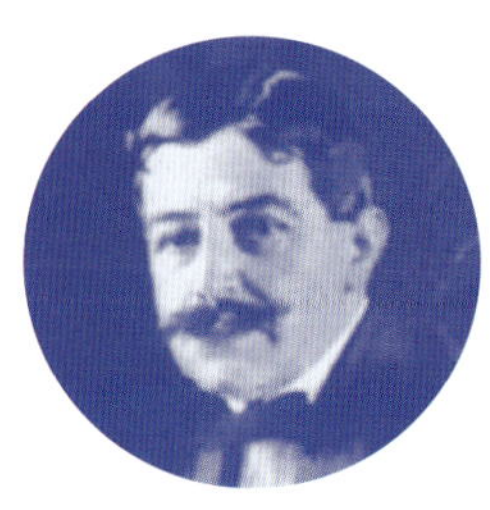

American financier Edgar Speyer (1862–1932) was German-Jewish by descent but became a British subject. He met Charles Tyson Yerkes in Chicago, succeeding him as UERL chairman in 1906 and becoming involved in the purchase of the CLR and CSLR. A keen arts supporter, he funded the Promenade Concerts (1902–14). Despite being knighted in 1906, he was accused of trading with the enemy during the First World War (allegations the prime minister insisted were 'baseless') and he returned to America (1920), selling his UERL shares for almost £30 million (at today's prices).

installed at every station. Ornate, slanting glass canopies had been used over entrances since the 1860s, but a 1907 innovation was the three-sided version with a flat roof jutting out over the street and featuring side panels specifically designed to carry signage (often etched onto glass, and illuminated at some stations, p. 95). These served a dual purpose: projecting the station out onto the street so that it was more visible, making it much easier to find at night and protecting passengers from inclement weather. The wordmark was to be included in these canopies too.

The wordmark gets printed

One of the earliest, if not the first, appearances of the enlarged U and D in print can be precisely dated to the publication on 1 April 1908 of the folded pocket map (p. 80), of which 6 million were printed for distribution to hotels, theatres and even ocean liners. A later version, printed on a small folded card with cloth backing (p. 104), was even handier for travellers. Another early example of the U and D wordmark was seen on a poster commissioned by Frank Pick. Designed by up-and-coming commercial artist John Hassall (p. 81), it was to prove the defining document of the entire rebranding exercise and has become central to the early 'corporate identity' history of the London Underground.

The very earliest examples of the enlarged U and D seem to have been deemed offensive to the eye, hence horizontal strips or dashes were quickly added (as early as May 1908) around the letters 'ɴᴅᴇʀɢʀᴏᴜɴ', framing them above and below, on a level with the top and bottom of the larger 'U' and 'D'. Where the word was displayed vertically, the dashes appeared to the left and right of each letter (p. 80). These devices – the 'ᴜɴᴅᴇʀɢʀᴏᴜɴD' word with enlarged U and D, the totem-pole vertical signs and the stylized skyline, together with slogans, lamp shields, poster frames and glass canopies – were manufactured quickly (which may account for slight irregularities in style between them), before being installed on every UERL station from late spring 1908 onwards. Though they performed their intended task admirably in being highly visible, they made somewhat ungainly additions to many otherwise beautifully designed buildings, appearing at best 'tacked on' and at worst downright unsafe, potentially rickety in a high wind and altogether rather intrusive (p. 82). But they worked.

Other lines strive for independence

The CLR would not play ball, however, rejecting the UERL's new signage in favour of their tried-and-tested (and simpler) 'ᴛᴜʙᴇ' moniker. In this spirit, they erected copycat, vertical totems outside many stations (such as Notting Hill Gate, p. 96) and even made their own glass canopies with 'ᴛᴜʙᴇ' and the CLR logo etched on (such as at Bond Street, p. 96). A few of the new 'ᴜɴᴅᴇʀɢʀᴏᴜɴD' poster frames were permitted, but only around the system map (produced in enamel for this purpose from about 1909, p. 94). The CSLR played a similar game – only the new Underground poster frame and maps were allowed. The LSWR would have none of it on 'the Drain' but the little GNCR did consent to the vertical UNDERGROUND totems at Highbury and Essex Road.

Oddly, it was the fiercely competitive Met which acquiesced more readily in certain instances to the installation of the new signage. At some stations (Kilburn & Brondesbury in 1910, for example, Euston Square by 1911, Aldersgate, and at Edgware Road too) gargantuan versions of the vertical totem were embraced with such vigour passengers would be forgiven for thinking the Met had been entirely subsumed by the Underground! Elsewhere, by contrast, many suburban surface Met stations (certainly most of the more far-flung outposts like the Uxbridge, Richmond and Barking branches), and even the majority of the Met north of Baker Street, seemed to sail majestically into the First World War without even so much as installing an Underground system map, let alone adopting the branding for their more central stations, ones that were more literally 'underground'.

However, with these notable exceptions, plenty of evidence for the 'UNDERGROUND' name could be found around the capital; an impressive feat of marketing that certainly had the desired effect of 'increasing awareness' (to use a modern term) and boosting passenger numbers and hence profits for the UERL. The point being that Pick and his team at the publicity office were now conscious of something that was only just dawning on other companies: that a logo can be applied to almost any surface or object as part of a branding exercise. Although there was a degree of over-exposure, the lesson they learnt is key to the formulation of the concept of corporate identity (p. 155).

Competition inspires design improvements elsewhere

Construction of the deep-level tubes was not the only exciting new development during this frenetic period. The Met, CLR and CSLR were also expanding, albeit at a slower rate than before, but undoubtedly with an eye to learning from the UERL in design terms. In 1907, for example, the CSLR achieved its goal of extending from Angel to Euston via King's Cross and erected an impressive building at the former (p. 75). CSLR signage was also improved and looked suspiciously similar to that of the CLR (p. 75). The CLR achieved a long-held ambition of opening a station beside the massive Wood Lane exhibition grounds, just in time for the major events of 1908 (p. 93). Here too there was evidence of learning from the UERL; the station frontage was the company's first to include the new logo.[16] Elsewhere the CLR remained, somewhat ill-advisedly, staunchly independent, continuing to produce its own publicity posters, which were nonetheless quite striking (p. 97). The Met, too, was opening new stations,[17] but these were little more than wooden shacks on remote halts until rebuilt some years later. The publicity machine for the Met, however, was in full swing after the appointment in 1908 of a new general manager, Robert Hope Selbie (p. 69). Though he wisely agreed to limited use of the 'UNDERGROUND'

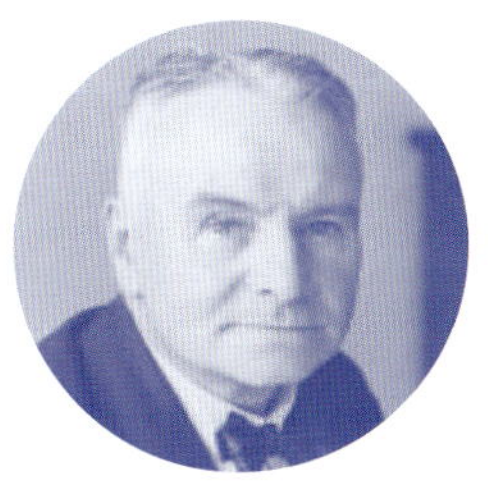

English architect Stanley Heaps (1880–1962) became Leslie Green's assistant in 1903, succeeding him in 1908. His designs for Maida Vale and Kilburn Park pay tribute to Green's tiling. Heaps rebuilt Wood Lane (1915), but shifted to a suburban style on the Edgware extension. His designs for Charles Holden influenced Osterley, St Johns Wood and Boston Manor, were masterpieces.

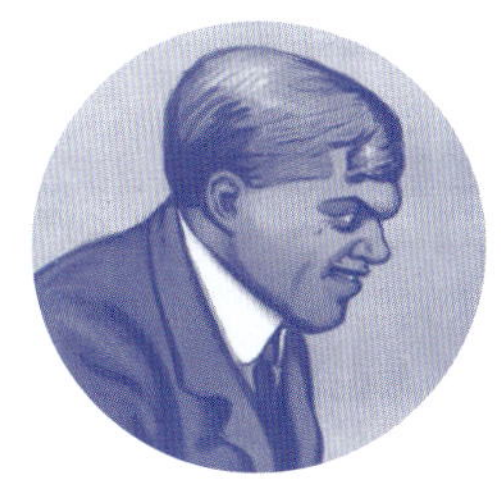

Kent-born John Hassall (1868–1948) created theatre posters. By 1900 he had launched a poster-design school and was spotted by Frank Pick, for whom he created a chubby 'P'liceman' in 1908 (p. 81). Hassall's 1910 Kodak Girl became a stalwart of that company's advertising into the 1960s, but it was a kitsch 'Jolly Fisherman' (1908) which shot him to fame.

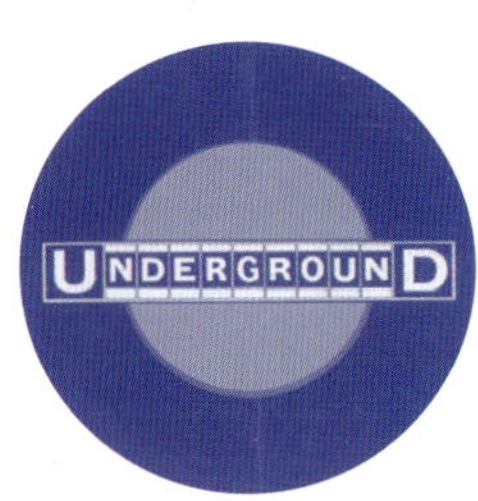

Little is known about Charles Sharland except the venerable record of eighty-six posters he made for the UERL. Most were charming and inventive, both in their technically perfect use of light (as in 'Light, power and speed', 1910) and their use of witty angles. His 1912 solar eclipse poster (detail pictured; in full on p. 98) is not just an outstanding juxtaposition of celestial bodies/Underground red disc; it is possibly the first instance the enlarged U and D appearing in combination with the 'bull's-eye' sign.

wordmark, his publicity office developed their own logo, with a direct replication of the UERL's enlarged U and D.[18] The Met's independent stand would, however, bear other fruit in years to come (pp. 68–9).

Progress below stairs

The one area in which the UERL signage did not yet reflect much progress was on the platforms. That was all about to change with moves that would give birth to an enduring emblem for London. Early in 1908, Stanley made a reconnaissance trip to the Paris Métro, noting how the station name was repeated along each platform wall.[19] Signage there consisted of blue paper or enamel strips with lettering in white condensed sans-serif capitals (a style borrowed from the street signs above ground). Advertising hoardings were not permitted in 1900, so station name signs were left clear of neighbouring clutter and stood out well. All this made a profound impression upon Stanley, who upon his return ordered a series of signage trials at St James's Park (beneath the UERL company offices) while the District was undergoing refurbishment. Spaces were cleared by removing some advertising and white panels were inserted along the platform at intervals equal to the length of one train car. On top of these was placed a long blue sign with the station name in white capital letters, thus effecting an approximation of the Paris Métro signage.

The station inspector at St James's Park, William Cleal, suggested to Stanley at a meeting that the blue signs needed to be even more distinctive and it was at this point that Joseph Carter informed them of his earlier experiments with discs. Card mock-ups were produced by W. Lowe, and Frank Pick selected the final design. Red paper semicircles were subsequently applied either side of the blue bar at St James's Park (p. 84). They were evidently deemed so successful that by the June of 1908 a large order of blue enamelled nameplates and accompanying red semicircles were made for the entire UERL group. The process of installation began that summer – even the Leslie Green platforms were provided with them: the bar and circle – or 'bull's-eye' – device was born (p. 86).

Culverhouse, Ford and Sherrin go a bit Green

Harry Wharton Ford was still busy designing fine stations for the District, his work often echoing the Arts and Crafts style (p. 104). The lettering on station exterior walls, for example, was reminiscent of Green's designs – albeit slightly chunkier and perhaps a little more authoritative. At Barons Court (1905) the lettering on the outside consisted of a decorative serif on a frieze set between balustrades topped by spheres (p. 79). The joint District and Piccadilly stations at Hammersmith and Earl's Court (both 1906) also benefited from Ford's style of lettering under their respective parapets.[20]

Commercial pressures forced all companies to examine how their stations could be made more profitable, hence several were reconstructed to expand retail space and

London Underground by Design

increase entrance widths. To this end, architect George Sherrin (p. 68) was commissioned
by the Met to reconstruct several busy stations between 1905 and 1909. Sherrin introduced attractive wrought-iron grilles above entrances that incorporated station name and
operating company (an example of which survives in situ at South Kensington, p. 106).
During the period 1907–9, architect P. E. Culverhouse was rebuilding the HCR station at
Hammersmith into a fine terminal complete with shops and a canopy the entire length
of the frontage which featured the most exquisite leaded-glass display of the operating
company's and station name in petit-serif capitals. The triangular roof also framed a fine
clock (p. 106).[21]

    The Met's biggest project, however, was at Baker Street, where George Sherrin
constructed a combined station with the Inner Circle (1907–11), which would also become
the company headquarters.[22]

Platform signs become a logo

The crucial point at which the existing U and D wordmark (p. 80) was merged with the
station nameboard bull's-eye (p. 85) is somewhat lost in the mists of the Edwardian era,
and several contradictory theories exist.[23] The first time the U and D logo and red disc
appeared together may have been on a tram poster from late 1911/early 1912 (p. 98).
But this could have been preceded by a poster from Charles Sharland (a studio artist at
Waterlow Printers, p. 98), known to have been issued in March 1912 as part of a publicity
drive to get people to use the Underground to watch the solar eclipse in mid April that
year. It then appeared on a map cover (dated July 1912, p. 99). A poster by Alfred France
advertising all the virtues of the system portrayed as Greek gods (p. 98) was also produced
in 1912, though it cannot be proved conclusively if this appeared before or after either
the tram poster, the Sharland poster or the map cover. Metal or glass signs featuring the
combined logo started appearing from 1913 onwards (pp. 102–103) and by the start the
of First World War[24] they were popping up all over the city. Although the evolution of this
device did not stop here, it is the laying of the U and D wordmark bar across the face of
the red bull's-eye disc (previously only station names were written in the bar) that was
the defining moment in the creation of the bullseye – what is now called the 'roundel'.
It is no unhappy coincidence that this shape appeared a hundred years ago, making the
approximate centenary of this most iconic logo (2011–13) coincide nicely with the 150th
anniversary of the world's first underground railway.

Diamonds but not for ever

Instead of the red disc, the Met chose a diamond shape (seen on signage in embryonic
form perhaps as early as 1909, p. 108), appearing in outline on stationery and fliers (around
1912), and coloured solid red from 1913. The diamond shape did not appear on Met

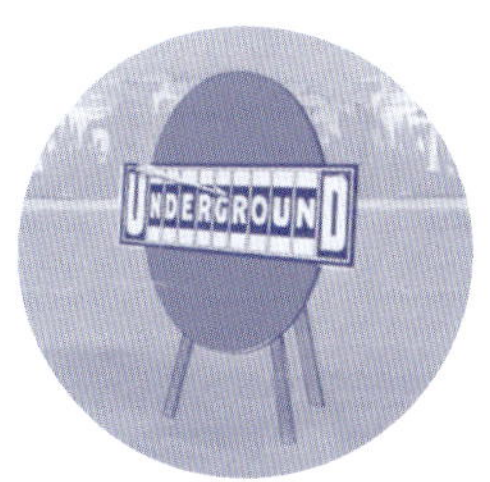

Alfred France's 1912 poster
(detail pictured; in full on
p. 98) may have helped
establish Underground
corporate identity. 'Hermes
for Speed, Eros for Pleasure'
was commissioned to
advertise the new brand,
summarizing its benefits
as attributes of the Greek
gods, including 'Chronos
for Punctuality' and 'Pan for
Countryside' – quite what
scholars of Charon (the
ferryman) would have made
of him being dubbed the
god of 'Cheapness' is not
addressed. The combined
logo is the target into which
the gods fire their arrows,
the 'bull's-eye' nickname
possibly emanating from
this poster.

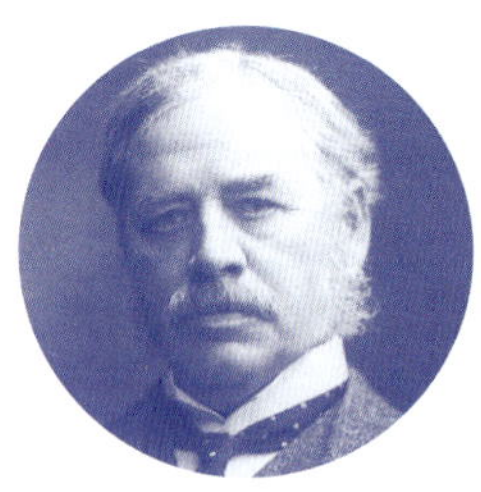

George Campbell Sherrin (1843–1909), born in Essex, was an architect and a sculptor who worked for the Met from 1893 on almost a dozen stations, some of which had to be completed by his son Frank after his death. His finest designs include the arcade at South Kensington (p. 106).

Met platform signage until after the war[25] (p. 137). The District's engineers, who had also been working on new signage for the ELR following its conversion to electric traction, coincidentally had plumped for a green diamond (p. 100) during 1912. The signs were erected in 1913,[26] much to the annoyance of Pick, indicating that the use of the green diamond device in ELR signage actually pre-dated that of the Met's red diamond, on stations at least, a fact that has only recently emerged. ELR station names were in black sans-serif condensed capitals on a white/pale background. The Met nameboards featured a blue plate with white sans-serif capitals (slightly more condensed and squared off than the letters being used on UERL nameboards). All the diamonds were gradually replaced with bullseyes from the 1930s, though some stayed in place right into the mid 1970s (for instance, at Highbury & Islington).

Unity leads to better publicity and a combined logo

The UERL was on an expansionist mission and its publicity needed to reflect this. In 1912 the group purchased the largest bus operator, the London General Omnibus Company,[27] and in 1913 it finally got its hands on the CSLR and the CLR. That same year the Met took control of the GN&CR, leaving London with just two major urban-rail operating groups (and the two smaller independent lines[28]). Because of the new 'combine', as the UERL became known, Pick demanded that greater emphasis be placed on advertising each grouping e.g. for passengers to take a bus to the Underground to get to a new destination. Crucially the publicity would be used on all modes; encouraging passengers to swap between trams, Tube or bus. The poster was at the heart of this publicity drive and one of its leading exponents was Sharland, who produced eighty-six for the combine between 1908 and 1922.[29] Indeed, it was he who was the chief advocate for merging the bull's-eye nameboard shape with the U and D wordmark into a unified emblem for the system. Sharland was evidently fascinated by the circle as a motif, as can be seen from his first poster for the Underground in 1908 ('Valley of the Thames', p. 88), the aforementioned poster for the solar eclipse, his annual publicity for Whitsuntide and later posters (p. 99). While different designers continued to use the U and D wordmark, it was the quality of the posters commissioned by the publicity department under Pick, and artists such as Sharland's frequent recourse to the combined logo, that gave rise to improvements in mapping (pp. 90–91 and 104–10), signage (pp. 102–103) and other printed ephemera (p. 82).

The smart marketing concept that transformed London

In response to this flurry of publicity, the Met, under Robert Hope Selbie, came up with a different strategy: a slogan. Despite its simplicity it proved one of the most successful marketing concepts; it effected a geographic change, expanding the boundaries and altering the very shape of the capital. The idea of railway companies promoting the

London Underground by Design

virtues of living out of town was nothing new (as exemplified by posters for the District's Osterley station in 1908, p. 89),[30] but the Met went a step further, buying land adjacent to its lines and flogging it off at inflated prices for speculative housing development, enabling it to recommend its own fast train services to London, luring people to live away from the grime of the city. While the use of this single slogan – 'Metro-land' – seems to have been the driving force behind the success of the project, it was backed up by glorious brochures with images of women strolling carefree around beautiful gardens surrounding palatial yet affordable homes.[31] The unimaginatively titled *Guide to the Extension Line* had been published by the Met in 1904, partly to promote Cecil Park, a new housing estate in Pinner, but this had limited effect; it was not until 1915 that the revamped guide, called simply *Metro-land* (p. 109), grabbed the public's imagination and kick-started an unprecedented migration of inner Londoners to the newly created suburbs along the edges of the Met's line through Middlesex and into Buckinghamshire. This was possibly the first time an advertising slogan had such a marked effect, inspiring people to move house and commute to work. Paradoxically the consequent urbanization destroyed the very bucolic countryside the advertising had sought to promote, as Sir John Betjemen wryly observed in the BBC documentary *Metro-land* (BBC, 1973): 'Why not buy these orchards and farms … turn out the cattle, and fill the meadowland with houses?'

Although a number of smaller developments from this period are also noteworthy,[32] what had been implemented during the Edwardian era were some of the most radical leaps in design introduced by any mass-transit organization in the world. Yet even these were to pale into insignificance next to the tumultuous changes about to occur as transport in London entered its most radical phase of design improvements yet.

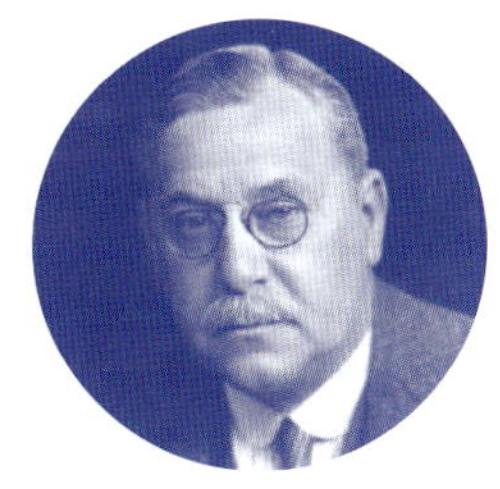

Robert Hope Selbie (1868–1930), born in Manchester, did not take over as general manager of the Met until 1908, but was the saviour of the line, responsible for establishing the mock-Tudor 'heaven' in previously empty north-west London. Marketed under the slogan 'Metro-land', the green fields between Willesden Green and Northwood Hills were hidden beneath stone, creating new suburbs, ticket-sale fodder and huge profits, while obliterating the idyllic countryside being promoted.

Green's red legacy, 1906–8

The architecture of Leslie Green's station buildings was exemplary in every detail, each location with its own architectural features, including cartouches and relief work in the Arts and Crafts style (seen in his drawings, 1). While the stations were essentially built from a kit (p. 60), no two were identical. Apart from the slightly unusual Great Central (where the ticket hall was located below street level so there was no need for a second floor), all the stations had two storeys consisting of arched windows (on the first level) above ground-floor bays comprising either shopfronts or wide exit/entrances (with the exception of the tiny entrance at Waterloo). Some additional smaller windows peppered the sides, usually in between each arch: they were either square (e.g. Goodge Street, 2) or, more often than not, circular (e.g. Gloucester Road, 3). The Leeds Fireclay Company provided the ox-blood tiles (sometimes also referred to as 'Burmantofts Faience'), with gold lettering on some and relief-moulded letters on others. Knightsbridge (5) had the most delicate faience work, executed in the Arts and Crafts style, and almost every station sported a decorative cartouche (4).

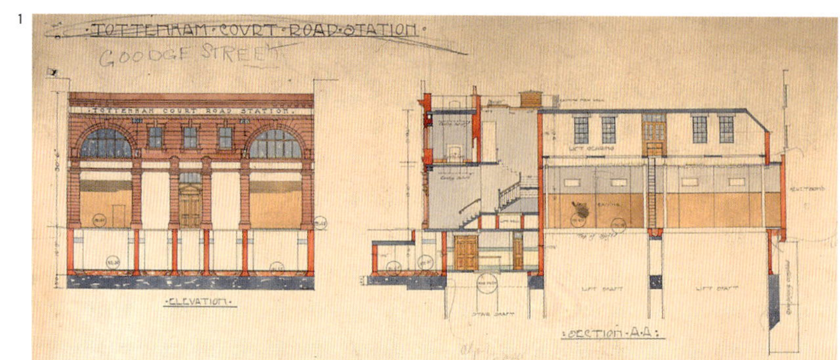

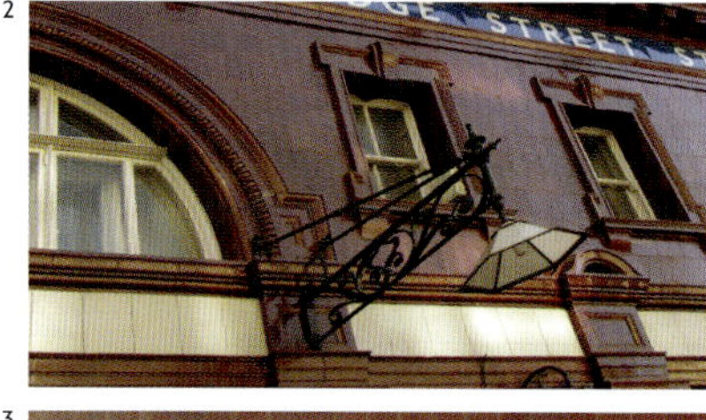

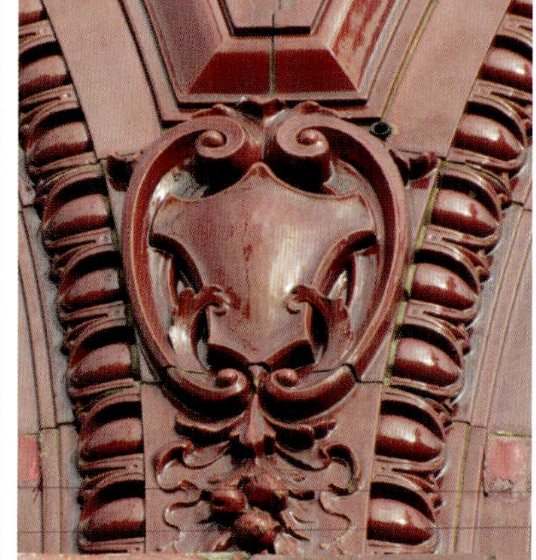

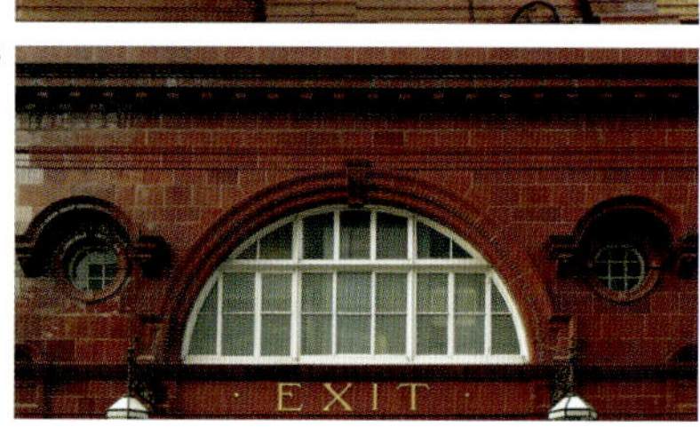

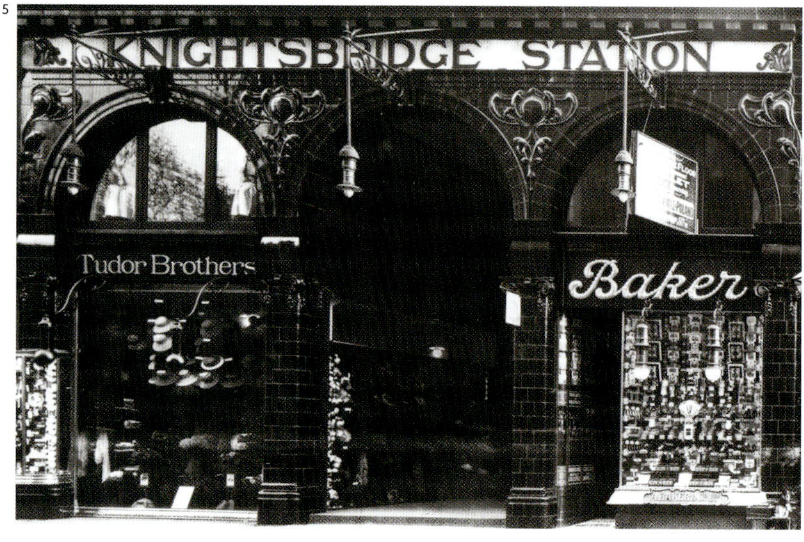

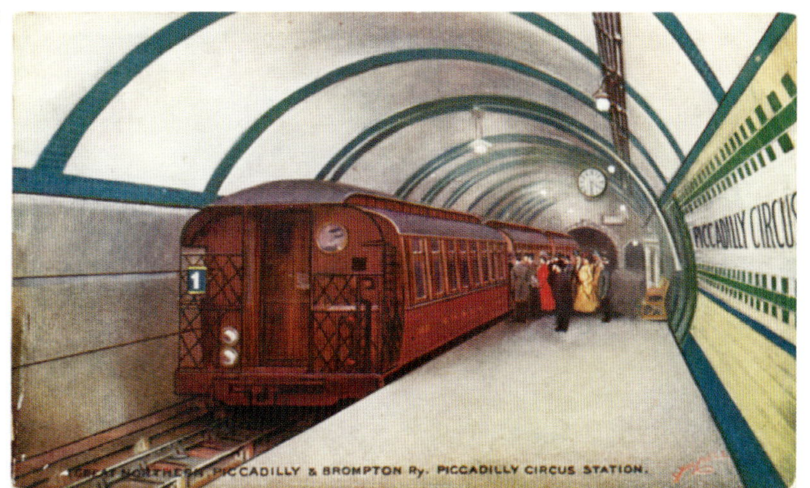

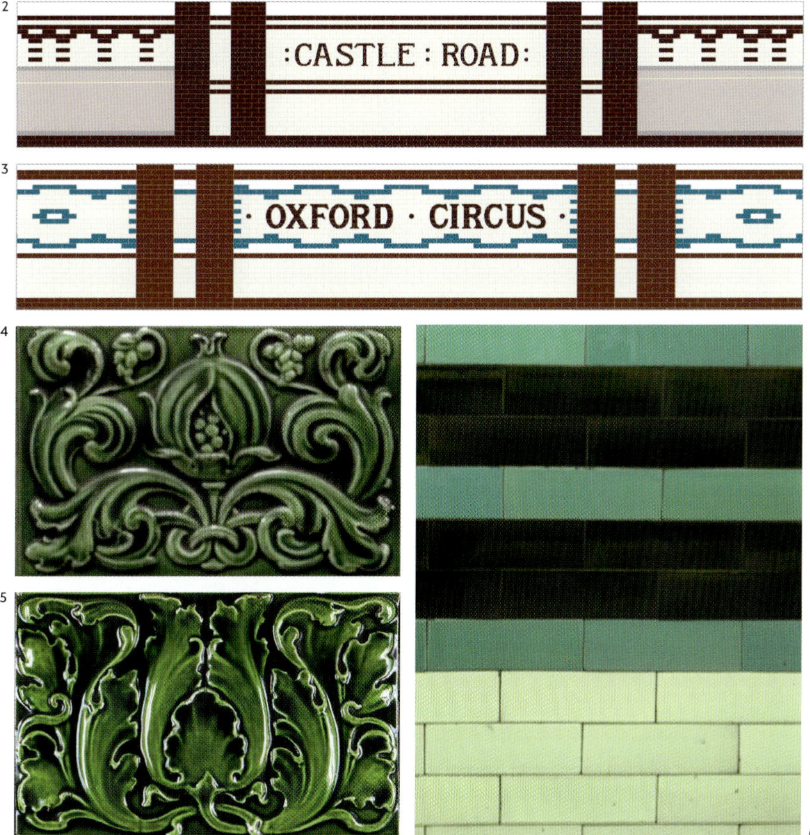

Green on the inside, 1906–8

Aside from his architectural skills, Green was the first station designer to pay close attention to interior decor and signage right down to the platform. For a start, the interior of each of his stations had its own unique colour scheme. Aside from the bands of coloured tiles that ran across the platform tunnel roof (seen on a postcard featuring Piccadilly Circus, 1), the whole near side had a matching tiled frieze that ran the entire length of the platform, with white-tiled frames for the station names (p. 73) and 'WAY OUT'/'NO EXIT' cartouches (p. 74). The unique combination of tile colours for each station (2 and 3) may have been designed to assist the illiterate or give the identity of the station if the name sign was hidden. Most passageways (especially those around the lifts) and many stairways also had a colour scheme, where the entire lower half of the wall was tile-covered to a height of about 1.5m from the floor. The ticket-hall dado rail was in a bright green tile featuring one of two designs, a pomegranate leaf (used at stations with tiling by Woolliscroft, 4 and p. 73) or an acanthus leaf (utilized in booking halls with Simpson tiling, 5 and p. 73) – the latter being slightly rarer. Dado rails elsewhere were simpler tiled bands in different colours (such as at Russell Square, 6).

Green's golden letters, 1906–8

The exterior lettering on Green's first batch of stations used relief-moulded serifed capitals in a form that may have been designed by Green himself. First seen on the Bakerloo (April 1906, 1): it sometimes appeared in more spread-out form ('GNP&BRy', 2) or condensed ('PICCADILLY CIRCUS', 3) and occasionally with unique flourishes and elongated tails. The gold-painted letters on a red background were stylish but not perhaps as legible as Green had intended and experimentation was soon underway – a handful of the panels were painted white and the serifed letters given a darker colour (South Kensington, 4). Many others retained the same lettering as the original Bakerloo stations for years, however. Elsewhere (especially on the Hampstead Tube) a new idea was tried: Green's serifs were abandoned in favour of a rather harsh condensed sans-serif: first white on red (e.g. Holborn, side entrance), then black on white (e.g. Belsize Park, 5). That style became the 'HAMPSTEAD TUBE' sign stand-ard. These letters were relief metal mounted on plain backgrounds – much cheaper than serif tiles. This cruder form of lettering also appeared on enamels around the interiors. Ironically, the less condensed capital used for the station name (e.g. Tottenham Court Road), and at almost every other of Green's stations from Great Central (27 March 1907) onwards, had the white bands with sans-serif black lettering, which looks uncannily similar to railway standard letterform dating right back to the first Met nameboards (p.22).

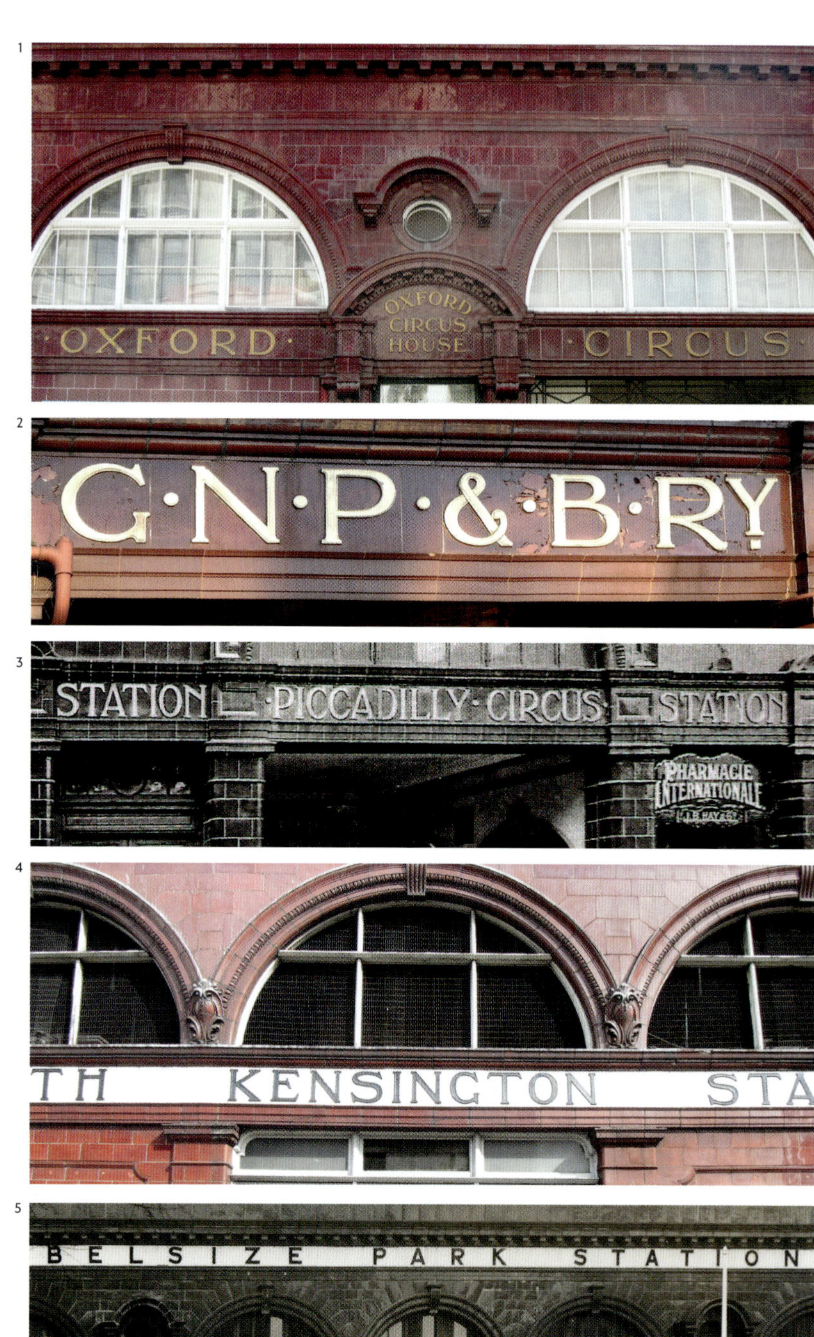

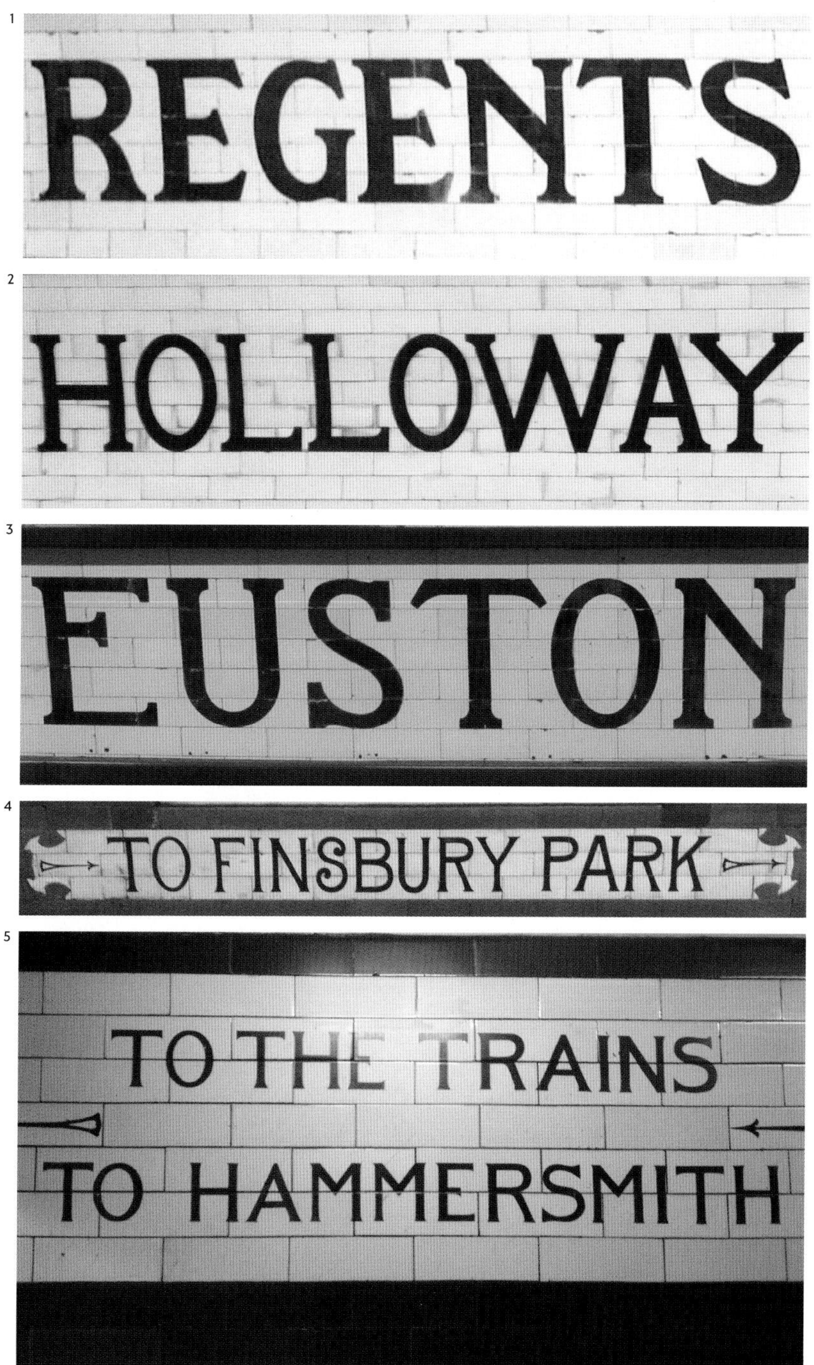

A conscious move towards a co-ordinated lettering style, 1906–8

For the first time in Underground history, station names were to be integrated into the overall platform design. But the lettering detail evolved even during two brief years. As Douglas Rose suggests in his book on tiles (Bibliography), this was primarily due to the different manufacturers, W. B. Simpson (agents Maw & Co.), G. Woolliscroft & Son and the Permanent Decorative Glass Company. The Bakerloo opened first (April 1906) with a brown serifed lettering for the station names – similar (but bolder) than that on the surface buildings (e.g. Regents Park – pictured in 2005, but now replaced, 1). Maw/Simpson letters were quite chunky and serifs triangular – a much more delicate version at Waterloo (not shown) was unique. By the time the Piccadilly stations were opened in December (most tiles by Woolliscroft), this shape had evolved into a blockier, squared-off serif (though Holloway Road, 2, was by Simpsons). On the Hampstead Tube six months later (using Permanent Decorative Glass tiles), letter shape had been further clarified (e.g. Euston, 3). Internal direction signage was also in this serifed letterform but generally a lighter version (e.g. 'to the trains', 5) and sometimes with more flourishes (e.g. 'to finsbury park', 4). Sadly no style guide has been found (though Rose has painstakingly reverse-engineered one), so it seems that any differences were probably due to the tile-makers rather than any conscious attempt to refine lettering for increased legibility or on aesthetic grounds.

Corporate identity trials, 1906–8

The importance of Green's contribution to an overall unified style for the Underground is often overlooked. It was not simply a question of some nice architecture and pretty tiling; his pioneering wayfinding work permeated every step of the passengers' journey. On entering the station, they would find the ticket hall filled with colour. About 1.5m from the floor a vibrant green dado rail with a leaf motif (p. 71) ran around the room, the wall beneath it covered in dappled green tiles. At intervals were the beautiful ticket windows (inspired possibly by those first seen on the CLR in 1900, p. 49) with the words 'IN' and 'OUT' (3) set in relief on tiles either side (in an exotic condensed version of Green's letterform) and 'TICKETS' (in a letterform much like those of the direction signs) curved overhead, with letters also in relief. The words 'BOOK HERE' (not shown) were also displayed in a separate panel and the lettering was consistent with that used for other signage. The window shape and lettering were echoed at platform level in the 'WAY OUT'/'NO EXIT' cartouches (installed later and not at every Green station, 1 and 2). Even the air vent above each lift had a stylish wrought-iron grille featuring flamboyant Art Nouveau emblems (4) and also seen on some other railings (5). This reflected Green's desire to project the idea of linking everything up, from the entrance to the platform, and to improve the passengers' experience. The only downside was that the styling could not easily be retro-fitted to older stations and that it did not incorporate the new collective name 'Underground' (p. 63).

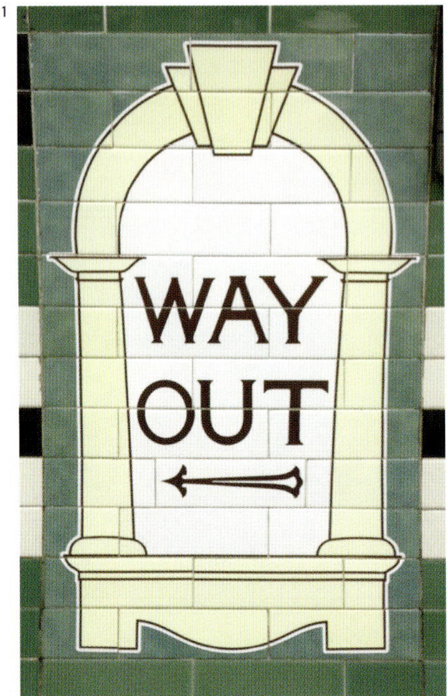

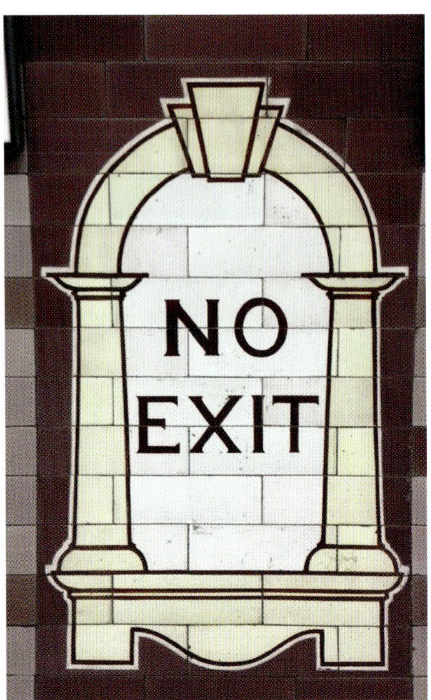

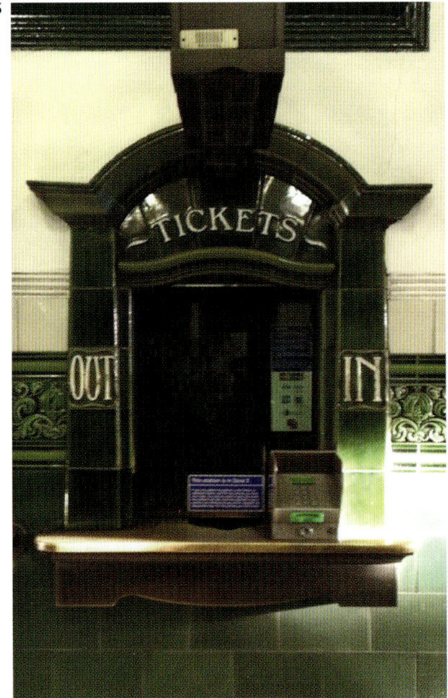

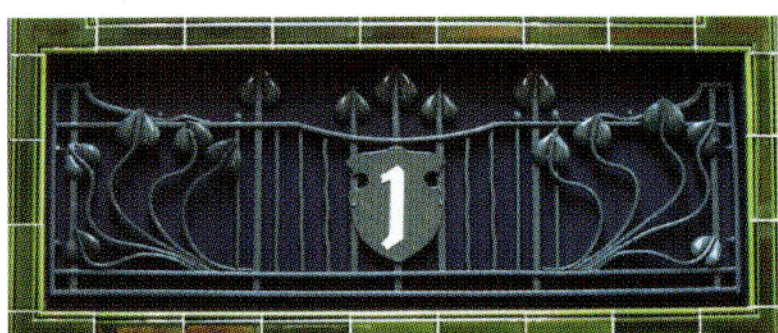

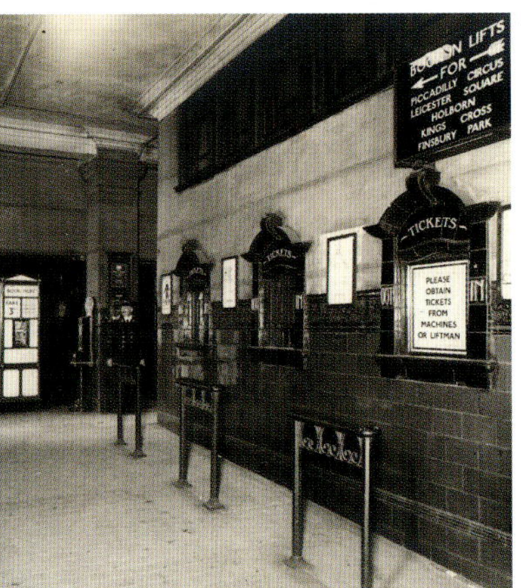

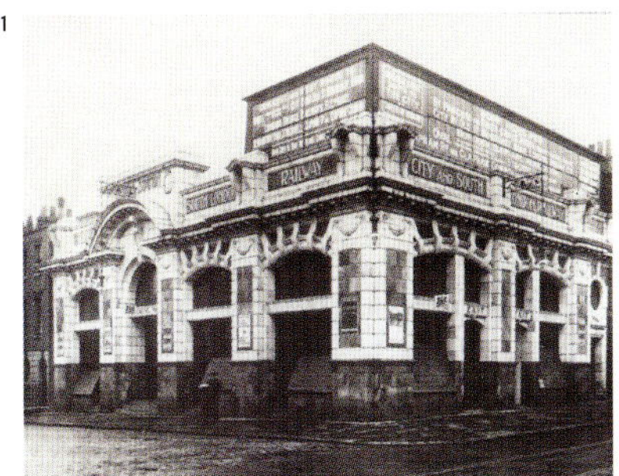

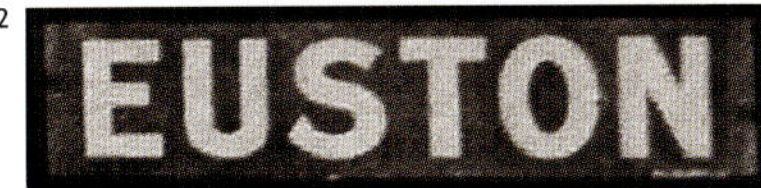

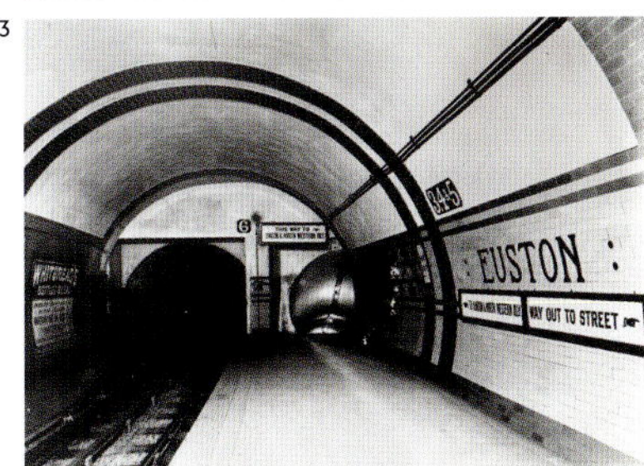

Euston, we have a problem, 1907

Both the CSLR and UERL's Hampstead Tube wanted to serve busy Euston. By May 1907 the CSLR's short but crucial section from Angel to Euston via King's Cross was open. The platforms at the latter were accessed from the mainline concourse, but at Euston a rather grand surface building, designed by Sidney R. J. Smith, was erected on Seymour Street (1). Using a steel frame and faience cladding, the structure was similar to the Measures and Green stations, but instead of using terracotta Smith employed green and white Doulton carraware with florid detailing, as described by David Lawrence: 'segmental arches had projecting voussoirs [wedge-shaped stones at the top of an arch] and swags decorated with pilasters' (1994, Bibliography).

Lettering on the pediments was in a serif so similar to Green's that a passer-by would have found it difficult spotting the difference. It was planned to be topped by several storeys but the air rights were never sold and the station entrances fell into disuse and were eventually demolished when Euston mainline station was rebuilt. Underground there was an island platform, and signage was so alike that of the CLR that again passengers may have been thrown by the similarity: blue enamel panels with bold capitals in white sans-serif lettering announced the station names (e.g. 'euston', 2). The Hampstead Tube station (on the corner of Drummond and Melton streets), not ready until June 1907, had to accommodate links to the CSLR and the mainline station (see technical drawing, 4, and directions from the platform, 3).

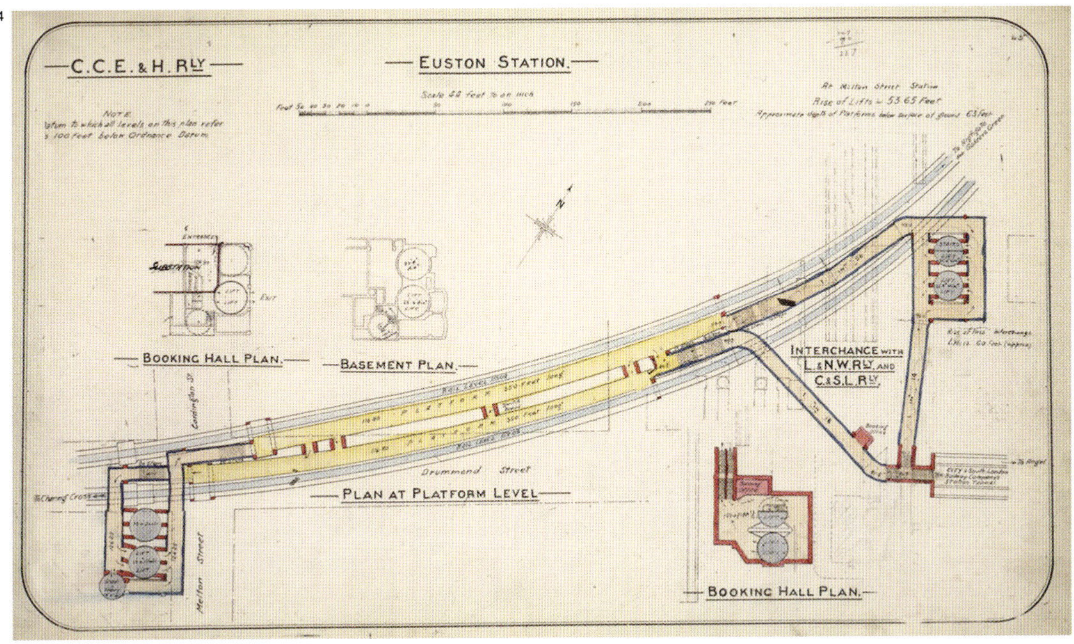

Too many little logos, 1906–7

As each of the new deep-level tube lines opened, they added signage to their stations and rolled out their own publicity, almost oblivious to the hard work of Green and the existence of the other lines. To be fair, this was a period when all railway companies were fiercely independent and the concept of a 'network' was barely beginning (though somewhat better understood in Paris owing to the fact that the Métro had been built from scratch and was run by one operator, until 1910 at least). So the

Bakerloo had a beautiful logotype with interlinked 'O's (4) and the Piccadilly seemed to have at least two (one using the word 'Tube' and the other 'Railway', 2 and 3), while the greedy Hampstead Tube sported three: one for posters, one for maps and a third yet more detailed version for map covers (1). Railed stairwell entrances in central London (5 and 6) looked even more dislocated, visually, from the rest. It was this duplication of effort and unnecessary clouding of the overall picture that Stanley and Pick were keen to overcome in their upcoming publicity drive.

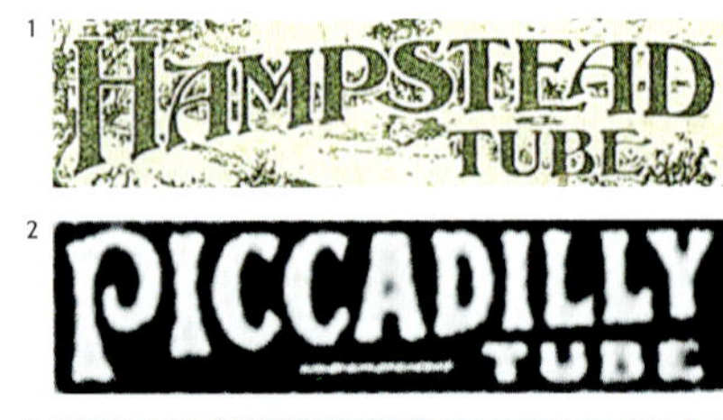

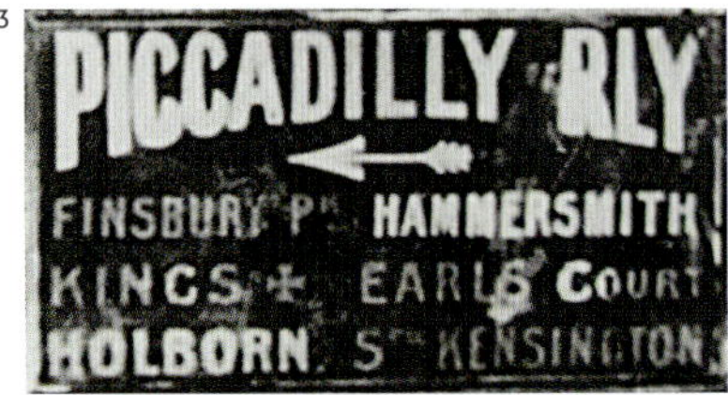

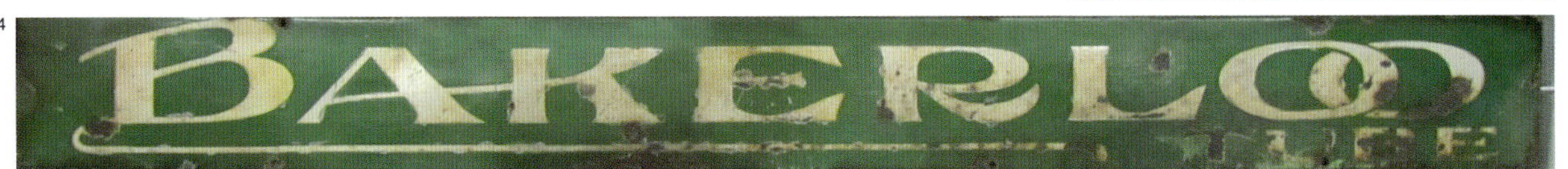

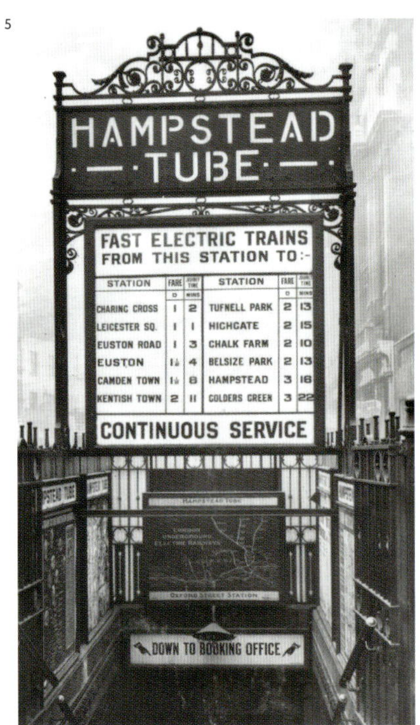

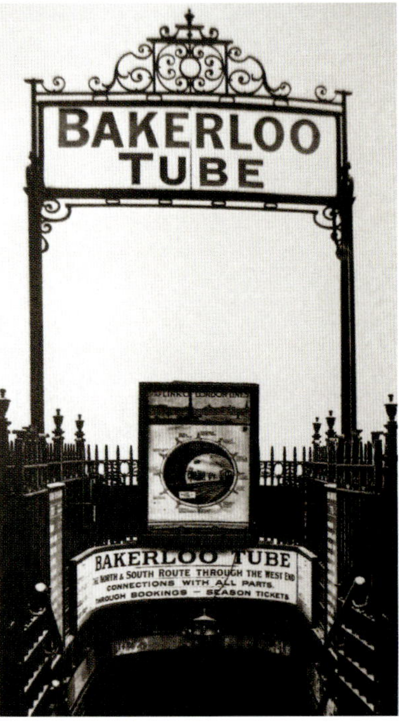

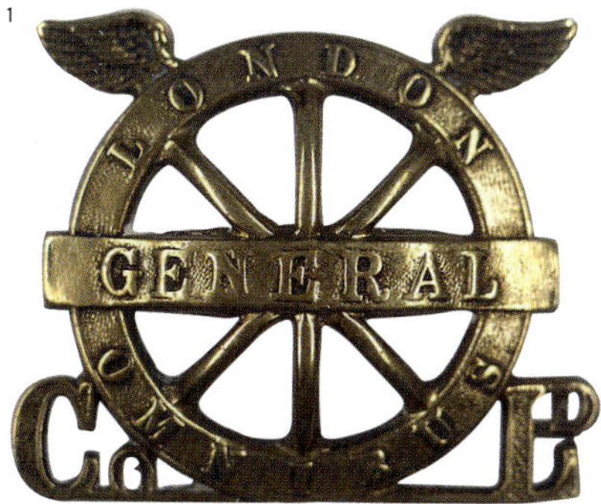

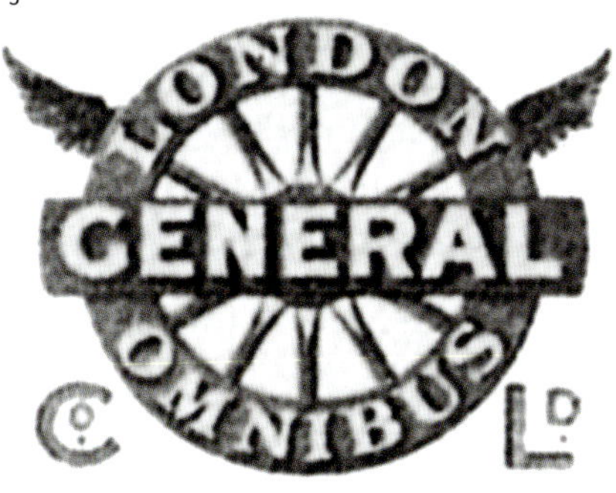

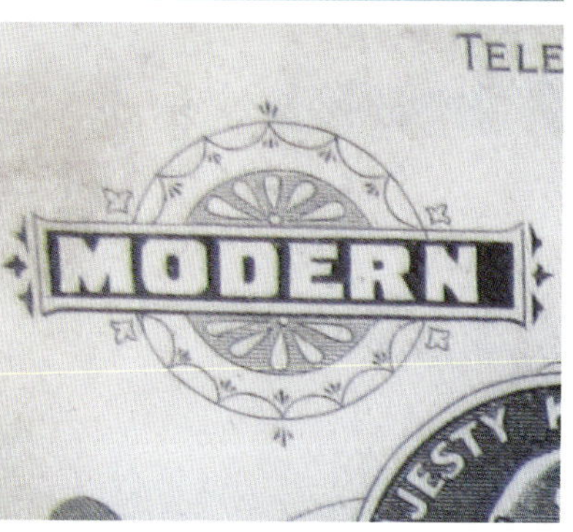

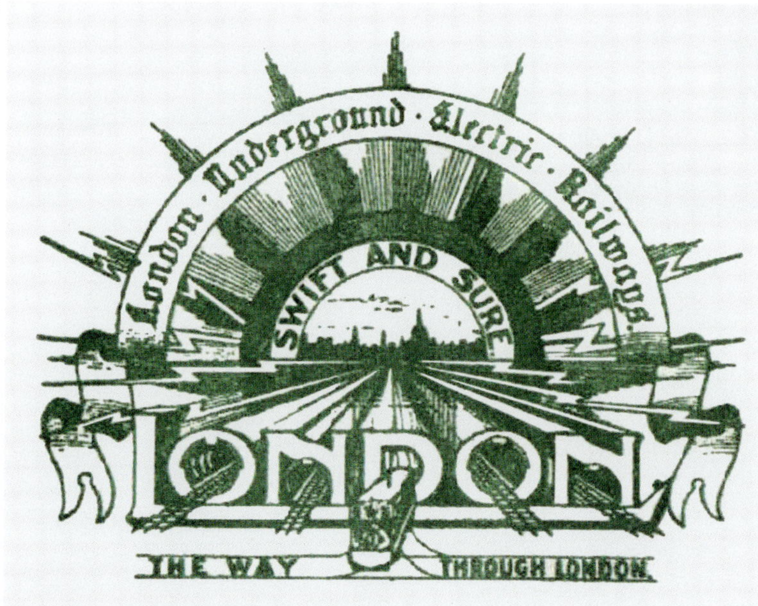

Too many big logos, 1906–7

During the first years of the twentieth century, a plethora of logos was on display among London's transit operators. While each of the deep-level tubes was trumpeting its own identity (opposite), so too were London's bus companies. The most vociferous of these was the London General Omnibus Company, which had as early as 1905 been using a 'winged wheel' device with the word 'GENERAL' set in a crossbar, the one appearing on uniform badges (1) being slightly different from the one used on bus sides (3). It may well have been the prevalence of this 'bar and circle' shape or perhaps other commercial publicity which inspired the UERL's Walter Gott – such as the one that appeared on Bartholomew map covers (2), or the National Gas Engine Company's four roundels, each with a different word on the bar (4). In early 1907 Gott was tasked with devising a trademark to advertise the combined Tube and tram services. His design of the sun rising over the word 'LONDON', with Tube and tram lines running through each letter (5), was used for some months on posters and maps. His slogan, 'Swift and sure the way through London', the horrendous Gothic lettering for the company name, and his overly fancy arcs of lightning were soon consigned to history, but the overall shape (a semicircle with a bar of writing across) and the stylized silhouette view of London at the centre were due for greater exposure (p. 83, 98–9).

The first photo-design survey, 1907

Given the swarm of new logos and letterforms invading London in 1906–7 and cognizant of the forthcoming Franco-British exhibition (due to attract vast crowds to Wood Lane in 1908), the UERL decided quite wisely that something had to be done to unify its collection of disjointed looks and lines. As the choice of a brand name was being ruminated upon, the first job was to conduct a photographic survey of station exteriors. This was carried out between July and December 1907. The second was to devise a way of linking them to the new deep-level tubes (and later the CSLR and CLR). This would be achieved by the combined use of an over-arching operating name, a slogan, a logotype and a silhouette of the London skyline (pp. 80–86, 94–5, 98–9). Artists then painstakingly (possibly hurriedly, it would appear in some cases) hand-painted these photographic prints to show the positioning of the new signage and poster-holding frames. This is so far the earliest known co-ordinated attempt to apply a graphic 'makeover' to existing public transport buildings. And it worked. Stations shown are Monument (1), High Street Kensington (2) and South Kensington (3).

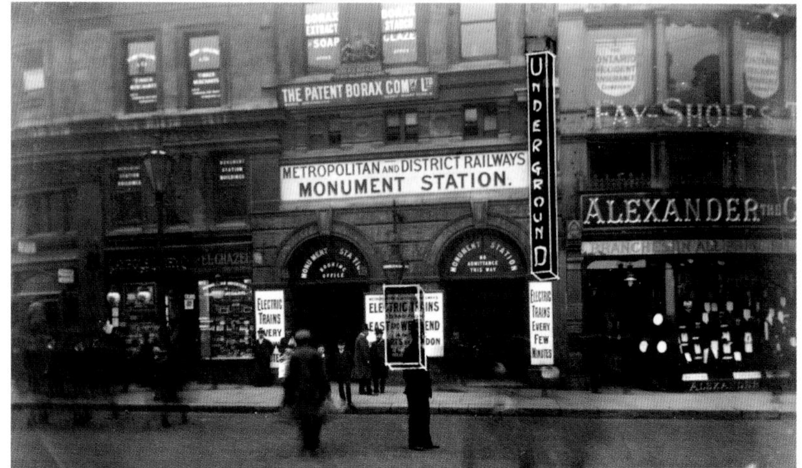

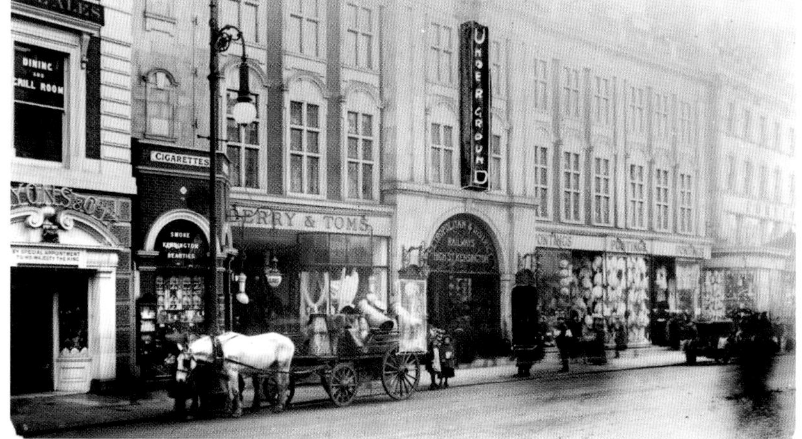

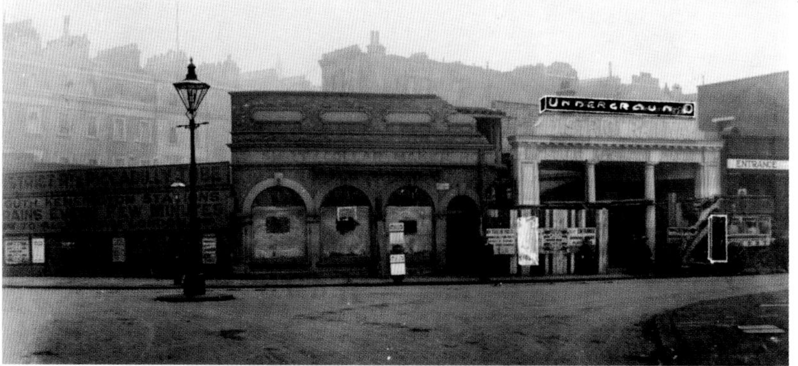

London Underground by Design

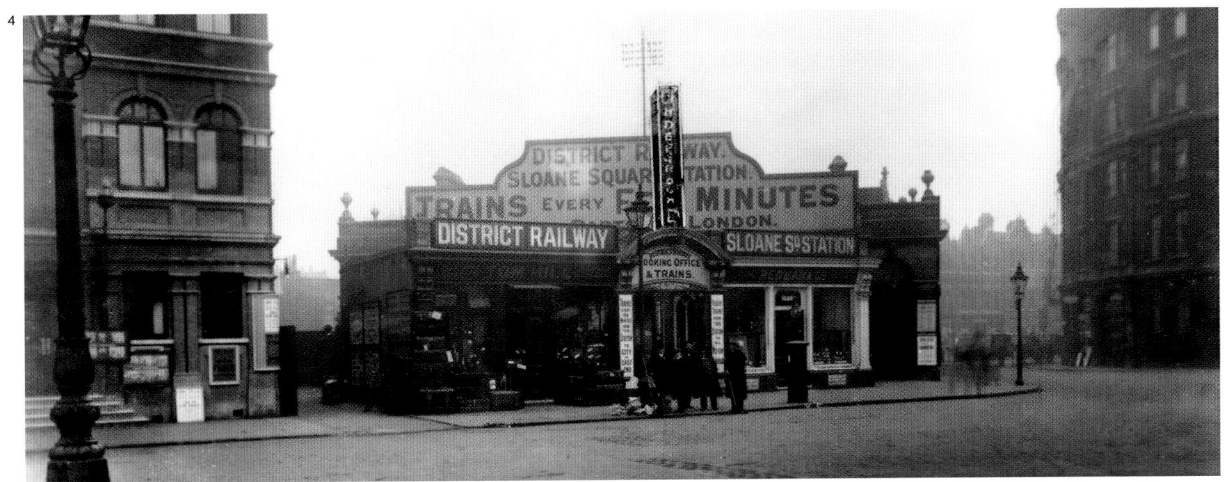

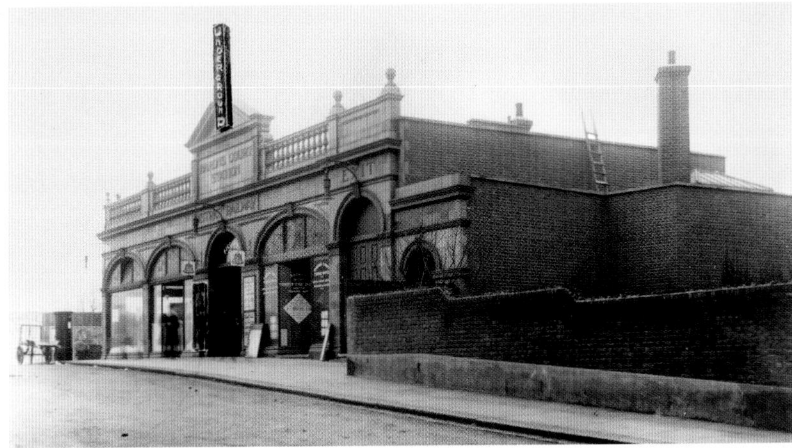

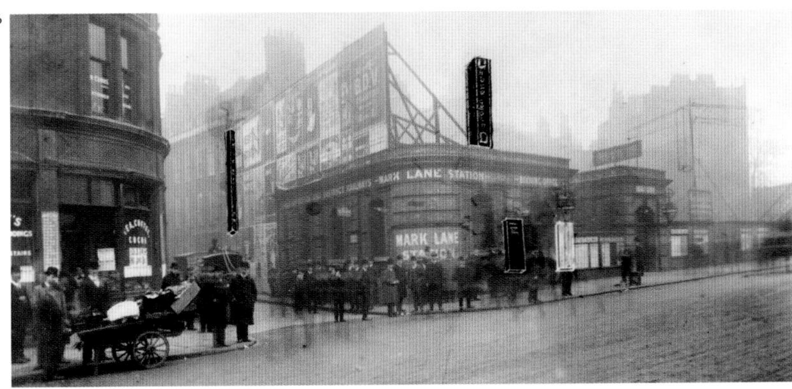

At Sloane Square (4), a free-standing vertical totem was also planned, which would have to stick up in front of pre-existing signage. At Barons Court (5) a totem was proposed, looking somewhat out of proportion with Ford's delicately crafted frontage. And two new poster frames and two illuminated 'totem'-style vertical signs (p. 82) were envisaged at Mark Lane (later re-sited and renamed Tower Hill, 6). While the photographic archives of the London Transport Museum has at least one of these touched-up images for every District station, few such photos have survived showing a suggested makeover for the newer Green stations. It is not known why: perhaps it was not deemed necessary precisely because they were so new. They did, however, receive one relatively soon as most of the new signage was already in position, across all the UERL stations and some Met ones, by the end of 1908. A remarkable achievement by any standard.

First appearance of the enlarged U and D, 1908

In early 1908 the word 'Underground' was chosen as the collective term for all UERL, CLR and CSLR rail services (p. 63). For display on stations and in all publicity, the name was to be set in capitals. Few trade names of the period were not (Pear's Soap, Coca-Cola and Rowntree's being notable exceptions), but while Harry Wharton Ford later claimed the logo as his invention, the reasoning behind the (quirky) decision to use an enlarged U and D has never been fully explained. One theory is that when sign-reading at speed it is only necessary to see the first and last letter to get the word. The Underground wordmark first appeared in print on a map cover (1) dated 1 April 1908 – albeit in an unconventional serifed typeface. A postcard-size map dated May 1908 also used the enlarged U and D (2) as well as a serifed letterform. But it was not until the John Hassall poster (opposite) that sans-serif capitals were used, the distinctive dashes above and below the middle letters appearing after the first official map (May 1908, 3). A monochrome map was provided for guide books in 1908 with the words 'LONDON' and 'RAILWAYS' around the wordmark (4). The logo began to be seen on posters from 1908 (5, and p. 88) and was quickly plagiarized on other official publications like this later 1908 guide to London (6) and a beautiful cover to a street and railway map from the same year (7).

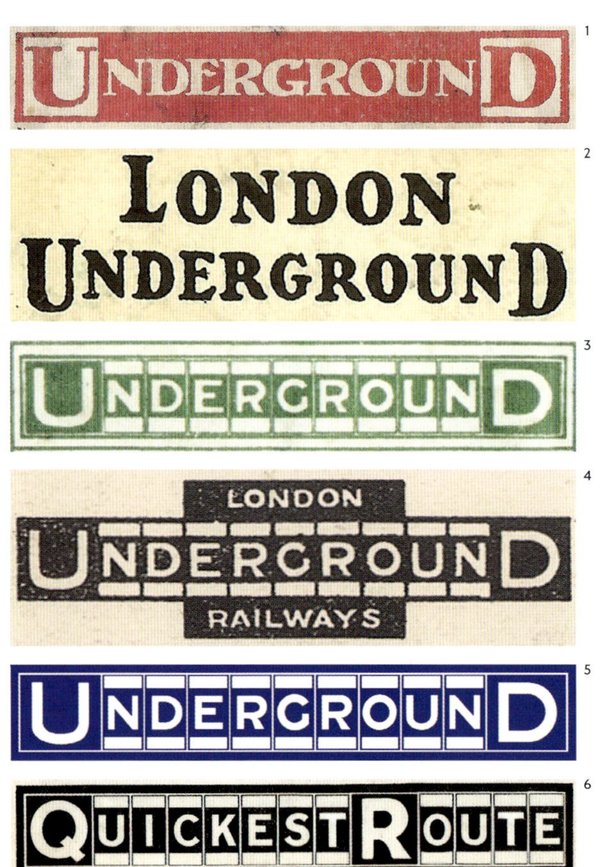

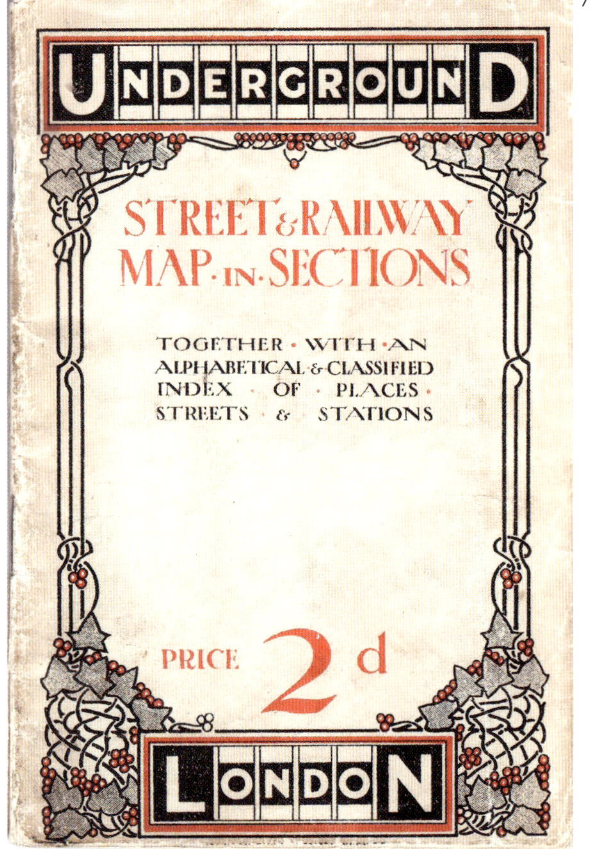

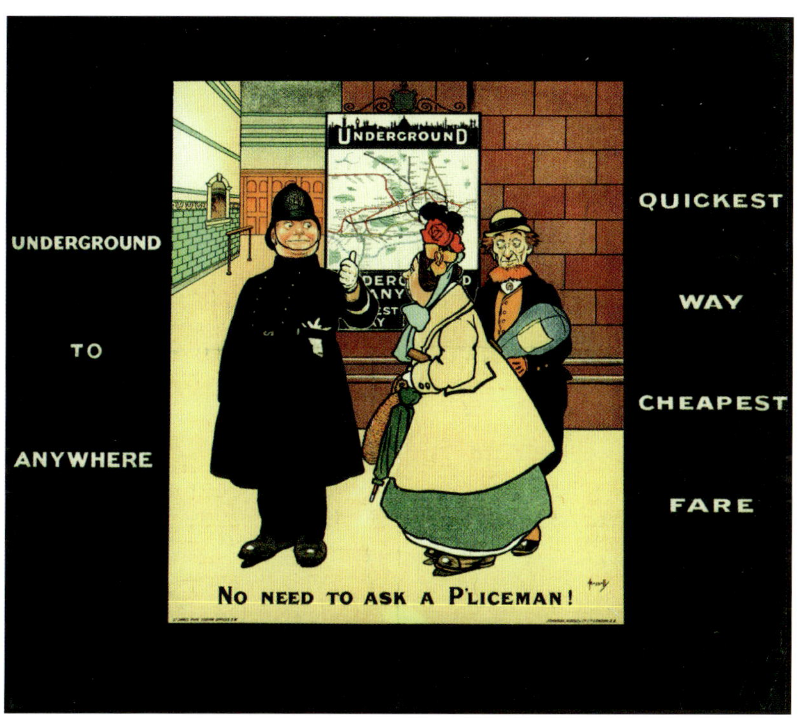

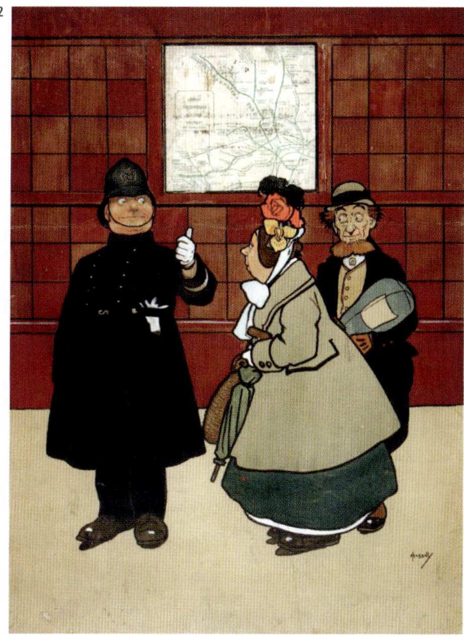

A seminal work in branding, 1908

A poster (1) commissioned by the UERL early in 1908 encapsulated almost every aspect of the group's thinking on what is now termed 'branding'. Here are not only the icons from the newly opened Green stations (the ox-blood tiles, the booking-office ticket windows, the ceramic decor), but the recently devised Underground wordmark with the enlarged U and D and, just visible at the top of the map, the silhouette of the London skyline (running left to right from the Houses of Parliament, Big Ben, St Paul's and the Monument to Tower Bridge). The skyline and logo form the top of a poster frame in which the latest official map is displayed; the lower part of the frame contains the new company slogan (adopted following a newspaper competition won by a young boy): 'Underground to anywhere, quickest way, cheapest fare' (p. 94). Comparing the poster with Hassall's original artwork (2), it can be seen that the background was deliberately amended to include the ticket hall, the poster frame (with ironwork topping), the new multi-coloured map (p. 91) and, most importantly, the Underground logo and skyline motif (p. 83). Apart from it being an attractive and witty poster in its own right, a clearer compendium of all the elements of the 1908 branding would be hard to find. Hassall also designed one of the quintessential railway posters of all time – 'Skegness is so bracing' with a fisherman bouncing along the sands (first issued by the GNR around Easter 1908).

A vertical logo, 1908–9

Having so many new elements with which to regale the passenger visually, it is surprising there was room for much more. Yet more there was. To produce a sign that could occupy tall thin spaces (for attaching to the side of poster frames, for instance, or to create a landmark towering above the entrance), a vertical version of the logo was devised, a novel departure for station signage. The individual letters of the word 'UNDERGROUND' were to be stacked one on top of the other (as seen in the initial technical drawing, 1), the first and last letter both amplified as in the horizontal version of the logo. To make the sign more visible, it would be made up of two, three or even four sides and electrically illuminated from within to give a kind of back-lit, totem-pole effect (2). These light boxes may have been crude and ungainly but they were without doubt innovative and made distinctive beacons, easy to spot on the streets of Edwardian London, and particularly effective at night. In printed versions, the dashes would appear vertically too, on either side of the central letters (1909 map cover, 3). The vertical logo, complete with dashes, was also to be used on the edge of poster frames, in deep blue enamelling with the letters in white capitals (4).

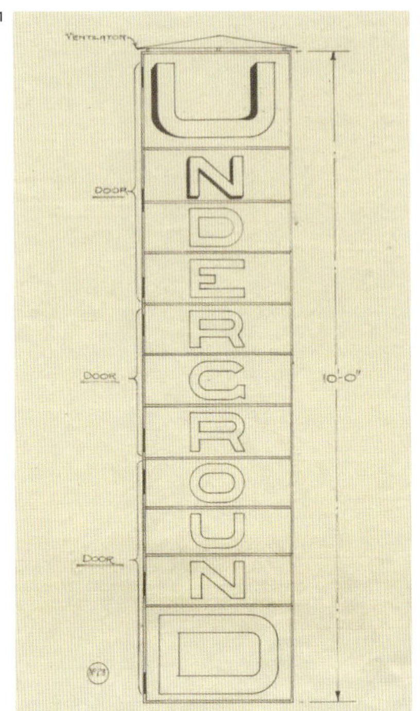

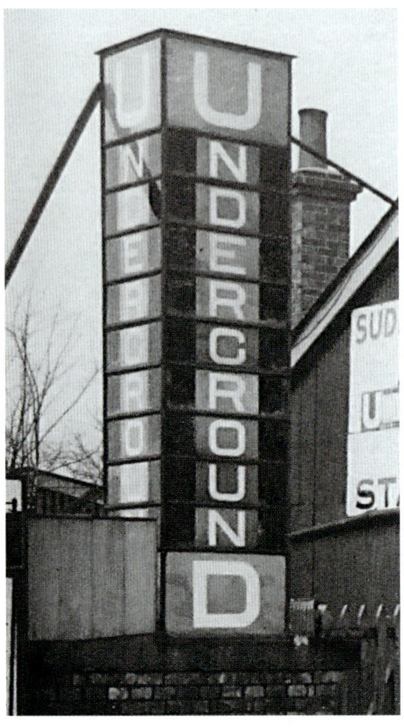

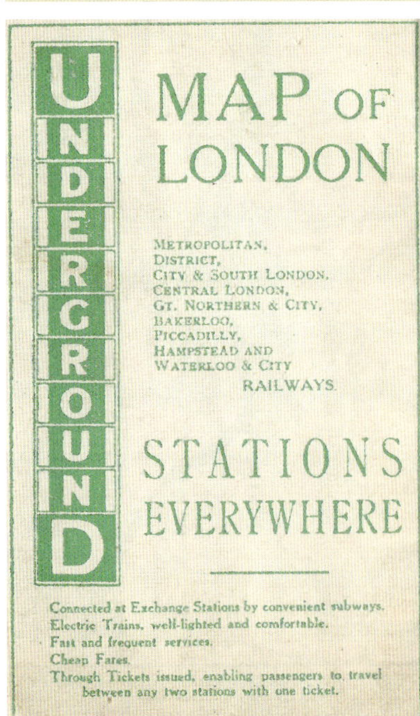

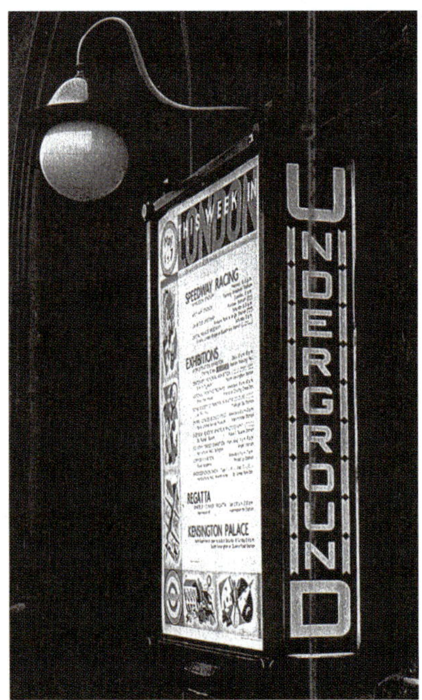

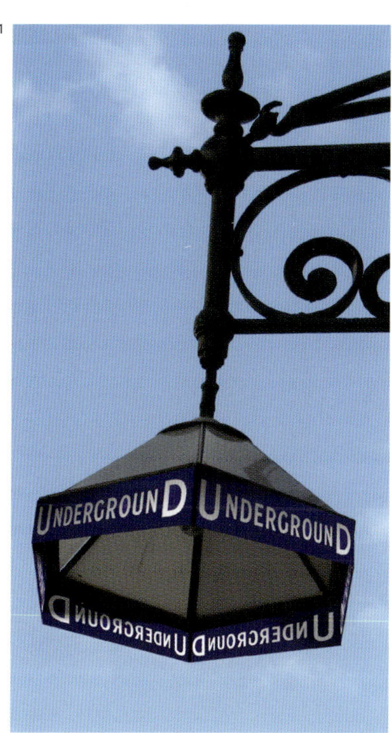

A skyline and some lampshades, 1908–10

In addition to the horizontal and vertical Underground signs with the enlarged U and D at either end, a third concept was introduced simultaneously across the system: a stylized silhouette of the London skyline (2). The idea can be traced to John Hassall's celebrated poster for the Underground (p. 81), first seen in print from spring 1908 (but having been commissioned earlier that year, at exactly the same time the other items were being studied/made). Hassall's poster was not the first time a skyline had been used to advertise the Underground; it was also used for a newspaper illustration (3, date uncertain, but possibly 1907), and on the 1907 UERL logo (p. 77), but Hassall's was the more simplified version on which Big Ben was clearly visible with a white-faced clock. Pick pulled the skyline from Hassall's poster, removing some of the finer details, and added it to subsequent publicity above the 'UNDERGROUND' arrangement, making an early combined emblem: a logo with a pictogram. The skyline device was not used much elsewhere, however. The 'Tiffany' lamps, on the other hand, were ubiquitous. Green's original lamps were circular and bare, but Pick's team introduced a smart hexagonal shade which had a small glass shield on each of the six sides with the UNDERGROUND wordmark etched on to produce a back-lit effect. These lampshades were used across the system, though sadly none have survived, so a digital reconstruction of how they may have looked has been provided (1).

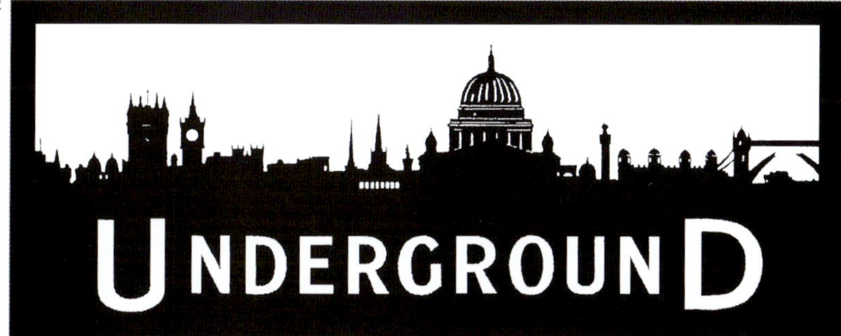

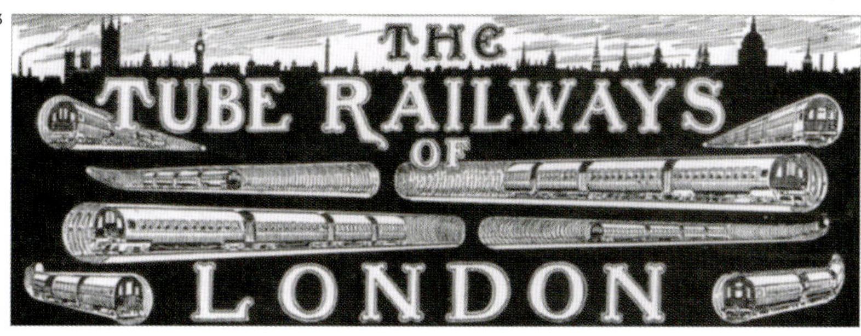

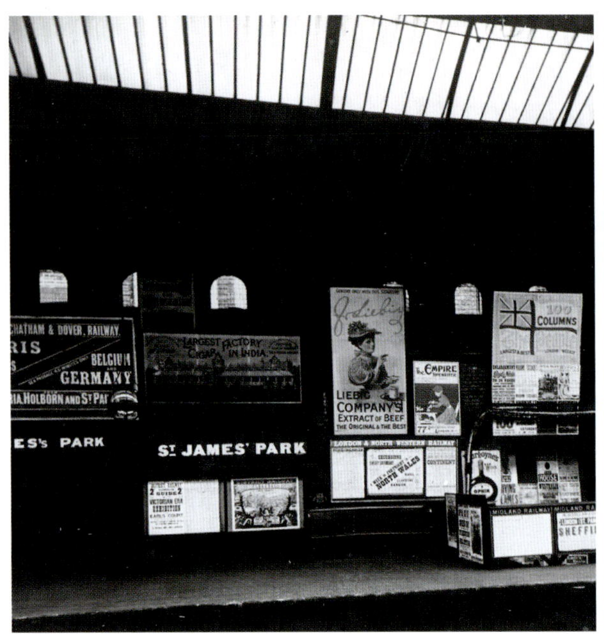

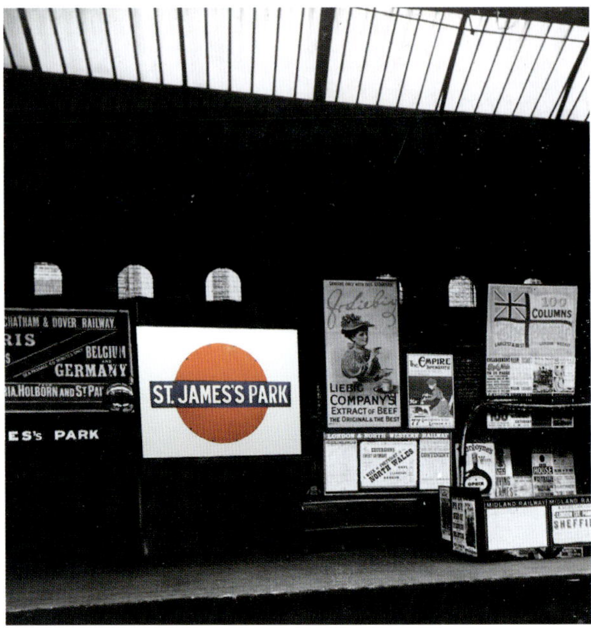

The first bar and circle, 1908

On his return from Paris in early 1908 (p. 66), Albert Stanley met with District superintendent W. E. Blake and William Cleal, the inspector at St James's Park station (directly below the UERL offices). Pick and publicity officer Henry T. Carr were also involved. At the meeting it was agreed to clear spaces among the commercial advertising boards (seen before space was made, 1), about one car-width apart, right down the platform, to make room for large white panels onto which a long blue strip would be affixed with 'ST JAMES'S PARK' written on it. It was certainly a big improvement, but then the signage concepts drawn up by William H. Hilton between 1906 and 1907 (p. 62) were brought to Stanley's

attention. Stanley and District railway secretary Joseph Carter could see that adding a semicircle on either side of each blue strip and setting this against a white background might have a kind of 'bull's-eye' effect, drawing the attention of passengers to the station name. A series of card mock-ups produced by W. Lowe were presented to Pick, who selected the final design and half-moon discs in red paper were pasted above and below the St James's Park nameboards (digitally mocked-up to illustrate the likely effect, 2). They were evidently so successful that by June 1908 an order was placed with Chromo of Wolverhampton for enough sets to be installed at each of the UERL's stations over the next six years. The iconic 'roundel' as it later became known, had almost arrived.

London Underground by Design

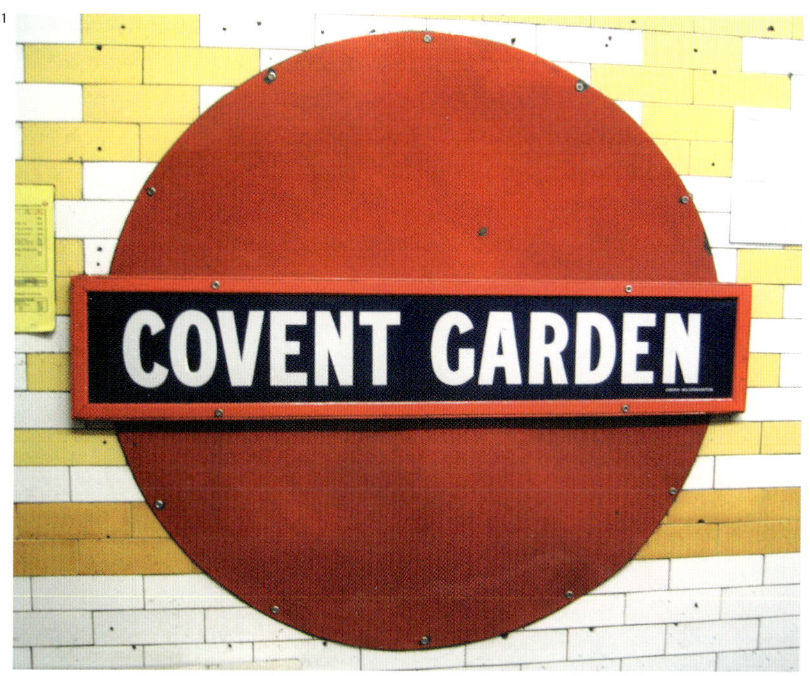

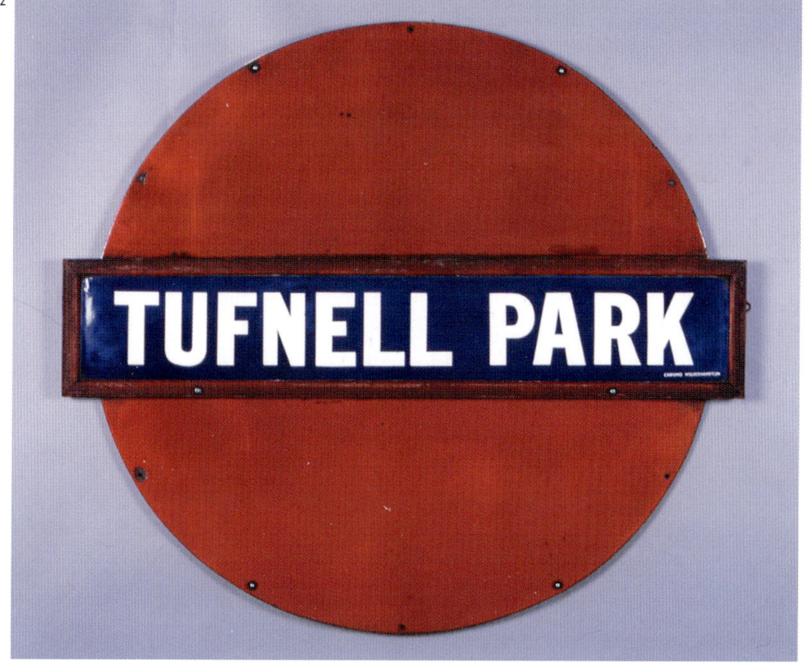

Deep-level difference, 1908

Cut-out versions of the new 'bull's-eye' signs were also supplied for the UERL's deep-tube lines in summer 1908 and placed along the platforms with scant regard to the effect they might have on Green's overall design. One saving grace, perhaps, was that without the large white backing they were fairly simple in style: measuring 137cm in diameter, they were supplied as two red enamel semicircles and a blue enamel bar (30cm high by 152cm wide) displaying the station name, together with a red-painted wooden frame (with a 2.5cm border) to hold the nameplate. It is interesting to note that Brasso (launched in 1905) also had a large red disc with blue writing in the centre, and there were certainly other brands with vaguely similar combinations of shapes (such as the American YMCA logo – a triangle with blue bar across it). The letterform used for station names – a white sans-serif condensed capital – was a modern Gothic with some similarity to the new typeface Franklin Gothic Condensed, which first appeared in 1906. They were mostly positioned at alternating heights (55cm and 150cm from the floor) and there would have been as many as 500 of these outline signs made – two survive in situ (at Covent Garden, 1, and Caledonian Road; at Ealing Broadway a slightly later, larger example on white is visible, p. 86), plus there are a dozen others in the London Transport Museum collection (including this one for Tufnell Park, 2).

Rolling out the red discs, 1908–15

The variation of these new bull's-eye signs used on the District had exactly the same dimensions but were displayed on a large white enamelled metal sheet (152cm square), though the frame holding the blue bar was still made of red-painted wood and glued on. Why the District versions had such a large area of white may be down to the simple fact that they had a better chance of standing out from the murk on platform walls caked in soot from the previous four decades (by contrast with the clean white-tiled walls of the new, electrically powered deep–level tubes). A number of these, with a taller white surround, also survive at Ealing Broadway (1). These are in a Franklin-style lettering, but the letters on most (such as at South Kensington, 3), while also set in condensed sans-serif capitals, look more like the typeface Akzidenz-Grotesk Condensed Bold. The District used smaller circles (e.g. Westminster, 2) but in the same style and occasionally, where space allowed – for example, at Wood Lane (possibly the very first put up in time for the 1908 exhibition) and King's Cross (on the Piccadilly platforms) – a wider, chunkier letterform was used. (This could equally have been based on the Akzidenz family or another standard Grotesque lettering).

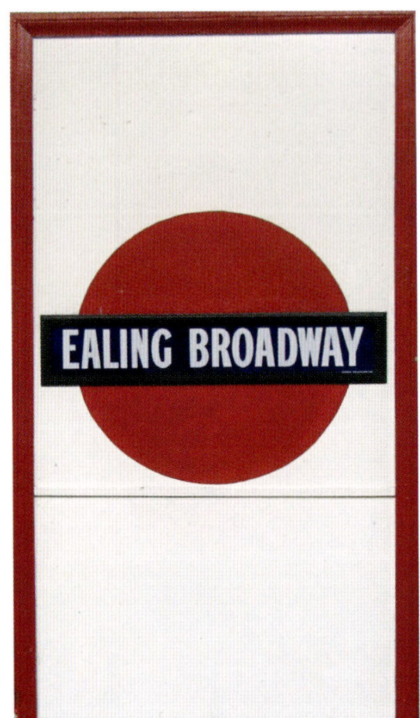

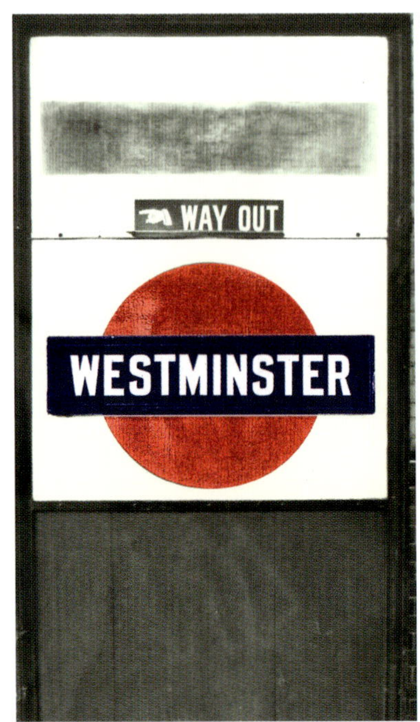

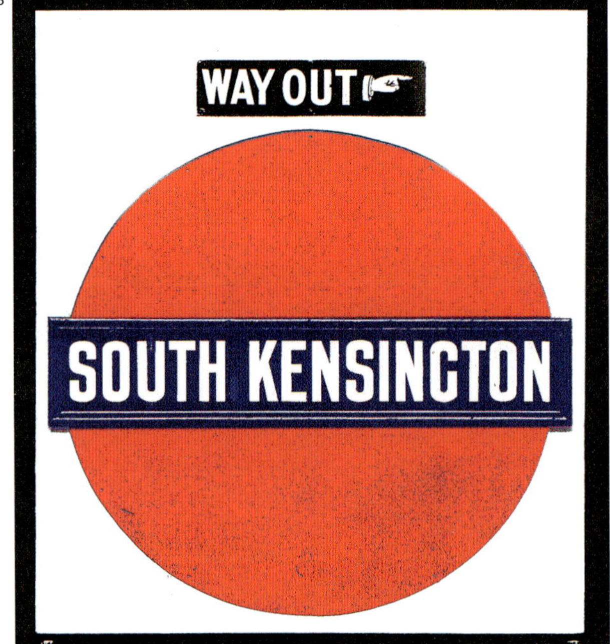

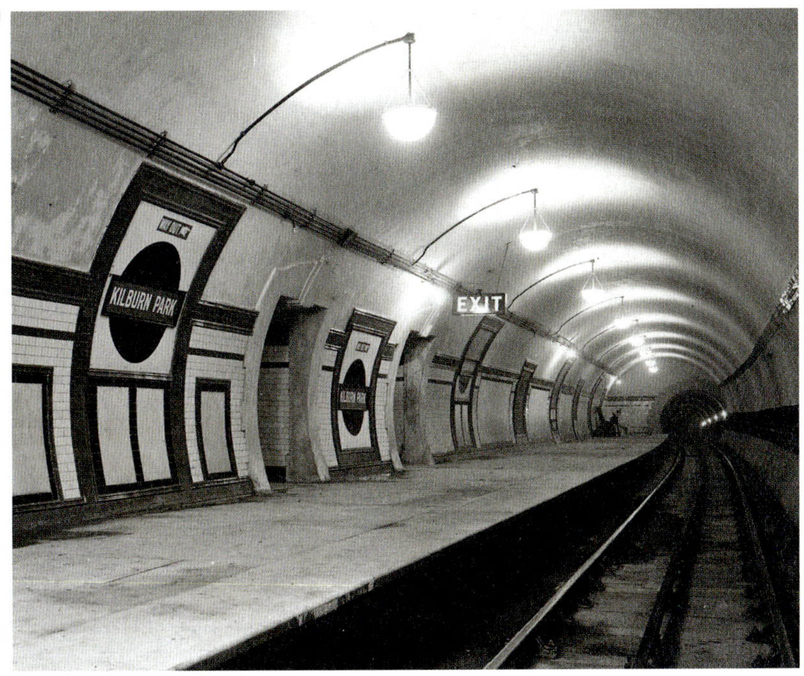

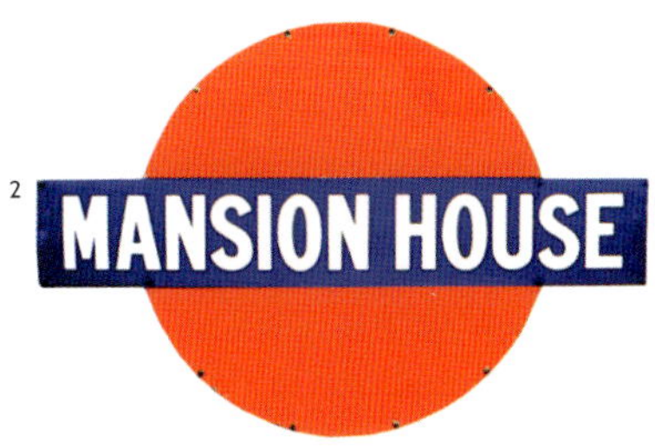

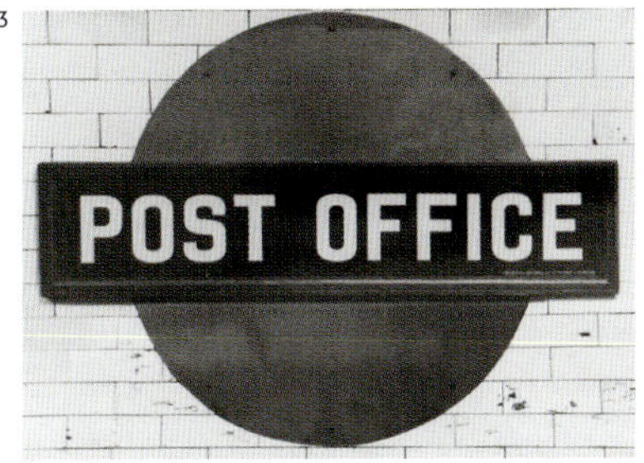

A new version of the cut-out 'outline' sign dispensed with separate parts. The station name and red semicircles were fired onto a single piece of pre-cut iron (no wooden frame needed), for instance at Mansion House (2), where space was made for it following a 1913 rebuild. These had a smaller disc (91cm in diameter) and blue bar (23cm high x 137cm wide) but with text still in the Franklin-style letterform. The next batch comprised two parts, one holding the red disc, the other directions (e.g. 'way out' or interchange details). The disc section consisted of a white enamel sheet (112cm high x 152cm wide) with the smaller red disc and was used primarily on the District, while a 122cm-diameter disc appeared on the 1915 extension of the Bakerloo to Queen's Park (1). Both versions had the same-sized blue name bars as the two previous models but were surrounded by a larger red-painted wooden frame (with a 4cm border), the lettering being white sans-serif capitals in the Akzidenz style. (Lettering on some District nameboard signs was slightly different, possibly made by another manufacturer). When the CLR was taken under UERL control in 1913, another variation of the one-piece outline was utilized, comprising the smaller-diameter red disc and blue bars with both the Franklin-style (not shown) and Akzidenz-style lettering (Post Office, 3); unfortunately none of these have survived. Wooden frames were not crucial to their integrity, being simply glued on top.

Posters, 1908–11

It seems clear from the physical evidence and records of the period that Stanley, Pick and the publicity office had become enthused, to the point of obsession, about the potential of commercial art to boost passenger numbers on the then somewhat underachieving Underground, which was losing passengers to cheaper buses. Pick had grasped the benefits of using posters – bearing the new logo – to increase revenue quite significantly by luring Londoners out to its hinterland, encouraging those who might not normally use the Underground to travel at off-peak times. Taking his cue from the mainline railways, Pick commissioned a whole series of posters urging people to pop on the Tube to sample the green spaces at the edge of the city – a dozen at least were produced in 1908. Works of art in their own right, these were affixed to the new, standard in-house poster frames, which were manufactured to include thin side panels to hold the stacked vertical Underground wordmark (p. 82), creating a type of branded signage that was quite advanced for the period. Various artists were employed for the purpose but, apart from Charles Sharland (1), the identity of those shown on this page is no longer known.

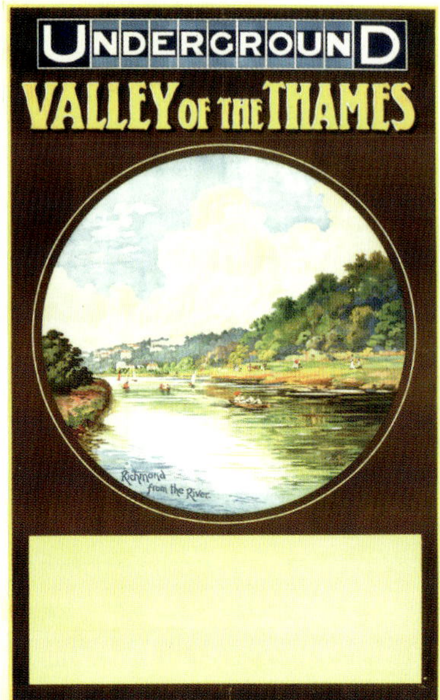

1

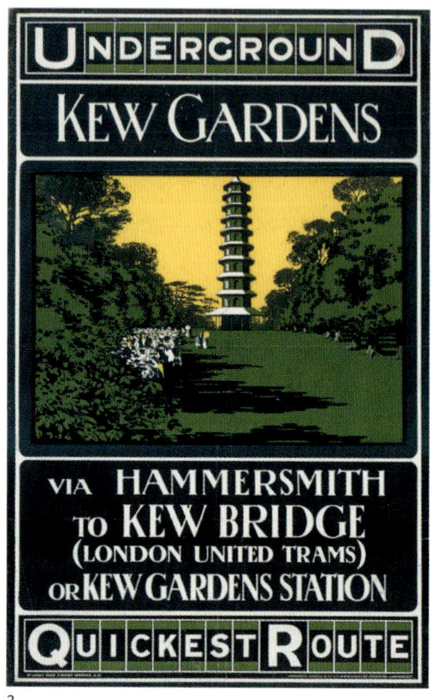

2

3

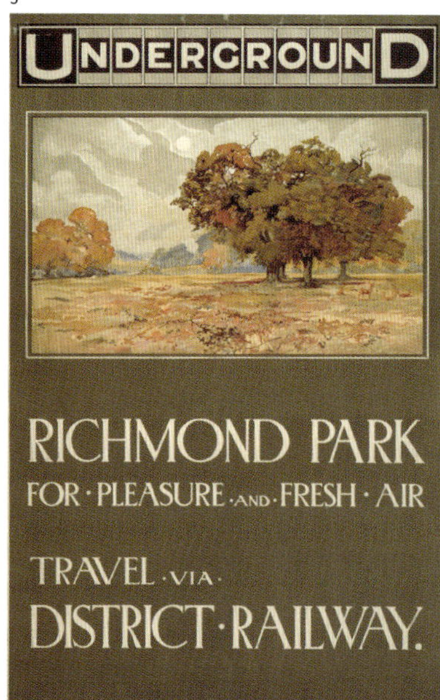

4

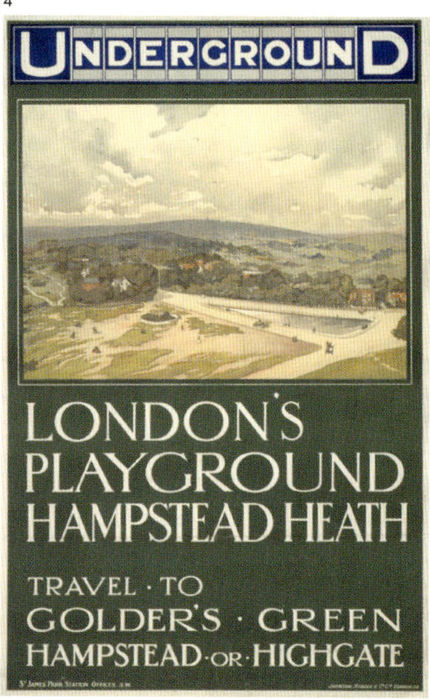

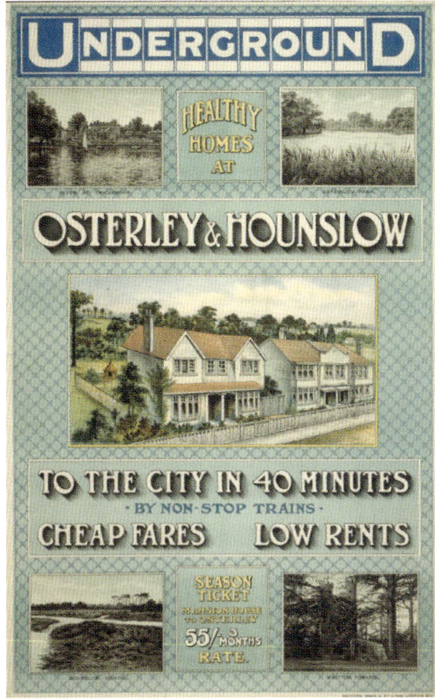

1

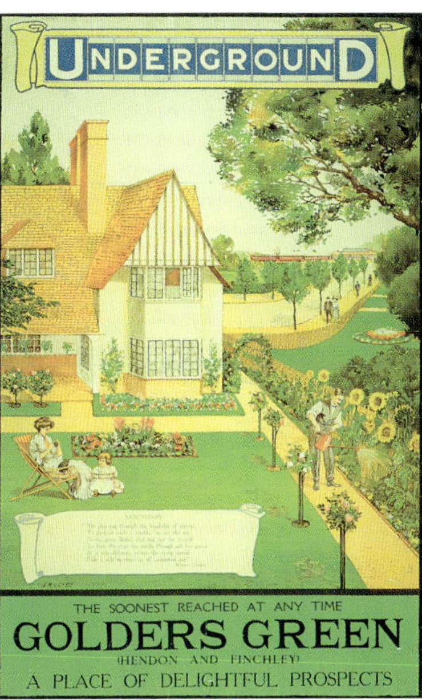

2

3

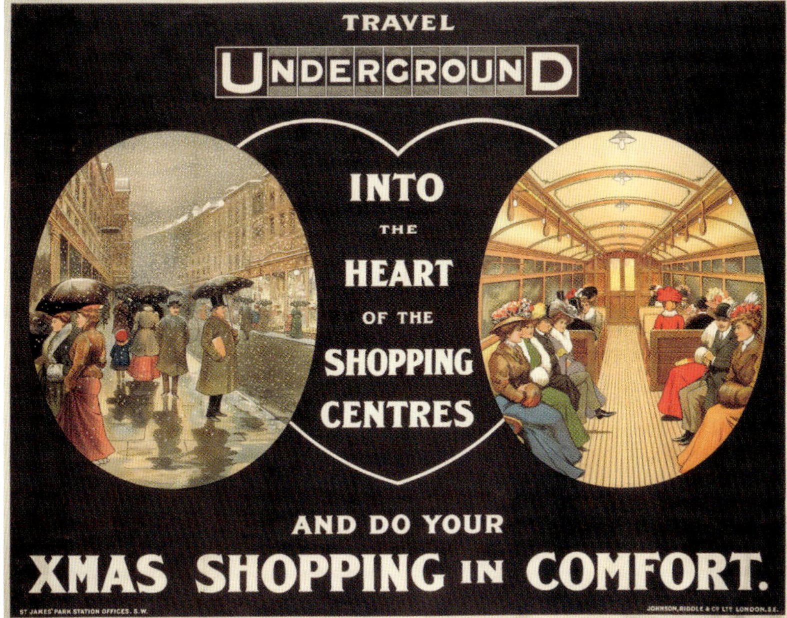

Underground posters promoted other benefits besides out-of-town leisure activities; Frank Pick commissioned stylish images to encourage people to go shopping, see shows and pageants, avoid traffic jams or even, as early as 1909, to buy a 'healthy house' (1) far from the pollution of London and commute 'to the city in 40 minutes'. A poster from 1908, for example, claims how an idyllic Golders Green may be 'soonest reached at any time' (2). This concept of moving inner Londoners out to the expanding suburbs was to take off and transform the city in the next decades. Encouraging shoppers to use the Underground in the off-peak hours has always been a major source of extra income (3) and a wise use of the system in 'down' time. Such colourful artwork adorning otherwise bleak or blank walls had the added benefit of making the stations feel brighter and more welcoming.

Cartographic advances, 1906–8

In conjunction with the other improvements in graphic design, maps were not forgotten during this crucial period. The UERL's pocket map of 1906 (1) was quite well thought out; the Piccadilly was shown in green and the District and Bakerloo in red — the Hampstead Tube and other sections under construction had to make do with a broken line. Other railways (including the Met) were shown in fainter lines. London United Tramway routes, also owned by the combine, were shown too. Just a year later, in 1907, the pocket plan gained a smart green border (2), which it kept for some years; the Hampstead Tube is shown as open but all the UERL lines are depicted in the bolder black, the District sports an attractive red, LUT trams get a thin blue (while other lines seem relegated to the background; cartographic evidence, if it were needed, of company rivalry and somewhat unhelpful as a navigation guide).

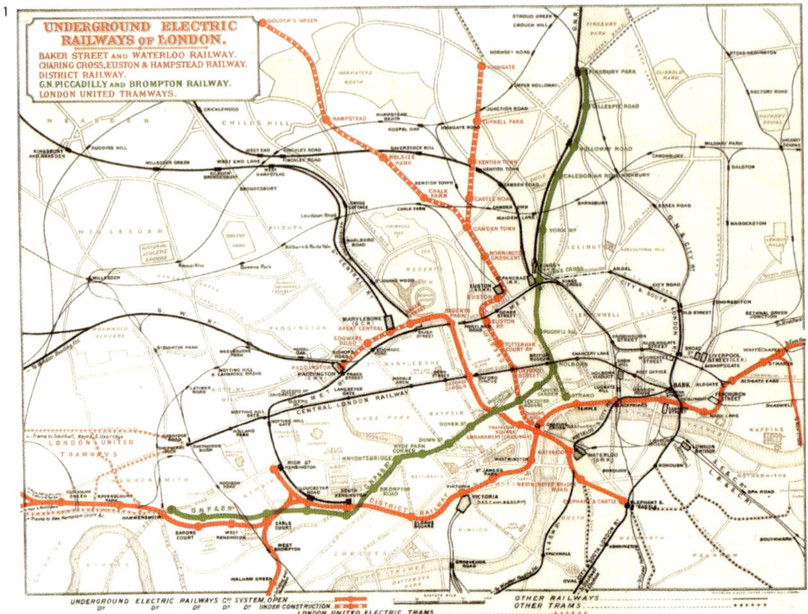

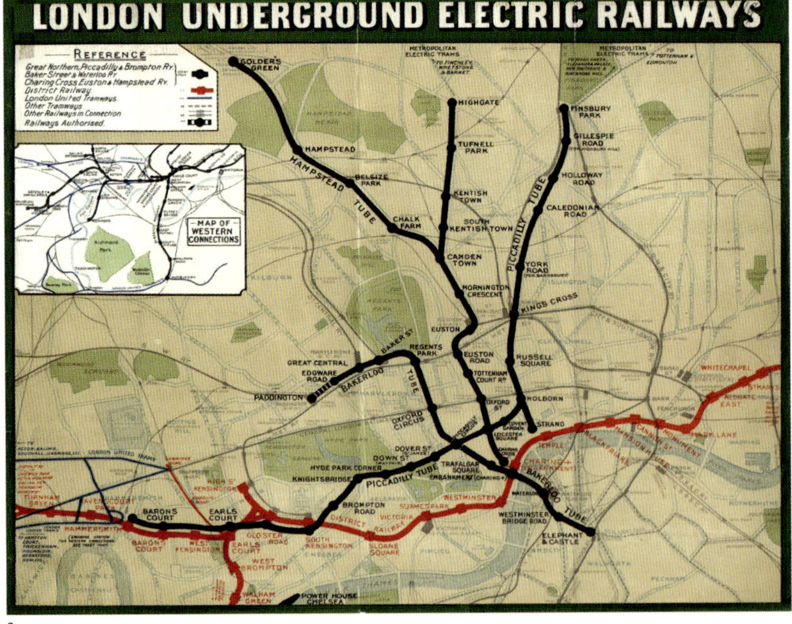

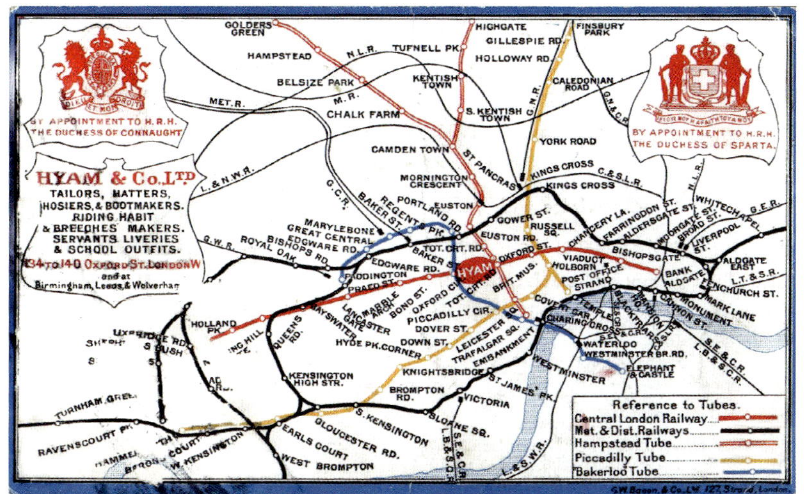

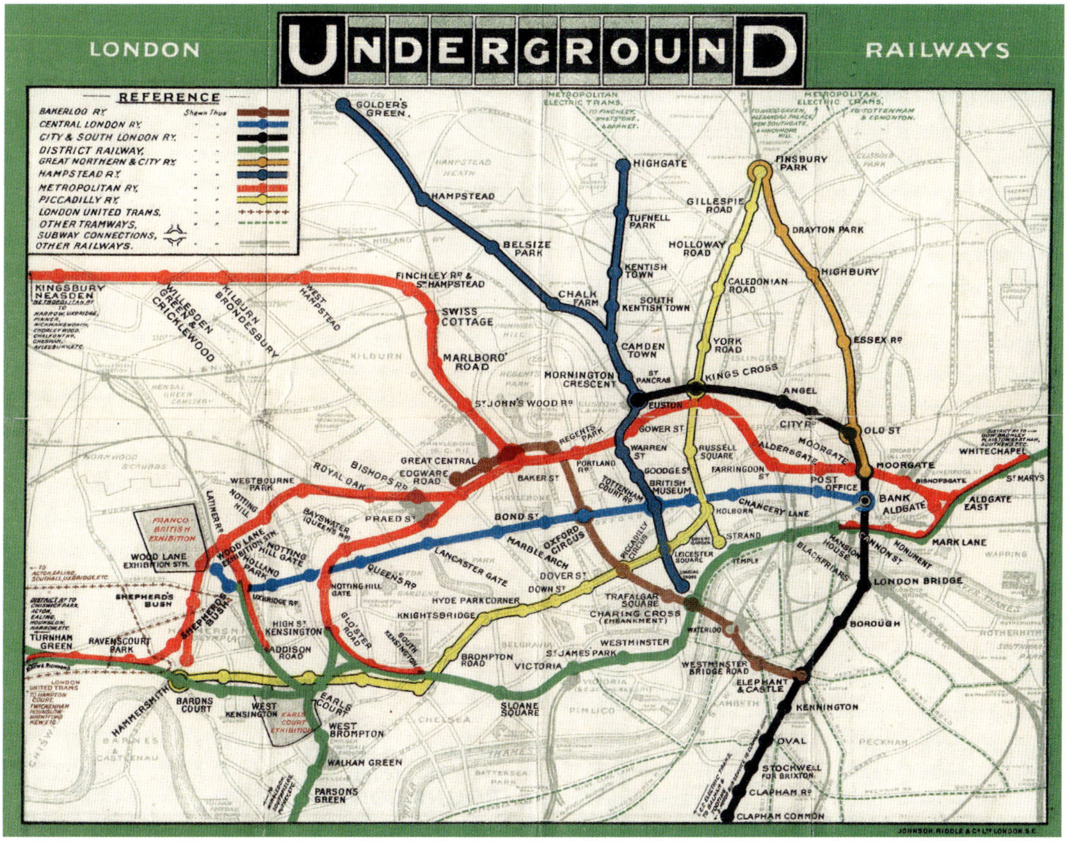

Colour had been used to indicate particular features on a map, but it was not until this period that railway cartographers began to use it to differentiate between different lines. A 1907 postcard (1) produced by a printers called G. W. Bacon for Hyam, a West End tailors exhibits possibly the widest range of line colours so far seen. But the 1908 UERL pocket map (2), resplendent with the new U and D logo, represents a step change in clarity: the colour coding of each line set the tone for Tube map-makers up to the present.

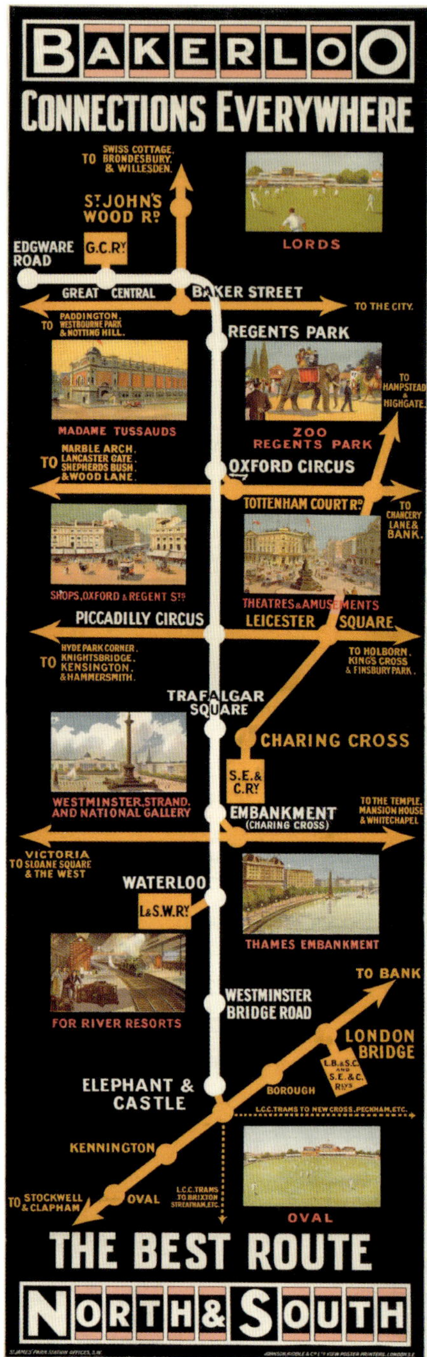

Early moves to simplify the lines, 1908–12

The most iconic map of the Underground is a diagram but it did not emerge in its present form until the 1930s (p. 169). Other attempts to simplify individual lines or parts of a whole system appeared sporadically before then. In 1908, for example, the Bakerloo produced a beautifully executed elementary diagram with exquisitely drawn vignettes (1). Almost 2m high, it featured in the London Transport Museum's 2012 exhibition 'Mind the Map'. In its efforts to promote all services, the UERL also produced a number of advertisements for taking the tram to get to the Underground. A 1909 poster with stylized tram and Tube tracks is an early example (2).

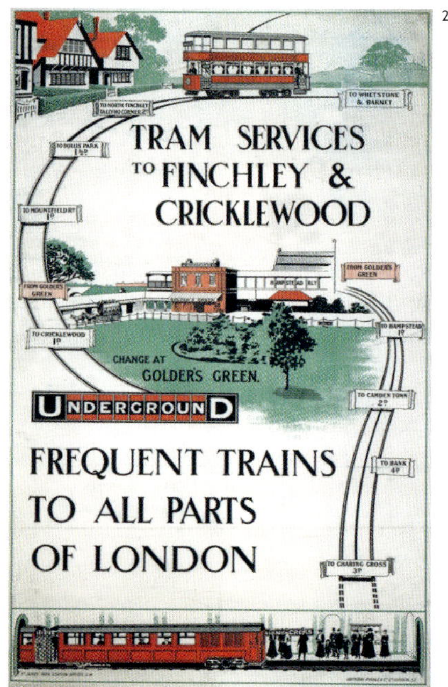

London Underground by Design

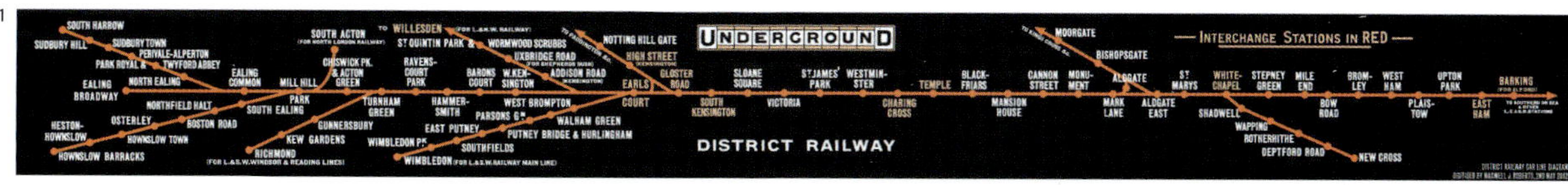

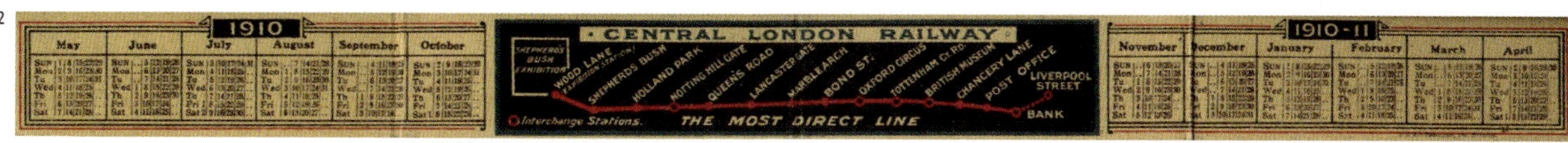

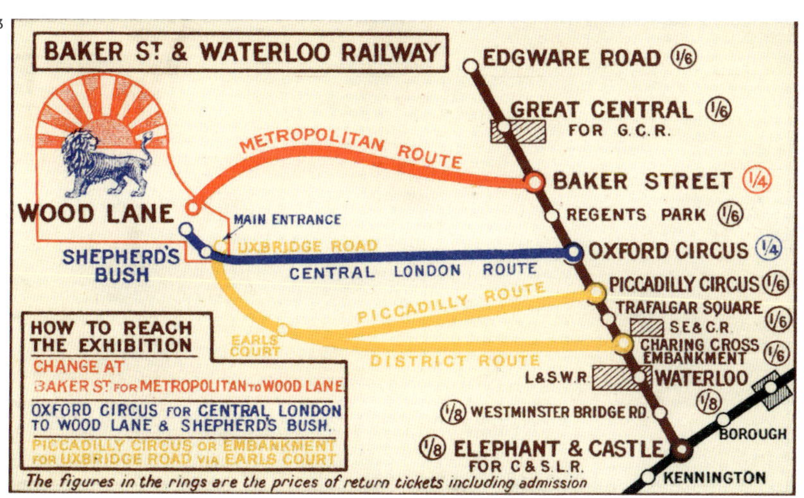

The same year, 1908, the District installed what is understood to be the first in-car 'strip map'; a highly simplified horizontal representation of its services (in a 2012 digital recreation by Max Roberts, 1). Though some similar line maps had appeared on mainline railways (in Lancashire in 1904, for instance, according to Andrew Dow – Bibliography), this was the first on the Underground and it set a trend: they are now in every car. Meanwhile, a 1910 strip map of the CLR (2) was designed to be folded up like a tape measure to advertise the directness of the route. A 1908 postcard for the Franco-British Exhibition uses more simplification to illustrate the handiness of the Bakerloo line for connections to the grounds (3). While a 1909 UERL fold-out map tries removing all the streets and numbering selected landmarks (detail, 4), two years later, the streets are reintroduced and the trajectory of the lines smoothed out (detail, 5).

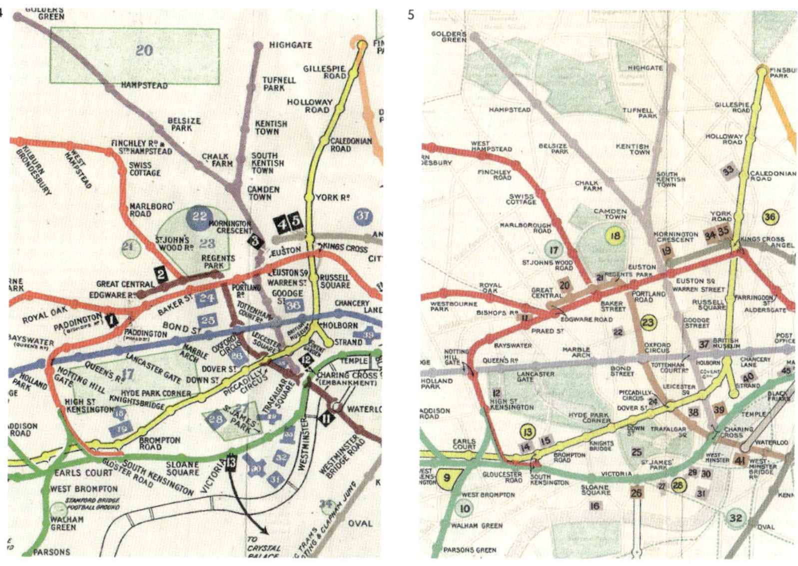

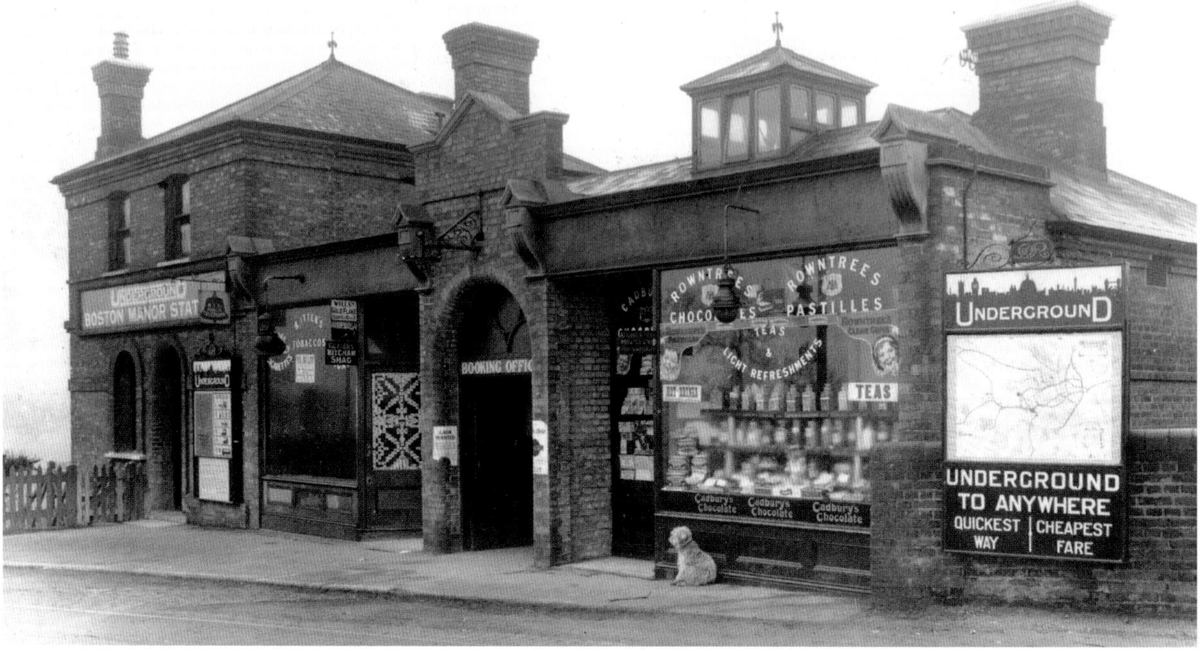

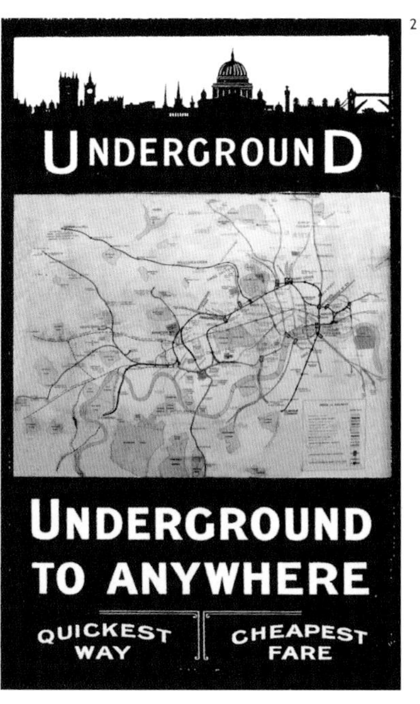

A slogan to anywhere, a logo for everywhere, 1908–16

Because of their unique styling, the Green stations posed a problem for the branding exercise, so, along with the other devices, a ceramic panel featuring the large U and D with one white letter per blue tile was designed exclusively for them. These were inserted on the station fronts of most deep-level tubes, and several survive (such as Chalk Farm, opposite, 2). There is even a theory that it was the design of this tiled feature that gave rise to the one-letter-in-a-box effect of the U and D logo. As if all the signage were not sufficient, the UERL also employed slogans, clearly designed to be used as part of the 1908 branding. 'Underground to anywhere' and 'Quickest way – cheapest fare' appeared all over London. The poster frames holding maps were the largest (150cm wide x 200cm high, 2, and slimmer versions were seen too (opposite, 1). The order of sections top to bottom was invariably: skyline device at the top; 'UNDERGROUND' logo beneath (no dashes above or below the letters); enamel system map below that; then on the next line 'UNDERGROUND' and 'TO ANYWHERE' on the next, followed by: 'QUICKEST WAY | CHEAPEST FARE'. Shown in situ at Boston Manor (1916, 1), this is identical in layout to John Hassall's poster (p. 81), lending credence to the supposition that it served as an early style guide.

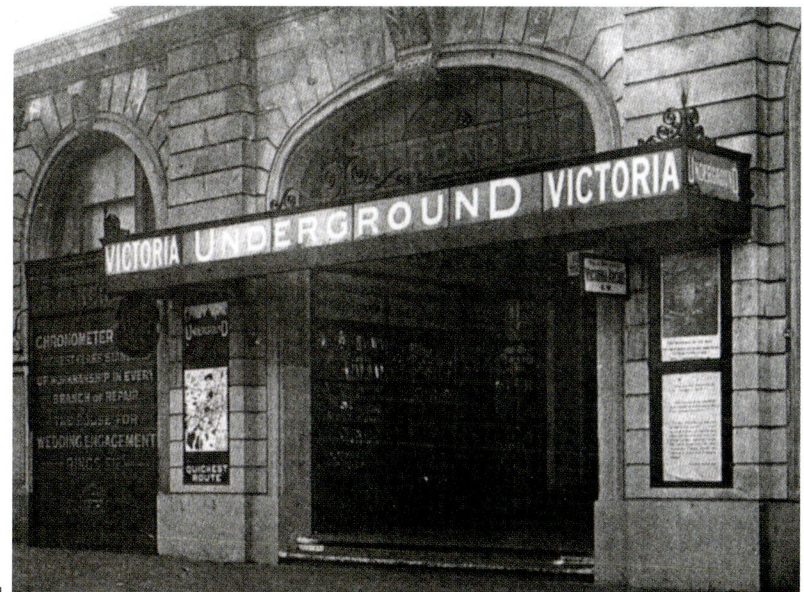

1

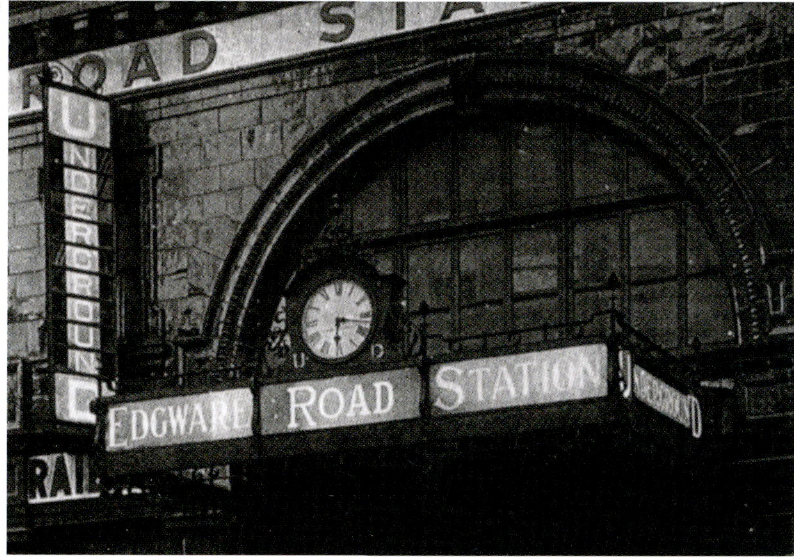

2

3

Enlarged U and D becomes a ubiquitous device, 1909–14

After the initial rapid roll-out of the U and D signs, further adaptations and variations were found for the logo, from posters, to fliers, to company notepaper, uniforms and yet more signage. The metal and glass canopies that were installed across the network from 1908 were useful for projecting the station out into the streetscape; they created a 3D elevation over the pavement which could not be missed by pedestrians (1, 3). But they were odd in that the serif lettering used initially did not always match the sans-serif style employed elsewhere. It is now believed that they were possibly ordered first, using the serifed style of lettering similar to the 1 April 1908 map cover (p. 80), which matched more closely Green's lettering style. Taking longer to manufacture, they arrived after the decision was taken to move to a sans-serif elsewhere and therefore looked somewhat out of place. Closer inspection of photos, however, reveals that while the Green stations sported this serifed lettering (Edgware Road, 3), most of the District canopies were made in a variety of sans-serifs (e.g. Victoria, 1) – although there were exceptions to this rule; for example, Stamford Brook, a District station, had the serif letters, whereas Camden Town, a Green station, sported the sans-serif canopy lettering. This relative mayhem, typographically speaking, was certainly part of the reason Pick decided to investigate an entirely new typeface for London Underground operations (pp. 112, 122–3).

Tube trumpeting, 1908–13

Nothing galvanizes a company into a bit of shameless self-promotion more than a winning campaign by a competitor, and the CLR realized very quickly after the UERL's installation of the U and D logos all over London that it had better pull its finger out. Ticket sales were falling, so an investment was made in fairly copycat branding – glass canopies over entrances and large vertical totems outside stations, but all boasting the word 'TUBE' (all images on this page). Its poster campaigns were most distinctive too, promoting everything from the amount of ozone in the tunnel air (opposite, 1) to a parcel delivery service (run between 1911 and 1917, opposite, 2). Two extensions were opened, the first to Wood Lane (in 1908, p. 93) for the exhibition grounds, the second – more useful for regular passengers – to Liverpool Street, which opened in 1912. The CLR remained the most effective marketeer of the non-UERL companies until 1 January 1913 when the Underground Group officially took control of the line. After that, the red discs were added to the existing blue nameboards on platforms (p. 87) and the 'TUBE' totems were replaced with 'UNDERGROUND' ones to give CLR passengers the impression that they were travelling on a more united system. The CLR made a feature of its loop at the new Wood Lane station (which opened on 14 May 1908), turning it into the head of a 'key' to London (opposite, 3).

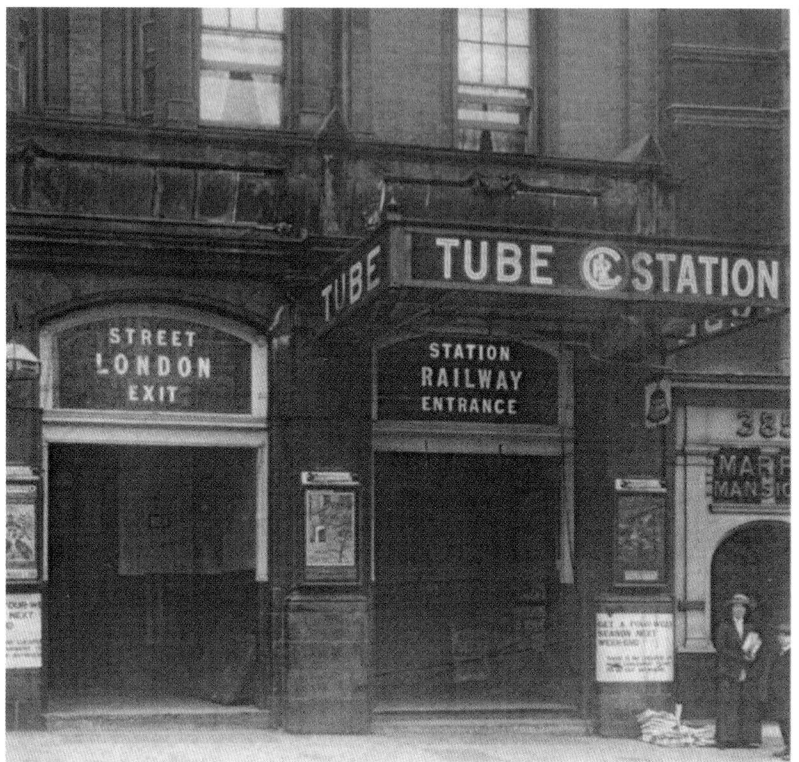

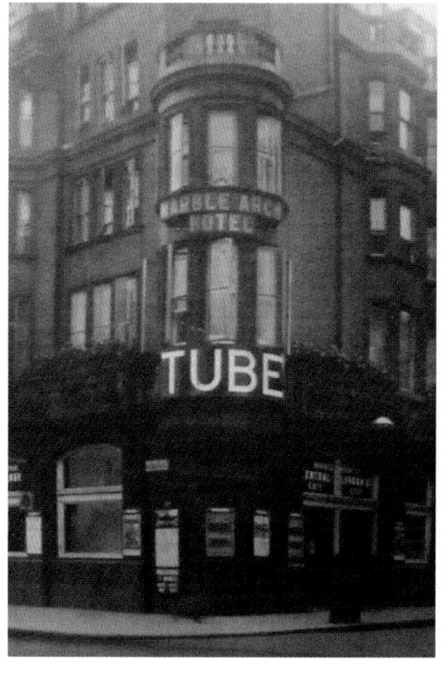

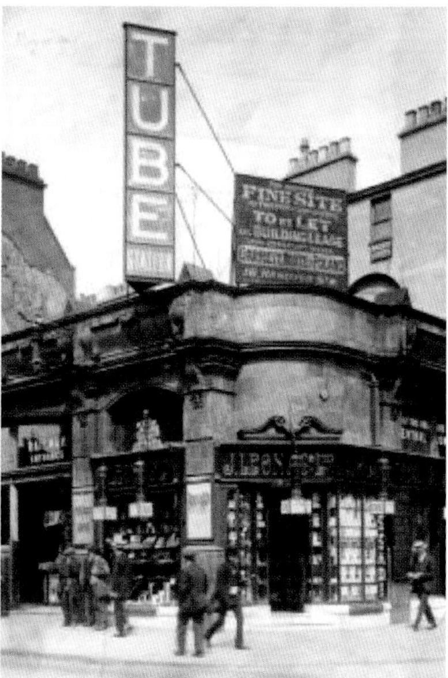

London Underground by Design

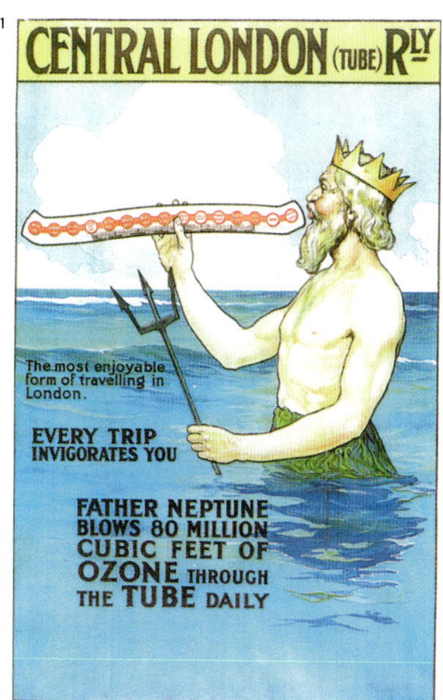

CENTRAL LONDON (TUBE) R^LY
The most enjoyable form of travelling in London.
EVERY TRIP INVIGORATES YOU
FATHER NEPTUNE BLOWS 80 MILLION CUBIC FEET OF OZONE THROUGH THE TUBE DAILY

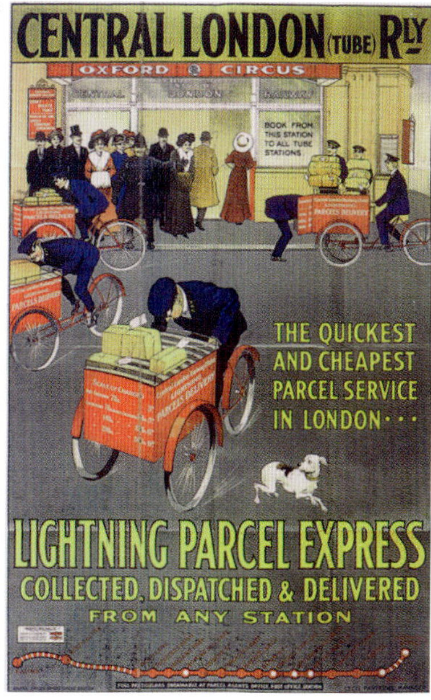

CENTRAL LONDON (TUBE) R^LY
OXFORD CIRCUS
BOOK FROM THIS STATION TO ALL TUBE STATIONS
THE QUICKEST AND CHEAPEST PARCEL SERVICE IN LONDON •••
LIGHTNING PARCEL EXPRESS
COLLECTED, DISPATCHED & DELIVERED
FROM ANY STATION

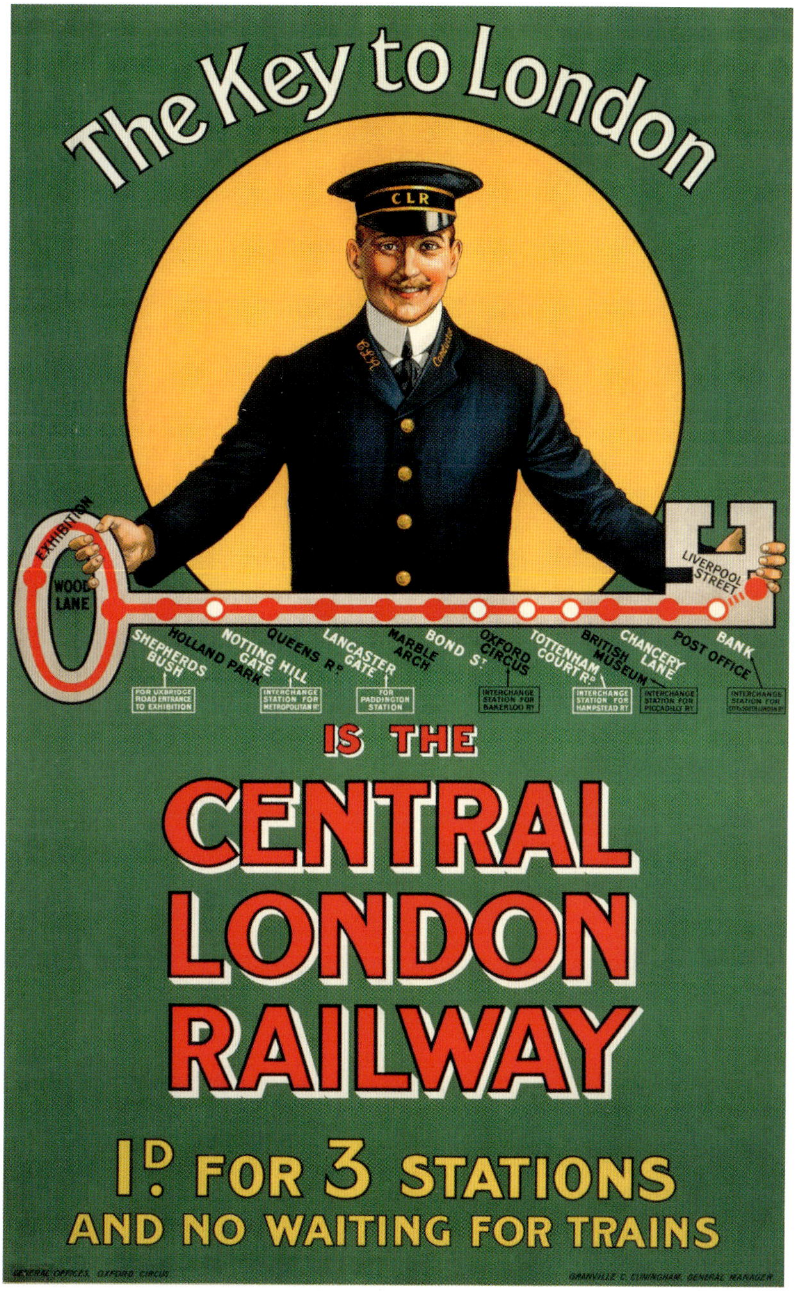

The Key to London
CLR
EXHIBITION
WOOD LANE
LIVERPOOL STREET
SHEPHERDS BUSH
HOLLAND PARK
NOTTING HILL GATE
QUEENS R^D
LANCASTER GATE
MARBLE ARCH
BOND S^T
OXFORD CIRCUS
TOTTENHAM COURT R^D
BRITISH MUSEUM
CHANCERY LANE
POST OFFICE
BANK
FOR UXBRIDGE ROAD ENTRANCE TO EXHIBITION
INTERCHANGE STATION FOR METROPOLITAN R^Y
FOR PADDINGTON STATION
INTERCHANGE STATION FOR BAKERLOO R^Y
INTERCHANGE STATION FOR HAMPSTEAD R^Y
INTERCHANGE STATION FOR PICCADILLY R^Y
INTERCHANGE STATION FOR CITY & SOUTH LONDON R^Y
IS THE
CENTRAL LONDON RAILWAY
1^D FOR 3 STATIONS AND NO WAITING FOR TRAINS
GENERAL OFFICES, OXFORD CIRCUS
GRANVILLE C. CUNINGHAM, GENERAL MANAGER

Bar and disc combine, 1912–14

The evolution of the enlarged U and D into a united wordmark can be traced back to 1908 (p.80). But the first time the red bull's-eye disc shape (on station-name signs) was overlaid by the U and D wordmark was around 1911/12. John Henry Lloyd's tram poster (2), from late 1911/early 1912, may be the first outing for the combined device. But Charles Sharland's invitation to witness the solar eclipse of April 1912 (3) is the first item that can be precisely dated with the merger. Whether he or Lloyd were instructed to marry the Underground wordmark with the disc by Pick or Ford is not known, but the matching shape of red disc and celestial body presented an opportunity clearly too good to miss. And so emerged the world's most recognized transport logo. In May 1912, Sharland used the device again, adapting it slightly, while a map cover from July 1912 (artist unknown, opposite, 1) featured the combined logo as a guiding star. Alfred France's poster, 'Hermes for Speed, Eros for Pleasure' (1912, but month unknown, 1), promoting deity-like attributes, seemed perfect for launching a new visual identity and suggests the publicity office considered the device a fait accompli. If France's poster came after the tram and eclipse posters, then Lloyd and Sharland must be credited jointly as creators of the new logo because from mid 1912 it stuck — although the U and D wordmark continued to appear without the red disc for some years.

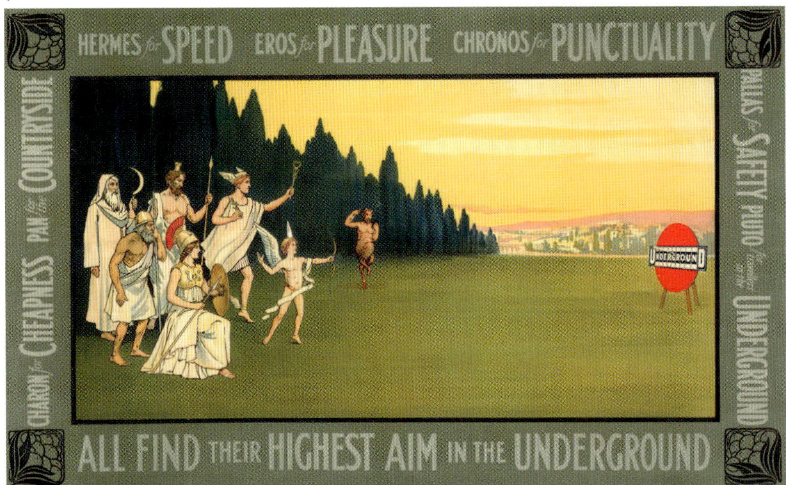

2

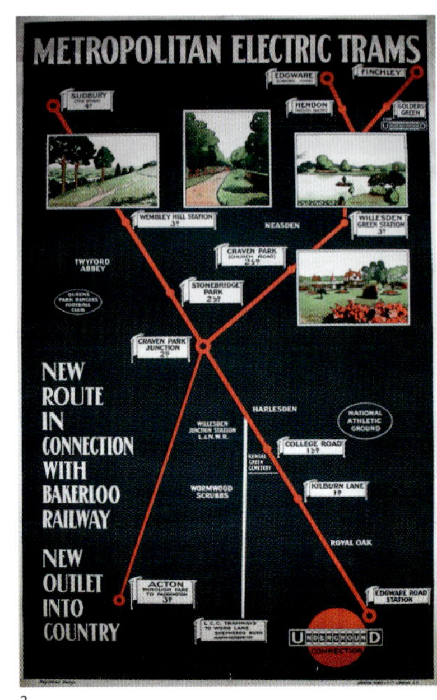

1

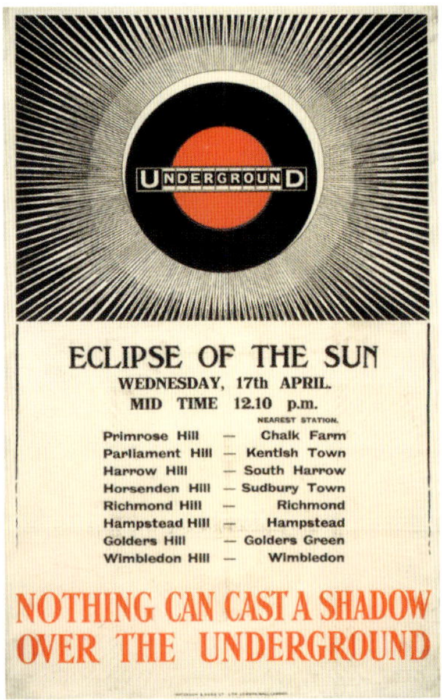

3

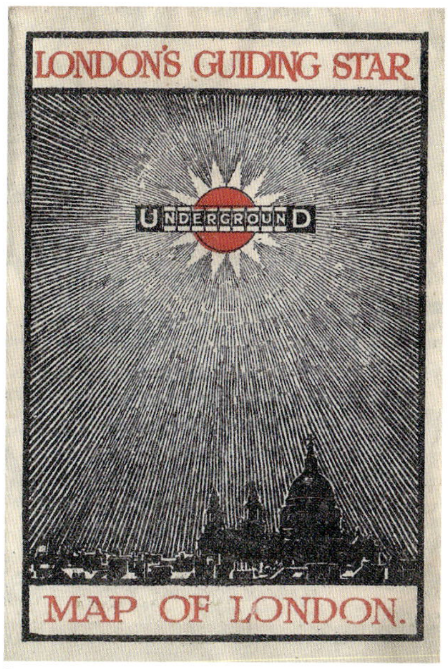

1

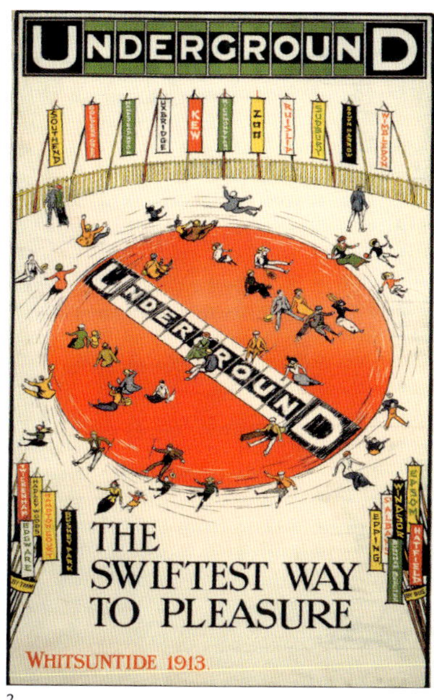

2

3

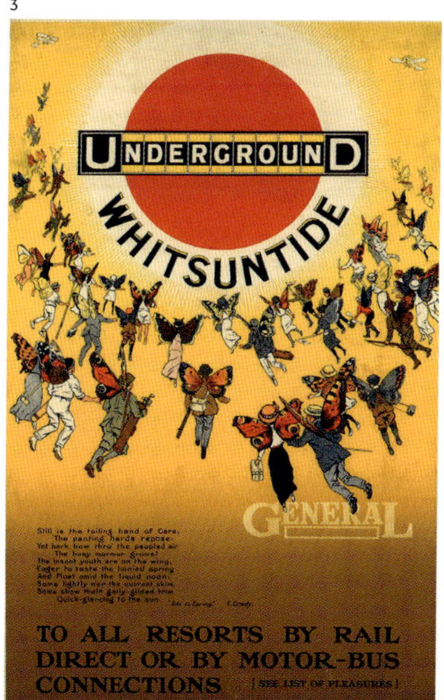

4

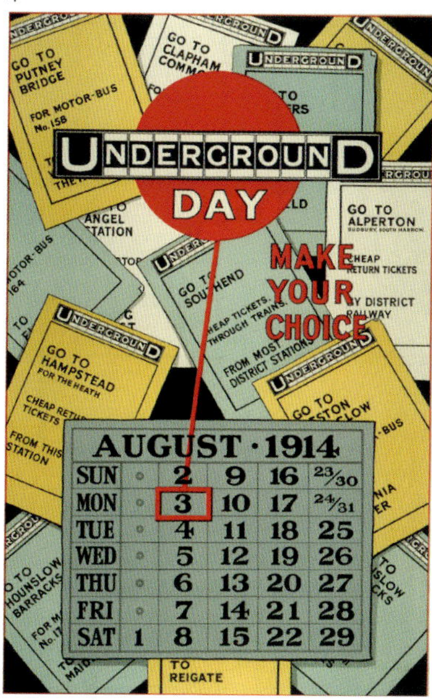

Before the exact dimensions of the combined logo were finalized, Sharland tried slight adaptations — for example, with the Underground bar completely engulfed by the red disc, which appeared on two Whitsuntide posters in May 1912 and 1913 (2). By Whitsun 1914, the disc was back to its original dimensions (3), but just a few months later its diameter was again shrunk — the point being that a definitive design had not quite been established (this had to wait until just before the end of the war). It is interesting to note how this August Bank Holiday poster (also by Sharland, 4) was encouraging people to use the system for a day out in the country just a week after the outbreak of the First World War in 1914. Sharland, whether by happenstance or great foresight, was also responsible for another adaptation of the logo in 1915 that was to have even further-reaching design implications (p. 126).

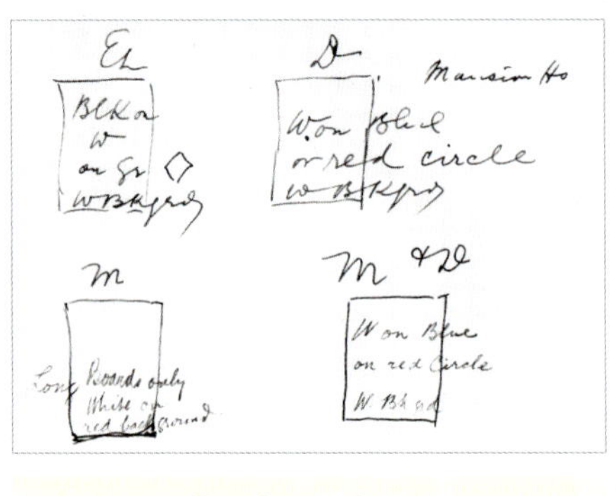

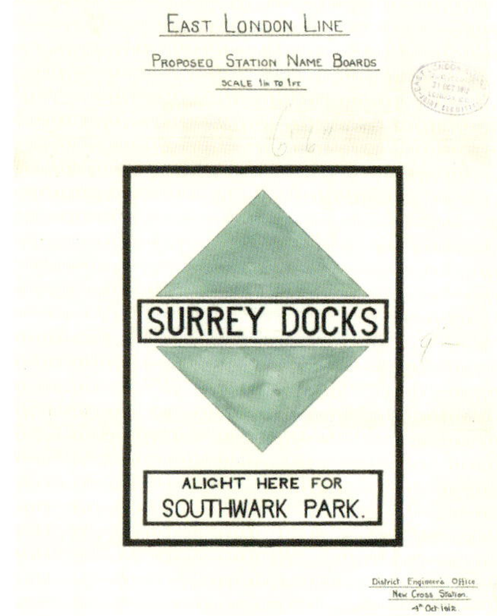

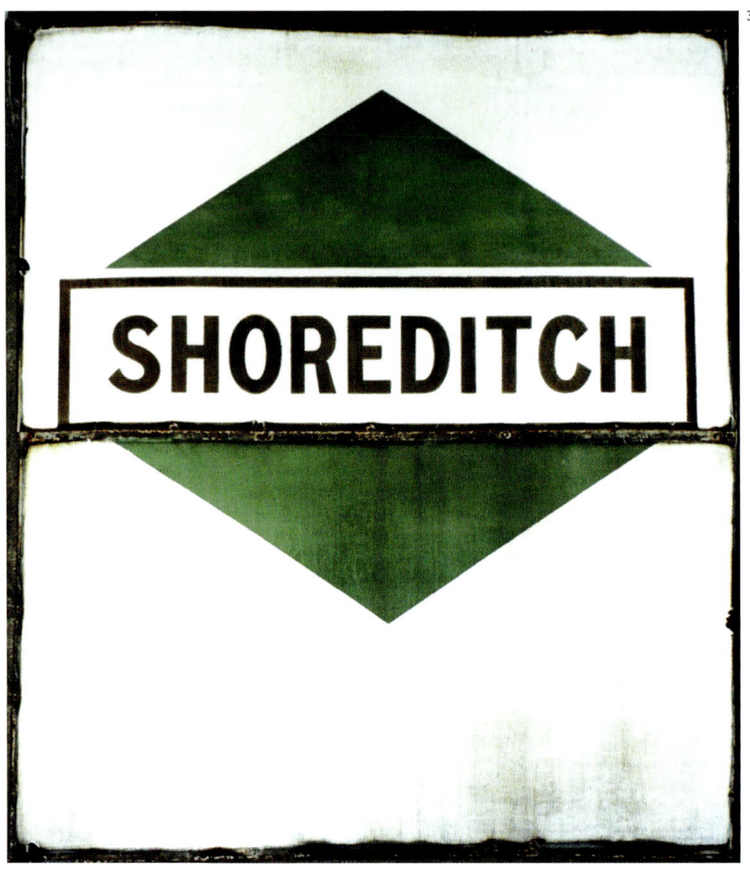

East London diamonds, 1912–13

The ELR was closed in 1905 for a protracted time during which it was electrified, not re-opening until March 1913. The District Engineer's Office was tasked with equipping the stations with new signage and, in 1912, W. H. Parsons drew up plans for a unique design – overlooked by previous studies of the London Underground identity. His sketch (1: never previously published) compares name signs of the District ('W on blue or red circle'), Met ('long boards only') and Met/District ('W on blue on red circles') with his idea for the 'EL' (East London Railway: 'Black on W on Gr' accompanied by a diamond). He commissioned designs (2: also published here for the first time) incorporating a green diamond rather than the red disc which was already established on the rest of the Underground Group's lines. These were installed, despite Pick's advice, along the East London Line (ELL) in 1913. However, only one sign and a grainy postcard photo of Whitechapel survive. The sole surviving specimen from Shoreditch (3) is now in the London Transport Museum's Acton depot collection and has been digitally restored specially for this book. Though the production version had a fatter diamond than the plans proposed, it nonetheless played an important role, coming as it did in advance of the Met's red diamond (p. 137).

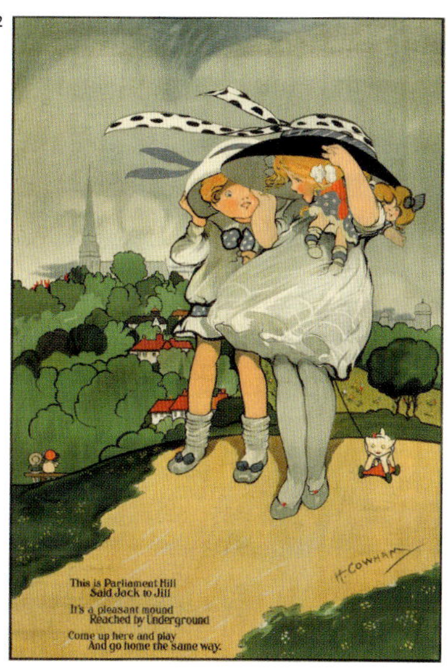

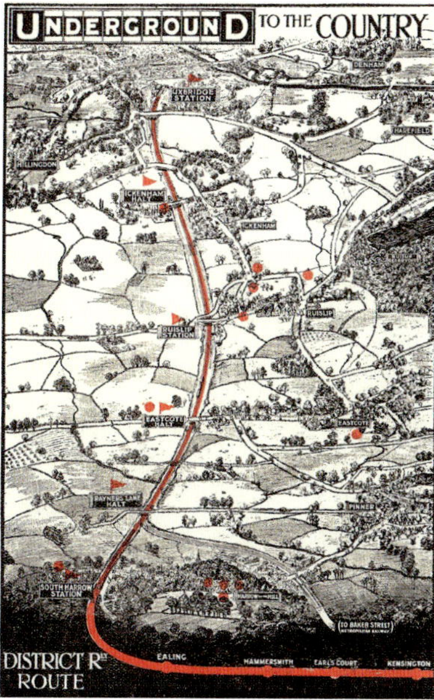

Indulging idyllic images, 1913–15

Some of the posters produced in the run-up to the First World War featured images that were so charming and idyllic it might be wondered if the artists were indulging their imagination in order to distract themselves and others from the heightening drama of the international crisis. Not uncommon in Edwardian illustrations, they allude to a child-like, magical, fantasy world where nothing can ever go wrong. Mabel Lucie Attwell exemplifies this with a sentimental poster, dated 1913 (1) as does Hilda Cowham (also 1913, 2). Reginald Rigby's cartoon-like animals (1915, 3) encouraged visits to the zoo while the District, much like the Met at this time, was heavily promoting its lines through leafy Middlesex (1913, 4) — again using a healthy degree of artistic licence in its utopian portrayal of the countryside.

Combined logo on signage, 1913–15

The UERL's new logo combination was slower to appear on signage than the quick roll-out that positioned the U and D wordmark alone all over the system in 1908. But two important developments happened towards the end of 1913. The Bakerloo Tube was extended to Paddington in December of that year, for which this delightful little entrance (1) on Praed Street was built in the Green style (Leslie Green having died in 1908). It featured a tiled mosaic representation of the combined logo and was arguably the first Underground Group sign like it. Here it is digitally re-coloured to give an idea of the effect (2). Meanwhile Ford's drawings (3) for the reconstruction of Charing Cross (opened in April 1914, 4) clearly show a U and D bar with a (somewhat diminutive) red disc in the centre – this may have been forced on him by the limited space of the pediment (4).

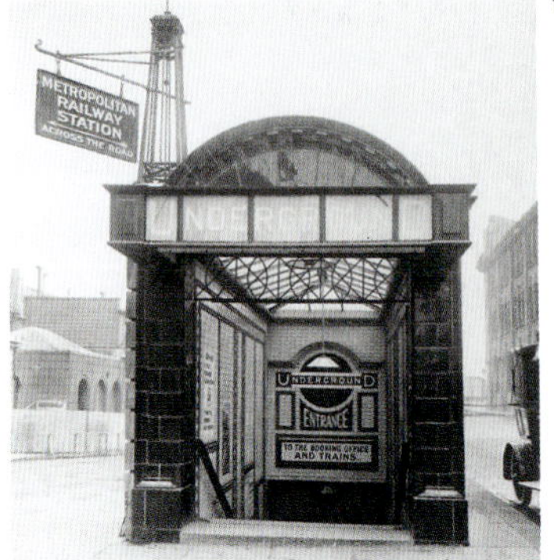

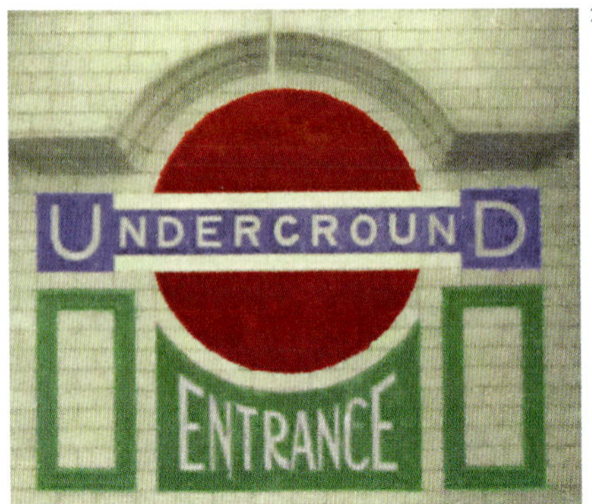

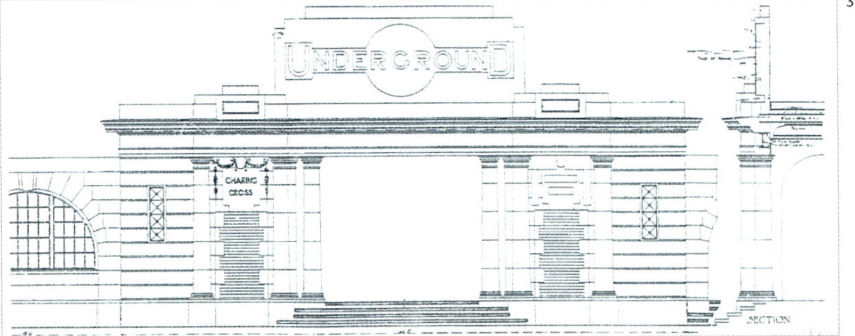

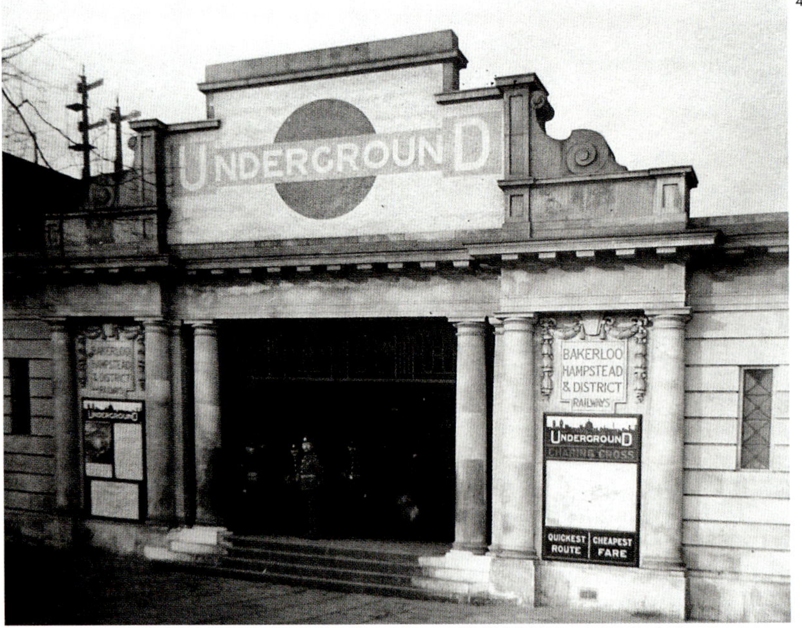

London Underground by Design

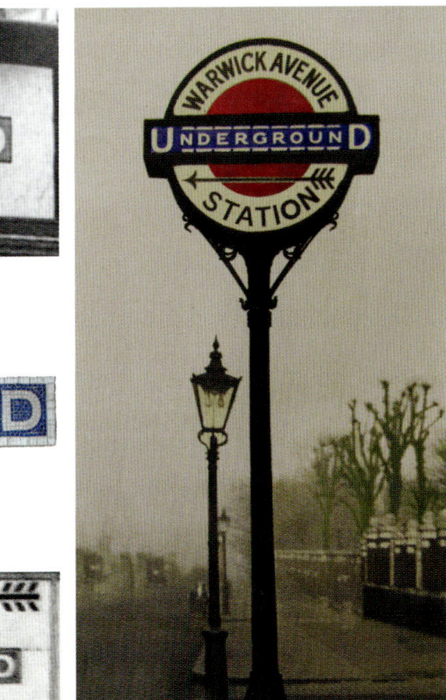

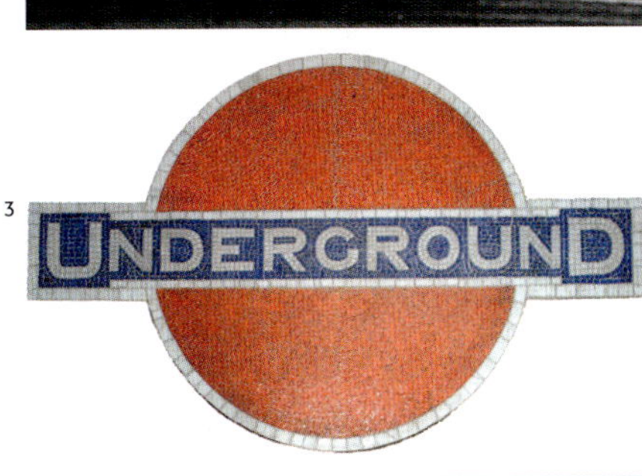

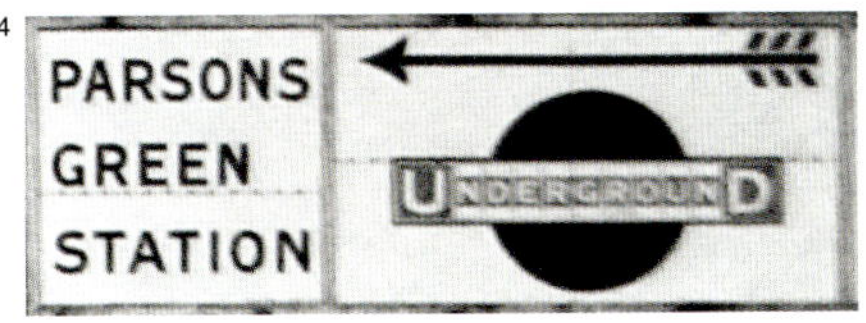

Trafalgar Square (now Charing Cross, 1), Oxford Street (now Tottenham Court Road) and Regents Park, where station entrances consisted of railed stairwells, all acquired the new combined logo signs during 1914. It is thought Bank also gained an external sign with the logo that year (2). The large sign above the entrance to Highgate (now Archway, not shown) appears to have been so big it was manufactured from ten smaller iron sheets. The device was made into an illuminated sign, by positioning two etched glass plates either side of an existing lamp at Strand (later known as Charing Cross). On the District, Parsons Green gained a large sign on the overbridge (1915, 4) when the combined logo was applied to stations all over the system. Just after the junction with St John's Wood Road and Maida Vale, a unique lamp-standard-mounted sign pointed pedestrians to Warwick Avenue station (circa 1915, 5). The CLR's Wood Lane station, though opened in 1908, went through several changes, possibly in recognition of its role as a flagship for exhibition traffic. In the 1915 rebuild by Stanley Heaps, an enormous 1m-wide mosaic version of the logo was added (mercifully rescued by dedicated London Transport Museum staff just days before the demolition was scheduled in 2003), is now back on display at the re-sited Wood Lane (3).

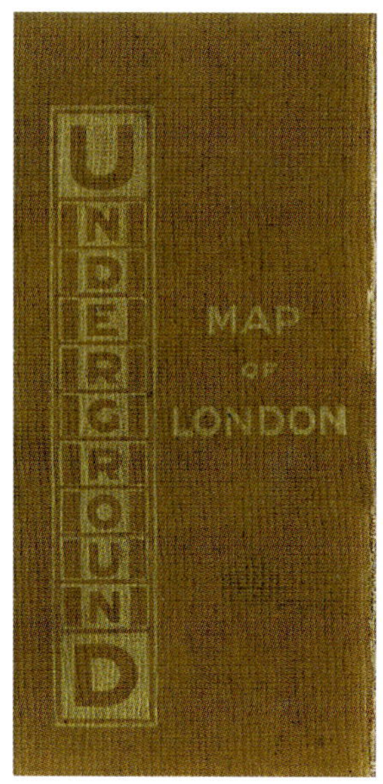

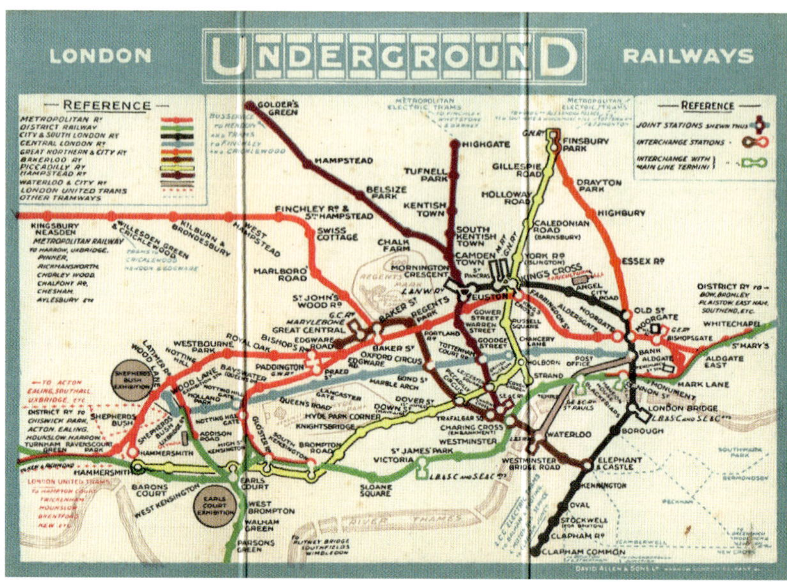

Improving cartography, 1910–14

The most useful map for travelling is self-evidently one that is easily portable. Though many were produced (by commercial publishers and the operators themselves), described as 'pocket' guides, one would have needed commodious spaces to keep these in, not to mention rather more room to unfold them on a crowded train. Since 1906 the UERL had been making smaller sheets that could be folded down to about 145 x 85mm (with a map face of 339 x 428mm, p. 91), but in 1908, while the rebranding operation was in full swing, the decision was taken to produce much smaller maps on card. Emerging at the end of 1908 and distributed in early 1909, the first of these (1) was minuscule compared with earlier maps and therefore the first truly 'pocket'-sized one. Linen-backed

for sturdiness and sporting the U and D wordmark, it could be folded down to 109 x 52mm, (map face: 109 x 148mm, 2). This shrunk the network so much that enhanced legibility was crucial, hence most geographic details were omitted (just the river and parks left on for orientation) while white 'line connectors' marked complex interchanges. Line colours in use today (District green; CSLR – became Northern – black; Bakerloo brown) appeared first on this 1908 map. By contrast, the 1912 fold-out map (opposite, 3), despite having a trailblazing cover (p. 99) and being the first stacked logo on the map face, was much more detailed, but looks cluttered. If the pocket map and branding marked a step change in how the system was promoted, the 1913 fold-out paper map (5), along with large enamel versions erected outside stations, took

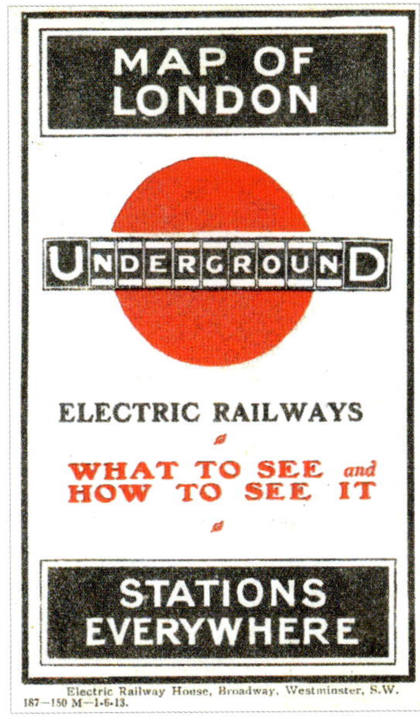

the design to a new level. The most noticeable changes are the background geographical details, which have been placed in fainter hues so as not to fight so much with the line colours. Coverage has been expanded to easily include the ELR (without missing it off altogether or just squeezing it in, as previously). There is much more of south London (allowing the District to be shown all the way to Wimbledon) and west London is expanded too: Hounslow, Sudbury and Rayners Lane are now easily accommodated. The cover (4) features the combined wordmark and red disc which had emerged in 1911–12 (p. 98). More of the lines gain the colours they have now (Central marked in red, Piccadilly in blue) and the thick dark blue border was first introduced here. Colour printing was curtailed during the war, however, giving maps made in 1914–18 a somewhat sombre look, fitting perhaps for the era.

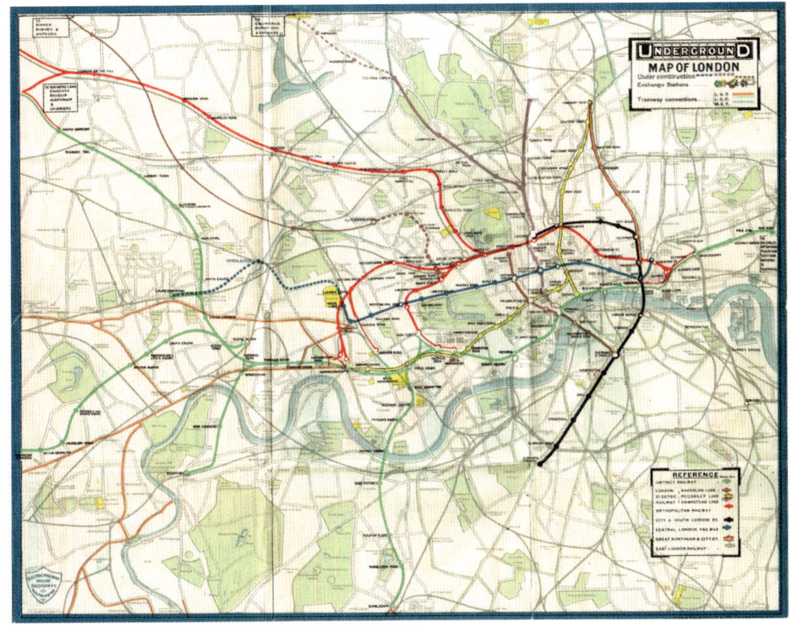

Redesigned for retail, 1906–14

Commercial pressures haunt the history of the Underground. Architect George Sherrin (p. 68) had been employed by the Met to rebuild Liverpool Street and other stations with shopping arcades incorporated into them. As well as generating much-needed extra income, the work was generally elegant. At High Street Kensington, for instance, passengers passed through a beautiful glazed octagonal ticket office (recently restored) to reach Derry & Toms and Pontings department stores. At South Kensington the ticket hall was relocated to provide space for a joint facility with the Piccadilly and the pedestrian tunnel to the Museums, allowing room for a new arcade of shops flanked by huge wrought-iron grilles in the entrance ceilings (still in situ, 2) with the station name in serifed Green-style capitals. At Victoria and elsewhere, the company initials 'D. R.' were shown in an arcade ceiling cartouche (still visible today, 4). The GWR architect P. E. Culverhouse rebuilt the HCR Hammersmith terminus with shop units in 1907–9, the large gable end featuring a fine clock (1), but it was still not directly connected to the District and Piccadilly station. District architect Harry Wharton Ford was busy enlarging stations for commercial units too; Walham Green (now Fulham Broadway) was redesigned in 1910 with a steel frame clad in light buff terracotta. Grade II listed, the building is now a market (cake and drinks served in the former ticket hall, 3), while the new station entrance is reached via an even bigger modern shopping arcade.

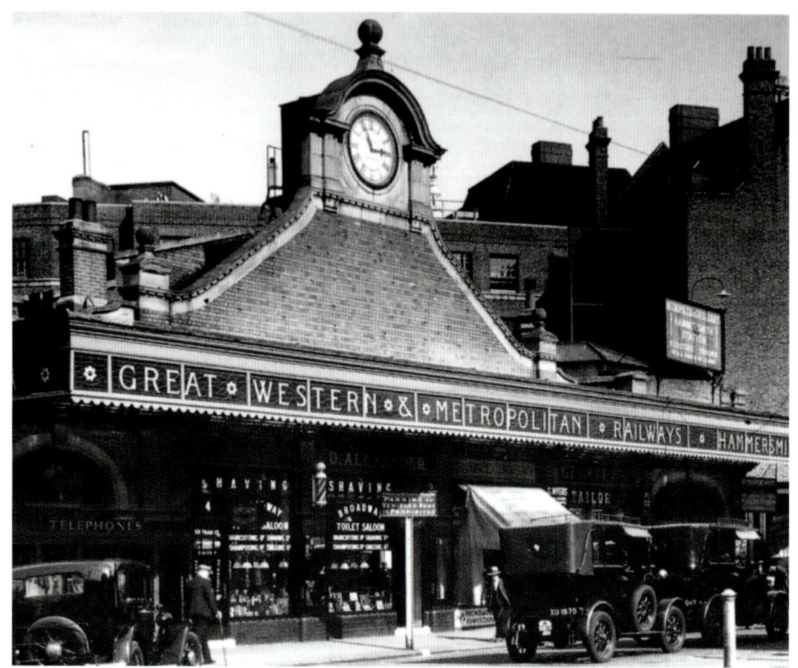

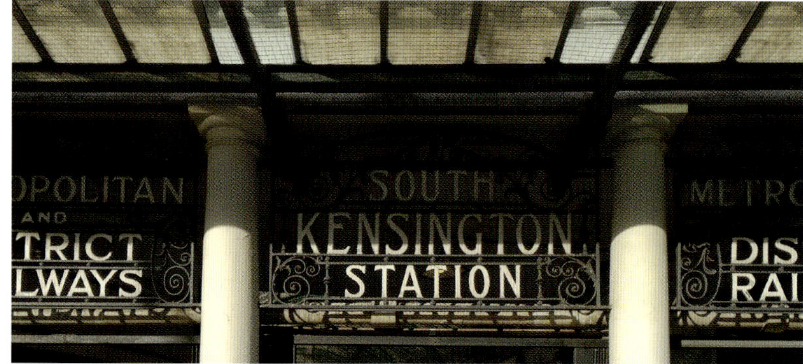

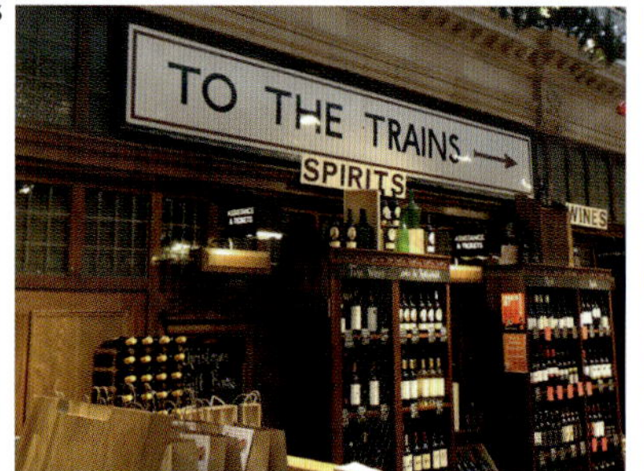

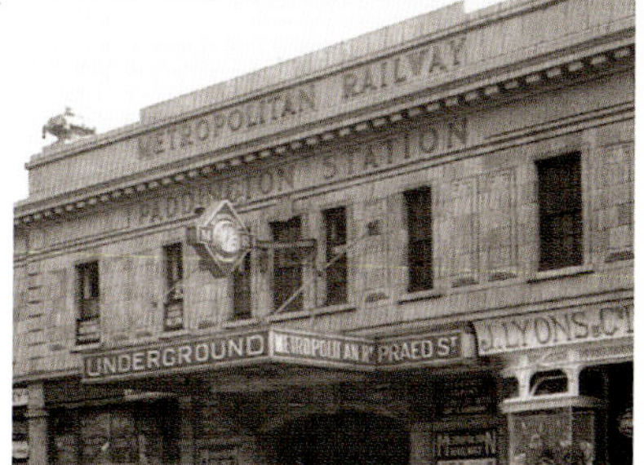

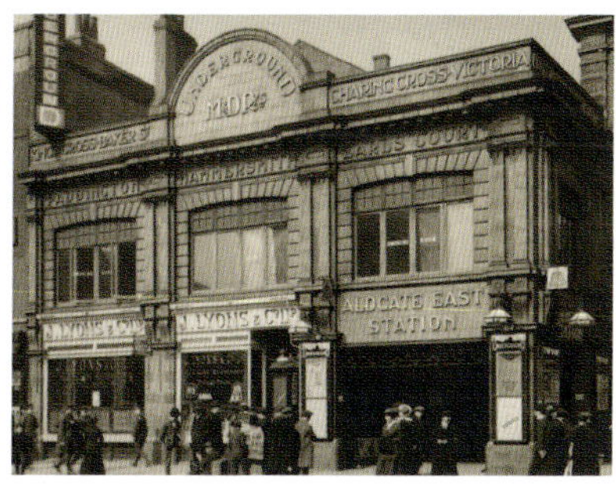

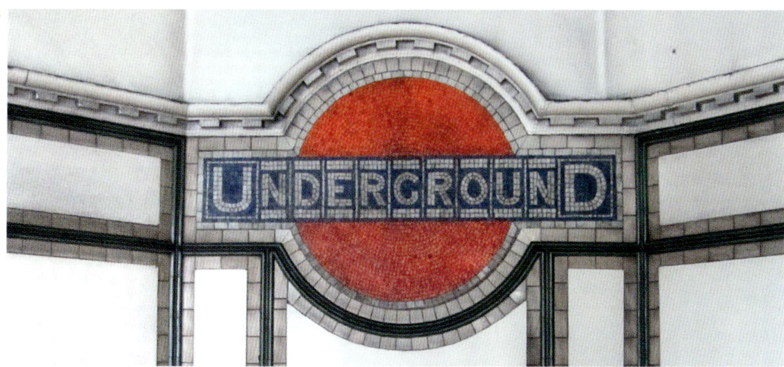

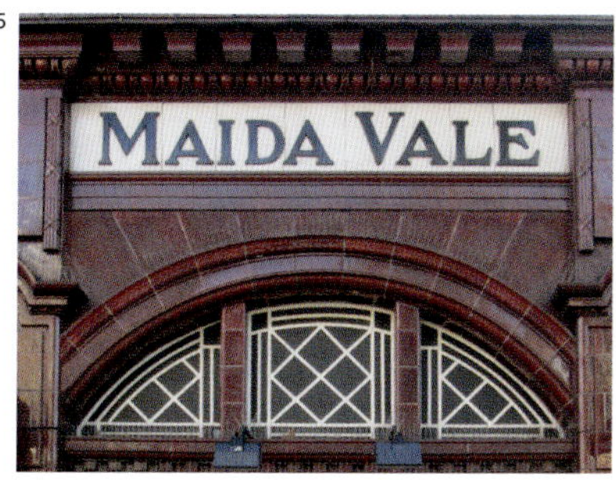

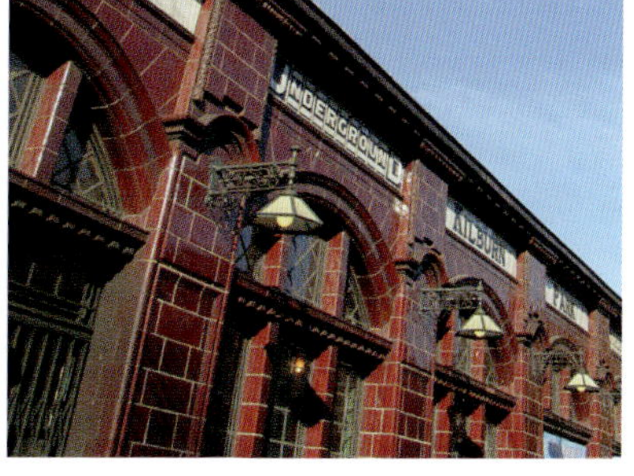

Retrograde splendour, 1907–15

Though the Underground is resplendent with significant and beautiful buildings, some designs were less successful; the CLR's 1912 Liverpool Street entrance (1) was a fairly bland piece of architecture, for instance. The Met's head offices at Baker Street were implemented by Charles W. Clark and not finished until 1913, but at Paddington (Praed Street), rebuilt in 1913–14 (2), and later at Farringdon (1923), Clark embraced a neo-classical style and used a serifed letterform, with letters mounted individually onto the pediment and other parts. Though not entirely identical at each location due to varying manufacturing techniques, Clark's illuminated canopies and wall-mounted letters were used by the Met right into the early 1930s. Ford's 1915 Aldgate East (3) provides a better example, although its fine, carved stone lettering was lost for ever in 1938. As the Bakerloo pushed from Paddington into the north-western suburbs, two exemplary stations were constructed in Green style with ox-blood red faience. Both opened in 1915, Kilburn Park (6) on 31 January and Maida Vale (5) on 6 June. Kilburn has a splendid (recently restored) span of six bays. Maida Vale features a magnificent mosaic tile Underground logo (4) — an identical one at Wood Lane (270 x 180cm) was painted over, but salvaged in 2003 and recently restored (p.103). Incidentally, the Queen's Park extension stations were the first to be purpose-built for housing escalators as well as featuring alternate-height nameboards (p.87).

Met diamond, 1909–15

A 1909 photograph (1) shows the smaller Baker Street entrance sporting not just the new Underground logo with the enlarged U and D (for its UERL lines) but also a Met sign flanked by two squashed diamonds. While diamond shapes had been seen on Met maps in the 1890s (surrounding a depiction of Edward Watkin's never completed 'Great Tower' (p. 14, 2), it was probably coincidental that the Met later adopted a diamond shape for its emblem. An order was placed in January 1913 for a sign at 'Praed Street Underground' and also one at Bayswater – both for the cost of £16 – although it is not clear from the Met's records what style of lettering the signs contained. The more square-shaped diamond can at least be traced to printed ephemera from 1914 (flier, 4), and a timetable cover from 1916 has the diamond in red (5). It is clear from a photo of women pasting up publicity at Willesden Green and Cricklewood (3), and dated precisely to 1915, that it was in use on another poster promoting the *Metro-land* guide (opposite, 1–3). The red diamond did not make the leap to signage until during or just after the war (p. 137), however.

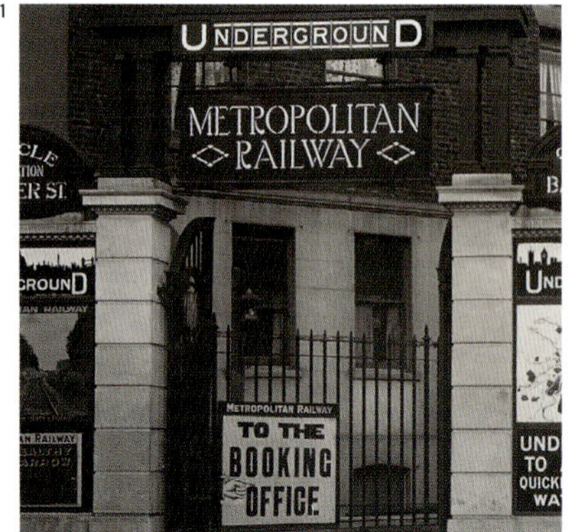

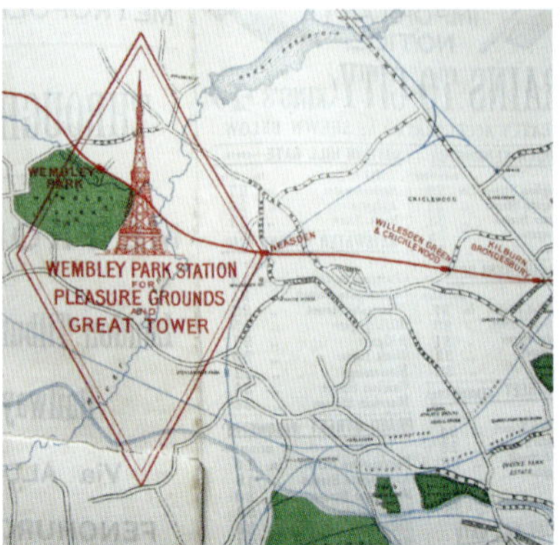

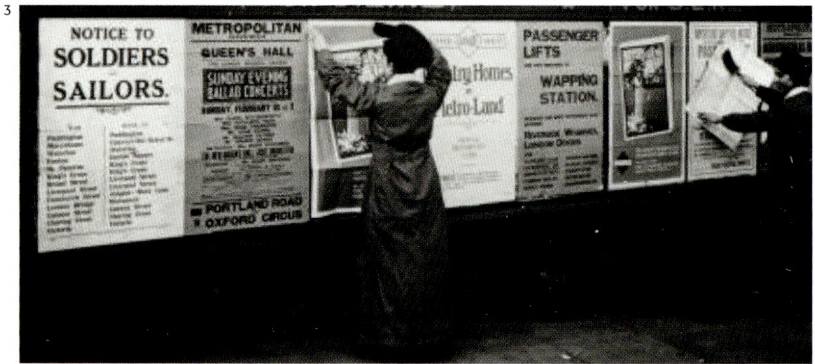

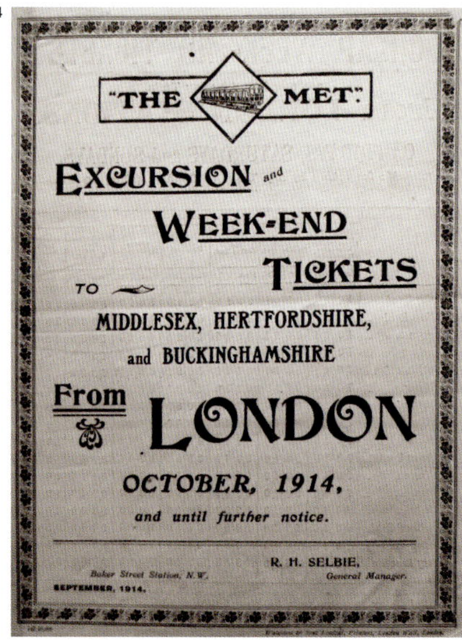

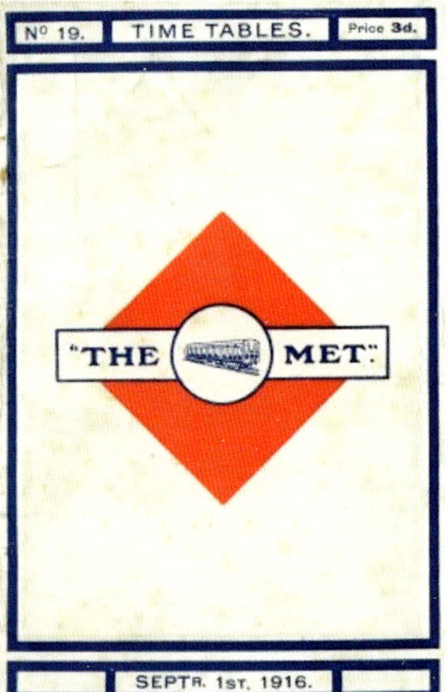

London Underground by Design

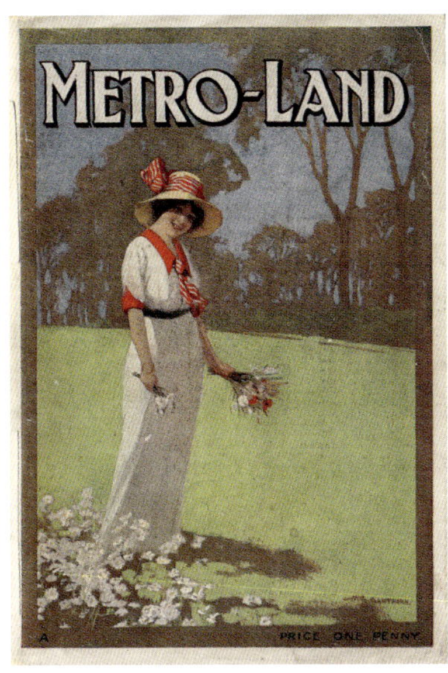

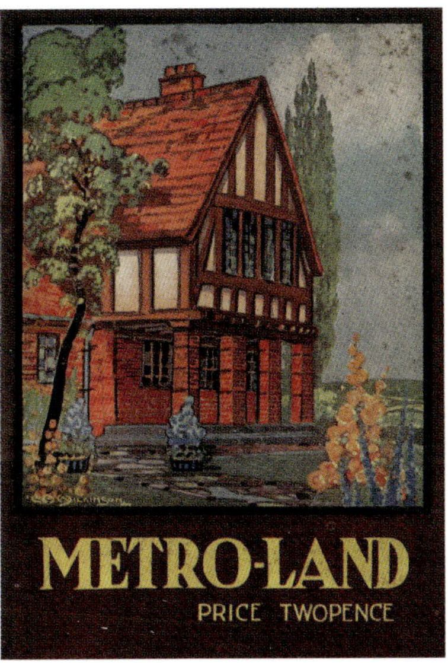

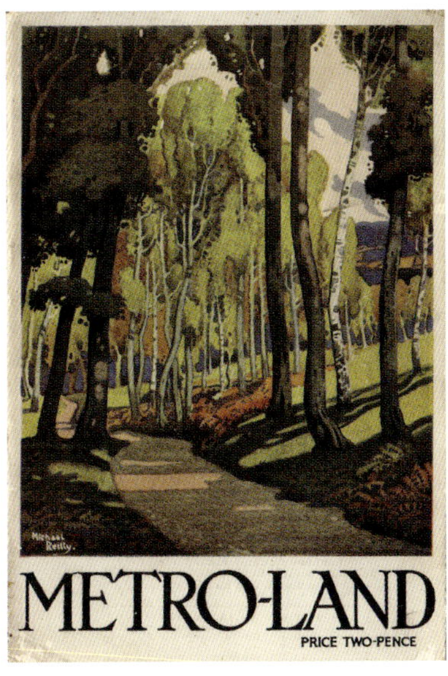

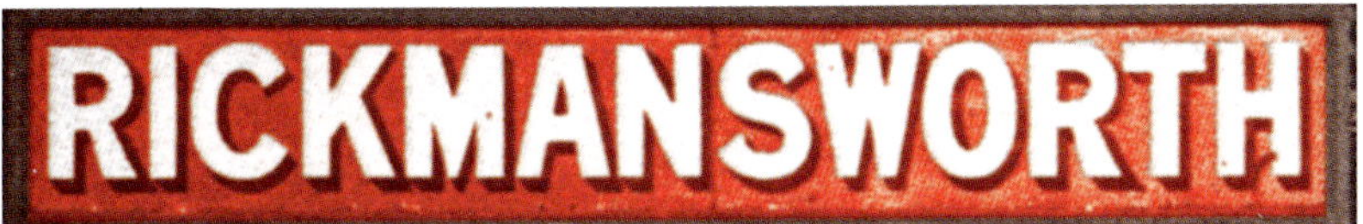

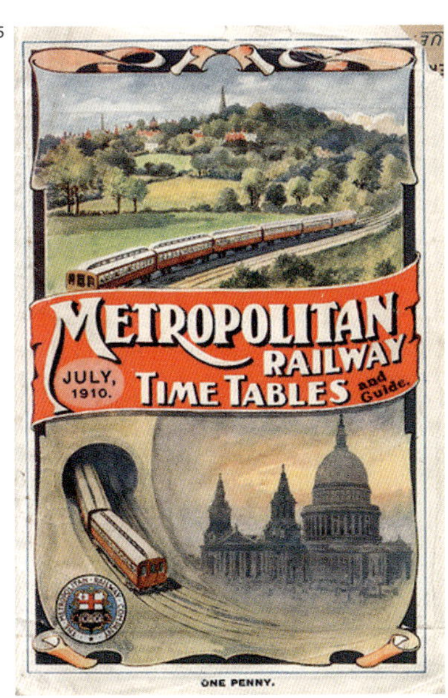

Met stands alone but creates a winning slogan, 1908–15

Despite agreeing in 1908 to use the Underground term and wordmark (though not the full combined logo), the Met remained fiercely independent, developing a strong identity through its own publicity, logos and style of architecture. Met station names had been seen on bright red backgrounds from the early 1900s (an example shown in a digitized approximation of the colour, 4). Timetable covers provided a useful canvas for the latest marketing concepts, a 1910 version (5) showing an early example of the distinctive bright red used by the Met until 1933. The first edition of an annual guide, issued in 1915 and simply called *Metro-land* (1), was a harbinger for the huge expansion of suburban north-west London (p. 68). This simple slogan was responsible for the Met's unprecedented success in changing lives, adorning covers of the eponymous guide (1–3) for many years.

IV.

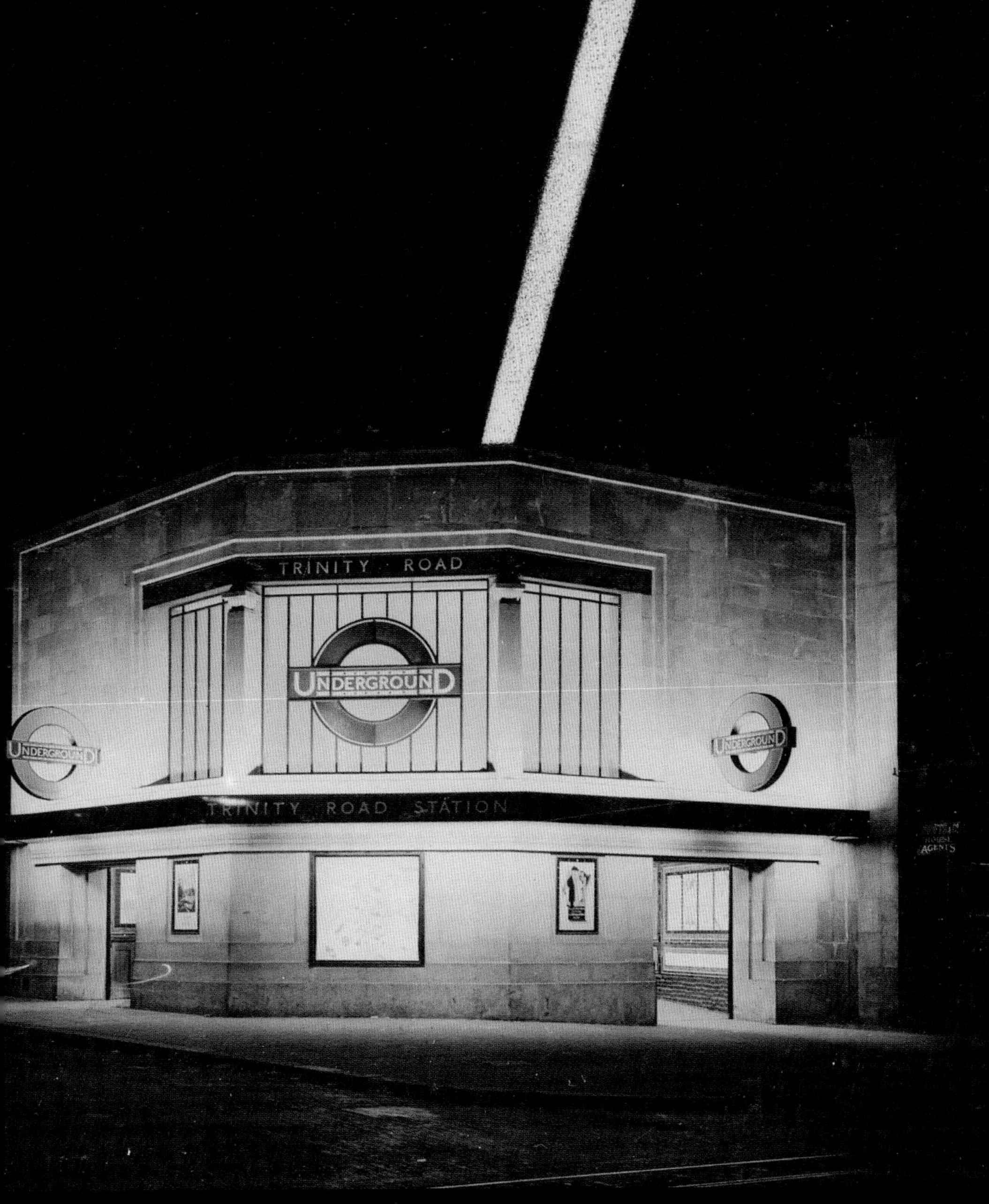

Unification by Architecture and Design
1916–29

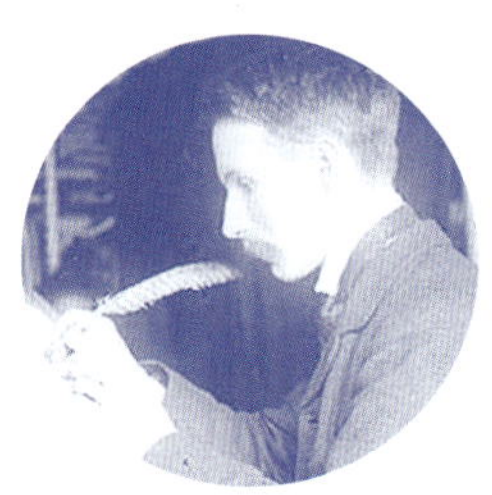

Edward Johnston (1872–1944), born in Uruguay, is one of the fathers of modern calligraphy. Influencing student Eric Gill, the pair worked together on banknote redesign, both relocating to Ditchling, Sussex. In June 1913 the publisher Gerard Meynell introduced Johnston to Frank Pick, who wanted a new typeface. At a second meeting Pick, Johnston, Gill and Meynell discussed 'monoline' block letters. Gill left the project so Johnston produced his first set in 1916. The letters were applied to printed publicity in 1916/17. An updated form of the typeface is still in use today, over a hundred years after its creation.

PREVIOUS PAGES: Holden's Trinity Road station (which became Tooting Bec) just after opening around 1926.

IV. Unification by Architecture and Design, 1916–29

Though Britain was gripped by war, development of the Underground in 1914–18 was still occurring, albeit at a slower pace than the frenetic rate of change leading up to it. Yet one of the most fundamental aspects of Underground design was already in gestation during this period. First emerging in 1916 and quickly spreading throughout the system, it had a profound effect, with repercussions still felt today.

London's letterform

Following meetings with Frank Pick during 1915, Edward Johnston (now sans Gill, pun intended) had delivered his first set of block (or 'monoline') letters to Electric Railway House, the UERL headquarters, on 15 December of that year[1] (p. 122). A trial poster was assembled in February 1916 but never issued. Commentators have cited Caslon, Figgins and other monoline typefaces like Akzidenz-Grotesk as influences on Johnston (p. 122).[2] He refined the letters during February and March 1916, delivering his finished upper case, which he called 'Underground Alphabet', in June (p. 122). He had been working on the lower-case letters at the same time and had a second drawing ready (in March) and a final design, including numerals, by July (p. 122). Howes (Bibliography) and others argue that some of the letters owe more to Johnston's original profession as a calligrapher than to modern type design, and some idiosyncrasies have stuck ever since.[3] The upper-case alphabet designs were then sent to a type foundry to be cut from wooden blocks.

One of the first posters issued using Johnston's letters (a list of tram fares to riverside destinations) and an in-car strip map for the Piccadilly line were probably produced from a mix of lithographic reproductions of his early designs and some hand-drawn parts. It was not until June 1917 that one of the Underground's preferred printers, Waterlow's, ran off a complete set from the wood blocks (p. 123), defining it as the 'Standard Alphabet (Johnston Sans)'. After this date, posters and notices and some of the myriad printed ephemera began to appear in the new face (pp. 124–5), although spacing was still not defined and early attempts at setting it lacked the requisite care and attention needed for laying out sans-serif lettering – much to Johnston and Pick's exasperation.

Refining the bullseye logo

As seen in the previous chapter (pp. 98–9), the amalgamated U and D wordmark with the red disc had started appearing from around 1911–12. In early 1912, the UERL's General bus division issued a handbill with the company name in the central bar surrounded by a ring (p. 126). The shape caught on, and soon appeared on bus map covers and posters. The Underground began emulating this neater ring style as a modification of the solid disc by about 1915 – indeed, one notable example on a Charles Sharland poster seems

London Underground by Design

to foreshadow the hollowing out of the disc into a ring (p. 126). The problem for the Underground was that while sterling efforts were being made at creating a recognizable look for the network, standardization was limited at best and often poorly executed. Therefore in 1917 Pick commissioned Johnston to create an official version of the modified Underground logo, better proportioned and using the ring[4] (p. 126). By March of that year, Johnston had prepared a drawing which included a black outline (or 'keyline') around the red ring. It also had a black keyline around the centre bar containing the Underground word, now set in his own alphabet.[5] The white letters were too fine to stand out against the black background so Johnston completely redrew them (by 1919) in a slightly heavier weight – though he never completed the range of weights desired.[6] He did reduce the width of the ring, though not before several examples of the wider version escaped, reproduced on posters and in other forms (p.131).

Registering the design

Given that the red disc had been used extensively since 1908, it is surprising that it took the Underground Group so long to register the design, but with Pick/Johnston's re-proportioning of the 'bullseye' (the combined ring and name bar) and the move to use this signage for the station nameboards, it was finally registered in 1917.[7] Hedley Clarke's meticulous recording of station nameboard signs (Bibliography) gives the dimensions of these early new enamels[8] but is not able to trace precisely where the first of these were installed.[9] Other early examples of Johnston lettering in use on signage are believed to have been displayed between 1917 and 1925 (p. 128). From the mid 1920s the use of the Johnston typeface became almost ubiquitous on the Underground, despite several periods when it was refined (pp. 228, 250), reprieved (pp. 232) and, in the 1960s and 80s, even threatened with retirement.

The Bakerloo goes north

Before the war, the UERL had been involved in fruitful discussions with the LNWR about a route to Watford. The electrified new track between there and Queen's Park was subsequently opened as a joint venture in stages between 1915 and 1922.[10] Although this made sense commercially, the design of the stations suffered as a result, being a little pedestrian, lacking in the distinctive style of their predecessors, and the line (which has experienced numerous changes of service pattern) has never attained the integrated look of the rest of the network.[11] Chiefly used by commuters, the line could not even be promoted by lush posters enticing off-peak travel to, for example, 'sunny Carpenders Park'. With the exception of a poster by Sharland in 1917 for the entire line (p. 124), and the obvious lure of Wembley for football and sporting events, not a single station on the route was immortalized by beguiling publicity.

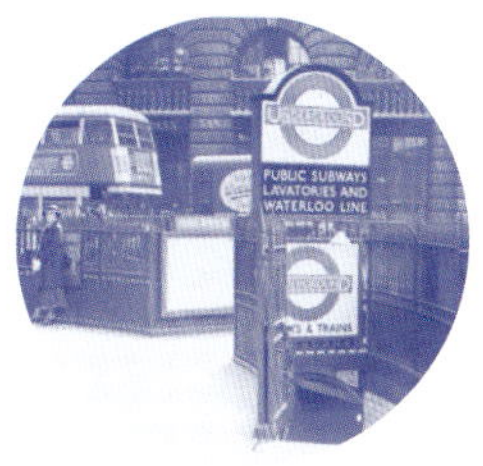

F. H. Stingemore (1890–1954) designed Underground information posters from 1914 – a job he continued until 1942. His cartographic skills were spotted by the publicity office and he was commissioned to redesign the card folder pocket map in 1925. He was a keen photographer (one he took of Bank is pictured above): over 7,000 of his images from 1909 to 1939 recently discovered in Radlett are now kept by Hertfordshire Libraries.

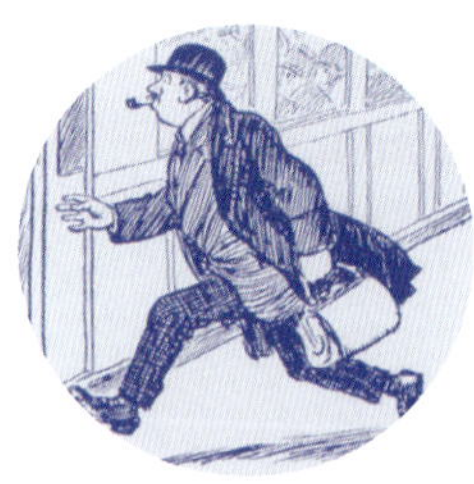

George Morrow (1869–1955), born in Belfast, was an illustrator and cartoonist. He studied in Paris and exhibited in London between 1897 and 1904, including at the Royal Academy, an institution which he often parodied. Morrow was a regular artist for *Punch* from 1906, joining the staff in 1924 and working as art editor 1932–7. He contributed over 2,700 cartoons in his career and designed seven posters (detail from one pictured) for the Underground (1918–31).

Designing for expansion

As Britain emerged from the war, mothballed schemes for Underground expansion into the inner suburbs and further afield were revived.[12] The extension of the Hampstead Tube from Golders Green towards Edgware (for which preliminary work had been tentatively started before the outbreak of hostilities[13]) was recommenced and there were public calls for the Piccadilly to be pushed north.[14] While engineers surveyed the land north-west of Golders Green, in-house architect Stanley Heaps (p. 65) and his assistant Thomas Bilbow (p. 117) started designing stations for the extended line. These were relatively large, built in brick with long Portland stone colonnades and Doric columns supporting a pitched pyramidal roof, resembling a cricket pavilion in style (p. 129). Construction began in 1922 and seeing these grandiose buildings rise from the fields of Middlesex must have been quite something, for almost every one – Brent (now Brent Cross), Hendon Central, Colindale, Burnt Oak and Edgware – was erected in wide open country. But this was intentional: they were planned to be at the heart of the new communities that the Underground envisaged would rapidly grow around them.[15] According to David Lawrence (1994, Bibliography), Heaps wanted 'buildings that blatantly advertised the railway … sufficiently dignified to command respect and sufficiently pleasing to promote affection'. Had the ensuing rows of samey suburban housing been as stately as the stations, how splendid might this sliver of north-west London have looked.

The interiors of the new stations were equally impressive. Self-confident and imposing, they each had a large, light-filled concourse with chequered flooring and wooden-framed glass doors leading to such facilities as shops, cafés and station offices. Wooden 'passimeters' for issuing tickets were installed as standard[16]. The Johnston alphabet was used for all signage from the outset (the first time this had been done), the re-proportioned Johnston 'bullseye' taking centre stage – carefully positioned and with some restraint. There were other nice touches too: clocks, door plates and even railings had echoes of the bullseye – another trick to be repeated countless times in future developments. The nameboard signs were of the 659,814 design but the first to be made with a convex curve at the upper edge, echoing the rounded shape of the logo beneath it (p. 131). Nicknamed 'tombstone' signs, these were another feature from this period to be retained for many years.

The Edgware extension showed how much easier it was to incorporate branding into a newly designed station rather than trying to retro-fit it into an old one. The project proved that bigger schemes still on the drawing board could work, and though a little grandiose for their surroundings, the stations have, as predicted, become much-loved centrepieces within their communities, the unsung pioneers of a new trend – corporate architecture.

Clark's retrograde styling

In a not dissimilar way, an architect at the Met was also trying to impose a sense of architectural uniformity upon the stations of that company. Charles W. Clark had already completed an impressive reconstruction of Baker Street in 1913 and Paddington (Praed Street) in 1914 (p. 107), but his plans for rebuilding Farringdon Street were scuppered by the war. With little regard for changing fashion, the drawings were simply dusted down and work completed on Farringdon in 1923, followed by a dozen other stations.[17] Light-coloured faience was used for cladding, and lettering for station names took the form of individually mounted relief capitals in a serif that became the Met house style (p. 139). Protective glass canopies, not unlike those on the Underground, were installed at most stations, featuring a similar (though not identical) serifed letterform, using letters cut out of a metal panel with stencil-like strips supporting the central portions (p. 139). This was used extensively on shopfronts and for signage giving directions or indicating facilities such as tearooms or toilets (p. 139). Though Clark's neo-classical design was perfectly sound, as time passed and the Underground employed more radical forms elsewhere (p. 148), his fussy detailing started to seem dated – on the later stations, even before they were finished.[18]

It was during the 1920s that the Met also built its own new branch (the first for some years), from Moor Park to Watford (with an intermediary stop at Croxley Green). Instead of seizing the opportunity to produce something more avant-garde, Clark embraced the Arts and Crafts trend for suburban houses with tall chimneys and pitched roofs; take away the heavy iron canopies bearing the station name and any of them might resemble a large domestic dwelling. The crowning glory of Clark's work was the gargantuan Chiltern Court – a combined hotel, entertainment centre, apartment and office block, completed in 1930, that was to sit over Baker Street station (p. 140). The impetus behind this massive development was the success of the Met's 'Metro-land' campaign that had started in 1915 but not reached its peak until a decade later (p. 136).

How to create a 'modern' style

While the Met was stuck on rustic, the Underground's plans for modernization of the CSLR[19] and for its own new headquarters building were fixed firmly on the future. The Edgware line stations were certainly distinctive – the first to be designed from the outset with Johnston Sans and bullseye (p. 128) – but not exactly groundbreaking. Pick had been contemplating how a station could combine an impression of authority and modernity with functionality – the need to move large numbers of people quickly and unimpeded through the entrances. Now that they had been in operation for almost six decades, it was increasingly clear that passenger flow was the chief area in which mass-transit stations differed from their mainline cousins. The person Pick chose to put all these lessons into

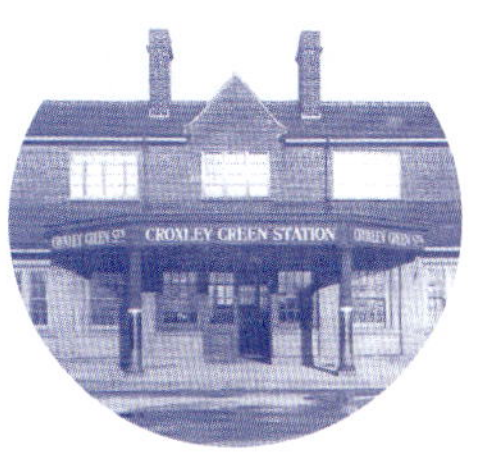

Charles W. Clark (1885–1972), born in London, was appointed by the Met as architectural assistant in 1910. His style encompassed urban and rural settings and was described variously from 'classical' to 'fussy', yet it defined the look of the line from the heart of the City to deepest Hertfordshire. In addition to over twenty stations, he went on to design 130 'Metro-land' cottages.

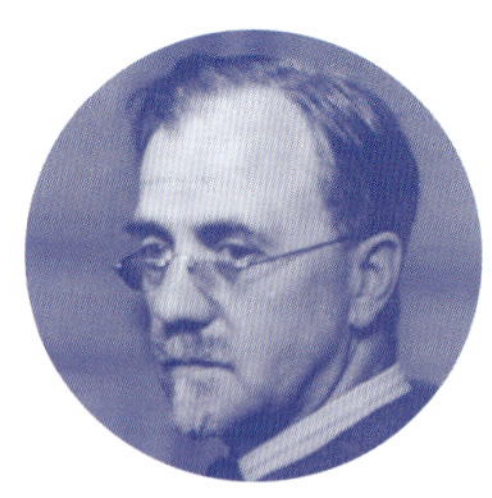

Charles Holden (1875–1960), born in Bolton, moved from a Manchester architects practice to London in 1897. During an unparalleled career he designed over fifty stations and much station furniture (1924–47) and is credited with revitalizing design in the railway environment, his approach to architecture being 'to throw off its mantle of deceits; its cornices, pilasters, mouldings'. Holden was a member of the Royal Institute of British Architects (RIBA), which described his contribution as 'the largest building programme in the capital shaped by a single architect since Christopher Wren rebuilt the City churches destroyed in the Great Fire'

effect was an architect he had met during his involvement with the Design and Industries Association (DIA) in 1915. Charles Holden had become a partner at architects Adams, Holden & Pearson and it was he whom Pick selected in the early 1920s for the remodelling of a single side entrance to Westminster station. The result (opened in 1924, p. 132), encouraged Pick to award Holden and his firm the commission for some improvements to older sections of the CSLR to accommodate the forthcoming long southwards extension[20] (pp. 134–5). With the exception of a decorative dome at Clapham Common (p. 133), Holden's style was again minimalist – almost austere. But the restrained (yet stylish) use of signage and logos, wide entrances and smart cream-coloured tiling reflected prevailing taste – sleek, contemporary and with an air that all would run smoothly and efficiently. Holden's emphasis on flat surfaces with fine geometric detailing and the widest possible opening in the facade not only met Pick's requirement for unobscured entrances but provided a neat, unmissable 'shopfront' for a modern railway, guaranteeing a working partnership that would endure for many years.

Holden emboldened

Pick gave Holden one more test before committing fully to him for the Morden section; at Bond Street, Measures's 1900 station needed replacing and Holden, building on his earlier success, was even more radical in his approach (p. 133). Designed in 1924 (opened in 1927), the two-storey facade was, like Westminster station, dressed in Portland stone and the entire ground-floor elevation made into an entrance with the canopy running the whole length of the frontage. To accommodate traffic, Holden removed 'doorways' (although the ground-floor facade was broken up by the necessary steel supports, these were stone-clad and neatly disguised as poster holders). The width greatly improved passenger flow – though this and later stations designed in the 'open' style were regarded by staff as notoriously breezy and in winter quite chilly. The first floor featured a huge glazed wall with vertical leaded panels incorporating a very large bullseye in stained glass. As if all this would not help it stand out sufficiently, the building was floodlit. It was without doubt the most streamlined Underground station of its day and it had the desired effect on Pick: Holden was commissioned for the entire run of stations to Morden.

The suburban Morden style

The eight new stations south-west from Clapham formed entrances to the longest stretch of tunnel since the creation of deep-level tubes in 1908,[21] so giving them an appropriate look was the main priority.[22] Sketches were made in September 1924 (p. 134) and a model was constructed, followed by a full-scale mock-up (at an Earl's Court exhibition hall, p. 134). Work started on the chosen design not long afterwards. Although the site shape of each station varied, Holden's solution (not dissimilar to Leslie Green's two decades

London Underground by Design

before) was a similarity of style which could be tailored to fit each location. Thus the frontages had three sections that could either be flat, set back, or bent to fit corner sites. There were no 'doors' at ground level, it was all entranceway, and the first-floor middle section, as at Bond Street, featured the glass frieze and central bullseye, which looked as impressive during the day as it did illuminated at night (p. 135). Topping the stone pillars on either side of this were three-dimensional bullseyes while a Venetian mast was added to each side of the entranceway in many instances, supporting a bullseye that projected out over the street. Set into the canopy, which ran the entire length of the frontage, as at Bond Street, was the station-name sign in blue glass and internally lit. This was mirrored by a smaller, enamel blue band set above the first-floor glazed section. Attention to detail was meticulous, right down to the metal poster frames studded with outline bullseyes.

While design of the station interiors was mainly handled by in-house teams, they were nonetheless sympathetic – with black and grey-green frames around white tiled panels (p. 135). Many had polygonal concourses with ticket offices, shops and other facilities around the edge (as on the Edgware line). Hanging above was a chandelier with exposed bulbs which helped to throw light through the glazed upper floor of the vestibule. At platform level, nameboard bullseye signs were set at alternating heights to aid visibility.[23]

The line to Morden opened on 13 September 1926 to great critical acclaim, *Architectural Review* describing the stations as 'prophetic beacons of the new age'. Holden was immediately commissioned for the rebuilding of Piccadilly Circus (pp. 144–5) as well as given the hugely prestigious task of designing the new headquarters for the UERL at 55 Broadway (pp. 146–7). A tour of the Continent in 1930 has been credited with inspiring Holden's style, but, as David Lawrence argues (1994, Bibliography), much of what Holden was trying to achieve in his 'unadorned geometric pavilions' had been evident in his earlier works such as the 1902–4 extension of the International Law Society building on Chancery Lane, the 1909 Bristol Royal Infirmary, and several French and Belgian cemetery pavilions (e.g. Buttes New British Cemetery memorial). He went on to design many more Underground stations, becoming one of Britain's best-loved architects.

Underground erects tallest overground building

Preparatory work began in 1925 and construction started in July 1927 on the biggest surface building the Underground Group had ever undertaken: somewhat paradoxically for an operator of tunnels, their new ten-floor headquarters at 55 Broadway (pp. 146–7) became London's tallest steel-framed building.[24] It was the first project over which Holden had complete control and, given the awkward nature of the site, he decided to try a radical approach. Straddling the platforms of St James's Park station, the resulting building was cross-shaped, the ground floor made into a thoroughfare for travellers and passers-by – an appropriate touch for a transit operator. Opening on 1 December 1929,

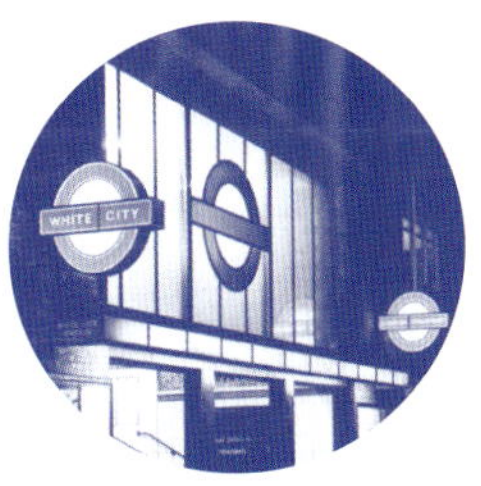

Thomas Bilbow (1893–1983), born in London, joined the Underground in 1922 as assistant to Stanley Heaps. In 1933 he became deputy architect of London Passenger Transport Board's railway division and took over Heaps's job in 1943. Appointed architect to the London Transport Executive in 1945, he headed the design team for White City (1946–50) as well as Sloane Square (1951) and Notting Hill Gate (1959). He also designed the reinforced concrete Stockwell Bus Garage in 1952 – now a Grade II listed building.

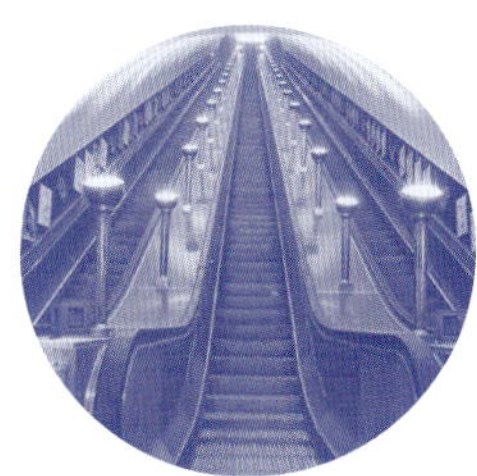

Harley Hugh Dalrymple-Hay (1861–1940) was resident engineer on the Waterloo & City in 1894. He worked with Heaps and Holden, especially on the installation of escalators (pictured), and consulted in 1928 on the Post Office Railway project.

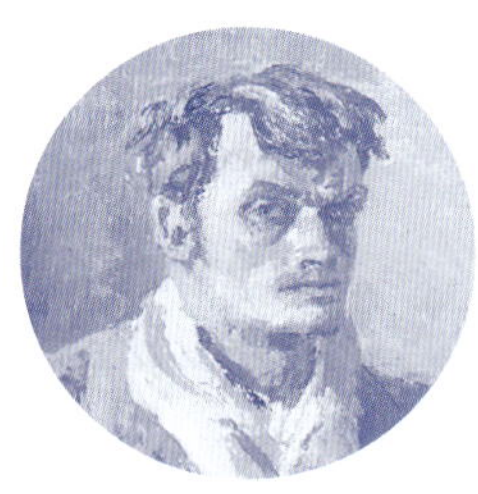

Stephen Bone (1904–58), born in London, was a painter, illustrator, art critic and broadcaster who exhibited at the Royal Academy and won a gold medal at the Paris Decorative Arts Exhibition (1926). He was commissioned to paint five murals for Piccadilly Circus (1928–9) and appointed a naval war artist (1944).

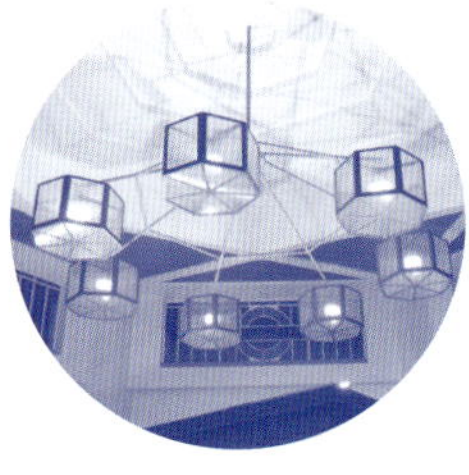

Basil Ionides (1884–1950), born in Scotland, was influenced by Art Nouveau at the Glasgow School of Art. He created station interiors (e.g. Hounslow West, pictured) and redesigned the Savoy Theatre (1929). He also designed Claridge's and the Savoy Hotel restaurant (sculpting the black cat statue Kaspar in 1926). He wrote two books on interior design and became a RIBA fellow in 1938.

the new UERL headquarters — still occupied by TfL — won Holden the prestigious London Architecture Medal and is now a Grade I listed building.[25]

Although Holden must have been working flat out at this stage, he was given the additional task of rebuilding Post Office (now St Paul's) and Mansion House stations. The frontages of both (opened 1928–9) have since been replaced, but they acted as useful models for future projects Holden and his team were to work on.

Holden creates a flagship subterranean space

While 55 Broadway was still under construction, a major redevelopment of the Underground's busiest ticket hall, at Piccadilly Circus, was in progress. Adams, Holden & Pearson worked with in-house architects (including Stanley Heaps and engineer Harley Hugh Dalrymple-Hay) and builders John Mowlem & Co. from 1925 on a vast concourse directly below the Circus.[26] The resulting design — from the suspended ceiling, ventilation and lighting to the positioning of the eleven escalators — was the most imaginative yet seen (pp. 144–5). Detailing included an enormous mural over the escalators by artist Stephen Bone depicting the lives of passengers at work, and brass uplighters in the Art Deco style[27] (p. 144). The surface entrances were simple yet stylish, consisting of black railings with the Underground logo mounted on a crossbar supported by two poles topped with diamond-shaped lampshades in frosted glass. Piccadilly Circus entrances from the street were later widened, allowing space for a three-dimensional, illuminated bullseye above the stairs, supported by the original poles and distinctive diamond-shaped lamps (p. 145). Every feature, outside and in — right down to the train indicator showing arrivals and departures on all six lines and a linear world clock — contributed to the impression of this being the hub of a thoroughly modern and smoothly operating transit system, making Piccadilly Circus the landmark Underground station of the age when it opened 10 December 1928. The design was so inspirational, in fact, that it led to the building being listed in 1983.

Pioneering Piccadilly

Discussions had been taking place before the war and throughout the 1920s on extending the Piccadilly line. Following passenger pressure from about 1919 onwards (a 30,000-signature petition was delivered to the Ministry of Transport in 1923 calling for the line to be extended northwards), a public inquiry was held in October 1925 to examine options for taking it north of Finsbury Park. The opportunity for extending westwards also presented itself due to latent capacity on the lines between Hammersmith and Turnham Green and the District's need to rebalance its services.[28] A plan was therefore devised to take Piccadilly trains along the District and LSWR lines to Acton and from there share the Hounslow branch along with the somewhat moribund route to South Harrow. Holden's

partnership began working in 1929 with Underground architect Heaps on the reconstruction of two key stations: Ealing Common (which opened 1 March 1931) and the terminus
Hounslow West (5 July 1931). The main ticket hall at both formed a glorious heptagonal
shape with light pouring in from glazed panels on every side. Portland stone was used
for the first-floor facade up to roof level, the signature stone usurped by grey Aberdeen
granite for the lower storey, giving a pleasing two-tone effect. The canopies had blue
glass frontages, possibly the first to be illuminated for their entire length. Interior designer
Basil Ionides, who was commissioned for the ticket halls, favoured the ziggurat shape (a
terraced pyramid where each level is smaller than the one below). He incorporated this in
the Hounslow West frieze, with tiling in pink, red and yellow – the colours repeated in the
dado. At Ealing Common a more traditional key shape appeared in the frieze, rendered in
various shades of grey, plus green and cream – colours mirrored in the dado. At Hounslow
West the star-like shape of the roof-support structure was echoed in the floor tiling and
in an enormous chandelier of seven heptagonal lanterns. Open-air platforms, meanwhile,
were covered by split roofs separated by clerestory windows and supported on square
concrete pillars – a design element that would feature heavily in Holden's future projects
and which would transform the look of suburban London.

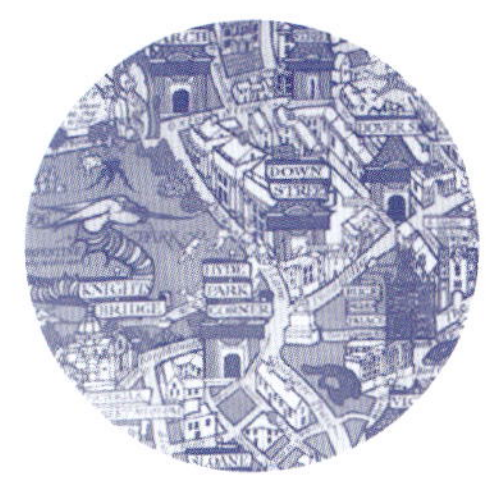

MacDonald (Max) Gill (1884–
1947) studied at the Central
School of Art and Design
where he was influenced
by the Arts and Crafts
movement. His lettering
was used by the Imperial
War Graves Commission
to engrave headstones. He
created the Wonderground
Map of London Town
(1914, detail pictured) and
several other maps for the
Underground. Gill received
greater recognition abroad:
a map of the North Atlantic
for the Cunard group still
survives on the *Queen Mary*
in Long Beach, California.

By the mid 1910s, so much expansion had taken place, in such a piecemeal fashion and by so many different rail companies, that the cacophony of graphic 'noise' was almost too much to bear. Signage and posters were the least consistent, with a variety of serif and sans-serifs. One of the most common letterforms in use – appearing on many of the glass canopies erected from 1908 – was a somewhat peculiar serif which seems to bulge in odd places (e.g. p. 95). It was not unlike the District letterform of the 1880s and the style of lettering on a map cover from April 1908 (p. 80). Even so it was tenacious – remaining on unaltered canopies way into the late 1920s/early 1930s. The Leslie Green serifs also remained in situ (pp. 72–3). There were various sans-serifs in evidence, from canopies (5) to direction signs (1, 2, 3). 'way out' and 'no exit' signs in a nondescript condensed sans-serif (used on the deep-level lines and the CLR, 4) hung on even longer – one remains at Holland Park (p. 48). Train indicators (e.g. St James's Park, 2), while practical, could be the worst culprits in terms of multiple weights of letter-ing. Pick had first asked calligrapher Edward Johnston to look at this issue in 1913 and his solution, a clear block letter, arrived between 1915 and 1917 (pp. 122–5).

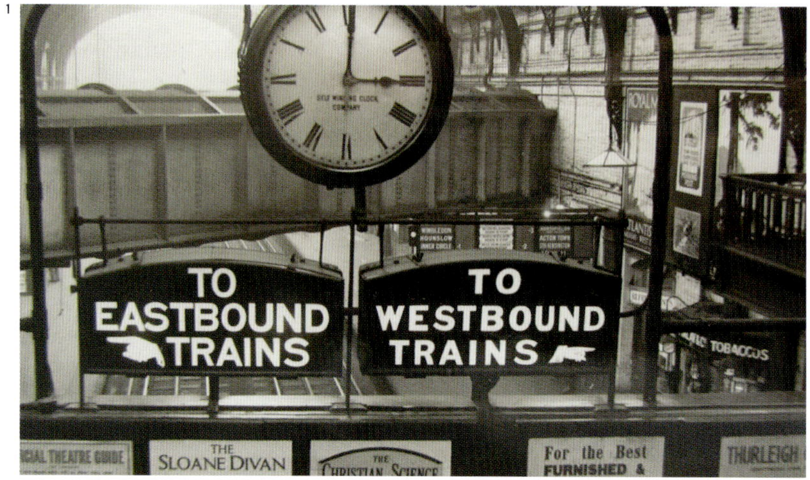

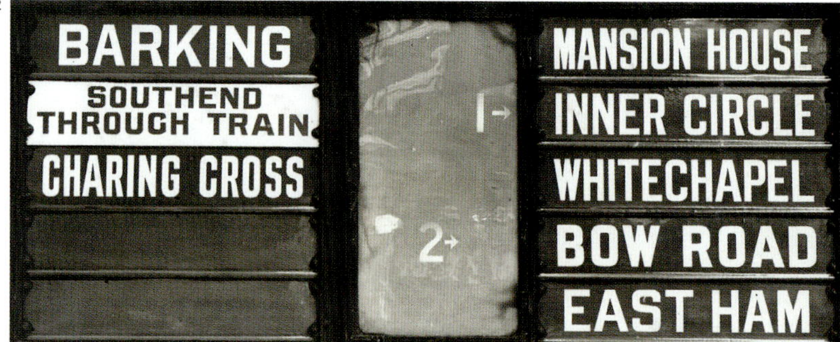

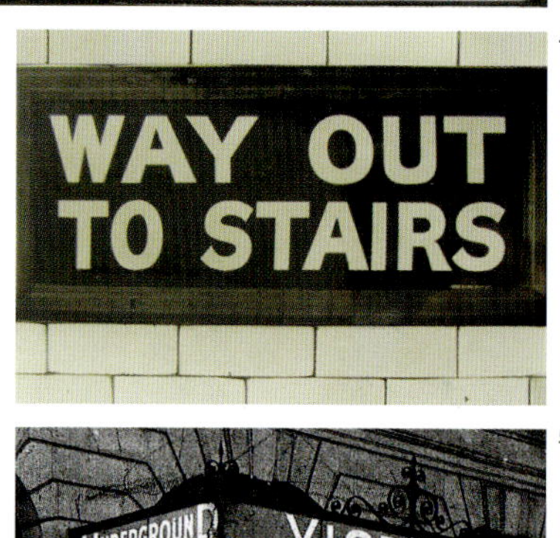

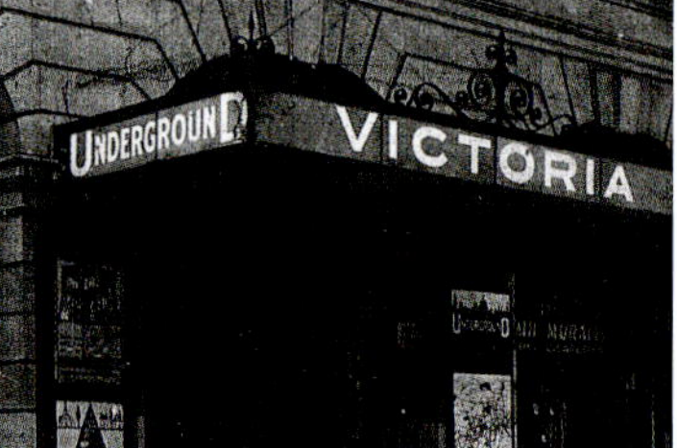

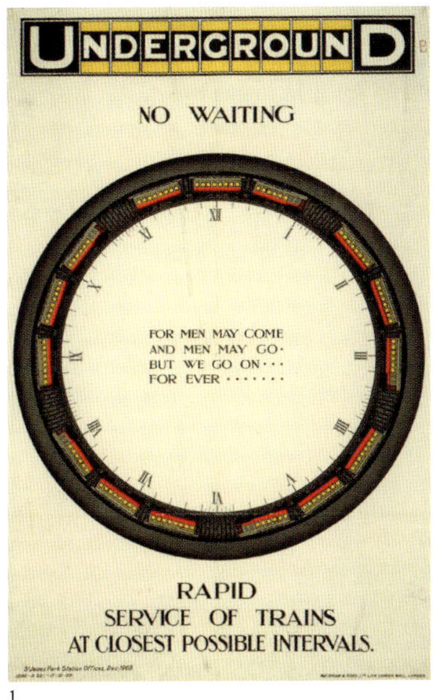

1

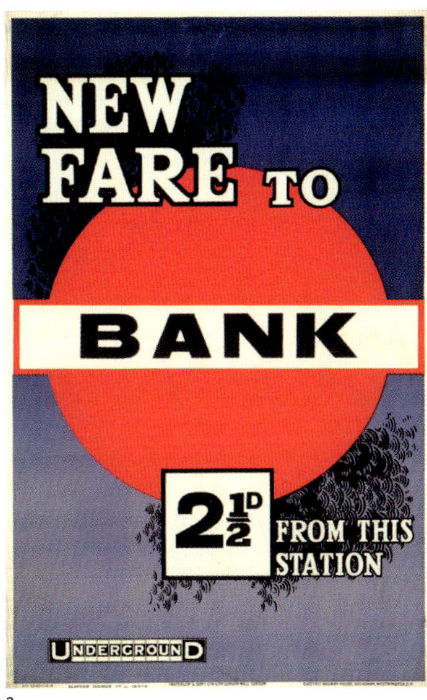

2

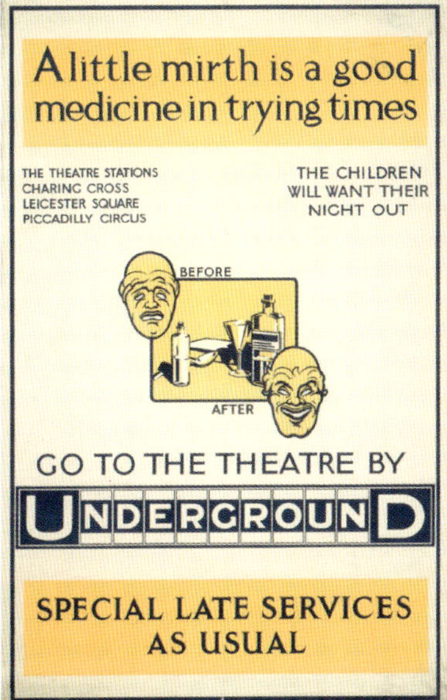

3

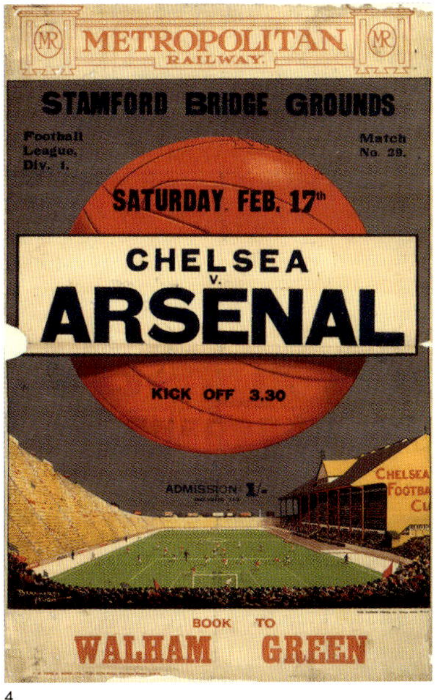

4

Though by no means the worst offenders, the examples on this page give an idea just what a mixed bunch of letterforms were displayed on posters. On an early Underground poster from 1910 (1), aside from the logo, only one type style has been used, but by the mid 1910s things were becoming a little more mixed up. An example from 1915 (2), using a variety of lettering, was designed to have different station names/prices overprinted on it. Another, also from 1915 (3), has a hodge-podge of serif and sans-serif faces. The same phenomenon is visible in posters for the Met. It is not known whether this 1923 poster for the Chelsea/Arsenal match (4) was a generic one with red or black overprints for station/operator/match details, but apart from the inelegance of the type, what is noteworthy is the clever pastiche of the Underground bullseye as a football, indicating that the logo was being freely adapted by the Met.

A brand new face for London, 1916–17

Sans-serifs were not new. Caslon's 'English Egyptian', first seen in 1816 (2), the nineteenth-century 'Grotesques' (of which every decent printer had a set) and such clear, clean faces as Morris Fuller Benton's Franklin Gothic (p. 24) may well have influenced Johnston in his creation of a new typeface for the Underground (p. 112). According to Howes (Bibliography), Johnston's lettering 'owes so much to Caslon [Old Face] (3) that in some respects it is virtually a monoline sans-serif version [of it]. Johnston was a calligrapher not a type-cutter, so he drew the entire alphabet

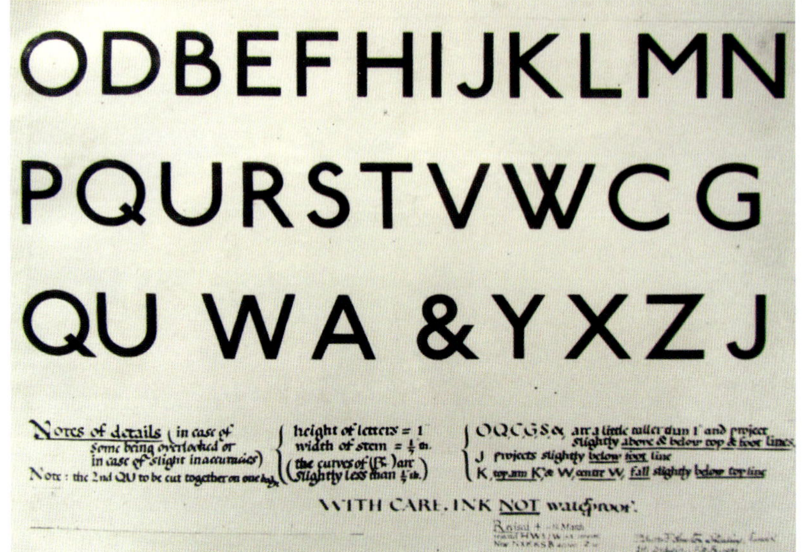

by hand (notice his warning 'WITH CARE INK NOT waterproof', 1). When finished in March 1916, several attempts were made to copy the letters by hand, but it was not until June 1917 that wooden blocks were made. Lower case, numerals and punctuation followed soon after (4). Waterlow's printed three double-crown sheets (76 x 50 cm) from which others could make copies (5). A special condensed version was made for the roller blinds of buses (1922) and a 'bold' capital was produced by Johnston in 1929, by which time Johnston's lettering had become ubiquitous across London.

Return to F.P.   (used p 7. Vol 24)

Rough pull of final U.D. Alphabet
Caps (enlarged from 1")

A B C D E
F G H I J K
L M N O P
Q R S T U
V W X Y Z
1 2 3 4 5
6 7 8 9 0

Johnston gets printed, 1917

Although wooden blocks of Johnston's type had only just been made, two colour posters for the Bakerloo extension to Watford were issued around the opening date (16 April 1917), both of which featured the new lettering, creating a much more unified look than previously. Charles Sharland's clever mix of a line diagram and the relief cutaway of Middlesex landscape shows the gradients in the run up to Hertfordshire, with some artistic licence (1). The other, more cartographic example (2) marks one of the first appearances of Johnston's lower case in print.

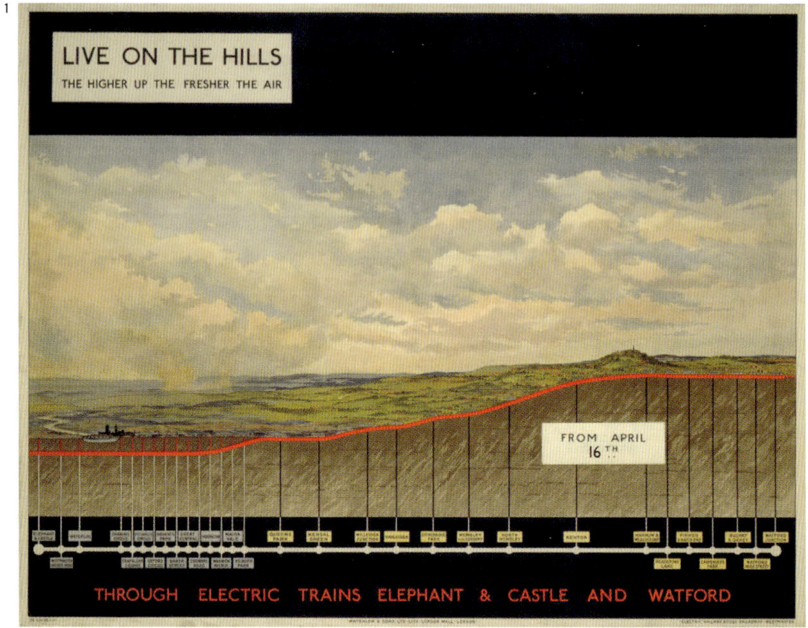

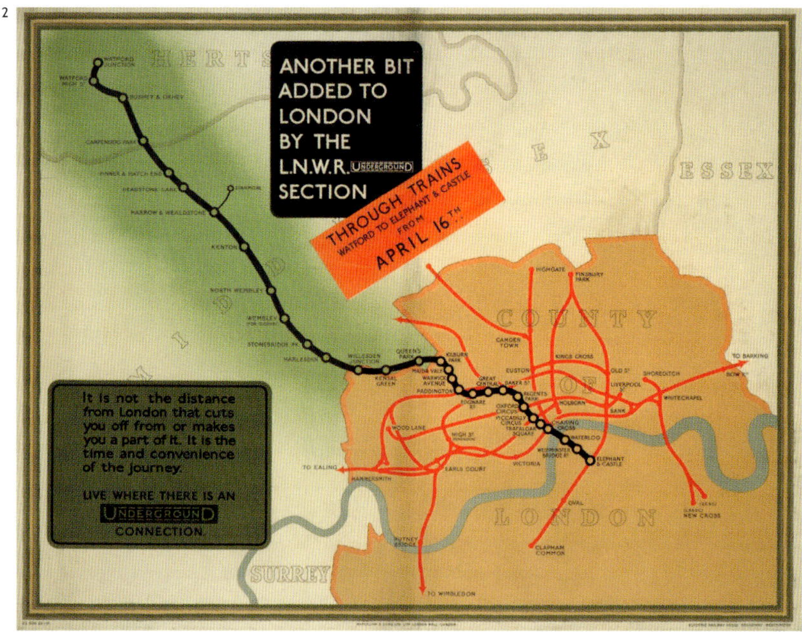

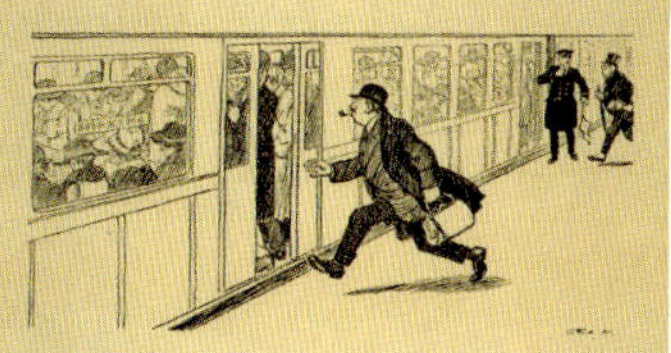

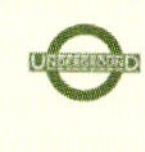

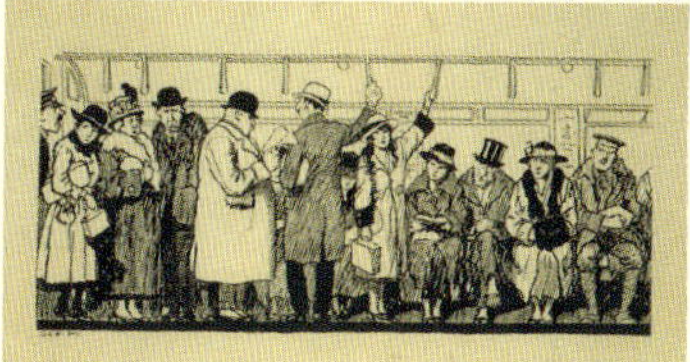

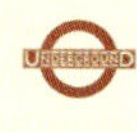

Celebrated cartoonist George Morrow (p. 114) was commissioned in 1918 for these witty posters. The amusing illustrations were combined with the clear Johnston Sans lettering, used in both upper and lower case, to create some of the most effective posters on Tube etiquette produced up until then, and paradoxically, still relevant to the modern tube almost a century later. All show evidence of the typesetters trying to get to grips with the letter spacing.

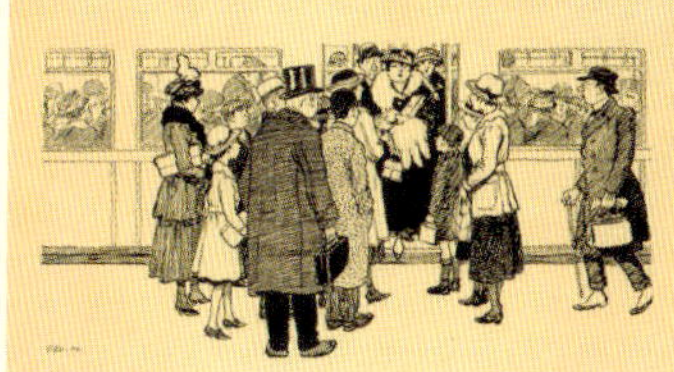

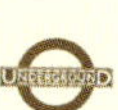

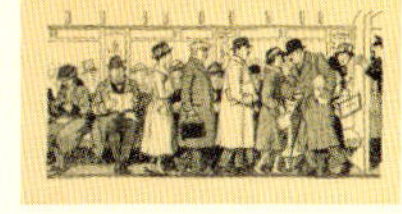

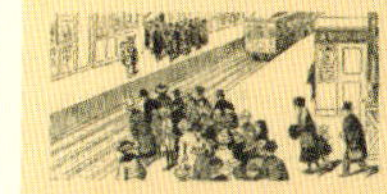

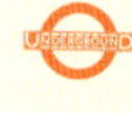

Disc becomes ring, 1915–20

The combined bar and solid disc logo
which had evolved between 1911-12
(pp. 98–9) had without doubt served
a purpose in giving a graphic identity
to the Underground, but Pick increasingly saw it as rather cumbersome.
By the mid 1910s, several circular
logos crossed by a text bar were in
circulation both in Britain and abroad
using a ring as opposed to a solid disc.
The General bus company had issued
printed material from 1912–13 sporting
a ring (1). A 1913 map cover from the
Chicago 'El' showed a similar device
(2). Made into a 'sticker' (though its
exact purpose is unclear), the ring had
even been used by the Underground
itself, in the form of an image overlaid
on a disc (possibly from as far back
as 1909, 3). It was the ever innovative
Sharland (p. 66) who conjured up 'ring-
like' devices for a series of station
names looking like segmented panel
windows in a 1915 poster (5). Frank
Pick then commissioned Johnston in
1917 to marry the new typeface with
the ring disc (opposite, 3). The design
was registered as a trademark that
year. It was soon appearing in posters,
such as 'A cue for Easter', by Albert
E. Fruin (1920, 6).

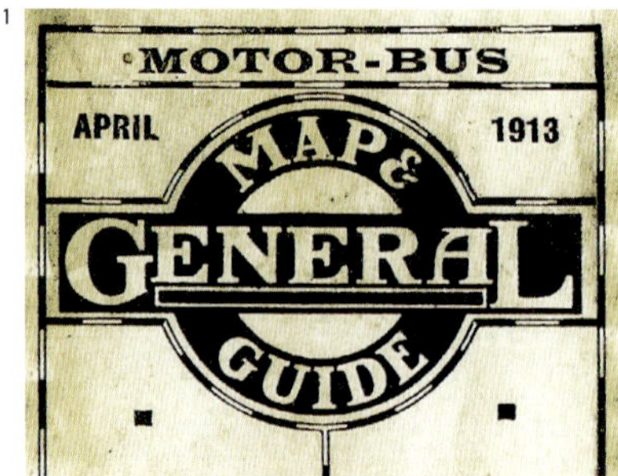

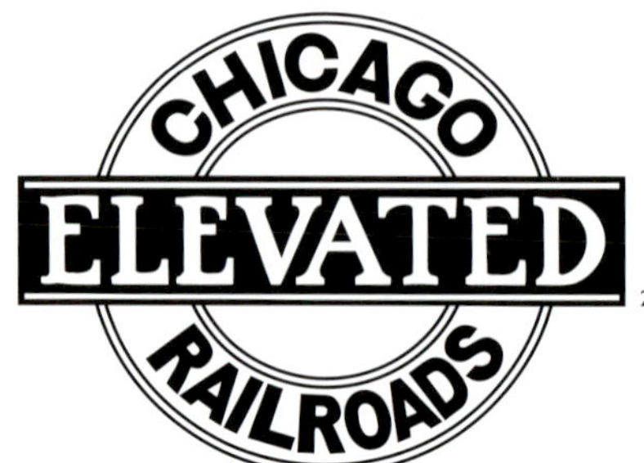

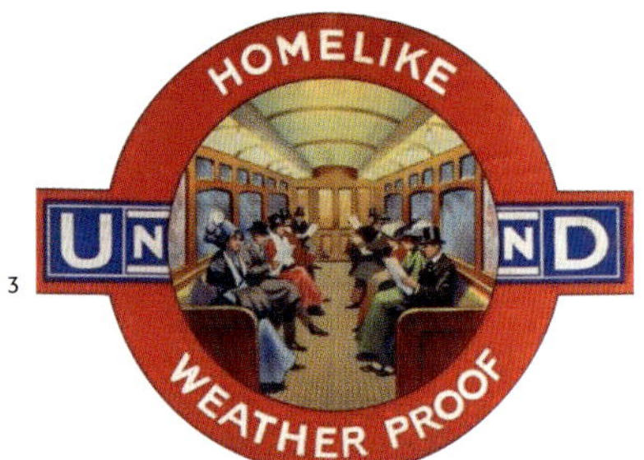

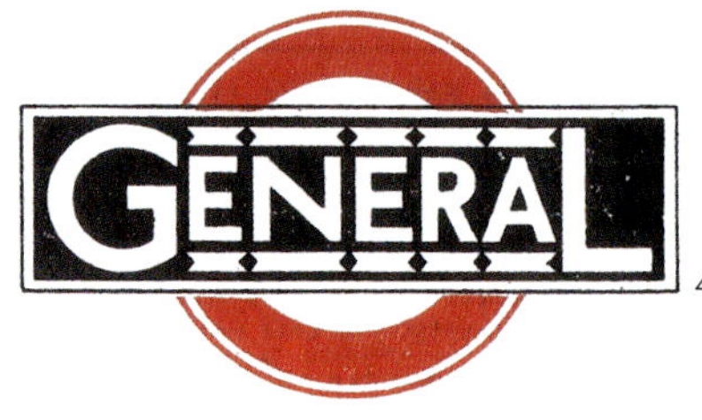

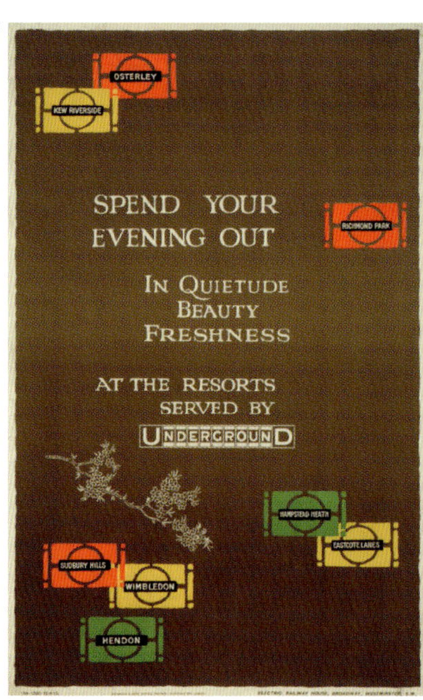

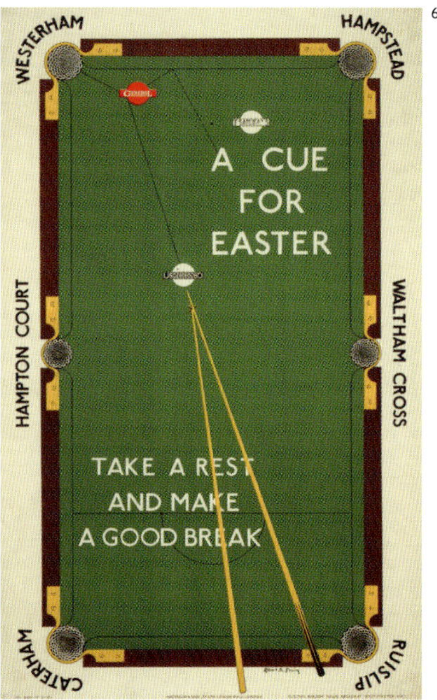

London Underground by Design

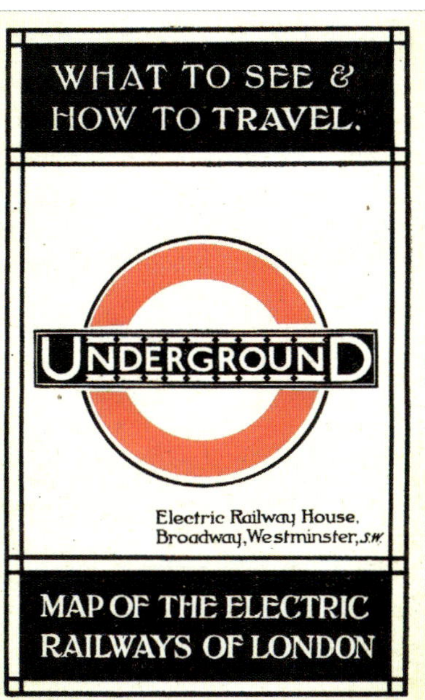

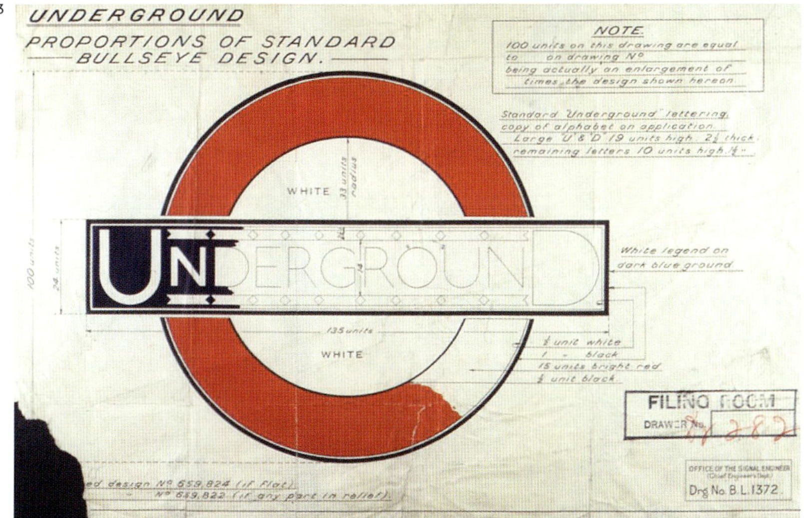

Johnston's standard ring, 1919–22

Johnston's bar (using his own typeface) and the new ring (as opposed to solid red disc) – now collectively known as the 'bullseye' – were printed on map covers for the first time in June 1919. By October, post-war print restrictions had been lifted and the ring was printed in red for the first time (1). The new design included the replacement of the somewhat clunky dashes above and below the middle letters by what Johnston termed 'ribbons' separated by 'chevrons'. This decoration remained on the logo until 1939/40. Johnston was not satisfied with his first attempt, however, and in 1920 he modified the ring, widening its diameter so that it was more in proportion with the length of the bar (3). Only the enlarged U and D now projected over the edge of the ring, giving a more balanced feel. The modified bullseye was first seen on a 1921 map cover (2) and just as the General bus logo influenced the Underground symbol, so the wheel turned full circle and Johnston redesigned the bus logo as part of the 'Combine' family (opposite, 4). He also designed the logos for the Tramways and Green Line coaches (p. 186) and later Trollybuses.

Johnston on signage, 1917–25

Johnston's 'bullseye' was not only intended for printing but designed for signage too. On 19 March 1917 it was registered for five years by the London Electric Railway Company as a 'sign board or name plate – shape of', numbered 659,814–25. The registered signs were first seen on the Edgware extension (such as at the terminus, p. 131). The new bullseye was also used on signage around the construction works though Johnston was not always employed for all lettering (such as at Brent, 1922–3, 1). At West Brompton the white enamel sheeting for the registered nameboards (2) had to be cut to fit the staircase sides, but more noteworthy is the use of a rudimentary version of Johnston Sans (with tell-tale early 'crossed W'). Clearly hand drawn, these signs (three still in situ) appear to be the first of their kind, in the author's view, dating to as early as 1917–20. West Kensington had them too, with similar 'hand-drawn' Johnston. The new style of signage was also installed at Borough in or before 1922 – another very early example. Trial application of the Johnston lettering on signage can be seen from as early as 1917 when, on 15 April, Westminster Bridge Road station was renamed 'Lambeth (North)' (4). Non-standard signs were still to be seen, however, such as this one over a stairway entrance at King's Cross in 1925 (3).

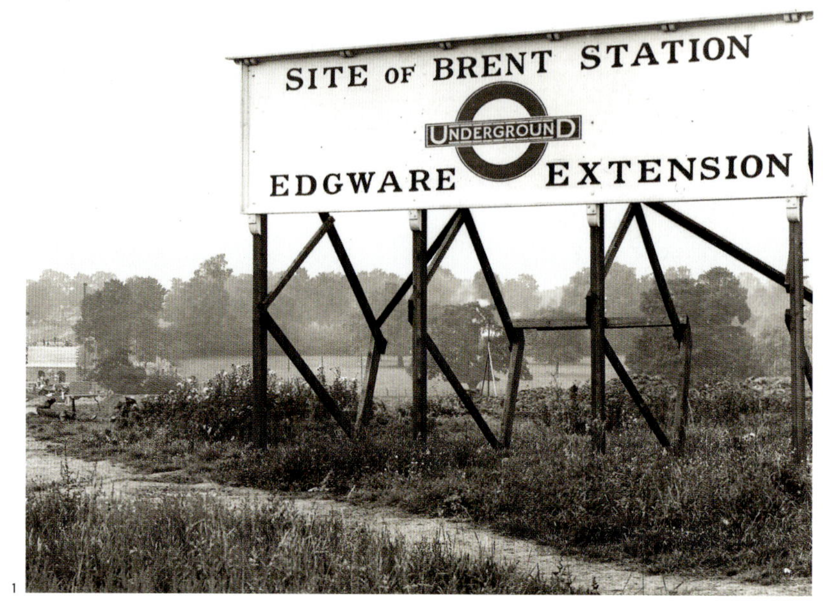

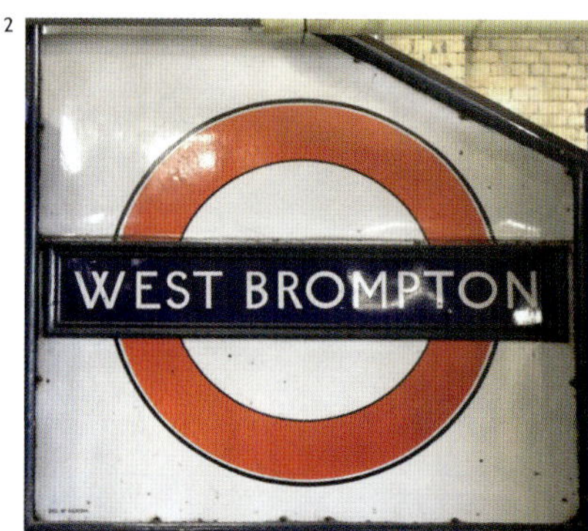

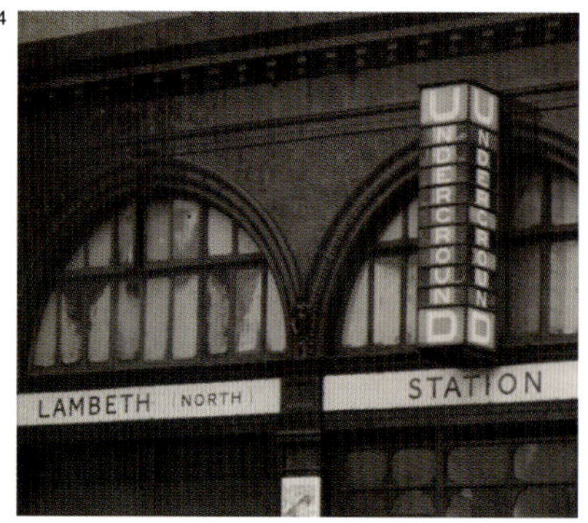

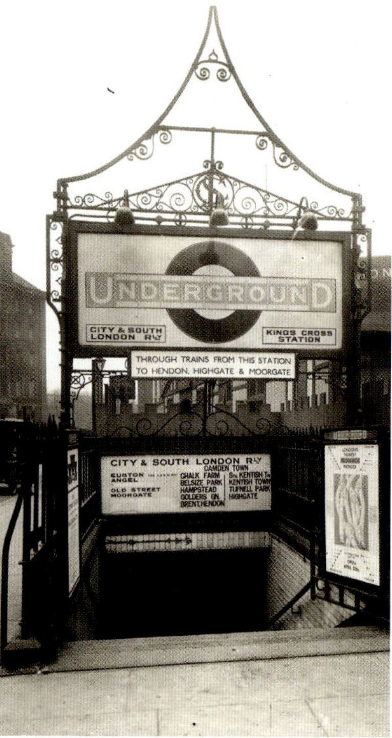

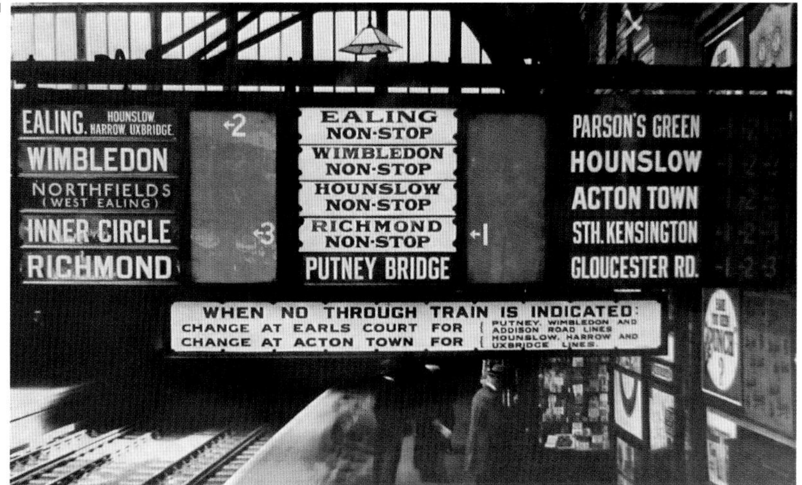

Three words set in Johnston crept onto the electrically operated train indicator at St James's Park '(Northfields (West Ealing'), 1921, 1). It was displayed on the glass canopy at Golders Green (1921, 2); above stairs leading to the Underground at Euston mainline station (1924, 4); for exterior and interior signage at Edgware line stations; at Charing Cross for the bullseye (1923, 5); and on experimental signage. By the early 1920s, Johnston was seen inside cars on maps and signage. The lettering – especially the reliefs on station frontages (such as at Brent (3) and Hendon Central, plus Borough and Angel, p. 130) – was so skilfully executed as to be indistinguishable from Johnston's own drafting of the letterforms.

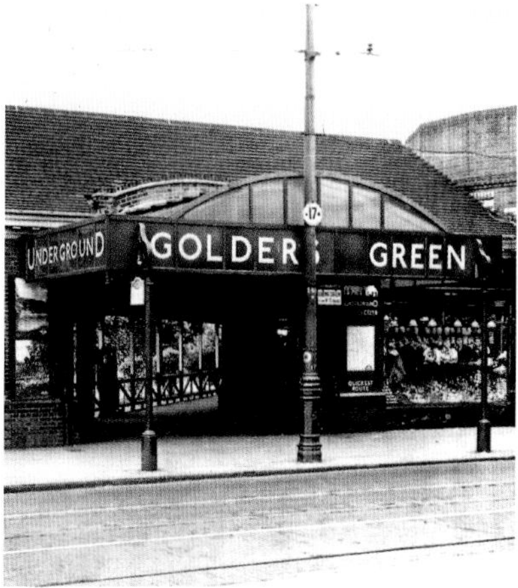

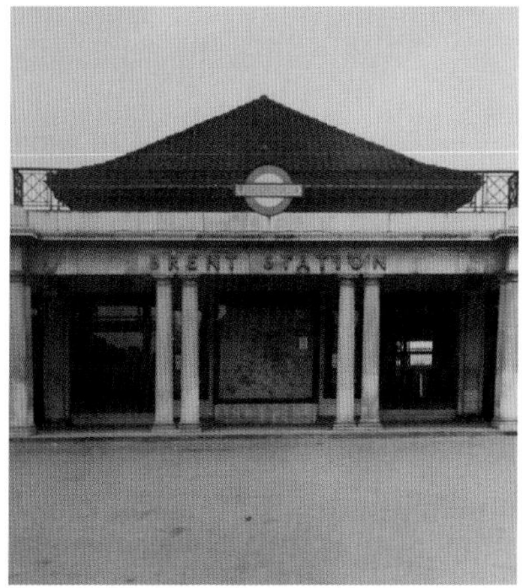

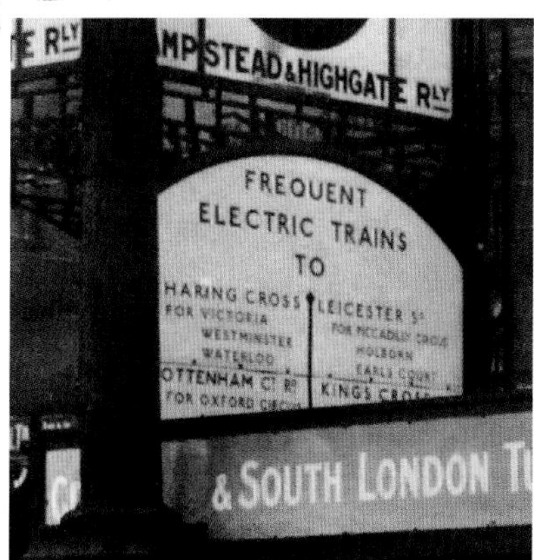

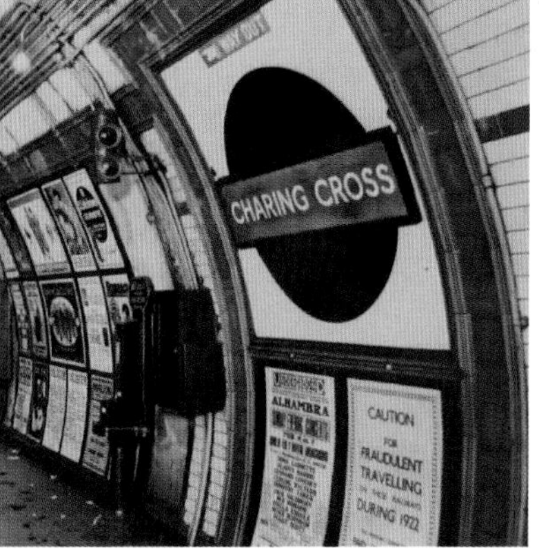

Refurbishment of the CSLR, 1922–4

During the early 1920s considerable work was undertaken on the existing CSLR to lengthen platforms and widen tunnels (e.g. Borough, 1924, 1) in preparation for extending the line at both ends. The station rebuild there by Charles Holden and at Clapham North and Angel (2) in 1924 included Johnston Sans signage in the glass canopies – the latter two with beautifully executed Underground wordmarks made using individually mounted metal letters. The logo was also added to entrances at Stockwell (1924), Elephant & Castle (1925) and Moorgate (1925; modified again in 1926). The success of Bond Street, however (p. 133), moved Holden away from light-coloured faience, at least for the forthcoming period. Standard (1923 Stock) cars were used for the CSLR and were fitted with leather straps for standing passengers and featured in a 1924 poster (3). The entire poster features Johnston Sans typeface with the notable exception of the station name plates – there is no photographic evidence that bullseyes were ever mounted at that height above the advertising posters.

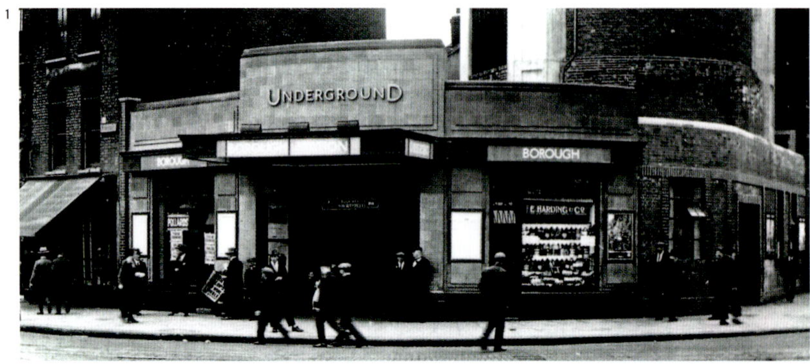

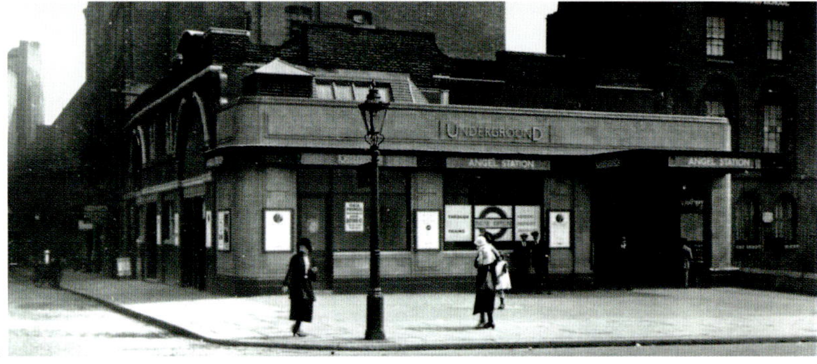

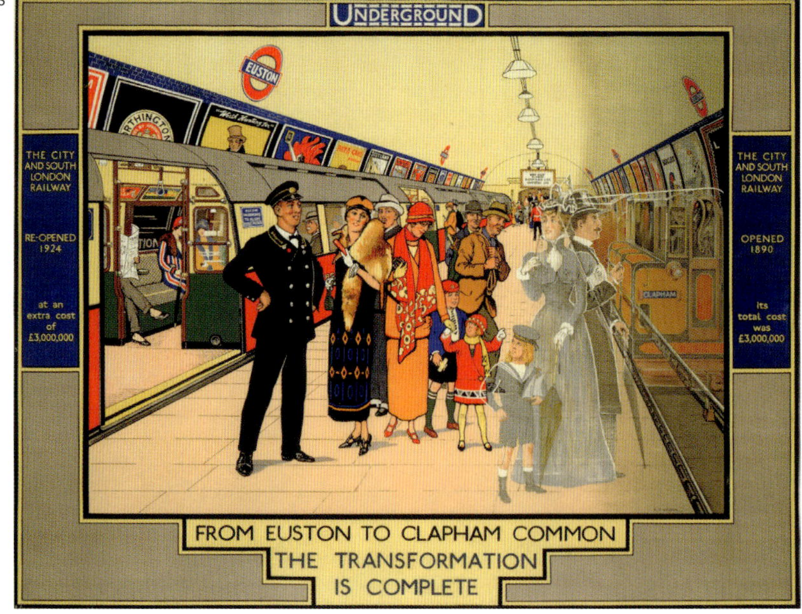

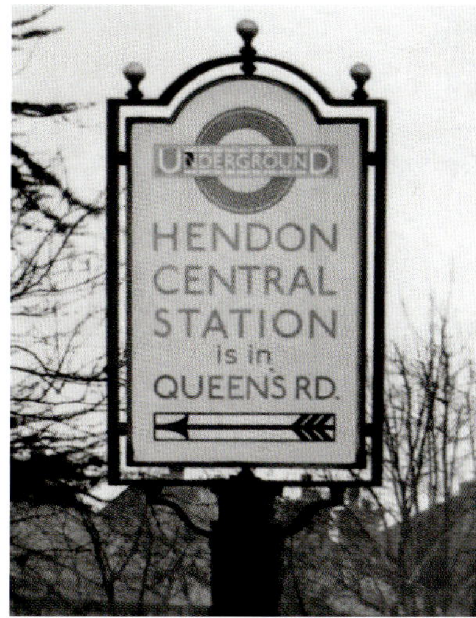

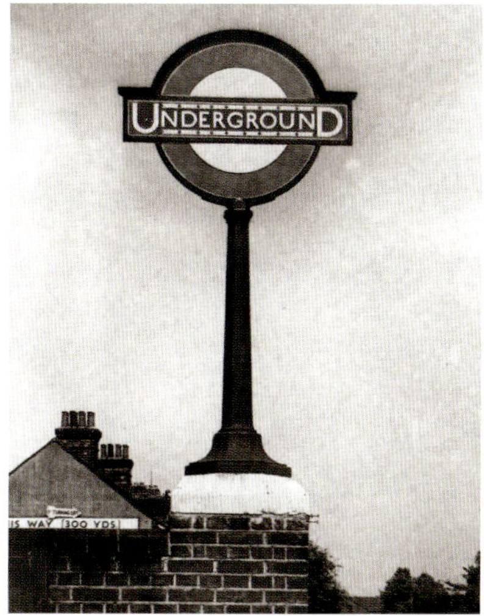

Johnston 'tombstones', 1920s

A bright idea occurred to someone (perhaps Heaps?) while designing signage for the Edgware extension: the curvature at the top of the bullseye could be echoed in the top of the sign itself. A curved shape was adopted on the street for the squat 'totems' (e.g. Colindale, 1924, 2) and directional signage, such as at Hendon Central (1923, 1). At Osterley (date unknown, 5) the logo was so high it almost leaps out of the sign. 'Tombstone' signage appeared above platform seating at Golders Green, Burnt Oak and elsewhere along the new route to Edgware and on nameboard signs (4). Illuminated double-sided 'tombstone' boxes were positioned over stairways at Bank (1926, 3) and Mansion House (1928). The shape continued to be utilized on signage right across the system until the late 1930s at least. It even appeared as a stop flag for the General bus company (6), manufactured by Birmingham Guild Limited and installed from 1924 onwards.

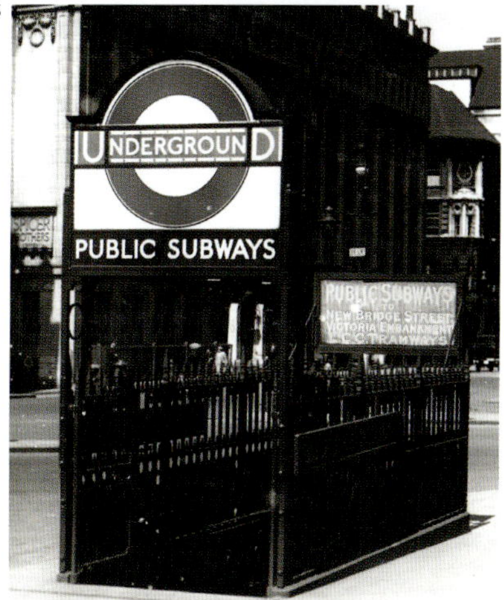

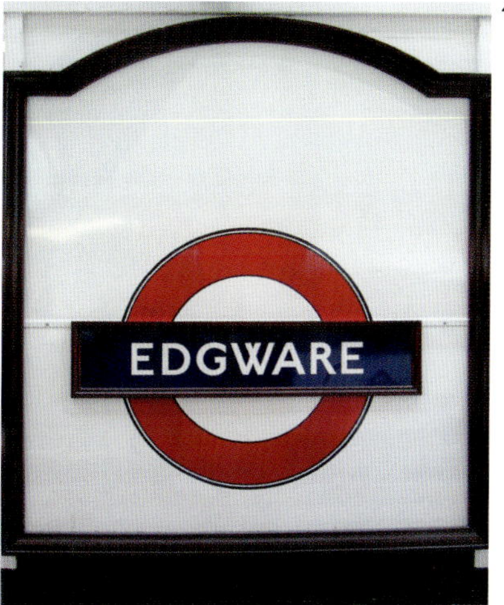

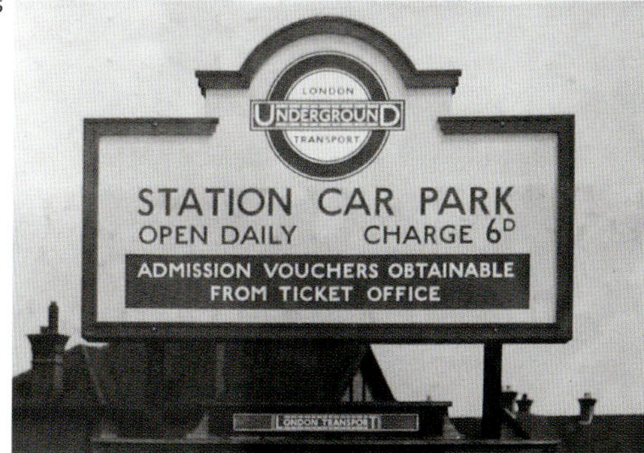

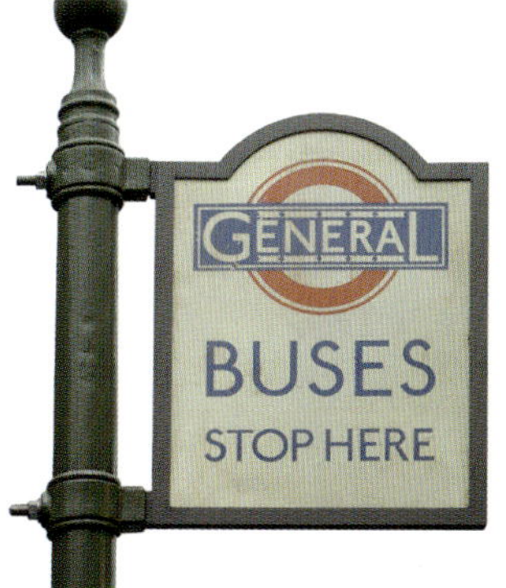

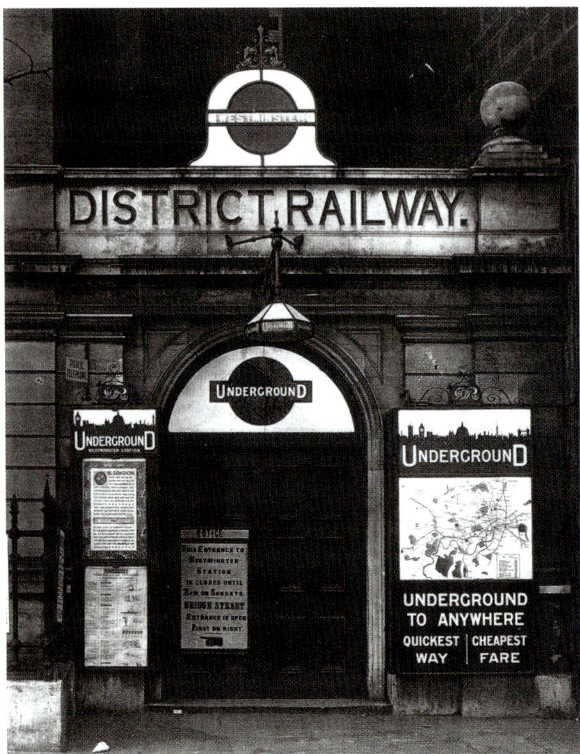

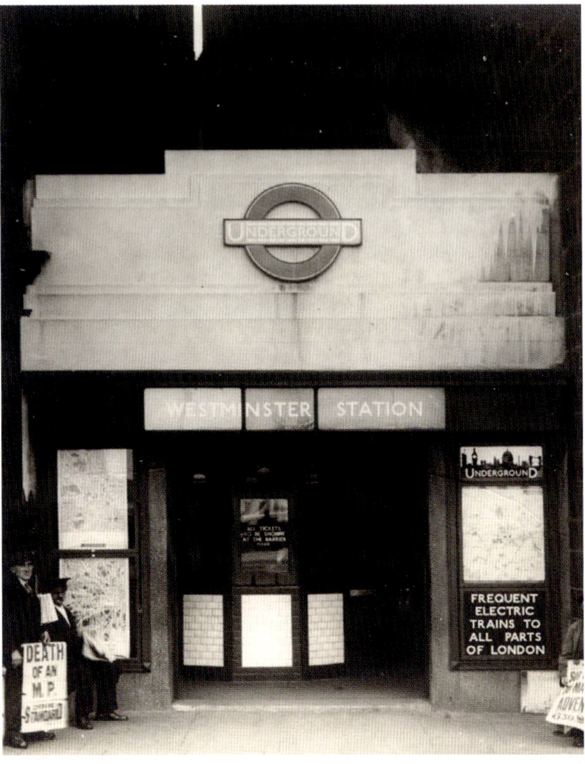

Holden's first Underground project, 1922–4

This tiny side entrance to Westminster (on Bridge Street, demolished in 1999 during work on the Jubilee line) was significant for two reasons. Firstly, the original entrance (photographed in 1916, 1) displayed two unique features: a combined Underground logo with solid red disc, without the customary dashes above and below the central letters, making it more akin to the later design and the bell-shaped station-name roundel above not seen elsewhere (according to photographic evidence). Secondly, the restructuring of this entrance (2) was the first project given to architect Charles Holden by Frank Pick in order to test his suitability for future schemes. Here in nascent form are many of the signature features of his later work: the dark band running the entire length of the station frontage; the wide, uncluttered entrance and pediment in flat but stylish Portland stone; the discreet placement of logos and passenger information. All beautifully proportioned, elegant and simple. It won him more commissions from Pick and changed the course of architectural history in the capital.

London Underground by Design

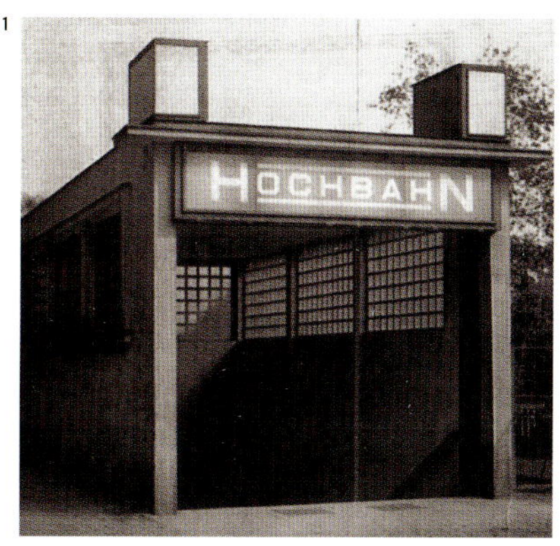

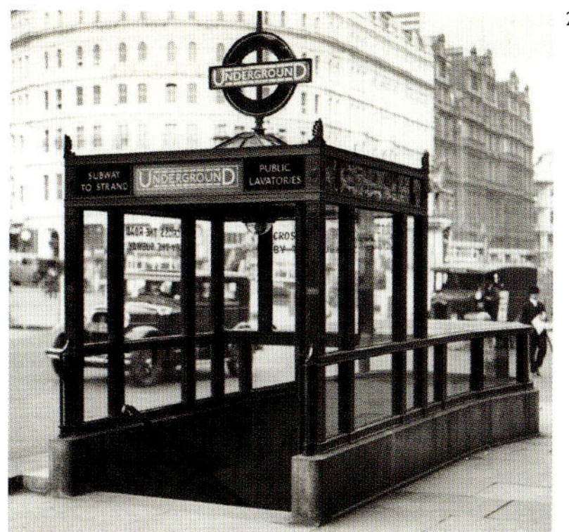

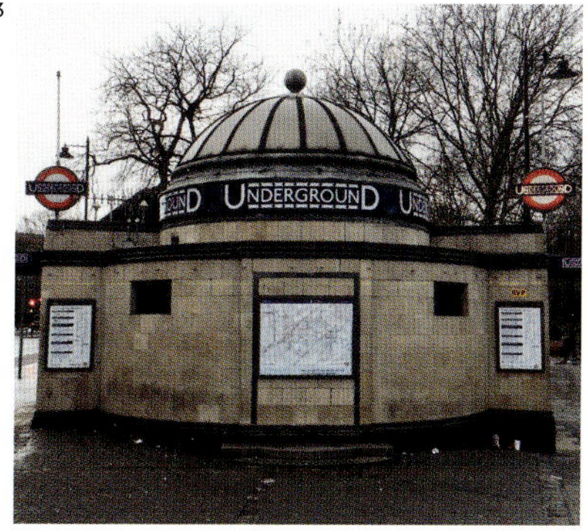

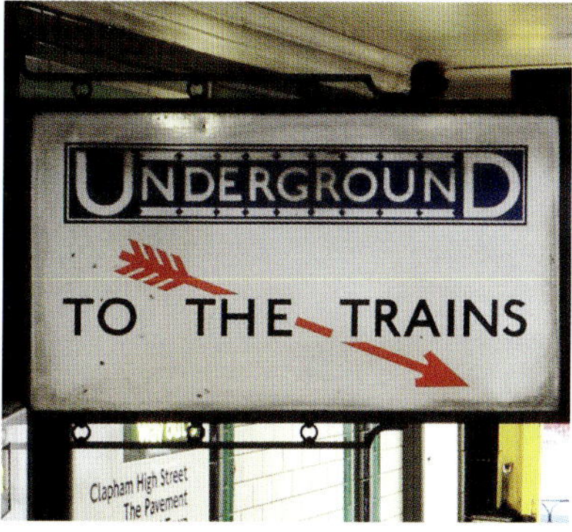

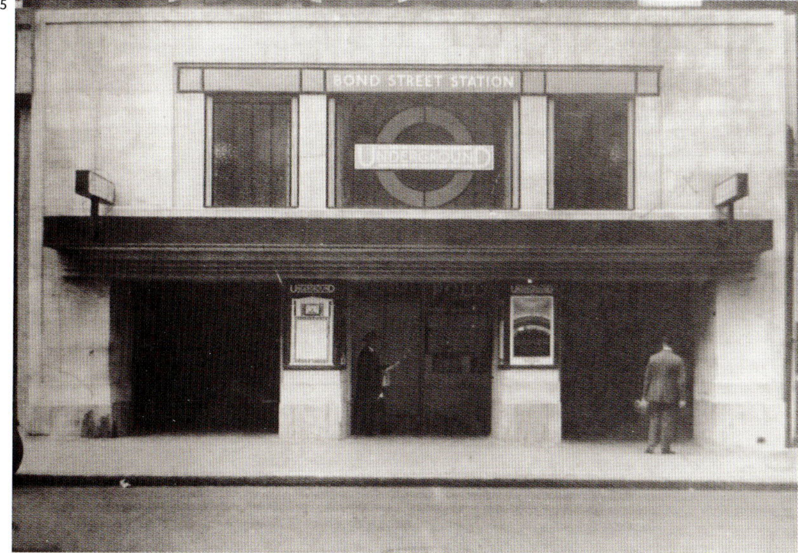

Holden's first classics, 1924–5

The 1920s was an age of new architectural thinking: skyscrapers were shooting up in Chicago and New York, the Bauhaus was in full swing in Continental Europe and le Corbusier was knocking out radical designs from villas to whole cities (including the complete rebuilding of central Paris, 1925, although the plans were never realized). In this spirit, the Hamburg Hochbahn (opened in 1911; Hallerstraße station, built in 1929, 1) – which adopted the idea of enlarging the first and last letters from the UNDERGROUND wordmark – had entrances constructed in what Robert Schwandl calls 'functional' style (2004, Bibliography). Holden had already been moving in this direction with a glazed entrance to Trafalgar Square (1925, 2). That and his beautiful glass dome over Clapham Common (3) and signage (4) were resplendent with subtle use of the Johnston Sans lettering. At the Bond Street rebuild (5), Holden went all out for the clean-cut, authoritative feel of unadorned Portland stone, wide entrances and a glazed wall on the first floor featuring an embedded bullseye in the glass. Such was its success, Bond Street became the template for the CSLR Morden extension (p. 116).

Thoroughly modern Morden, 1924–6

Holden's adaptable frontages (pictured on the drawing board, 1924, 1) for the seven stations to Morden (p. 116) were made into wooden mock-ups in 1925 (2) and construction on-site began the same year. The end result looked very similar to the trials. The exquisite architecture of these stations remains virtually unchanged to this day: refurbished in original style, Balham (3) and its sister stations look as resplendent now as they did when they first opened, especially at night when light fills the large windows from the ticket-hall chandeliers (5). Passageways and platforms were clad in white tiles with simple borders in grey, black and green (4), while bullseyes of the new registered design '659,814' (p. 128) were placed at alternating heights along each platform. These consisted of two white enamelled sheets, the bottom one displaying the lower half of the red ring and blue bar incorporating the station name in Johnston Sans, the top one the upper half of the red ring and often with directional information above, such as 'WAY OUT' and an arrow. The entire red ring was outlined in black and a painted wooden border glued around the blue bar. The effect against the tiling was striking. All other signage — including suspended illuminated boxes, lists of destinations and notices about escalators — was in Johnston Sans.

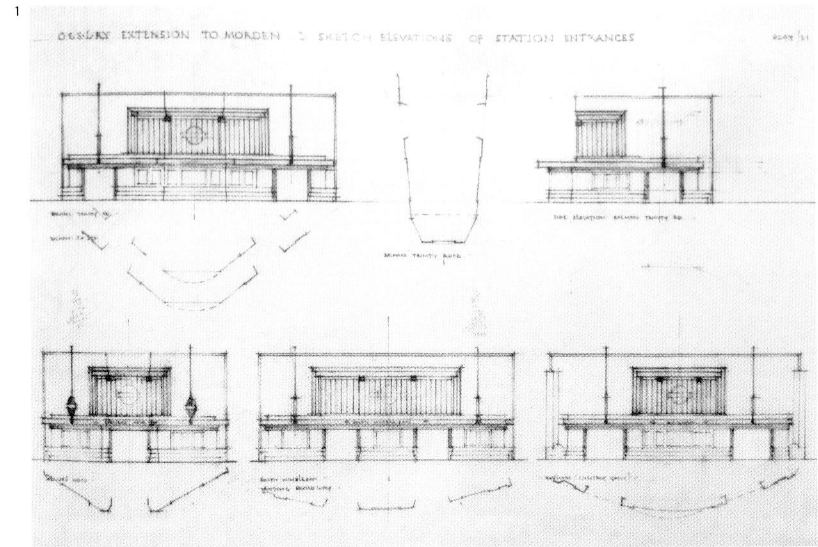

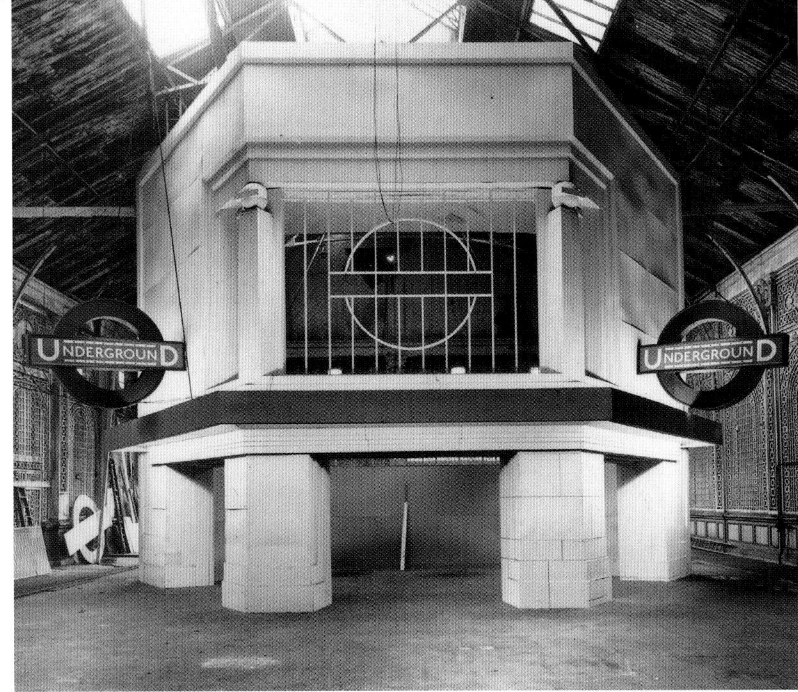

When the extension opened in 1926 (the world's longest stretch of underground railway at the time), the unified effect of the architecture, signage, logo and printed matter all using the Johnston Sans lettering would not have been lost on passengers. It was an absolute triumph of best design practice.

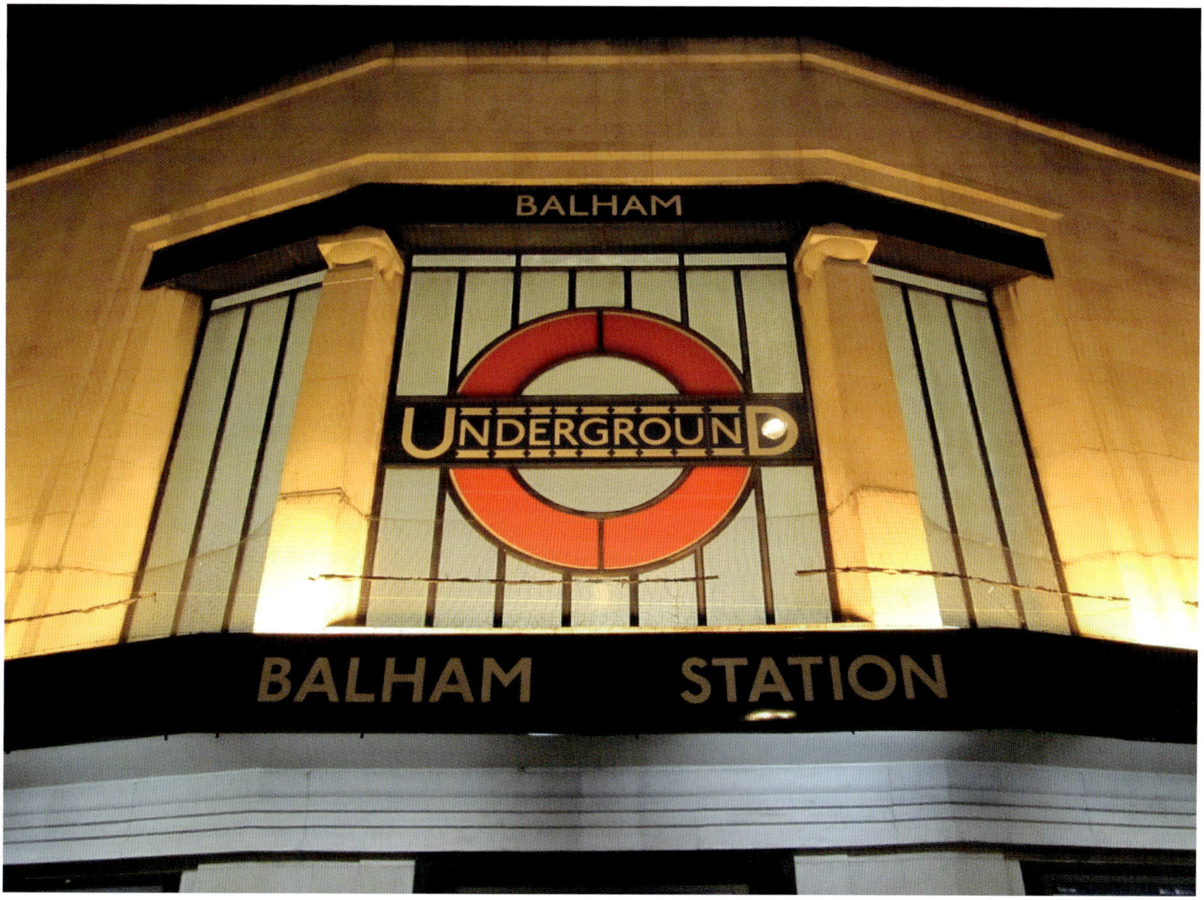

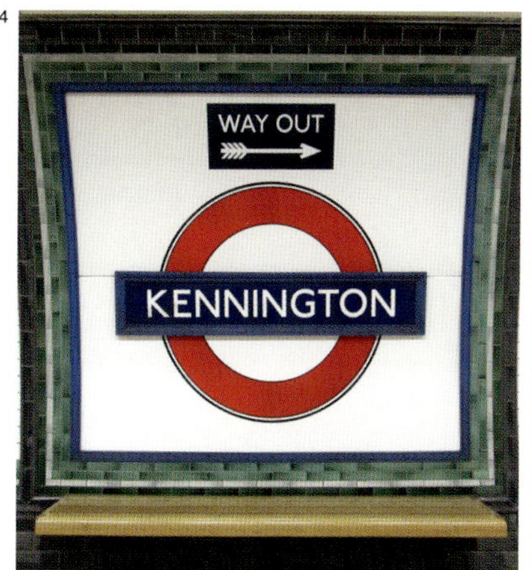

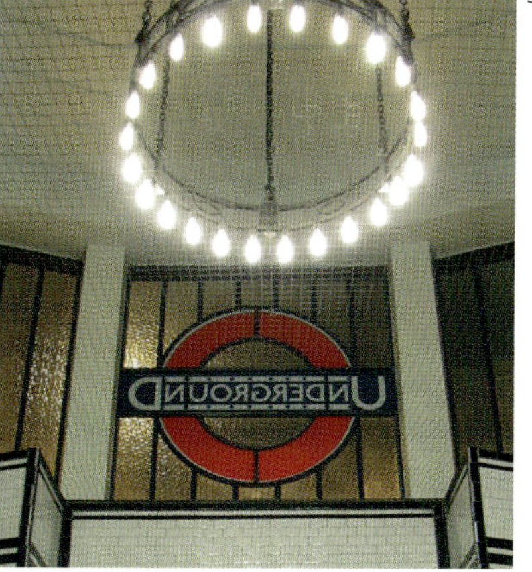

Promoting 'Metro-land', 1916–25

Much has been written about the unprecedented involvement of the Metropolitan Railway in the development of north-west London, but the role played by the company's use of design, if not as groundbreaking as that of the Underground, was equally significant in its own way. The chief reason for its success lies in the succinct slogan, 'Metro-land', which summed up the allure of escaping cramped inner London for the rolling open countryside of Hertfordshire and Middlesex, while linking it indelibly with the rail company's name (pp. 68–9). Though its publicity was less stylish than that of the Underground, the Met recognized the importance of a co-ordinated look – such as using white lettering on a red background (p. 109). Elsewhere, the emphasis was always on the countryside and its proximity to the city. Hence posters (1), brochures (pp. 108–109), signage, maps, property developers' ads (2) and even door handles (3) all reflected the clarion call, 'Live in Metro-land', to the extent that it became engraved in the contemporary psyche.

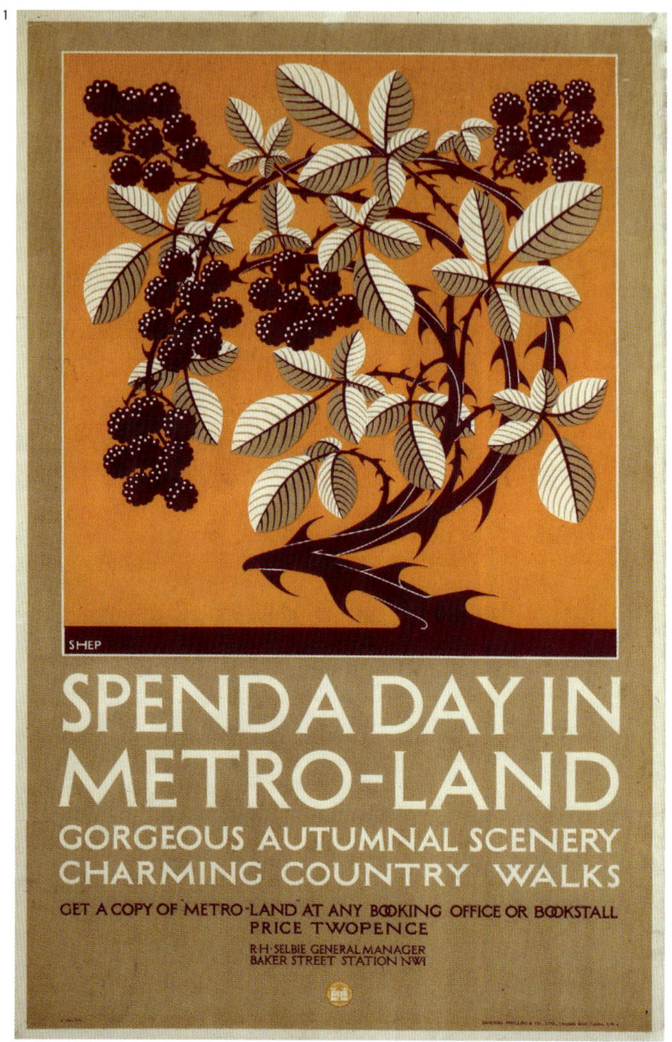

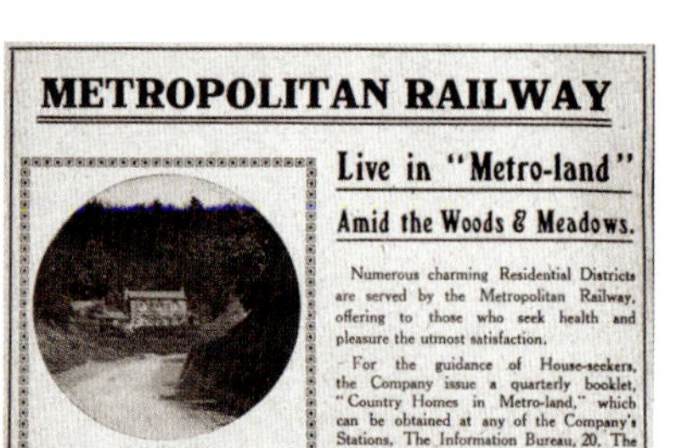

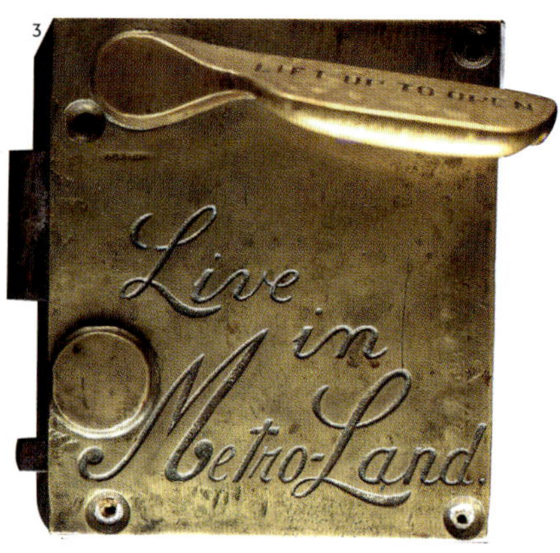

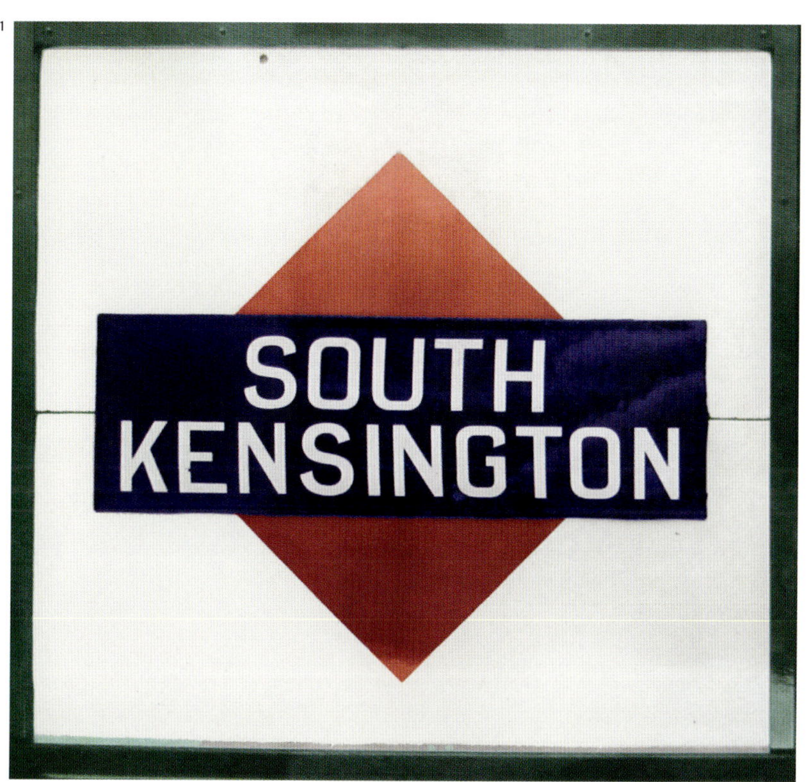

1

The Met's red diamond, 1917–29

Around sixty stations are thought to have displayed the Met's red diamond on nameboards. These ranged from Watford and Rickmansworth in the north-west to Hammersmith in the south-west, and from Uxbridge in the west to Farringdon and Aldgate (3) in the east. They were present at Inner Circle stations like South Kensington (1), where they jostled with Underground bullseyes (p. 86), and Great Portland Street and Regent's Park (2), where the station name was so long (between 1923 and 1933) it needed *three* lines of text. The first of these signs were installed just after the war, from about 1919, and the last of them came down when a rogue sign was removed from Highbury & Islington in the early 1970s. Although the ELR's green diamond (p.100) and the Met's red were second and third logos out of the starting gate (p.67) and therefore unlikely to have won the race, it is intriguing to imagine how Underground stations might have looked had this shape dominated rather than the bullseye. In the Met's final years, a few red diamond logos were given the Johnston lettering in the centre blue bar (p. 181), though never on a station nameboard.

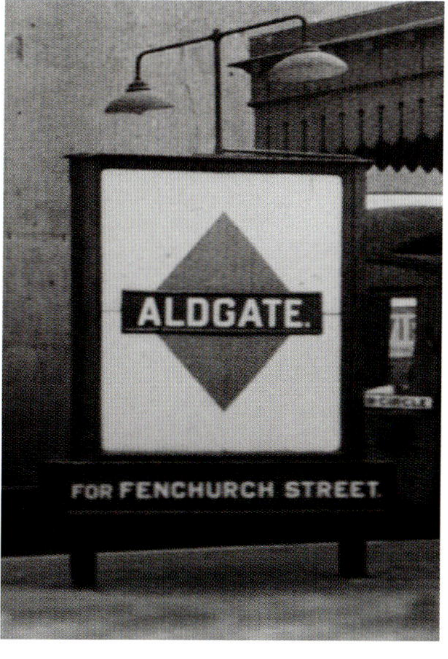

2

3

Met styling behind the times, 1923–9

The Met's plans for rebuilding key stations (put on hold during the war) were resumed in the 1920s. Architect Charles W. Clark had employed a traditional style at Baker Street in 1913 and Paddington (p. 107) a year later, but did little to modernize the look for the first few stations that he rebuilt: Farringdon (1923), Paddington (original drawing, 1923, 1), Willesden Green (1925, 2), Aldgate (1926), Edgware Road (1928), Notting Hill Gate (1928), St John's Wood and Swiss Cottage (1929). Only for the final three, Great Portland Street, North Harrow (both 1930) and Euston Square (1931, 4), did he simplify his style with a nod to the modernist look emerging on the Underground's new and rebuilt stations. Clark's station interiors featured wooden-framed ticket sales windows and stylish green-glazed bricks (3). He also embraced the Met's diamond, which can be seen on everything from signage, clocks and their holders (5 and 6) to mosaic friezes. If Clark's 'new' stations seemed dated in town, they were positively old-fashioned in the country; Watford and Croxley (both 1925, p. 115) were more like branch-line halts or domestic dwellings with station awnings attached. The one place where Clark's fussiness felt comfortable was the exquisite segmented glass canopy over Euston Square entrance (4) – a clear nod to Guimard's entrances on the Paris Métro.

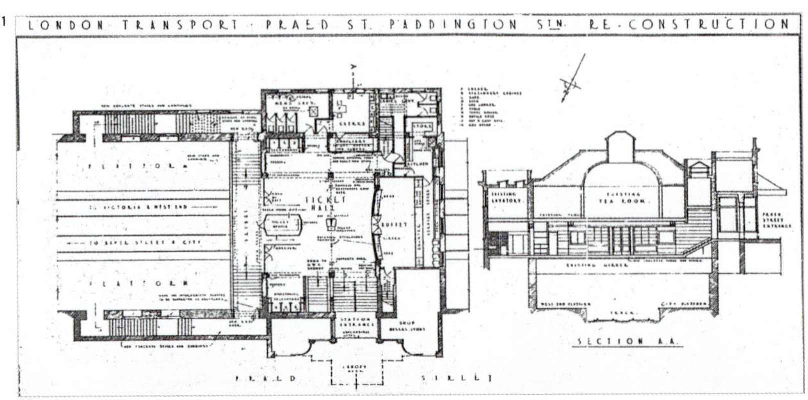

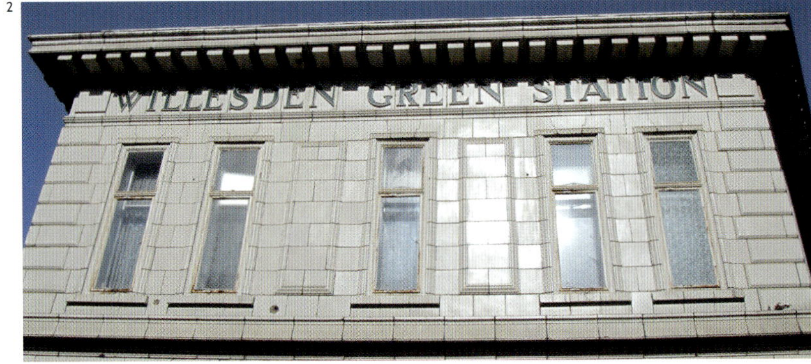

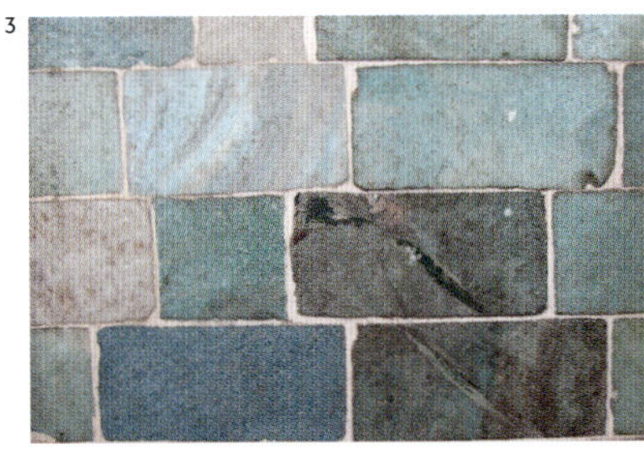

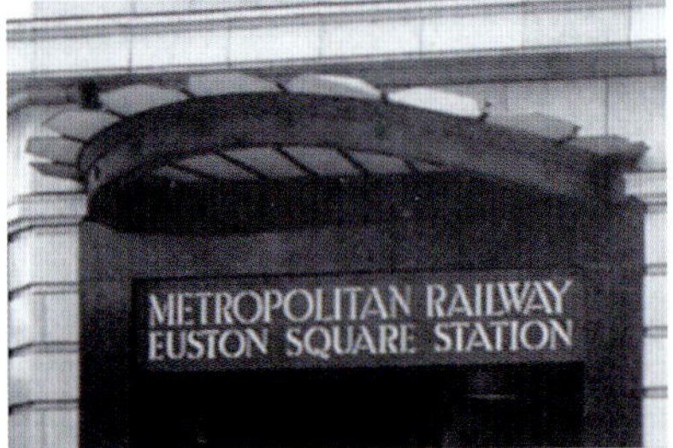

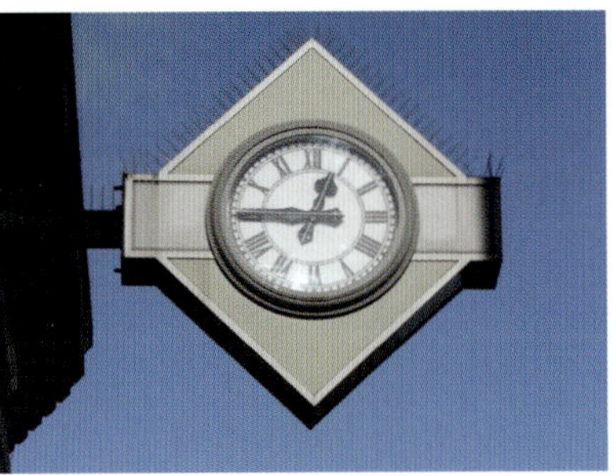

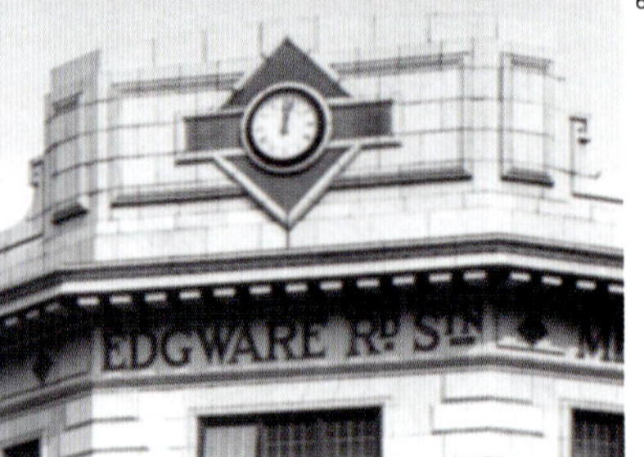

London Underground by Design

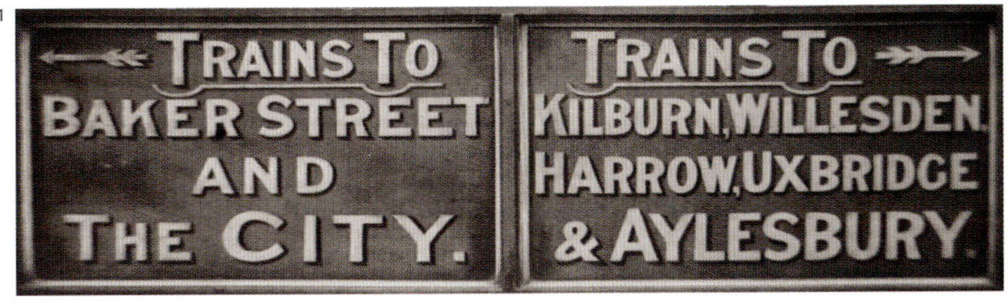

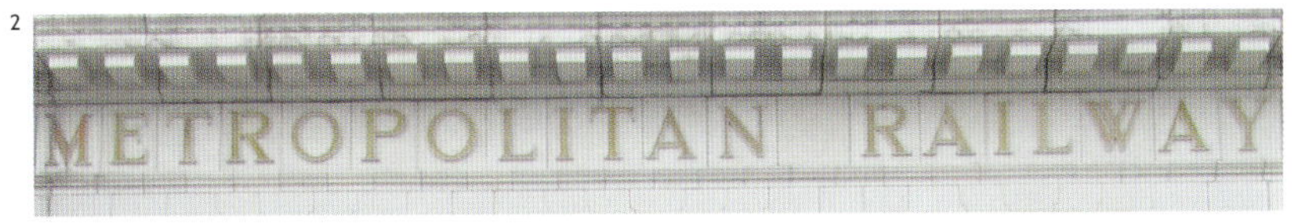

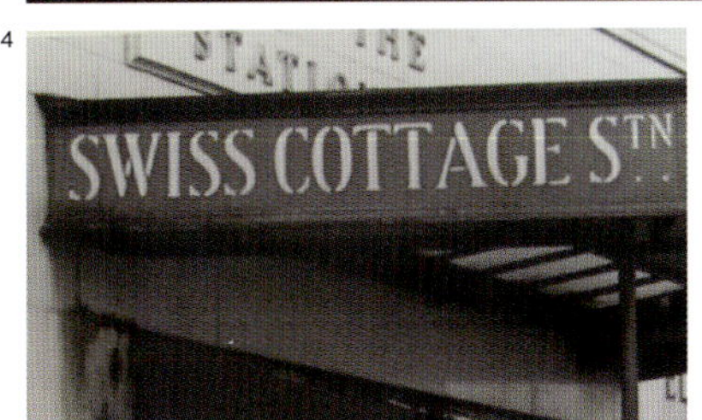

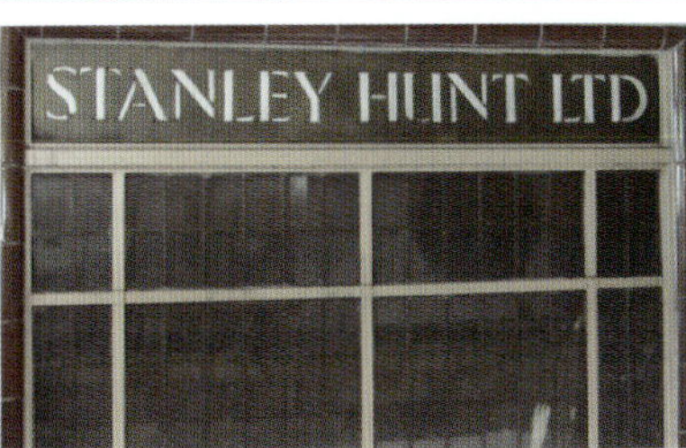

Met serifs, 1920s

Up until 1913 most signage on the Met consisted of adaptations of the first styles of sans-serif lettering (1 and p. 22), but Clark introduced a serif at Paddington and Farringdon in 1923 (2), which continued to be employed after the war on the pediment and as a stencil letter on the steel-framed canopy projecting over the street (4). Signage for waiting rooms, buffets, ticket windows, toilets and directions (3) were all made using this stencilled letterform. Even shop units had signage in it (one of the few still visible today at Great Portland Street, 5). By the 1920s, however, far from having a traditional feel, the letters seem obsolete by comparison with the confident modern styling of the Underground stations, with its clear, authoritative sans-serif. Towards the end of its time as an independent company, some effort was made to modernize the Met's styling (6 and p. 180), but it was unlikely to ever win out over the power of the Johnston type and was progressively obliterated as new signs replaced old. Only a few isolated examples of original signage remain on station frontages (Farringdon, p. 275, Paddington and Willesden Green, and restored at Baker Street).

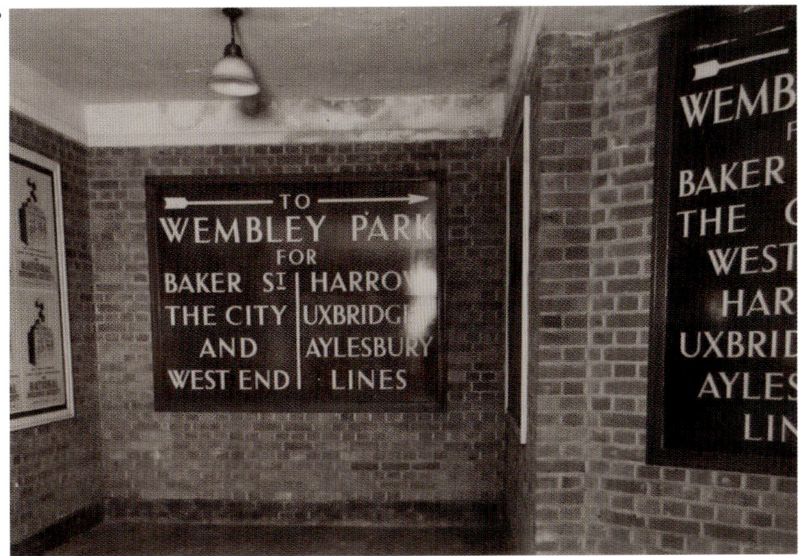

The Met's flagship headquarters and iconic train, 1924–30

Clark's grandiose 'porte-cochère' to Baker Street (1) with stone pillars and a handsome clock was completed in 1924 (serif letters were made like stencils with holes cut into the metal and space left for connections to central parts of the A, B, O and R). But the Met had even bigger plans for the site. Some initial work was done at platform level, including pleasant brown and blue tiling and a new overbridge at the east end. Then, on 2 August 1927, construction began on what would be the Met's biggest building (1): the company headquarters combined with a residential block, restaurants, shops and even a ten-room bachelor penthouse. Completed in 1930, Chiltern Court had a 122m-wide frontage and contained almost 200 flats of the highest modernity. It was a valiant effort and ahead of its time in the provision of refuse collection, pre-cabled phone and radio points. The Met was to have its headquarters there but, as the building was only completed in 1930, the company enjoyed just three years' occupancy before it too was absorbed into the Underground (p. 154). Back in the Met's heyday, the Bo-Bo electric trains of 1925 became iconic emblems of the company (2), appearing on posters and other printed ephemera (3).

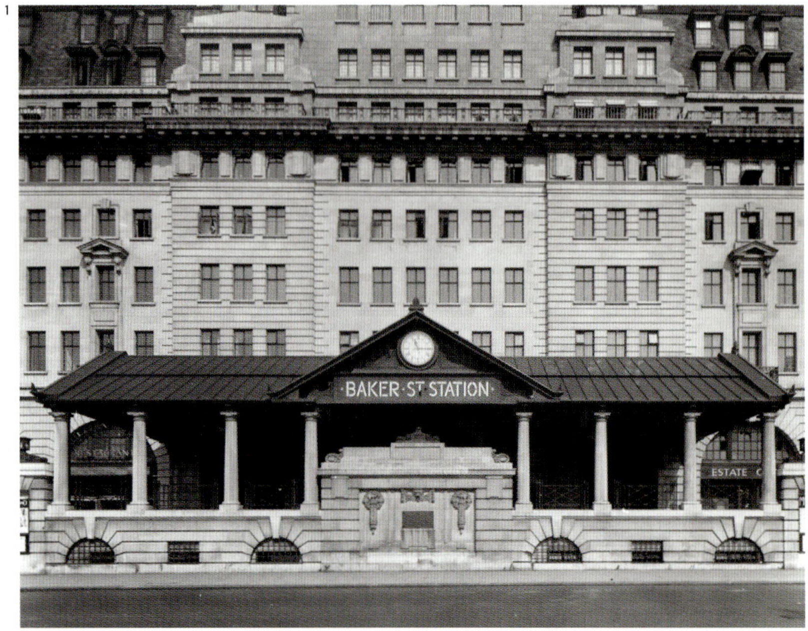

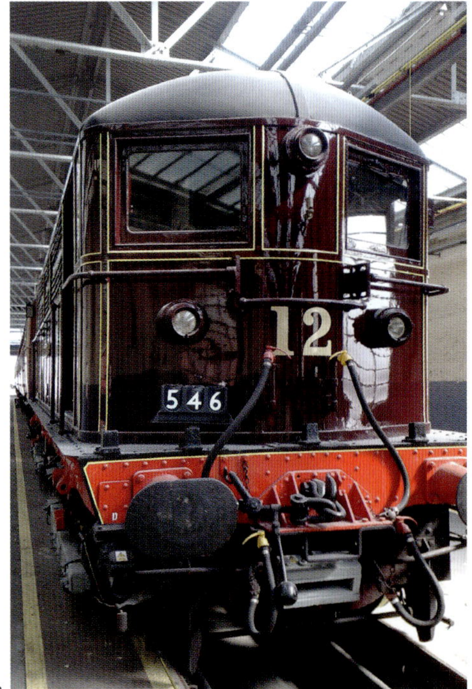

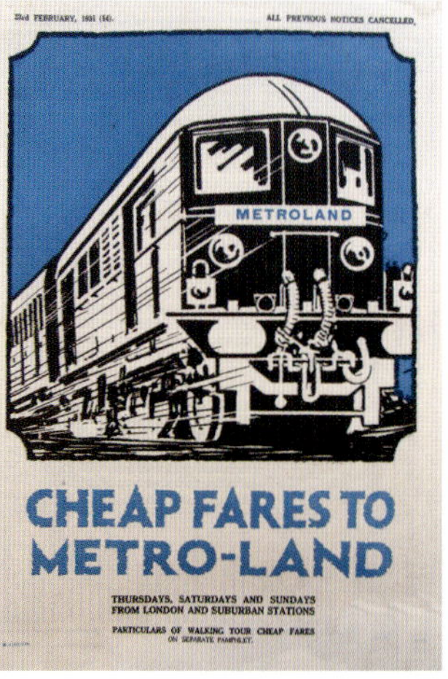

Mapping the Met, 1924–9

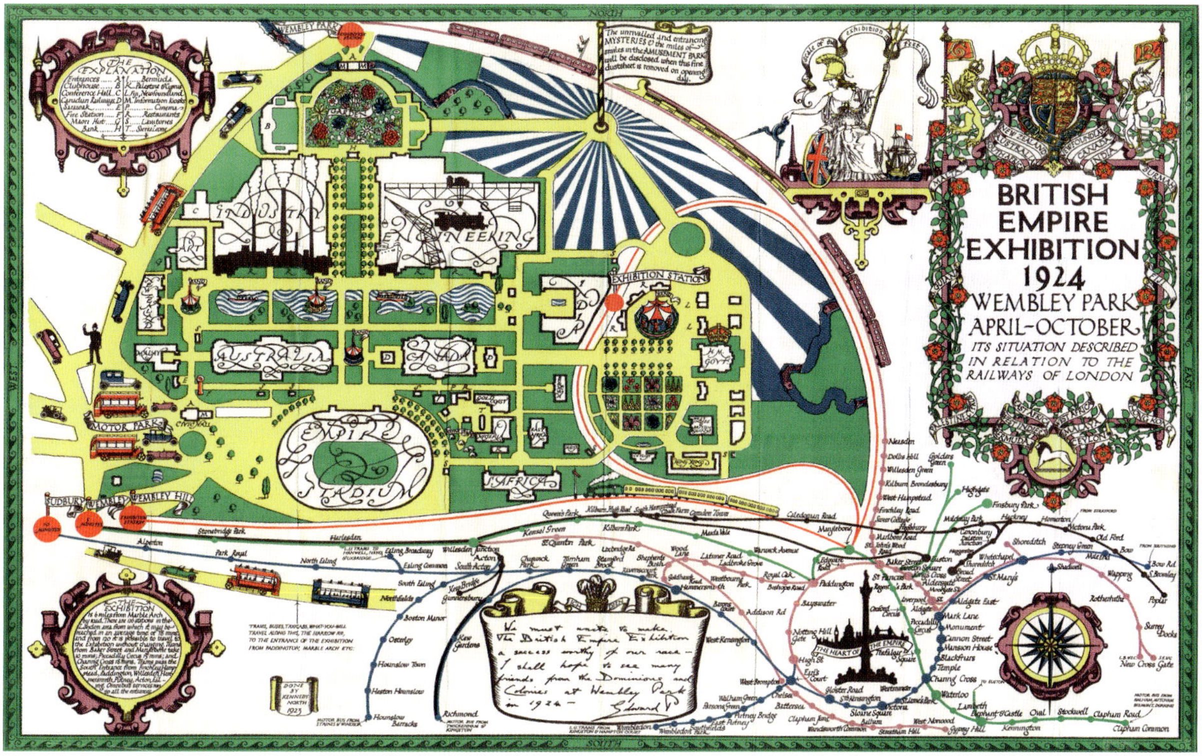

Just as Britain once occupied the heart
of a pink-shaded cartographic empire,
so the Met's Inner Circle at the heart
of London and its stations at Wembley
are presented as key to the 1924 Empire
Exhibition in this map by Kennedy
North (made for Thomas Cook, 1).
It was a clever and very beautiful (if
not exactly accurate) portrayal of the
company's services, North's calligraphic
annotations were no doubt inspired
by MacDonald Gill's map (p. 142), and
in turn North's caricature of London's
geography inspired others to play with
spatial relationships on the map of the
Underground. The 'ovalization' of the
circle (2) was made for a carriage map
around 1924 (and issued to commercial
attractions like Madame Tussaud's
to include in publicity leaflets), but
the standard pocket map of the Met
retained its traditional geographic
format until 1933, when the company
was taken over by the Underground.

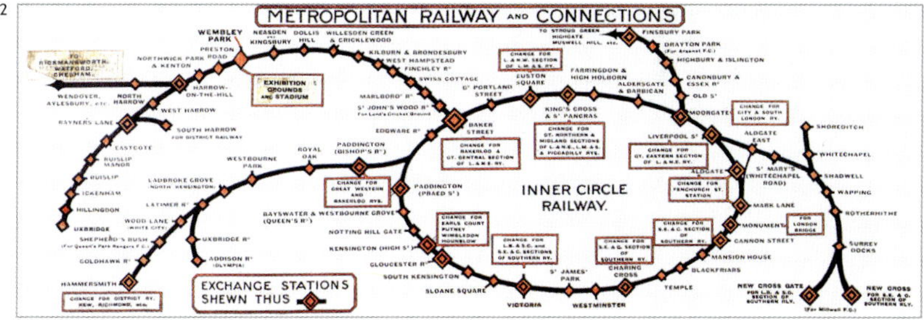

New hands on the map, 1921-9

The fold-out maps had done their job, but the smaller card maps from 1908 onwards (p. 91) were popular. In March 1921 the Underground issued a new 203 × 152mm fold-out series which, like the pocket maps, had no background geographic details – not even the River Thames. It was designed by MacDonald Gill. Known as an artist more than a cartographer, his previous work the Wonderground Map of London Town, of 1914 (detail, p. 19), was an intricate patchwork of the West End as cartoon-style vignettes; his 1921 map, by contrast, could not have been more different. Gill was allowed to use his own fine calligraphy for station names – an odd decision given the introduction of Johnston lettering – but it was illegible when squashed into the confined spaces of central London, requiring awkward arrows and shrunken letters (compare, for example, Goodge Street or Moorgate with Westminster or any of the stations south of Kennington). This illustrated only too well why another solution would be needed for the map.

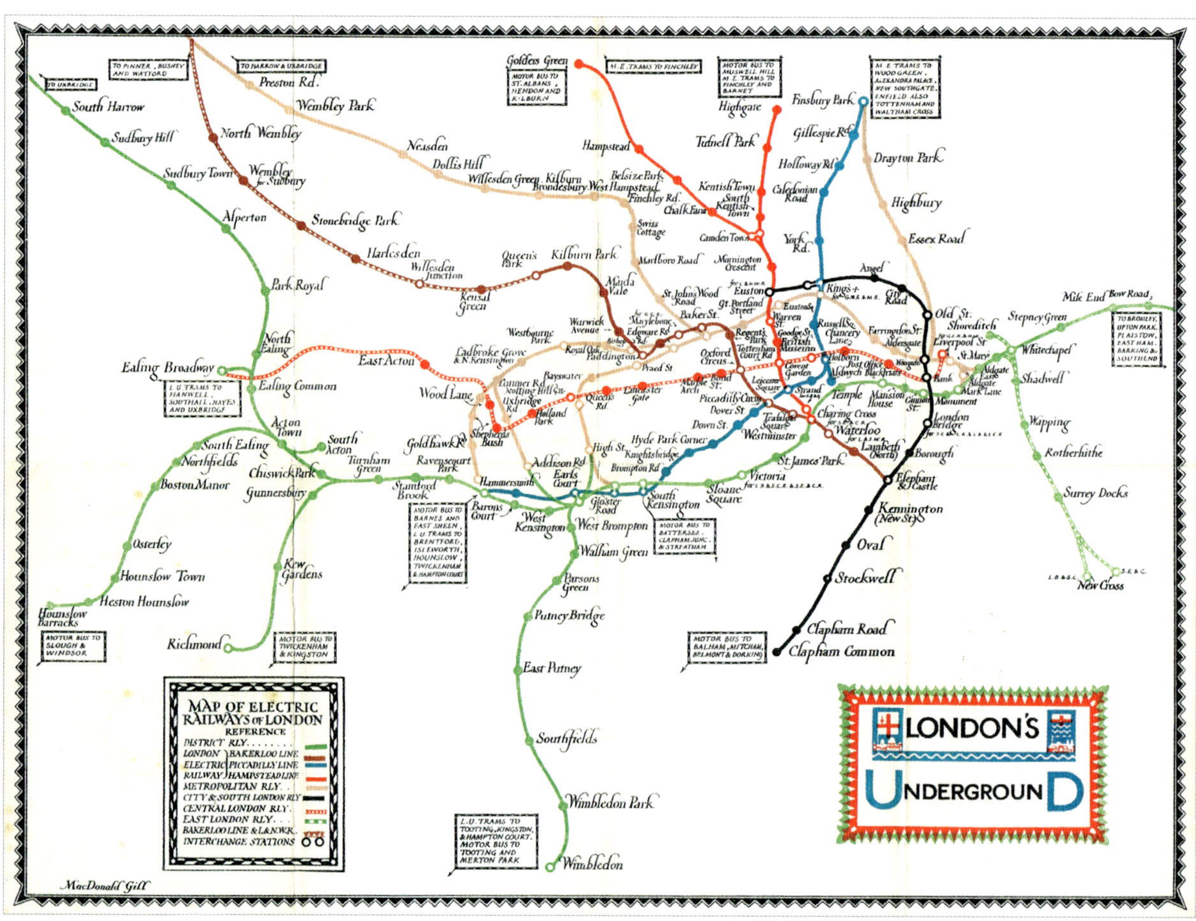

London Underground by Design

The 152 × 137 mm card folder pocket map of May 1925 (below) was produced by another new hand. F. H. Stingemore (p. 113) had designed posters for the Underground since 1914, several of which had included cartographic elements, so he was asked to tackle the 1925 edition of the map. It built on Gill's background-less idea but allowed space for both ends of the extended CSLR/ Hampstead lines (which would become today's Northern line). Unfortunately this was at the expense cartographically of the ELR and the Hounslow branch of the District (a problem that would take almost a decade to solve). Stingemore's lettering was a step in the right direction for clarity. Hand drawn rather than printed in Johnston Sans, which seems odd to modern eyes, it is still a tad squashed (poor Goodge Street suffering again), but Stingemore seems to have at least learnt the trick of not allowing the text to slip over onto the coloured route lines.

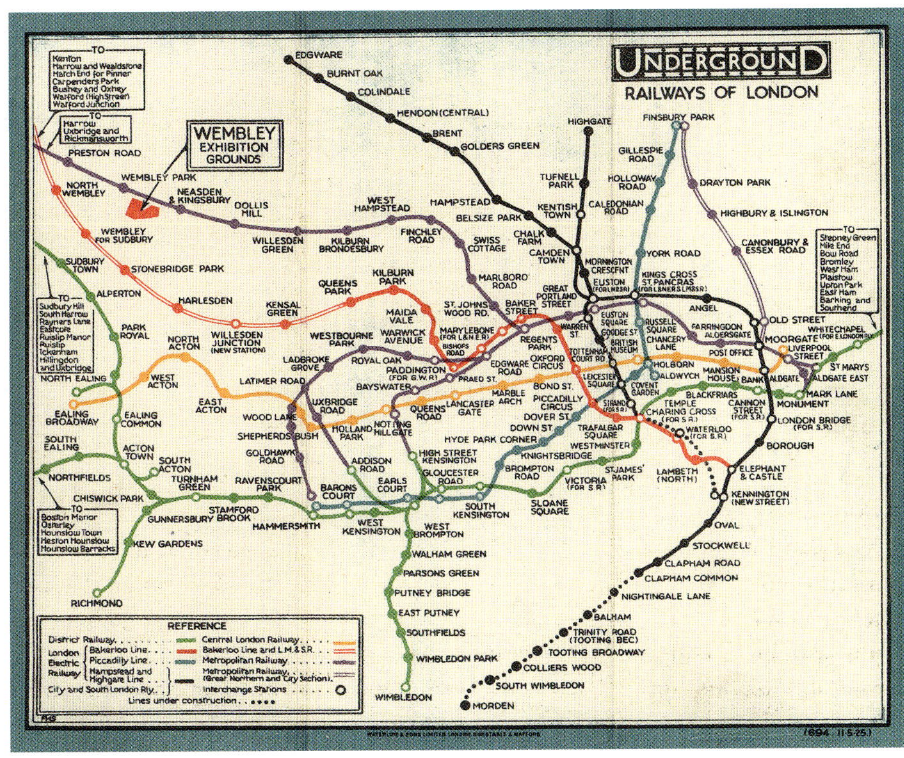

It's like Piccadilly Circus in here, 1928

Described when it opened as a masterpiece of opulence and chic, the reconstructed Piccadilly Circus (designed by Charles Holden), with its new booking hall concourse/circulating area and escalator shafts, was without doubt one of Britain's defining Art Deco buildings. On a par with such other gems of contemporary architecture as the Carreras Cigarette Factory (Camden, 1926–8), Ideal House (Argyll Street, 1929), Broadcasting House (built between 1928 and 1932) or even Battersea Power Station (started 1930), Piccadilly Circus was a celebration of the age. First mocked up at Earl's Court (1), the result was modern, sleek, stylish as well as functional. Every corner screamed attention to detail: from the cream-coloured Travertine marble walls to the faceted pillars clad in red scagliola (opposite, 1), Art Deco mouldings and bronze trims, it all combined to give the hall a bright, spacious and yet sumptuous feel. Signage was in cream Johnston Sans on brushed dark bronze (opposite, 3). But Holden's pièce de résistance was undoubtedly the Art Deco bronze uplighters installed along the escalators (3). Similar details featured on many subsequent stations and although a large number were removed following the conversion to fluorescent lighting, many have been restored during recent station renovations and are now regarded as architecturally important.

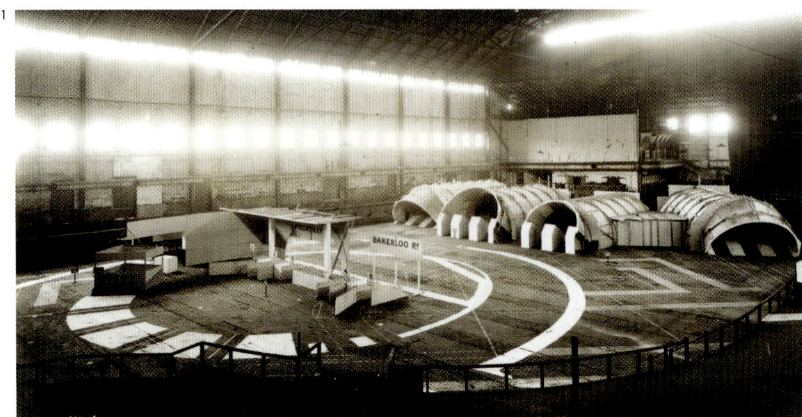

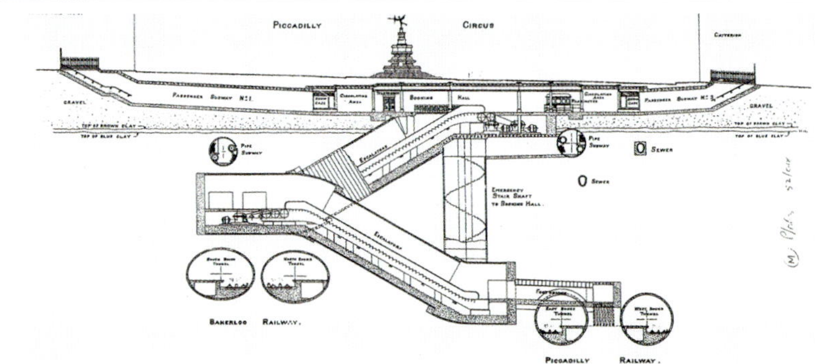

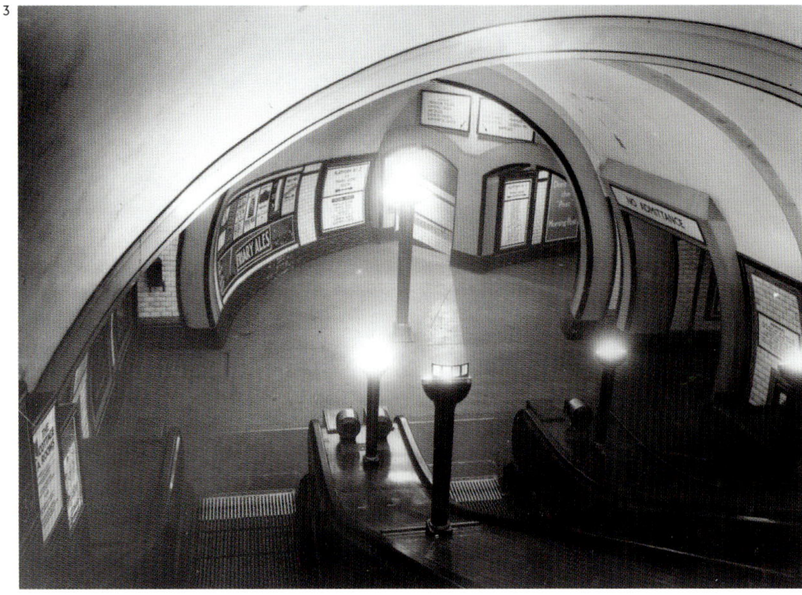

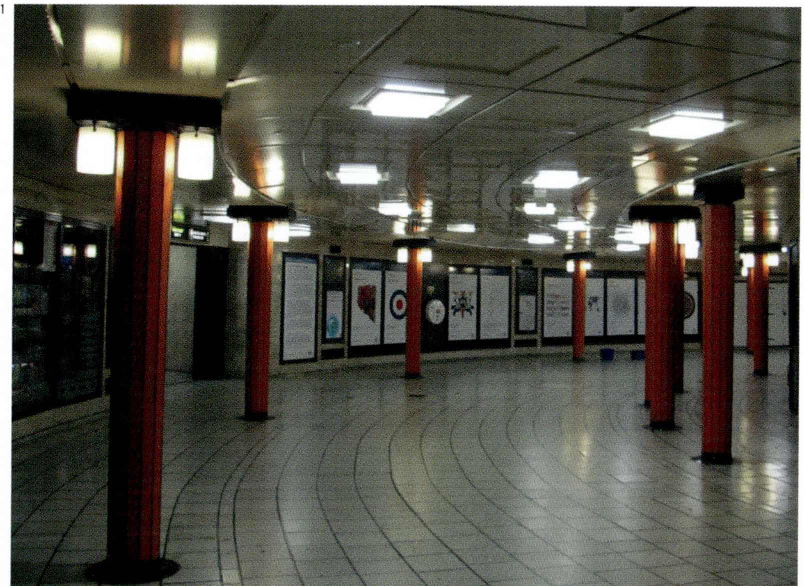

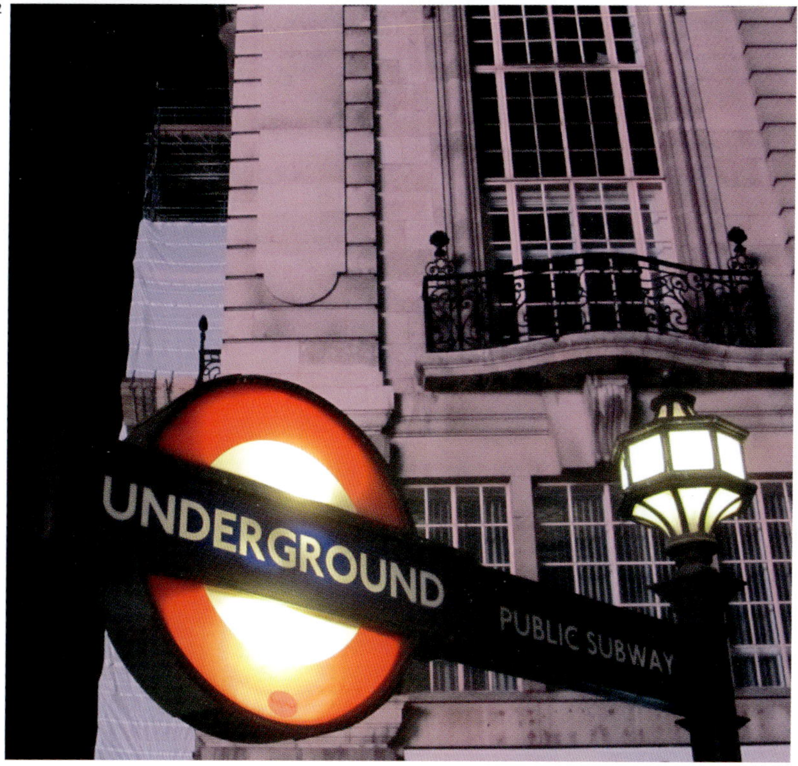

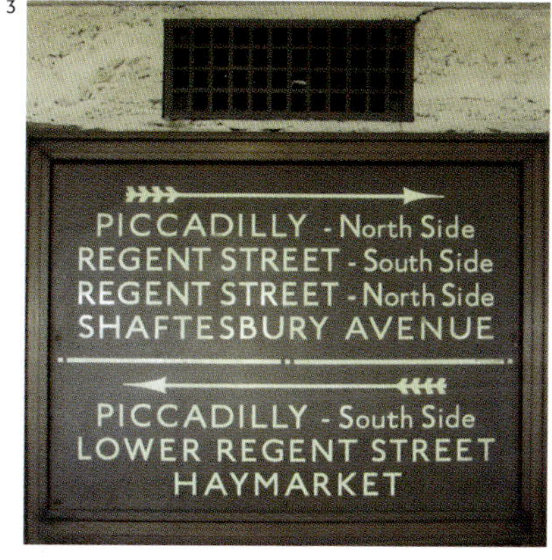

Constructing the new ticket hall and escalator shafts underneath the statue of Eros and one of London's busiest road junctions strained the technology of the time (1928) to the limit. Drawings (opposite, 2) and publically issued posters illustrated the complexity of the design below ground. Painter Stephen Bone (p. 118) was commissioned for five mural panels to sit above the escalator shafts, depicting the people of London and Britain's place in the Empire. Exterior lighting consisted of diamond-shaped lamps (still in situ, 2) which have become a landmark of Piccadilly Circus itself. A memorial to Frank Pick was installed in the concourse on the 75th anniversary of his death, in 2016.

A landmark for London, 1929

Having outgrown previous office space
and with plans to expand the network
further, the Underground needed a
new headquarters building. Charles
Holden was chosen by Frank Pick to fill
an oddly shaped site above St James's
Park station (1 and p. 118). Constructed
on a 'cruciform' plan (previously
used by Holden's firm for building
hospitals, albeit on a smaller scale),
'55 Broadway' was clad in Holden's
favourite material, Portland stone,
each elevation decorated at sixth-floor
level with a relief representing one
of the four winds (each 'wind' being
repeated, making eight in total) by
contemporary sculptors Eric Aumonier,
A. H. Gerrard, Eric Gill, Henry Moore,
Samuel Rabinovitch and Allan Wyon.
Jacob Epstein made a separate pair
of sculptures, Night and Day (2 and
3) set over the entrances at first-floor
level. The building opened in December
1929 to critical acclaim – although
the stark style and graphic nakedness
of the statues (especially Epstein's)
aroused controversy initially – and
was immediately featured on a poster
with the confident slogan: 'London's
Underground – Always at Your Service'.

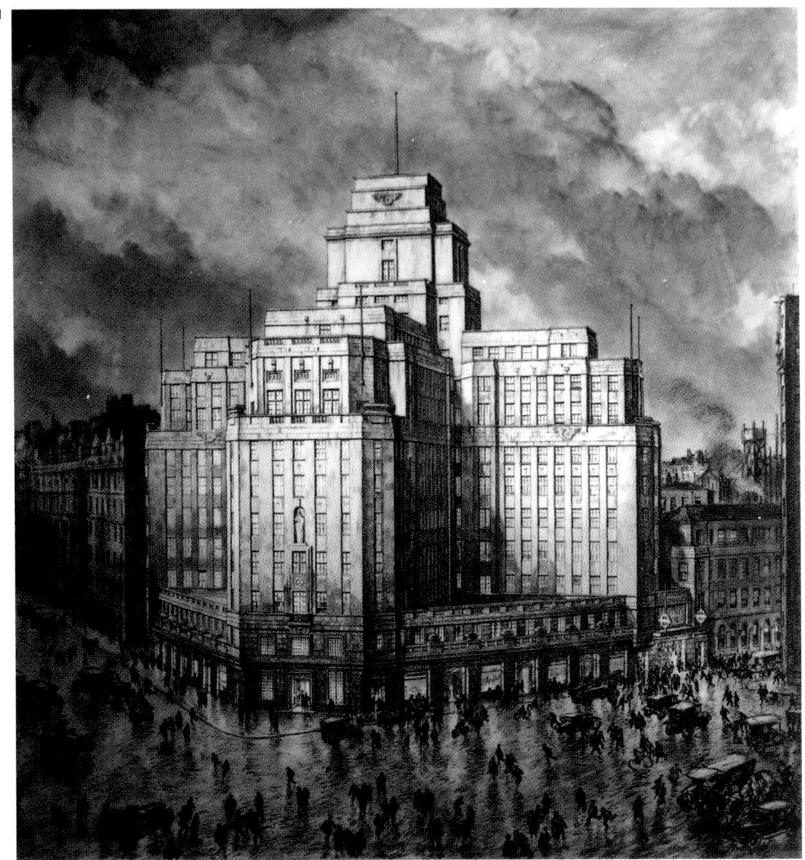

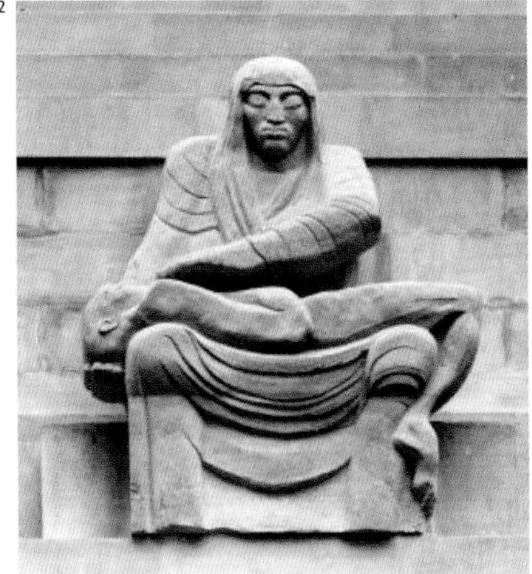

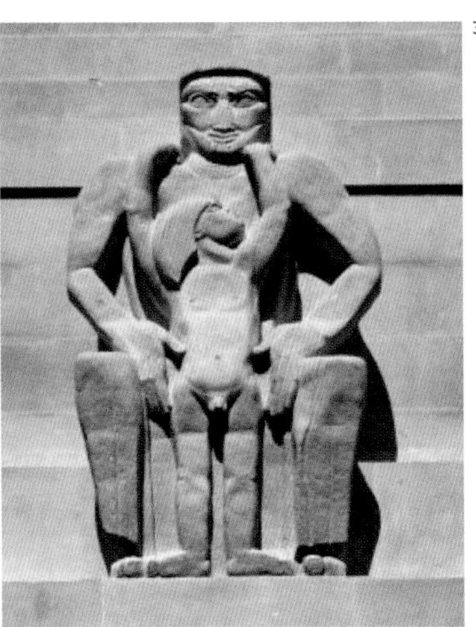

London Underground by Design

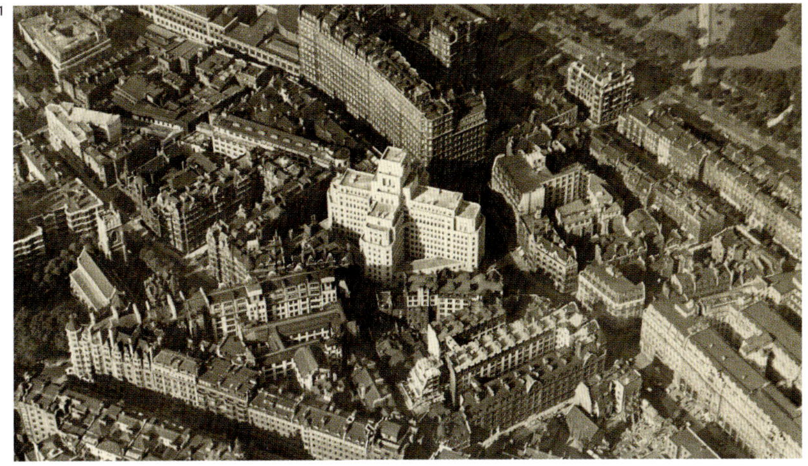

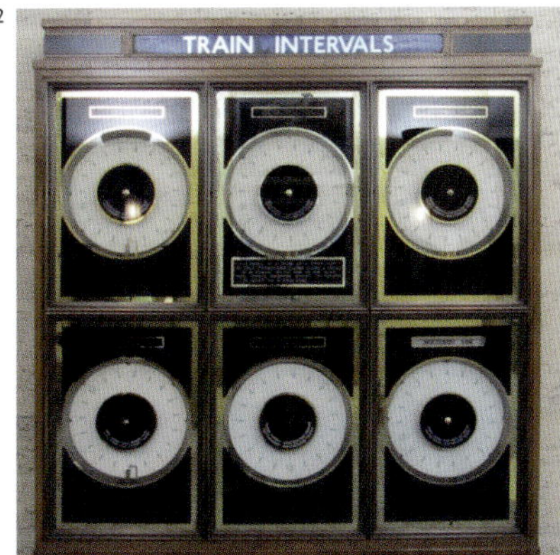

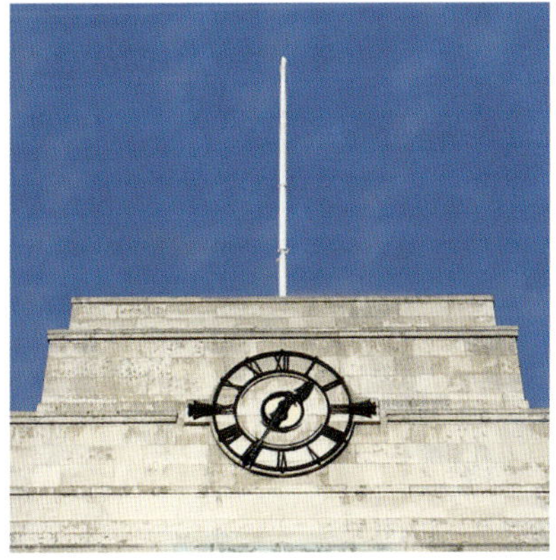

Every aspect of the building's design reflected the overall aesthetic, from the Travertine marble flooring and bronze panelling to the lift shafts and even the guttering. The company lettering and logo were omnipresent, though never overdone. The clock face on the tower, for example (3), was in the shape of a bullseye. Though internal signage was restricted to directions only (4), it had a unique feature: instead of being executed in the obvious plain Johnston Sans, lettering had a tiny elegant serif, designed by Percy Delf Smith (p. 165) and later used on the Piccadilly extension. Johnston Sans was, however, used for the bronze-edged 'TRAIN INTERVALS' display case (2) in the reception area which showed train frequency on each of the six lines, the same style of indicator being installed at Piccadilly Circus. Simple and stylish yet eminently practical, such touches summed up Holden and Pick's approach for the building and the system as a whole, 55 Broadway becoming a landmark for London – its height though was soon topped by Holden's own Senate House (completed in 1937).

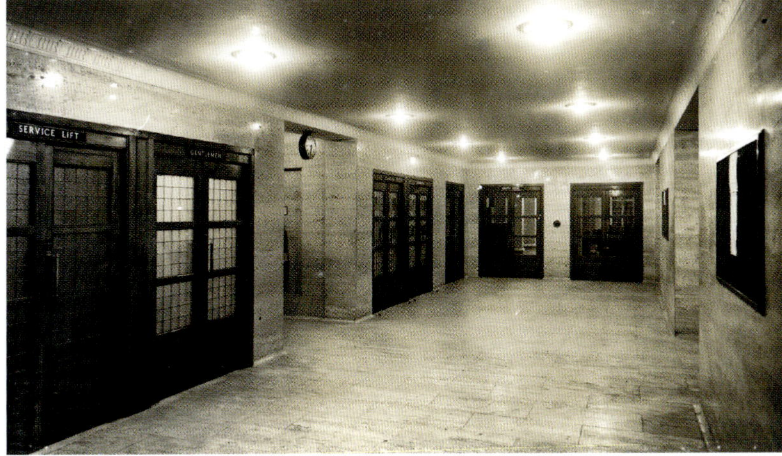

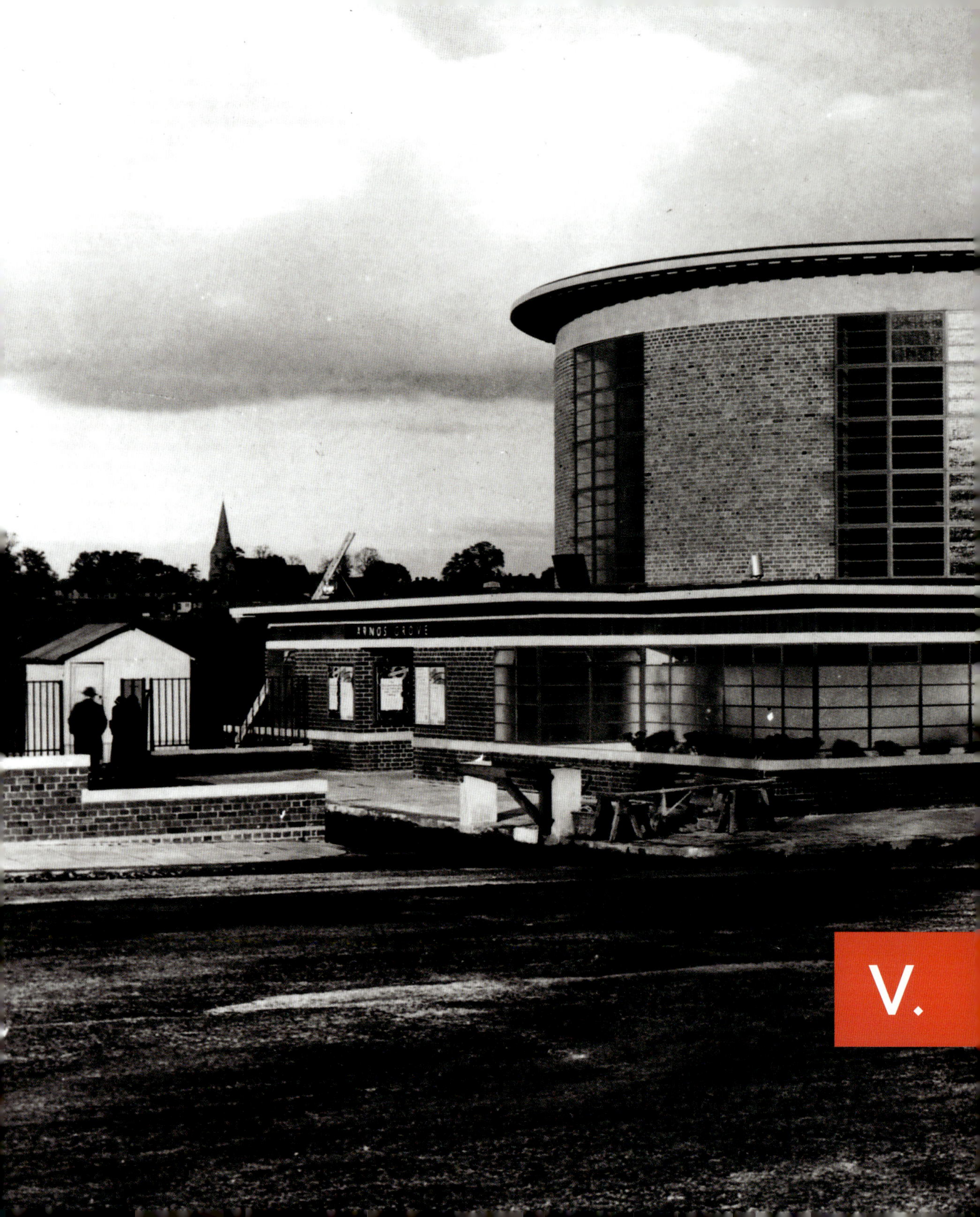
ARNOS GROVE
V.

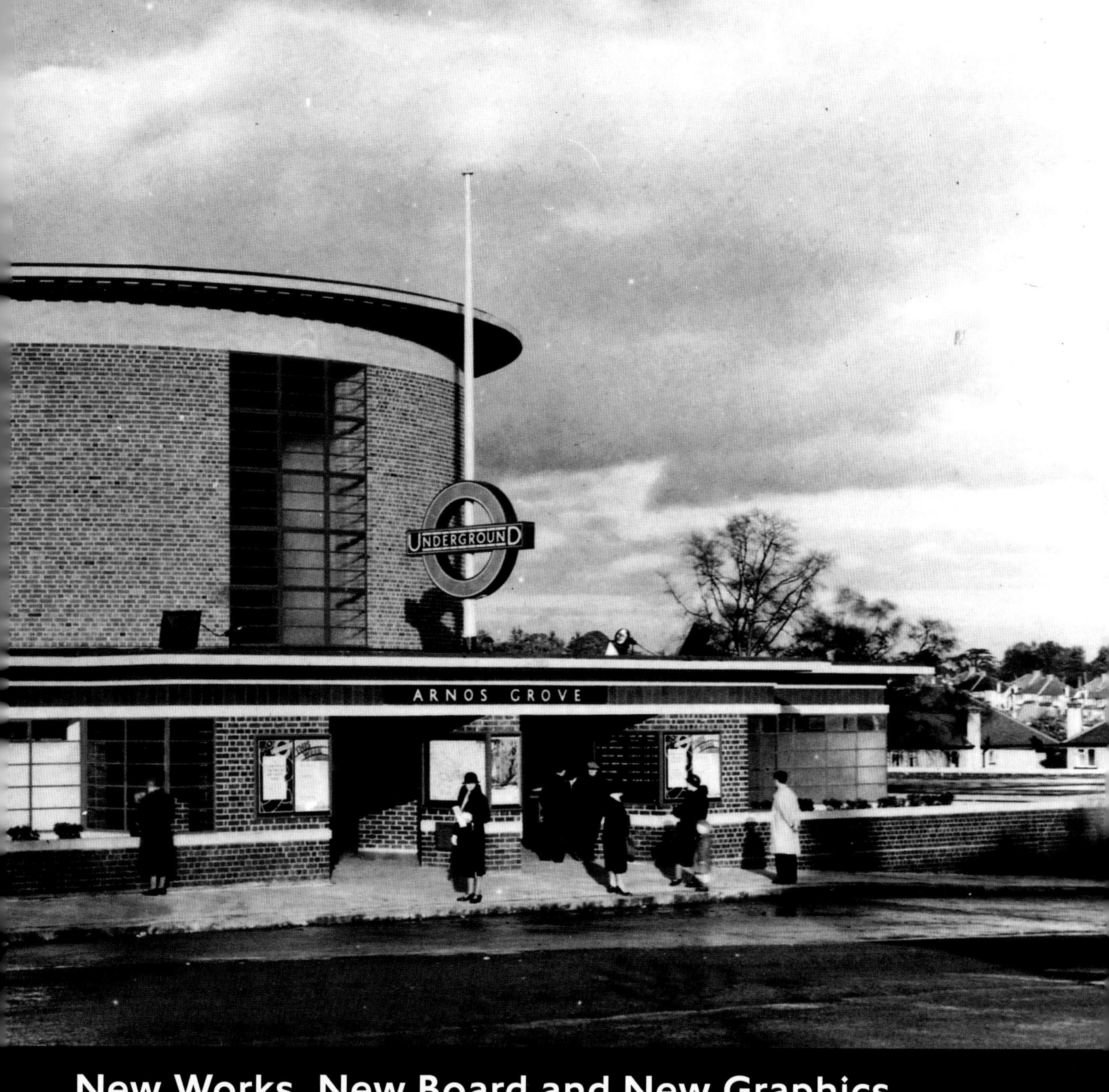

New Works, New Board and New Graphics
1930–45

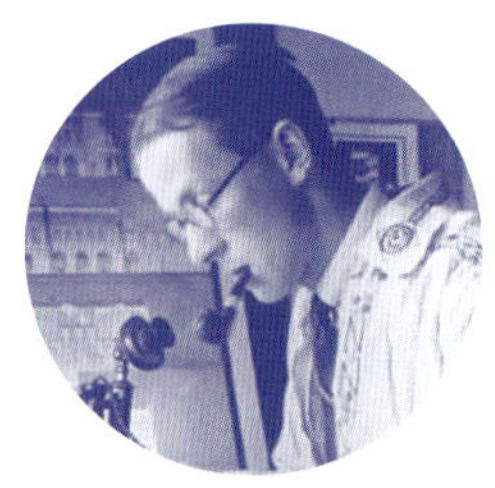

Charles Holloway James (1893–1953), born in Gloucester, worked with Holden as well as other prominent architects, including Sir Edwin Lutyens. He contributed to Letchworth Garden City and provided early designs for Welwyn Gaden City.

V. New Works, New Board and New Graphics, 1930–45

It would be no exaggeration to say that the expansion of the London Underground in the 1930s helped change the face of Britain. Design played a crucial part in this, and that was down to two individuals in particular; Frank Pick (p. 62) and Charles Holden (p. 116) are rightly credited with creating a look for the transport environment that reverberated across the country and around the world.

It was clear from the outset that the Piccadilly expansion would be an even bigger job than the Morden extension (p. 116). Not only would it involve the creation from scratch of eight new stations north of Finsbury Park,[1] but almost all the old District infrastructure that the Piccadilly line would inherit in north-west and south-west London needed rebuilding — much of it substantially. Given the scale of the task, Pick decided to look abroad for architectural inspiration (p. 162), taking with him Holden and Ashfield's secretary W. P. N. Edwards. From 20 June to 7 July 1930, they visited Denmark, Germany, the Netherlands and Sweden, looking at new buildings and an architectural style becoming known as the 'Amsterdam School'[2]. What they gleaned during their tour had a profound effect on the design of London Underground stations for the next decade and beyond (p. 213), creating a new lexicon in British architectural style and inspiring the look of many other buildings, both public and private, across Britain.

Designing around passenger flow

The first project was a complete rebuild of Sudbury Town (p. 164), which Holden then used as a prototype for subsequent stations. Taking his cue from those built for the Edgware extension (p. 129) and his last two out-of-town stations (Hounslow West and Ealing Common), with all facilities (ticket sales, offices, shops and cafés) leading off a large circulating area, Holden prepared graphs of passenger movement and designed each station around the flow of people passing through it. Arguably the first time a proper, scientifically based study had been conducted for such a purpose, it demonstrated an appreciation of what would now be called wayfinding, regarded as crucial in the planning of any public building. Once the circulating area had been established, and bearing in mind the function of the station as the hub of a multi-modal transport system connecting with buses, trams and taxis, Holden then fused what he had learnt from the European tour with local materials to design what he called his 'brick boxes with concrete lids' (p. 166). Using Sudbury Town as his blueprint, Holden created a 'kit of parts' for all the Piccadilly line stations, based upon what would nowadays be termed an MESR (modular, extensible, scalable and reconfigurable) system that can be adapted to each location.

Sudbury Town sets the standard

Taking only seven months to build, Sudbury Town opened in July 1931. The station included so many pioneering design features that it merits close attention; it was like nothing previously seen in Britain — even the signage was unique on the Underground. The front and rear elevations, for instance, had a neon name sign — a nice touch, although expensive to maintain and so removed in the 1950s.[3] The use of Delf Smith's 'petit serif' version of Johnston for directional signage (p. 165) was unusual, seen at only a handful of other Piccadilly line stations,[4] and the station nameboards in the same typeface were unique and never repeated. The station building itself with its exposed-brick booking-hall area was so spacious and well lit that by day it was a shrine to masonry[5] and by night it was equally welcoming, the internal illuminations shining through the large glass panels intersected with steel glazing bars. Two flared, square Art Deco uplighters dominated the booking hall (p. 164), similar in design to those at Piccadilly Circus[6] but not repeated elsewhere. On the platforms, Bauhaus-style hoop and sphere lamps are still in evidence, while the building, first listed in 1971, is now categorized as Grade II*.

The height of Holden

The years 1931–9 were a frenetic time for building new stations. In addition to eight on the Piccadilly extension to Cockfosters (pp. 170–177), Adams, Holden & Pearson was working on no less than twenty others.[7] There were so many projects that Holden could not possibly design and supervise every one (as he had done previously), so other individuals — colleagues, assistants, trainees and the Underground's in-house architect, Stanley Heaps — became involved at different sites. This team approach had already led to some successful designs at Hounslow West and Ealing Common (both begun in 1929) and opened in 1931. At Enfield West (now Oakwood, p. 176), while Holden was at the helm for conceptualizing the 'brick box with concrete lid', it was Charles Holloway James who oversaw much of the project and Heaps who designed the platform canopy. James also supervised the Bounds Green site following Holden's specifications (p. 171). Heaps was responsible for the distinctive 8m-high 'mushroom' shelters or 'pylons', comprising a round canopy over circular seating, with standard lamps and the bullseye sign (p. 198).[8] After outstanding praise for Sudbury Town, neighbouring Sudbury Hill was given the Holden treatment (p. 166), featuring a well-lit stairway with stepped glazed enclosures down to the covered shelters at platform level (opened 1931). Northfields, Alperton and Acton Town followed during 1932 in Holden's now recognizable style (p. 166).

Three more central London rebuilds were also in hand during the early 1930s, all based upon Holden designs and with Heaps assisting: Knightsbridge ticket hall and platforms (opened 18 February 1934), Hammersmith (Queen Charlotte Street entrance — ready by June 1932) and Highgate (renamed Archway in 1939, p. 184). Both the latter featured

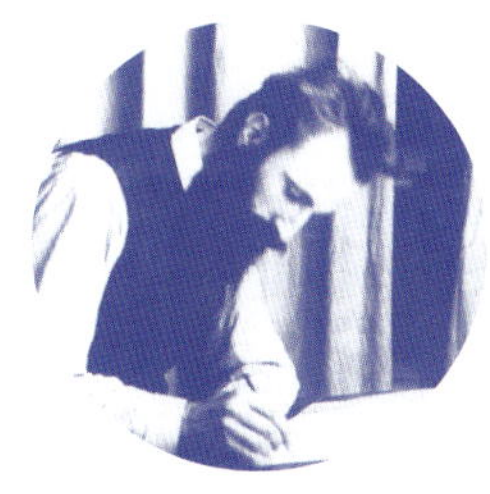

Pieter ('Piet') Lodewijk Kramer (1881–1961) was a Dutch architect and Amsterdam School member. His design of the De Bijenkorf store in The Hague (1930, p. 182) probably had the greatest influence on Holden.

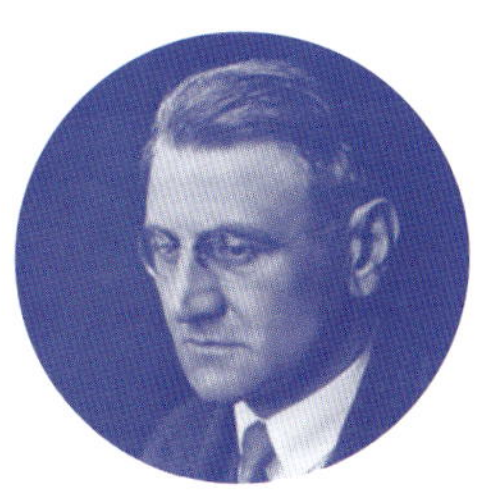

Jan Frederik Staal (1879–1940), Dutch architect and member of the Amsterdam School, designed brick buildings with high clerestory windows such as the newspaper offices of *Kantoorgebouw de Telegraaf* (p. 182) that inspired Pick and Holden on their 1930 visit to Holland.

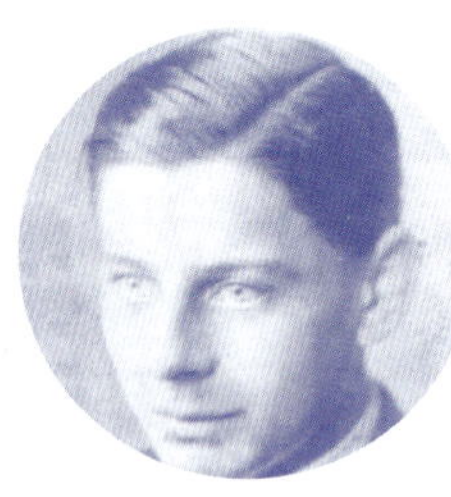

George Dow (1907–87), born in Watford, was a railwayman, draughtsman and author of railway history books. He joined the LNER as a clerk at King's Cross (in 1927) but following his successful diagrammatic maps ('Dowagrams') was appointed press relations officer (1939). He remained with the railways until his retirement in 1968. His numerous 'Dowagrams' (1929–41) influenced Beck et al.

relatively narrow frontages which were almost entirely in glass with Holden's signature steel glazing bars; sadly both have since been demolished.

By contrast for the rebuild of the old Leslie Green station at Gillespie Road (renamed Arsenal in October 1931), no glass was used at all, the concrete facade being decorated instead with a large mosaic Underground bullseye (p. 184). More radical designs like the drum-shaped building at Arnos Grove (p. 172) and Chiswick Park, which opened in April 1932 (p. 167),[9] were inspired by the Stockholm Public Library (p. 162) and Krumme Lanke U-Bahn station in Berlin (p. 162), which Pick and Holden had seen on their tour. This shape was also used for Warren Street for a rebuild needed to accommodate the escalators (1933) – an Adams, Holden & Pearson design executed by Heaps.

While Holden's remaining Piccadilly line stations were largely cubic (or octagonal in the case of Bounds Green), Southgate – on the second stage of the Piccadilly extension to Cockfosters – took the circular concept into the next dimension (p. 174). One of Britain's quintessential Art Deco buildings (constructed in the 'Streamline Moderne' style[10]), it sums up the forward-looking spirit of the age. At Cockfosters itself, although the station entrance was less remarkable, the train shed is notable for its cavernous size and textured concrete (p. 177),[11] its first outing in Britain. Public enthusiasm and rave reviews from the trade press encouraged Pick and Holden into performing yet more daring feats but not before a monumental shift in the organization of transport in London had taken place, one that would also have a profound effect on station design, as will be shown (p. 154).

'Tidying up the lines'

Meanwhile, radical ideas were surfacing elsewhere on the Underground, not just in the architecture and signage, but in the cartographic representation of the system. Each Underground line had for many years been represented inside the cars by a line diagram or 'strip map'.[12] Railways were experimenting with schematics in other parts of the world,[13] while in Britain the cartographic simplification of mainline and commuter networks owes much to pioneering draughtsman George Dow.[14] The problem for the Underground was that the official pocket maps of F. H. Stingemore (p. 143), while adequate for the 1920s, looked somewhat dated alongside the new streamlined trains and stations. Furthermore, any new extensions to the system could not be accommodated without the map looking cramped. It was this that inspired Underground employee Henry ('Harry') Beck to think about how to simplify the map and create a more legible diagram of the network.

Working as a junior draughtsman in the engineers office, although not a designer per se, Beck came up with a sketch (p. 168) that was to change both his life and the way Londoners viewed their city, not to mention the mapping of transit systems around the

London Underground by Design

world. In his initial drawing Beck presented the Central London Line (as the CLR had then
become known) as a straight horizontal baseline, other Underground lines being shown
vertically, horizontally or at an angle of 45 degrees. He explained that he imagined he 'was
using a convex lens or mirror so as to present the central area on a larger scale' (Garland,
Bibliography); suburban stations, by contrast, were set much closer together, evenly
spaced along the clean straight lines out of the centre, so that the entire network would
fit onto a pocket map-sized piece of card. Beck drew the lines only *loosely* in the correct
geographical location, hence distorting the geography of the capital; but that was his
point. The opening out of central London allowed all the interchanges to show up more
clearly so that the station names did not need to be so squeezed in. Beck spent many
hours making a 'presentation visual' (p. 168) from his initial sketch and after encouragement from colleagues (including Stingemore, according to Garland), he submitted it to the
publicity office in 1931. To Beck's astonishment and dismay, the idea was rejected.

Luckily for London, Beck was persistent and resubmitted the idea a year later. He was
sent for after a meeting of the publicity office and told by a Mr Patmore: 'You'd better sit
down: I'm going to give you a shock. We're going to print it.' Over the next few months
Beck's idea was refined,[15] and the first card folder was issued in January 1933 (p. 169). A
quad-royal poster version was made in March of that year. Though the diagram has been
fiddled with and endlessly tweaked – for almost thirty years by Beck himself, and by many
hands since – the 1930s design is still used in essence to this day. Given the millions
produced every year, it is arguably the most recognized cartographic item in the western
world. In 2001 the tag 'This diagram is an evolution of the original design conceived in 1931
by Harry Beck' was added to the map face. A fine tribute for an outstanding design.

A final far-flung fling for the Met

The Met had long planned its swansong – a 6km run towards Stanmore (p. 180).[16]
Following the unparalleled success of 'Metro-land', Robert Hope Selbie (right up until his
death in 1930) had been on the lookout for other undeveloped areas adjacent to his lines
to expand into. In fairness, there were not that many options as urban growth was now
occurring at a breakneck speed around all the edges of London (peaking in 1934), but aside
from some industry at Kingsbury[17], this sliver of Middlesex was relatively undeveloped.
Despite the popularity of the Underground's emerging modernist style, the Met stuck
with Charles W. Clark as the main designer of the stations on this line.[18] Clark had been
having a little flirt with the modern look at his rebuild of Northwick Park in 1931 (p. 180)
and at Northwood Hills (1933). Consequently he had what can best be described as a
'tinker' at Canons Park Edgware (later just Canons Park, p. 180). Needless to say, despite
these nods to modernization, his services were not called upon again.

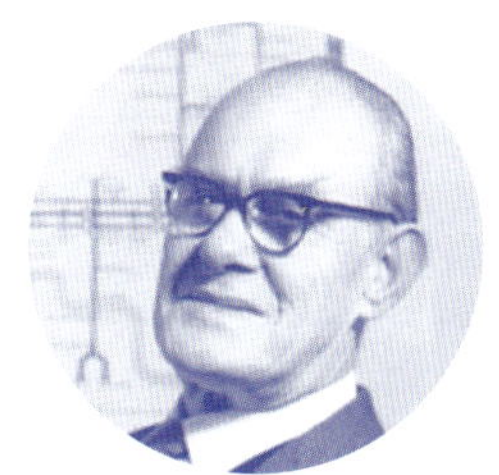

Henry ('Harry') Charles Beck
(1902–74), born in Essex,
was a draughtsman who
worked in the Underground's
Signals Office in the 1920s.
He became fascinated
with 'tidying up' the old
Underground map. His work
not only changed the way
transport maps are designed;
in 2006 it was named one
of Britain's top three design
icons.

When the London Passenger Transport Board was formed in 1933 a new 'winged' logo was commissioned from Cecil W. Bacon (1905–92), a well-known illustrator whose work appeared regularly in *Radio Times*. The device was used on some early publicity material, and at one point it threatened to replace the bullseye, but this thankfully did not happen.

The Board is born

On 1 July 1933, a new body came into being which would have unprecedented powers over the capital and the Home Counties. The London Passenger Transport Board (LPTB or 'The Board') effectively nationalized the Underground group and the Met, with Lord Ashfield as chairman and Frank Pick as his deputy.[19] The Board, which operated under the overarching name 'London Transport' (LT), was allowed a complete monopoly within a radius of approximately 50km from Charing Cross. With a budget of £120 million (£6.5 billion at today's prices), it was able at last to strategically design and plan services for this vast and diverse area. Following a quick updating of the logos (p. 186) and some rebranding of services, various projects left over from before the Board was formed were completed, including the new 'jewels in the crown', Boston Manor (designed by Holden) and Osterley (a Holden/Heaps collaboration), which both opened during 1933–4 (pp. 182–3). Three others (Holden's reconstructed entrances for Leicester Square and Knightsbridge and the complete rebuild of South Harrow, p. 185) also opened during 1935 and were among the first stations to sport the new London Transport branding on the bullseye signs.[20] The last stations planned before the Board came into being, but not opened until 1936, were the colossal Park Royal (designed and built by a new entrant: Welch & Lander, p. 185) and South Ealing, where waiting rooms with rounded ends in the Streamline Moderne style[21] would influence the design of platform buildings for years to come (e.g. Dollis Hill, p. 198). The final pre-Board design was the exhibition entrance rebuild on Warwick Road for Earl's Court. This was a glazed rotunda by Heaps not completed until 1937.[22]

The New Works Programme, 1935–40

Meanwhile, Pick had already embarked on preparation for a major scheme of expansion and rejuvenation. Published by the Board on 5 June 1935, the 'New Works Programme'[23] (NWP) provided major investment – £40 million (£2.25 billion today) – for a host of improvements on the Underground,[24] including extensions and station rebuilds which Adams, Holden & Pearson would be involved in along with new architects and designers. One of the first of these projects to come to fruition was the reconstruction of a former smallish station at Rayners Lane (p. 193) – an important junction between the Met and the Piccadilly and close to an area of rapidly increasing population. The final design was made by Reginald H. Uren, an architect at Adams, Holden & Pearson. Fully opened on 8 August 1938, it seemed to combine all the Holden features: the 'brick box with concrete lid' towered over the hill it was set upon while the elegant Streamline Moderne curved windows beneath (and at platform level) felt fitting for the age – a perfect companion for the nearby Grosvenor Cinema.[25]

London Underground by Design

Inheriting buildings from other railways

One of the easiest and least expensive methods of expanding the Underground was to simply route trains over existing suburban or commuter lines. 'Running rights' is a practice dating back to the earliest days of railway history and it was as much a part of the NWP as it was during the heady days of the District routing trains to Windsor (p. 17)! But the lines first needed to be electrified. Along with other mainline companies,[26] the London, Midland and Scottish Railway (LMS) provided electrified tracks to Upminster in 1932 (the Underground having used the LMS line to Barking for many years) and rebuilt stations between 1932 and 1935. The company designed a number of tasteful brick buildings in the Art Deco style,[27] which fitted in with the Board's buildings of the same era even if it took many years for LT signage to appear on the platforms.[28]

The Carr–Edwards report, 1938

Now that the Board was established and major improvements were planned for all services, a co-ordinated approach to signage was urgently needed. W. P. N. Edwards and the assistant publicity officer, Henry Carr, had been working with publicity boss Christian Barman on 'a report upon the standards which should, in our opinion, be adopted governing the location and types of direction signs, notices and maps upon the railways'.[29] The Carr–Edwards report (Bibliography), as it subsequently became known (including the accompanying drawings), was arguably the first attempt to compile a manual of graphic standards – certainly in any transit organization (p. 192) – and was rigidly adhered to for almost every sign erected as part of the NWP.

The report recognized with some prescience that 'the Board's stations are the railway's shop windows', recommending the installation outside every station of Underground bullseyes, the name of the station (including the word 'station'), the name of the line(s) and a system map. Inside the station the report recommended 'Use of the bullseye symbol on all signs and notices'. This suggestion was somewhat rigorously applied, leading, it could be said, to slight over-exposure of the device (such as in the passageways at refurbished Earl's Court).[30] The report also acknowledged, quite rightly, that signage was crucial at any 'bifurcation point' (such as the circulating area at the bottom of an escalator) where 'a complete list of the stations on the line concerned' should be displayed, 'with a line diagram incorporated into it and interchange stations shown in the colour of the line with which interchange is effected'. It did also point out with a vague hint of regret that 'Complete standardization of signs is unfortunately impossible without a standard design of station'![31] Given the popularity of Beck's recently introduced diagram, there was an interesting recommendation running counter to this: 'the map on the outside of stations should be in geographical form. Passengers requiring to make use of maps outside stations are normally strangers, who may not even know

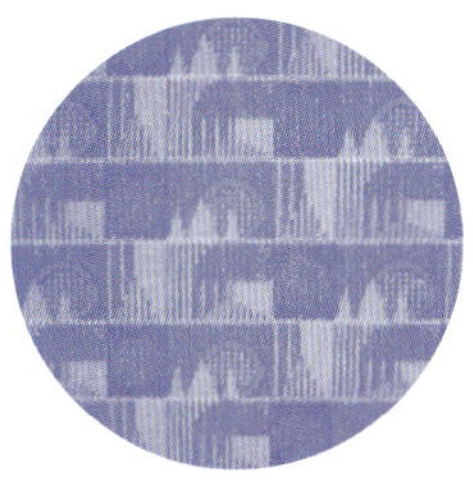

Christian August Barman (1898–1980) was a Belgian architect and industrial designer who produced various iconic items (1934–8), such as an Art Deco 'beehive' electric fan heater. He was London Transport's publicity officer 1935–41. In 2011 Transport for London issued a new moquette (pictured) in his name.

the name of the station they require, but merely have a rough idea of the neighbourhood which they wish to visit.' This proposal was not carried out with much rigour in London, perhaps because the Board had invested so much in Beck's diagram.[32]

The signage erected following implementation of the thoughtful and well-reasoned recommendations of this report was soon to be seen all over London. Indeed, the corporate branding of today stands firmly on the shoulders of this outstanding contribution to wayfinding and graphic design.

Converting the Met to LU design standards

Now that the fiercely independent Met had been brought into the LT family, the important task of assimilating it into the corporate brand was begun in earnest. From 1933 onwards, Met locos and carriages were painted with the LT wordmark in Johnston Sans. A planned station at Queensbury on the Stanmore branch was opened in 1934 (p. 198), but constructed in the modern Underground style. Following a study by Pick of the Met, he concluded that the majority of it should be electrified.[33] Inevitably some services were rationalized,[34] and stations between Finchley Road and Baker Street were closed when the Bakerloo took over the Stanmore branch in 1939 (p. 198) so the Met could operate as an express between Wembley Park and Finchley Road. The red diamond signs began to be replaced by Underground bullseyes with Johnston Sans nameplates. In-car strip maps sported the typeface too, although the Met logo with its enlarged M and N briefly survived the conversion to the new signs in Johnston lettering.[35] Later on, the need to repair war damage would accelerate the replacement of old Met company signs and logos.[36]

'Friezing' for freer flow

One problem that designers had been trying to get to grips with was how to make the station name sufficiently visible on crowded platforms where signs were frequently obscured by people waiting for the next train. Placing name signs at alternating heights (since Kilburn Park in 1915, p. 87 and along the Morden extension, p. 135) had helped, but in the streamlined 1930s was regarded as untidy. A concept that may have been inspired by signage on underground systems in other parts of the world [37] was therefore trialled during 1937 at several busy West End deep-level Tube stations. This consisted of a paper frieze positioned at a height of 2m along the platform wall, with the name of the station repeated at intervals (in Johnston Sans, of course, p. 190). The idea was simple yet so effective that enamelled signs were soon ordered and used universally on platforms underground. Ceramic friezes were introduced on the new Bakerloo stations two years later (p. 196) and also on some Northern and Central line stations, but the practice was short-lived and enamel became the norm.

Pick takes umbrage about Uxbridge

As part of the renovations on the former Met, the station at Uxbridge needed re-siting closer to the centre of the town, but as Charles Holden was completely taken up with his new project for the University of London,[38] Adams, Holden & Pearson subcontracted some of the work to a new architect, Leonard Holcombe Bucknell. Perturbed by the exclusion of Holden and the expense of Bucknell's designs, Pick insisted that Holden should be involved or his firm would receive no further commissions. After this was agreed, the company was asked to prepare some designs for the proposed extension from Edgware to Aldenham.[39] Holden's design for the train shed at Uxbridge was effectively a carbon copy of the concrete structure at Cockfosters, but the rest of the building was unique and much grander, incorporating shops and offices. Opening on 4 December 1938, the final design consisted of a two-storey brick facade with sculpted 'wheel' motifs above the curved entrance (p. 193) and sporting a stained-glass mural by Ervin Bossányi. In the forecourt was a new type of totem sign[40] which would be adopted at other stations: this was a square concrete pillar with a double-sided, illuminated Underground bullseye and three internally lit blue strips showing the station and line names (p. 193).

Aiming for the Heights and naming the Northern

Despite the deteriorating international situation, the NWP was optimistically pushed forward. Rebuilding the small halt at Ruislip Manor to a Holden design had begun in 1936 and was completed in 1938; this featured a unique ticket-hall clock with numerals replaced by orange circles fired into the cream-coloured tiles (p. 191). A similar scheme to rebuild the Eastcote halt, also completed in 1938, resulted in a wonderfully well-balanced design – another Holden 'brick box with concrete lid', incorporating on this occasion two exquisitely proportioned shop fronts complete with Streamline Moderne curved windows and mast-mounted bullseyes on each retail unit. But it was the design of three major projects that dominated the period: the Bakerloo was to have new tunnels north of Baker Street and take over the Stanmore branch (p. 198); the Central was being extended outwards with new tunnels in the east and electrification of suburban steam lines both east and west (p. 199); and the Northern line was to be extended north of Highgate (now Archway) via a tunnel and with further conversions from steam (p. 194).

Proposals were so far advanced before the war that building work was already well under way and new trains (the so-called '1938 Stock', p. 189), signage (p. 189) and even destination roller blinds had been ordered. In anticipation of the complex arrangements for the full Northern Heights plan (so named because the areas to be served, such as Alexandra Palace, were on high ground), the poorly named 'Morden–Edgware' line, as it had by then become, was rechristened the 'Northern'.[41] Two of the line's largest new stations were to be at East Finchley and Highgate. Bucknell worked with Adams, Holden

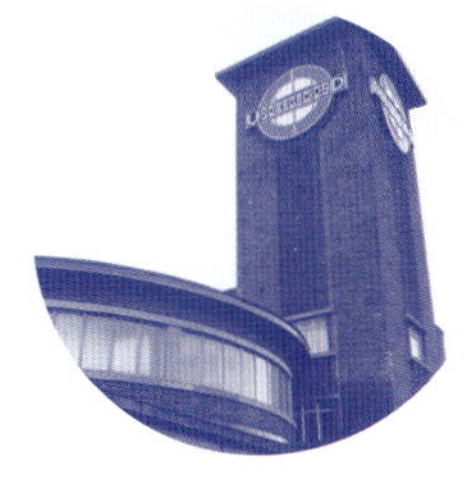

Felix James Lander (1897–1960), born in Berkshire, was a draughtsman who worked for Adams, Holden & Pearson. Here he met N. F. Cachemaille-Day, going on to form a partnership with him and Herbert Welch. Park Royal station (pictured) was designed by his firm.

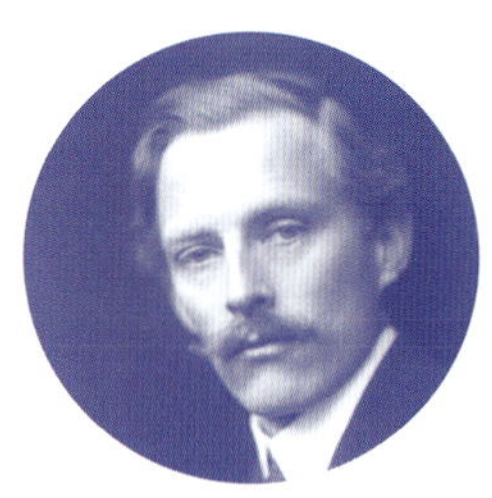

Harold Stabler (1872–1945), born in Cumbria, was a ceramic and metalwork designer influenced by Art Nouveau who produced a series of eighteen relief-moulded tiles depicting counties and landmarks served by the Underground (p. 197). They were employed at Aldgate East, Bethnal Green, Swiss Cottage and St. Johns Wood to such great effect that his name has become synonymous as a style on the system.

& Pearson on the East Finchley station, which opened on 3 July 1939 (p. 194). The building is now listed and with its curved, two-storey glazed stairwells and beautiful bronze sculpture by Eric Aumonier, its easy to see why.[42] Highgate, by contrast, never achieved its planned potential: re-modelled on the site of the original 1860s station, it was designed to have two levels, but the majority of the planned station was not built on account of the Alexandra Palace branch never being electrified.[43]

The appliance of faience

To relieve congestion and speed up services, an extension of the Bakerloo was proposed north of Baker Street in new tunnels rising to the surface at Finchley Road and taking over the Met stations to Wembley Park and the newish branch to Stanmore. The tunnelled section, begun in 1936, included two new stations, St John's Wood and Swiss Cottage (p. 196),[44] which opened on 20 November 1939. Their tile-lined platforms were designed by Harold Stabler and set the tone for more in this style.[45] As Clark had only recently substantially rebuilt Swiss Cottage, all that was required were escalators between the new platforms and the older ticket hall. No substantial surface re-modelling was needed but the ticket hall was matched with the cream coloured tiling style (though the station was later built over, leaving only stairway entrances). These Stabler platforms, recently restored to their 1939 glory, epitomize the streamlined neatness of the age.

At St John's Wood, comprising the only wholly new surface building serving the Bakerloo tunnel, a fine rotunda was constructed in the Holden style by in-house architect Stanley Heaps. Direction signs at the top and bottom of the escalators were of the illuminated bronze bullseye shape on fluted, squat brass columns (p. 192). Other stations along the new Bakerloo branch were tarted up and improved; Kilburn, for example, was given a re-modelled side entrance (1939) and curved windows in the Streamline Moderne style were installed in waiting rooms there and at West Hampstead and Dollis Hill (p. 198).

Trains with flares

The streamlined look of the 1930s not only encompassed stations and signage; funky new rolling stock was also designed during this period. The first to appear was in January 1933, in the form of an experimental high-speed Tube train. Consisting of a 'Standard Stock'[46] car affixed to a 'streamlined' cab with windows surrounding the driver, permitting a much wider field of vision, this was the brainchild of deputy-chief mechanical engineer William S. Graff-Baker. Though it ran at night for six months on the western end of the Piccadilly line, it was never in active passenger service, but it did lead to the production of eighteen high-speed trains. Instead of being tapered in at the front, they each had a flared prow (front end) and sported an Art Deco 'feather' ventilation grille on the domed roof (p. 188). This design caused some controversy between the LPTB and officials at the Ministry of

Transport, who did not see the point of the flared edge, and indeed Pick himself was not entirely convinced by the look. When they were brought into service (April 1937), people took to them at once, not least because the interiors were so plush, with comfortable, coach-style seats, sprung ball-ended strap-hangers and even a crude form of air-conditioning! Though the streamlined cabs were replaced, the trains proved the inspiration for the celebrated '1938 Stock', which became the archetypal design of Tube train (p. 189), remaining in service for *fifty* years.[47] The same shape also inspired other train design such as the larger, sub-surface 'O Stock' of 1937 with a flared *side* (p. 188), which stayed on the system until 1981.

War halts works but hones publicity

After the Bakerloo, the Northern was extended to High Barnet in 1940 with East Finchley as a hub, though apart from Mill Hill East (1941), work on the rest of the Northern was halted. On the Central line some work was accomplished, including a 4km section of tunnel between Gants Hill and Wanstead – used as a deep-level factory by Plessey during the war – and the rebuilding of stations at Loughton and West Acton (both 1940, p. 199). But the shortage of materials and workers caused by the conflict inevitably put the brakes on construction elsewhere until after 1945. The war had one benefit however: it helped hone the skills of the publicity office. Aside from numerous warning and information signs (p. 201), it issued a large number of posters – effectively propaganda for boosting morale – during the six years of hostilities (p. 200), including outstanding pieces by such respected artists as Edward McKnight Kauffer. And it learnt valuable lessons in the process that would greatly assist in the mammoth task of rehabilitation and rebuilding following the outbreak of peace in 1945.

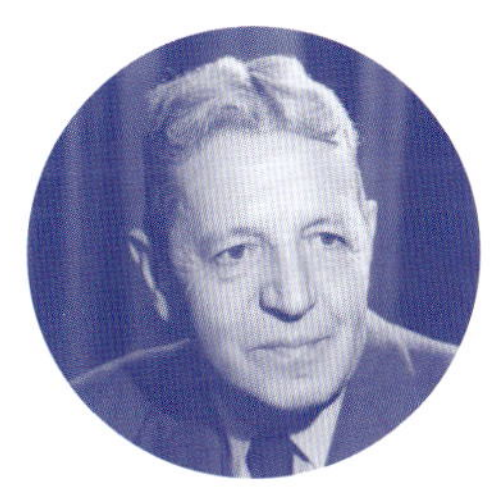

William S. Graff-Baker (1922–2009), Underground deputy-chief mechanical engineer, said that for a design to succeed, the answer must be 'yes' to each of the following: 1. Will it work? 2. Is it as simple as possible? 3. Can it be easily maintained in service? 4. Can it be readily manufactured? 5. Does it look well?

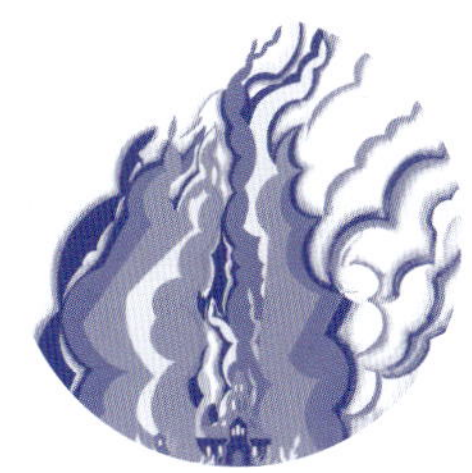

Edward ('Ted') McKnight Kauffer (1890–1954), born in Montana and moving to London in 1914, was one of the twentieth century's most influential commercial artists. A champion of Futurism, Cubism and Surrealism, he received commissions from the GWR, Shell and the Underground. His 1922 poster commemorated the 1666 fire (pictured).

Burton's event posters, 1929–34

The 1930s was a golden age for commercial artists and poster designers. The Underground commissioned over a thousand works during this decade, giving exposure to some of the world's most influential designers as well as many newcomers. Just as Charles Sharland dominated the early twentieth century, so the work of several other artists called 'Charles' (Atkinson, Baker, Brown, Cundall, Mozely, Paine, Pears, Shepherd and Frederick Charles Herrick) played an important role in the 1930s and 40s. Outstanding among them is Charles Burton, who between 1929 and 1934 created a series of exquisite event posters (all images below) for setting above the windows inside carriages. His simple cartoon-style images seem to epitomize the Streamline Moderne age, while lettering is a hand-drawn approximation of a decorated sans-serif as Burton chose not to use Johnston Sans — a concession that only a handful of other artists (including Edward McKnight Kauffer, posters shown opposite, Austin Cooper, Margaret Calkin James, and Clifford and Rosemary Ellis) were permitted.

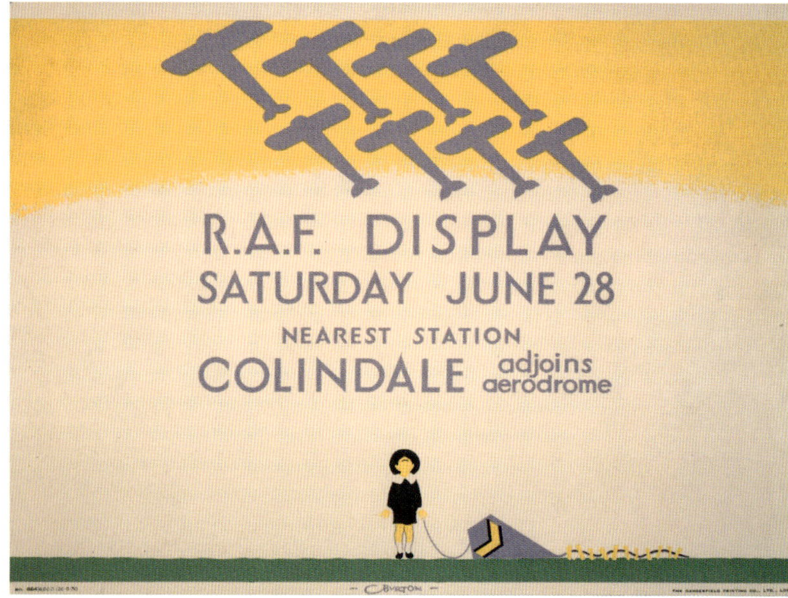

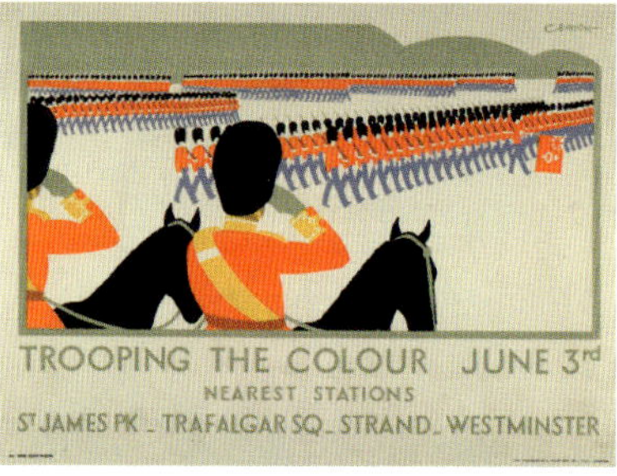

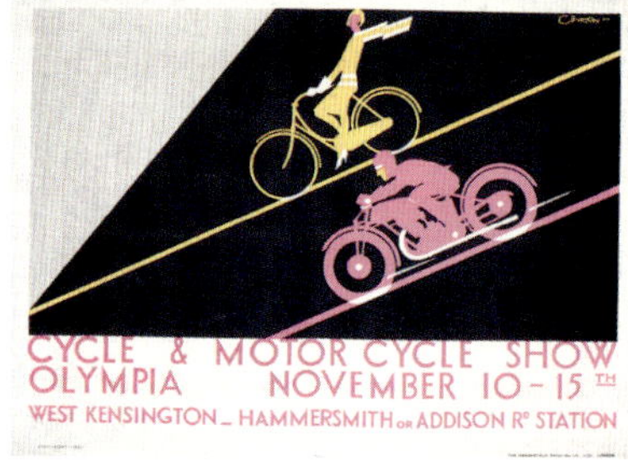

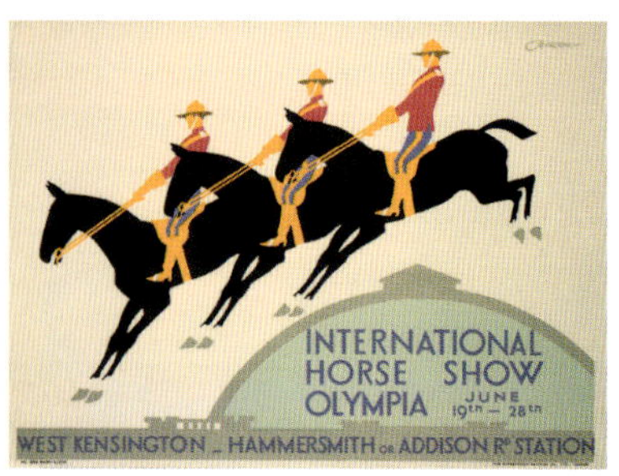

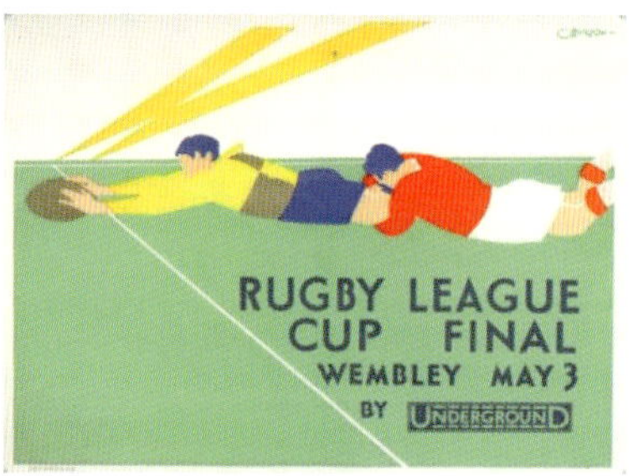

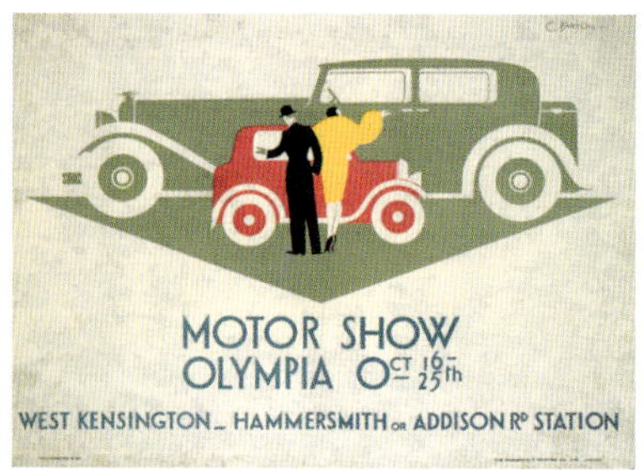

London Underground by Design

McKnight Kauffer posters, 1930–38

Cited as one of the twentieth century's most influential artists, Edward McKnight Kauffer (p. 159) produced over 100 posters for the Underground (including those pictured, from 1930 to 1938), ranging in style from Cubist to Surrealist. His first commissions in 1915 were mainly idyllic country scenes but during the 1920s his posters show an increasing degree of abstraction, culminating in the 1930s in some of the most witty and imaginative yet seen on the station walls of the capital.

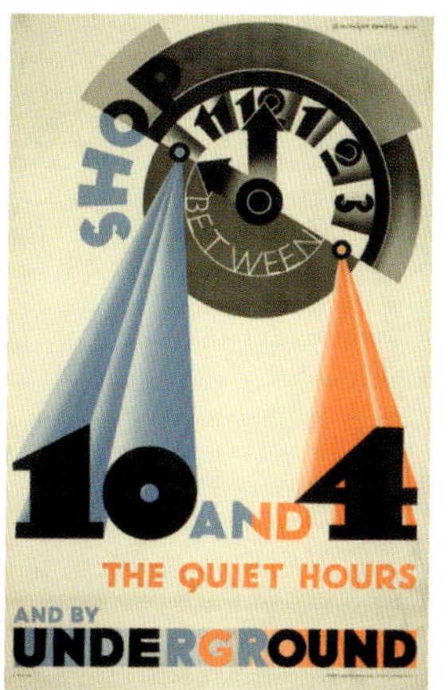

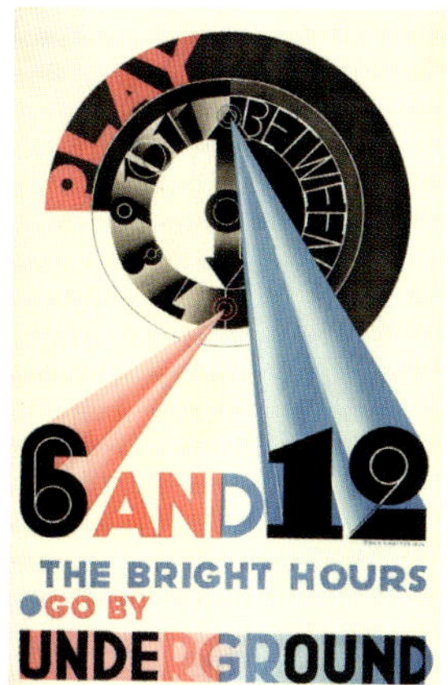

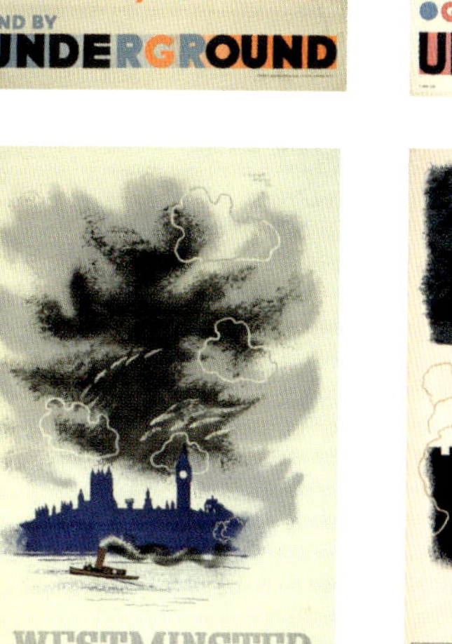

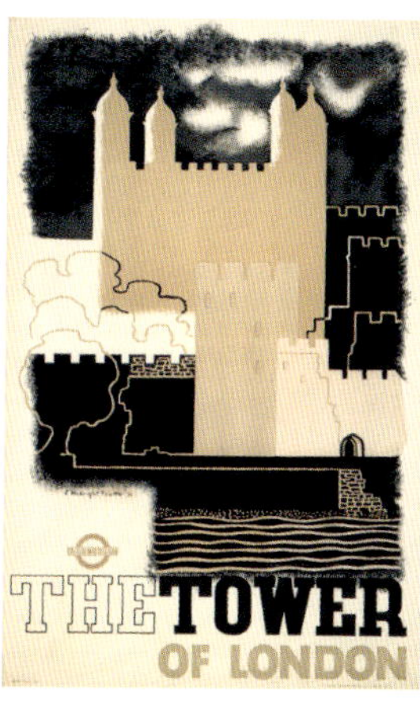

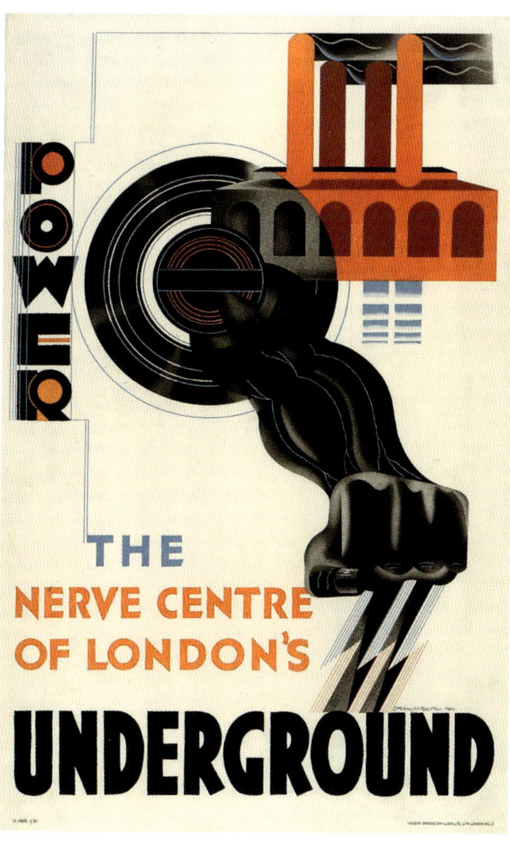

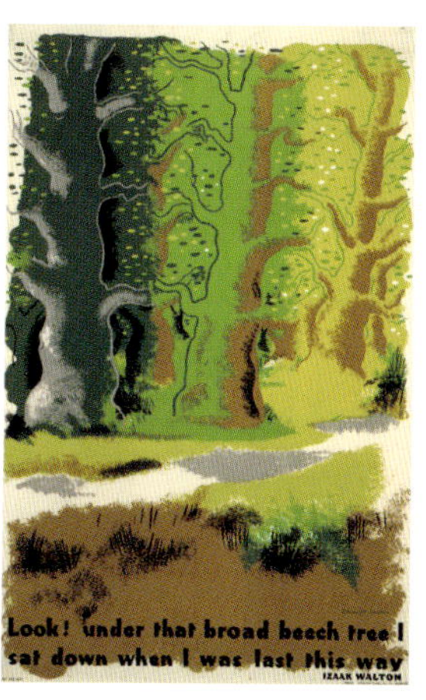

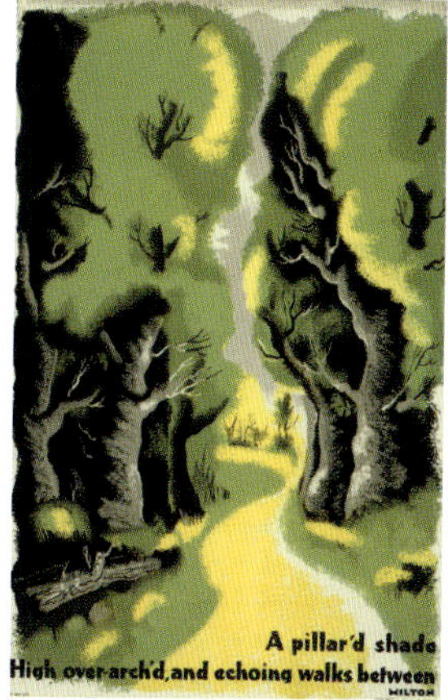

Pick and Holden's visit to the Continent
(1930, p. 150) took them on a tour of
some of Europe's most striking new
public buildings, which had a big impact
on their thinking for the Piccadilly extension. Square towers like W. M. Dudok's
1928 Hilversum Raadhuis (City Hall, 1)
and the Kantoorgebouw de Telegraaf
in Amsterdam (p. 182), designed by
J. F. Staal and G. J. Langhout in 1930,
inspired Holden's design for Osterley
(p. 183). Rotundas like the Stockholm
Public Library (1928, 2), by Erik Gunnar
Asplund, and the Berlin U-Bahn station
at Krumme Lanke (1929, 3) by Alfred
Grenander (both possibly inspired
by the 1784 Rotonde de la Villette in
Paris) influenced Holden's plans for
Arnos Grove (p. 172) and Chiswick Park
(p. 167). The glass curtain wall of Piet
Kramer's De Bijenkorf department store
in The Hague (1930) and the trademark
exposed brick and curved edges of
the Amsterdam School (exemplified
by Michel de Klerk's Het Schip, or
'The Ship', in Amsterdam, 4 and
E. Mendelson's textile factory 'Krasnoye
Znamya', built in St. Petersburg from
1925) were replicated on stations like
Sudbury Town (p. 164) and Holden's
other 'brick boxes with concrete lids'.

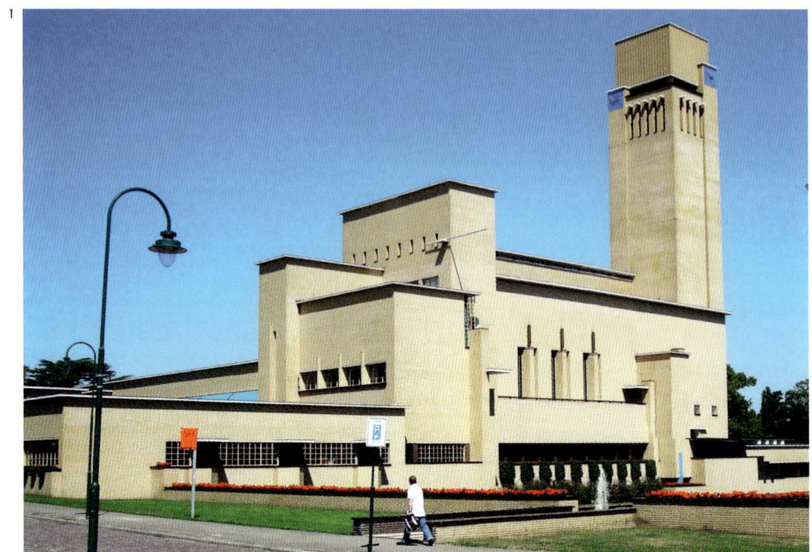

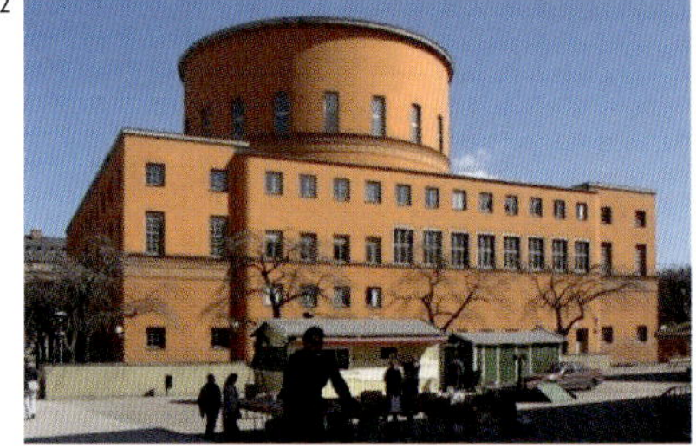

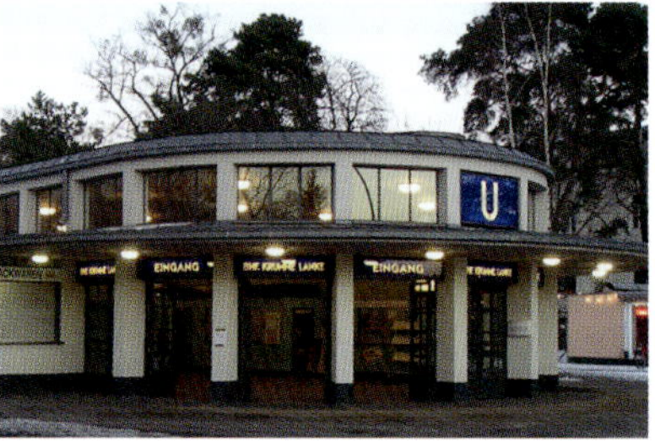

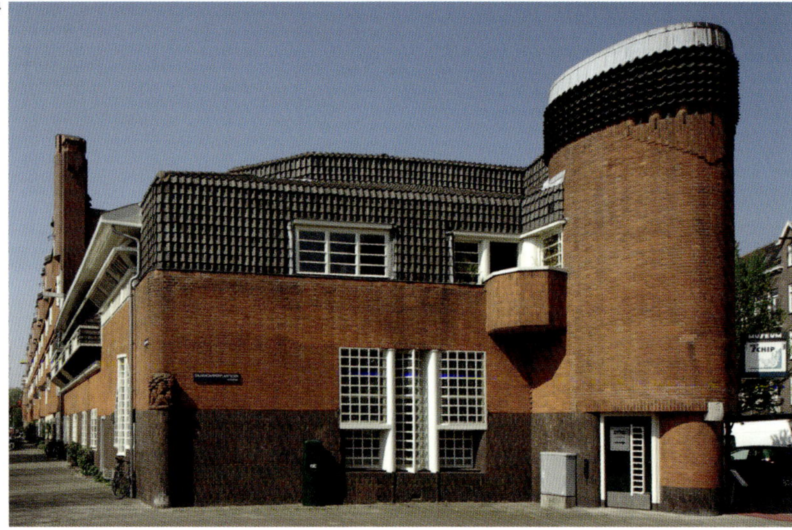

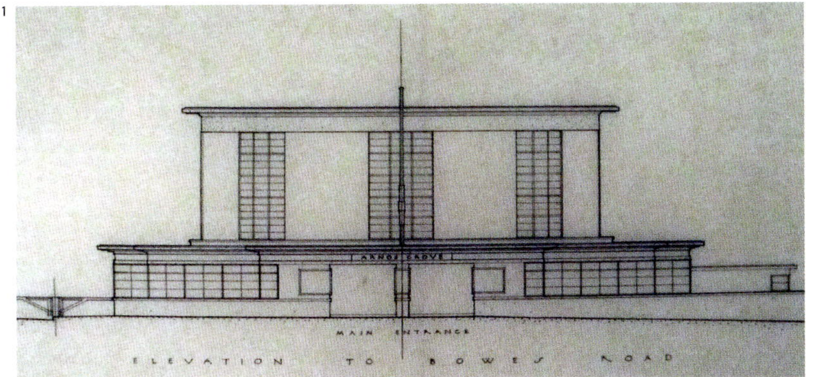

On his return from the tour of Europe, Holden began work on designs for the stations of the Piccadilly line extension. The influence of the various features he and Pick had observed — the towers, rotundas and brickwork — is evident in his drawings: Arnos Grove (1), Chiswick Park (2).

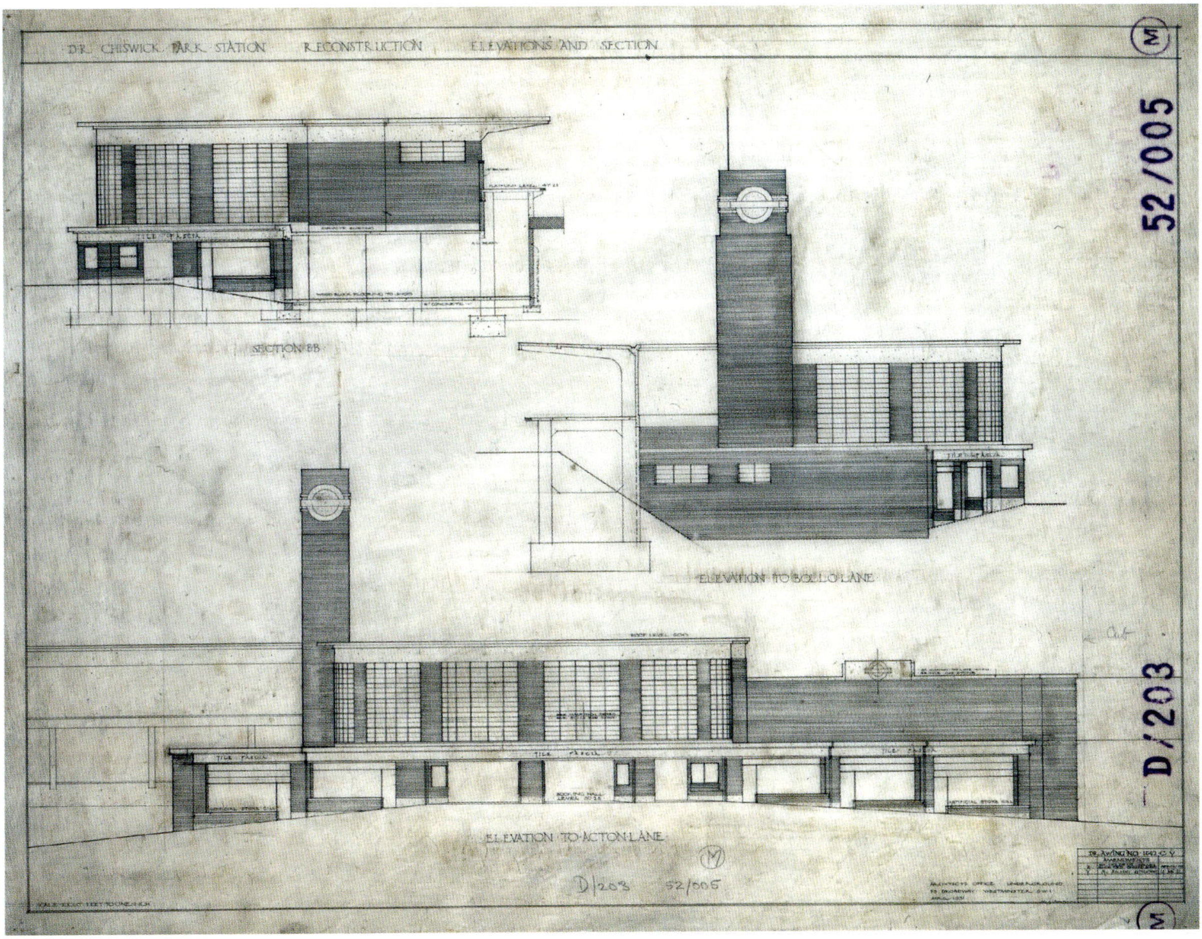

Sudbury Town sets the standard, 1931

Although not built to the original design for the station, Sudbury Town was the first reconstructed in the new style to open (19 July 1931). What emerged shook the British architectural establishment: taking just six months to build, the station contained almost all the elements that would find their way into most of Holden's subsequent designs, ideas that would resonate throughout the land, replicated in numerous public buildings, from hospitals to schools, benefit offices to power stations. This station was the original Holden 'brick box with a concrete lid'. So simple, yet so effective, with its double-height ticket hall and brick-and-glass curtain wall (1), rounded platform buildings alongside Bauhaus-style 'hoop and sphere' lamps, concrete fencing, and unique square uplighters (2). Dubbed 'rationalist', it is a style whose descendants (and antecedents in the Amsterdam School, p. 150) spread throughout Britain and mainland Europe.

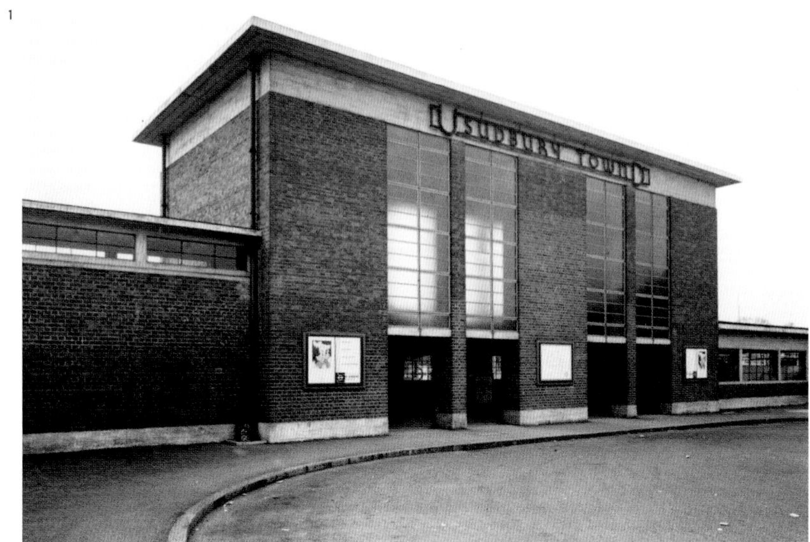

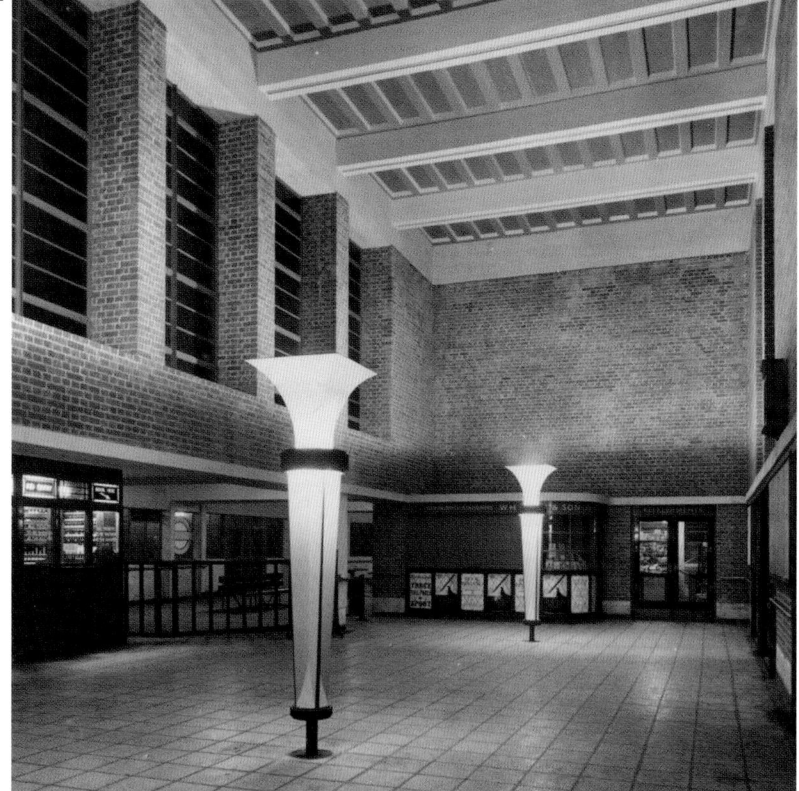

London Underground by Design

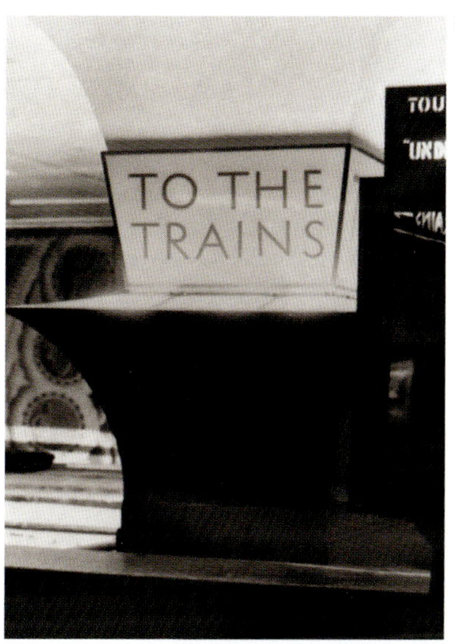

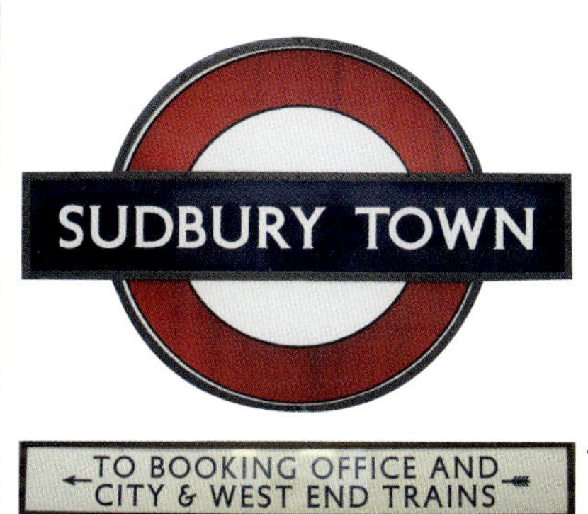

Peculiar to the Piccadilly: petit serifs, 1931

Though the elegantly formed Delf Smith 'petit serif' version of Johnston Sans (1) was originally intended for use at 55 Broadway (p. 117), Holden had included the lettering in a few select places at the Piccadilly Circus rebuild (2). At Sudbury Town, all of the signage was in this style (3, 4, 5, 6, 7). There is evidence that it was also used elsewhere (pp. 170, 176), though not universally, Pick possibly limiting exposure for fear that it might creep into other parts of the system. Hence the only places where it can still be seen in situ today are at Sudbury Town.

Holden's 'brick boxes with concrete lids', 1930–32

As the Sudbury Town model was being refined and developed, so the plans Holden's company had prepared for the other stations began to come to fruition. Work began in late 1930 on Northfields (opened 18 December 1932, 1 and 2). Set in the middle of flat-roofed, single-storey buildings occupying a relatively wide footprint, the double-height ticket hall appears set back. With glazing on all four sides of the tower, daylight floods the interior (opposite, 6), while a stained-glass bullseye in the Bond Street style is centrally mounted on the front elevation. The ticket hall features larger versions of the fluted brass uplighters (opposite, 6). Platform furniture includes a three-faced concrete mount for the station-name bullseye, flanked on either side by a poster holder (2). The 'brick box with concrete lid' was repeated at Sudbury Hill (4), with a covered stairway, inset with clerestory windows, down to each platform (3). At Acton Town the street frontage was on the overbridge, curving round to a side road at a slightly lower level included a rounded, single-storey corner unit used as a shop. At Alperton the platforms are on an embankment, which the generic design was altered to fit. Chiswick Park (opened April 1932, opposite, 5) was a drum-shaped sister of Arnos Grove (p. 172), but with a squat tower to one side.

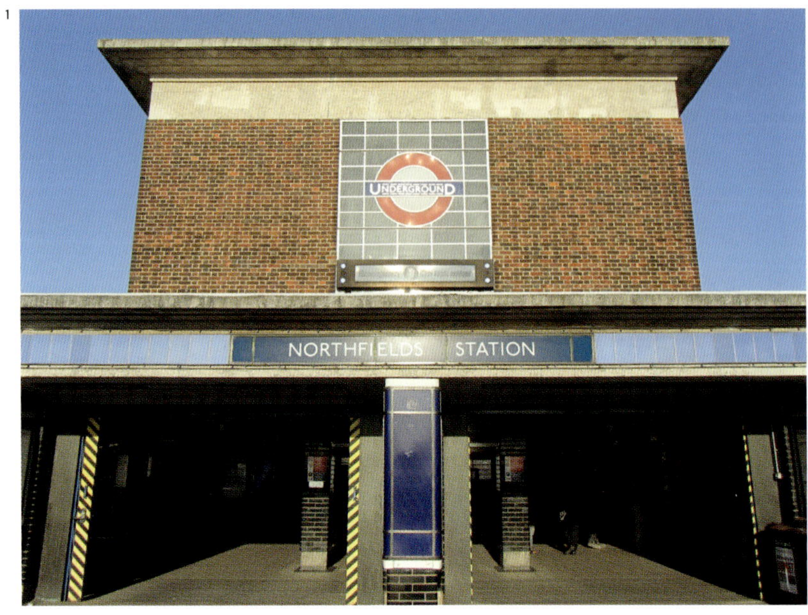

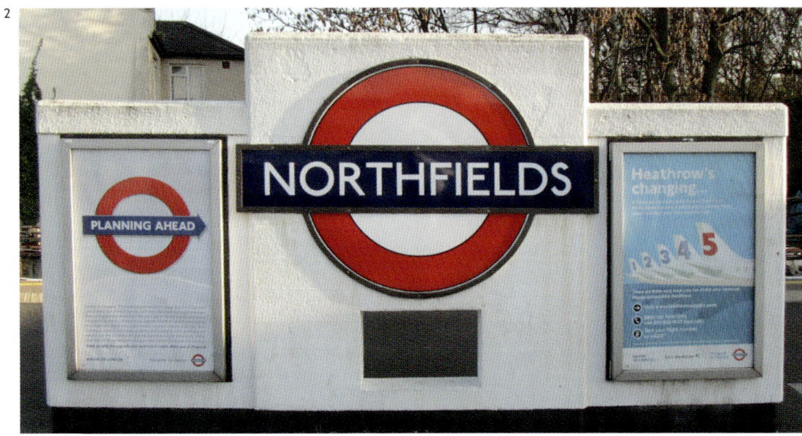

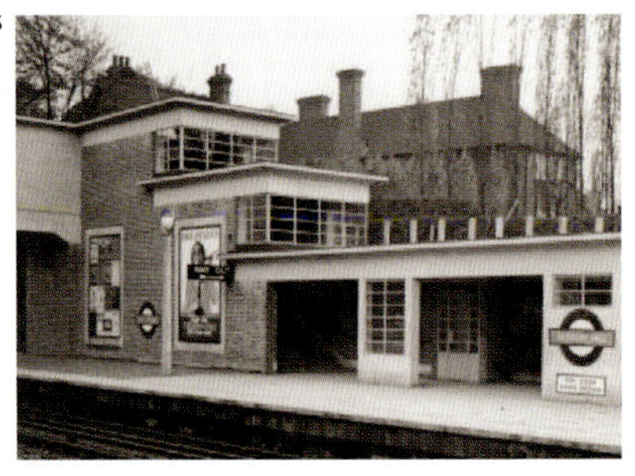

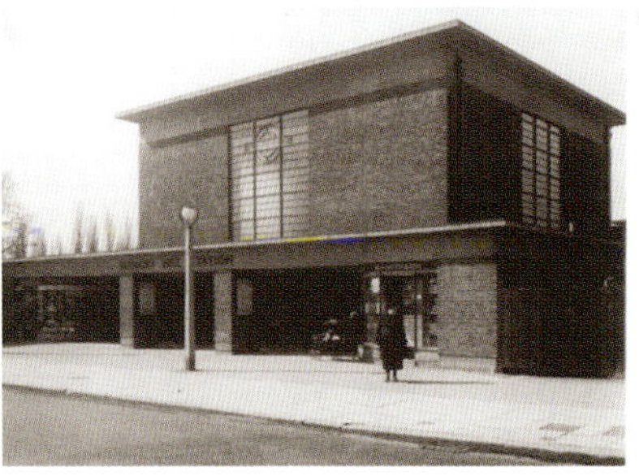

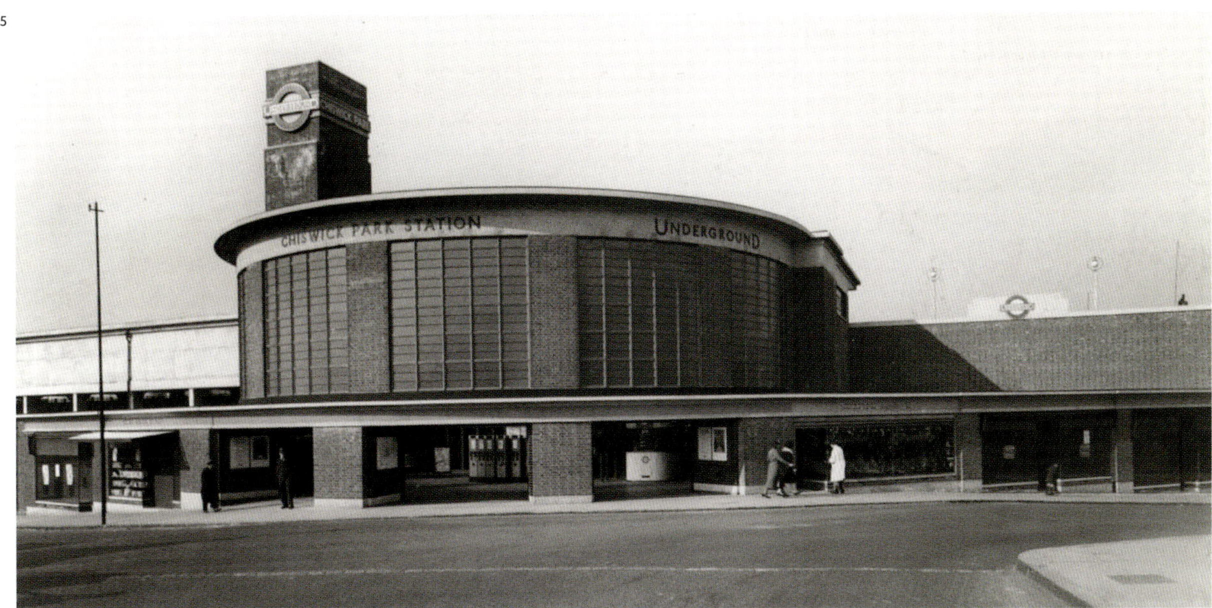

6

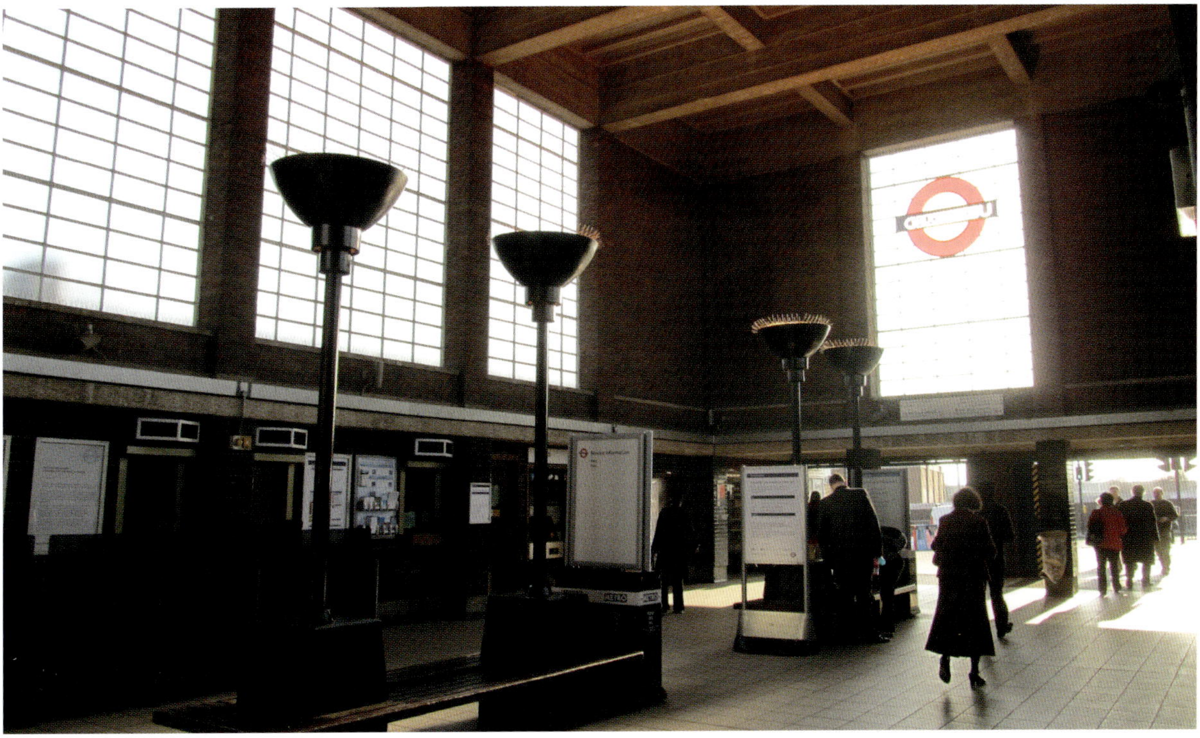

A sketch in time, 1931

The contribution of a single individual to something that changes the course of history is usually pretty minimal, just one of many, but occasionally someone comes up with a concept so remarkable that it alters things completely. A few lines scribbled in a cheap exercise book in 1931 (1) certainly come into this category. Though now generally accepted that schematic representations of rail services had been circulating previously, what Underground engineer Henry Beck (p. 153) sketched in 1931 represents one of the most radical leaps in cartography since the invention of triangulation. While his idea for a simplified map of the Tube network was based upon what had gone before (in-car strip maps, for instance, and George Dow's LNER schematics, p. 152), his expansion of the central area, equalization of station spacing and, crucially, use of only horizontal, vertical and 45-degree diagonal lines – plus his tenacity in resubmitting his idea after the rejection of his visual (2) – demonstrates the confidence Beck had in this breathtakingly simple yet wholly practical concept.

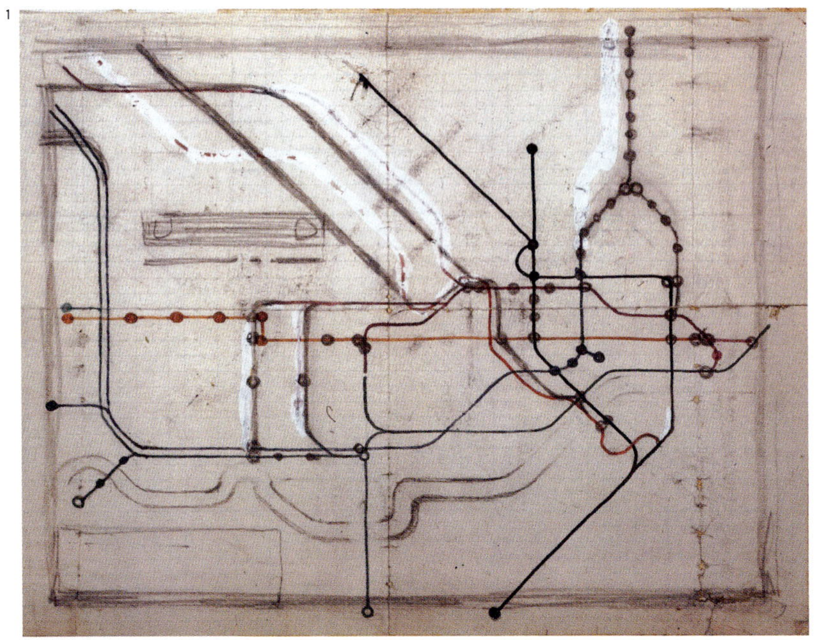

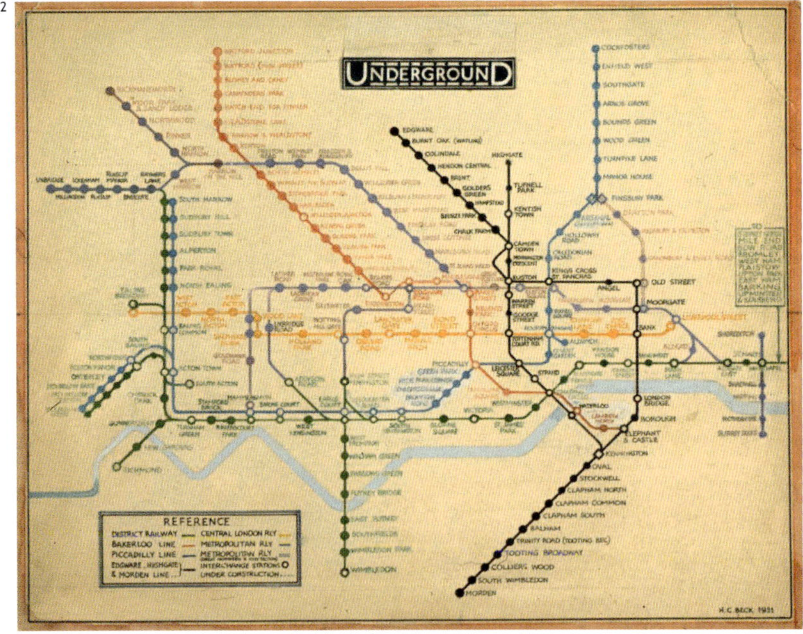

London Underground by Design

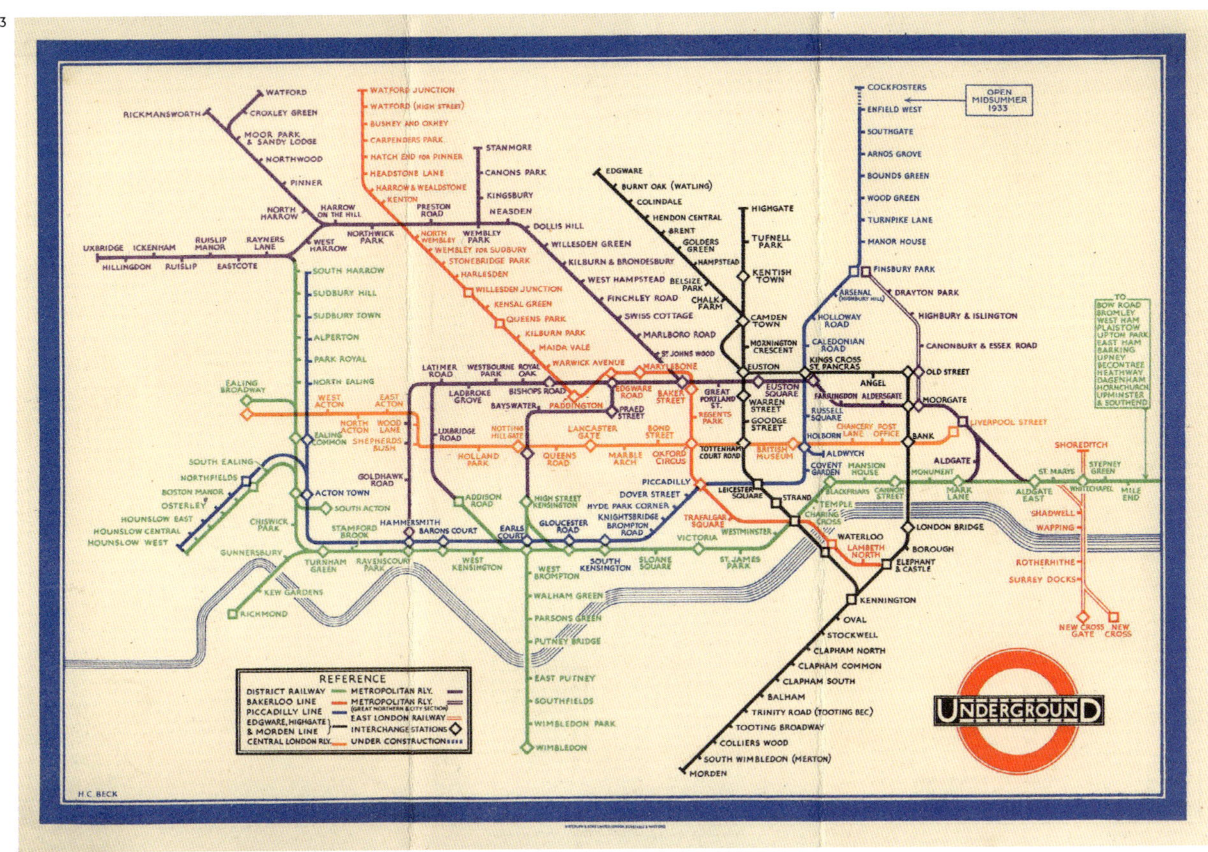

Forty-five degrees of separation, 1933

Five hundred trial copies of Beck's diagram were issued in 1932, followed by a print-run of 700,000 for release in January 1933 as a card pocket map (3). The map face (158mm high x 226mm wide) was folded over twice to create a 'cover' 75mm wide on which the following was printed: 'A new design for an old map. We should welcome your comments.' A quad-royal poster was produced in March the same year and issued in July. The clarity and innovation of the design went down so well that, for generations of travellers, its quirky distortion of London's geography has supplanted the real shape of the capital. Millions have been produced annually since then, leading to this magnificent work becoming one of the most iconic pieces of British graphic design. Its ingenious solutions have been adopted by the overwhelming majority of metro/subway system maps the world over. Though the design has been tweaked and tinkered with, new lines and extensions have been added and a plethora of extra details included (too many, in the opinion of Maxwell J. Roberts – 2005, Bibliography – and others), the card folder in use today is virtually identical in size and in the overall look.

First out from Finsbury Park, 1932

The inaugural section of the Piccadilly's extension north from Finsbury Park opened on 19 September 1932. The first station reached, Manor House, was a bit unusual at the surface as it had only one fairly nondescript entrance (1) and several railed stairwell entrances. It was nonetheless a major intersection for trains, trams and buses and so a unique octagonal totem column (3) was installed with three-fingered flags on four sides pointing to the further-flung destinations of north London. It also featured a unique interlaced U and D (rolled on to its side) atop the finial. The circulating area/ticket office, by artist Herbert Felton, resembled that of Piccadilly Circus and Leicester Square with its suspended ceiling, passimeter and circular display board showing ticket prices (2). The words 'fares' and 'litter' on this column and some of the direction signage here (4) were in the Delf Smith petit serif.

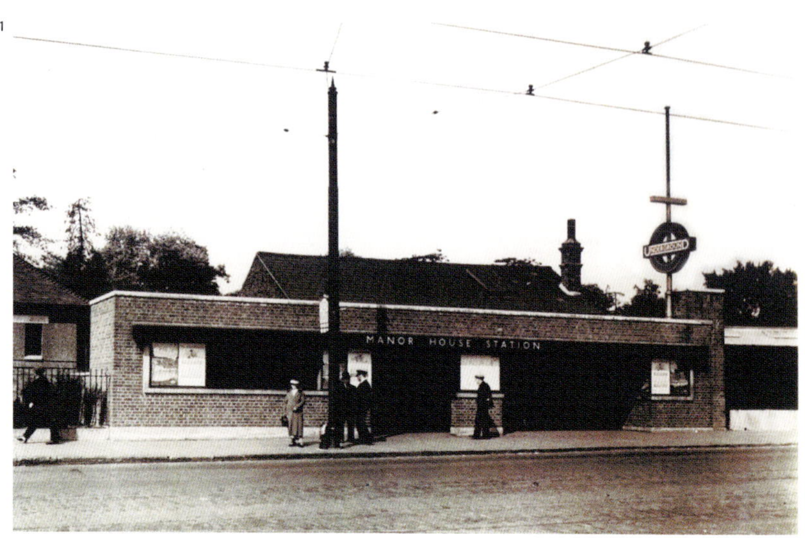

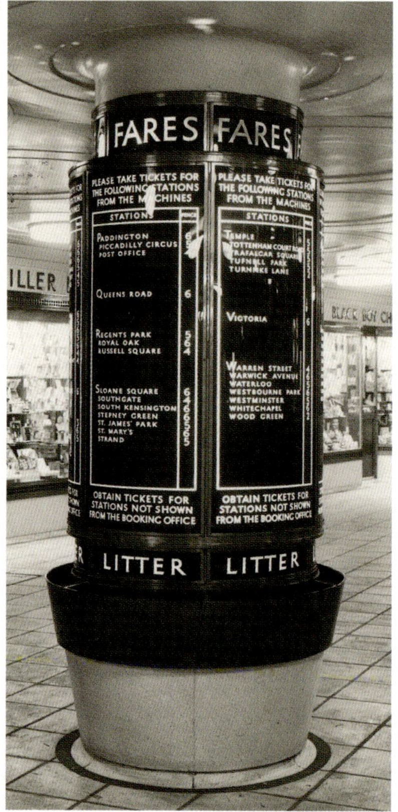

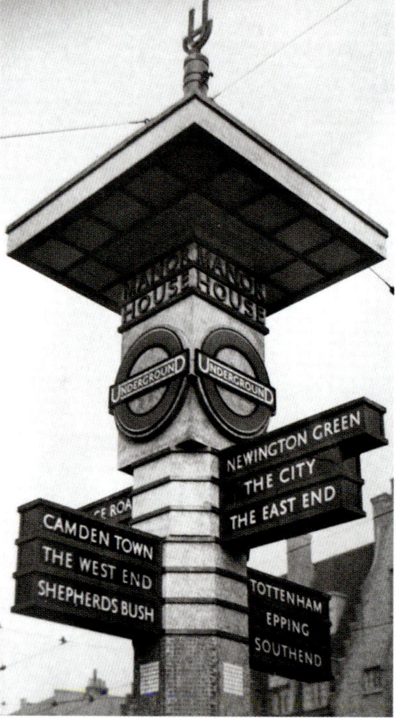

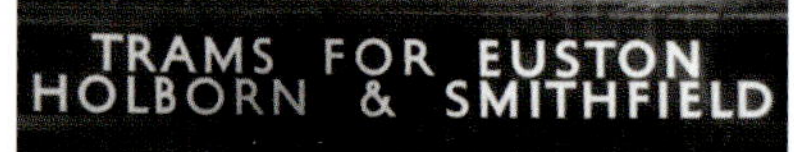

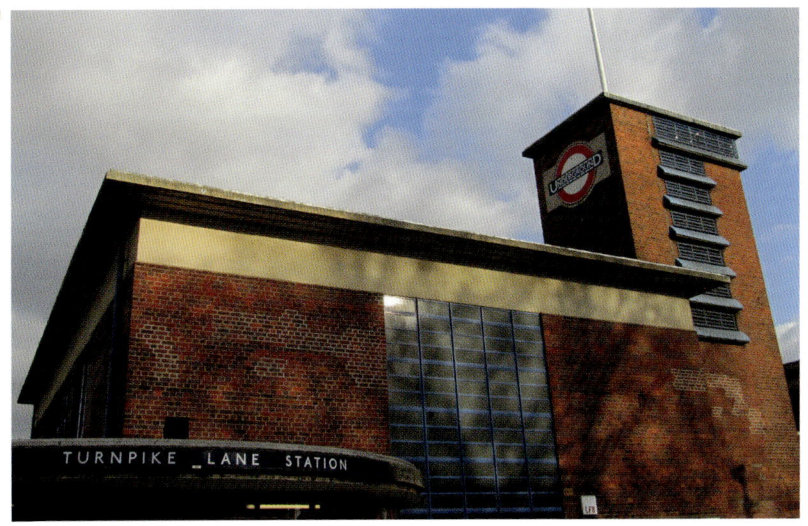

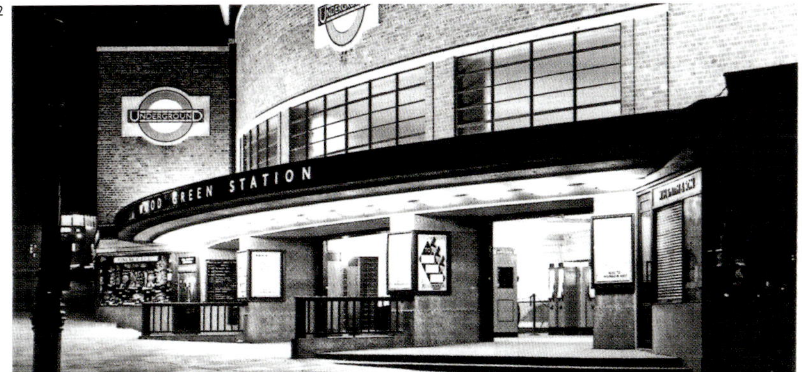

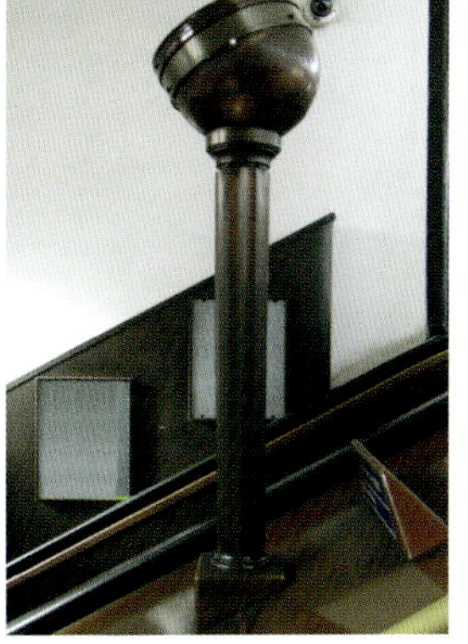

Turnpike and two Greens, 1932

The next station, Turnpike Lane (1), was another Holden-designed 'brick box with a concrete lid' with characteristic window panelling and a ventilation tower. Due to its corner location, Wood Green (2) had a variation on the theme with a curving frontage and vent towers either side. At the next station, Bounds Green (3), for which the lead designer was Charles Holloway James (p. 150), the brick box became octagonal with glazed 'sides' and a brick frontage. The ticket halls at all three, like those on the west side at Sudbury and Northfields (pp. 164–6), benefited from being double height with inset windows, making them light and airy. Here and on the escalators and in the circulating areas below were the signature Piccadilly line Art Deco bronze uplighters (4).

Around Arnos Grove, 1932

Arnos Grove was the first cylindrical ticket hall to be erected in Britain. Inspired by Stockholm Public Library (p. 162), Holden drew up (with his assistant Charles Hutton) a design for what was to become one of the most quintessential Underground stations ever built (front in 1933, 1). Although Chiswick Park (p. 167) was under construction at the same time, Arnos Grove opened first as the temporary terminus of the Piccadilly extension. The flat concrete roof of the drum is supported by a sixteen-sided central column with a circular passimeter at the base (2). Its shape has inspired many other stations, such as the 1936 rebuild of Berlin's Olympia-Stadion by Alfred Grenander, Park Royal (1936), Hanger Lane (1949, p. 216) and, in modern times, Canada Water (1999, p. 269) and Walthamstow (2005, p. 274). Described as 'an architectural gem of unusual purity' by the *Observer*, Arnos Grove was listed in 1971 and is now a Grade II* building, sensitively restored in 1990 and again in 2005. Station furniture included double-sided wooden seats holding the bullseye.

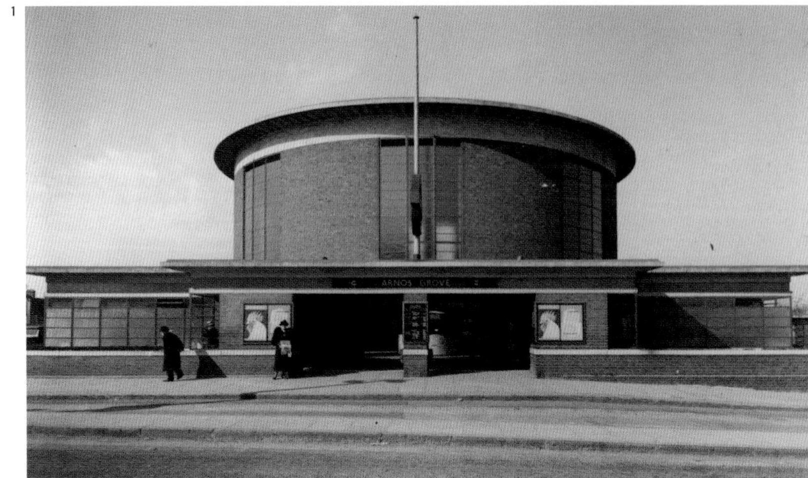

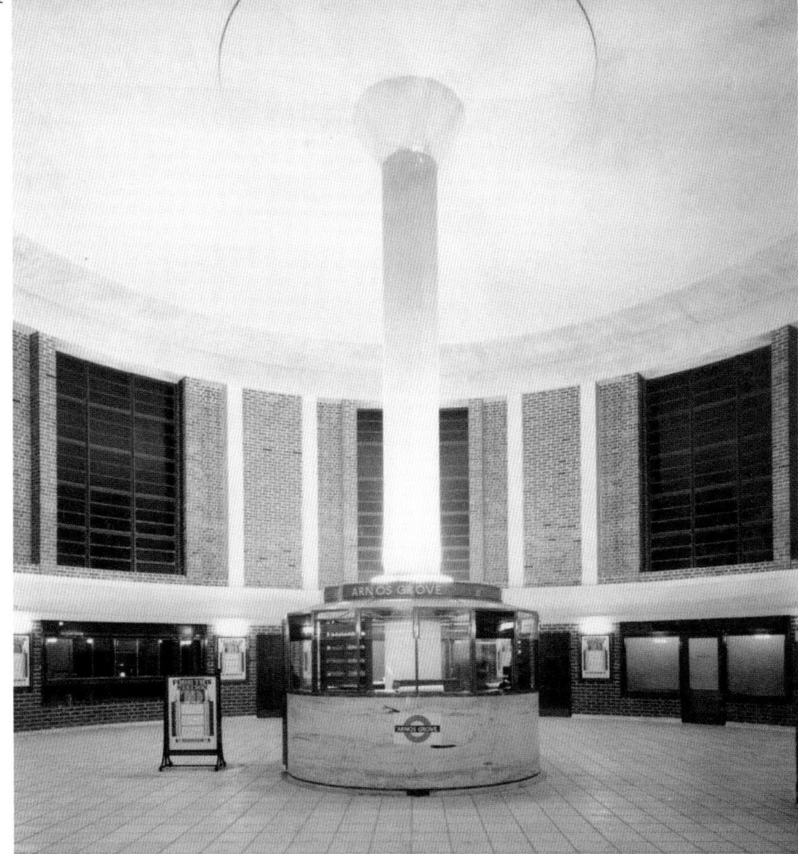

London Underground by Design

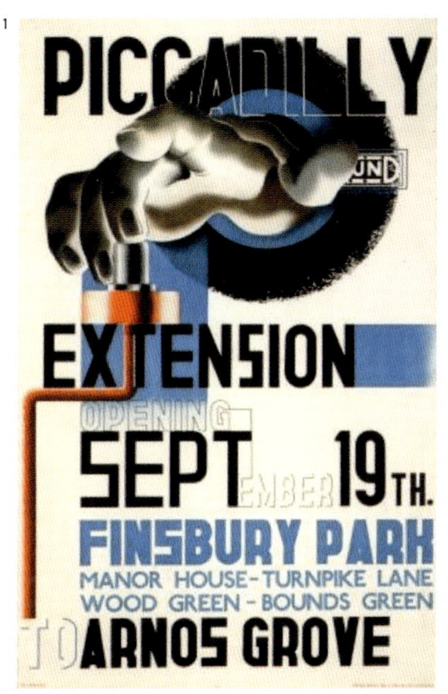

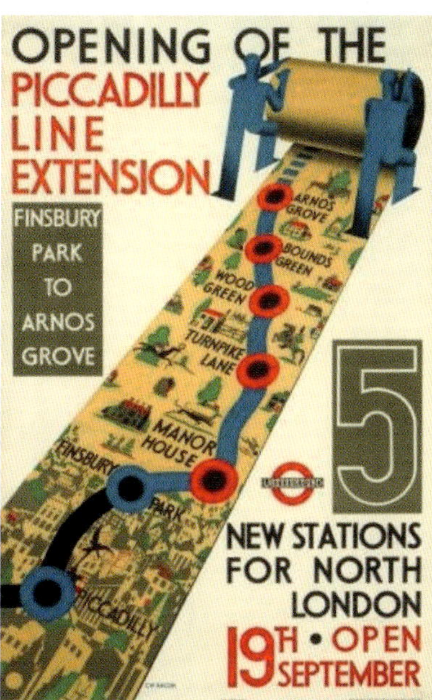

Stations as destinations, 1932

Pick's publicity office lost no time in promoting the new stations as destinations in their own right. These beautiful, streamlined buildings represented some of the sharpest architecture in Britain at the time, on a par with the finest modernist buildings of the era. In the words of *Architect and Building News* (10 November 1933), they 'revolutionised our idea of suburban stations'. Posters advertising them varied in their degree of sophistication, from (crude) new-build photos (3) to more imaginative designs like Cecil Walter Bacon's beautiful paper roll (2) or McKnight Kauffer's giant hand poised over a button that would switch on the new line (1).

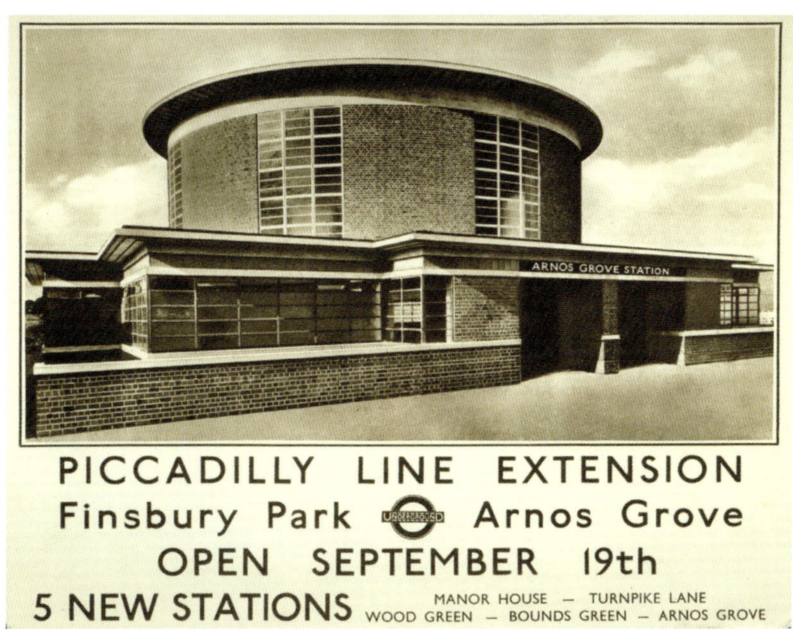

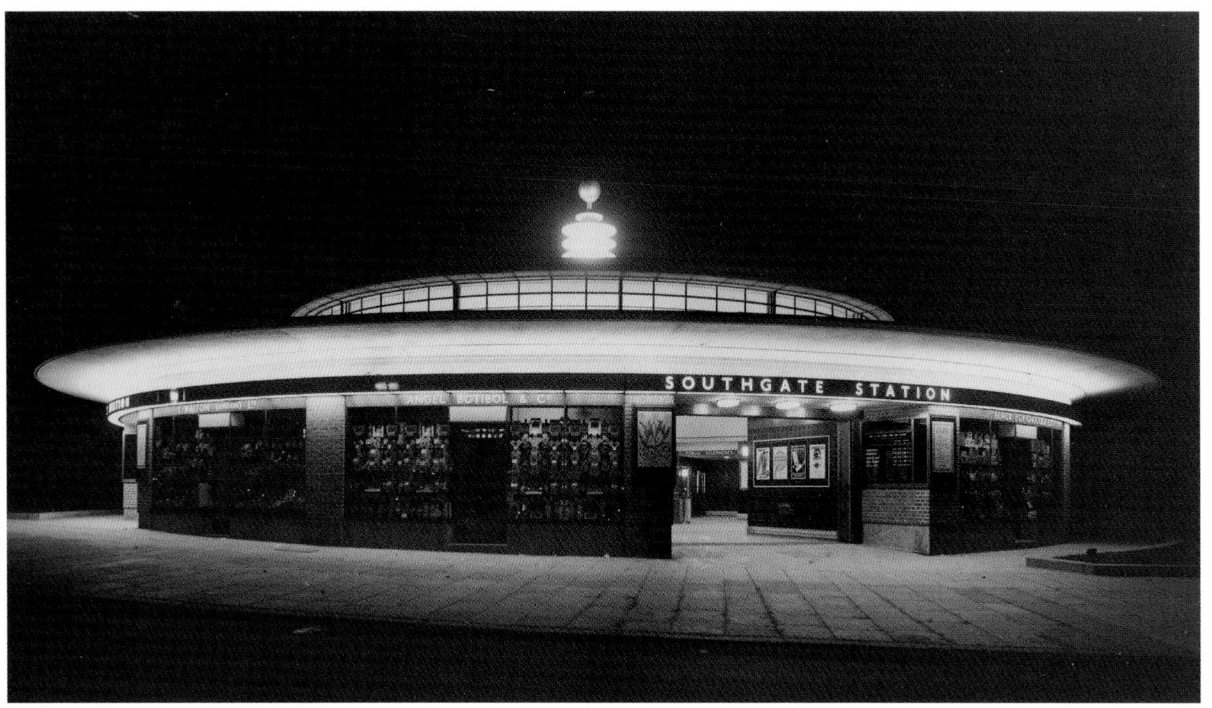

Southgate spaceship spawns sinister sci-fi stars, 1933

What Holden envisaged on paper (1931) for Southgate, the first station after Arnos Grove on the extension to Cockfosters, was extraordinary. Constructed as a bus/train interchange from the outset, Southgate was a spectacular circular celebration, the most revolutionary station yet. Possibly taking his cue from the Berlin U-Bahn station at Krumme Lanke (p. 162), Holden took the island setting of the ticket hall to its logical conclusion, constructing an edifice so gracefully balanced and geometrically perfect that in many ways it is still unequalled. The design is so futuristic that at night (1) the building resembles a kind of spaceship; indeed, its lighting beacon (2), based on a Tesla coil, is said to have inspired Terry Nation, a screenwriter for the *Doctor Who* TV series, when designing the top half of the Daleks. The huge roof is supported by the retaining walls and a single central column with the ticket office beneath. Interior decor followed that of the other Piccadilly stations, with squat uplighters on the escalators and full-height ones at the foot of the shaft. A shopping arcade wraps around the ticket hall, its curved units echoing the main building. One of the finest surviving examples of Art Deco/Streamline Moderne style, the station is now Grade II* listed.

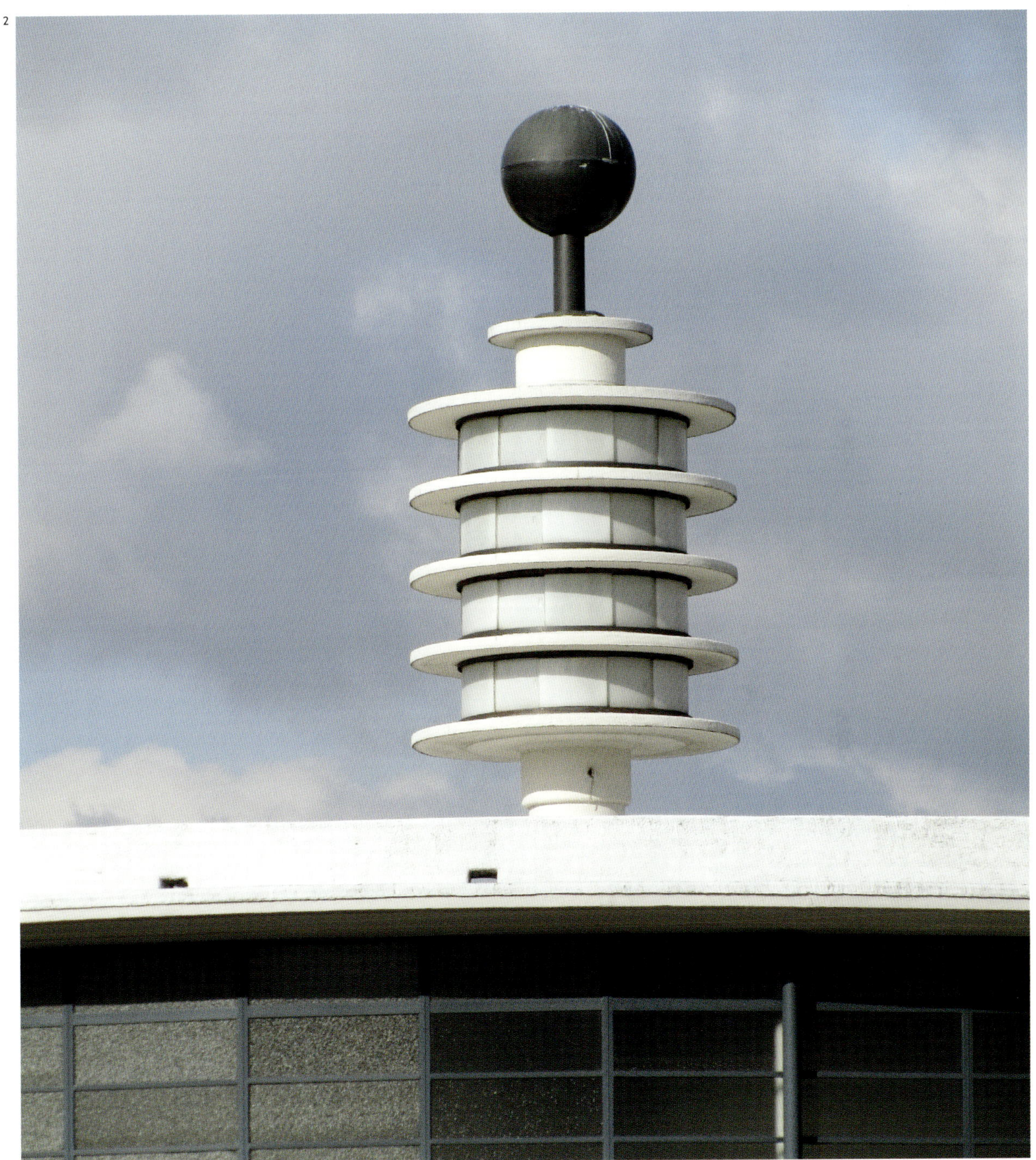

Mushrooming Oakwood, 1933

Designed by Charles Holloway James (p. 150) under Holden's supervision, Enfield West (now Oakwood) had a very large ticket hall with glazed panels in the curtain wall – the longest 'brick box with concrete lid' built so far, its ceiling supported by concrete beams (1). Devised as an interchange, like the other two on this extension (Southgate and Cockfosters, p. 174 and opposite, 1), the long frontage facing the forecourt doubled as a bus shelter. Heaps was called in to design the concrete platform canopies (here and at Cockfosters), which featured built-in seating between piers (3) and station-name panels flanked on either side by poster frames set under the distinctive Bauhaus-style circular lamps. Apart from the modern style of trains, posters and electrical fittings, the platforms are little changed since the 1930s. Outside, a stylish 'mushroom shelter' still stands (2), although the long enamel plate for the station car park (4) in the Delf Smith lettering has long since disappeared. The shelters were practical touches with their steel halo of lights at the summit of a tapered concrete pole, first used here and at Southgate and Turnpike Lane but quickly copied by 1935 for Queensbury (p. 198 and elsewhere), some with information poster frames; these days they seem more decorative than functional.

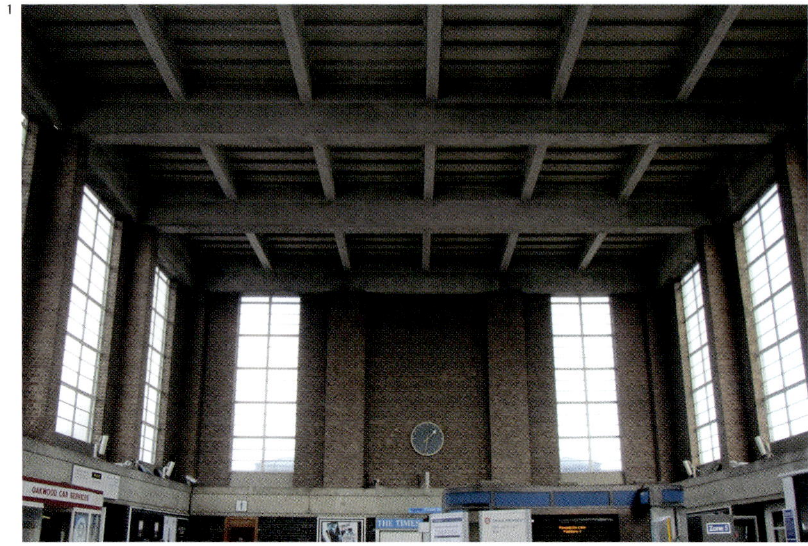

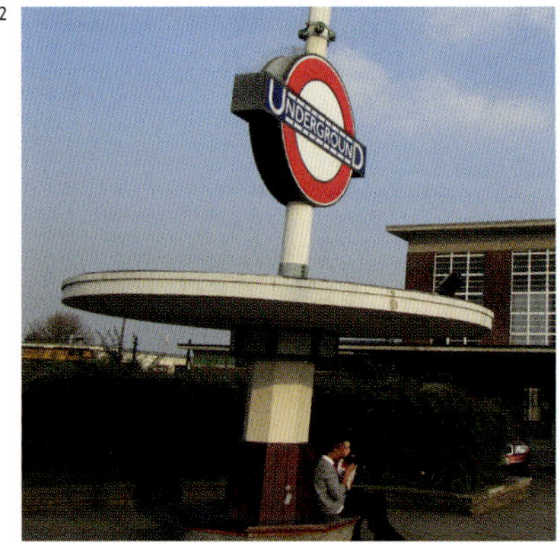

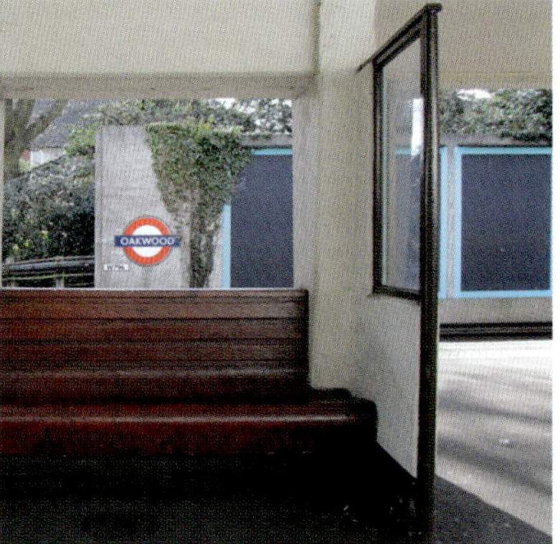

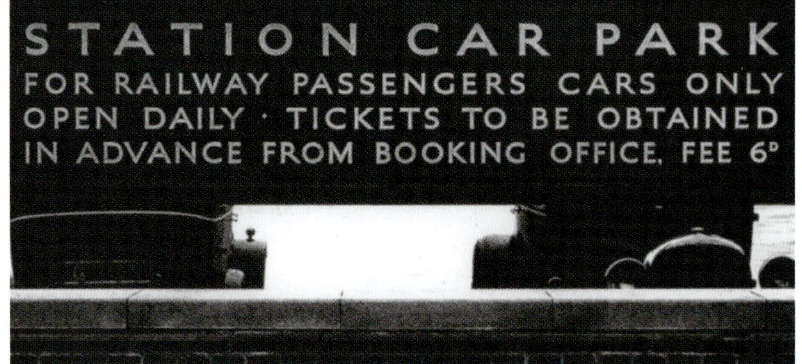

London Underground by Design

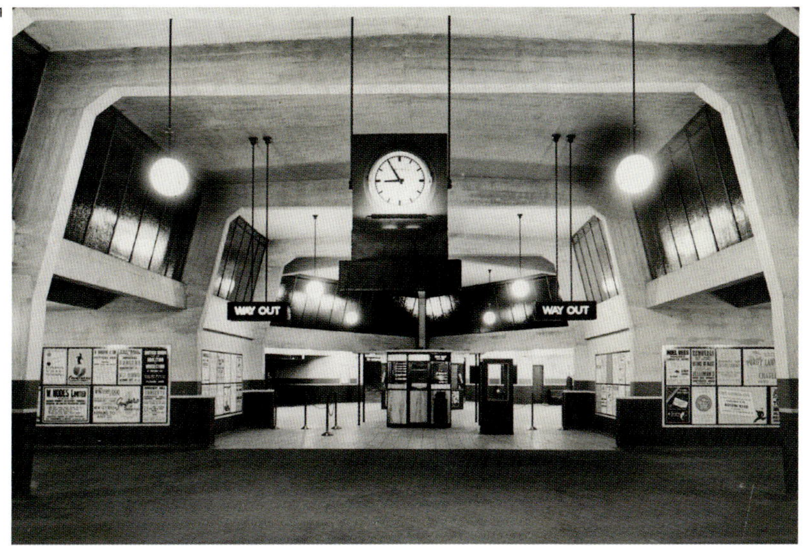

Cockfosters of the north, 1933

The opening of the last station on the mammoth northerly extension of the Piccadilly line was designed to coincide with the inauguration of the new authority, the LPTB, on 1 July 1933 (p. 154). Though perhaps less aesthetically pleasing than some of the stations to the south of it, Cockfosters was nonetheless a major feat of structural engineering with its vast concrete train shed (1) – necessary for a terminal. And while the surface entrance buildings seem a little understated, they were originally designed with bigger things in mind: flats, cinemas and offices were to top the station entrance with a second structure mirroring the first on the other side of the road. As these were never constructed and the building has been faithfully restored, the station retains the feel of its opening day – even the unusual *black* background fascia still remains (2). The passimeter has also been kept, though it is not used for its original purpose. Hollowed-out bullseyes (5), restored signage (3) and seating between concrete piers (4) all add to this air of authenticity.

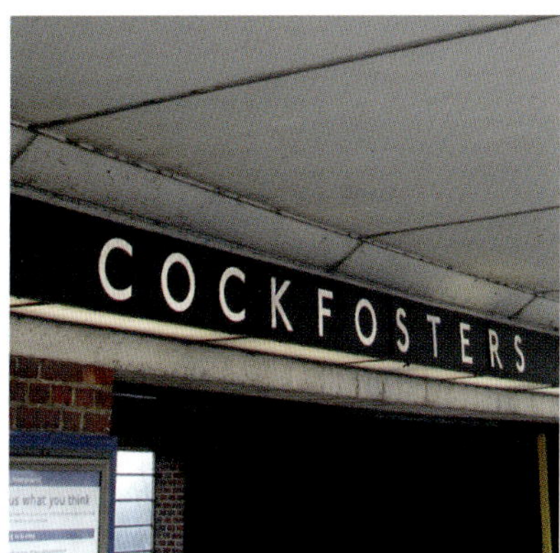

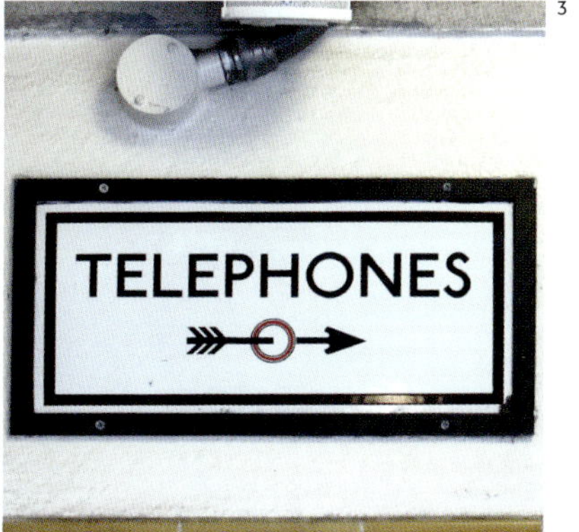

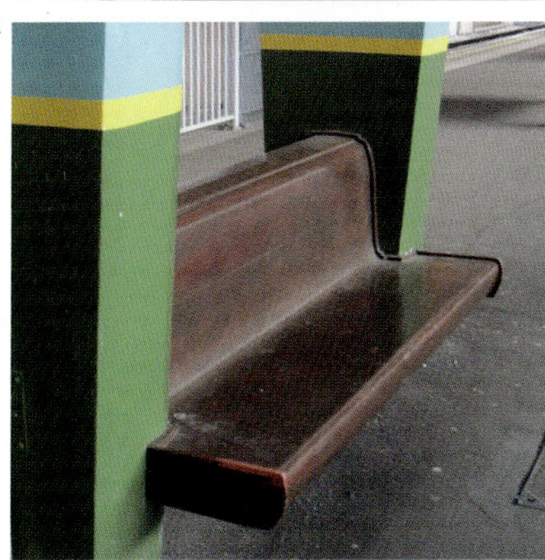

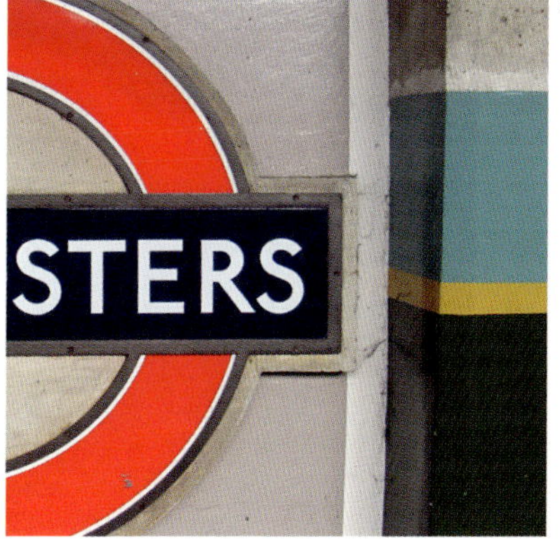

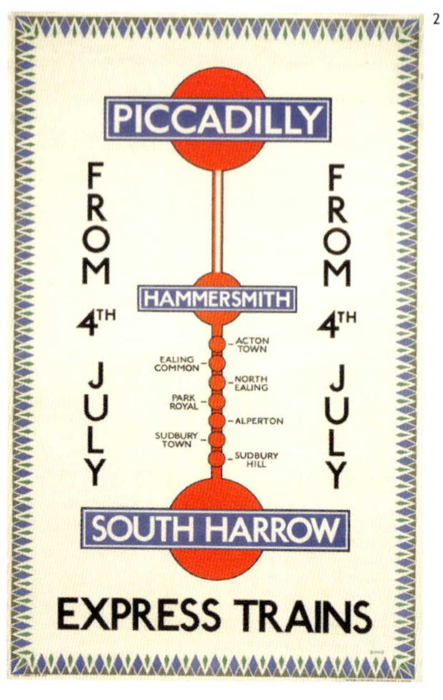

PICCADILLY LINE
EXTENSION
FINSBURY PARK
TO COCKFOSTERS

Promoting Piccadilly-land, 1932

For the opening of the second stage of extensions (to Enfield West and South Harrow) posters were once again out in force to promote the new sections. Most sensibly included maps (1 and 3) and there was a focus on the latest 'express trains' (4) which skipped certain quieter stations. One (2) featured old-fashioned solid red circles with oversized blue station-name bars — not particularly in keeping with the house style but eye-catching nonetheless. McKnight Kauffer was again called upon for a few more posters, one featuring a globe (4), possibly foreshadowing the top of the Southgate finial (p. 175).

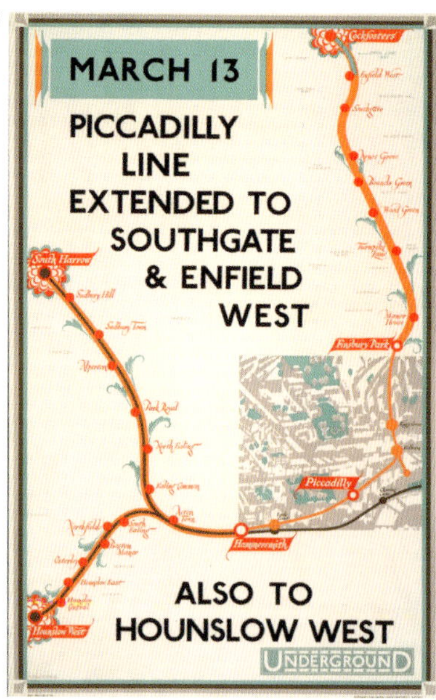

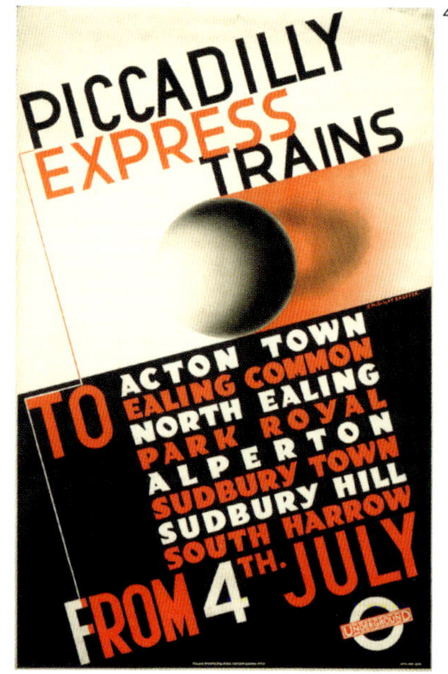

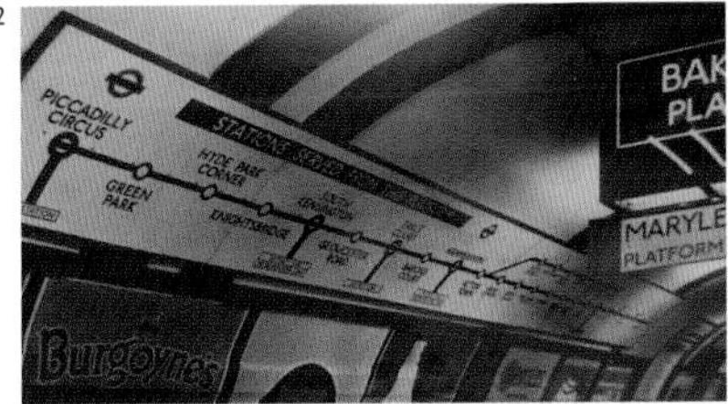

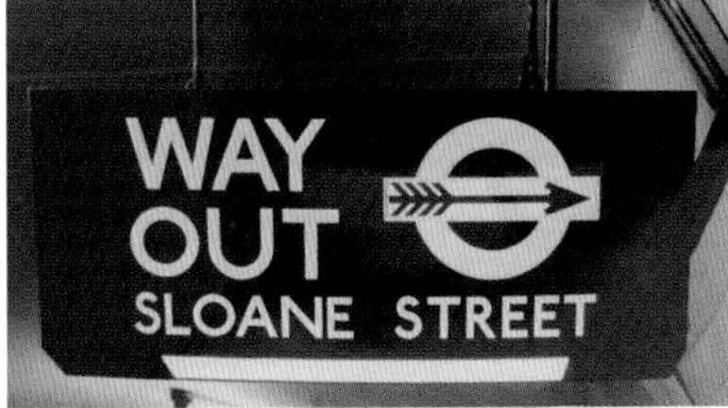

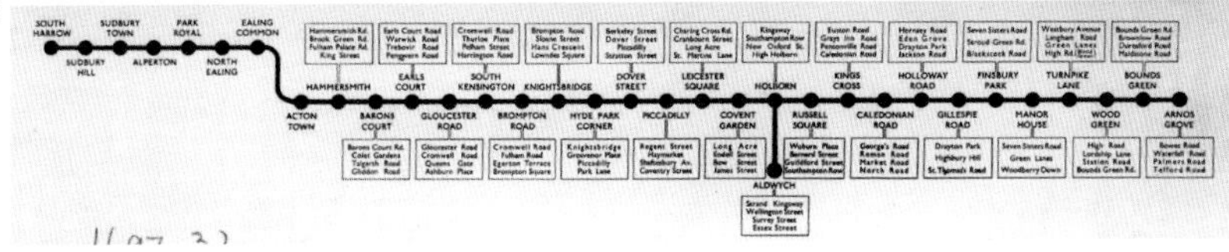

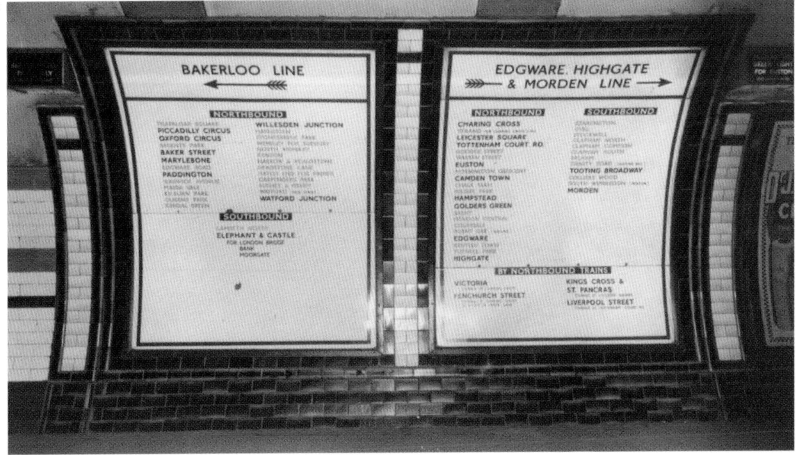

Passenger information, 1932

With the backdrop of Beck's clear diagram (p. 169) and the opening of the new Piccadilly extensions, the publicity office began experimenting with new ways to inform passengers of the route. The humble in-car strip map utilized since 1908 (an odd example from 1932 included neighbouring street names, 4) was enlarged and added to all the Piccadilly stations as a long frieze on station exteriors and above the advertising posters on the trackside wall of platforms (e.g. Bounds Green, 1, and Piccadilly Circus, 2). These were put up in 1932 and tried at Charing Cross and other stations at around the same time. The experiment was evidently not deemed a success and the traditional enamel plates listing all the stations served from that platform were made and expanded upon (e.g. at Waterloo, 5). These were backed up by extra signs on white enamel above the entrances to some platforms which gave the destination and a summary of key stations, designed to be taken in at a glance by passengers hurrying past. The bifurcation panels retained their crucial direction-giving role. Illuminated direction signs like this 'WAY OUT' one at Knightsbridge (3) typified the 1930s style of combining bullseyes with arrows and these devices were not standardized until 1938 (p. 192).

Clark's last rural outposts, 1931–4

While other parts of Middlesex were gaining new Underground stations at a rate of knots, another small section of the county (now part of Greater London) was being linked to the network, though by the Met this time. The short 6km route from Wembley Park to Stanmore (3) opened on 10 December 1932, with Clark-style, rural-looking stations at Kingsbury (2) and Stanmore. At Canons Park (1) a slight concession to modernism was permitted by Clark. Queensbury, which was to open later, was left to the LPTB to complete, which it did in a more Holden-esque fashion (in 1934). Clark's last stations for the Met, at Northwick Park (1931, 4) and Northwood Hills (1933), both showed he was grasping for a more contemporary style – the lettering was especially advanced for the Met – but even these fell short of the LPTB's requirements and Clark was not taken on by the Board. Meanwhile, internal signage on the Stanmore branch reflected the company's standard serifed typeface (p. 139).

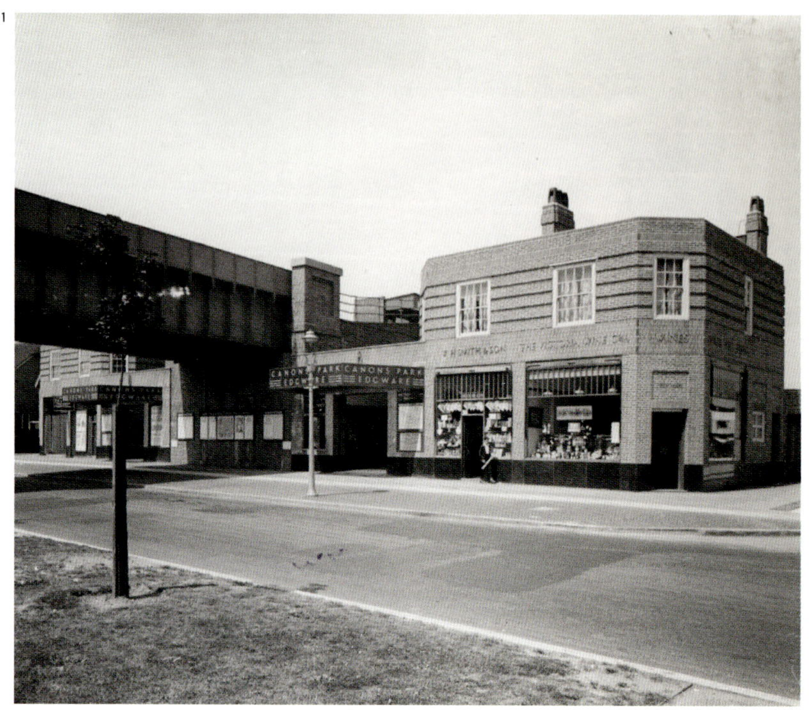

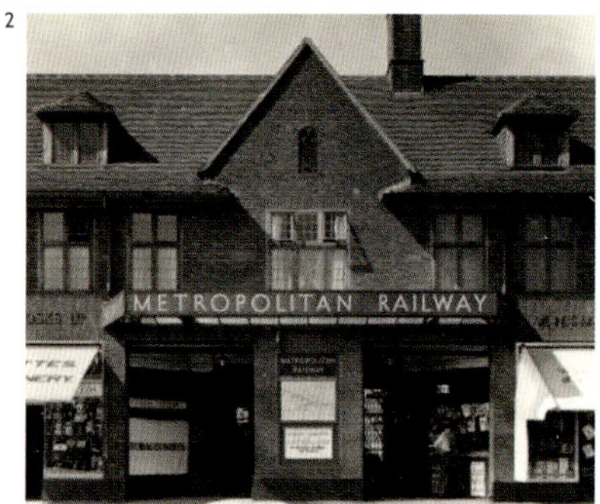

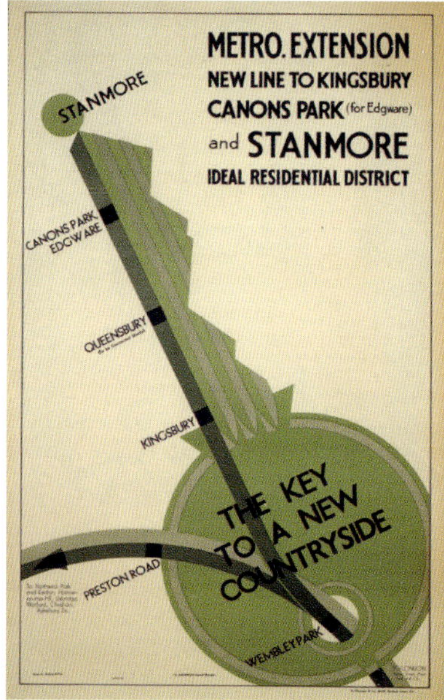

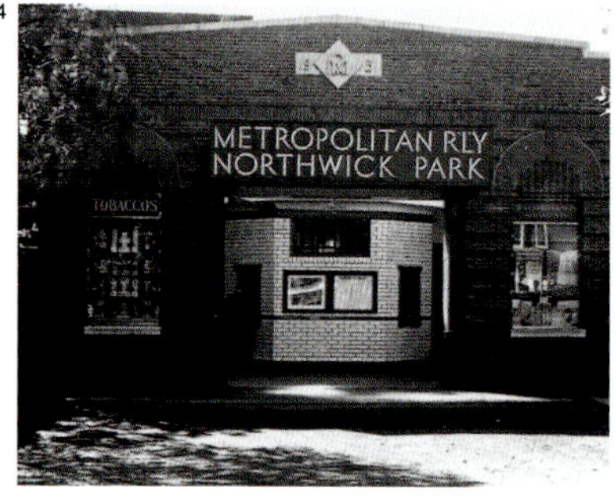

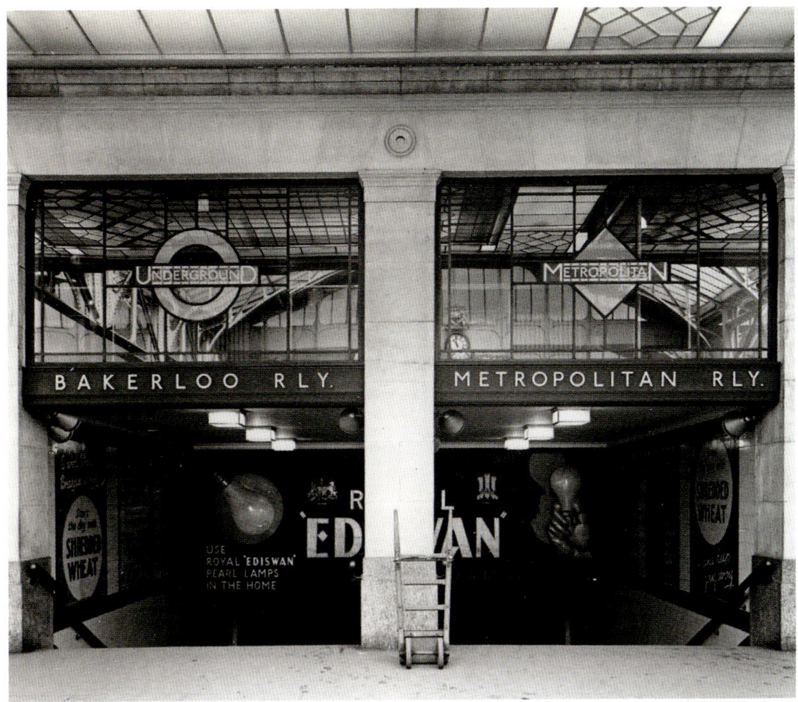

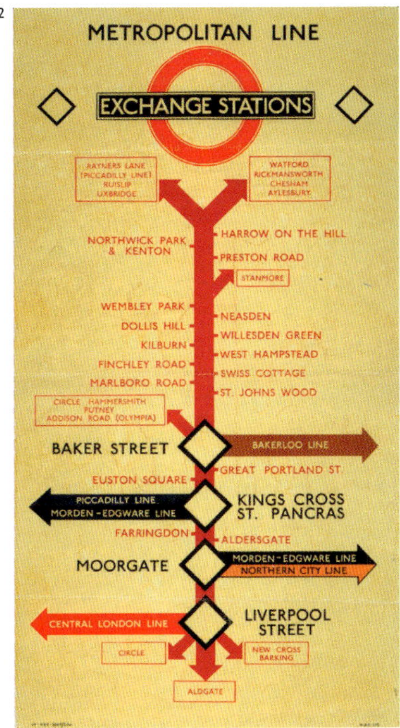

Mixed Met messages, 1931–5

As the Met was inexorably absorbed into the LPTB during 1933 and rebranding started to make it look like part of the Underground, Johnston Sans was the inevitable choice for signage and publicity. The very last Clark stations had already been edging away from their traditional serifed signage and Canons Park (opposite, 1) and Northwick Park (opposite, 4) were both given signs in 1931–4 that looked suspiciously sans-serif. Some minor concessions to the old red diamond logo were permitted (e.g. a Johnston Sans one at Praed Street, dated 1935, 2) and some train livery continued to sport the words Metropolitan linE for some years. The first of the red diamonds were removed from as early as 1934 (e.g. Uxbridge and Westbourne Park the following year), however, to be replaced with LU bullseyes. At least one 'hybrid' Met poster displaying their red diamond was used to promote the Arnos Grove extension of the Piccadilly line (1932, 3) – oddly using Gill Sans – but by 1934 in-car panels had migrated to Johnston Sans (2).

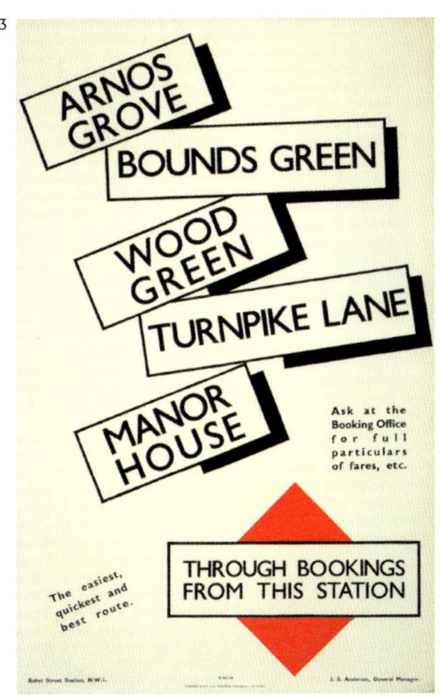

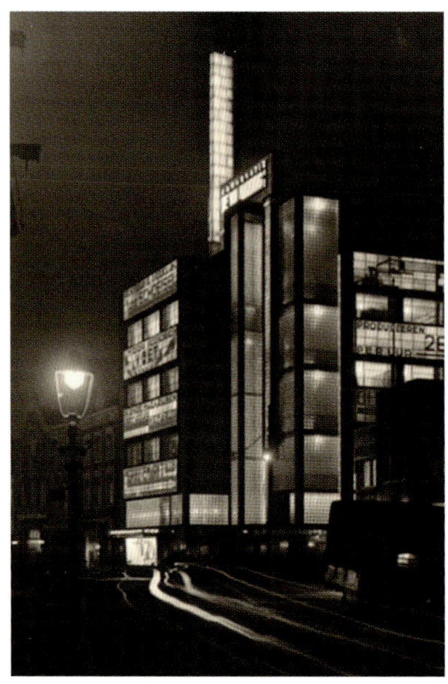

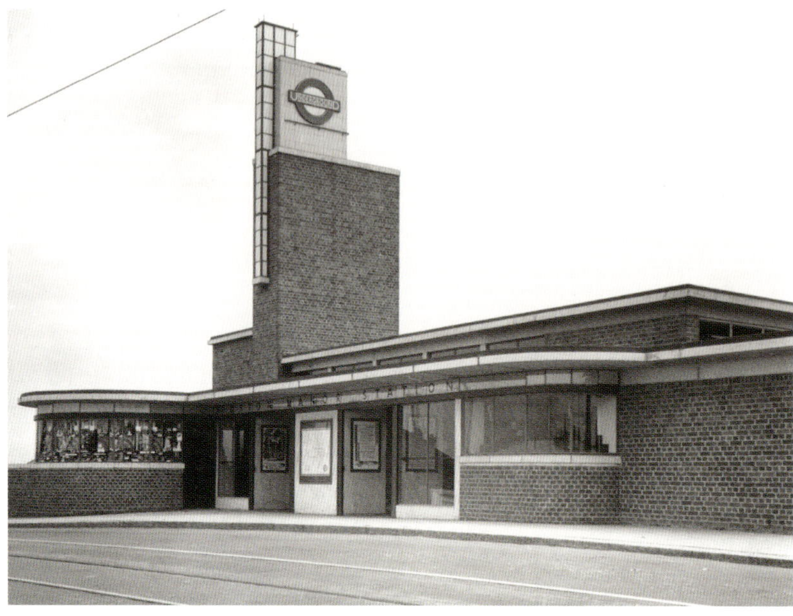

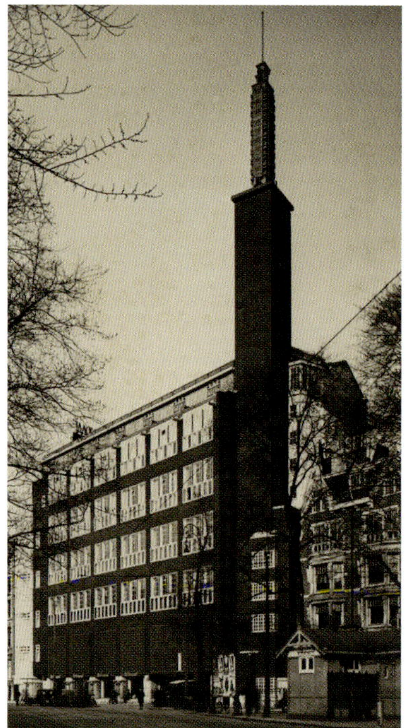

Boston manners, 1934

While the northerly Piccadilly needed new tunnels and stations, the takeover of the western District stations required the reconstruction of a number of dreary rural buildings dating to the 1880s. Although the Piccadilly began running to Hounslow in 1933 and both Northfields and Hounslow Central had been opened on time, Boston Manor and Osterley were not. The former, a dishevelled mess architecturally (p. 94), needed a complete rebuild due to a depot siting. What Holden designed (opened 25 March 1934, 2) was another jewel in the LT crown. The glass-and-steel casement (reminiscent of Bernard George's 1933 Barkers Department Store on Kensington High Street) is said to be based on the De Volharding Building in The Hague (designed in 1928 by Jan W. E. Buys and seen by Pick and Holden on their European tour, 1). Despite the Grade II listed status of Boston Manor, it has been marred by unsightly steel barriers erected for 'Health and Safety' reasons. A poor show for a London landmark, although they are hidden by night. At Osterley (4) the 1880s station was deemed badly sited so it was relocated further along the Great West Road. Designed by Heaps working with Holden, it is perhaps his finest contribution to the network. At 21.3m, it had the tallest tower on the system, topped by a unique concrete lighting spire, possibly inspired by Amsterdam's *Kantoorgebouw de Telegraaf* building (3). Osterley is also a Grade II listed building, serving as a beacon for drivers entering London's western outskirts.

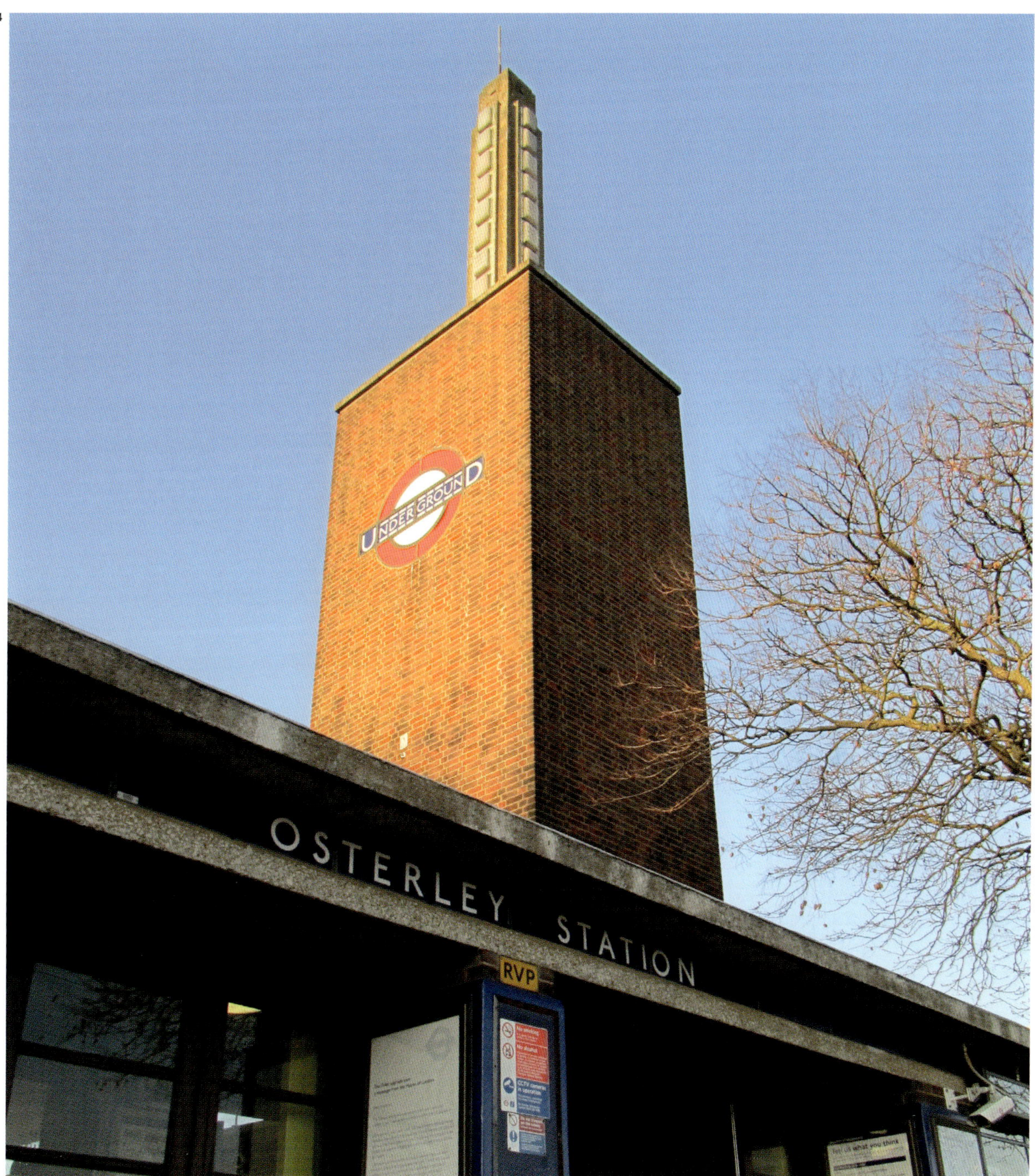
UNDERGROUND
OSTERLEY STATION
RVP

New stations for old, 1932–4

The renovation of older, more centrally located stations became necessary in the 1930s. One of the first to be upgraded (in 1930) was Highgate (renamed Archway a few years later). After several more radical plans were considered, Holden's huge glazed wall (1) was chosen for the frontage and when opened (3 April 1932) it became the first station outside the Piccadilly line to gain the fluted brass uplighters for the escalator shafts. A very similar glazed frontage was installed for the rebuild at Hammersmith, where the open-air platforms were supplied with cantilevered concrete roofing and distinctive seats with station-name bullseyes incorporated (3). Due to its high passenger numbers, Knightsbridge was given a spacious new sub-surface ticket hall, which opened on 18 February 1934. In addition to a sub-surface arcade of retail units, platforms were also retiled in a new 'biscuit cream' colour and featured enamels with bullseyes that had four-flighted arrows on the blue bar (p. 179). At Gillespie Road (2) Holden sketched an idea to replace the old Leslie Green entrance. This was enlarged and the station name changed to Arsenal (22 February 1934). In contrast to previous designs, the frontage was a huge wall of rendered concrete featuring a giant mosaic logo.

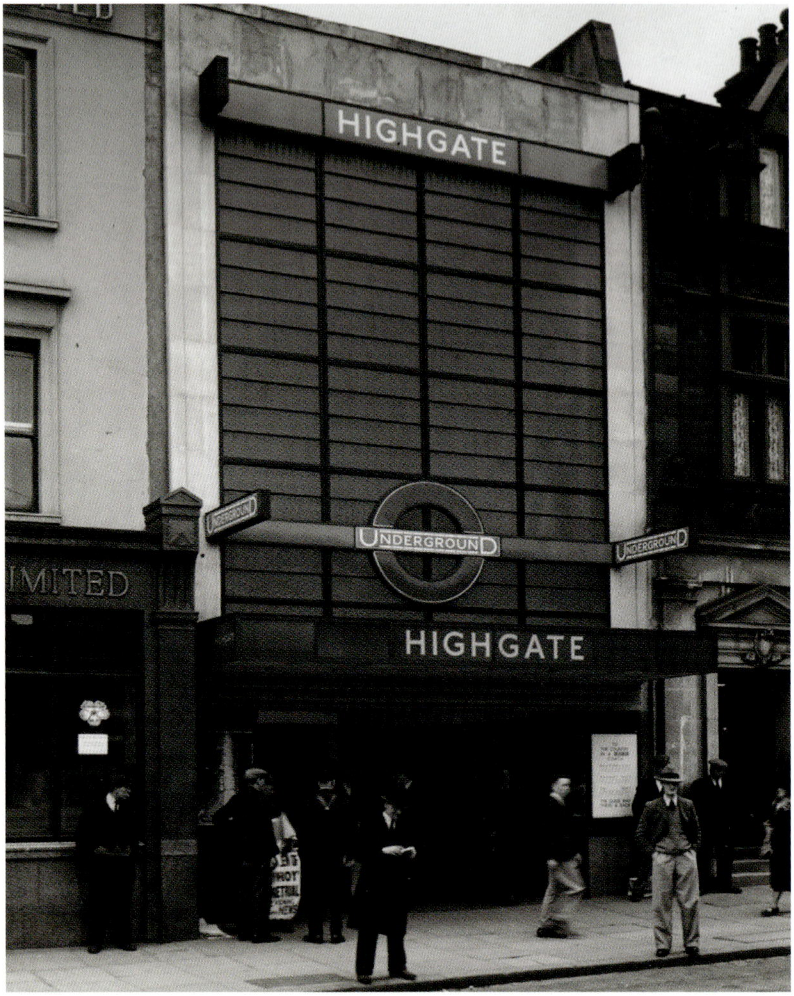

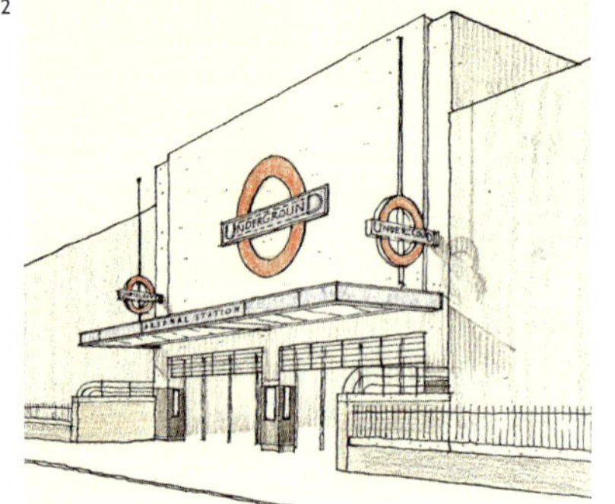

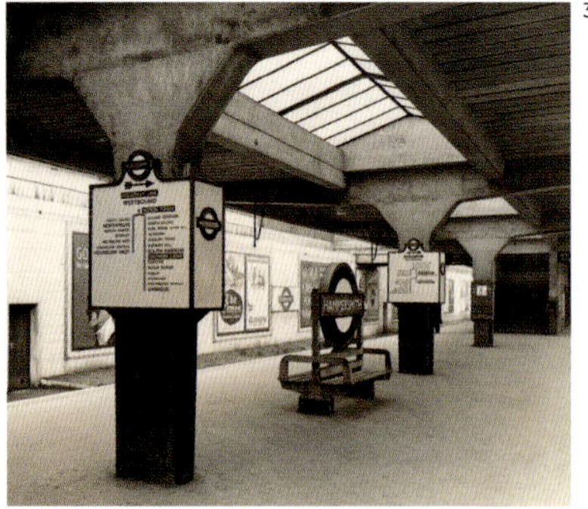

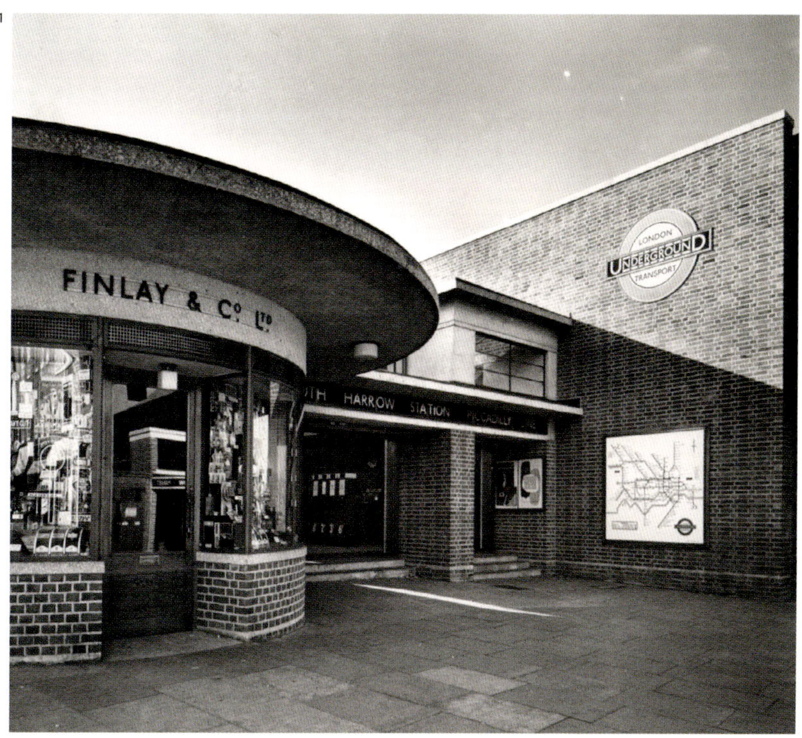

1

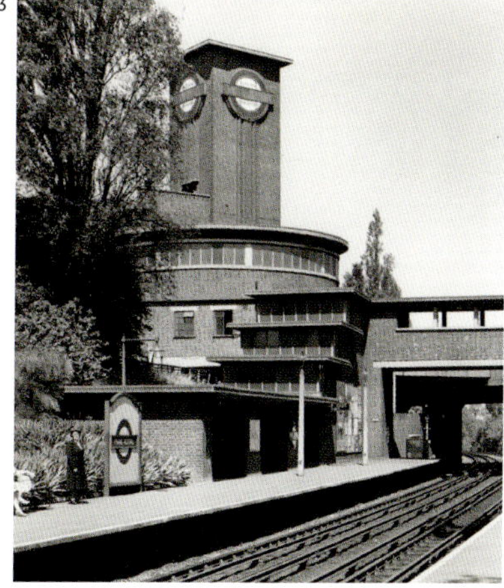

2

3

Changes in the round, 1933–6

The success of circular ticket halls had highlighted the need for improvements elsewhere, the most pressing being the installation of escalators. At Warren Street (opened in 1933) this process required the station (originally designed by Green) to be moved; the resulting drum-like ticket hall was made to support further storeys (duly constructed in 1939). Exhibition Road entrance at Earl's Court was given a circular ticket hall in 1935; a novel feature was the illuminated 'train describer' with route diagram. Also benefiting from a circular ticket hall was South Harrow, where the station was shifted slightly to provide entrances closer to the main road (1). Given the climb from the street, a separate covered stairway was created, inset with clerestory windows; a circular building beside the entrance was used only for shops when the station opened on 5 July 1935. South Harrow was equipped with 'neighbourhood' maps (2), captioned 'District within ¼ mile radius'; a similar style of map had been installed at Boston Manor in 1932, while its descendants can be seen at every station. The rebuild at Park Royal (3) by Felix James Lander (p. 155), in Holden style, opened on 1 March 1936. Here was another circular ticket hall, this time dwarfed by a 20.4m-high tower.

Logos for all London Transport, 1933-35

The creation in 1933 of an overarching body to co-ordinate transport in the capital (p. 154) called for a unified branding across all modes of transit. The LPTB therefore created a logo for itself and each of its operations, Underground, Tramway, General Bus, Green Line, Coach and Trolleybus (1), registering them as trademarks between 1934 and 1935. Each mode featured an enlarged first and last letter and the 'pecking' above and below the central letters. The artwork was again prepared by Johnston, who to begin with enlarged the inner white space of the circle, then placed the LPTB acronym above the bar inside the circle (from mid 1933). Lord Ashfield preferred the full trading name to the acronym, so on individual modes whose name was in the centre, 'LONDON' was placed above the bar and 'TRANSPORT' below (in 1934). The logo was to adorn everything, from annual reports to joint timetables. Until the Carr–Edwards report of 1938 issued stricter guidelines (p. 192), the bullseye became the base of numerous direction signs on the system, some more successful than others (2 and 3). The shape was also used for LT's power generator 'Northmet', in which the logo was somewhat loosely interpreted.

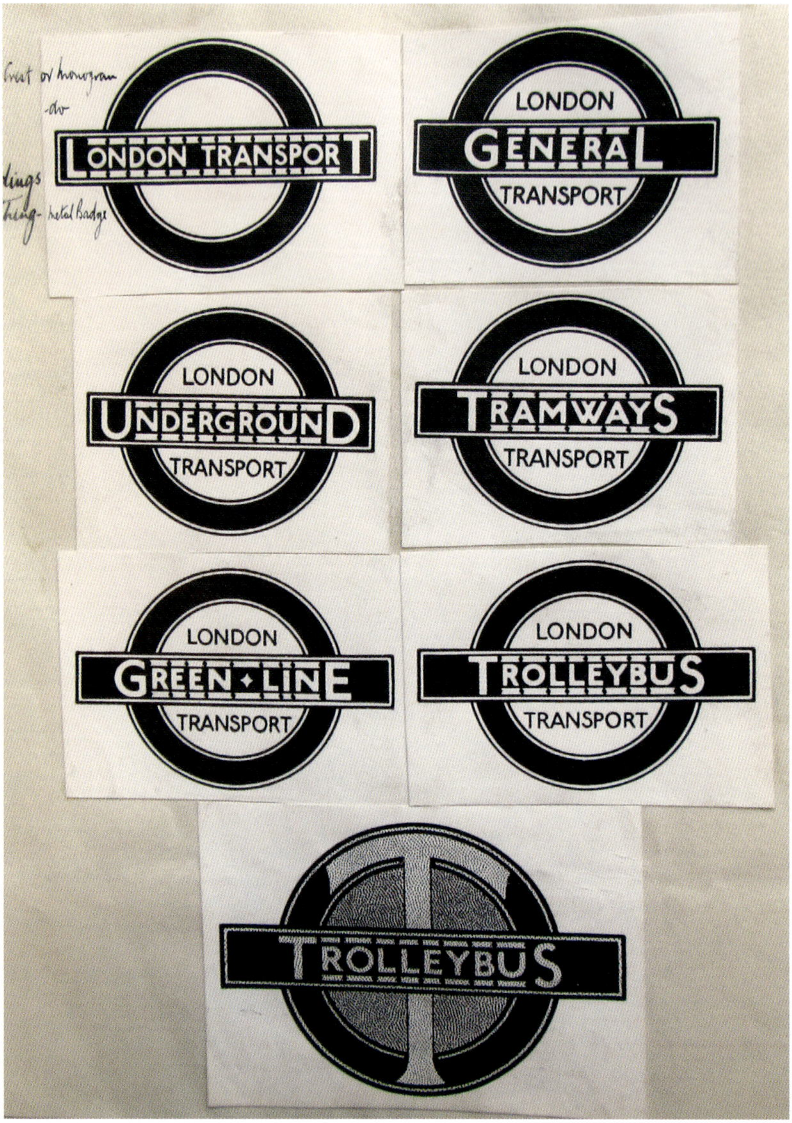

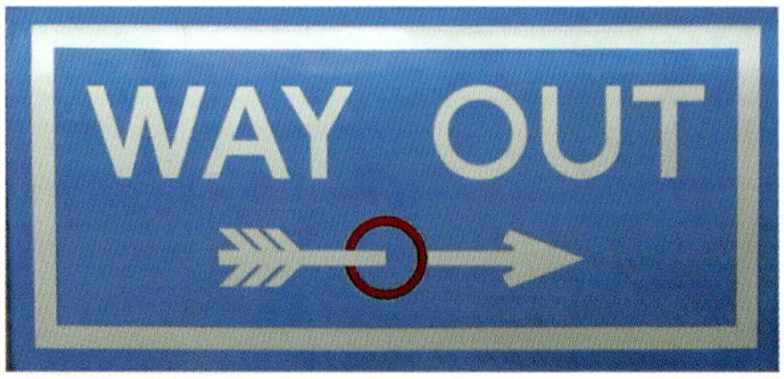

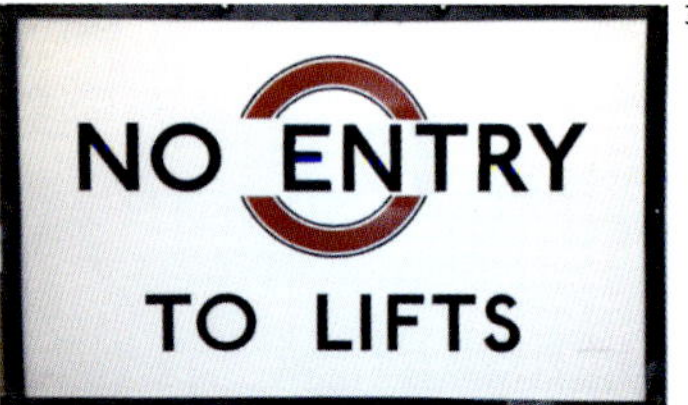

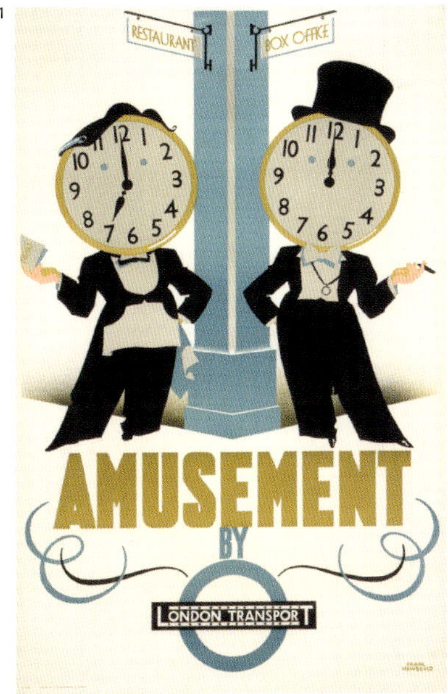

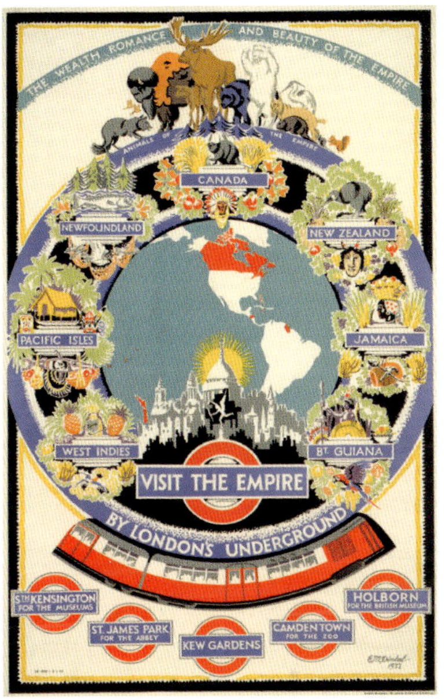

Leisure for pleasure, 1932–34

A well-known commercial artist, Frank Newbould, produced twenty posters for transport in London and just a handful for the Underground, including this 1934 one, (1) promoting off-peak 'Amusement' in a delightfully whimsical style. Ernest Michael Dinkel's pair of 1933 posters promoting the Empire (2) made great play on the bullseye logo. Marc Fernand Severin created only six posters for the Underground, all during 1938; those featuring the bullseye as a clock and encouraging use of the Tube for leisure activities (3) are particularly distinctive. Anna Katrina Zinkeisen designed twenty Underground posters between 1934 and 1944 and often on a theme of fun outdoor activities. Dora M. Batty designed more posters for LT than any other female artist – her 'Rose Garden' of 1932 being one of the most exquisite (4).

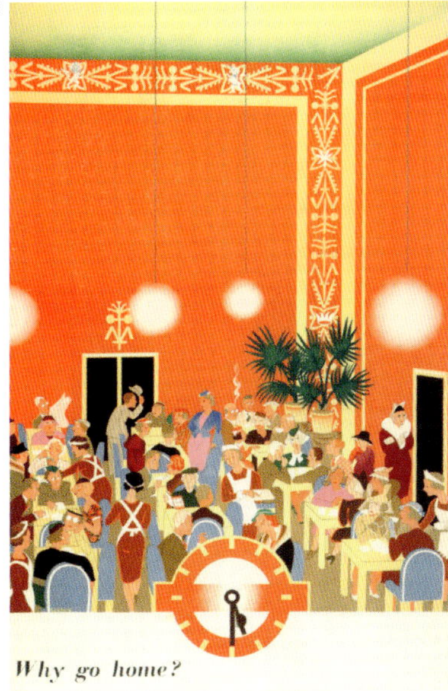

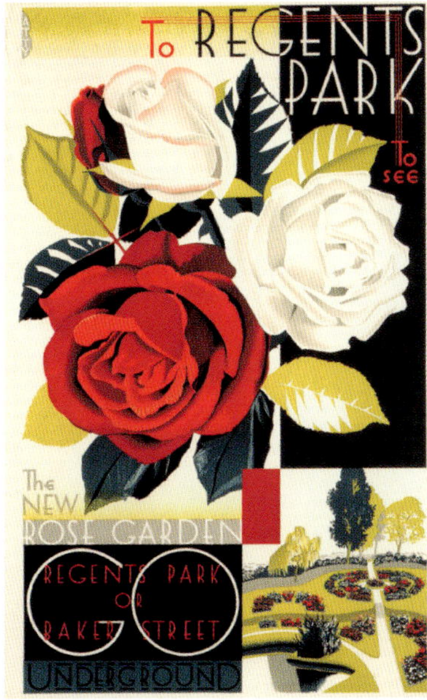

Streamlined trains, 1935–7

Art Deco and Streamline Moderne dominated design on the London Underground in the 1930s and even trains were not immune. An experimental vehicle tried in 1933 was deemed unsatisfactory (p. 158), but by 1935 another version was tested; instead of being tapered *in* it had a flared-*out* prow (front end) and a domed roof with a stylish ventilation grille (1). The trains began running on the Piccadilly on 8 April 1937, to great acclaim by the press. Interiors were comfortable with moquette in pink, grey and cream. They inspired the sub-surface trains called 'O Stock' which appeared in 1937 (2). These echoed the streamlining of the 1935 Stock but with flares along the *sides* as opposed to the front and were provided with a so-called 'Chevron' design moquette by Enid Marx (3). So many were ordered that they proved more enduring than their predecessors – the last of their splayed-out breed ('P Stock') being withdrawn in 1981 after forty-four years' service on the Met, Circle, District and East London lines. 'R Stock' was the last incarnation of the flared trains, with a batch built in the 1950s. Both the 1935 Streamline and 1937 'O Stock' (and their descendants) were classic pieces of Art Deco design, loved by Londoners for decades.

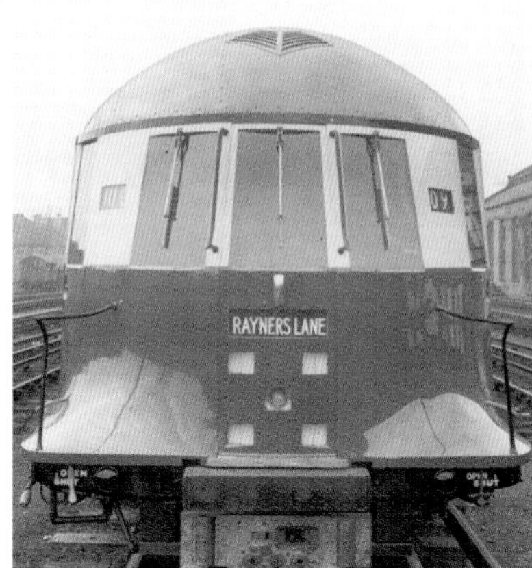

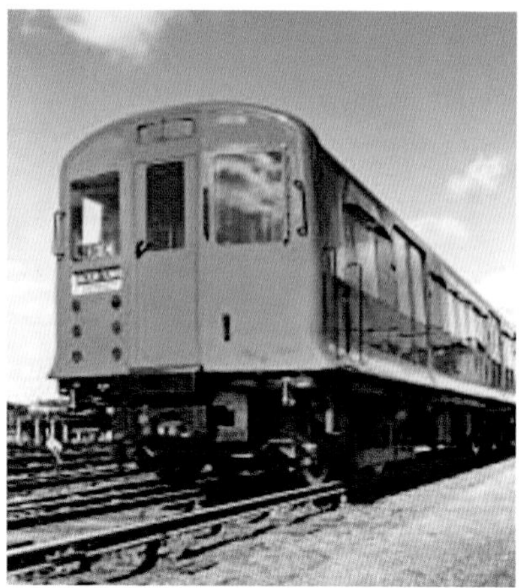

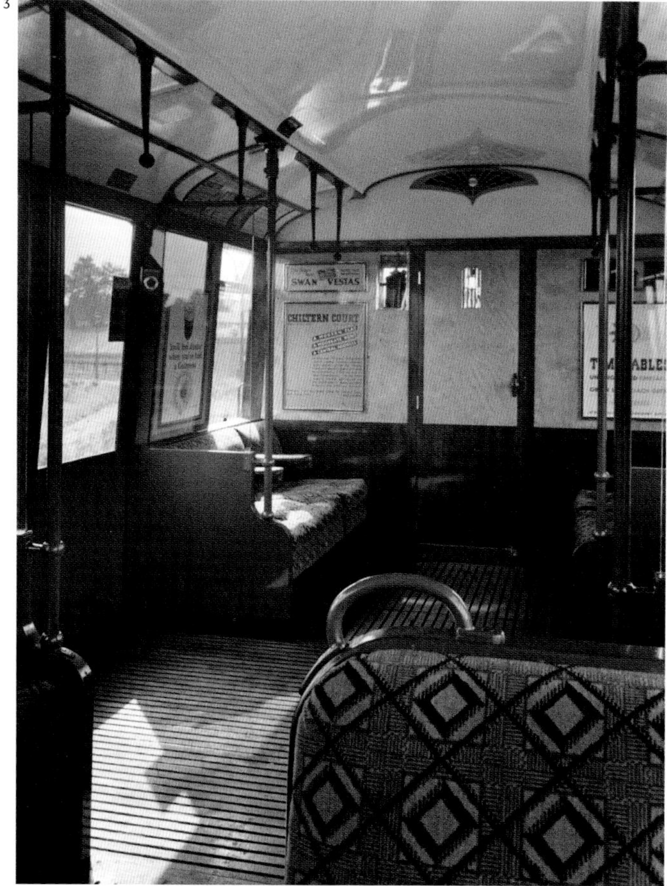

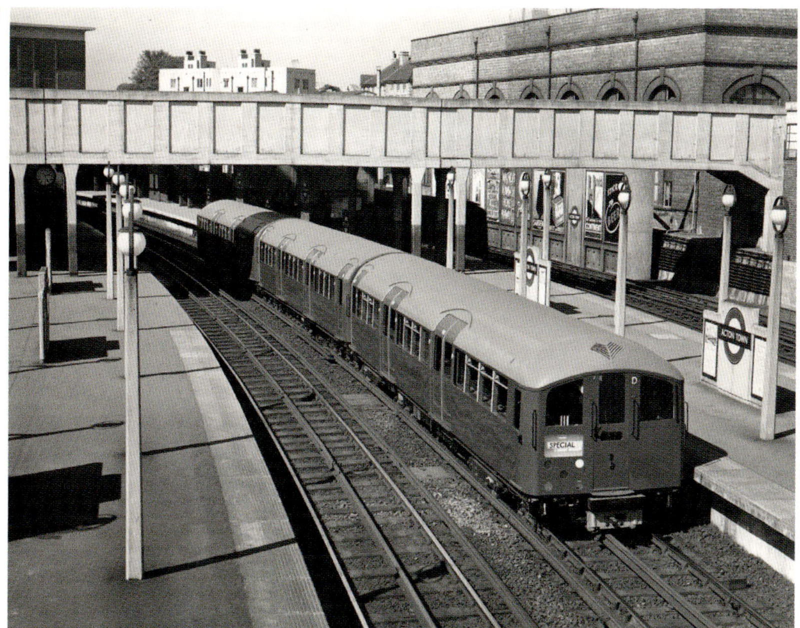

1

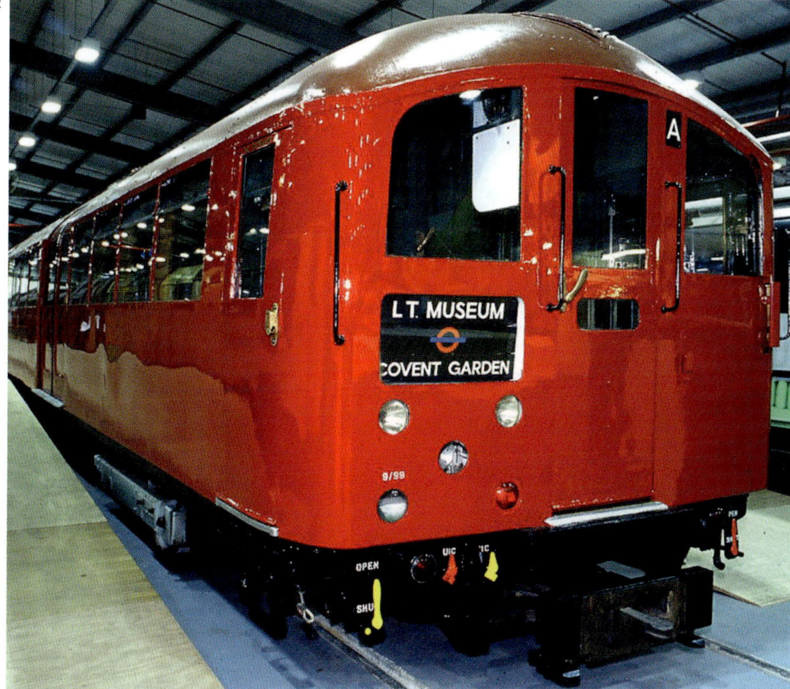

2

Birth of the 1938 Stock, 1935–8

Due to disquiet inside London Transport about the shape of the streamlined 1935 Tube stock, some of them (eventually all) were rebuilt with a flat front (1). The domed top of the cab and the stylish 'feather' ventilation grille were retained but the flare was removed and the cab end flattened out – prototypes were seen from 1937. The resulting design was so clean-looking and functional that it was applied to all the vehicles needed for the proposed expansions (over 1,100 trains in total). The style was named '1938 Stock' and is seen by many as the seminal Tube train, critically acclaimed by the likes of the *Architectural Review* (1942), which commented: '[it] puts the rolling stock of the Paris Metro to utter shame and makes the Berlin U-Bahn appear heavy and pedestrian.' Seating was upholstered in a new moquette, either Marion Dorn's 'Leaf' (also referred to as 'Colindale') or Enid Marx's 'Chevron', and there were new end-of-car ventilation grilles incorporating the car number in a bullseye (a much-sought-after collector's item now, 3), while the Art Deco 'shovel' lamp shades were the same as those used in the 1935 streamlined stock (opposite, 3). Every detail was carefully thought out: even the alarm pull was incorporated into the ceiling profile. Later moquette by Eddie Chapman featured a nested roundel in red and green and became the arche-typal seat covering for this stock (p.191).

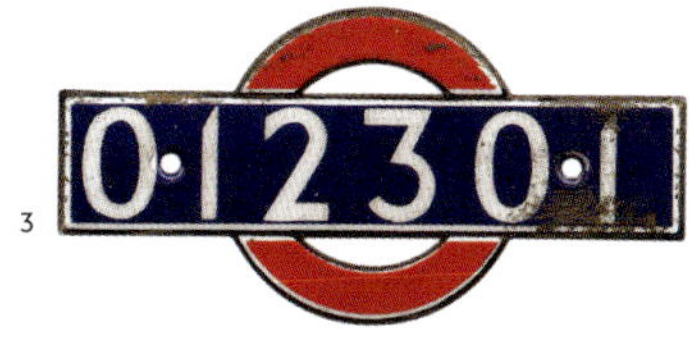

3

Paper trials for heavier metal, 1937–45

Tested for visibility at several busy West End stations (p. 156), paper friezes with the station name and bullseyes repeated along the strip were pasted on platform walls about 2m from the floor during September 1937 at Tottenham Court Road (1) and Strand. To indicate an interchange, a red panel with the words 'CENTRAL LINE' and an arrow was inserted at intervals along the Tottenham Court Road frieze. At Strand there were black panels with 'FOR THE SOUTHERN RAILWAY' printed on them, intended for passengers looking for directions to Charing Cross. Signs with the words 'NORTHERN LINE' in a black panel were also tried at Strand. The experiment was seen as a success and the idea incorporated into the Carr–Edwards signage guidelines (pp. 155 and 192), which stipulated that they could be made from enamel. Due to the steel shortage, however, paper rolls were initially used instead and glued up at most tunnelled stations. Platforms in the new Bakerloo tunnel (opened 1939, p. 196) were given ceramic name friezes, an idea adopted elsewhere after successful trialling. The first enamel frieze plates were positioned along the walls of Piccadilly Circus platforms in 1945, where, oddly, a mistake was made and only the word 'PICCADILLY' appeared (2). The line colour was later introduced in a band above and below the station names, which were in black. The line name was shown in the bar of the bullseye. Enamel versions were installed piecemeal and paper rolls were still being applied up until the late 1940s, many revealed during recent renovations. The name friezes have become a design feature of all tunnelled stations. Line diagrams were also trialled on the trackside wall (shown at Piccadilly Circus in 1947, 3) but these were not so successful.

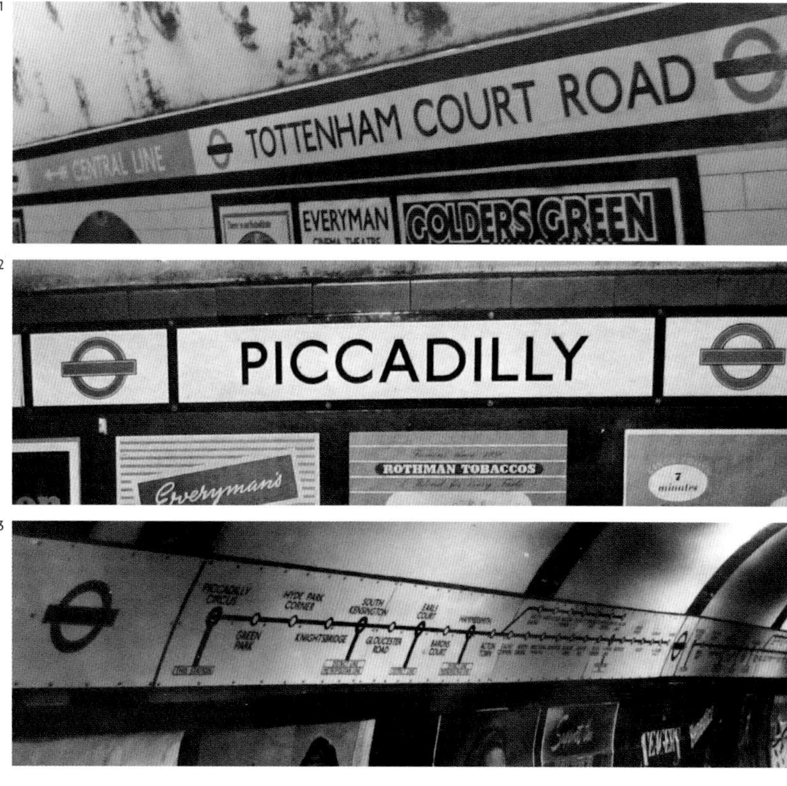

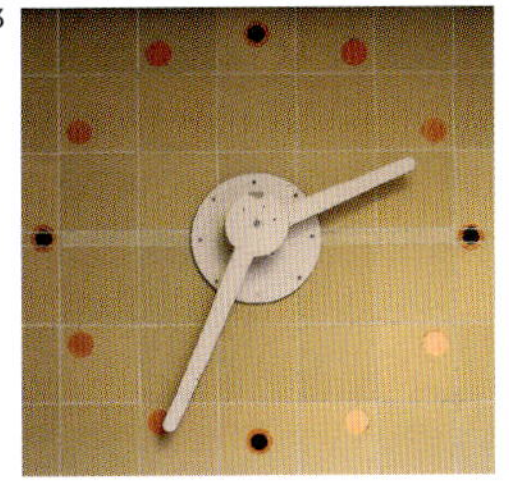

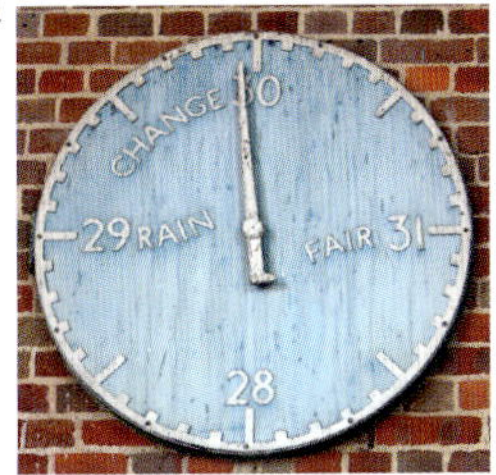

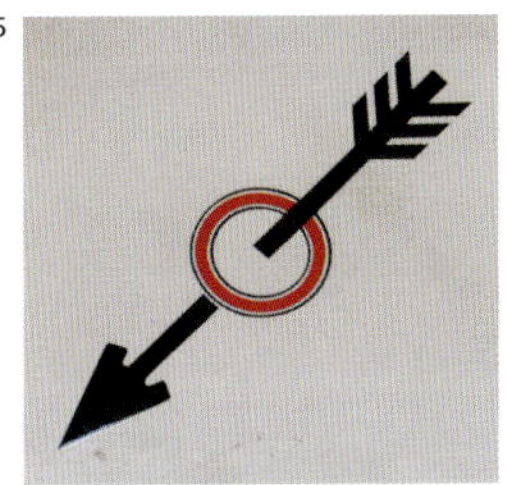

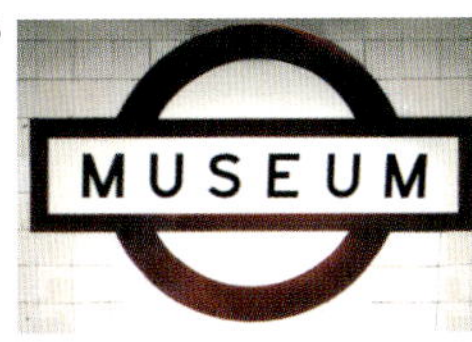

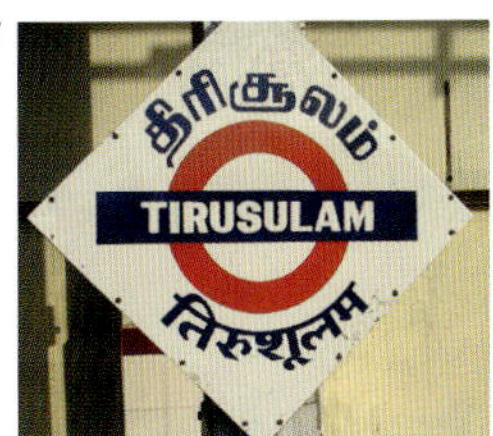

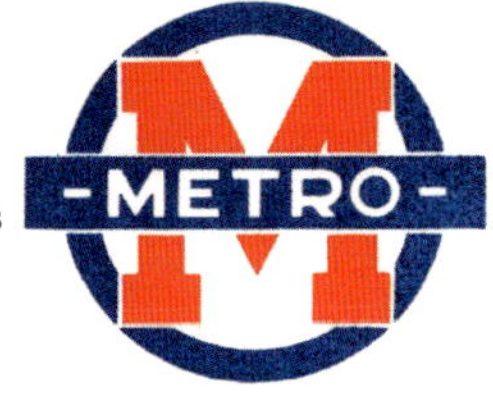

Bullseye replicated around the world, mid 1930s onwards

The bullseye was proving to be a design asset in so many ways, partly because of its simplicity as a logo. It found echoes in station clocks (Ruislip Manor, 3) a barometer (Sudbury Town, 4), moquette (Eddie Chapman's design, 2), signage (Kilburn, 5) and particularly in publicity material. No advertisement for the Underground plays with the bullseye shape better than the celebrated 1939 poster by Man Ray (1). Equating Saturn's rings with the shape of the familiar bar and circle was, like many great ideas, both immediately obvious and a stroke of genius. It is a perennial best seller at the London Transport Museum shop. The bullseye design was also gaining international recognition, imitation being, as ever, the sincerest form of flattery. The shape was adopted in the mid 1930s for logo and signage of the underground Sydney City Rail stations (6), for instance. The closest of all is the one used by Chennai Suburban Railway in India (7). In 1937 the Paris Métro adopted a design that was wholly inspired by London, but swapping the colours to make the ring blue and used red for a capital 'M' set in the centre (8). Variations of this shape lasted until the early 1950s and the system still uses an 'M' in a circle. Transit operators in other cities that have adopted bullseye-type logos include Salt Lake City, Osaka and Tokyo (though this shape has now been replaced).

Implementing standardization, 1938

The 1938 Carr–Edwards report (p. 155) reveals early insights into 'wayfinding', including: 'As the passenger enters the station, those who do not know how to make their journey will find the necessary information displayed in the ticket hall in the form of lists of stations served by the Board's trains, with directions on how to reach each station.' The accompanying 'portfolio of drawings' (1–5) was effectively the world's first known graphic standards manual and it was fairly rigorously adhered to as the resulting signage show (6, 7, 8). Some public-transit bodies took *decades* to comprehend the need for such simplicity (New York City Subway, for example, took until the late 1960s to tackle its hodgepodge of mismatching signs). A large order was placed for enamelled signage adhering to the Carr–Edward guidelines, some of it delayed due to the onset of war and some of it displayed even before line refurbishment was completed (in certain cases never finished, such as the Northern line extension to Bushey). Some innovations had begun while the Carr–Edwards report was in progress, such as these illuminated direction roundels mounted on squat brass columns at the head and foot of escalators (9, 10). This ingenious incorporation of the bullseye shows how flexible it was as a design; the much-loved signs have been restored at heritage stations, even though such whimsical games with the official logo would fall short of stricter present-day guidelines on how the logo may be displayed.

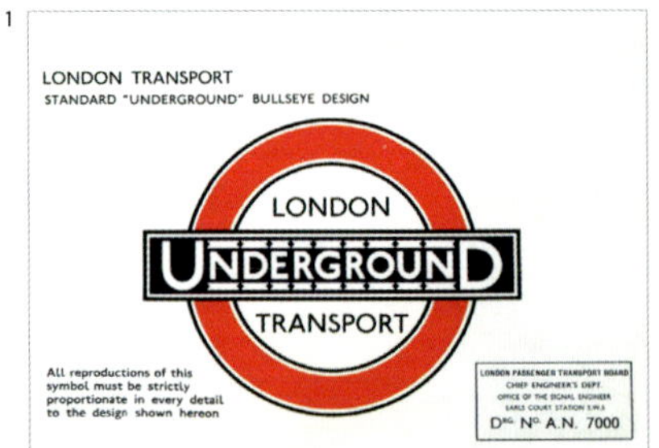

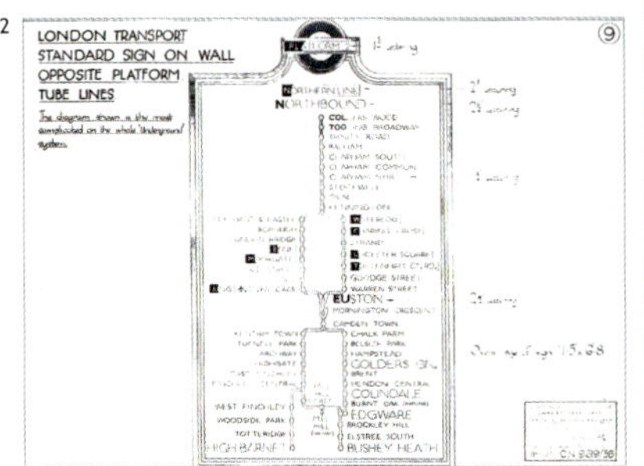

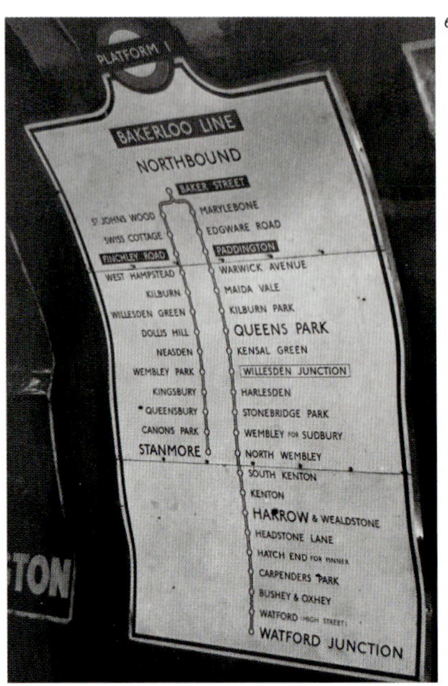

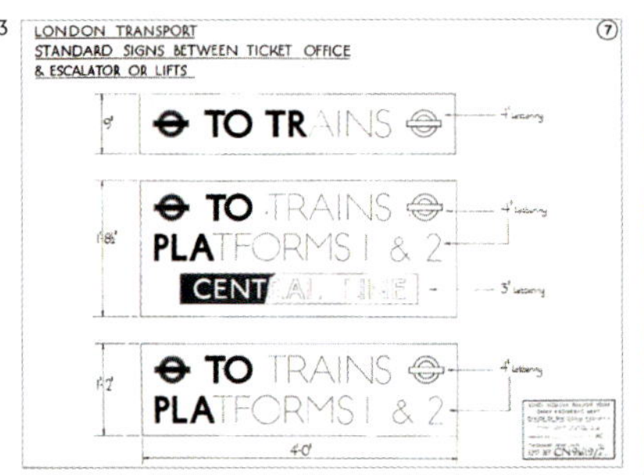

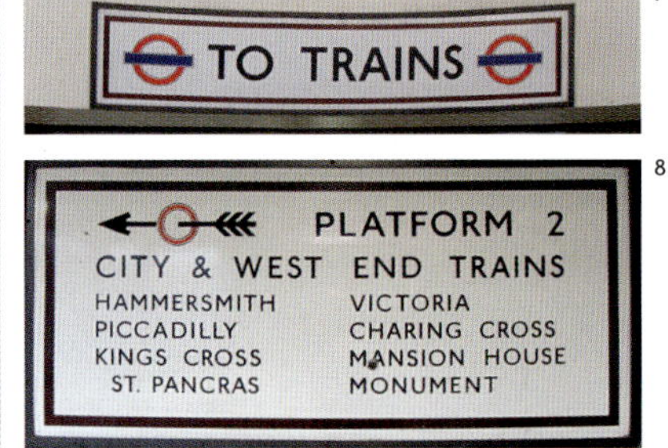

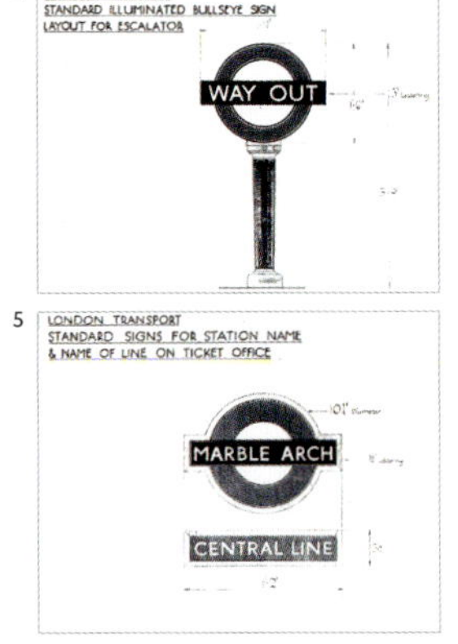

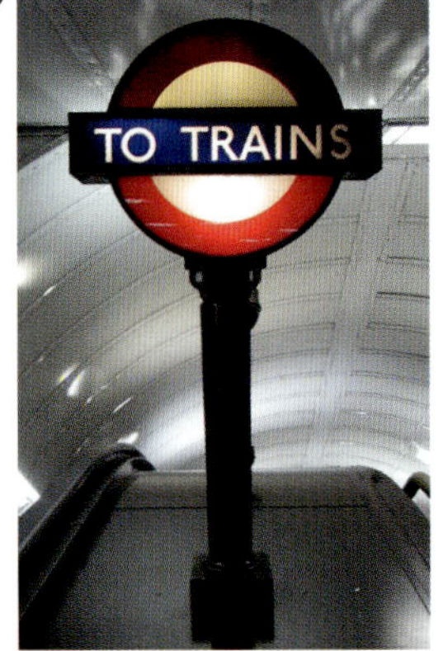

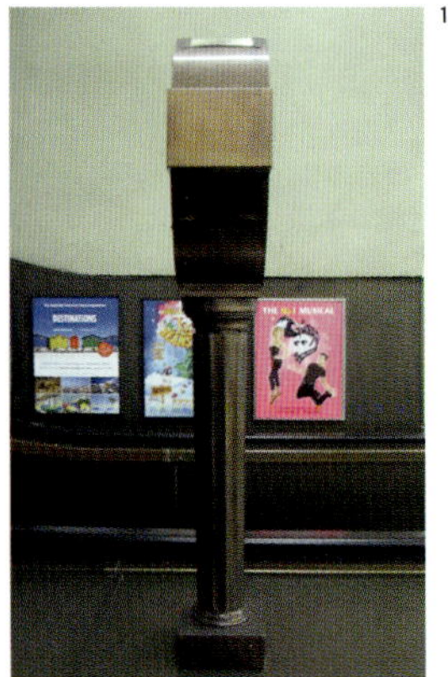

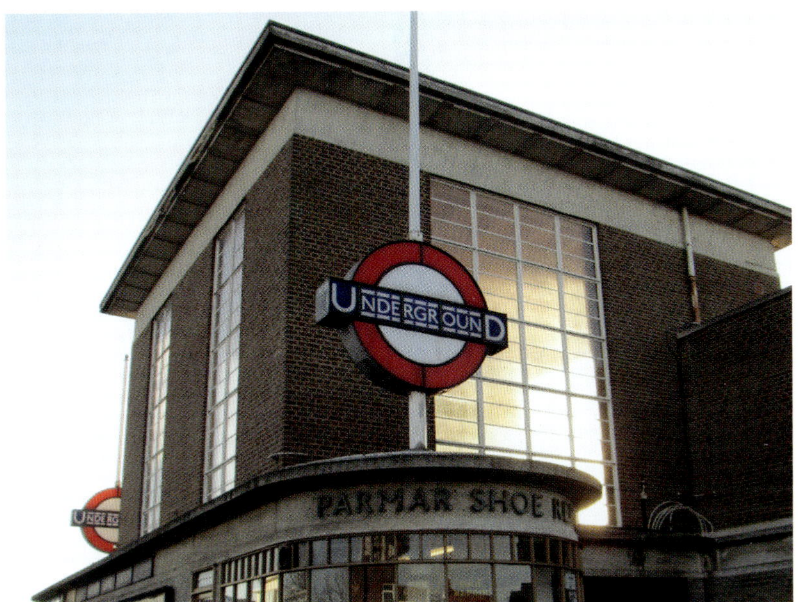

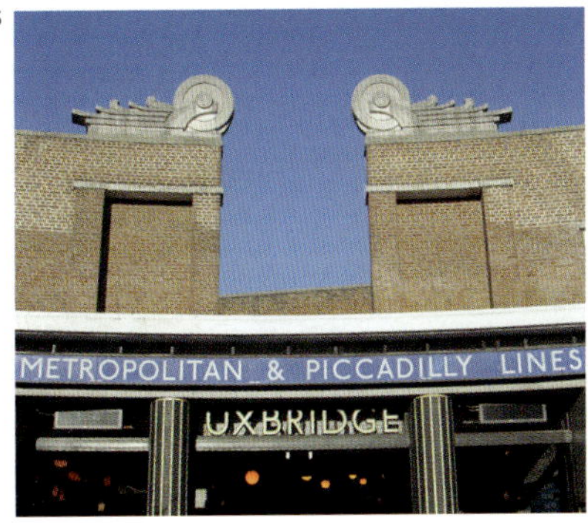

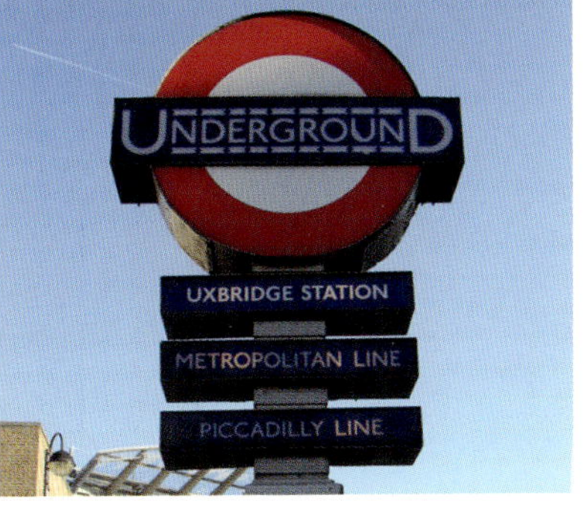

Perfect proportions and stylish statements, 1938

The first draft for a new station at Rayners Lane would have been made by the Met architect Charles W. Clark and doubtless in his somewhat dated rural style. Negotiations over the shared site straddled the handover to the LPTB, so it was bequeathed to Reginald Harold Uren of Adams, Holden & Pearson (p. 154), who came up with the final design. The resulting station, perfectly proportioned with its brick-and-glass ticket hall and flanking semicircular retail units (1), opened on 8 August 1938. At the end of the line from here, Uxbridge station needed re-siting and after rejecting an earlier scheme (p. 157), Pick insisted upon one by Holden, which featured a train shed (2) similar in design to that at Cockfosters (p. 177). But Uxbridge (opened 4 December 1938) had a much grander entrance, with stained glass and two sculpted wheel motifs on the roof (3). In the forecourt stood a new sign: over 4m tall, it was a double-sided illuminated silhouette bullseye, a metre wide and in a shiny bronze casing (4). It sat atop three other illuminated blue strips (also bronze-cased), showing the station and line names, all mounted on a four-sided concrete pole. Such impressive totem-style signs were subsequently installed for several years across the network. Two other schemes of the same era had mixed fates: a massive rebuild of Hillingdon never materialized, but a Holden plan for Ruislip Manor was completed in 1938.

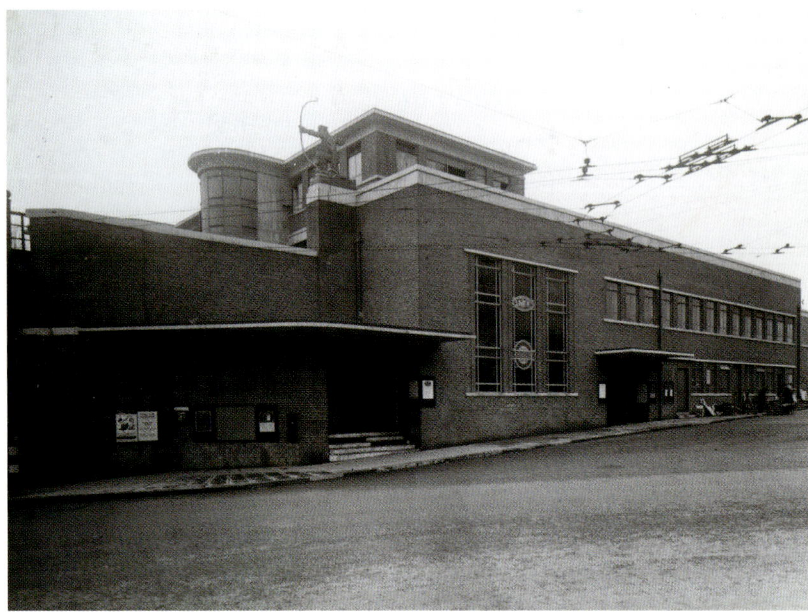

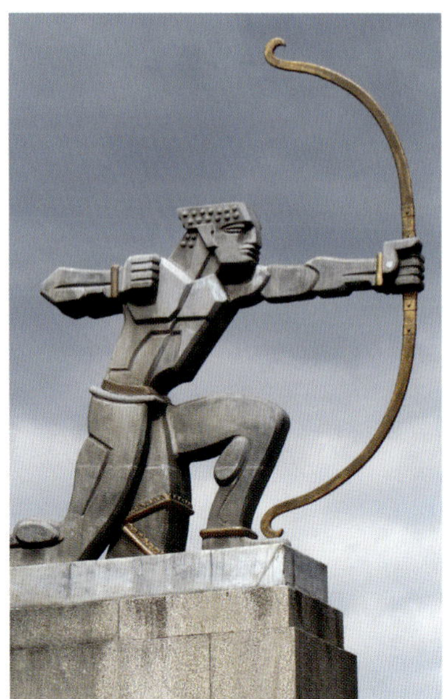

Northern knitting, 1937–9

Given what was planned for the Edgware–Morden line under the 'Northern Heights' scheme (still visible on the 1949 diagram, p. 220), one issue became problematic: what to call it. After many names were considered (including 'Medgway' and 'Edgmor'), and owing to the works being chiefly in north London (of which ironically half were never completed), the route was called the 'Northern line' from August 1937. A steam train LNER line was to be electrified between East Finchley and High Barnet but the first section needed was a tunnel from the original Highgate terminus (which was hastily renamed 'Highgate (Archway)' on 11 June 1939 and then again 'Archway (Highgate)' in 1941) to the surface at East Finchley, where a very large new station was designed by L. H. Bucknell working with Adams, Holden & Pearson (1). Double-height spiral staircases on the platforms led to offices over the tracks and the creation of a striking lead-cladded statue of an archer by Eric Aumonier (2), set on a plinth and with bow aimed towards London. Cast-concrete lamp stands doubled as station-name and poster holders (3). East Finchley, opened on 3 July 1939, has recently been tastefully restored, and is now a Grade II listed building, but it has never reached its full potential as an interchange station owing to the cancellation of the Northern Heights programme in 1953.

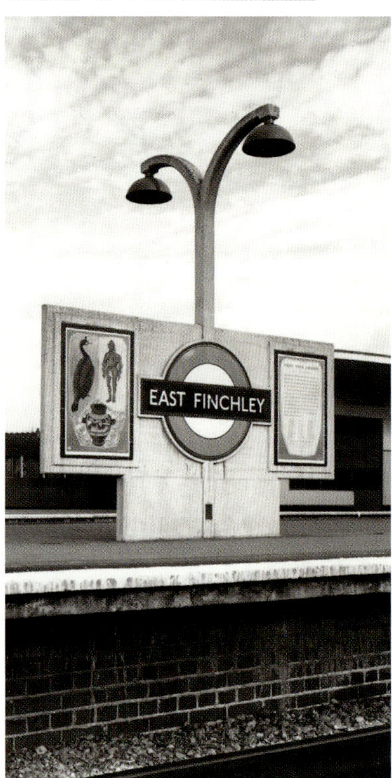

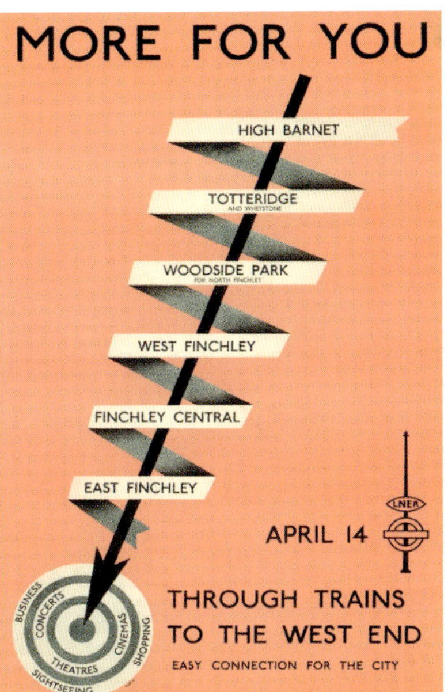

A stitch just in time, 1939–41

The station before East Finchley was to be named Highgate (forcing the older station just south of there to change its name). Built in the tunnel, it did not open until 19 January 1941 as it required complex work to link to the surface platforms that were part of the old LNER route from Finsbury Park (which was to be electrified for the Northern Heights plan). Highgate platforms featured biscuit-cream tiles and station-name friezes by Stabler (like the new Bakerloo stations, p. 196, 3). As the entire project was so complex and costly, very few of the stations being electrified towards High Barnet (with the exception of East Finchley, opposite, 3) had any major work done on them, hence they looked a bit disconnected from the network when opened on 14 April 1941, as advertised on several posters, (1 and 2). Holden did design stations for the entirely new section proposed from Edgware to Bushey, but this part was never completed. Yet more station rebuilds were ready just before the onset of war, for example at Eastcote – a Holden 'brick box with concrete lid' flanked by rounded shop fronts – and at St Paul's, where platforms were reconstructed (1939). Here new signage was installed on railed stairwell entrances and a wrought-iron figure of the saint incorporated into the metalwork (5). The totems outside (4) were similar to those at Uxbridge (p. 193).

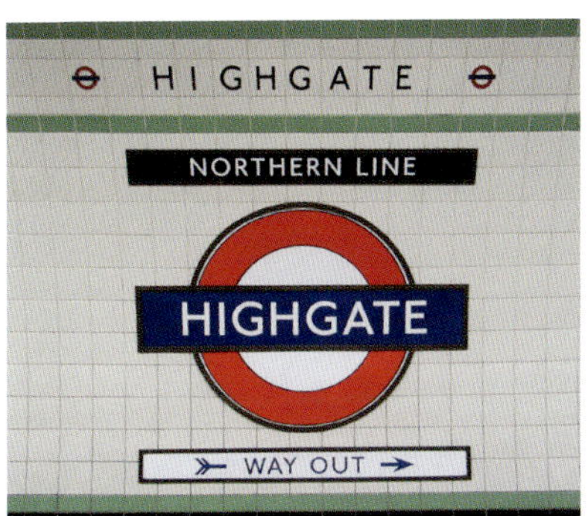

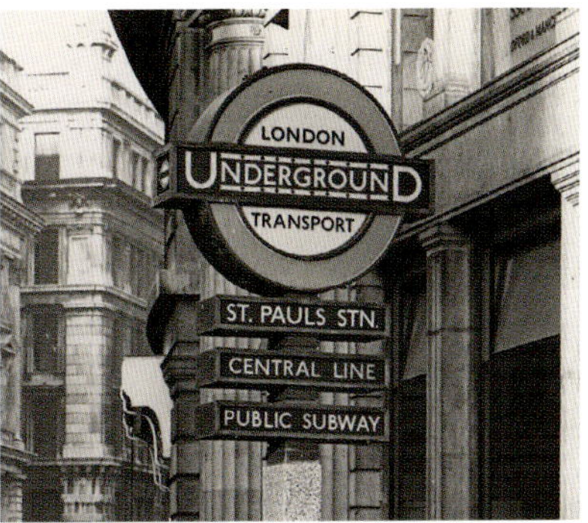

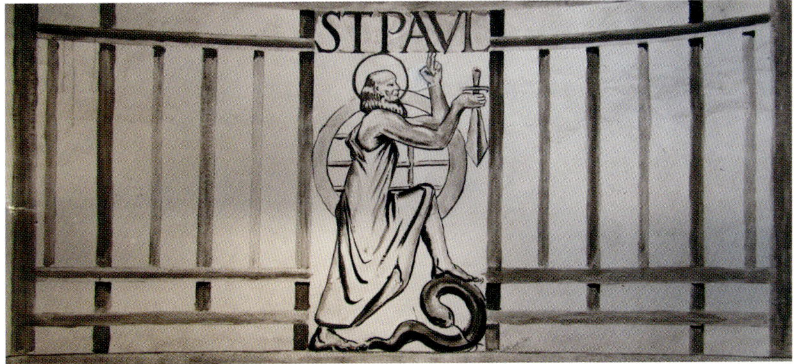

Stabler's stylish signage for new Bakerloo, 1939

Opening on 29 November 1939, the new Bakerloo section was streamlined, practical and stylish. The platforms built at Swiss Cottage and St John's Wood featured beautiful biscuit-cream tiles lining walls and had tiled station-name friezes (2, 3) — also installed on the new platforms at Baker Street. The station name alternated with tiles bearing plain bullseyes. Eighteen special relief-moulded tiles were commissioned from Harold Stabler (shown opposite) and set along the wall on the platform side, intermingled with plain tiles. Nameboard bullseyes were of the outline variety and above each was displayed the line name (and is now part of the Jubilee line, pp. 248–9), with a 'WAY OUT' direction sign below. The escalator shafts had the squat brass uplighters and at the top and foot were bullseyes mounted on stands with 'TO TRAINS' or 'WAY OUT' on the blue bar (p. 192). These stations are regarded by many as the epitome of the Holden/Art Deco era. Miniature bullseyes (30cm in diameter, 5) were placed on the trackside and on the passimeter in the ticket hall. It was Heaps, however, who designed the only new surface building at St John's Wood (provisional name Acacia Road) — a drum-shaped ticket hall flanked by curving wings housing retail units and station offices (1). Such was this station's appeal that it graced the front of a Puffin children's book (published 1946, 4).

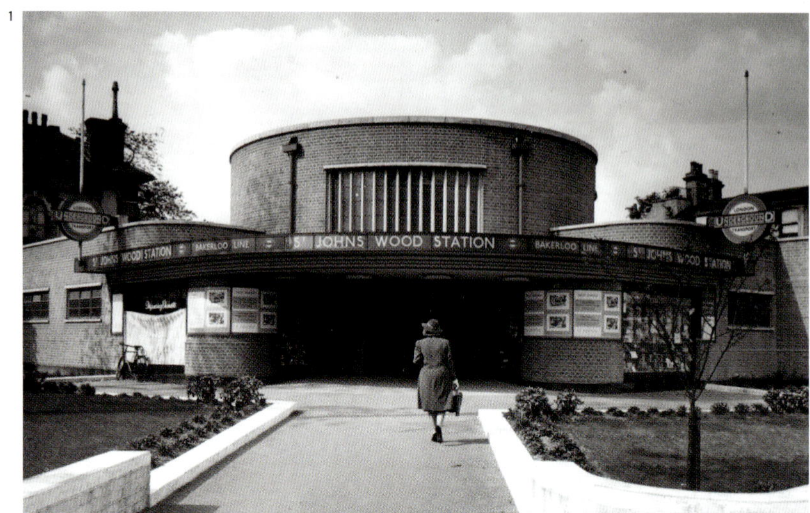

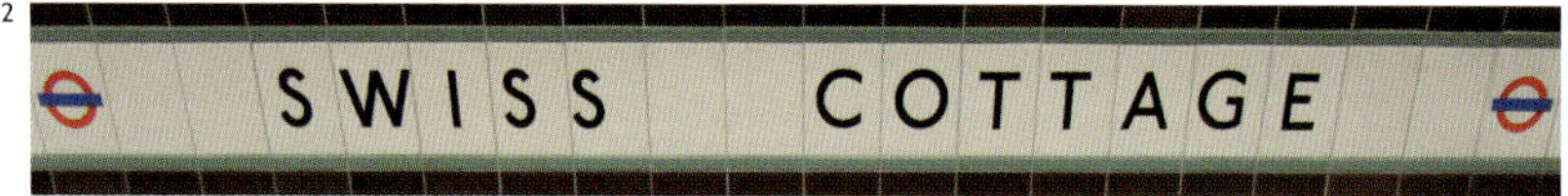

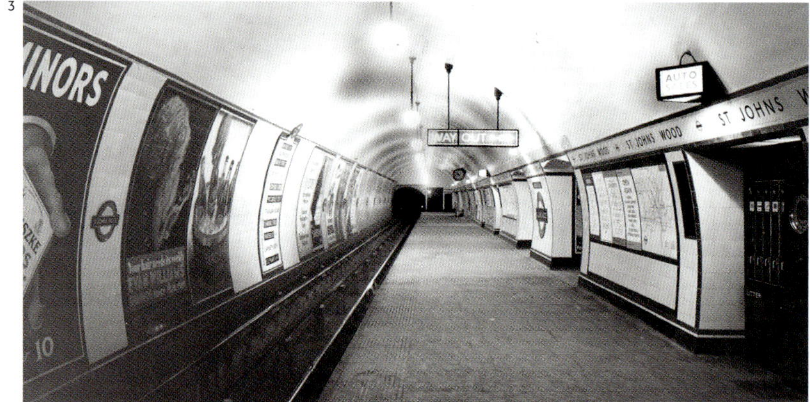

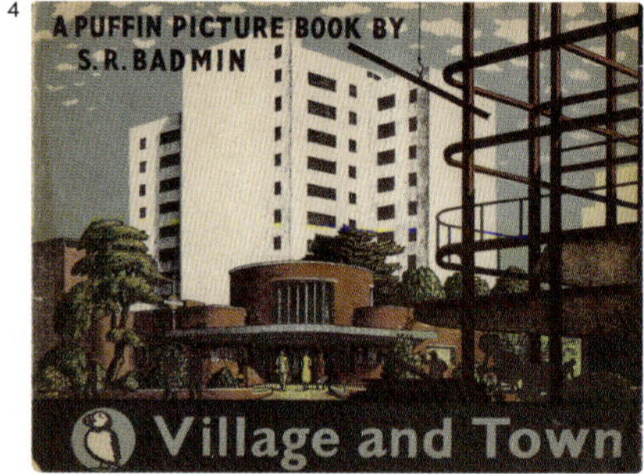

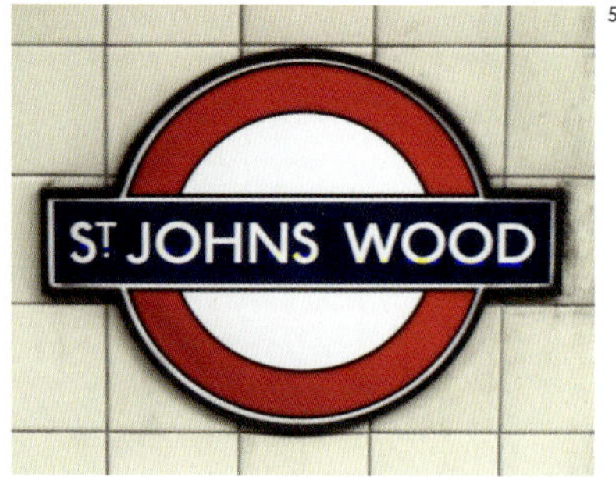

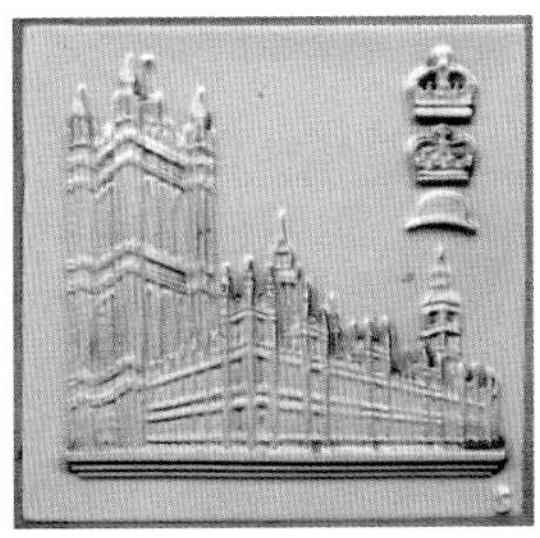
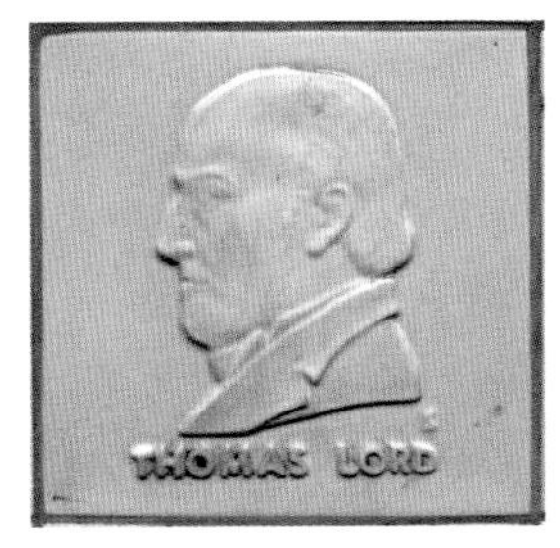
THOMAS LORD
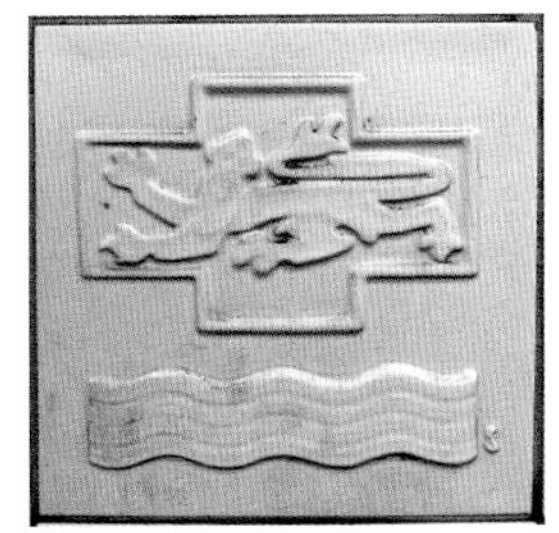
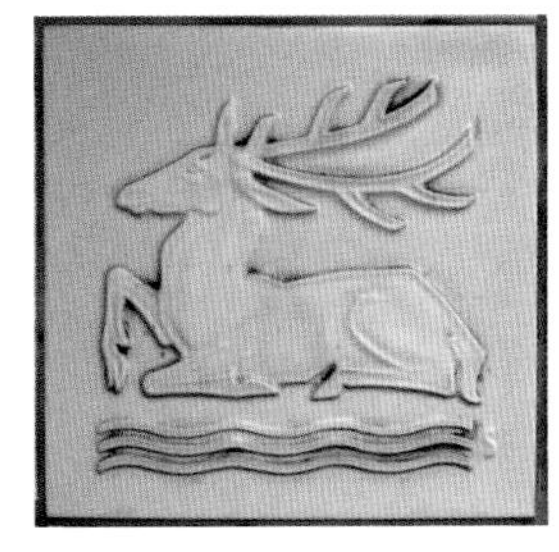
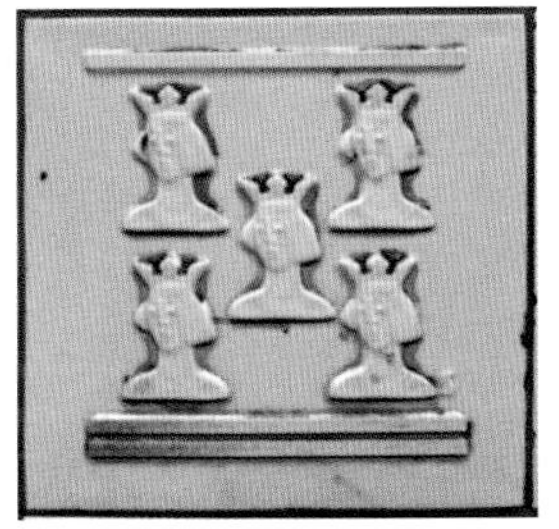
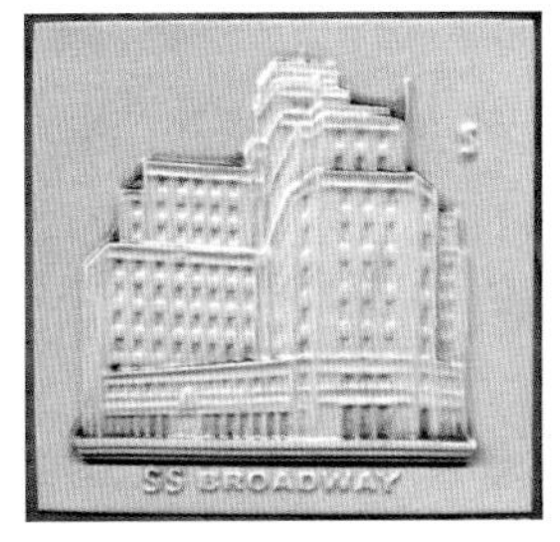
SS BROADWAY
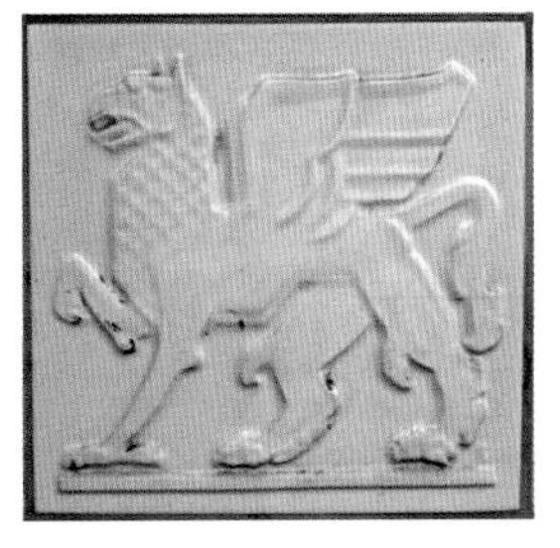
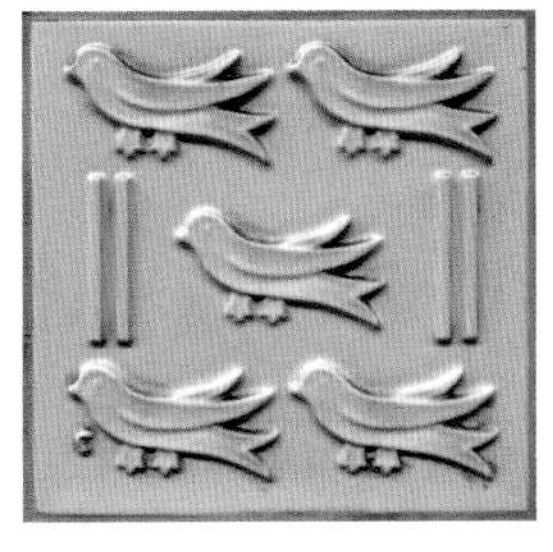
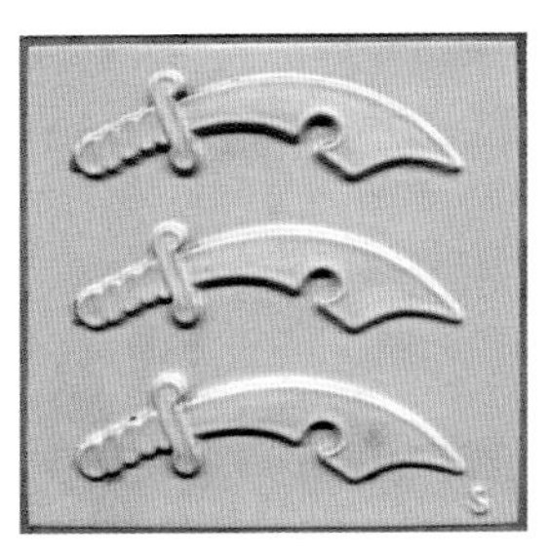
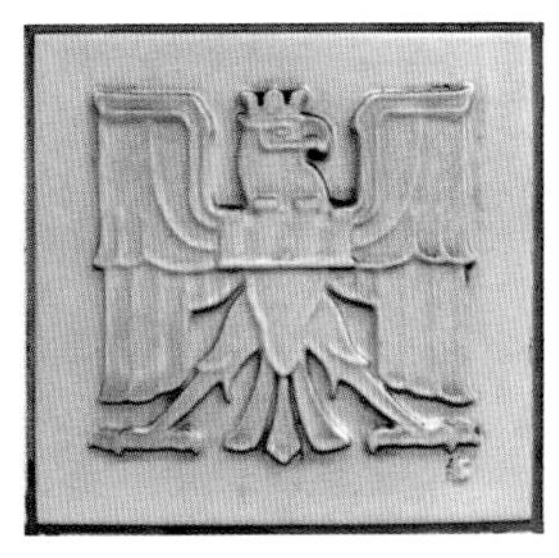
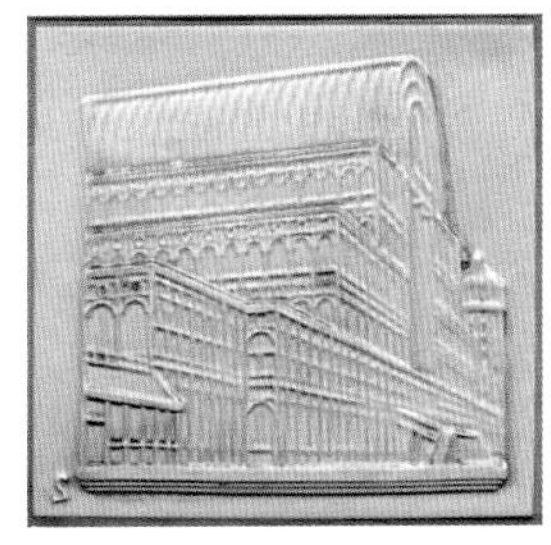
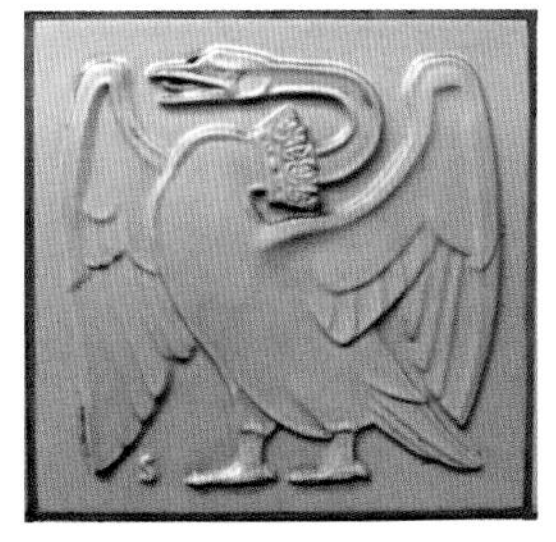
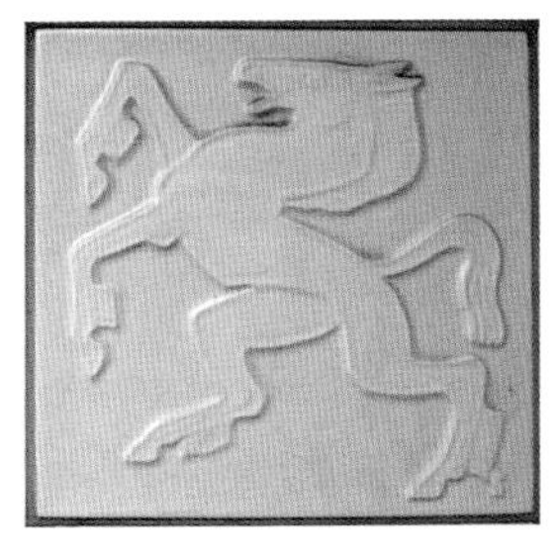
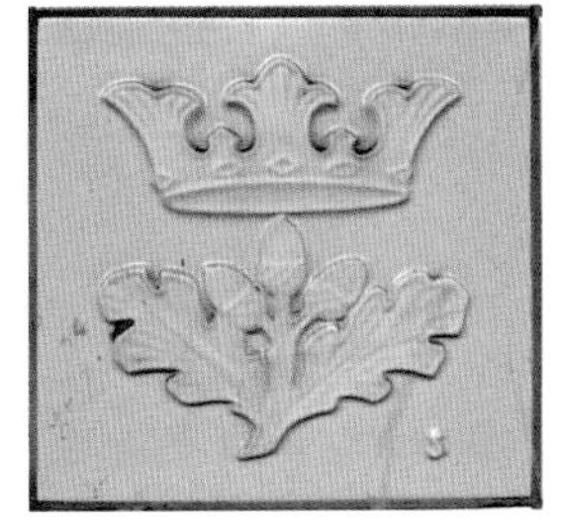
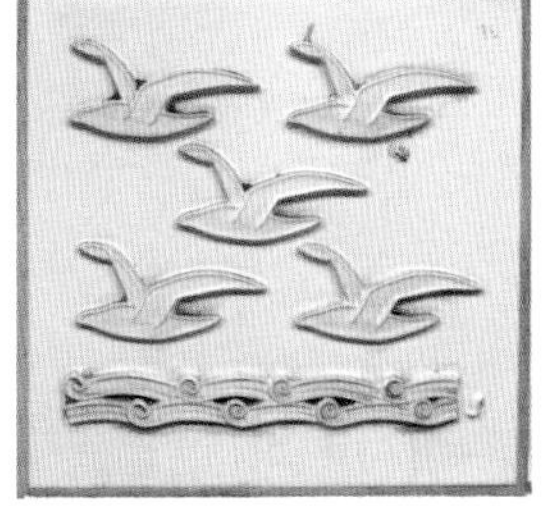
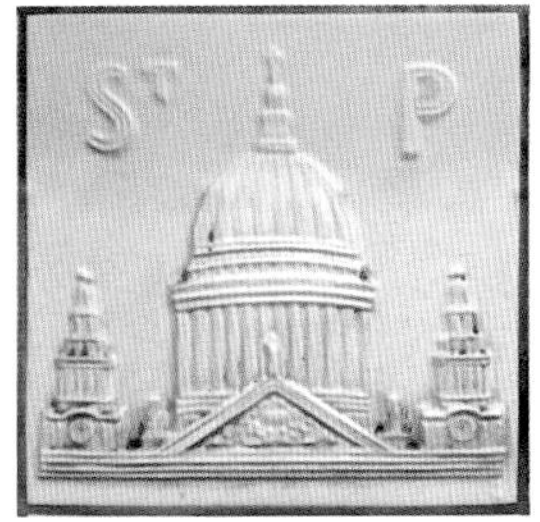
ST P

Bakerloo ballyhoo, 1939–40

Where the tunnels emerged at Finchley Road, the 'new' section of Bakerloo line took over all the stations between there and Wembley Park (while the Met ran as an express route alongside), then adopted the Met's former branch from Wembley Park to Stanmore (p. 180). Many stations received upgrades to bring them into line with the contemporary Underground style: elegant Art Deco waiting rooms with glazed rounded ends were installed at Dollis Hill (2); Kilburn was given a re-modelled entrance between the two overbridges; and Queensbury was provided with a 'mushroom' shelter (1). Multi-purpose concrete lamp standards with built-in station-name bullseyes and poster frames also featured on most island platforms. Any red diamond station-name boards left over from the Met were replaced with LT bullseyes, and all direction signage was updated to reflect the new identity of the route – three-flighted arrows being in vogue (p. 191).

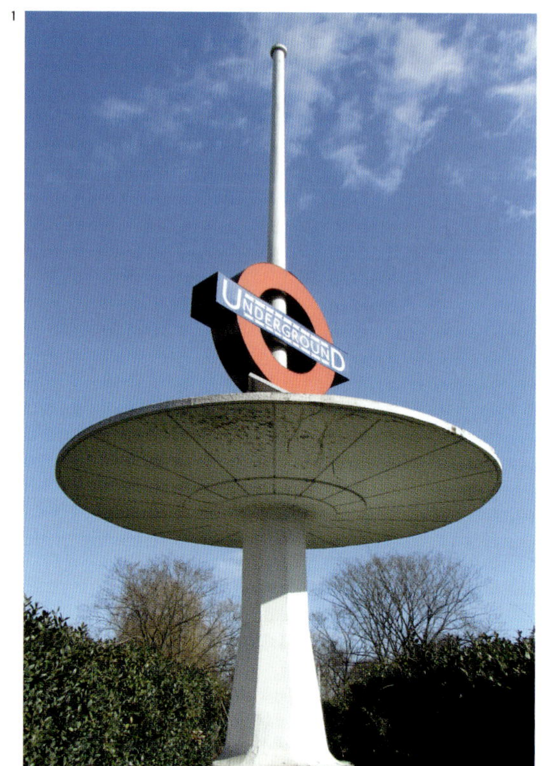

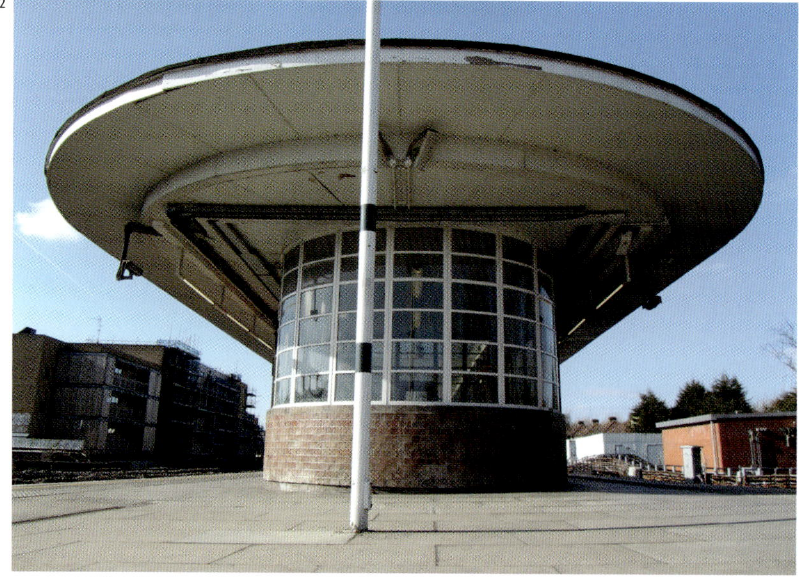

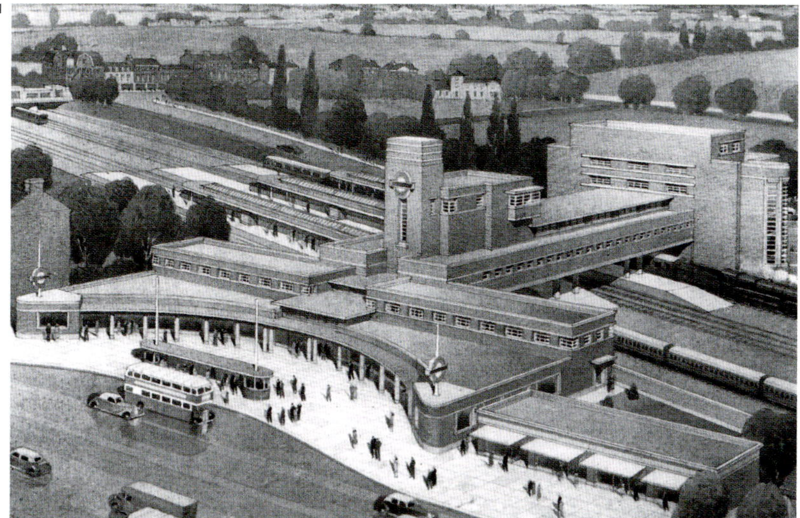

Lofty ambitions dropped, 1940–45

Despite the most valiant efforts of LT engineers and architects, the international crisis placed many of the NWP schemes on hold, some of them never making it back on the agenda after the war. One of these was the enormous project for Harrow-on-the-Hill, which would have created the largest suburban interchange station, combined with offices (1). Though a scaled-down version of it was made (south entrance by 1939 and the north side by January 1943), it was nothing like the imposing structure previously envisaged. On the other side of London, the LNER was working with LT to prepare its line to Epping for electrification and takeover by the Underground. John Murray Easton was commissioned to work on the stations between Woodford and Ongar, but only Loughton was completed, opening on 28 April 1940, although not served by Central line trains until 1948 (2). In preparation for electrification of the western Central line to Ruislip, Brian G. Lewis was to design the stations, but, as with Easton, just one of his designs was initially completed, at West Acton (3 and seating, 4) – opening in November 1940 and, like so much great design, looking equally good seven decades later.

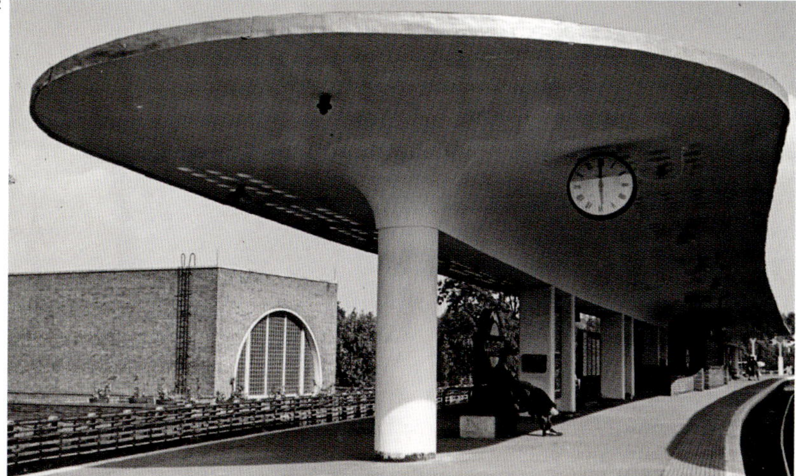

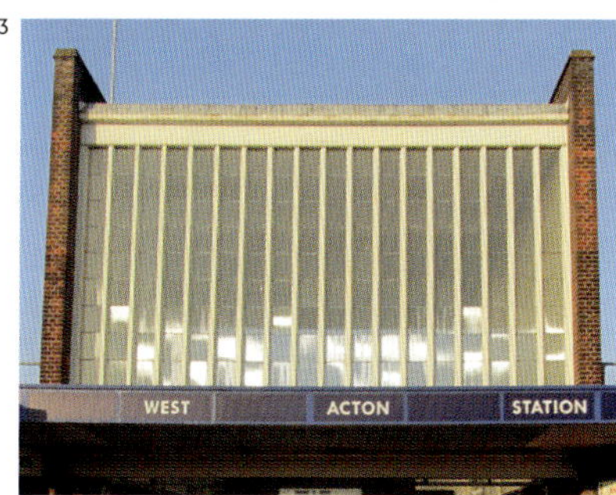

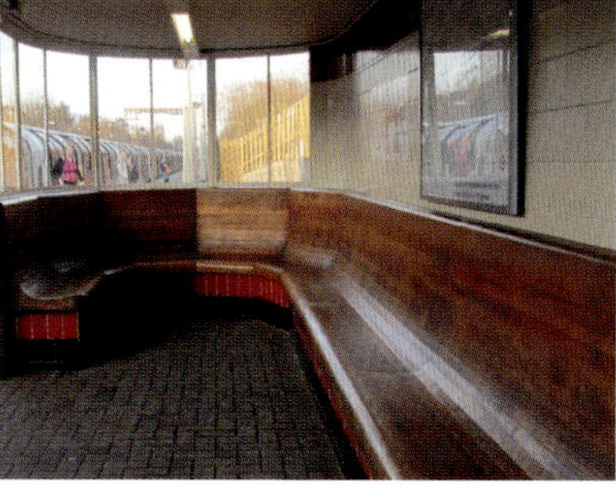

Propaganda posters, 1939–45

Bomb damage sustained by London and the Underground during the Second World War was horrendous (and is amply documented elsewhere – most books in the Bibliography include a section on it), but staff at the publicity office (like so many others) just kept on working, nothing daunted. Admittedly many of the items produced during this period were functional warning notices, especially for those sheltering in the deep-level stations which provided so much protection during air raids (opposite, 8, 9, 10), but the creative spirit was not dampened. Several series were commissioned, such as Fred Taylor's eight morale-boosting 'Back Room Boys – They Also Serve' (1942, 3); Hans Schleger's 'Blackout' set (1943, 2); 'The Proud City', Walter Spradberry's series of six (1944); and Eric Kennington's beautiful studies of individual workers, 'Seeing It Through' (1944, 6). A series by Robert Austin may have featured chiefly historical heroes, but his Churchill poster certainly summed up the mood of the age (1943, 1), as did Lowes Dalbiac Luard's fierce 'Spirit of 1943' (5). The series on Tube manners by popular cartoonist Fougasse are still best sellers (4), while Fred Taylor's evocative 1945 poster of the work needed to return the city back to some kind of normality summed up the 'make do and mend' ethos of the immediate post-war years (opposite, 7).

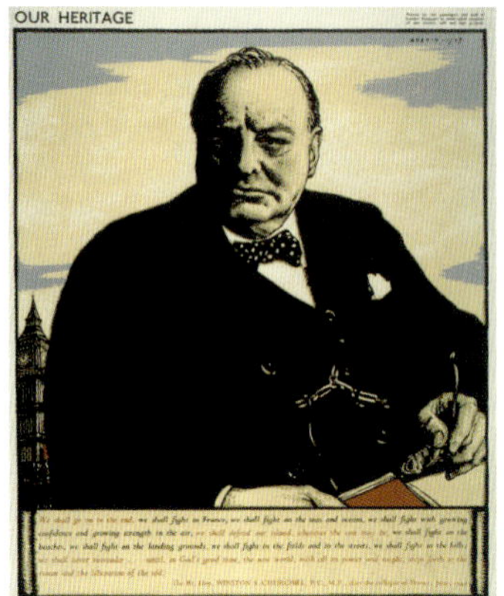

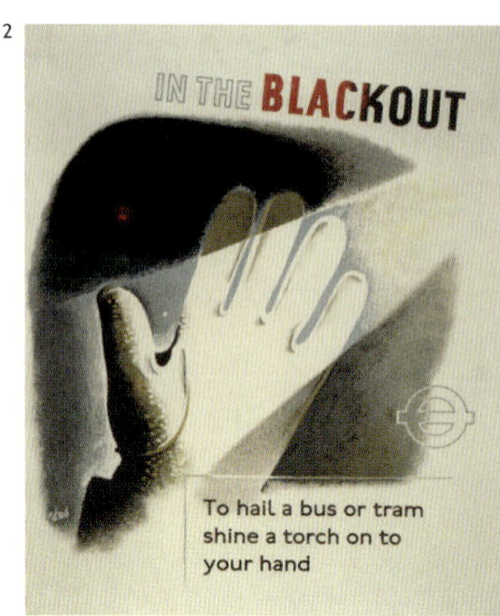

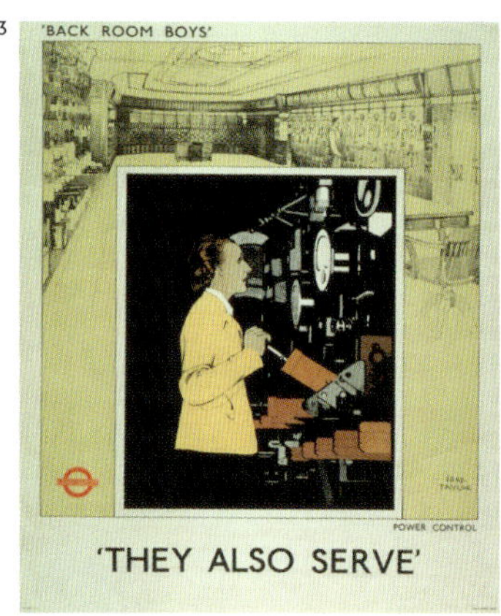

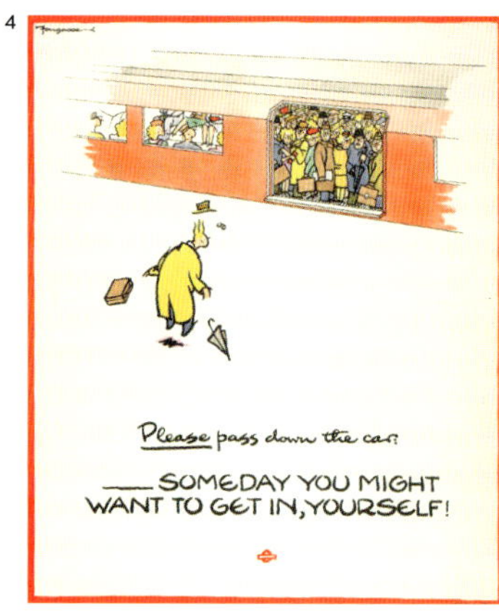

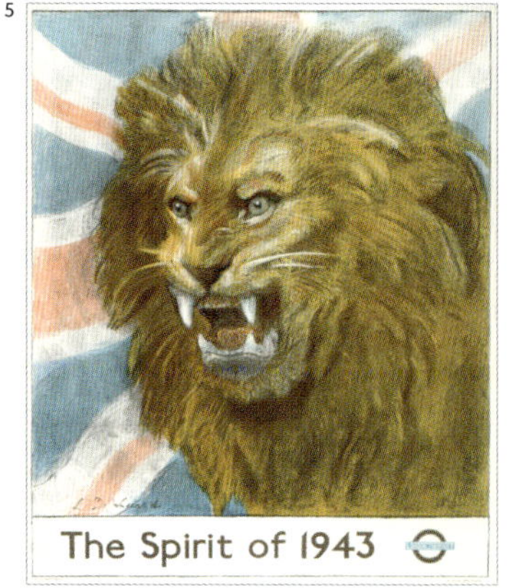

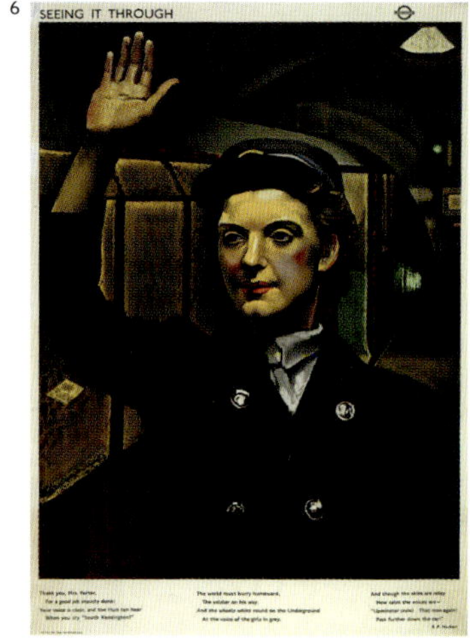

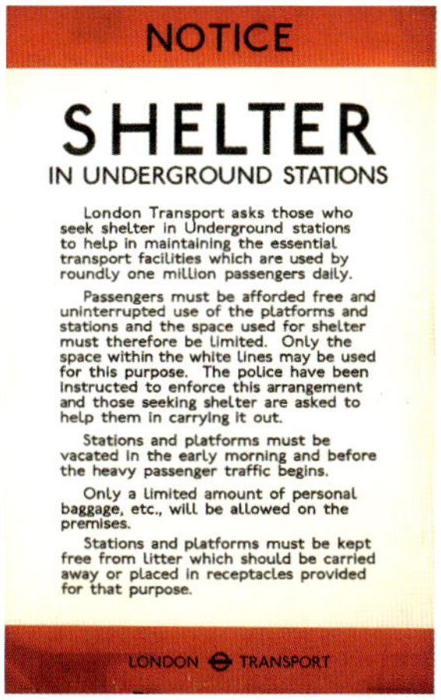

8

NOTICE

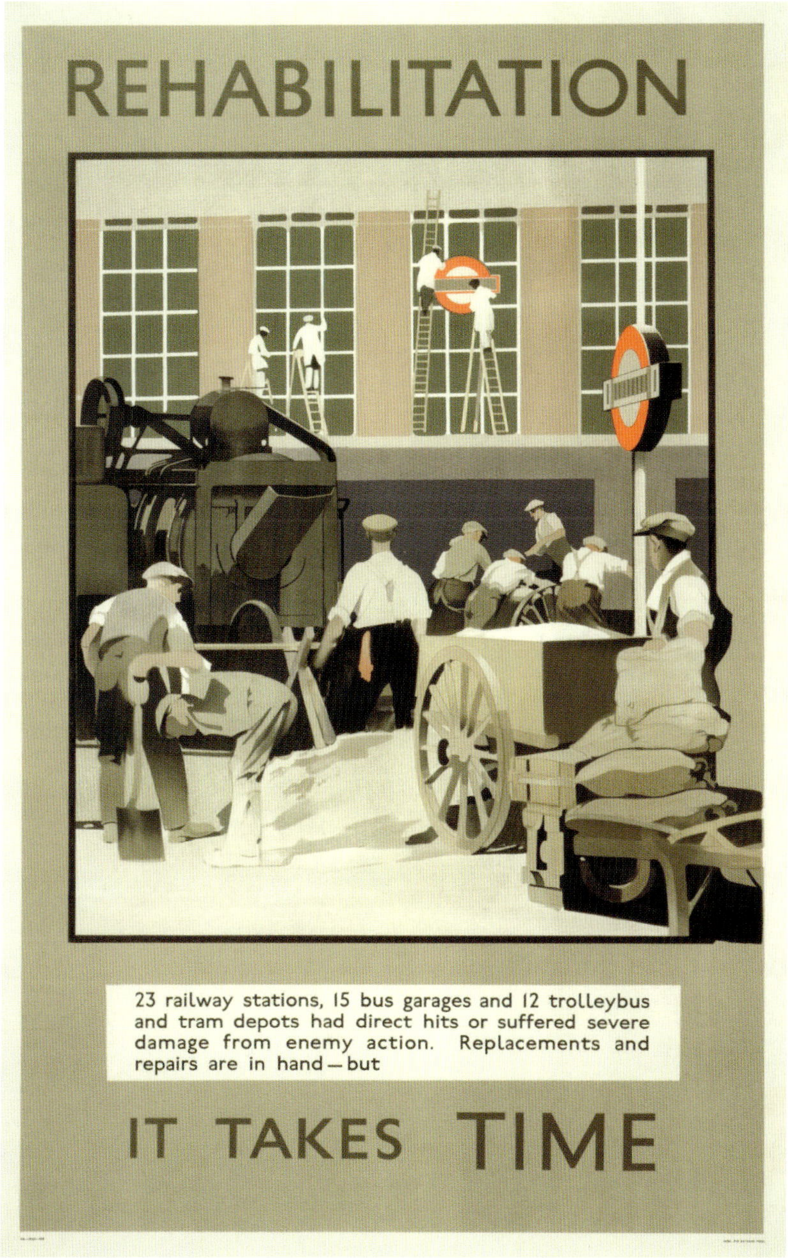

SHELTER
IN UNDERGROUND STATIONS

London Transport asks those who seek shelter in Underground stations to help in maintaining the essential transport facilities which are used by roundly one million passengers daily.

Passengers must be afforded free and uninterrupted use of the platforms and stations and the space used for shelter must therefore be limited. Only the space within the white lines may be used for this purpose. The police have been instructed to enforce this arrangement and those seeking shelter are asked to help them in carrying it out.

Stations and platforms must be vacated in the early morning and before the heavy passenger traffic begins.

Only a limited amount of personal baggage, etc., will be allowed on the premises.

Stations and platforms must be kept free from litter which should be carried away or placed in receptacles provided for that purpose.

LONDON TRANSPORT

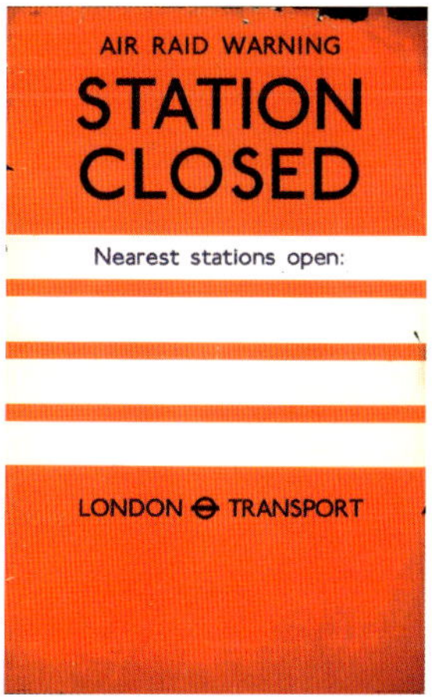

AIR RAID WARNING
STATION CLOSED

Nearest stations open:

LONDON TRANSPORT

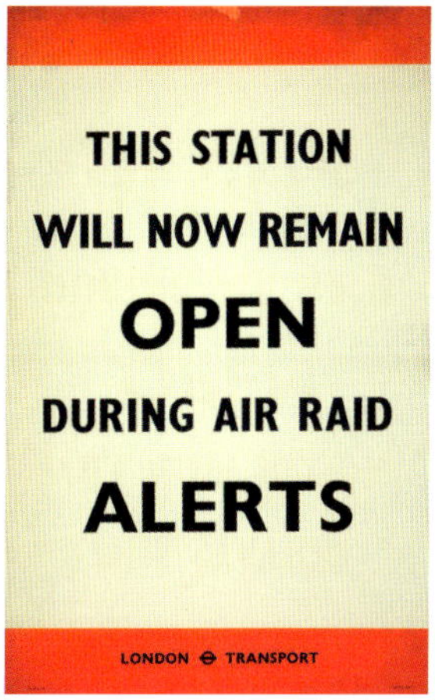

THIS STATION WILL NOW REMAIN OPEN DURING AIR RAID ALERTS

LONDON TRANSPORT

LONDON TRANSPORT
STANDARD ILLUMINATED SIGN FOR EN...
TO SUB BASEMENT STATIONS

"Public Subway" to be shown only where necessary

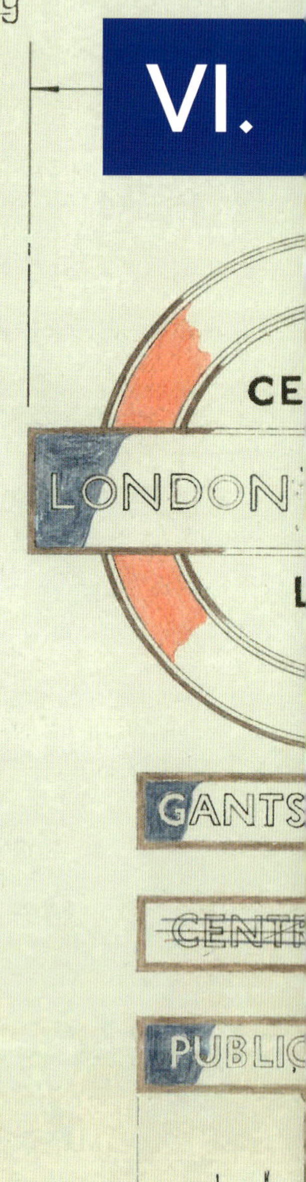

ANCE

SCALE OF $1\frac{1}{2}''$ TO $1'\text{-}0''$

Austerity, Nationalization and Celebration
1946–67

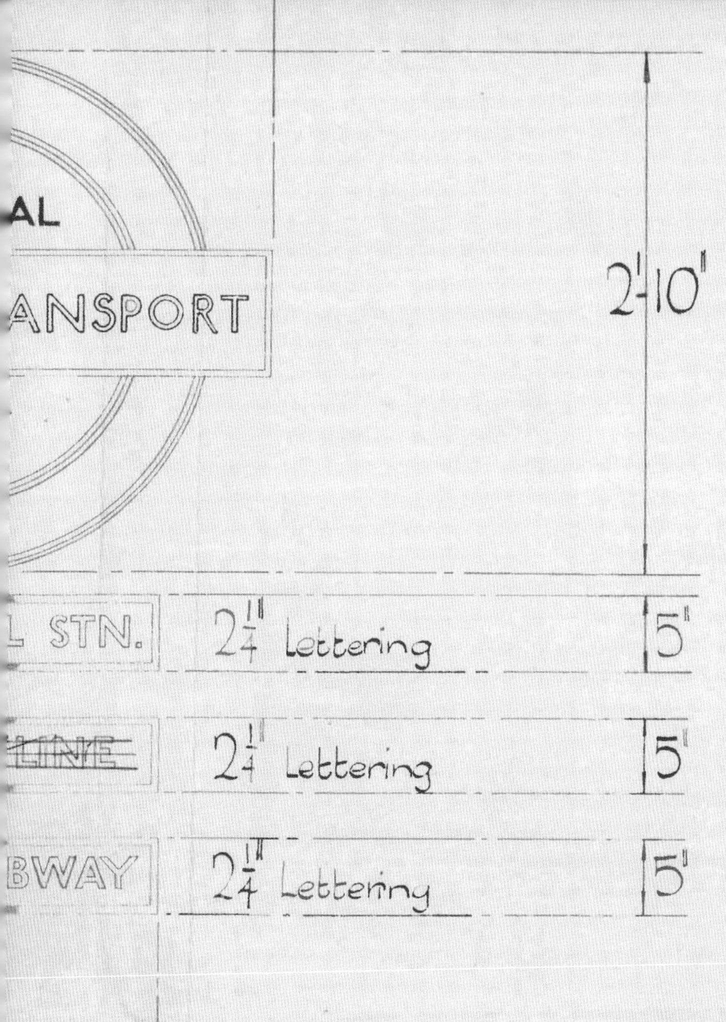

VI. Austerity, Nationalization and Celebration, 1946–67

The period immediately following the Second World War was hard for everyone, but London Transport operations had been particularly badly affected by the bombing and reconstruction would take some time. The New Works Programme, largely halted by the shortage of labour and materials, only partially recommenced in 1946 with schemes that had been planned before the war, notably lengthening the Central line.

Expanding the Central line

Though many of the station rebuilds along the former steam lines being electrified (north, east and west of the centre) had been started by the LNER and GWR respectively, the Board was permitted to oversee the work in recognition of its future role. By contrast, it had full control over rebuilds in central London, such as Notting Hill Gate (p. 228), and tunnel construction. New tunnels to bring the Central line east from Liverpool Street to meet with the District at Mile End (via a new station at Bethnal Green), and through to Stratford, opened on 4 December 1946 (p. 212). Mile End needed significant rebuilding to allow cross-platform interchange with the District, though at Bethnal Green no surface buildings were deemed necessary, just railed stairway entrances. At Stratford these tunnels merely broke the surface to allow Central line trains cross-platform interchange with the mainline station there and then dived straight back underground again to take the tracks to Leyton. The next sections, one to Woodford (by electrifying former LNER lines) and the other via another new stretch of tunnel to Newbury Park, both opened almost exactly a year later, in 1947. Most of the below-ground build had been finished before the war and was completed immediately afterwards. Brand new station buildings had been designed before the war by Adams, Holden & Pearson for the tube section between Wanstead and Newbury Park (p. 215), but after 1945 the schemes were simplified by a new architect, Oliver Hill, and only Redbridge with its circular ticket hall and tower retained many of the features of the original Holden design (p. 213).[1]

Architectural audacity amidst austerity

Holden had proposed several ideas for Wanstead (in the 1930s), but by the time his firm started work on it in 1947 (completed in 1950, p. 215), post-war economies rendered the surface buildings nothing short of bleak — a far cry from those fine monuments to brick and glass of the previous decade.[2] What was lacking at Wanstead, however, was amply compensated for by the outstanding platforms at neighbouring Gants Hill. During the 1930s, some LU engineers had been acting as consultants to the Moscow Metro (which opened with its opulent stations in 1935). Ever since then, the Board had been keen to design a Moscow-style platform area for a London station. That opportunity was taken up

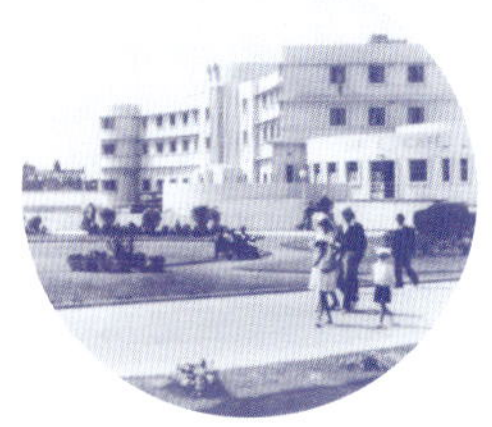

Oliver Hill (1887–1968) was an Arts and Crafts enthusiast who moved towards modernism. Apart from being the LNER's consultant architect and therefore overseeing the rebuilding work of its stations between Stratford and Hainault, he was also responsible for the Streamline Moderne LMS Midland Hotel in Morecambe (1932, pictured), a number of pieces of industrial and interior design and several private houses.

PREVIOUS PAGES: Most of the technical drawings for signs were prepared by the office of the signal engineer. Amended following 1947 guidelines, this one shows how 'Underground' was to be replaced with 'London Transport', with the line name in the bullseye either side of the blue bar (as opposed to being shown in the middle bar below). When the changes were applied in situ, these signs were dismantled and reconstructed minus a bar.

uniquely at Gants Hill (p. 214). Newbury Park with its striking arched forecourt was another architectural triumph (p. 215). The remaining stations on the loop,[3] which opened on 31 May 1948, were all previous LNER surface stations and, aside from a few waiting rooms with curved Art Deco-style windows and the installation of contemporary signage, very little was done to help them blend in with the Underground.[4]

Olympics west prove best for redesigns

Tunnelled Central line platforms in the east followed the Stabler style with biscuit-cream tiling on the walls and smart ceramic name friezes above head height (p. 214).[5] The work to extend the Central westwards was all above ground, hence the lack of Stabler-tiled walls on this section. The old GWR stations on this side of the city were reconstructed to a much higher spec than those in the east, however, resulting in a much more cohesive look. With the staging of the Summer Olympics at Wembley Stadium in 1948, west London was about to see one of its biggest influxes of visitors since the great exhibitions of the last century. The station at Wood Lane (on an odd loop), in particular, was just too awkwardly positioned for the services needed and the planned extension. Chief architect Thomas Bilbow (p. 117) therefore appointed two of his staff, A. D. McGill and Kenneth H. J. Seymour, to design a new station, White City, just north of the original site that could both accommodate the crowds and allow a correct alignment of the tracks for the westward extension. Their resulting design was very much in the Holden mould: the characteristic 'brick box with a concrete lid', incorporating all the best features from the earlier stations – the exposed brick, clerestory windows, biscuit-cream tiling and bronze fittings. Despite its 'crush hall' for peak-time overflows and planned (but never built) subway to the stadium, the station, which opened on 23 November 1947, rarely saw big crowds after the Games, although it won an architectural award four years later.[6]

The first part of the new western section opened on 30 June 1947, with stations at Hanger Lane[7] (another circular ticket hall in fine style), Perivale and Greenford, both featuring curved frontages (all pp. 216–17). The section from Northolt to West Ruislip opened on 21 November 1948, though reconstruction of the station buildings was subject to severe cost cutting and they are therefore of lesser architectural interest.[8] The sole features of any merit were the platform-roof concrete canopies and the station furniture.[9] Only the terminal station, West Ruislip, went one step better, with a large glazed frontage (p. 228).

The last section of the Central line expansion programme, Loughton to Ongar, was transferred to LT services on 25 September 1949, but although the tracks as far as Epping were electrified, the section between there and Ongar was only deemed worthy of being operated by a steam-powered shuttle.[10] Even less effort was put into restoring the old LNER stations than had been at the former GWR stations to West Ruislip, although the entrance at Debden was eventually rebuilt in 1974.

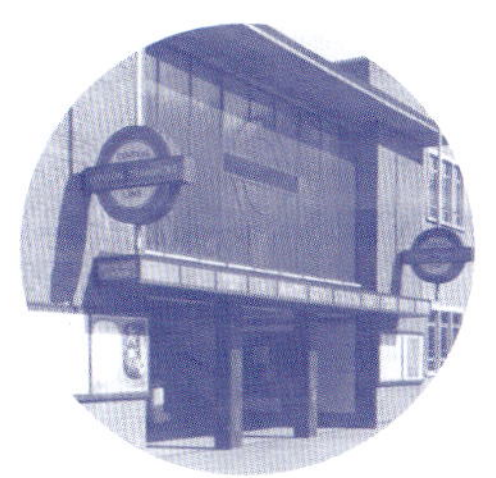

Kenneth James Hyde Seymour, born in London 1910, become the Underground's chief architect 1960–74. Although his only major credit is for White City station (pictured), he supervised the design and architecture of the entire Victoria line project.

Burgeoning publicity cut short by nationalization

Despite the unfortunate corner cutting at certain stations, the Central line extensions did include a handful of architectural gems and the new service was well received by the public as it brought large swathes of east and west London into the Underground network that had hitherto been unserved. One of the key drivers as ever was the LU publicity office, which produced a number of posters and pamphlets promoting the extensions (pp. 210–11), along with temporary signage directing spectators to Wembley for the 1948 Olympics. The new publicity officer was Harold Hutchinson (p. 208). Shortly after his appointment, however, the activities of the publicity office were put on hold following the nationalization in 1948 of the LPTB, renamed the London Transport Executive and now under the control of the British Transport Commission (BTC).[11] With so much rebuilding and modernization needed elsewhere (especially on the mainline railways, where design took centre stage[12]), improvement to transport in the capital – which by contrast had seen major investment in electric trains and new stations before the war – was somewhat curtailed. It was not until 1962, when the BTC was finally abolished, that the Executive, rechristened the 'London Transport Board', regained its autonomy and could push for much-needed improvement.

Revisions to the Carr–Edwards report

While publicity in general may have been more subdued during the post-war era, signage and maps came under close scrutiny following a list of amendments in 1948 to the 1938 Carr–Edwards report on signage. It chiefly recommended:

- Dropping the word 'Underground' (p. 218)
- Restoring lighting to pre-war levels[13]
- Adopting a system of coloured direction lights in passageways[14]
- Installing route-planning indicators (p. 219)[15]
- Adding the route diagram frieze above the tracks (p. 190)
- Placing geographic maps at station entrances
- Colour-coding circles for interchange stations on line diagrams (p. 226).

Oddly, of all the proposals made only one stood the test of time: using brighter, fluorescent lighting. The dropping of the logo was a serious error of judgement for a brand name which had taken forty years to build. The word 'UNDERGROUND' was removed from the blue bar on maps, publicity and a large number of station signs, to be replaced with the 'LONDON TRANSPORT' wordmark (or 'RAILWAYS')[16] (p. 218). While it was understandable that the Executive wished to stamp its authority on all services, it must have been confusing to visitors at some Underground stations trying to work out what mode of transport they might be entering.[17] This policy decision lasted precisely eight years before being overturned (p. 226).

Amendments to the 1938 report that stood the test of time were concerned with line colour/designation. The Met and District had both been shown in green on maps from 1937 – unhelpful, to say the least; the 1948 revisions wisely reintroduced purple for the Met. The Inner Circle was renamed the 'Circle line' and shown in yellow on frieze plates and maps (encased in a fine black outline to aid legibility, p. 226). Renewed emphasis was put on providing lists of stations next to ticket machines, with prices alongside. The previous arrangement of making terminal stations appear larger than others was overturned, thereby compelling London Underground to refer to directions by compass point rather than end-of-line terminus.[18] It was also recommended that beneath every station-name bullseye on the platforms there should be a 'WAY OUT' sign and direction signage to any exchange stations. This recommendation was carried out on surface and tunnelled stations, although not exhaustively.

The manual of graphic standards was revised as a consequence: the need to alter the logo to 'London Transport' meant the drawing up of several amended guidelines in 1949 and again in 1954, where further simplification was introduced to the bullseye and other outdoor signs (p. 219).

Major events test Underground design

Even though very little investment was made in the Underground during the 1950s – with the exception of the work at Notting Hill Gate (p. 228) – ongoing station repairs continued. Bomb damage at Sloane Square had destroyed a recent rebuild, for example, and the station was restored by 3 May 1951 (p. 222). With an eye to the upcoming Festival of Britain, a handful of improvements were carried out to reflect its forward-looking spirit. The south side of Charing Cross (now Embankment) saw the removal of Ford's 1913 mosaics and the introduction of more Portland stone, while architect Jack Howe redecorated a few centrally located District line stations and provided fashionable new platform kiosks (p. 228). All such projects delighted in the use of new materials, including lighter-weight tiling, asbestos suspended ceilings, melamine and perspex – if with mixed results (p. 228).

Planned originally as a centenary celebration of the 1851 Great Exhibition, the Festival of Britain was conceived as a 'united act of national reassessment', conveying a sense of progress and optimism following wartime devastation and the misery of rationing.[19] Permanent and travelling exhibitions were set up in (or toured around to) major cities all over the UK, but the focus was the South Bank (p. 222) north-west of Waterloo, where Sir John Burnet Tait and Partners built a temporary joint entrance to the mainline and Underground stations, known as Station Gate.[20] Located on York Road, it sat between the Royal Festival Hall[21] and a 90m-high futuristic-looking structure called the Skylon.[22] Abram Games's 'Festival Star' emblem and LT poster, meanwhile, seemed to sum up the design ethos of the age, with nods both to the nation's past and its future.

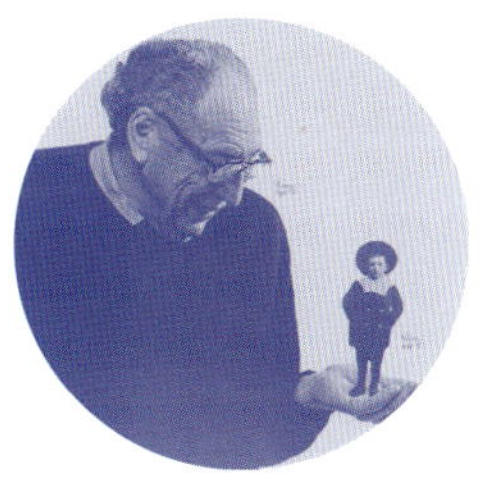

George Him (1900–1982) (pictured 'holding' his younger self) and Jan Lewitt (1907–91), both of Polish descent, set up a design partnership in Warsaw specializing in public-information posters. Known for its witty style, Him's work was used by numerous companies, including Schweppes, El Al Airlines, *The Times*, Thames TV and the BBC. Lewitt-Him made only two posters for the Underground but both were in their humorous and arresting style (p. 210).

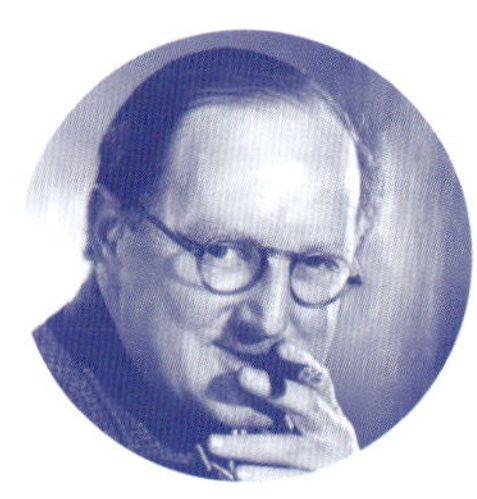

Harold Frederick Hutchinson (1900–1975) was LT publicity officer 1947–66 and Design and Industries Association chairman from 1951. An admirer of the 'pair poster' (one design made up of two), he commissioned many well-known artists but presided over a period when less than a dozen posters were being produced per year. He replaced Beck's diagram in favour of his own, described by Roberts as 'possibly one of the worst diagrammatic maps ever devised for any transport undertaking' (2005, Bibliography) – though he admits this was until Madrid's Metro map (2007–2013)!

If the Underground had been tested by the Festival of Britain, and the Olympics three years before that, these events were to pale into insignificance next to the strain placed on services on the day of the Coronation, 2 June 1953 (p. 223). *Three million* people attended the procession – the largest gathering ever assembled to that date – and the majority came by public transport. Planning for the day was led by the operating manager F. G. Maxwell and took months, placing huge strain on the organization. Two hundred stations opened at 3 a.m. to bring in the crowds. Colour-coded signage was used to mark specific routes around the West End and 2 million fold-out maps (which users were advised 'should be studied carefully') were issued to help guide spectators to and from their chosen vantage points, making it possibly the most practical souvenir of the occasion (p. 223).

Squaring the Circle

Meanwhile, improvements were being made to another map. Beck's first addition of the yellow Circle line to the 1949 diagram (p. 220) was a little inelegant, so he spent some time redrawing the central area to find a neater solution. The resulting design – an oblong with rounded ends – first shown on the pocket map in 1954 (p. 221) was ingenious, enabling him to fit in Upminster on the District's far eastern extremity, for the first time.[23] He remained in charge of the map until 1960, but Harold Hutchinson had secretly been working on his own version of the diagram (p. 227). Published in 1961, it had been made without a single curve; not only was the map jarring to look at, but it was full of inconsistencies. Hutchinson's map design was poorly thought through and ungainly. Bad layout causes one station name to be broken into two halves – 'Ald' and 'gate' are forced to either side of the route lines. The splaying out of Circle, Met and District station 'ticks' is inconsistent and effectively pointless – compare Tower Hill and Edgware Road. It lasted just three years before being jettisoned, replaced by Paul E. Garbutt's fine effort in 1964 (p. 227). Hutchinson's map did introduce some improvements, however, including upper and lower case for lettering and the black interchange symbol, features retained to this day. According to Roberts (2005, Bibliography), as well as finding a better solution for the Upminster branch, this was the first diagram to use lower case for most stations and single black interchange circles on parallel lines.

Rebuilds and renewals

By the late 1950s, major works had restarted. At Notting Hill Gate – where there had been plans to link up the separate stations since the opening of the CLR in 1900 – the rebuilding was so complex that it constituted the biggest Underground station reconstruction since the NWP. It opened on 1 March 1959 with a shiny escalator shaft in 'satin finished' aluminium, ceilings covered in plastic panels of yellow, pink and grey, and passageways lined with brightly coloured tiling in burgundy and sky blue (p. 228). It was such a contrast from the previous pale decor that it made a big impression. A revised, thinner version of Johnston was used in new illuminated suspended-box signage (p. 228).

During the process of adding two extra tracks to the Met in 1962, Northwood and Moor Park (p. 228) needed reconstructing. Though the latter is a small station, it was neatly executed with a raked clerestory roof, mosaic-tiled floor and wood panelling. The last stations to be finished on the western side of the Central line were between Northolt and West Ruislip but the pre-war designs of the GWR's Frederick F. Curtis seemed outdated, so architects John Kennett and Roy Turner were called in to simplify and modernize them. All were completed by the mid 1960s.

New line on the block

Along with rebuilds, something rather more radical was afoot. What Beck was making space for in his next (never published) diagram design[24] was the first new line under central London since the deep-level tubes of the early 1900s. Originally known as 'Route C',[25] it was proposed to run from Victoria to Finsbury Park,[26] and 1.6km of twin-bore test tunnels from the latter to Seven Sisters were made between 1960 and 1961. The project was approved in August 1962 and much of the preliminary work soon under way.[27] The entire scheme was planned in house by the London Transport design panel, which included Misha Black (p. 234) and K. J. H. Seymour (p. 205), now chief architect. The key feature would be the use of automatic trains, the first of their kind (p. 235). The project was originally referred to as the 'Victoria line' as early as 1955 and announced as 'under construction' in a 1962 poster campaign (p. 231) – and it was set to transform the way Tube lines were designed and built from then on.

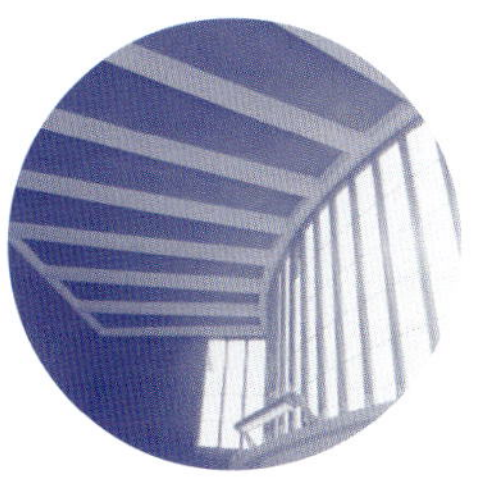

Dr Frederick Francis Charles Curtis (1903–75), German by birth, came to the UK in 1933, joining Southern Railway before moving to Adams, Holden & Pearson in 1936. In 1947 he replaced Brian Lewis as architect at GWR and when it was nationalized in 1948 was the Western Region's first chief architect. His LT credits include Hanger Lane (p. 216), Perivale (pictured) and Greenford (p. 217).

Abscratchy and silhouette posters, 1945–6

Given the popularity of Beck's diagram – it was already a teenager by the end of the Second World War – it is perhaps surprising that there was not much publicity for the design in its own right. One exception was this 1945 poster (1) by Jan Lewitt and George Him (p. 207), which, with its slightly whimsical, avant-garde figure formed from abstract diagram parts, invited passengers to be 'map conscious'. It was produced to broadcast the newly agreed colour for each of the five lines (though most line colours had been fixed for some time before this and indeed have not changed since then). Given the poster's aim, it seems odd that no actual sections of the diagram were shown, merely a 'pastiche' of Beck's central area in the lower right corner. Mary Le Bon also stylized the map (detail, 1946, 4). Outline forms seemed to be a theme in the late 1940s; Tom Eckersley used them frequently, as in this poster from 1946 encouraging considerate escalator usage (2), and other artists were keen on them too, as exemplified by a 1946 poster of the first eastern extension of the Central line, by Hans Schleger (issued under his pseudonym of 'Zero', detail, 3).

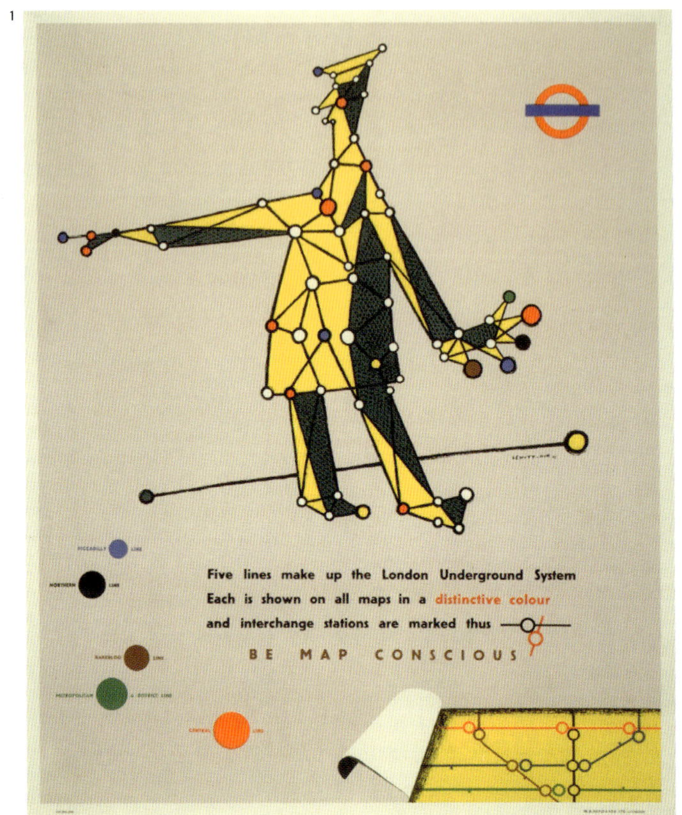

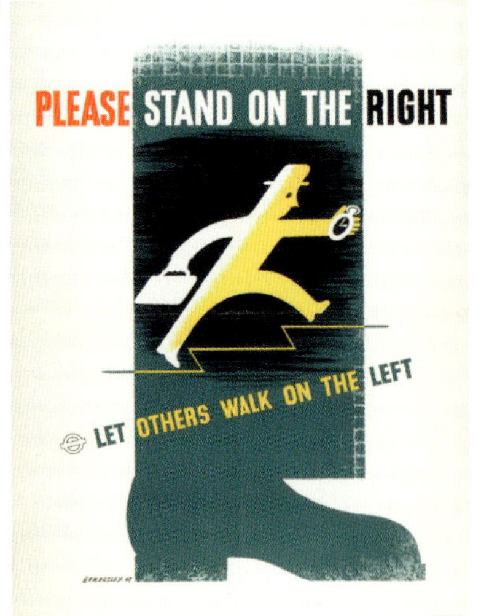

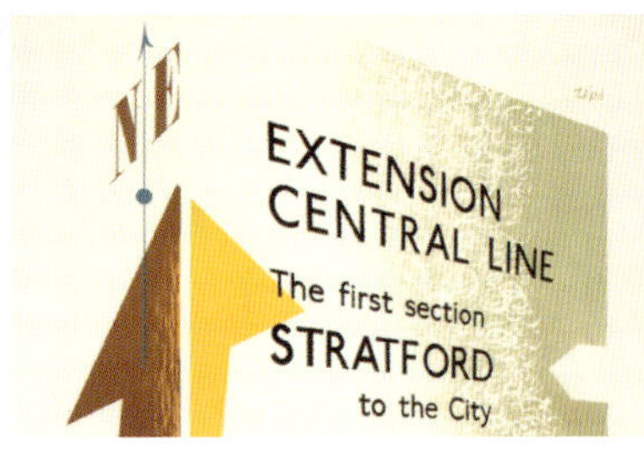

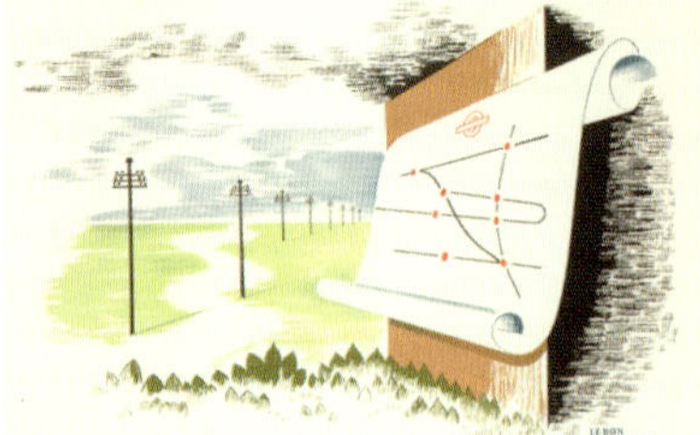

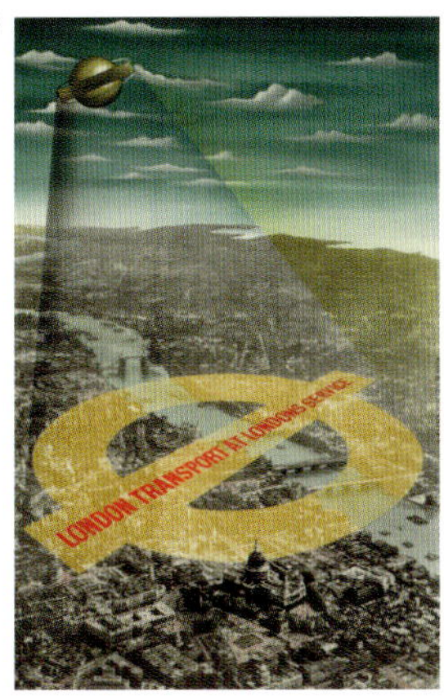

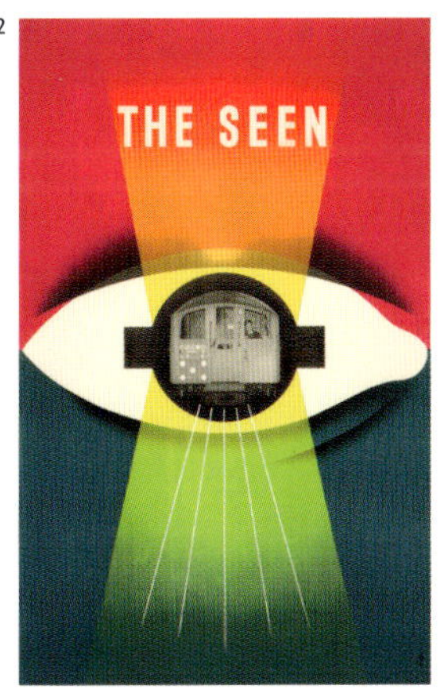

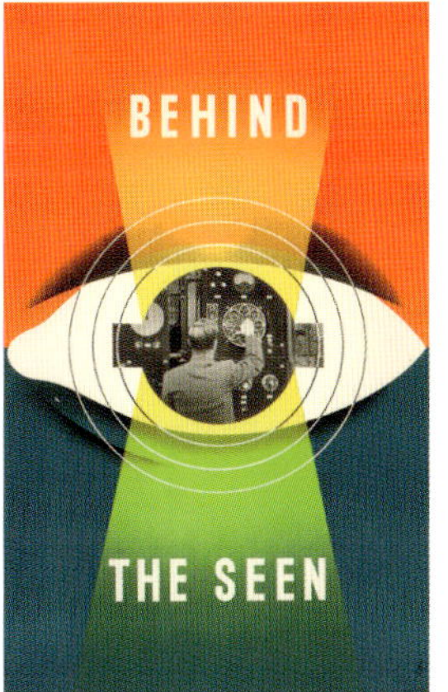

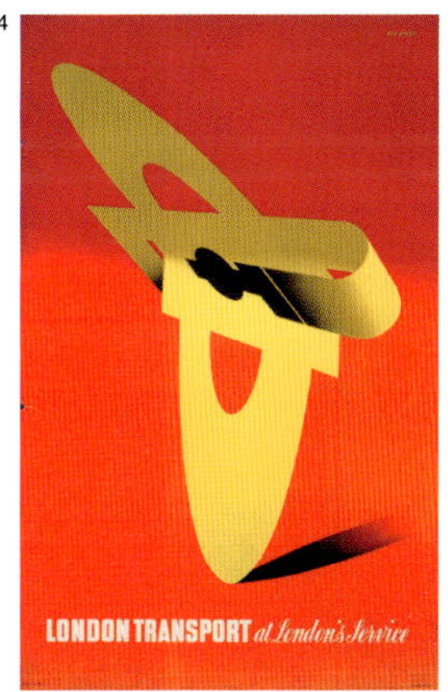

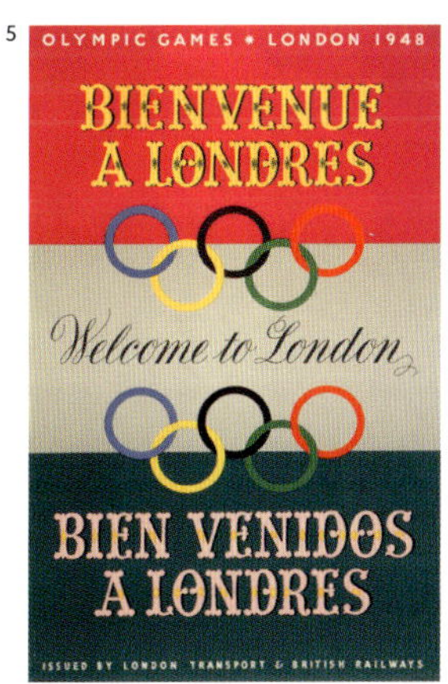

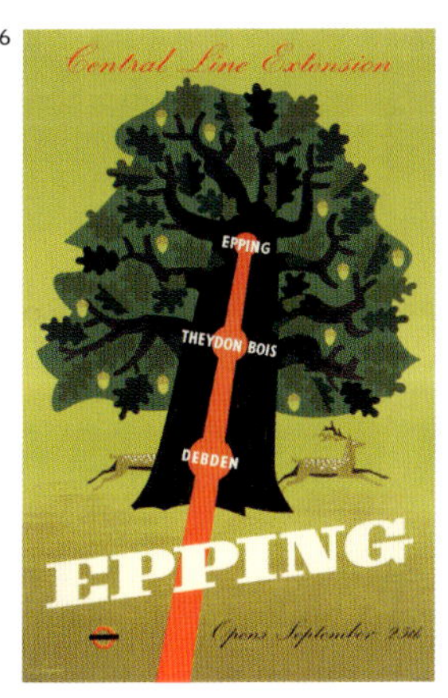

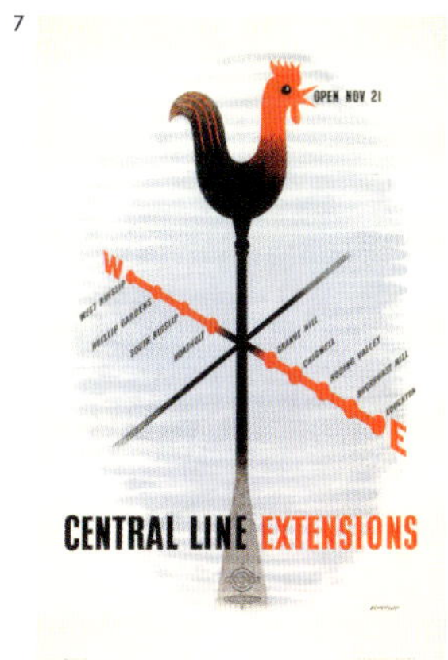

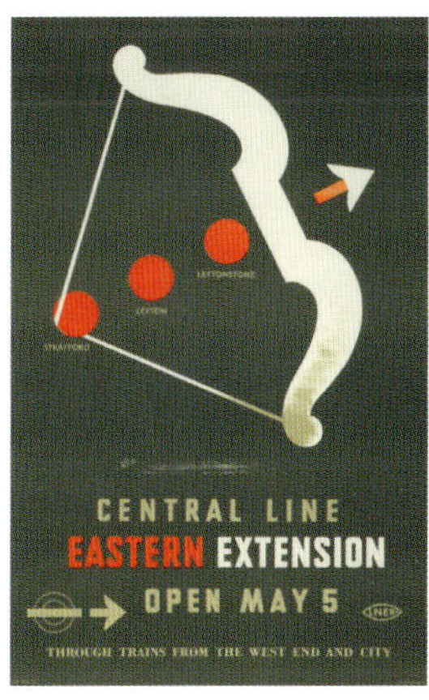

Post-war posters, 1947–8

Although the London Transport Executive did not take over until 1948 (p. 206), many self-promotional posters with the theme 'London Transport At London's Service', in which the bullseye featured strongly, were commissioned from as early as 1947. The subject was tackled by several artists, including Abram Games (1947, 4). One of the most effective images was Misha Black and Kraber's bullseye projecting down upon an aerial view of the city (1), originally issued as a pair with the other poster listing LT's attributes. Another pair set were four posters by James Fitton (2 and 3) promoting the back-room staff. The two biggest events of the late 1940s were the Olympic Games of 1948 and the opening up of the eastern and western extensions of the Central line. The Clement Dane studio produced this multi-lingual welcome to the spectacle (5), the only Olympic poster made by London Transport. The Central line extensions, on the other hand, required several posters as each section was opened at a different time. Artists were commissioned to integrate cartographic representations of the new sections in various ingenious ways, as exemplified by those shown here: K. J. Chapman (1948, 6), Tom Eckersley (1948, 7) and Hans Schleger (1948, 8).

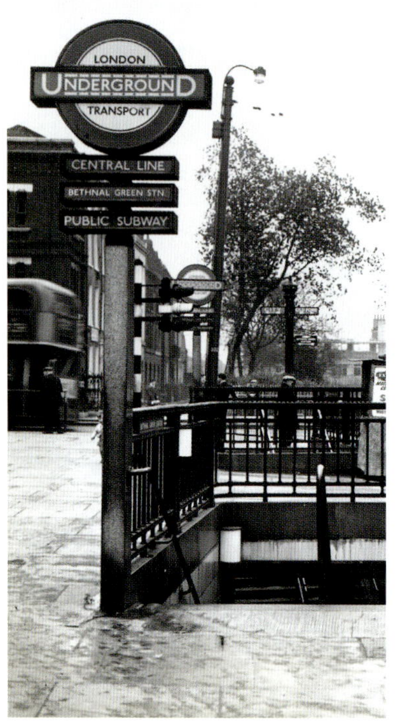

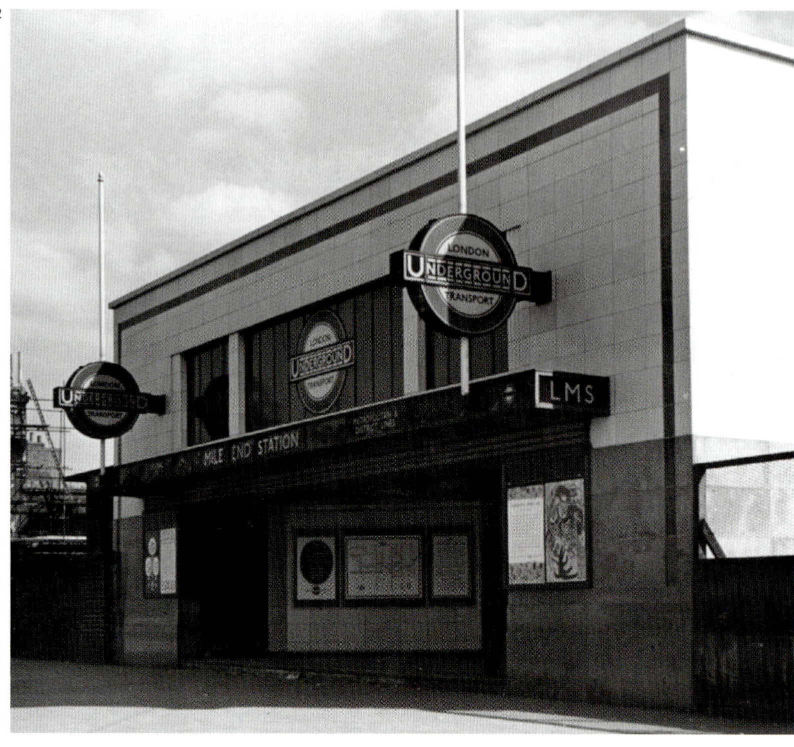

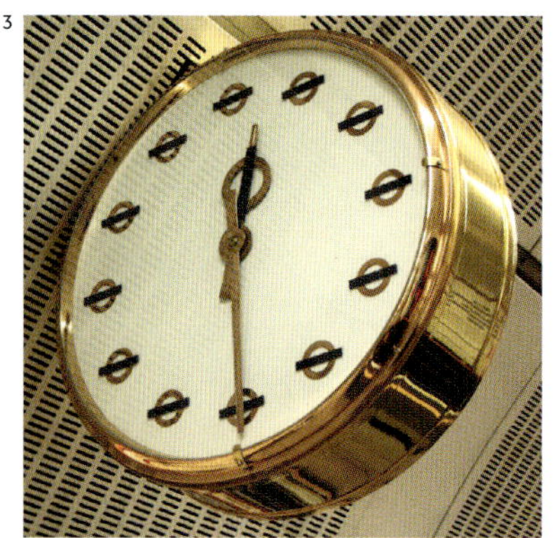

Central stretches to Stratford, 1946

The first major post-war opening was the Central line extension from Liverpool Street to Stratford (frontage rebuilt with the LNER) – made possible because much of the work had been completed before 1939. The only substantial surface building was the new ticket hall at Mile End (2); much in Holden's earlier style, it had a large glazed wall on the first floor with a coloured Underground bullseye inset into it. At Bethnal Green, platform walls were in the Stabler style with tiled friezes on a biscuit-cream background, but it featured one new item that was to appear at a handful of other Central line stations: a clock with the hours and hour hand made out of bullseyes – one of the nicest touches in the whole extension (recently restored, 3). At street level, Bethnal Green also had the pole-mounted bullseyes (seen in 1955, 1), originally with three blue bars below, showing station name, line name and 'public subway' (these were reduced to two bars in later years, the line name being removed).

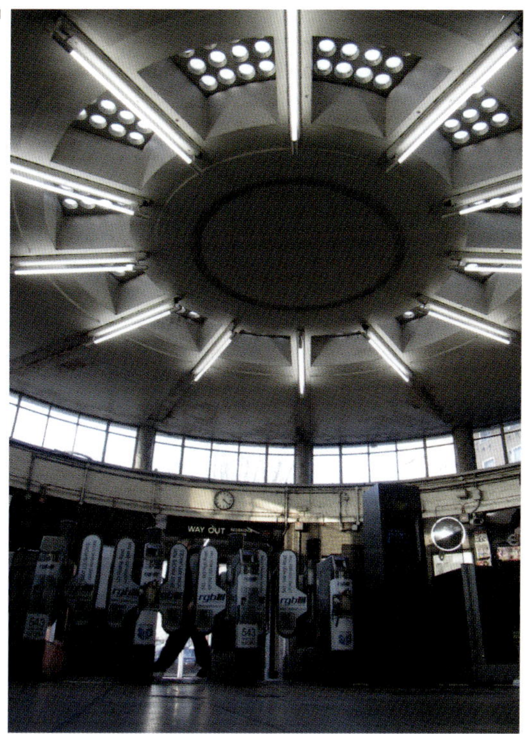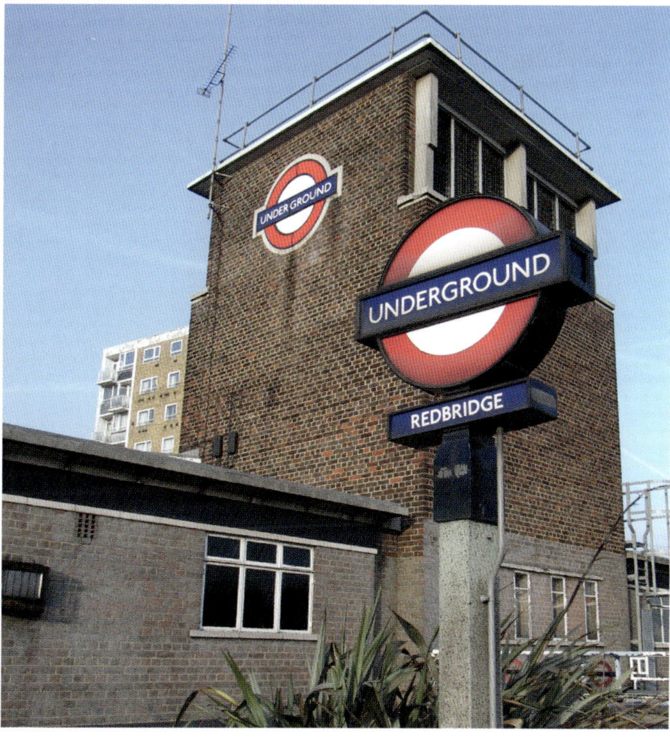

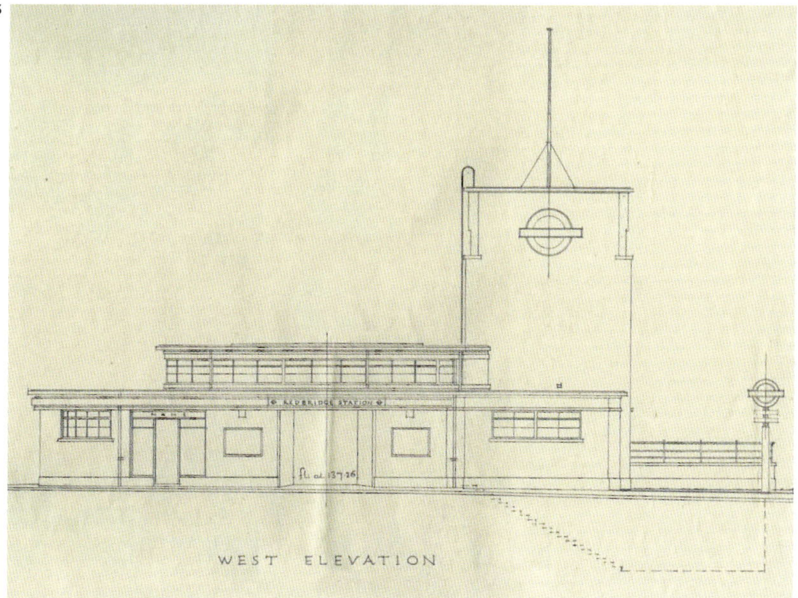

Eastern enterprise, 1947

The next raft of Central line stations to open pushed into Essex. Stations at Wanstead, Redbridge, Gants Hill and Newbury Park each had unique features. Wanstead (p. 215) was simplified from pre-war Holden designs to produce the first station in proto-Brutalist style. At Redbridge (all images on this page) much of the original Holden, Adams & Pearson design (3) was retained and improved upon to produce a glorious circular ticket hall (1).

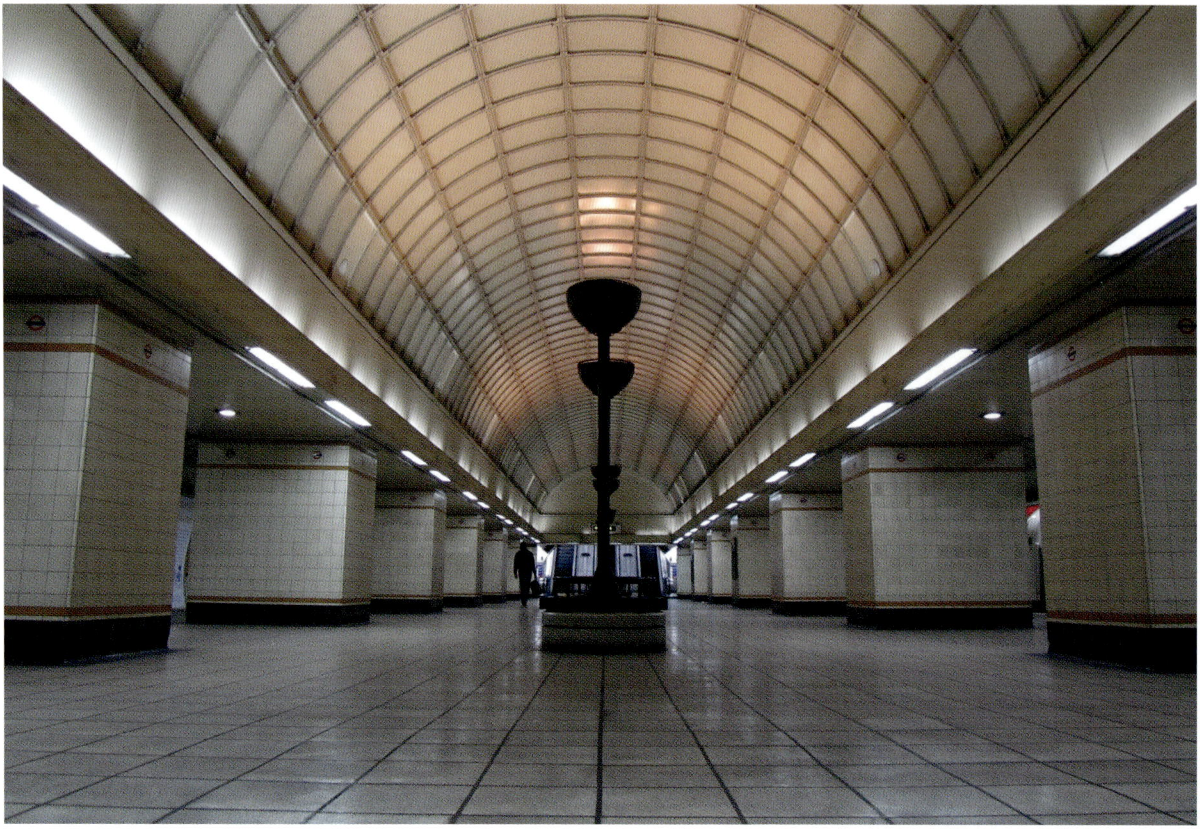

Must go Moscow, 1947

At Gants Hill a cavernous extra tunnel was built between each platform, allowing space for a 6m-high vaulted roof (with yellow chrome bands, 1). The resulting concourse, a homage to the early Moscow Metro stations (p. 204), must be one of the Underground's most spacious and distinctive.

What was lavished upon the platforms below ground with their stabler-style tiling and bullseye-faced clock (2) was spared at street level, however, and like Bethnal Green this station had no surface buildings. Instead the ticket hall beneath a roundabout is accessed by means of gently sloping ramps flagged by stylish totems.

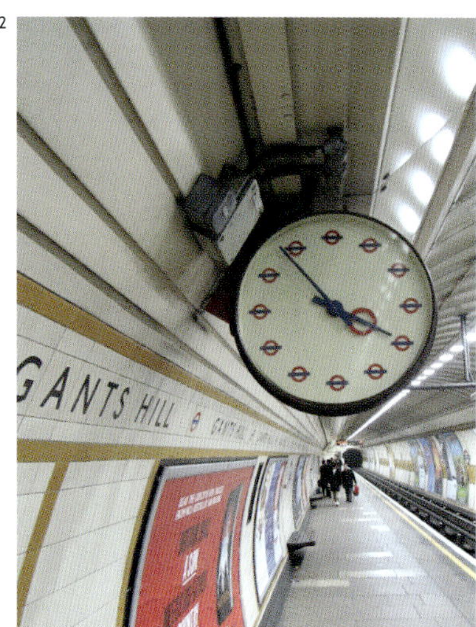

London Underground by Design

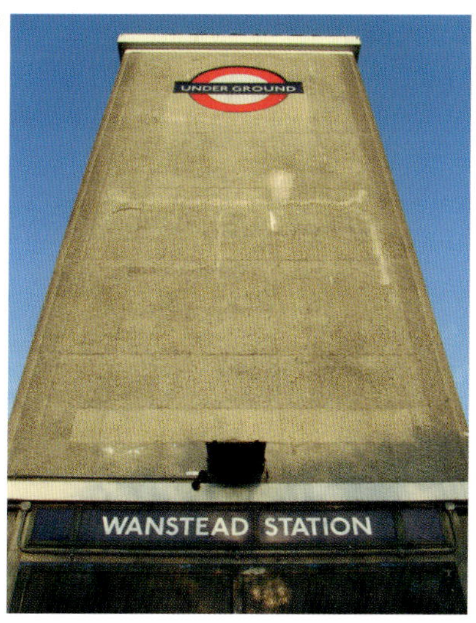

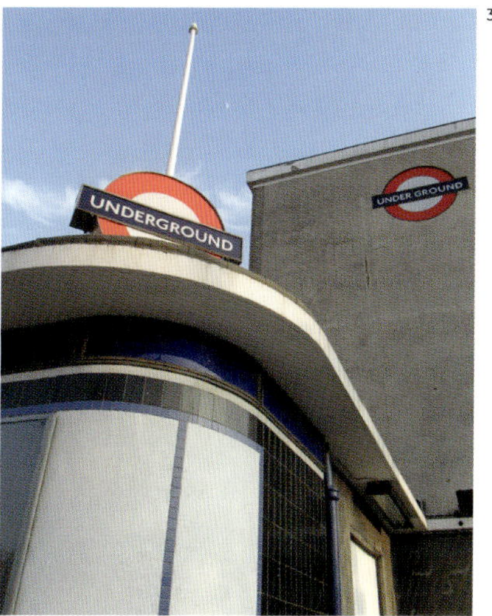

The stylish way is Essex, 1947–48

Newbury Park (1) was to have been another shrine to Holden-style curvaceousness, but architect Oliver Hill (p. 204) rejected these ideas and prepared (with his assistant Edward Dudley) the first post-war architectural masterpiece for London Transport, the stunning semicircular bus garage with its barrel-vaulted roof giving access to the Tube station. The structure won a Festival of Britain architectural award in 1951 and is now a listed building. Holden's plans for Wanstead, opened in 1947, were 'simplified', boiled down to a stark concrete tower (2), but the use of black glazed bricks for the ticket-hall entrance (3) did at least give the exterior a stylish finish at ground-floor level. Other Essex stations on the Central line had little done to them although Hainault, opened in 1948, received a beautifully proportioned curved waiting room.

Central great westerns, 1947

The first three western extension stations on the Central line were no less impressive than those in the east. Following the abandonment of a series of ambitious plans, Hanger Lane (1 and 4) was a tamed-down version of what had been envisaged. Similar to previous 'drum-like' ticket halls, the cylindrical structure embodies all the panache of earlier manifestations at Southgate (p. 174), Chiswick Park (p. 167) or Arnos Grove (p. 172) but with an eye to the 1950s preference for starker simplicity. Whether this was due to building materials shortages or the astuteness of BR's Western Region architect Peter MacIver may never be known, but the result was as clean and neat as any 1930s Art Deco Holden. Embracing Pick's prime directive of form following function, Hanger Lane is perhaps the lightest, simplest and most authoritative of the period. At the next stop, Perivale (2, 3), a rebuild of the former GWR station resulted in another unique design. Although Holden's team had proposed several stations with concave frontages, it was GWR architect Brian Lewis (p. 209) who designed the first one to be built.

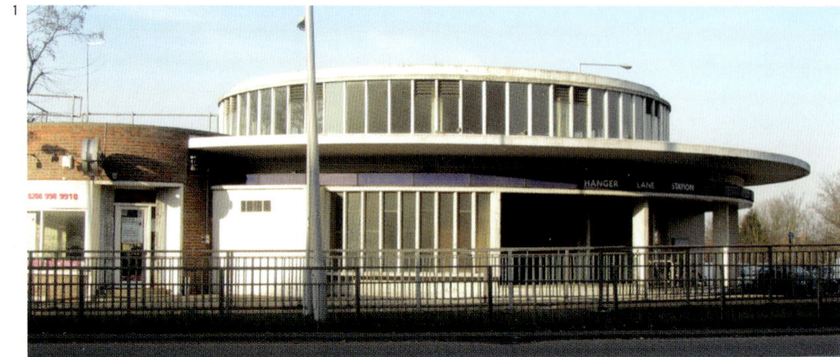

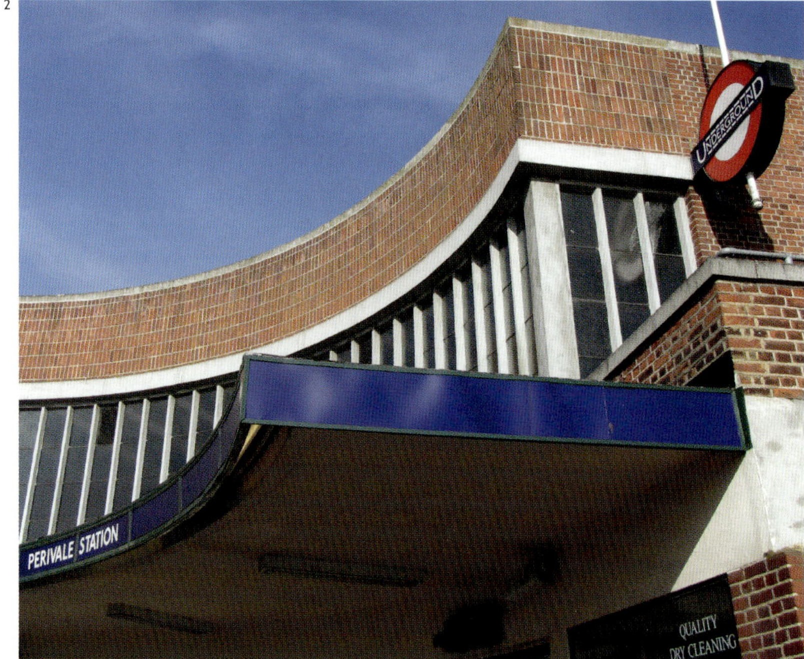

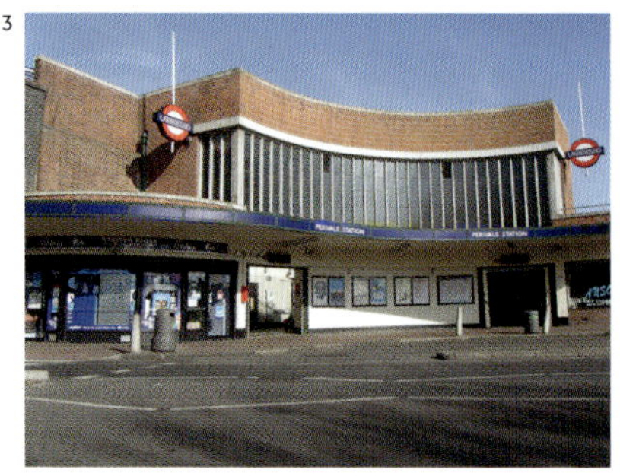

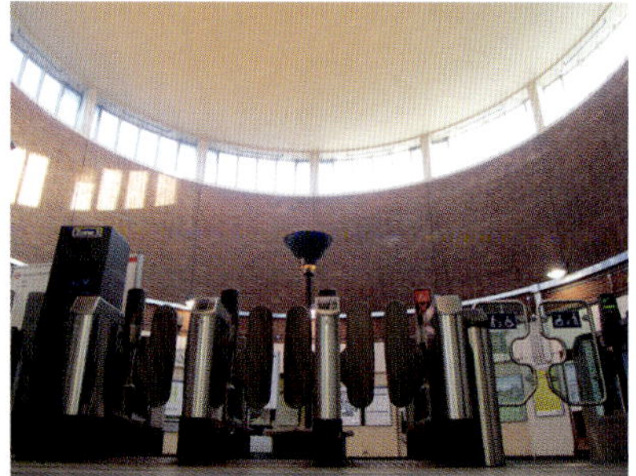

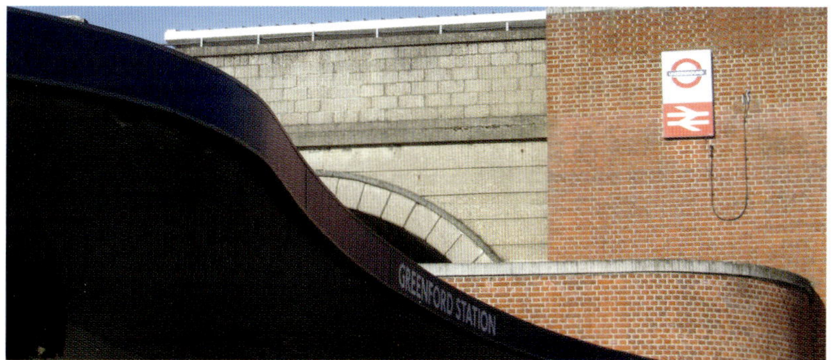

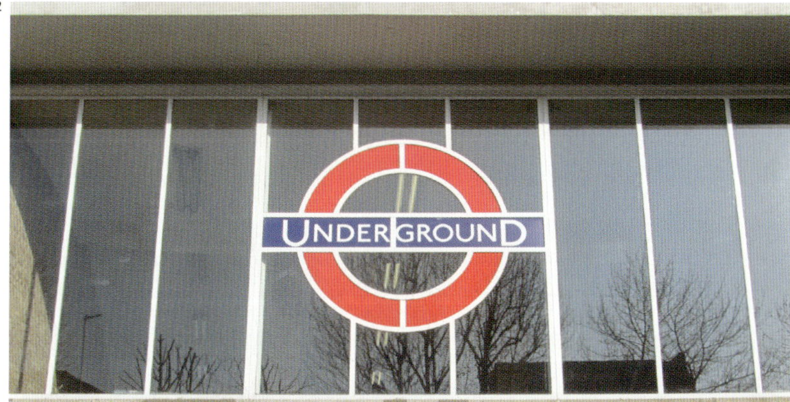

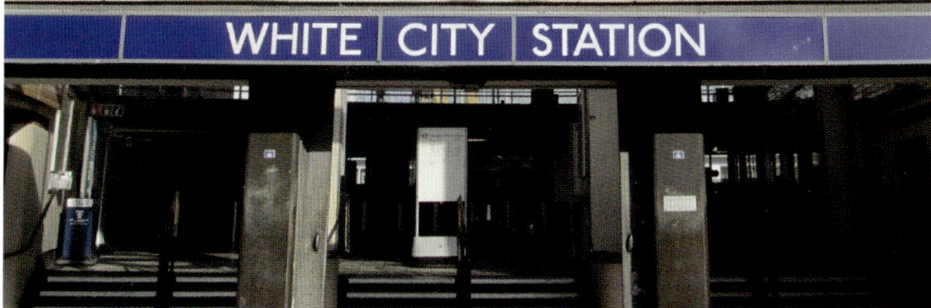

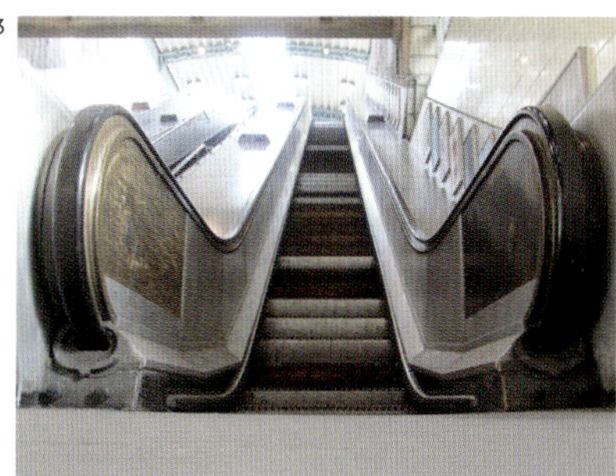

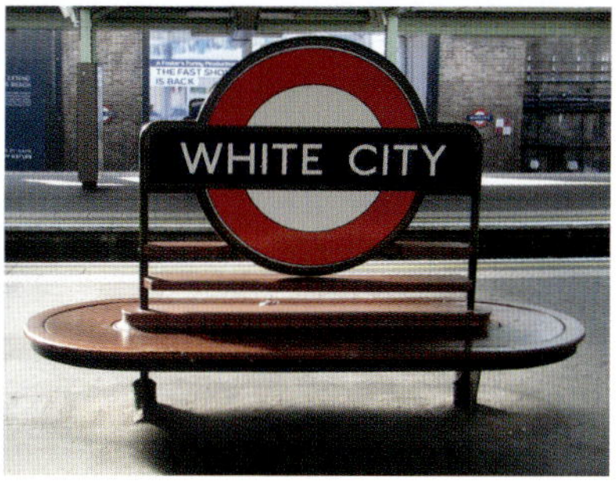

Next on the western extension was Greenford (1), also a Brian Lewis design (though he was not involved in its construction); an 'underground' station on an embankment that necessitated escalators up to the trains (the last wooden ones on the system, 3). Lewis's curving canopy must have given the engineers headaches, but the effect was a delicate undulation of brick and glass. During the same period the original buildings at Wood Lane were closed, superseded by a new station slightly to the north of there named White City (opened 1947). Architects A. D. McGill and Kenneth H. J. Seymour (p. 205), clearly inspired by Holden's classic works, made copious use of large glass walls (2) and exposed brick finishes. Station furniture included the bullseye with wooden oval seat (4).

Carr–Edwards veers off the rails, 1948

Despite the measurable benefits of the 1938 Carr–Edwards signage report (pp. 155, 192), its revised version a decade later could not be said to have scored the same success. The idea of 'branding' was still in its infancy and the 1938 report had helped unify signage across the system, but the 1948 amendments committed the cardinal sin (in modern terms) of throwing out a brand name which had taken four decades to build. The word 'UNDERGROUND' – deemed a 'legal misnomer and a factual error' in the revisions to the report – was to be universally replaced with the operator name 'LONDON TRANSPORT'. The photographs here show how graphic artists interpreted the new edict, but while it is true that only 40 per cent of the network is physically underground, Londoners and visitors recognized the brand and even those working on the recommendations must have questioned the sense in ditching the name, hinting at this in the report itself: 'it is a matter of judgement … as to whether this [signage] would clearly say "station" at a distance.'

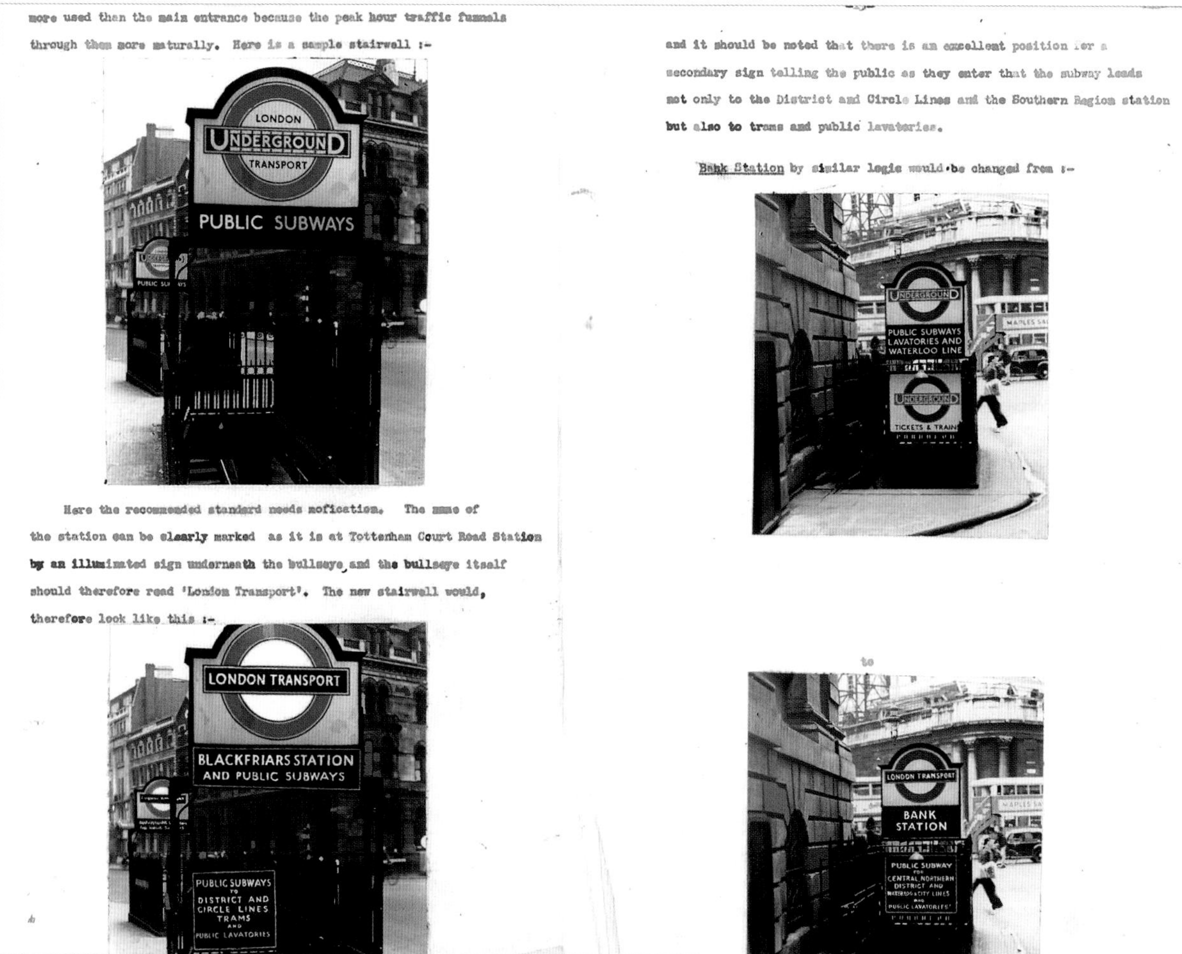

London Underground by Design

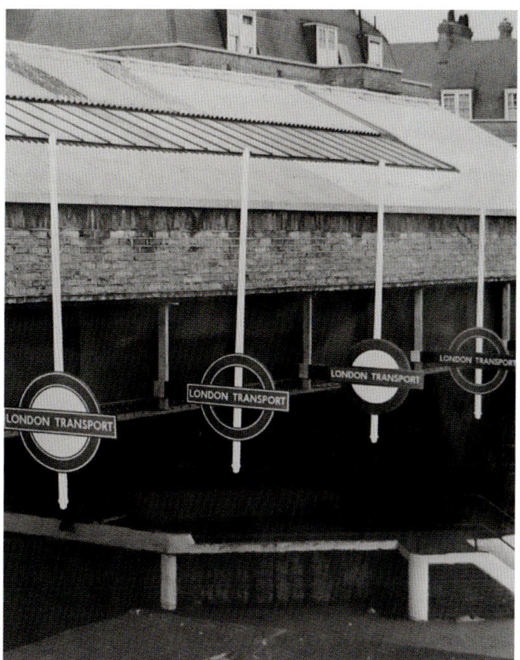

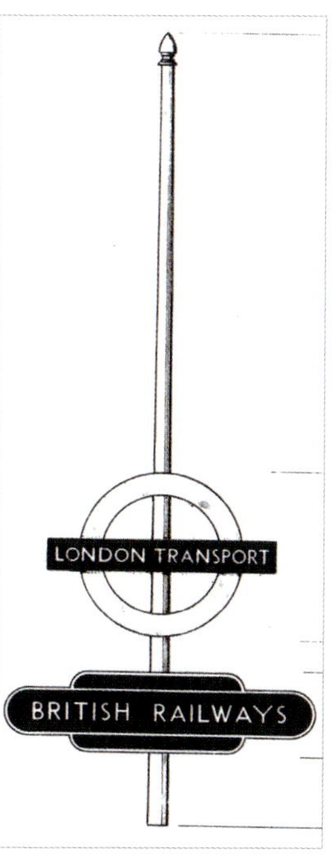

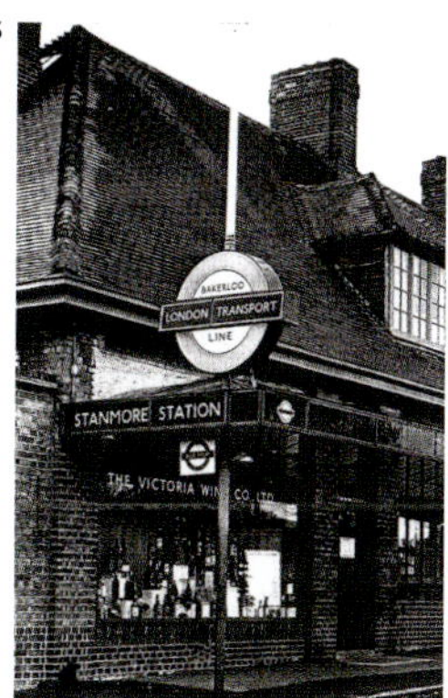

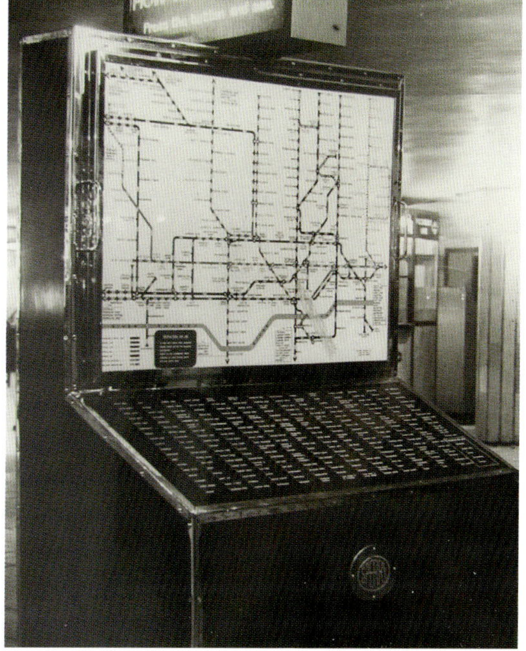

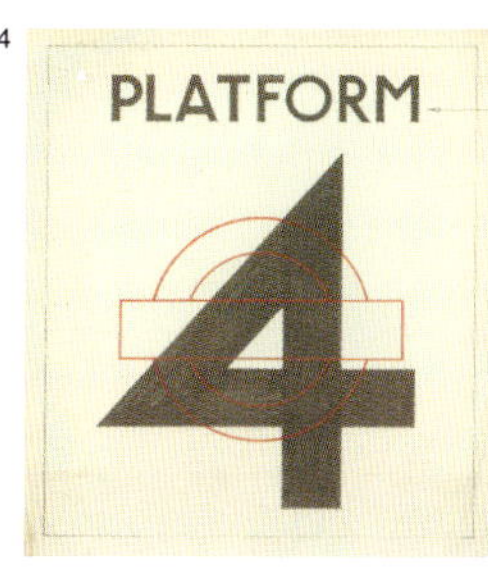

Pick a bullseye, 1949

This fascinating display of experimental signage at Parsons Green (in a rare photographic record, 1) was put up in 1949 to test the revised 'LONDON TRANSPORT' mast-mounted bullseye. Drawings were prepared for the latest graphic standards manual (issued 1949–54, 2). Despite the misgivings of losing the Underground word, a re-signed exterior at Stanmore (winter 1949, 3) shows how neat the new signage looked when carefully applied. Not all the suggestions of the 1948 Carr–Edwards design revisions were successful, however, and not all of them were implemented. The long trackside wall friezes – though a good idea and attempted in the Piccadilly 1930s extensions (p. 190) before being enshrined in the 1948 report – never took off, for instance, possibly due to cost. Instead, bifurcation diagrams were improved (p. 226). 'Sperry' indicators (named after the manufacturer, 5) would show the best route at the touch of a button and were more of a success – ever popular with children, young and old. (Similar wayfinders were used in Paris, but as happened in London, they proved difficult to maintain). By the time the Jubilee line was being built (1974–7, p. 248), they were being phased out (the last one at Oxford Circus was removed in the 1980s). One attractive design feature that was adopted were the platform number signs overlaid on outline bullseyes (4). There was a greater emphasis on illuminated 'WAY OUT' signage too, made by the lighting department to fit standard-sized lamp bulbs.

The Circle shows its true colour, 1948

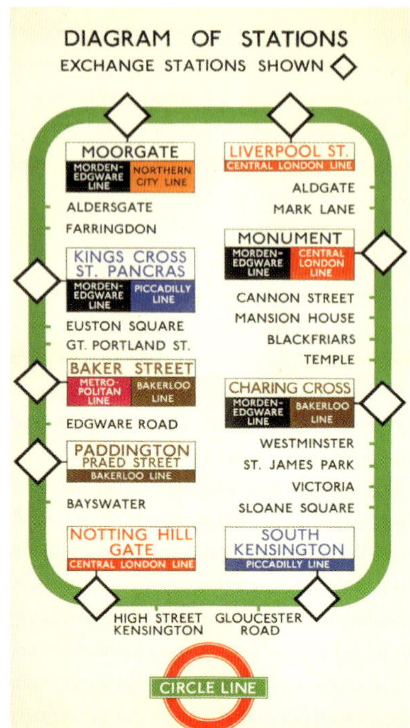

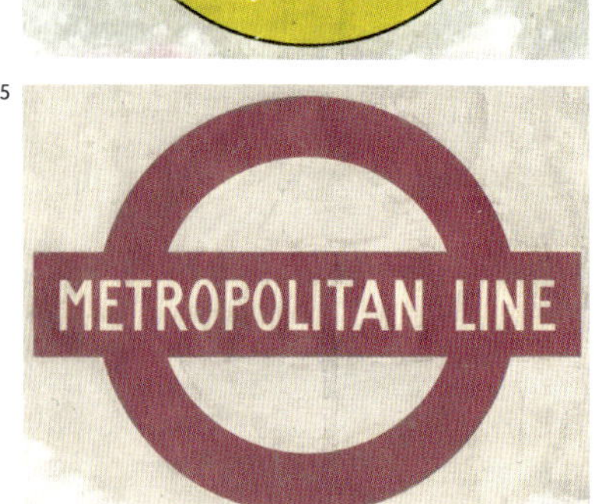

The operational running of trains around the 'Inner Circle' had been a constant headache for managers, but displaying its name clearly on maps from 1949 (4) was supposed to help matters (for passengers at least). Platform wall friezes were interspersed with a new yellow bullseye (1) to distinguish it from the District (green) and the Met (changed back to purple, 2) (p. 208). Interestingly, the 1948 official naming of the 'Circle line' was not the first outing for the term. It appears to have been in use from 1936, as can be seen from this in-car poster panel (3), possibly inspiring the Carr–Edwards revision.

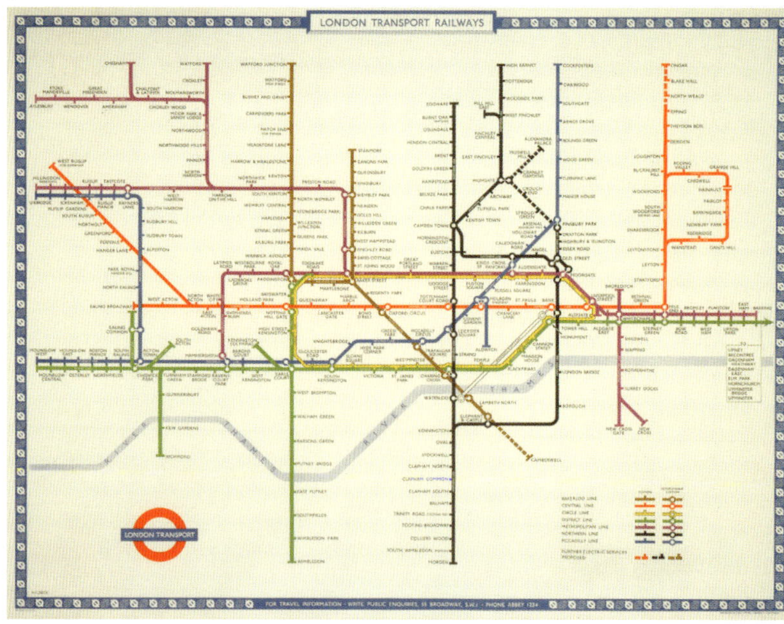

London Underground by Design

Beck's Circle solutions, 1949–54

Beck first added the Circle line to his map – coloured yellow with a fine black casing around it to help it stand out – in 1949, as can be seen in this quad-royal poster (opposite, 4). He may not have had much time to do this as it does feel a little tacked on to the previous artwork, unlike the complete redrawing he produced for the poster of 1953 (below) and appearing on the card folder pocket map the following year. Beck's widening out of the eastern end of the Circle gave more space for fitting in station names, but it clearly did not meet with the approval of Hutchinson, who squished the Circle back into an almost indecipherable tangle in his own self-proclaimed 'masterpiece' (p. 227). The redesign also allowed Beck to include Upminster, which had stubbornly refused to fit onto any previous versions of the map. In addition, Beck had whittled the entire system down to only five diagonal lines (four if the Waterloo & City is not counted), which clearly pleased him, but may have been his downfall as he was soon to be usurped (p. 227).

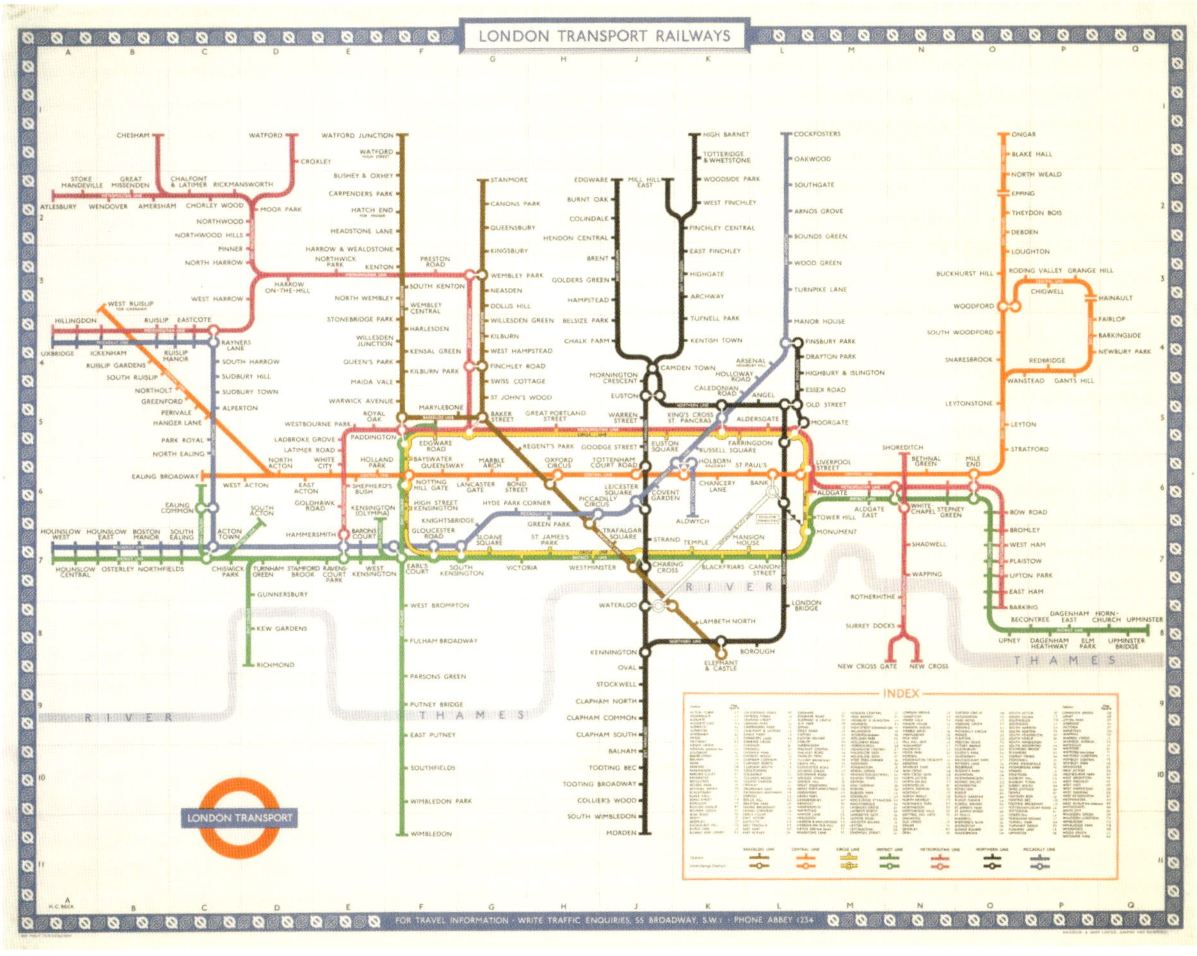

Fit for a festival, 1951

Recognizing that the country was in sore need of a collective tonic after the war, and keen to promote latest developments in science, technology and the arts, the government organized a nationwide celebration. Staged in the summer of 1951, the Festival of Britain was centred on a number of specially constructed exhibition buildings between Westminster and Waterloo bridges. Much of the South Bank was devoted to showcasing British design: Misha Black (p. 234) created 'The Land' exhibit, for instance, featuring a section on 'Transport' themed by George Williams. Abram Games designed an emblem (the 'Festival Star') and London Transport's event poster, incorporating it (4). A temporary structure called Station Gate (2 and p. 207) was constructed for passengers to access Waterloo from the Festival site. Several stations close to the South Bank were improved at this time, including Charing Cross and Sloane Square (1), which was completely rebuilt following bomb damage. The map (3) was produced as a poster and in a fold-out pocket guide.

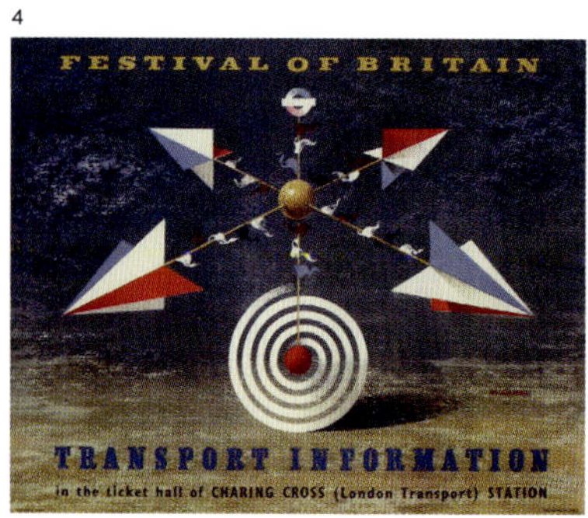

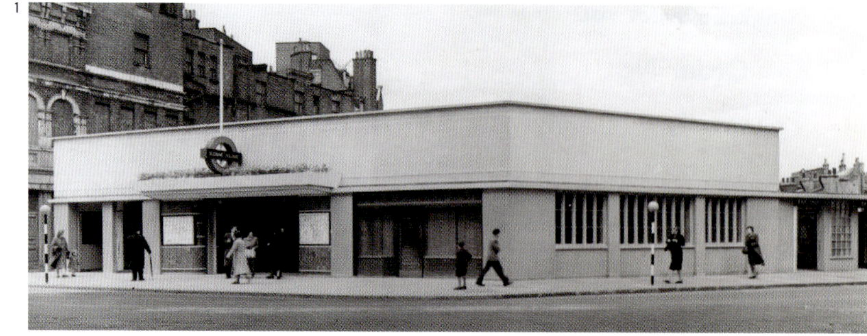

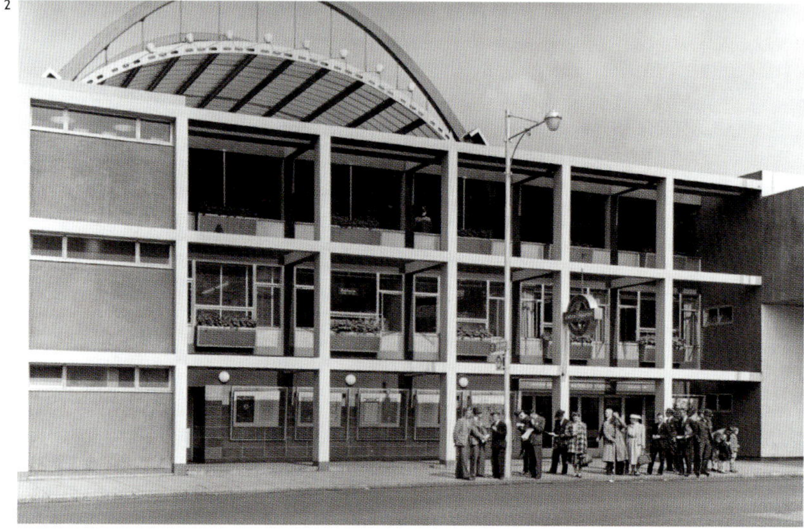

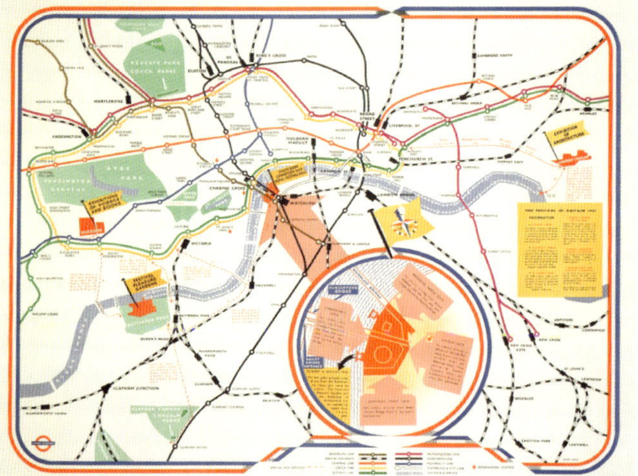

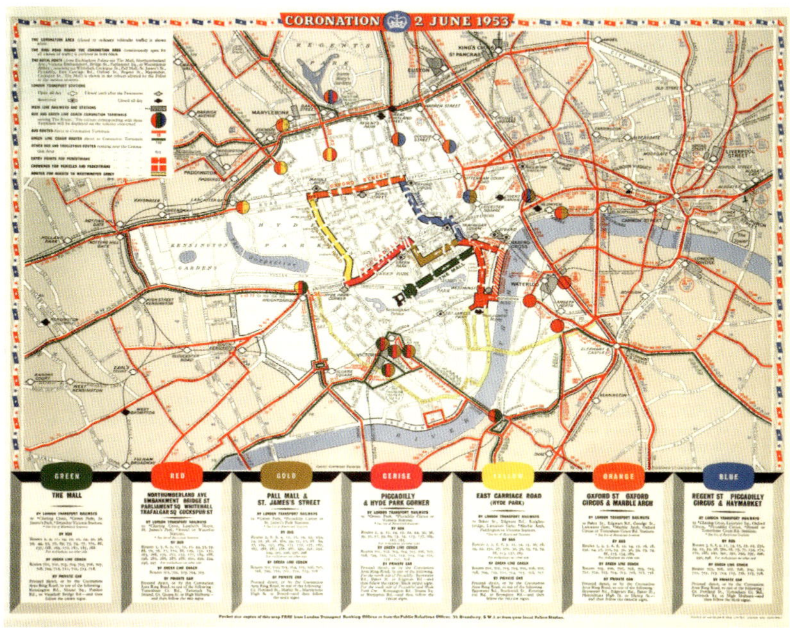

Fit for a queen, 1953

With so many people expected to congregate in London along the Coronation procession route on 2 June 1953, London Transport planners had to think very carefully about how to get spectators in and out of the city. Lessons learnt from the Festival of Britain two years before (opposite) convinced operations manager F. G. Maxwell to close certain West End stations, or restrict access to them, and open others in the early hours of the morning. A fold-out map showing joint transport services (1) was kept by thousands of people as a souvenir of the event, and recently reissued as a commemorative item. Hans Unger designed a striking poster for the Coronation year featuring a stylized Coldstream Guard (2), and publicity for the royal activities gave rise to numerous other posters and fliers. Certain key stations along and close to the route were decorated for the event with flowers and special canopies (e.g. Westminster, 3), where revellers slept on the street the night before in order to get a good view of the procession.

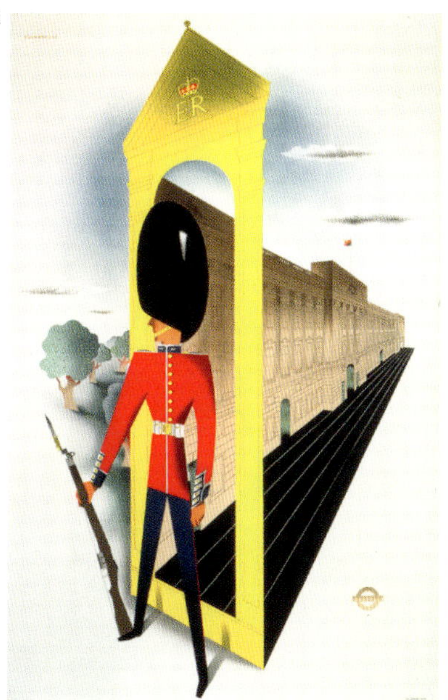

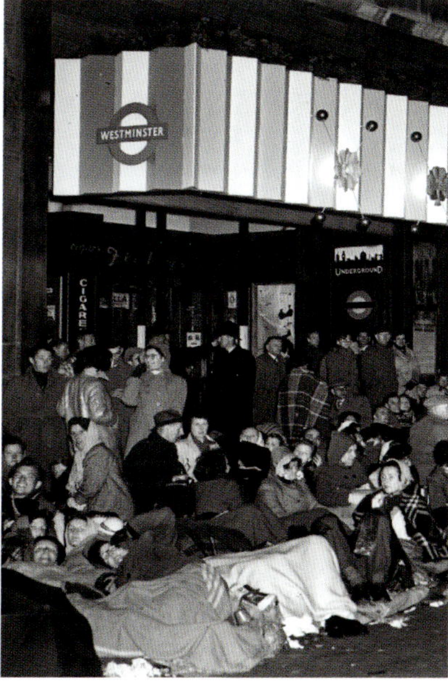

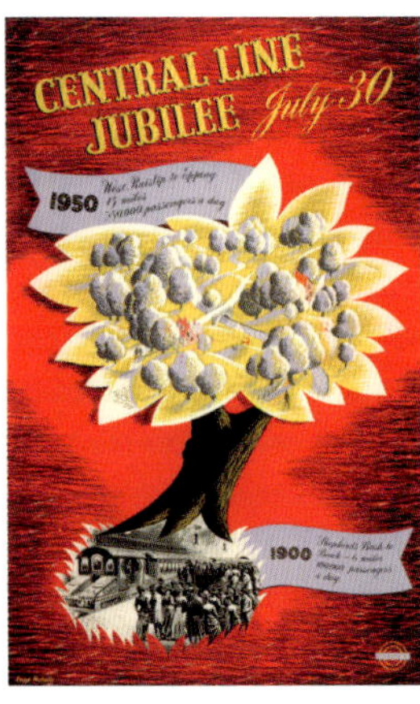

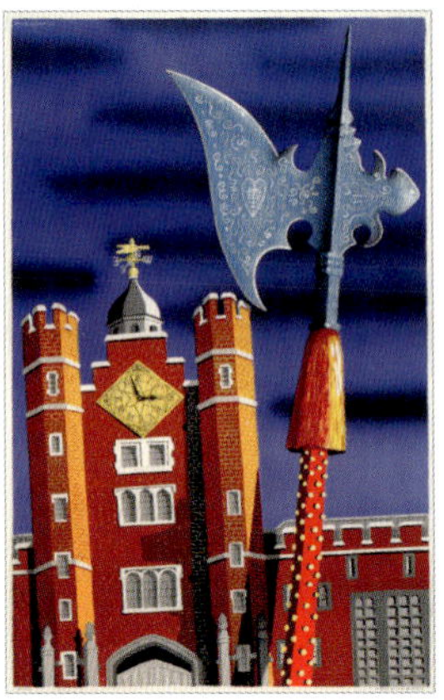

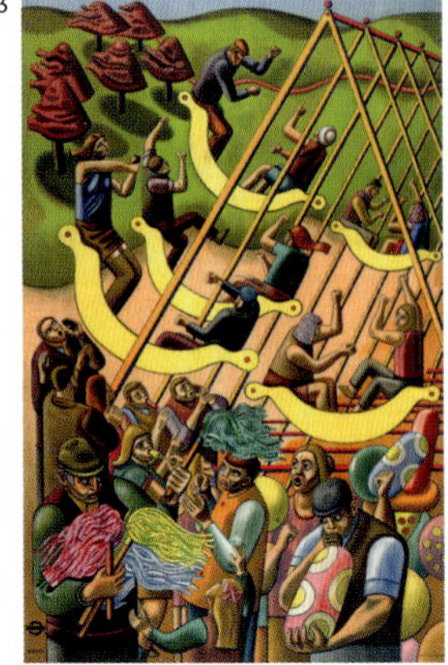

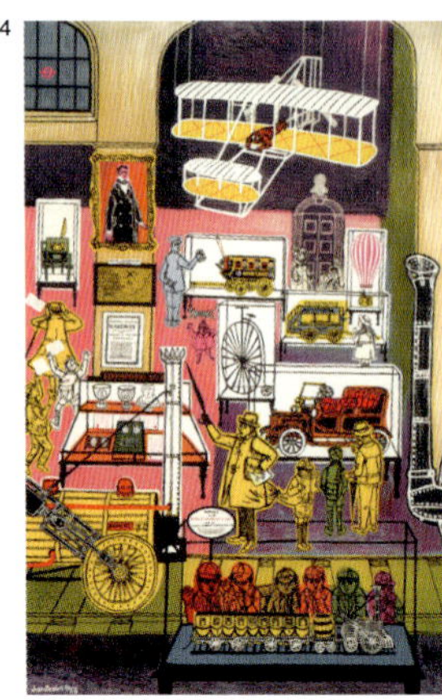

Underground lost, 1948–57

The decision in 1948 to focus on the London Transport brand (p. 206) meant very few posters were commissioned which promoted the Underground by name in the 1950s (up until the 1957 policy change). Denys Nicholls's 1950 design for the Central line's Golden Jubilee (1) was the last pictorial poster to refer directly to the Underground for several years. Instead a number were produced with no text whatsoever (because they were issued in pairs with the image one side and the text on a separate poster – though they were occasionally displayed separately), for example this invitation to 'Royal London; St James's Palace' by David Lewis and the Clement Dane Studio (1953, 2). In William Roberts's 'London's Fairs' (1951, 3), another pair set, the text (not shown) refers to travel 'by train' rather than 'Underground'. An internal poster calls for staff suggestions (1951, 5) – one of which might have been to ask why the typeface used was not in-house Johnston but Gill Sans Condensed. Joan Beales created a pair set for the cluster of museums around South Kensington (1955, 4). Peter Roberson's potty poster, also for the museums (1956, 6), was even more cryptic: rather than name the obvious South Kensington Tube station, it suggests people write to 55 Broadway for a leaflet! It was the graphic standards manual under Hutchinson that perpetuated the eradication of the 'Underground' word and the 1954 revision was no less harsh; the sole period when the word 'Subway' had greater importance than the system's traditional name.

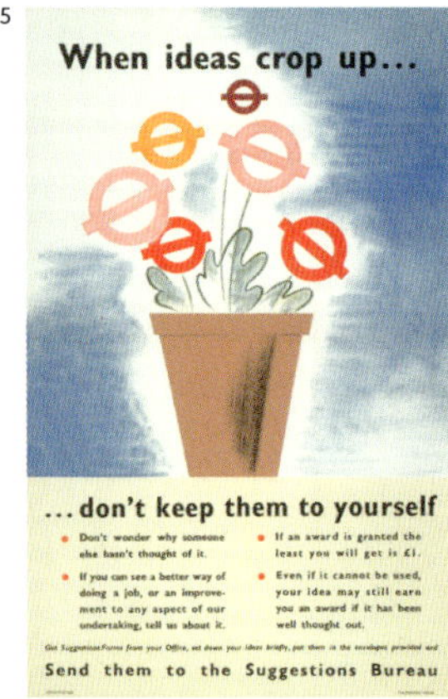

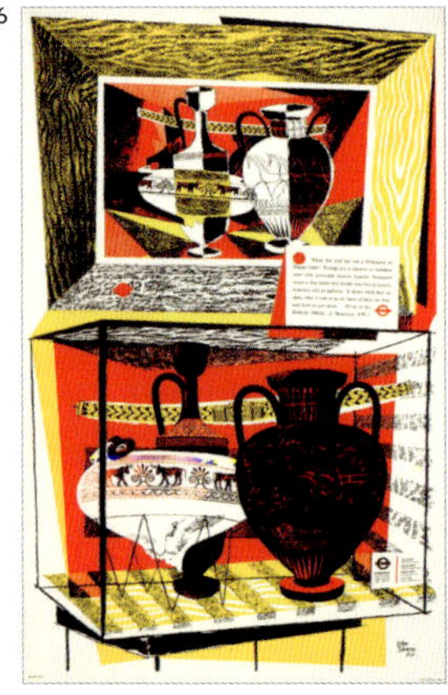

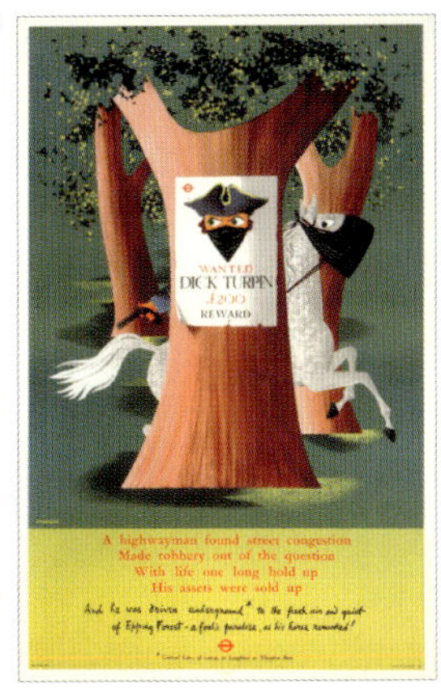 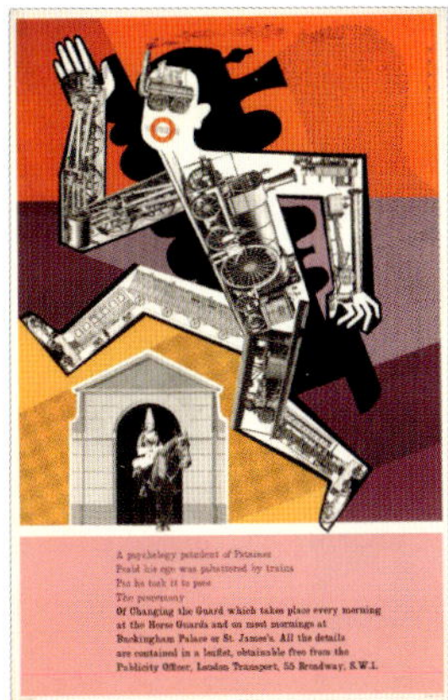 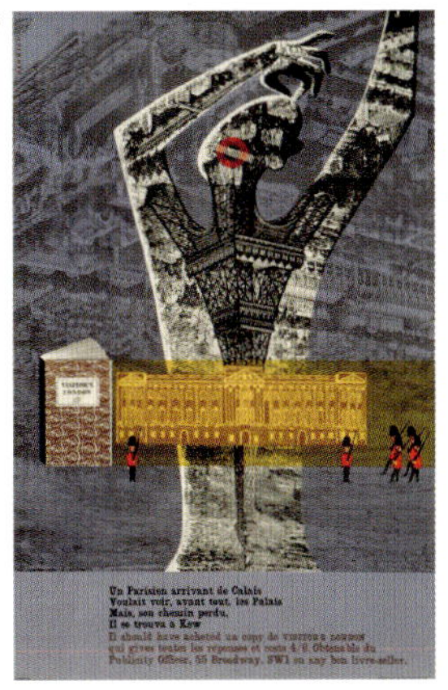 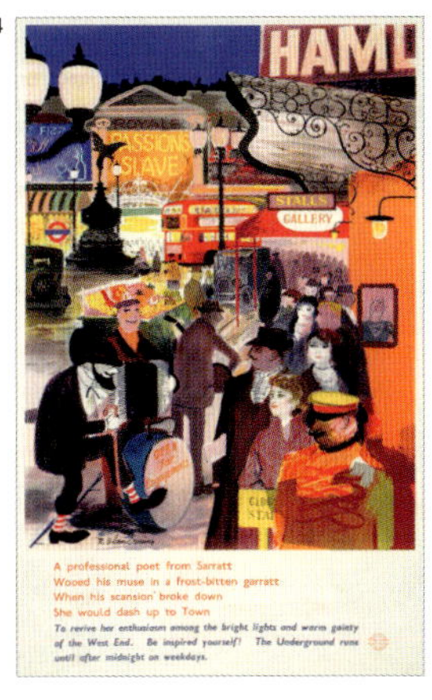

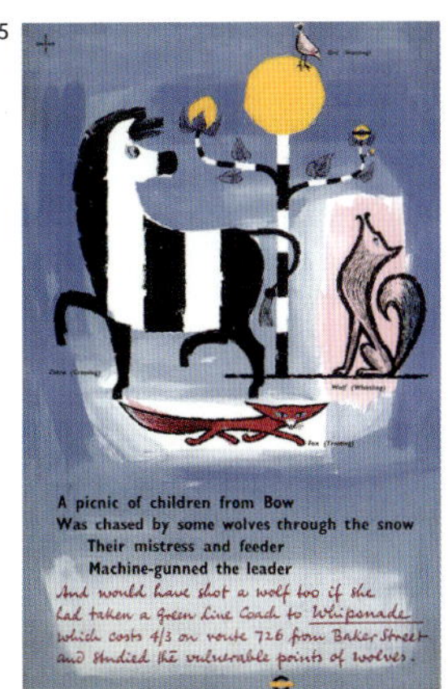 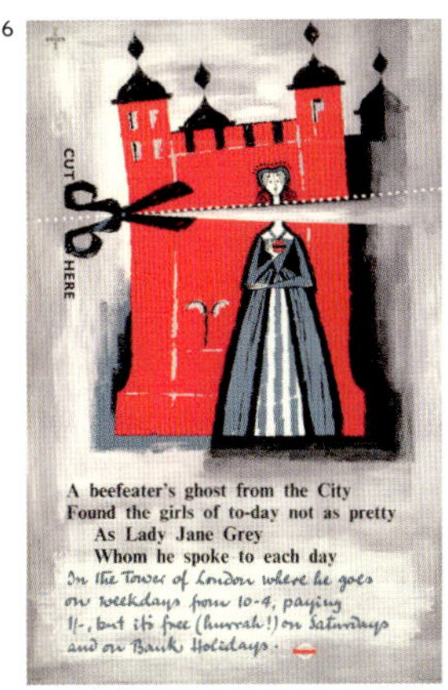 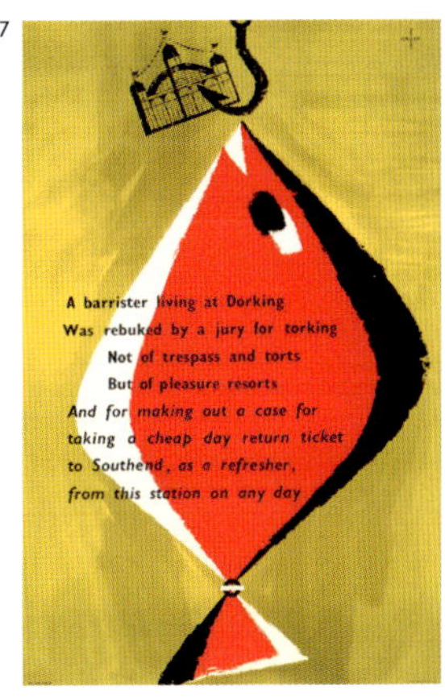 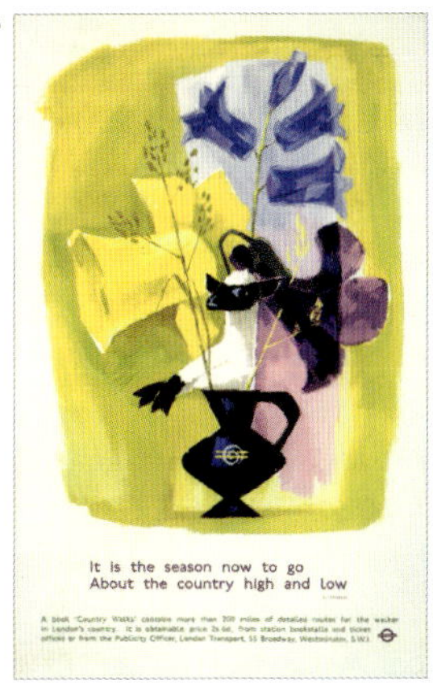

Landmarks, limericks and lamented logos, 1956–7

A wonderfully whimsical series of posters was issued in 1956, each including a different limerick in which the last line promoted a booklet called *Visitor's London*. These included strange and eye-catching photomontages and other images, including John Bainbridge's camouflaged Epping tree dress (1), what looks like a mad 1990s raver dancing over a Guard's sentry box in Frederic Henry Kay Henrion's collage (2) and, most bizarre of all, his upturned Eiffel Tower and jolly Franglais (3). Hans Unger, one of the most frequently commissioned artists during this period, produced a zebra-cum-crossing for travel to Whipsnade Zoo (5) and another witty juxtaposition for cut-price tickets to the Tower (6). His quirky fish poster (7) doesn't even mention the railway needed to take 'A cheap day return ticket to Southend' in 1956 (through trains on the District still offered this service). Unger also produced a somewhat bizarre sheep in a flower jug promoting country walks in the 'Spring' (1956, 8). Just as the limerick series drew to a close, Ronald Glendening was permitted to include the word 'Underground' again in his 1957 depiction of theatre-goers near Eros (4).

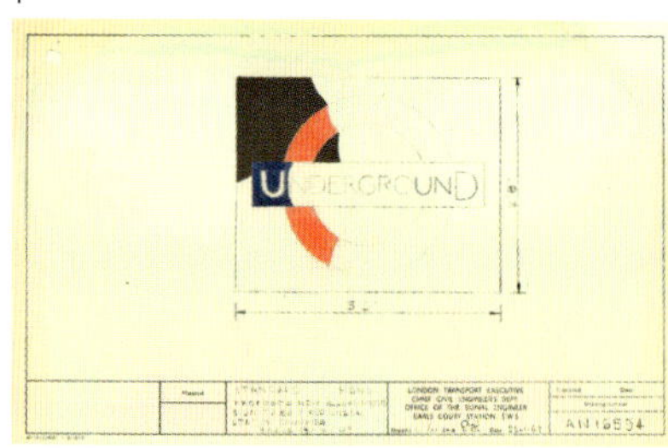

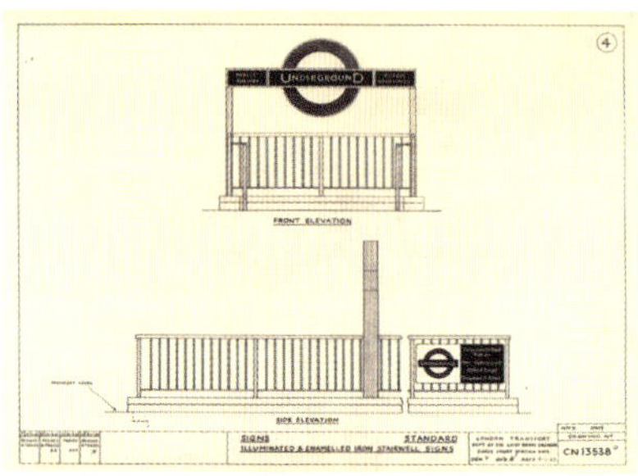

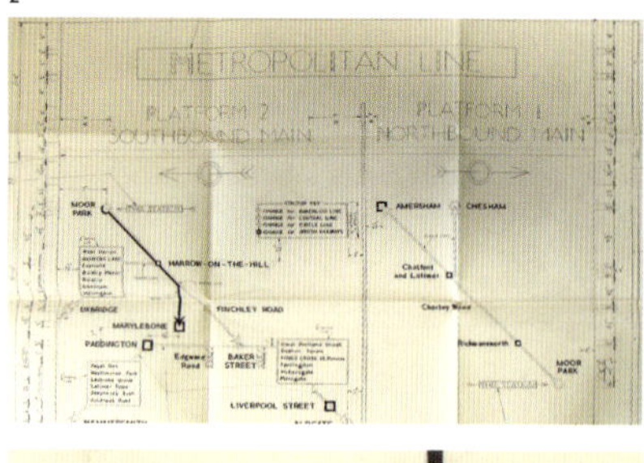

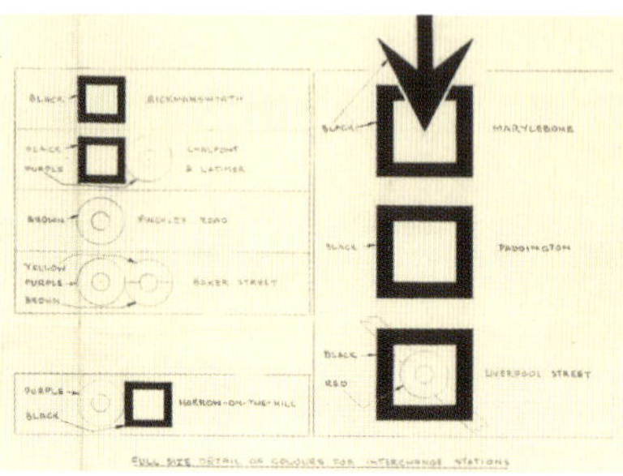

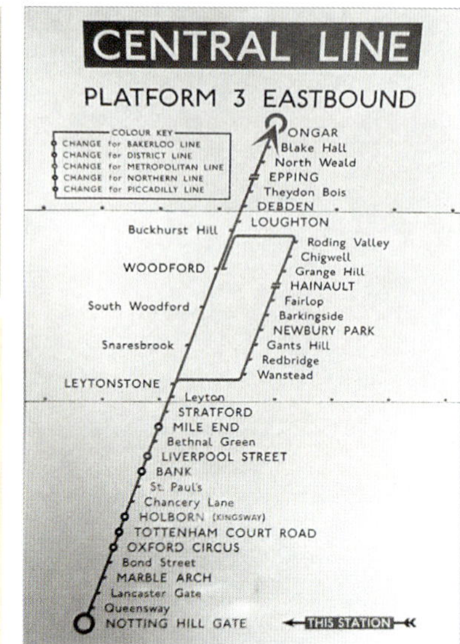

'UNDERGROUND' brand revival and signage, 1957–64

The colour-coded interchange symbols recommended by the Carr–Edward revisions of 1948 (p. 206) are shown on this detail from a Central line bifurcation route diagram sign (7) – these were not entirely successful but lasted well into the 1980s. Dropping the Underground brand in 1948 was perhaps the unwisest decision in LU's design history, but thankfully sense prevailed and in 1957 it was brought back into the fold. A revision to the Carr–Edwards guidelines was made, including this drawing from 22 January (1), which reveals plans to revive the enlarged U and D though without the pecking above and below the central letters. The reinstated logo was quickly added to the system – by a no doubt thankful staff; a direction sign to Gunnersbury joint mainline station (6) includes the contemporary lozenge-shaped BR logo (itself inspired by the original Underground bull's-eye). Hutchinson had ordered other changes to the signage by the late 1950s; they reflected his preference for upper- and lower-case letters, thinner lines, bigger arrows and sharp angles, with no curves. The 1954 revisions to the graphic standards manual compare to those from 1964 (4), with the lower-case lettering and large U and D in evidence. The 1964 manual also updated bifurcation signs, allowing angles (3), but technical drawings for Met signs (2 and 5) reflect the look of the Hutchinson diagram map (opposite, 1). The resulting enamels (3) were less pleasing to the eye and somewhat jerky compared to their predecessors; most of them were replaced during the 1970s and 80s.

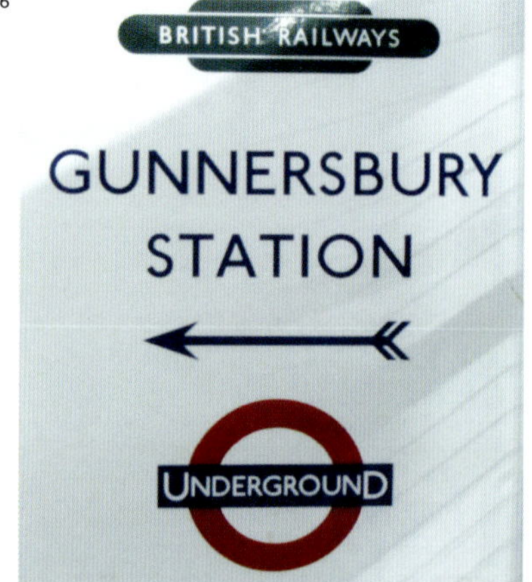

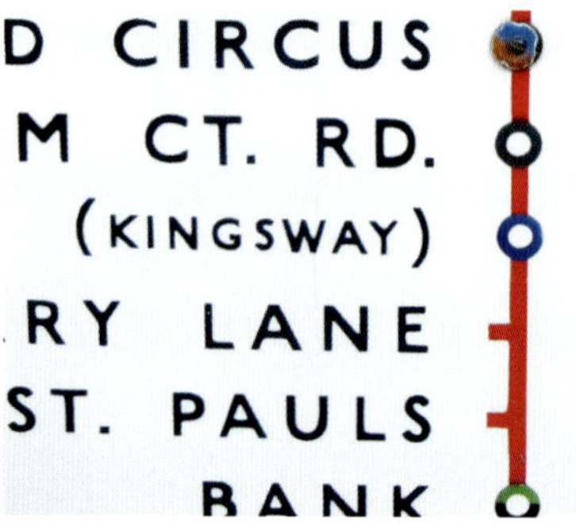

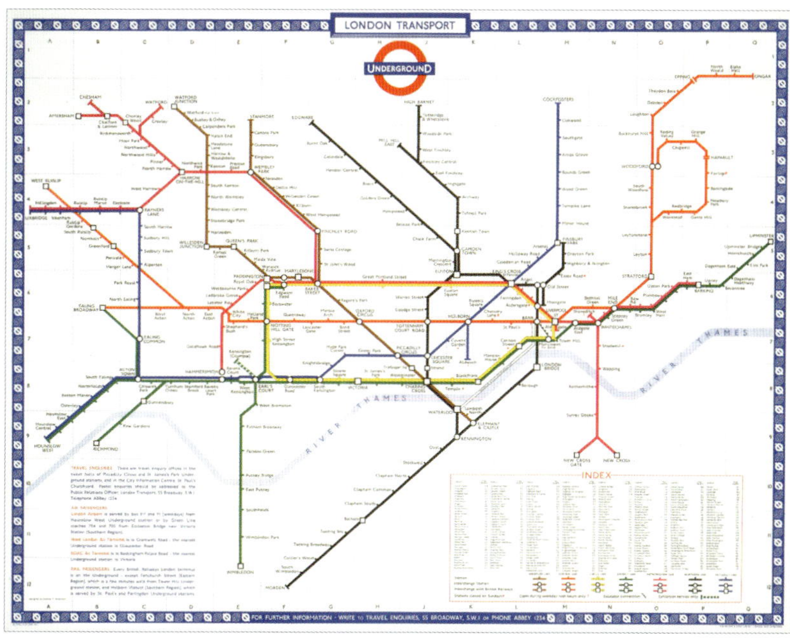

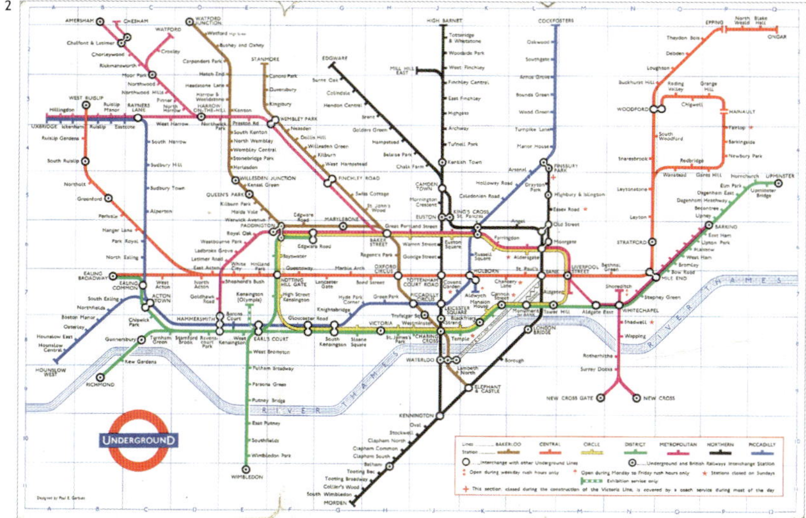

Healing Hutchinson, 1960–64

As head of publicity, Hutchinson was able to enforce his prejudice about curves on diagrams. All the grace and beauty of Beck's latest effort (p. 221) was eradicated by Hutchinson's rectilinear realization, first seen in 1961 (1). Promoted as a 'change of style after 30 years', it certainly was, if not perhaps in the way Hutchinson had intended. He was not a designer and it shows. Even if the outlying areas are at least legible, the eastern central section around Aldgate is unforgivably not. Eventually assistant secretary and works officer Paul E. Garbutt (p. 209), who had been working on what he called 'rescuing' the diagram, came up with a solution in his spare time, like Beck before him. Garbutt quite wisely submitted his concept straight to the top, circumventing Hutchinson who was known to brook no criticism. It was published in March 1964 (1965 card folder version shown, 2). As well as restoring the curves, which immediately gave it greater aesthetic appeal, Garbutt both opened out the crushed-up central area and restored a little more geographic accuracy. He did this by curving in the eastern end of the Circle line so that it formed what has been described as a 'thermos on its side'. Garbutt had relearnt the Beck rule that sufficient space must be made for station names as for the lines themselves; even so, he still needed a couple of arrows to indicate which name referred to which station (Strand, Blackfriars, King's Cross), although these had been eliminated entirely by 1970.

Widening perspex-tives, thinning Johnston, 1959–63

By the 1960s, most new public architecture was resolutely modernist in style (inspired in part by Holden's earlier pioneering work). This was reflected in the interior design too, with an emphasis on concealed (fluorescent) lighting and modern materials like melamine laminate, perspex and aluminium, which appeared smart initially but soon looked dated and at worst a bit tacky. There was a passion for chequered floor tiles, as seen at the new combined Notting Hill Gate station (1959, 1), the Colindale rebuild (1963, not shown) and the Shell building entrance to Waterloo (1964, 2). Note the illuminated shells above the escalator shaft. Externally, station buildings were generally uninspired. Moor Park (1961, 3) did benefit from an attractive slanted roof with clerestory windows, but elsewhere, for example at Northwood, inclusion of this type of glazing seemed an almost desperate attempt to enliven an otherwise lifeless design. West Ruislip (1966, 4) fared slightly better, with yellow and white concrete brick (now repainted) and a large glazed upper floor. The period also saw the introduction of the new thinner Johnston type (5) designed specifically for illuminated suspended signage, manufactured to a standard shape to accommodate fluorescent lamps. Such characteristic signage appeared across the system until phased out from the 1980s (though some is still in use, p. 250).

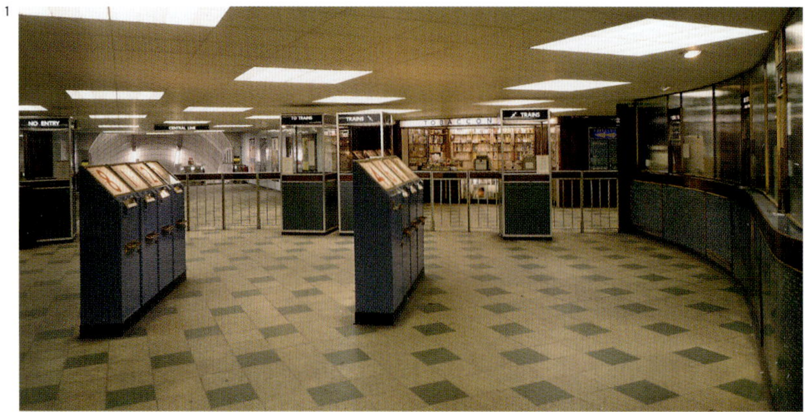

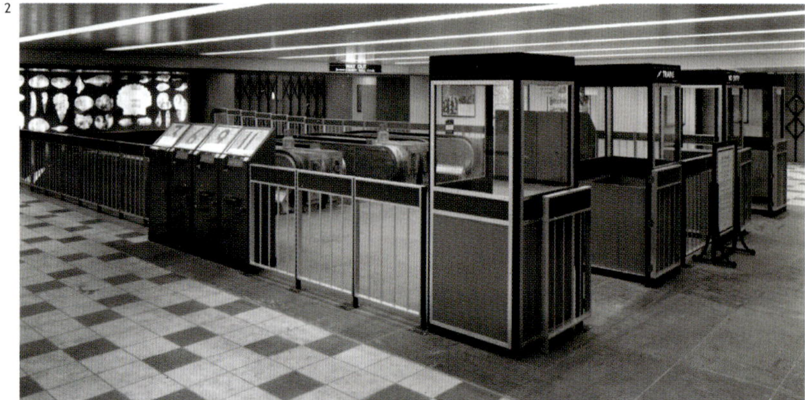

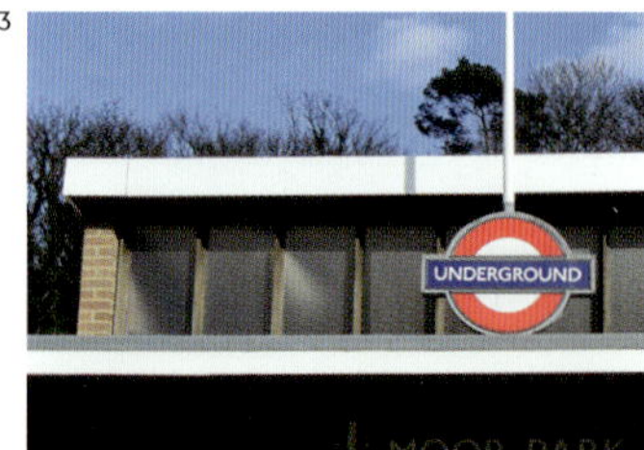

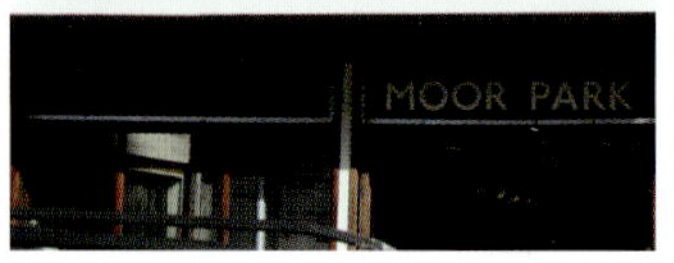

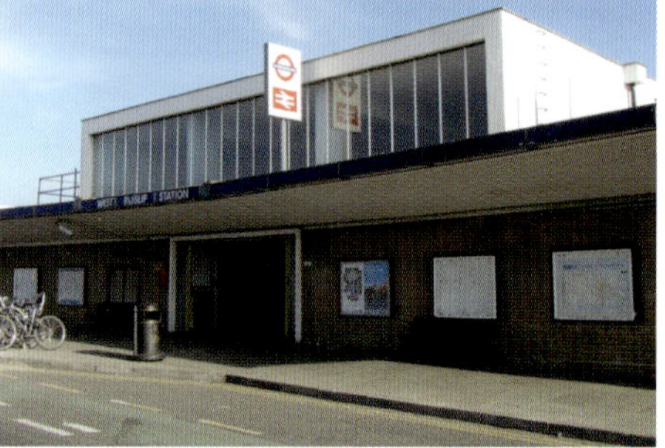

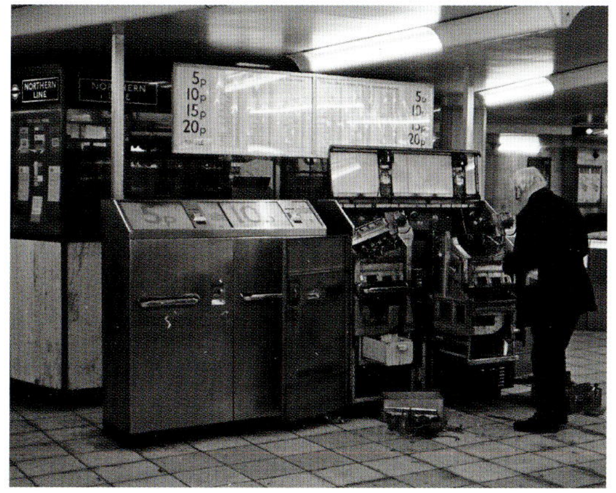

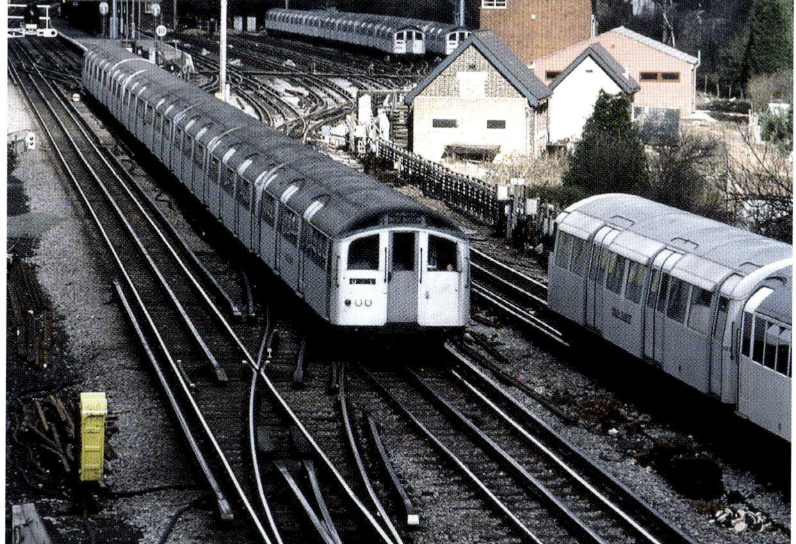

Silver lining and grey pride, 1952–66

Just as the 1930s and 40s had been about bus-red trains and biscuit-cream tiling, so the 1950s and 1960s were characterized by a different, more machine-like hue. The automatic slant-fronted ticket dispensers (2) – installed on the Underground since 1936 (a poster advertising their arrival, 1) and not phased out until the introduction of the Underground Ticketing System in 1987 – were a feature of every ticket hall in their characteristic blue-grey finish. The trains were now changing to match. Experiments had taken place as early as spring 1952 in leaving the sub-surface 'P Stock' aluminium cars unpainted. The biggest batch of 'silver trains' were promoted on 2 January 1958 with a special day trip and can be seen on a 1960 poster (p. 231). They were named '1959 Stock' (used mainly on the Piccadilly) and '1962 Stock' (numbering almost 620 vehicles, for use on the Central, 3). The last of these were withdrawn as late as 2000. Their automatically driven sister 'silver trains' for the forthcoming Victoria (pp. 234, 242) were promoted on posters in the mid 1960s (4).

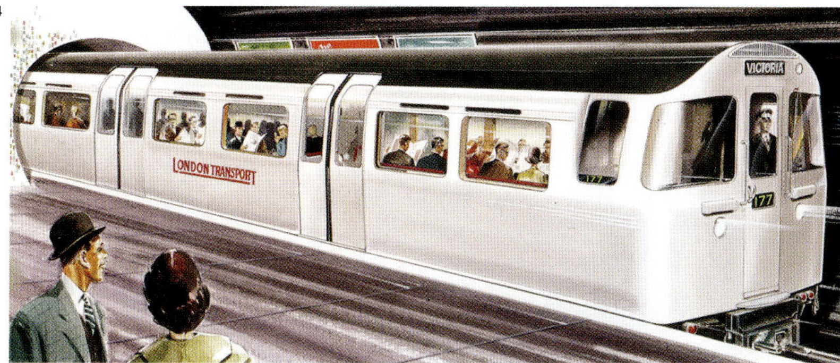

A new poster palette, 1959–65

While every decade has its extremes, 1960s publicity design for the Underground must be one of the most diverse, from the elaborate curlicues of the 1960 royal wedding poster (2), by Charles Shepherd, to Hans Unger's modernist vision of a skyscraper-filled 'Brave New London' (of the same year, 4). The ball was already rolling in 1959 when Tom Eckersley's panel poster 'For Traffic Enquiries; For Lost Property' (1) and Anne Hickmott's 'Boat Races' (3) both hit the streets. The 1960s was a decade of highly inventive and often outlandish poster design. Robert Scanlan's 'When did you last see your Picassos?' (1960, 5), for the Tate Gallery, mimics the style of the artist whose work it is advertising. John Griffiths's 'Rhubarb and Roses' poster for Covent Garden (when it was still a market, 1965, 6) reflects the era with its lyrical montage and slightly trippy characters, while Pat Keely's 'Sightseeing' (1962, 7) evokes London's architectural contrasts.

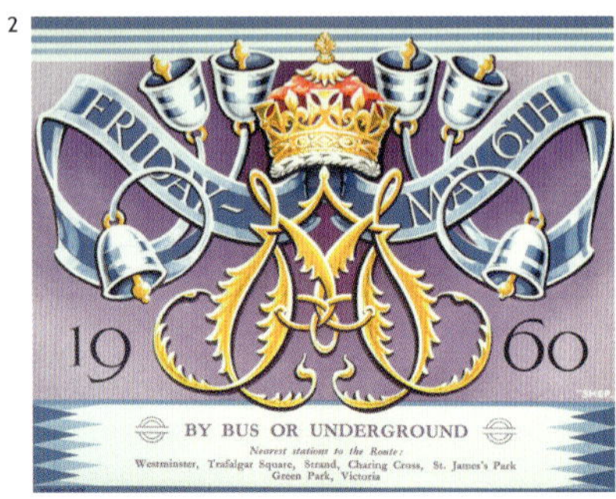

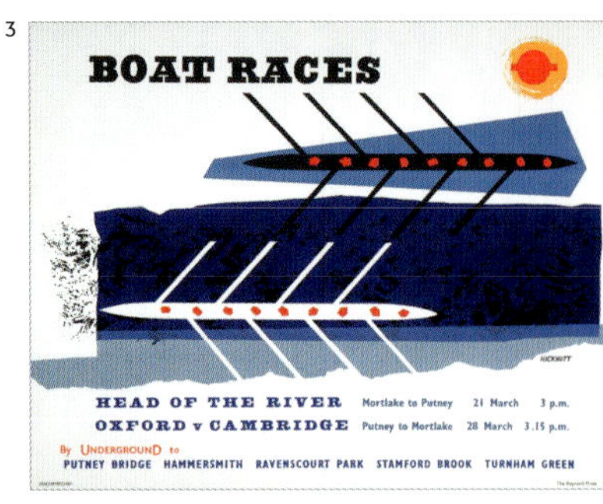

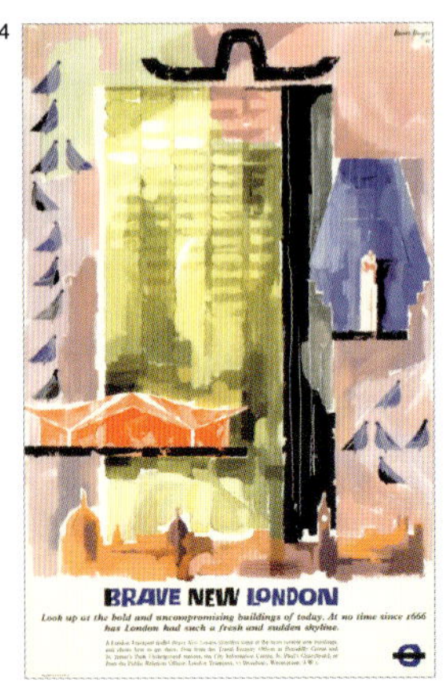

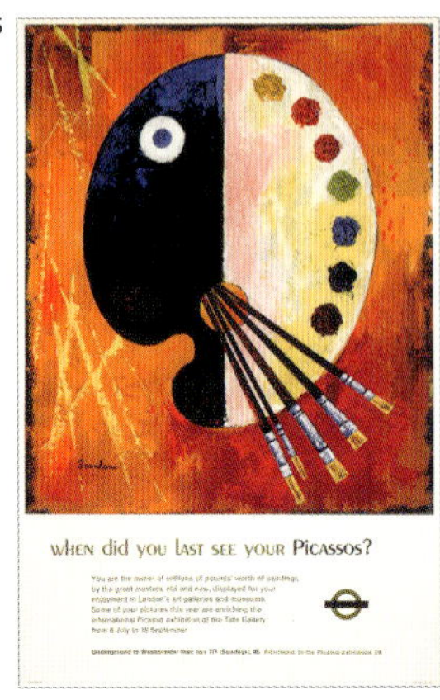

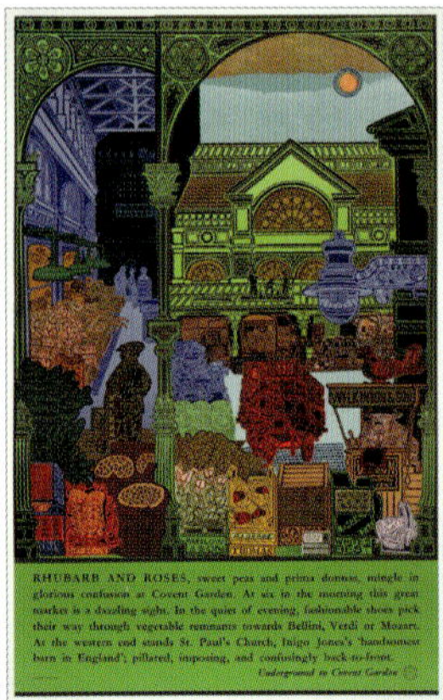

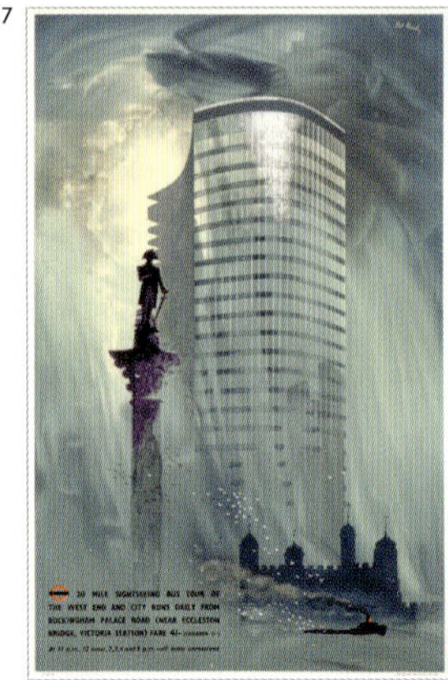

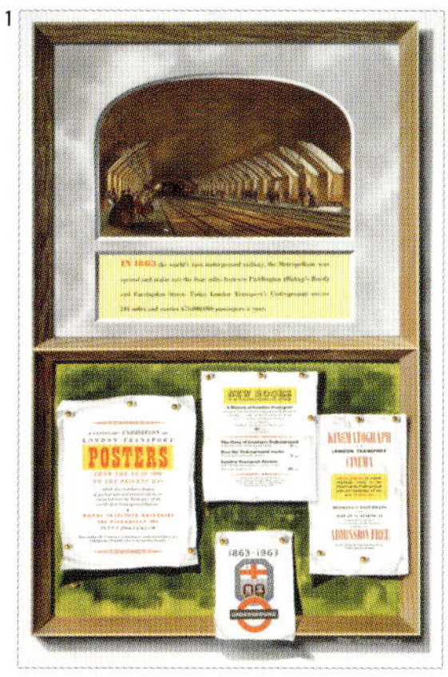

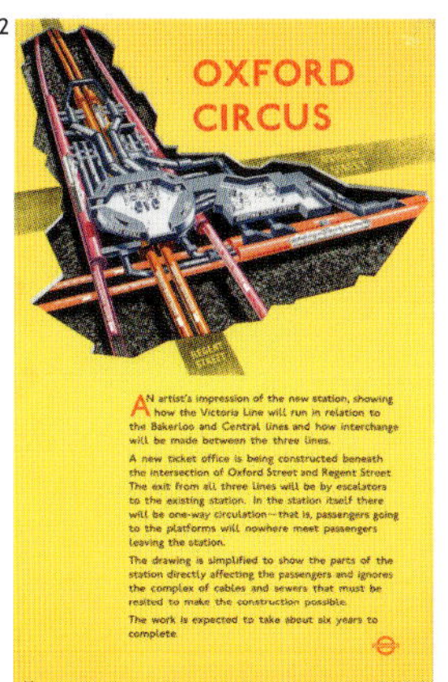

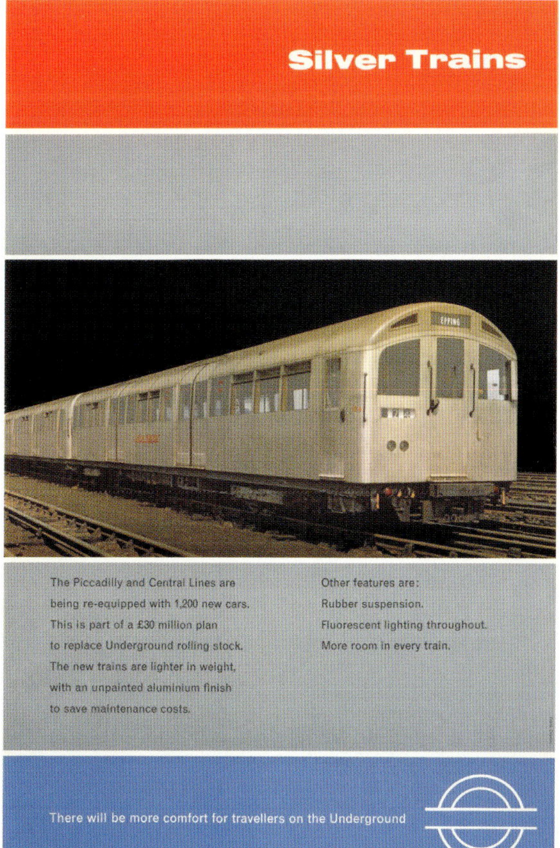

The Piccadilly and Central Lines are being re-equipped with 1,200 new cars. This is part of a £30 million plan to replace Underground rolling stock. The new trains are lighter in weight, with an unpainted aluminium finish to save maintenance costs.

Other features are: Rubber suspension. Fluorescent lighting throughout. More room in every train.

There will be more comfort for travellers on the Underground

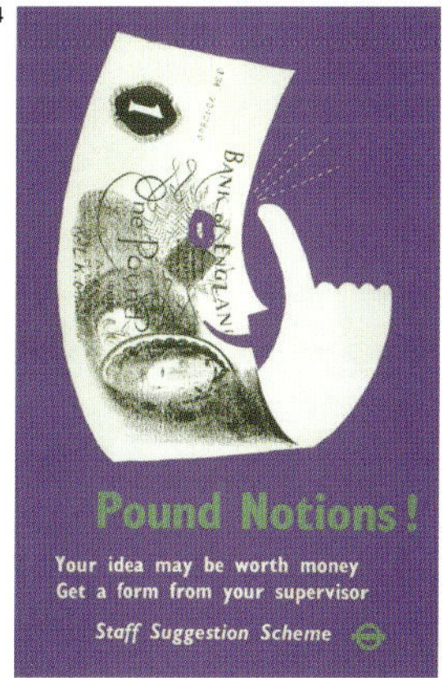

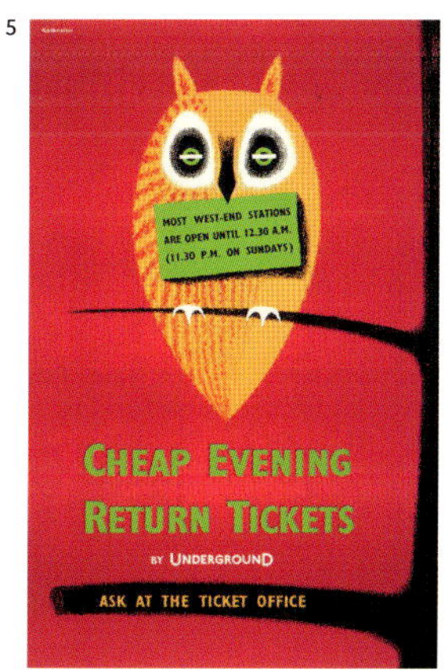

Johnston takes a break, 1960–63

Another aspect of 1960s poster design was a temporary move away from Johnston Sans. Gill Sans and Univers were tried, among others, although thankfully never adopted for lettering elsewhere, but the in-house face did not reassert itself fully until the early 1980s. Peter Roberson used anything but Johnston in his 1963 Met centenary poster (1), for example; perhaps understandable given the inclusion of 'Wanted'-style lettering, but a tad peculiar even so. Frank Overton's welcoming of the new silver trains (1960, 3 and p. 229) was set in Univers. Victor Galbraith produced two posters using a non-Johnston typeface — both in Gill Sans: 'To Town Tonight' (1962, not shown) and his wonderful roundel-eyed owl design for 'Cheap Evening Return Tickets' (1960, 5). The same typeface was used for two internal staff information posters: 'Pound Notions' (1965, 4) and a notice on 'load' safety by Alec Gorton (1961, not shown). Johnston was back for the Clement Dane Studio poster showing a cutaway of the station rebuild at Oxford Circus (1963, 2): a tantalizing early peek at the proposed Victoria line route.

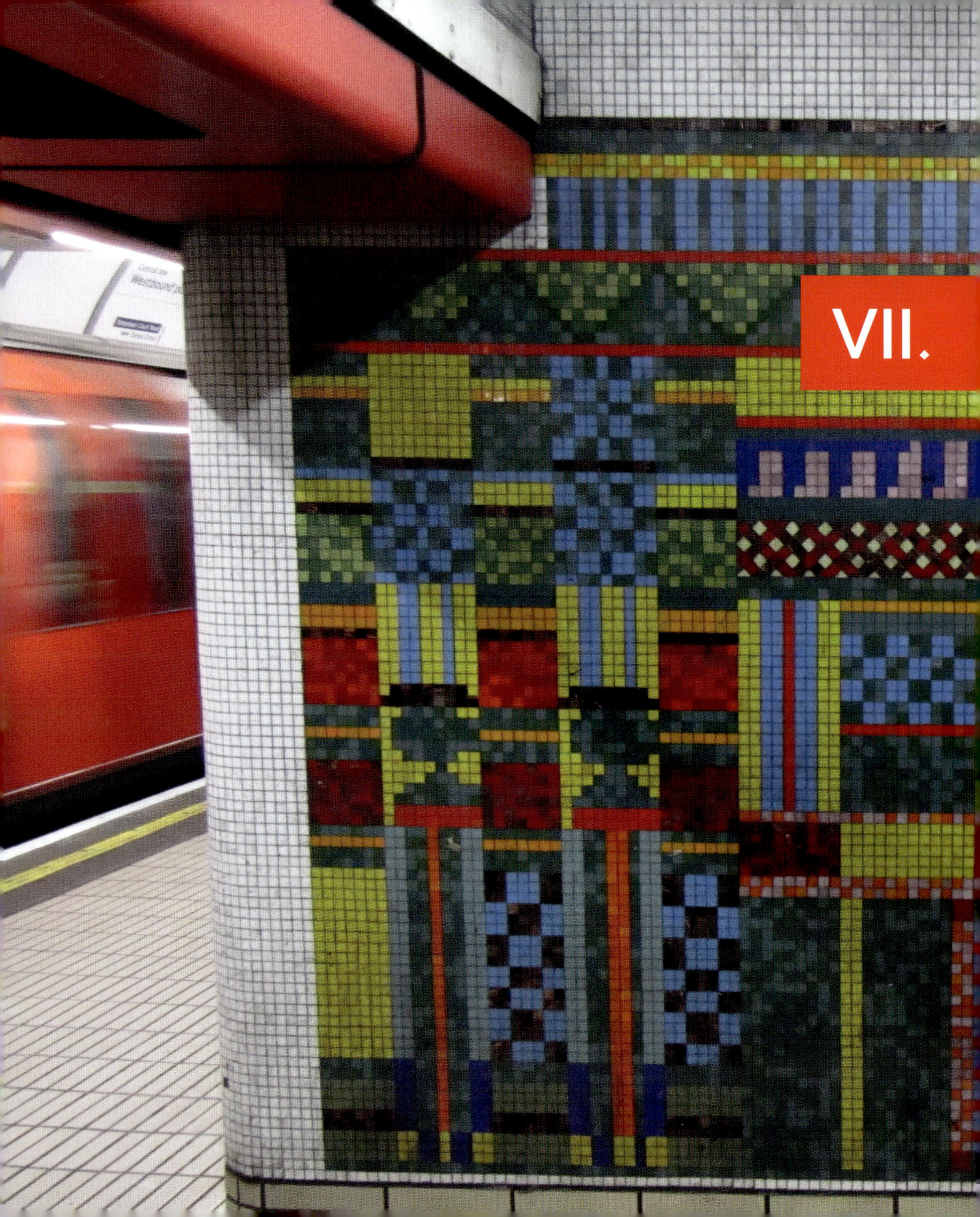
VII.

Automation and Regeneration
1968–99

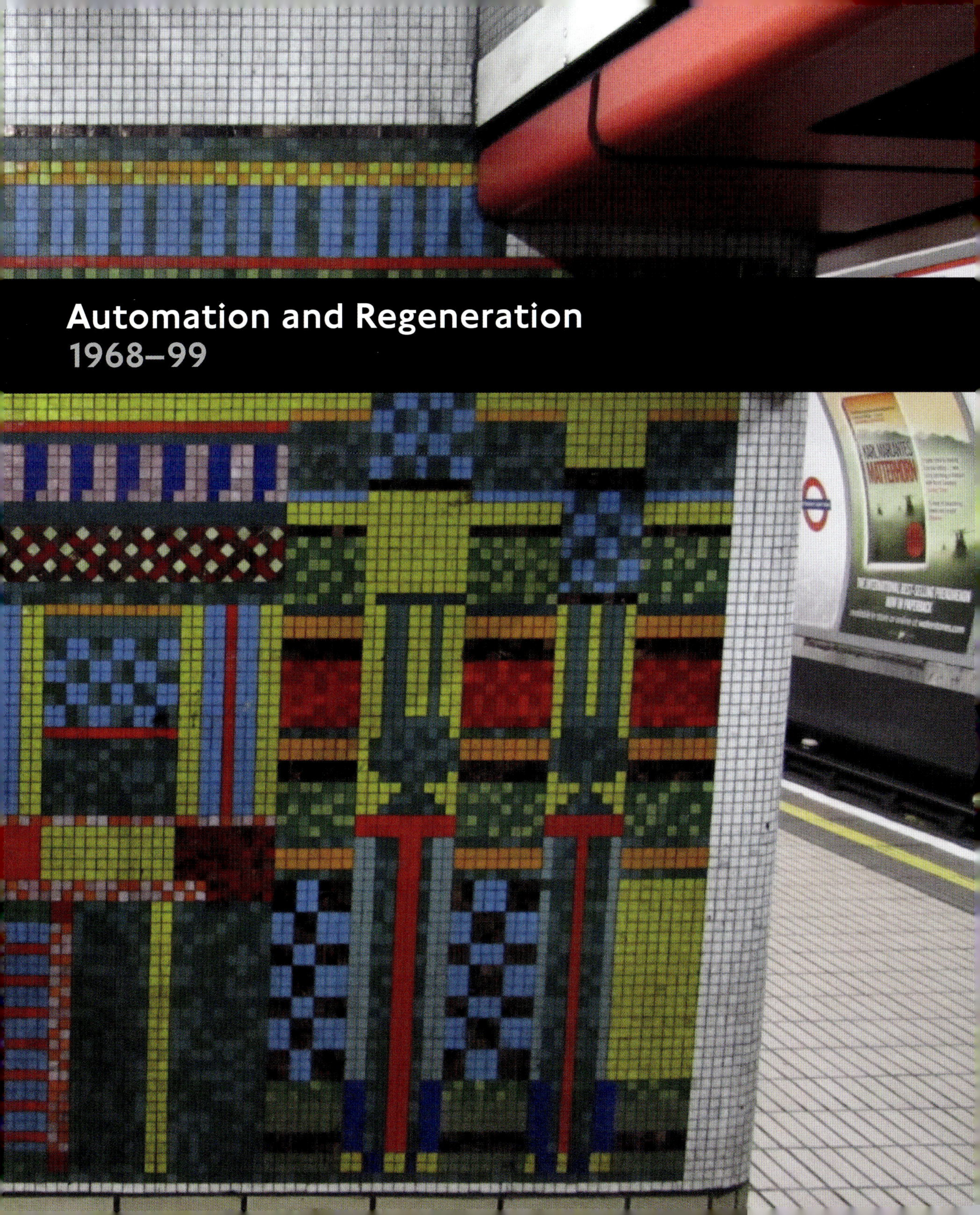

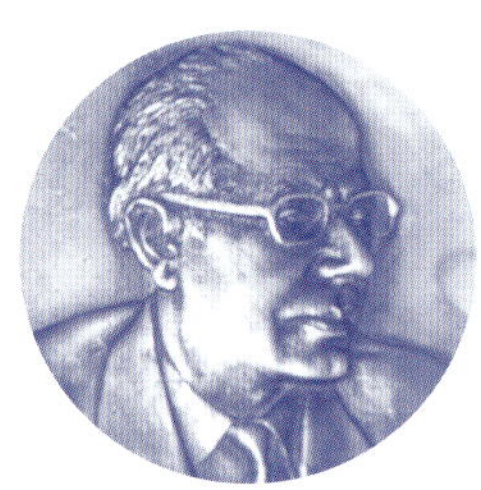

PREVIOUS PAGES: Though the opening of the Victoria line was the first major addition to the Tube network for many years – and also the last until work began at the end of this period on the Jubilee Line Extension (p. 241) – there were still many advances in design, particularly the station refurbishment programmes of the 1980s and 1990s. Here Tottenham Court Road is seen with some of the magnificent mosaic murals created by Eduardo Paolozzi and first put up in 1984.

VII. Automation and Regeneration, 1968–99

After thirty years of relative quiet, the three decades leading up to the millennium were, in comparison, a hive of activity, with major projects and station improvements being carried out. In 1968 the first new Underground route was opened since the deep-level tubes; the Victoria line revitalized a creaking system and, although some criticized the aesthetics, the coherent look for an entire line was a design milestone.

Victoria Black and blue

It's true that the decor was a bit austere – greys, blacks and blues – but according to Misha Black (of the Design Research Unit (DRU), hired by LT for the project), this was to help signage stand out and passengers would supply the colour in the monochromatic interiors. Much of what became the Victoria line had been mooted back in the 1930s. By the time Parliamentary approval had been given, a name chosen[1] and design begun, it was clear the line was going to be a very different beast from its predecessors. From an engineering perspective, it was to be the first automatic underground railway in the world: trains would be accelerated and braked electronically in a system overseen by a central control centre.[2] The genius behind this was the remarkable Robert Dell.

No new surface-level stations were required, except at Blackhorse Road where a single-storey building, in keeping with the rather stark style of the period,[3] was designed by Black's team. The entire line was to be in tunnel,[4] every station of the first section forming an interchange either with another Underground line, or, north of Finsbury Park, an existing mainline station – an extremely challenging engineering project.[5] At Oxford Circus a complete rebuild was necessary to create the circular ticket hall, similar in size to those at Piccadilly Circus and Leicester Square.

Experimentation with new signage

A new style of frieze, running the entire platform length, was chosen to display wayfinding information and station name (p. 242). Illuminated, flush-mounted boxes with bullseyes rear-painted on glass were used to display station names (these were badly maintained and despite being easy to read, they fell out of favour in the 1990s, replaced (except at Pimlico) with standard enamel signage). Walls above recessed platform seating were decorated with murals showing local attractions above ground (p. 243), the splash of colour helping to enliven otherwise bland platforms.[6] On the surface, signage was minimal because all the stations were shared with pre-existing services. Blackhorse Road featured a standard illuminated dark blue frieze along the canopy and a lone cantilevered bullseye projecting from the wall. If not for the horse relief and mosaic by sculptor David McFall, the building would have been entirely devoid of decoration.

Look, no hands!

It was not just the trains that were automated. For some years LT wanted to improve ticketing. Automatic ticket gates were trialled[7] in 1967 and subsequently installed on the Victoria line (p. 242), greatly speeding up the process and requiring less staff. The 'Automatic Fare Collection' system introduced small yellow tickets printed in magnetic ink that could be read by the 'magic eye' inside the gate. Fully automated, from train operation to ticket inspection, the section of the new Victoria line from Walthamstow to Highbury & Islington opened, without ceremony, on Sunday 1 September 1968, followed on 1 December by the next part to Warren Street. On 7 March 1969, by contrast, the stretch from Oxford Circus to Victoria was officially opened by the Queen.[8] The southern extension of the line to Brixton had been given Parliamentary approval but did not open until 23 July 1971.

Several stations connecting to or close by the Victoria line were rebuilt at this time. At Old Street, for instance, the Northern line platforms were reconstructed to blend in with those of the Victoria and the Holden-designed surface station was closed. The station entrance was instead relocated beneath the large road roundabout above between 1967 and 1969. Remodelling older stations to match the Victoria style partly inspired the DRU's 1971 design survey report, which recommended simplified signage across the entire bus and Tube network and renamed the bullseye to 'roundel'.

To Brixton and beyond … or not

Just as Walthamstow had never been the intended northern terminal of the Victoria line, so the southern section was cut off somewhat abruptly at Brixton.[9] There were intermediate stations at Vauxhall and Stockwell, but the addition of Pimlico had to wait until 14 September 1972. All had little in the way of surface buildings apart from Stockwell.[10] Pimlico had sloping subway-style entrances with pole-mounted, illuminated signs sporting a black background and a roundel with white semicircles.[11]

Enforcing a unified style

In 1973, Pimlico's blue bar was replaced with a red one to reflect the change of ownership of the Underground (the Greater London Council had taken over management of London Underground three years before via a new body). The desire for greater uniformity across all modes of operation (combined with the recommendations of the DRU report) led to the standardization of the logo for bus and Tube. One-colour roundels (usually white on red paintwork) were quickly introduced on buses and trains, appearing on publicity (pp. 244–6) and some signage. The blue bar was restricted for use only in station-name roundels on platforms.

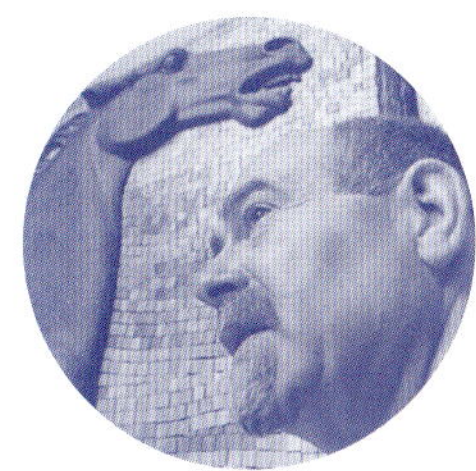

David McFall (1919–88), born in Glasgow, was a sculptor who became an assistant to Eric Gill (1939) and worked with Jacob Epstein (1944–58). He produced a horse relief in glass-reinforced polyester (pictured) and a mosaic (189cm high x 230cm wide) for Blackhorse Road Victoria line station in 1968.

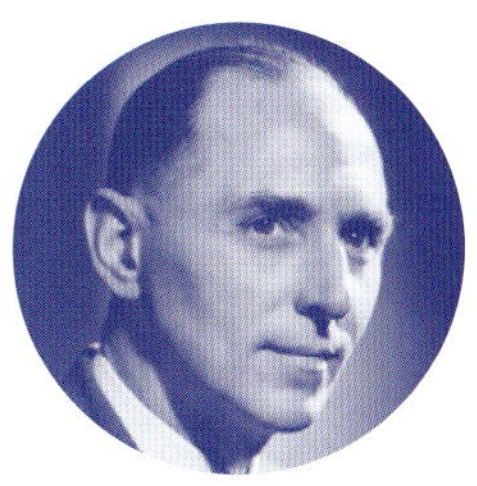

Robert Dell (1900–1992) was a signal engineer who worked for the Underground. He invented a 'Programme Machine' for automatic working at junctions (installed at several sites in 1958) and was the creator of the Victoria line 'Automatic Train Operation' (1968) and ticketing system. An apprentice award was created in his name in 1973.

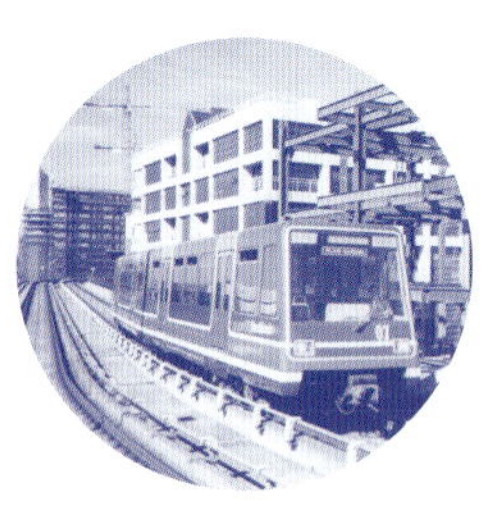

Bill Clarke, born 1934, joined LU as a graduate. He worked on the Victoria line and the Metropolitan improvements. In 1983 he became general manager of the DLR project (pictured just after opening), returning to the Underground three years later to work on the JLE, Crossrail and East London line extension.

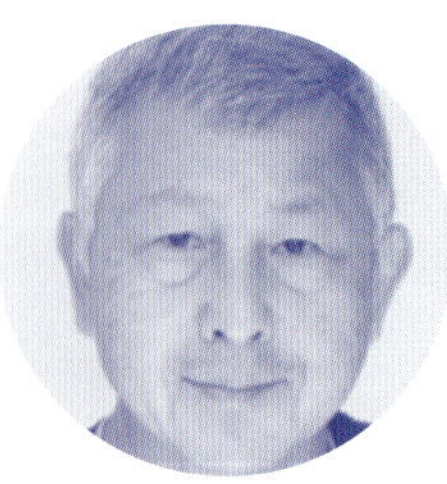

Eiichi Kono, born in Japan 1941, came to study in London during 1974, joining Banks & Miles in 1979, where he redesigned the Johnston typeface (1979) and the BT telephone directory (1984). He has taught typography at Middlesex and worked for Pearson, Toyota, *The Economist* and Microsoft.

Taking the train to the plane

It had long been an ambition to serve Heathrow Airport by Tube and work began in 1971 on projecting the Piccadilly in that direction. The first station to open was Hatton Cross, on 19 July 1975. The surface building resembled an aircraft hangar – appropriate maybe, but lacking flair, its sole redeeming feature being door handles in the shape of a split roundel (p. 244). The uninspired surface structure at Heathrow Central had been restricted by space, so the ticket hall was below ground, but platforms were more aesthetically pleasing, with Concorde tail motifs by Tom Eckersley (p. 244), illuminated station-name bull's-eyes and the first appearance on the Underground of airport-style pictograms (p. 244). The Queen was in the cab as the train cut through the ceremonial blue ribbon, which bore the words 'UNDERGROUND EXTENSION TO HEATHROW CENTRAL 16 DECEMBER 1977' in Johnston Sans.

Though the Underground as a whole was dilapidated and in need of repair, big projects were in vogue. They seemed to be happening faster too. While the Victoria line took thirty years from conception to opening, the Heathrow extension was far quicker. Although a British Rail line was mooted to the airport from Feltham in 1966, a 1970 study recommended an Underground connection. Design started on 28 April 1971 and the line was opened just six years later: a breakneck speed for the UK. The same cannot be said for the Jubilee line, however.

Fleeting jubilation

Gestated as far back as the 1930s as part of a second New Works Programme (1940–50), which never materialized, a north-west to south-east trajectory was outlined in the 1946–7 London Plan,[12] but even that was shelved until 1963. An idea emerged to extend the Bakerloo line south from Baker Street to Trafalgar Square/Strand and then east to Tower Hill/Fenchurch Street. Notionally named the 'Fleet line', because some of the tunnels would pass beneath Fleet Street and cross the (long buried) Fleet River, the potential location of its southerly terminal varied between Bexleyheath, Hayes, Lewisham, Addiscombe and later Thamesmead. A mid-1970s opening date was envisaged. Parliament approved the preliminary central London section, 'temporarily' terminating at Trafalgar Square/Strand. MPs decided on a Lewisham terminus (in 1973) but by 1979 the plan was changed to go beneath the Thames via the Isle of Dogs to Thamesmead, under a new name – 'River line'. Test tunnels were bored almost to Aldwych in readiness for that phase, which never happened. Boring the first tunnels between Charing Cross and Baker Street started in February 1971 and was mostly finished by the end of the following year. Cross-platform interchange was constructed at Baker Street (destroying the Stabler-style tiling), but while no new surface buildings were needed, Bond Street required reconstruction to cope with the expected Fleet line traffic. Little was done at Green Park, however, as it had recently been modernized for the Victoria. Trafalgar Square and Strand were remodelled into a single station. The new complex of tunnels was renamed Charing Cross and the station which formerly went by that name became Embankment (p. 248).

Prescient name change

Building was well under way when the new Greater London Council (GLC) leader Horace Cutler announced, without informing anyone at LT, that it would thereafter be known as the 'Jubilee line' – even though its opening would miss the 1977 celebration by at least a year. 'Fleet line' maps, publicity and signage (p. 248) had to be remade ready for 1 May 1979 when the Baker Street to Stanmore stretch was rebranded as the Jubilee line and the new section to Charing Cross opened. The grey line colour had already been chosen (in 1974), but luckily this fitted with the *Silver* Jubilee theme. In contrast to the Victoria, station decor was noticeably brighter, almost lurid, with tiling in acidic yellows, flame reds and neon blues (p. 249). New trains were designed – 1972 Mk II Stock (p. 249). The bodies were in unpainted, satin-finished aluminium, for the first time the doors were painted bus red, a colour scheme that lasted until the late 1980s. Meanwhile, Cutler's surprise renaming was to prove unexpectedly helpful when the proposed next stage of the route under Fleet Street was abandoned (p. 241).

Updating station design

Meanwhile, a programme of modernization elsewhere was proposed by the 1979 station update policy report. Compiled in consultation with LU architect Sydney Hardy, this was published in 1980 as *Initial Design Strategy for the Rail System*. Following successful renovations at Charing Cross that year and trials at Aldwych, £220m (at 2013 prices) was allocated to improve central area stations. These were permitted their own graphic identity relevant to the local area, resulting in some refreshing new designs (p. 252). The line colour would always be used for the station-name frieze on platform walls, but the dominance of the roundel would be downplayed (though still used for station names and at entrances). To conceal cables, line-coloured box 'trunking' doubling up as station-name friezes was also introduced[13] (p. 252).

Kono tackles Johnston

It was not just the buildings that would be modernized; even the Johnston typeface was updated. LT commissioned Banks & Miles for the purpose and the agency gave the task to new recruit Eiichi Kono, on his very first day, 2 July 1979. New Johnston, the first proper revision since 1917, comprised a slightly heavier 'Medium' than the original typeface, allowing a full set of weights: Bold, Condensed, Light and Medium – plus italics for each

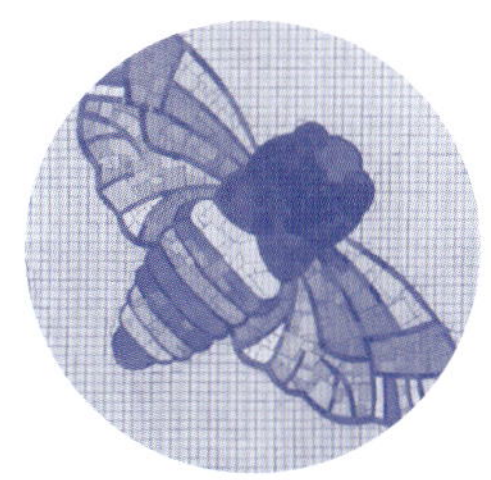

Sculptor Eduardo Luigi Paolozzi (1924–2005), born in Edinburgh, was one of the first Pop artists. He created mosaic murals for Tottenham Court Road station in 1984 (detail pictured; in full on pp. 232–3 and 253) and was knighted in 1988.

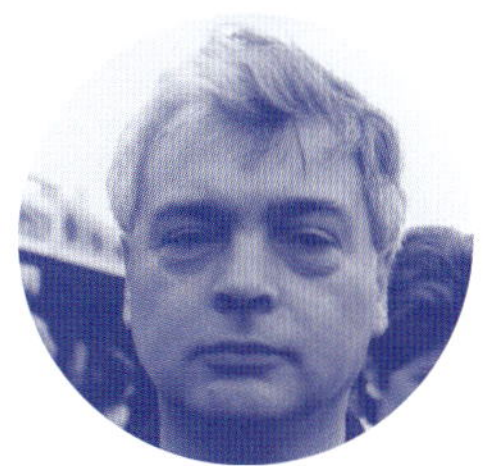

Tim Demuth, born in Surrey 1942, joined the LT publicity office from 1971, becoming art director and designing maps, timetables and posters. A fan of the diagrammatic style, he made the first official all-London rail diagram (1973).

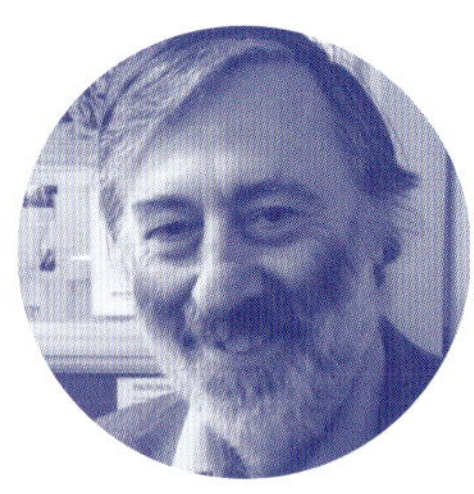

Doug Rose, born in London 1949, is an information designer who trained as cartographer, joining FWT (in 1979) which oversaw the LU diagram 1983-6. He has designed maps for transport authorities internationally and was involved with the development of the bus 'spider maps'. His history of line/stations (Bibliography) is invaluable to researchers.

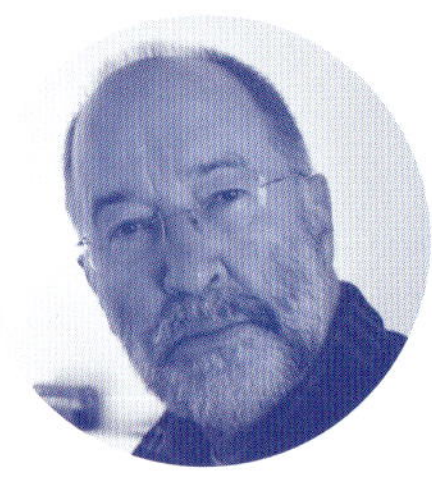

Chris Ludlow, born 1946, was a co-founder of Henrion Ludlow Schmidt. Its first major project evaluating Underground signage led to innovations still visible today. This work created a reputation for the consultancy and projects followed for Canary Wharf, BAA, Bluewater, Eurostar and the Millennium Dome, among others.

(p. 250). Book was added later, in which the body copy of this text is set. It remains the in-house typeface to this day (now called 'New Johnston TfL' and revived again in 2015 as Johnston100).

Ticketing zones and Travelcards

The Tube diagram was evolving too. Paul Garbutt's name had been on it since 1964, but on his retirement a new LT employee, Tim Demuth (p. 237), took over, producing a couple of maps (1979–82, p. 251) before the mantle was passed in 1983 to the FWT agency (David Penrose and Doug Rose).[14] Ticketing zones[15] were added to maps and in-car diagrams (4 October 1981), which enabled Travelcards to be issued (p. 251).

Back to basics for Baker Street

Baker Street station, built in 1863, had been unsympathetically knocked about ever since. In 1983–4 the oldest Met platforms were stripped to bare brick by LT's architect Alan Douglas; the former light-wells were reinstated and lined with white tiles. It was the most successful rebuild to date, gaining Grade II listed status (1987) and inspiring similar strip-back-and-restore projects at Great Portland Street (1985) and Gloucester Road (1993).

An outside agency with an inside eye

During the same period, LT commissioned renowned agency Henrion Ludlow Schmidt (HLS) to examine sign design. Its report of May 1984, *Underground Railway Signing Study for London Transport*,[16] focused on consistency. Critical of piecemeal changes, it urged an immediate return to core design values, stressing a coherent style, including uniform colour-coding of lines and incorporating elements of the Tube map in signage. It also stipulated that all signs should have white backgrounds and grey rims; station-name roundels should be the large 'tray' variety; and New Johnston should be applied universally (although heritage stations were exempt, such as Sudbury Town or those with Leslie Green tiling). Chris Ludlow of HLS recalls: 'Our proposals were eventually trialled at Victoria in 1989, centring round a rigorous logic for the order of information.' The first versions were made of aluminium but this attracted brake dust, so enamel (which easily wipes clean) was soon back. An alphabetical listing of stations lasted precisely one morning because, despite research favouring the idea, it completely foxed passengers. Alternative ideas were also tried at Holborn (1990, where outline roundels included in Allan Drummond's museum artefact friezes had a white rim to stand out against the black background, p. 253), and at Mansion House (1991), but the insistence on customer-focused signage (as opposed to what was easiest to do and make) won the day. Following the successful trials at Victoria, all new signage (with the exception of specially commissioned replicas for heritage signs) conformed to the HLS specifications. This was not plain sailing: implementing the HLS report caused a battle between Mike Duffie's architects department (who wanted signs to *blend in* with finishes) and the team of designers and marketeers like Helen Robinson, Raymond Turner, Roger Hughes and Jeff Mills (who insisted the signs *stood out*).

The end of the box

Box trunking proved impossible at Shepherd's Bush due to the pillars. At Paddington (Bakerloo line, 1984–7, p. 152), it would have vied with the Brunel architectural drawings fired onto the tiling. The same was true at Leicester Square (Northern line, 1985, p. 152), where the film-sprocket motif on the tiles and a neon cinema theme would have clashed with a black frieze box above, so a traditional enamel frieze with a white background was used instead at all three stations (cables being encased higher up). At Euston and Embankment (Northern line, 1987 and 1988) enamelled panels were used to hide cabling (p. 253). The suspended 'box' direction signs were also on their way out following HLS guidelines that signage should be 'modular by message' (one message per sign) rather than trying to fit everything into a standard-sized sign. Made by the LU lighting department and in use for decades, these illuminated glass signs with their black background and multiple messages, often in varying type sizes, did not fit the HLS ethos. Design refinements such as to trunking and box signage were subsequently incorporated in the new station at Heathrow Terminal 4 (opened on 12 April 1986).

London looks east

On the opposite side of the capital, major projects were in hand. The once thriving docks of London's East End had been decimated by 1970s containerization and a vast area along the Thames laid waste. Then in 1981 the London Docklands Development Corporation (LDDC) was created to revitalize it. Improvement to transportation was a prime objective with an extension of the Jubilee line to Fenchurch Street initially regarded an absolute priority, but then dropped due to lack of funding. 'River line' (a Jubilee 'branch', with four under-Thames tunnels) was deemed too expensive but a 'low cost' option for Jubilee extension (1980) was ignored, funds going to road improvements instead.

Plans to build a light railway went ahead, however, and construction began on this in 1985. In the meantime, two East London line (ELL) stations were rebuilt in 1983 (p. 253): Surrey Docks (renamed Surrey Quays in 1989) and Shadwell – both in brick but with none of the bright decor of the Zone 1 stations.

Docklands defies doubters

While light rail had worked for the Tyne and Wear Metro, there were doubts initially that it could cope with the much higher level of traffic expected in London. Despite this, the first

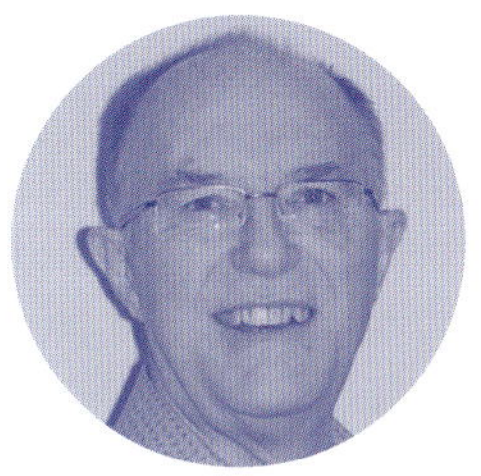

Jeff Mills, born in London 1947, was Underground marketing manager in the 1980s, overseeing HLS implementation, which he admits was an 'uphill battle' at times. He retired in 2007.

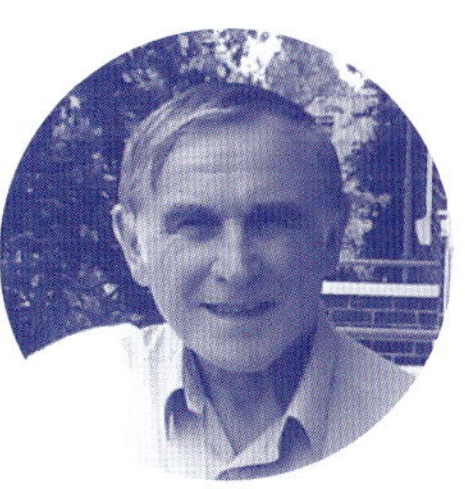

Paul Moss, born in London 1939, was an industrial designer who worked initially for Hoover. In June 1987 he joined LU, designing train interiors and working on station hardware (e.g. the circular 'Help Points') and sign construction.

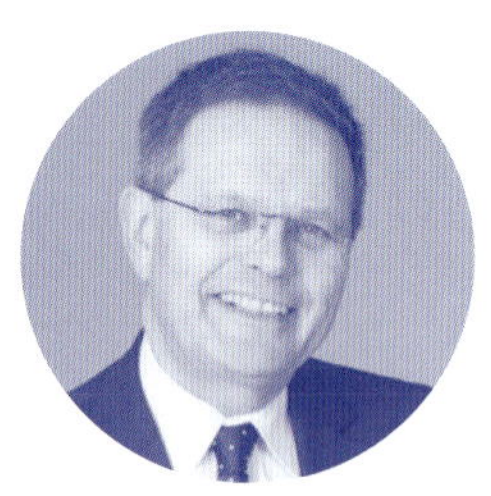

Stephen Jolly, born 1952, was the first PR manager of the Docklands Light Railway. He began work with the Design Research Unit and was a technical journalist and a bus company manager before working on major projects for the JLE, Crossrail and the Olympic Transport Plan.

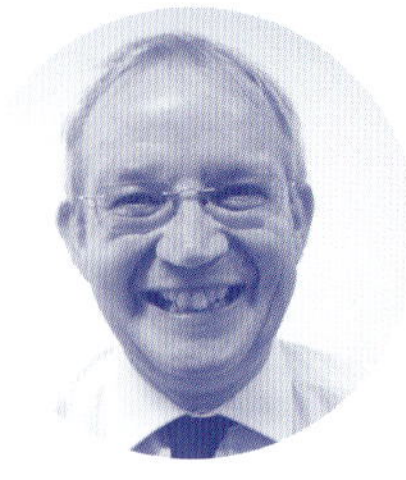

Nick Agnew, born in London 1950, left TfL in 2012 after a long career in transport which included safeguarding Chiswick Park and parts of Loughton station, protecting heritage signing at several others, recreating replica bull's-eyes at Aldgate East and saving LMS heritage features at Upminster Bridge.

13km of a fully automated, driverless line – the Docklands Light Railway (DLR) – opened in 1987, and has since become a real success story. The initial sections ran from Tower Gateway (between Fenchurch Street and Tower Hill) to Island Gardens with another branch running from Island Gardens to Stratford. Both mainly utilized abandoned rail alignments, or newly built elevated piers. A new style of lettering was selected (p. 254) and a competition organized to choose the livery design – won by a London student whose blue and red cars with white detailing were almost a direct reverse of the white, red and blue of LU. Platforms featured a signature tunnel-shaped glazed canopy reinforced with blue bands.

Regeneration of the Docklands took off spectacularly; as the Canary Wharf project unfolded in 1985, the LDDC realized that the capacity of the DLR would need to be increased and began investigating how to link Docklands with the rest of the Tube system. A plan crystallized to divert an extension to the Jubilee line through Canary Wharf, but it would take years to build, so instead the DLR was extended in tunnel to an interchange with Bank Underground station[17] in 1991. The entire Bank/Monument interchange was upgraded under HLS guidelines,[18] demonstrating how clever design could seamlessly integrate two systems (p. 240). By the time of the 1994 Beckton extension, the signage was looking scruffy, so a new style was introduced with a sans-serif typeface (p. 240).

Enter the salmon

For operational reasons (and without a single new station or extra metre of track), a new line, in salmon pink, was added to the system in 1990: the Hammersmith & City line (H&C). Though not an entirely new name (it was the original moniker of the 1864 line), it was affixed to existing signage (as so many name changes had been previously) by temporary means, using vinyl stickers, but from that date onwards permanent enamel signs had to be made and maps updated to include the new line.[19]

Preserving heritage

Following the devastating events at King's Cross on 18 November 1987, in which thirty-one died after a fire broke out beneath a 1940s wooden escalator, the Fennell report specified the removal of all combustible materials from the network. The remedial work messed up some stations and this, plus years of neglect at many others, meant that a total overhaul was needed. At the end of 1992 an audit was proposed by Nick Agnew, leading to the most thorough survey of the network ever undertaken; a team was sent to every single station.[20]

Published in March 1993, the *Station Design Audit* included a separate report for each of the 247 LU stations. These revealed how, despite overall structural soundness, repairs were needed on a huge scale, especially at the older 'heritage' stations. While

London Underground by Design

many features had survived intact, modernization (such as new wiring) carried out at some listed stations had been so insensitively applied that it would have to be redone. Other stations, meanwhile, were just wasting away from neglect/overuse. The dire state of some Holden and Green stations required immediate action, for which the HLS *Heritage Signing Handbook* was issued on 1 March 1993 (p. 255). Implementation of its recommendations came just in time; any later and some design treasures may well have been lost for good.

A marriage of convenience

Plans to extend the Jubilee – this time from Green Park to Westminster and Waterloo – were revived by LU at much the same time that the development company behind the biggest Docklands projects, Olympia & York, was proposing a new tube between Waterloo and Greenwich. A marriage of the schemes produced the Jubilee Line Extension (JLE) which was approved by Parliament in 1990 and internationally renowned architect Roland Paoletti appointed (p. 264), helping to eventually deliver London's most ambitious stations ever (p. 268).

Preparing for the noughties

As work began on the new line, renovation went on elsewhere. LU designers like Innes Ferguson (p. 266) continued working with HLS on refining existing signs, replacing outdated or inadequate ones and producing new material for refurbished stations and the DLR. As a result of the competitive tendering process, design of the Tube map was awarded to an agency called Clockwork, where, during 1996, under lead designer Alan Foale, its type and line sizes were refined to conform with recommendations in the HLS report.

Operational changes were underway too. The Waterloo & City line (p. 36) was transferred from British Rail ownership to LU in 1994 and restyled accordingly. That same year the Piccadilly stub to Aldwych carried its last passenger, as did the Central line's Epping to Ongar section. The ELL closed too, in 1995, but only to allow repairs to the old Thames Tunnel; it re-opened in 1998 with refitted stations in anticipation of an extension (p. 255). Another small section of line to close was the Jubilee between Green Park and Charing Cross – having been in service just twenty years – but it was all part of the JLE plan, which was to open for the last day of 1999 (pp. 268–9). By Herculean efforts it met the millennium deadline, leaving London the greatest set of new stations since Holden's day and providing a fine finish to an amazing century for the Underground.

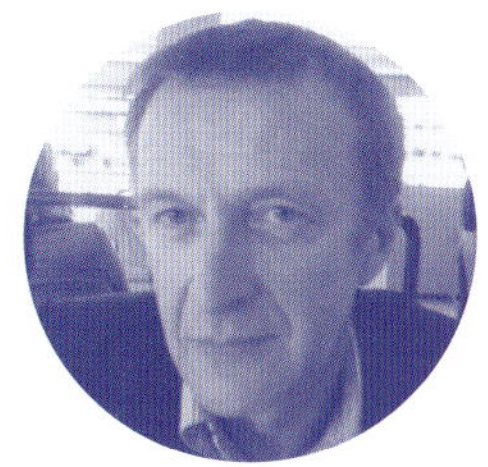

Mike Walton, born in Hertfordshire 1953, is the head of trading at the London Transport Museum. He joined the organization in 1980 and after commissioning a set of art to fill unused ad spaces (1995), he became increasingly involved in championing new artwork for posters. His tenure at the museum shop has led to an unprecedented rise in popularity of Underground art, books and ephemera.

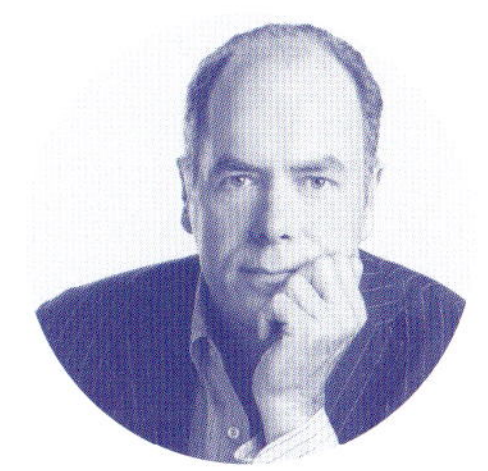

Allan Drummond, born in Essex 1957, won a competition to design the Holborn refit in 1983. His selection of British Museum artefacts presented as life-size monochrome images on a black enamel background (p. 253) is perhaps the most impressive of all the 1980s station murals.

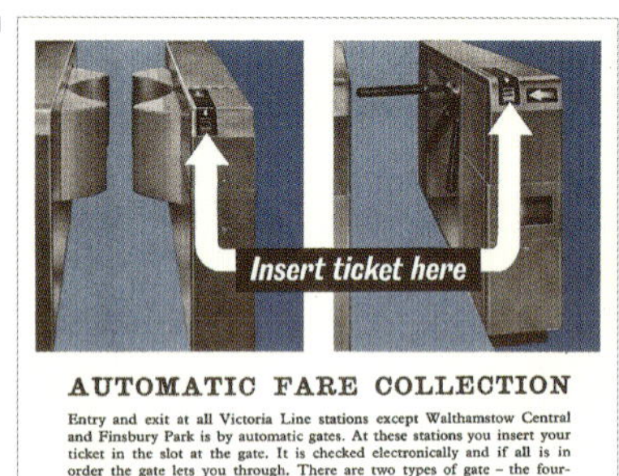

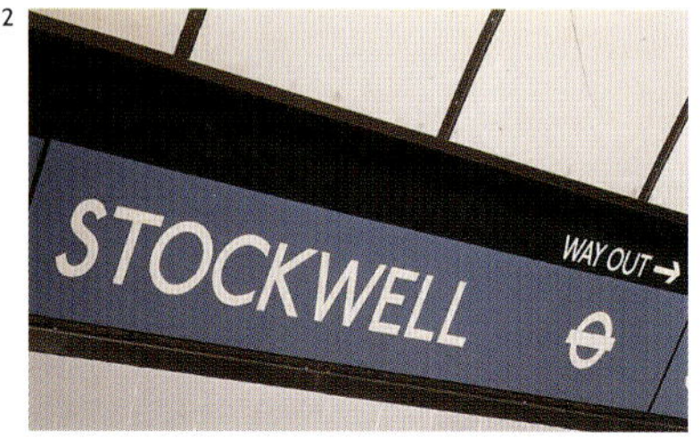

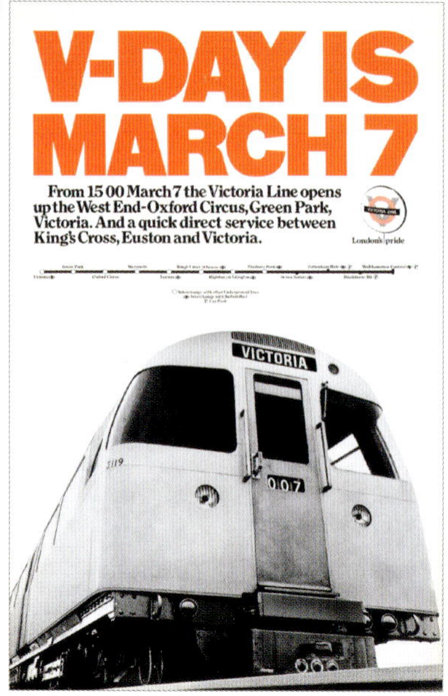

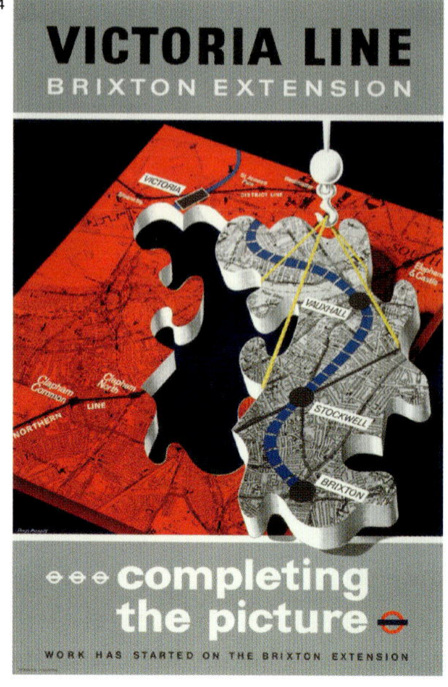

Victorious design, 1967–72

The world's first automatic metro line needed new trains as well as signalling. The DRU was heavily involved in the design of the former, creating what Paul Moss (Bibliography) describes as a 'superbly clean cigar tube styling' (1967 Stock, seen on 1969 poster, 3). Automatic ticket gates needed some explanation when they were first introduced (1). The emphasis on strong, clear signage was at the heart of the DRU's design ethos (p. 234); an unused platform at Aldwych was adapted for full-size mock-ups – some of which were spartan in the extreme. The two-toned frieze was new, the thicker lower section featuring the Victoria's blue line colour as a continuous backdrop for the station names (interspersed with outline roundels), all in white (2). Above this was a thinner black strip for directional information like interchanges and 'WAY OUT' signs, the lettering on this also in white. The line colour was originally to be 'Royal Purple', which apart from being perilously close to the blue of the bar on the Underground logo, and not far from the colour of the Piccadilly line, was not that different from the Met's purple. It also proved difficult to render correctly on enamel signs; hence the lighter 'Cambridge Blue' became the Victoria's hue – the first time line colour was selected with signage production in mind. A Brixton extension poster (1967, 4) meanwhile ignores DRU proposals to use the Johnston typeface for everything. Other Victoria line design features included litter bins concealed neatly beneath each name sign (all sealed since the 1980s due to various security threats). The most outstanding pieces of design, however, were the seat recess murals. Artists commissioned were Hans Unger – Blackhorse Road, Seven Sisters, Oxford Circus, Green Park and Brixton; Tom Eckersley – Finsbury Park, King's Cross, Euston; Abram Games – Stockwell; Alan Fletcher – Warren Street; George Smith – Vauxhall; Julia Black – Walthamstow; and Edward Bawden – Tottenham Hale, Highbury & Islington and Victoria. Pimlico had a theme of 'optical art' by Peter Sedgley to reflect its proximity to the Tate Gallery. The full set of the initial twelve stations was immortalized in a 1969 poster (5).

TILE MOTIFS ON THE VICTORIA LINE

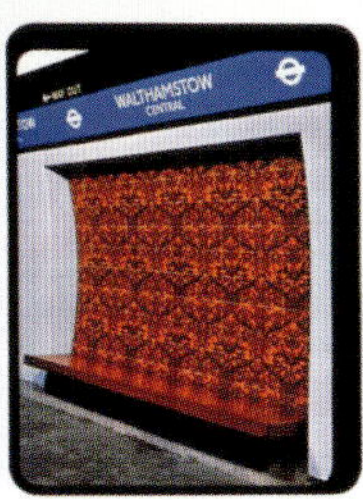

by Julia Black
An adaptation of a William Morris design. He was born and worked for a time in Walthamstow where a museum displays examples of his work.

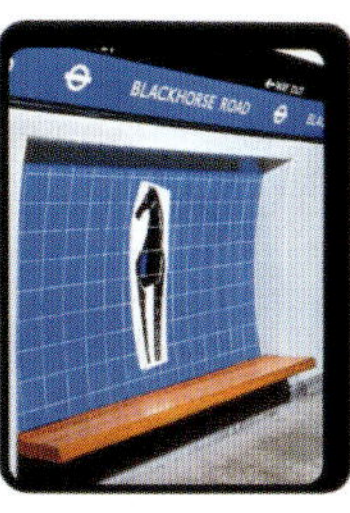

by Hans Unger
The black horse also appears as a sculpture, by David McFall, on the exterior of the station.

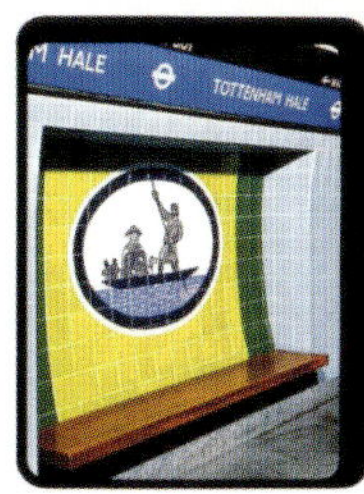

by Edward Bawden
The name is derived from a ferry over the river Lea in earlier times. The word 'hale' is said to be a corruption of 'haul'; or perhaps 'hail'.

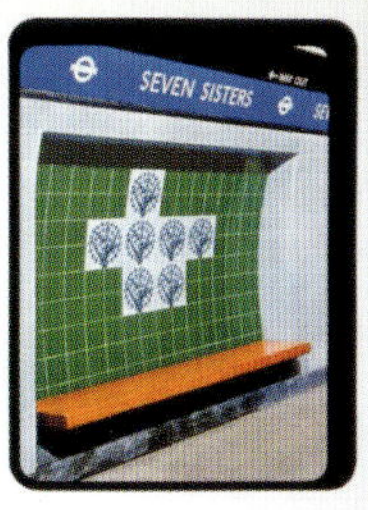

by Hans Unger
The seven sisters were seven trees which gave a name to the locality.

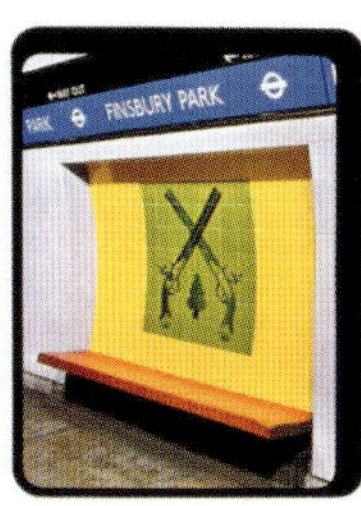

by Tom Eckersley
The crossed pistols refer to the duelling that took place here when this was outside the edge of London.

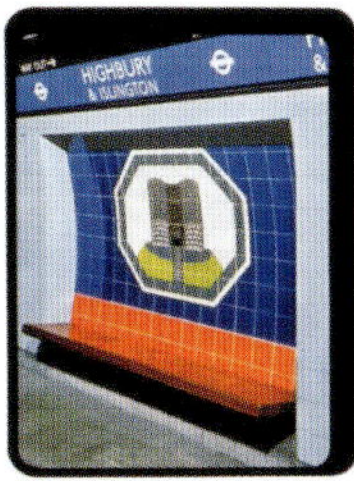

by Edward Bawden
The high bury, manor or castle, was destroyed at the time of the Peasants' Revolt (1381).

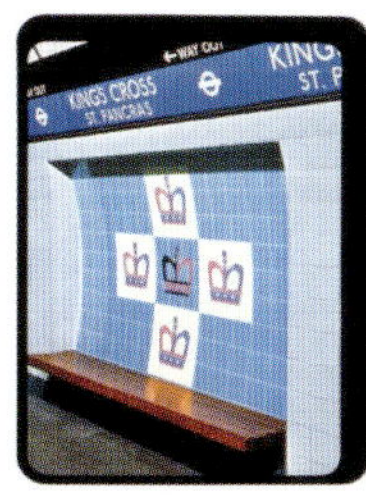

by Tom Eckersley
A literal design based on a cross and crowns. The King concerned (if there ever was one) is not identified.

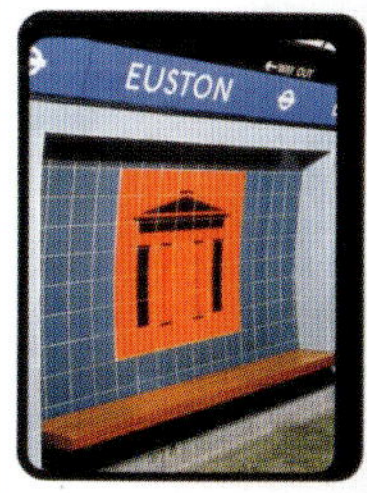

by Tom Eckersley
A reminder of the Doric Arch which stood on the station site.

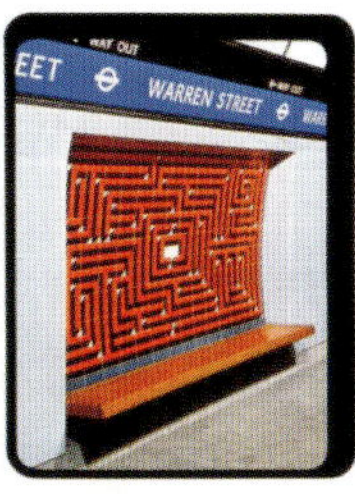

by Crosby/Fletcher/Forbes
A maze or Warren as a pun on the name. A solution is possible for the traveller with time to spare.

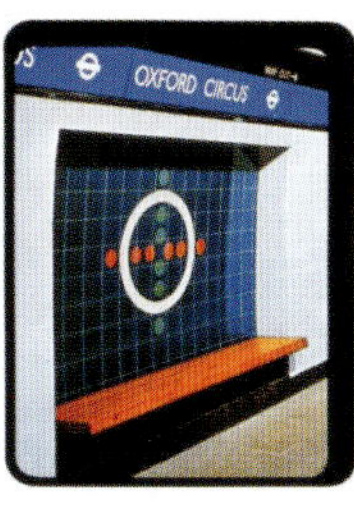

by Hans Unger
A device to incorporate the circle of the circus with the linking of the Bakerloo, Central and Victoria Lines.

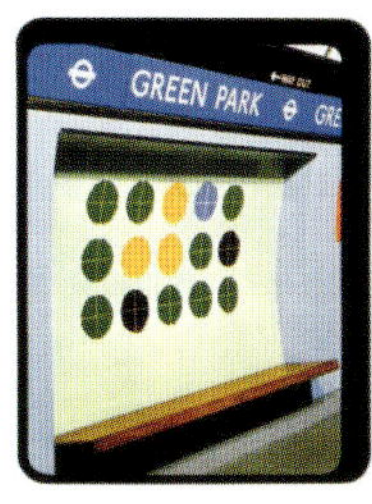

by Hans Unger
A bird's eye view of the trees in the park against the green background of the grass.

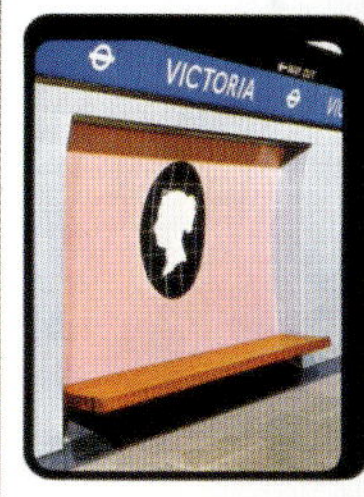

by Edward Bawden
The great Queen herself, from a silhouette by Benjamin Pearce. A plaque in the ticket hall records the visit of Queen Elizabeth to open the Victoria Line in March 1969.

All these motif designs, specially commissioned for the twelve stations so far open on the Victoria Line, are reproduced in full colour in a folder obtainable price 1/- at any main London Transport Travel Enquiry Office (including those on the Victoria Line at Euston, Oxford Circus and Victoria Stations). Or post free from the Public Relations Officer, 55 Broadway, S.W.1. Copies of this poster cost 12/6.

Flying the Tube, 1977–8

The Piccadilly extension to Heathrow, though short, was perhaps the network's most significant. To link a major international airport to its city's rapid-transit system was a landmark development. Advance publicity included Eckersley's clever 1971 poster (1), and, for the opening of Hatton Cross in 1975, Walter Brian's invitation to fly into the blue (2). The dreary surface building at Hatton Cross, the intermediate station, was alleviated by fun door handles (3), illuminated roundels and an impressive array of surface signage. Borrowed from the Victoria line were tiled motifs, here in the style of Imperial Airways' 'speedbird' (4), and a continuous frieze in the line colour displaying the station name (though the 'WAY OUT' words, interspersed with 'HATTON CROSS', looked too big). The name, incorporating that of the bus station, was also displayed high up on the parapet in individually mounted Johnston letters (6). For the surface signage at Heathrow Central (now Heathrow Terminals 1, 2 and 3), the station name was for the first time rendered in blue lettering on a white background, flanked by the plain red roundel. At platform level there were decorated seat recesses (Tom Eckersley's overlaid Concorde tail fins, 7). Illuminated station-name roundels included the internationally recognized airport symbol (5). The frieze was in the Piccadilly line colour with station name in white and above it, on a black background, a continuous reminder of the 'WAY OUT' in white lettering.

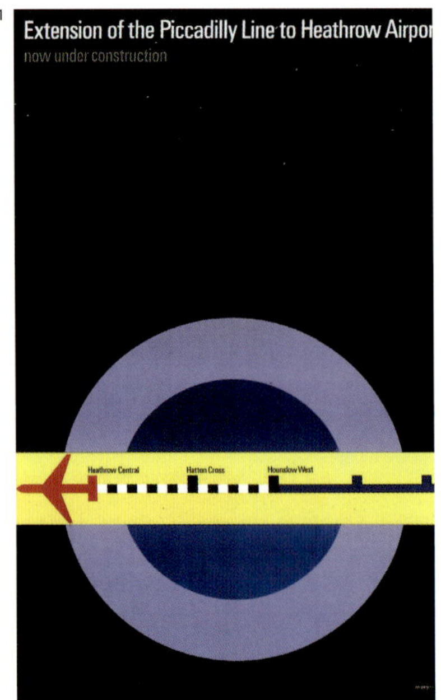

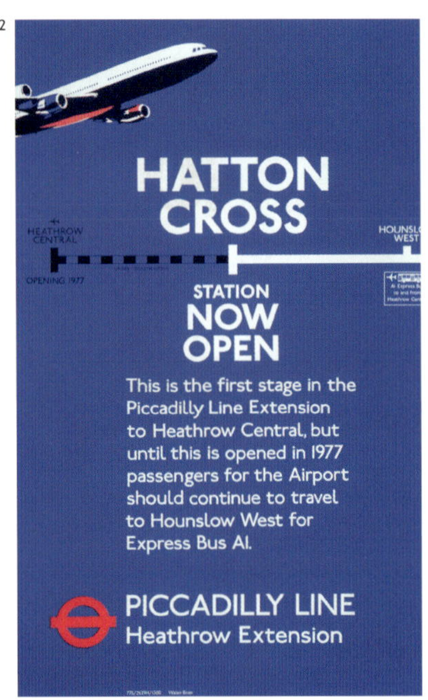

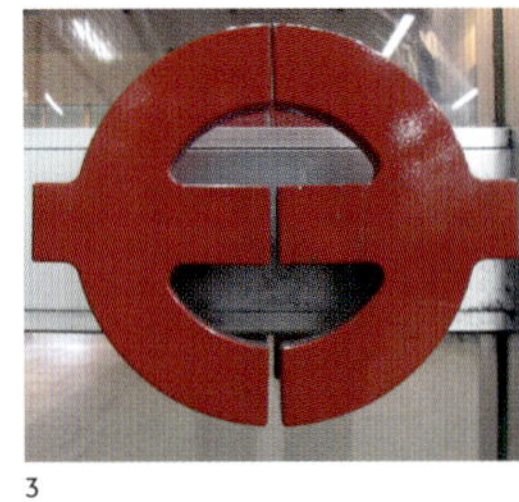

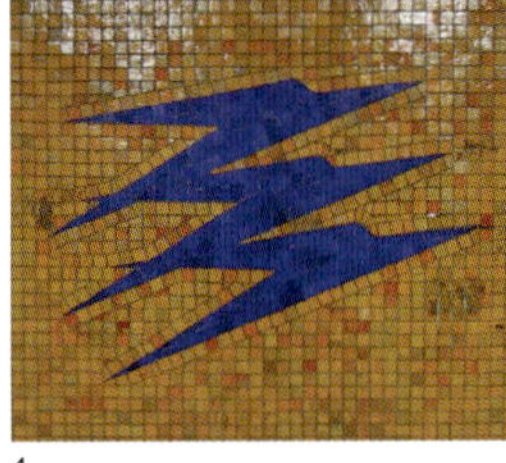

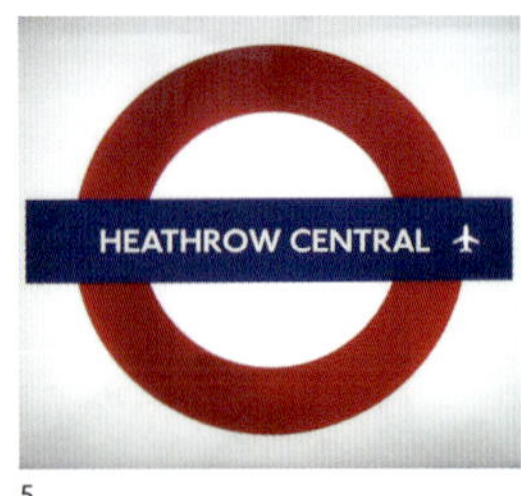

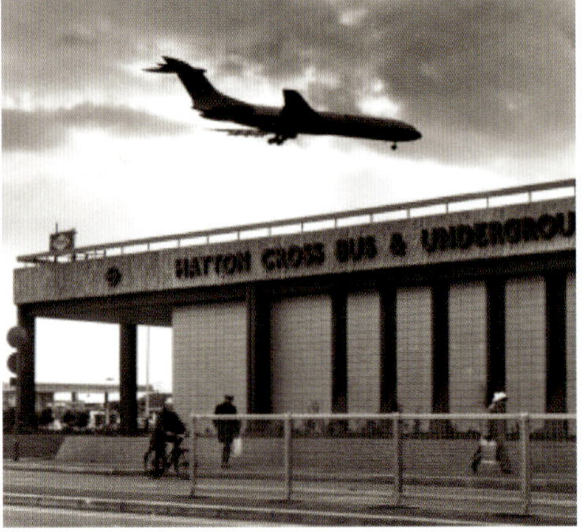

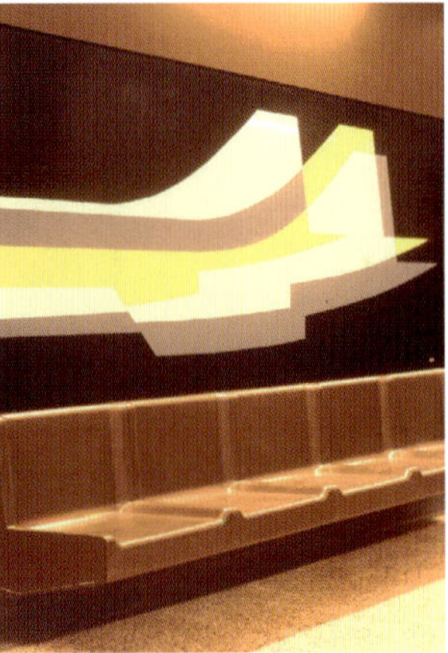

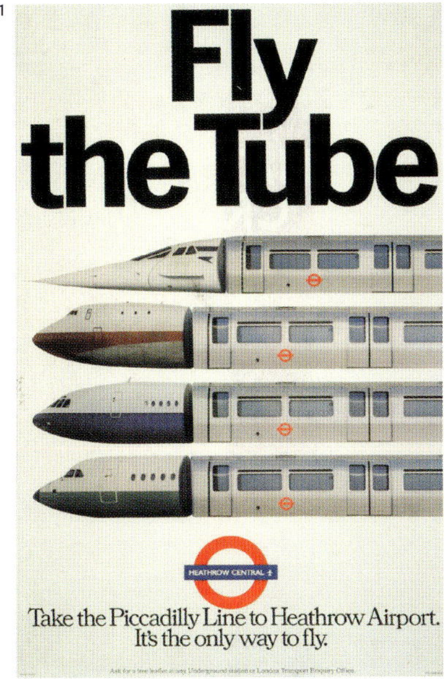

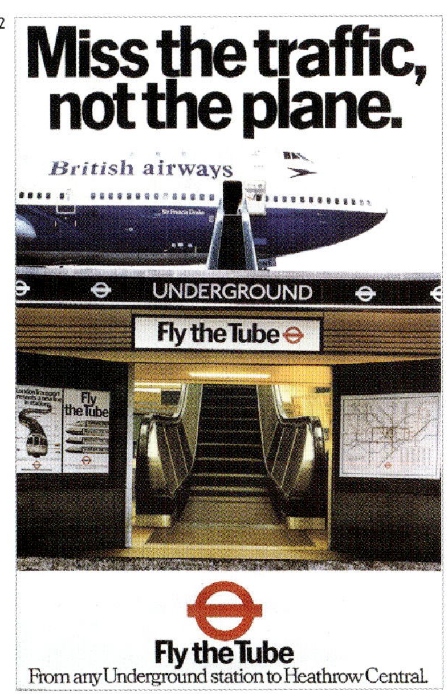

3

4

Flying the poster and looping the loop, 1977–86

The provision of a direct Tube connection to the airport was too good an opportunity for designers to miss; a plethora of posters were issued juxtaposing trains and tunnels with aircraft. The first, 'Fly the Tube' (1978, 1) by Geoff Senior (of Foote, Cone & Belding), gave birth to the entire ad campaign and has become a perennial classic in the London Transport Museum shop. 'Miss the traffic, not the plane' (1979, 2), 'Less bread. No jam' by Phil Dobson (1980, 3) and 'The Heathrow Connection' (1982, 4) followed the lead. The slogan has been used periodically up until 2007. The Queen inspected the new Piccadilly trains (1973 Stock) which are still in service. The Underground's first one-way loop was built in 1986 by in-house LU architects to get the Piccadilly to Terminal 4. The treatment here was elegant and classical yet modern (partly because it was completely new), resulting in one of the classiest new stations to date. Reconstructed marble clads the platform walls with the numeral '4' embedded. Note the lack of Johnston almost entirely (1 and 3) and its complete absence in the 1980 offering (3). It is only back by 1986 thanks to New Johnston (4) although even here Gill Sans Bold is used for the smaller text in the centre.

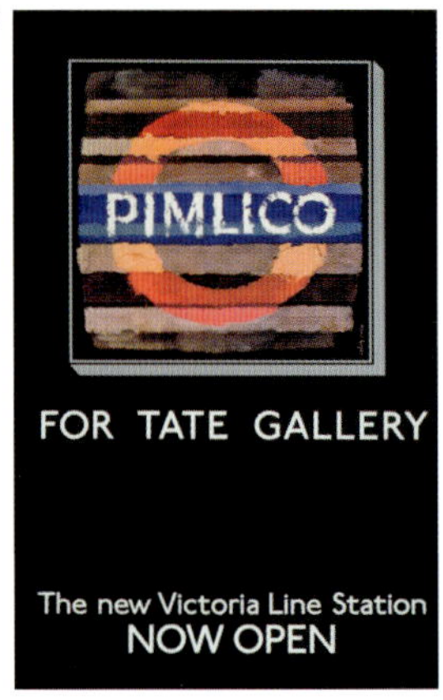
PIMLICO
FOR TATE GALLERY
The new Victoria Line Station
NOW OPEN

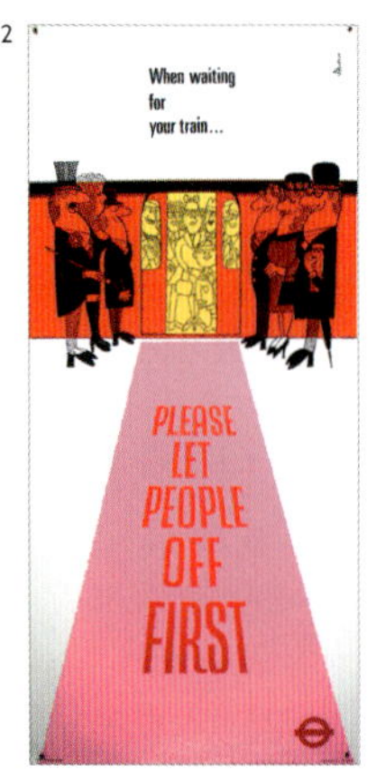
When waiting
for
your train...
PLEASE
LET
PEOPLE
OFF
FIRST

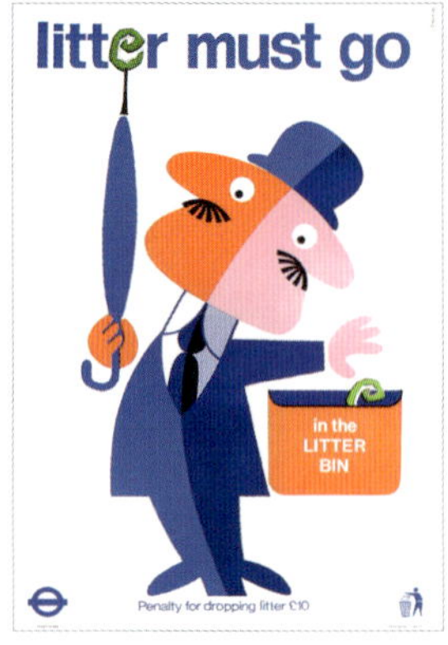
litter must go
in the
LITTER
BIN
Penalty for dropping litter £10

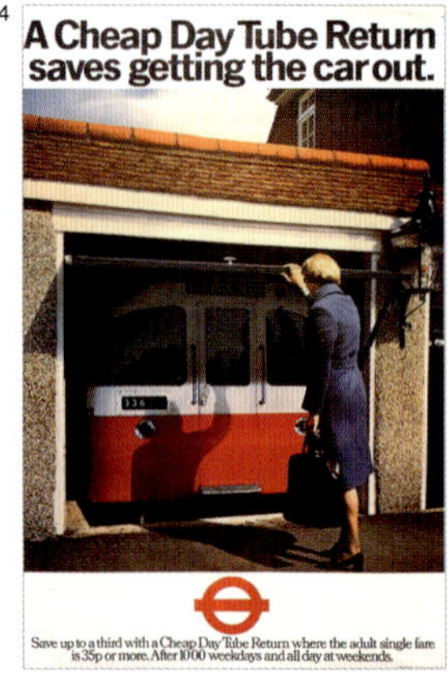
A Cheap Day Tube Return
saves getting the car out.
Save up to a third with a Cheap Day Tube Return where the adult single fare
is 35p or more. After 10.00 weekdays and all day at weekends.

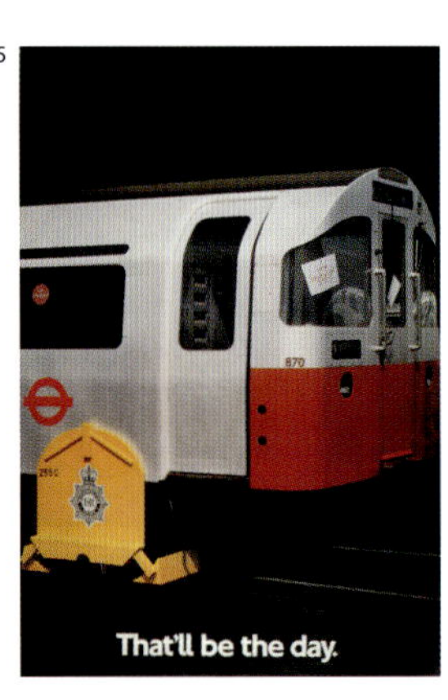
That'll be the day.

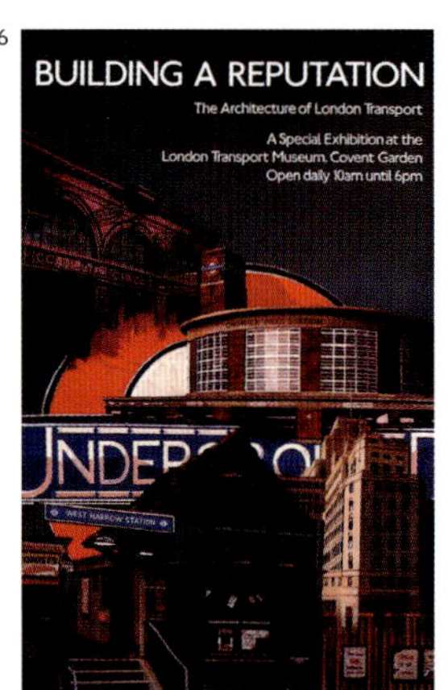
BUILDING A REPUTATION
The Architecture of London Transport
A Special Exhibition at the
London Transport Museum, Covent Garden
Open daily 10am until 6pm
UNDERGROUND
WEST HARROW STATION

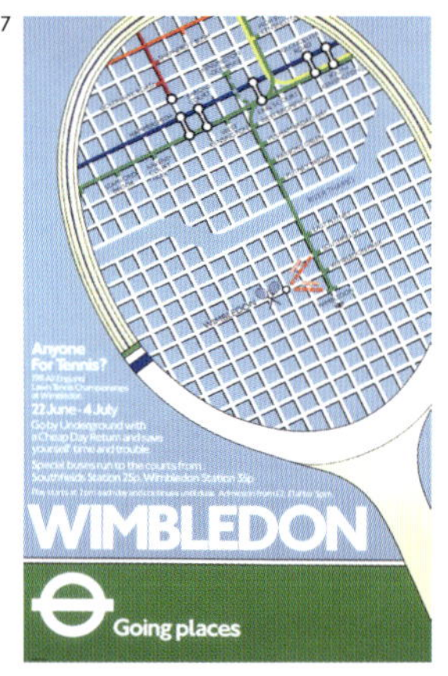
Anyone
For Tennis?
WIMBLEDON
Going places

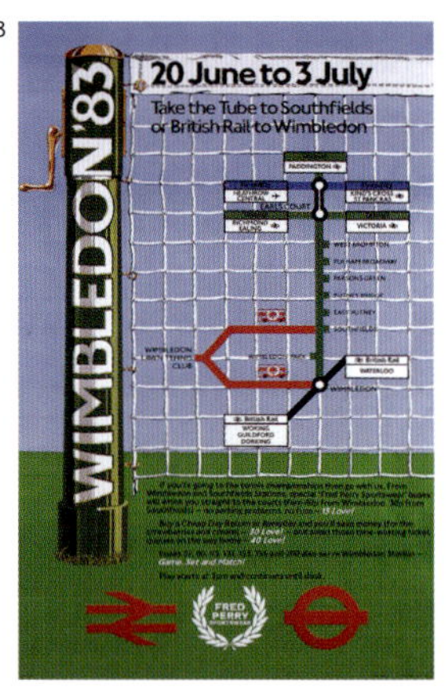
WIMBLEDON '83
20 June to 3 July
Take the Tube to Southfields
or British Rail to Wimbledon
FRED
PERRY

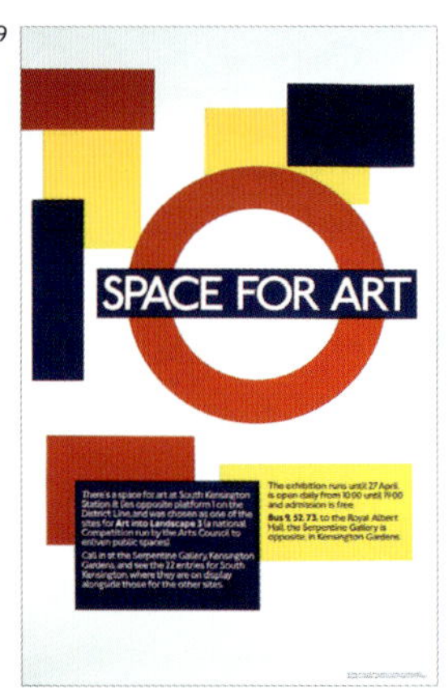
SPACE FOR ART

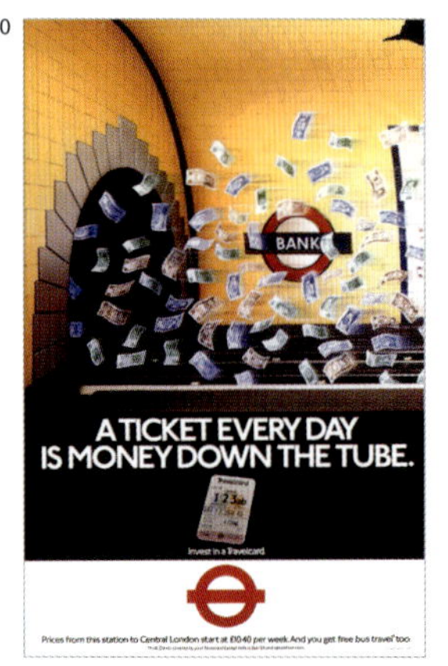
BANK
A TICKET EVERY DAY
IS MONEY DOWN THE TUBE.
Invest in a Travelcard
Prices from this station to Central London start at £6.40 per week. And you get free bus travel too.

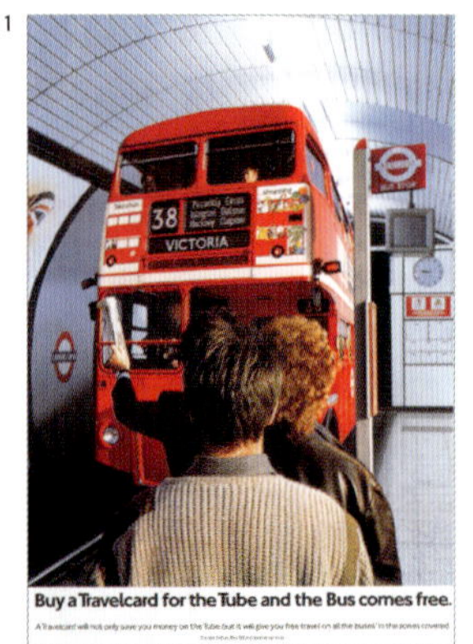
VICTORIA
Buy a Travelcard for the Tube and the Bus comes free.

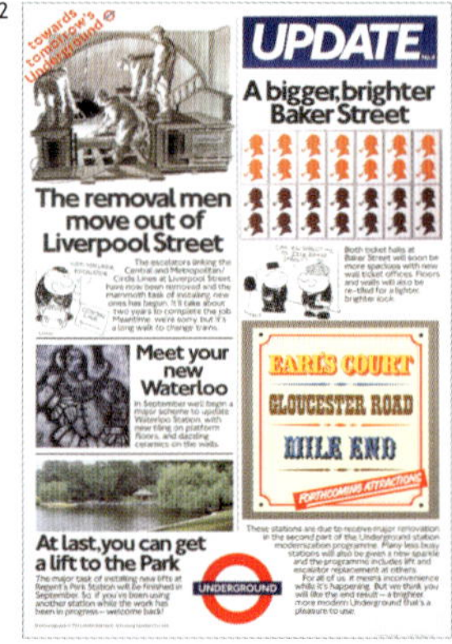
UPDATE
A bigger, brighter
Baker Street
The removal men
move out of
Liverpool Street
Meet your
new
Waterloo
At last, you can get
a lift to the Park
EARLS COURT
GLOUCESTER ROAD
MILE END
UNDERGROUND

Posters, 1972–85

OPPOSITE: In the 1970s posters ranged from the purely graphic (Hans Unger's promotion of the new Pimlico station, 1972, 1), through scratchy, retro-looking cartoons (Harry Stevens, 1975, 2) to powerful photomontage ('Cheap Day Tube Return', 1978, 4). Stevens's images are so evocative that anyone living in London during this period will immediately recognize his style (e.g. 'Litter', 1974, 3). Kim Wheater (of FCB Advertising) cleverly employed photomontage in this witty image of a Tube train being clamped (1984, 5), as did Lawrence Menear in his museum poster (1981, 6). The tennis at Wimbledon and the Tube diagram are both perennial poster motifs; in 1981 (7) and 1983 (by NN /Anthony Reid Partnership, 8) they were brought together. Adapting the roundel was another regular theme of LT posters, as featured on Mike A. Welch's homage to Mondrian, 'Space For Art', promoting a Transport Museum exhibition (1980, 9). After the success of earlier photomontages, the trick was continued in the 1980s with posters such as an eye-catching bus in a Tube station (1985, 11). For the mid-1980s station-upgrade programme, the publicity department issued a series of information posters called 'Underground Update' (12). While not of the greatest merit artistically, they show what was being achieved during this period of renovation.

THIS PAGE: Tom Eckersley's 'London Transport Collection' (1975, 2), 'Ceremonial London' (1976, 3) and 'The Museum of London' (1977, 4). Abram Games's last poster for the Underground 'London Zoo' (1976, 1).

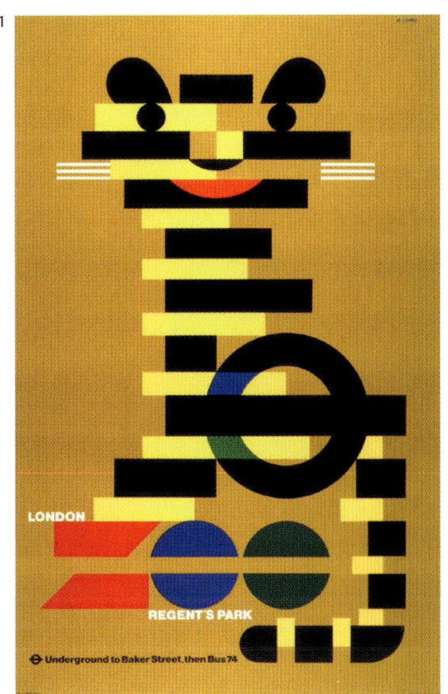

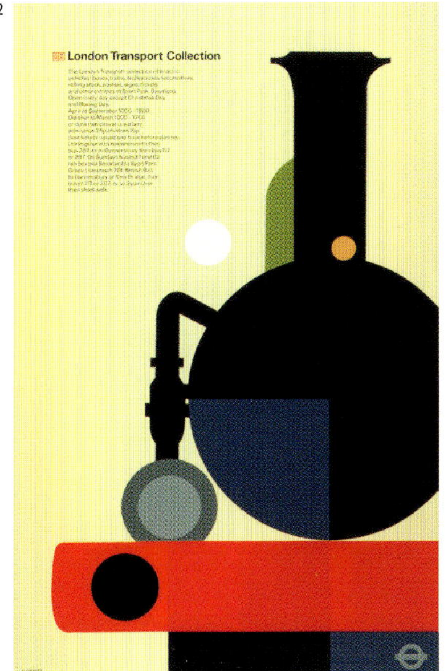

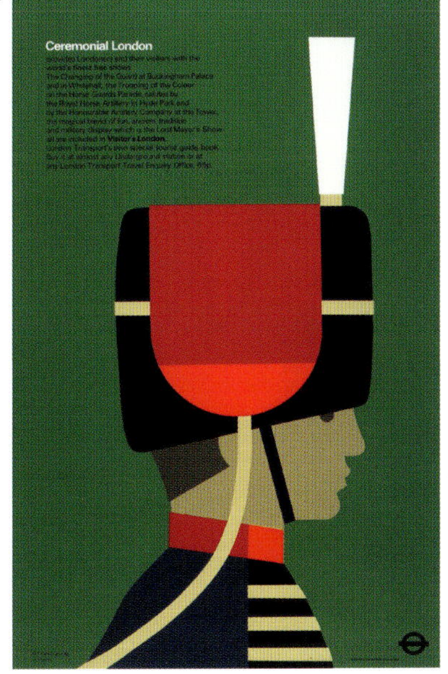

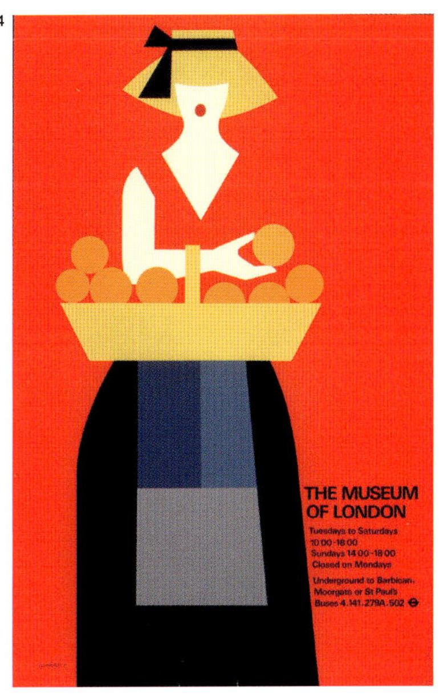

Bakerloo becomes Fleet becomes Jubilee, 1977–9

Proposals for the extension of the Fleet line from Charing Cross went through many different stages, including a route to Thamesmead (p. 236). By 1975 work was well under way on the new tunnels from Baker Street, rebuilding Bond Street station (2) and merging Trafalgar Square and Strand into the new Charing Cross (1). The 1975 London railways diagram described the 'Fleet line' as 'under construction'. During the whole of this time there was no question that it would be called anything but Fleet line – signage was even prepared with this name – but when GLC leader Horace Cutler rebranded it without warning (p. 237), this all had to be changed. The new Jubilee name was bolted over 'Fleet line' on signs to save having to remake an entire run of expensive enamels. In keeping with the palette of the era (and perhaps to contrast with the grey line colour), the four new Jubilee station interiors (opposite) were to be brightly coloured, matching, for example, the Munich S-Bahn stations of the same period, such as Marienplatz, which opened in 1971 with ultramarine and bright orange tiling. Metro systems all over the world were also renovating stations in bright colours: the Paris Métro and the Glasgow Subway both embraced orange – the latter in 1977 was so dominating that it became known as the 'Clockwork Orange'.

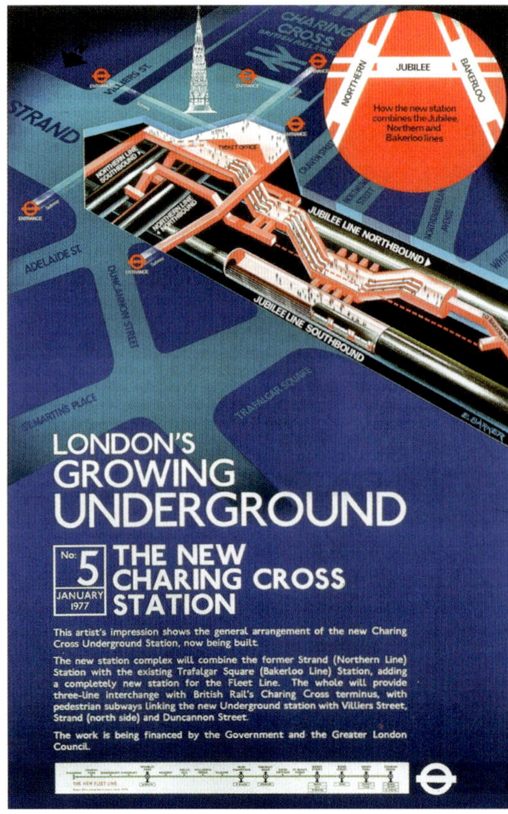

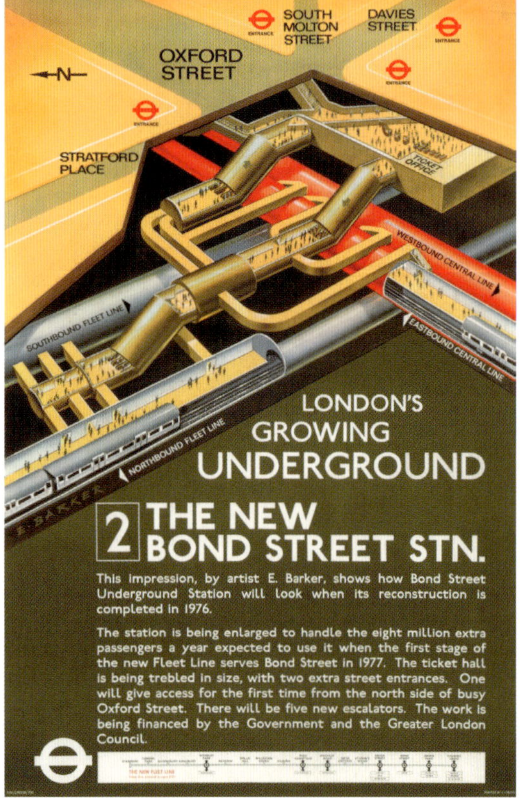

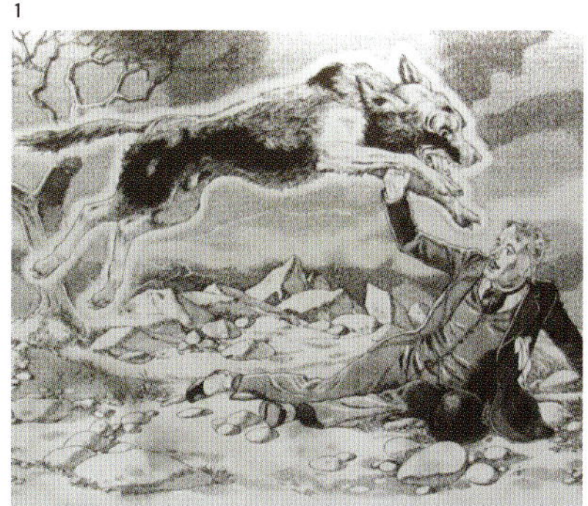

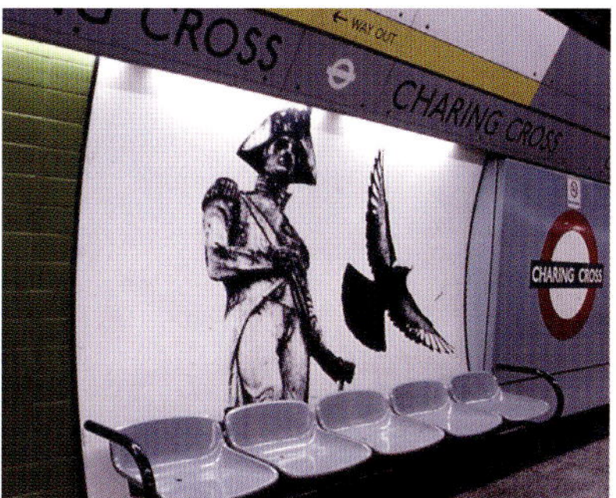

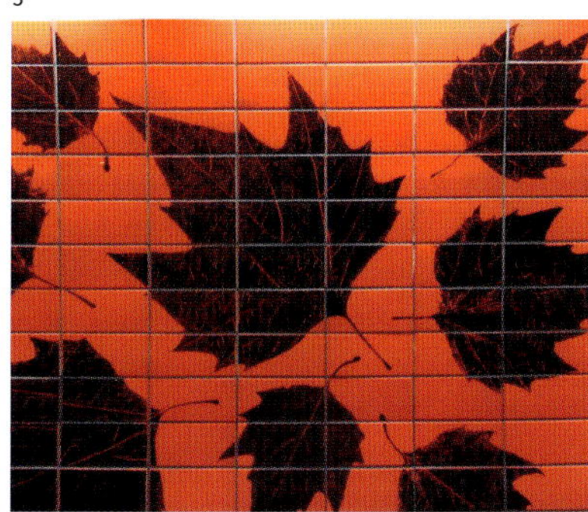

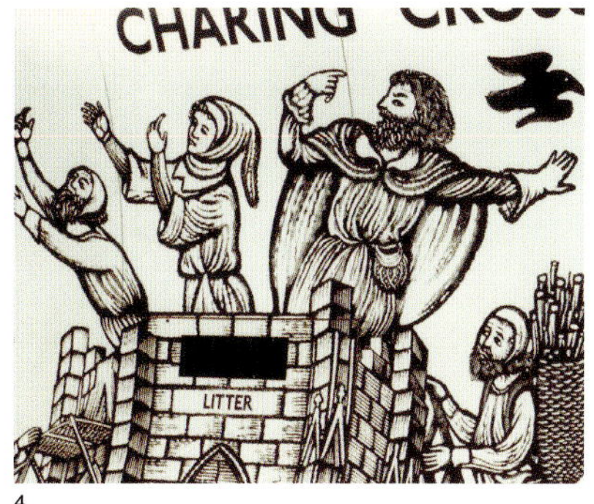

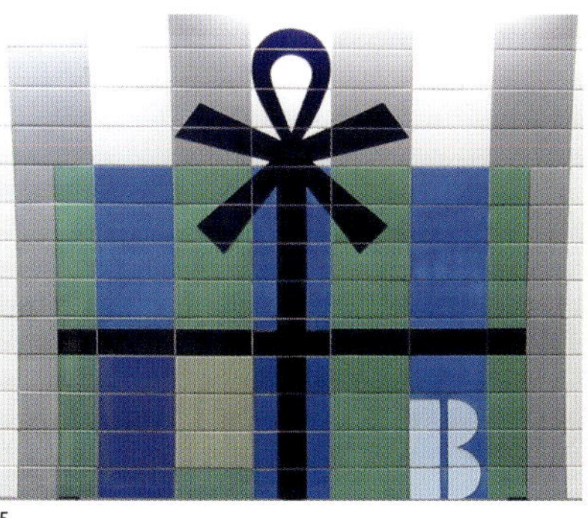

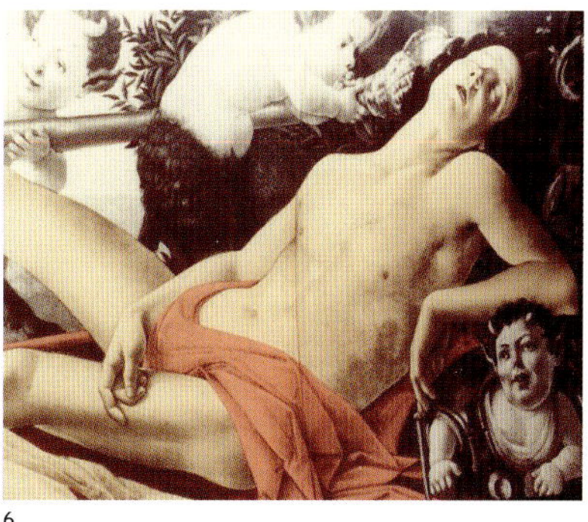

Lessons had been learnt from the perceived drabness of the Victoria; it was as if the colour tuning had been turned up to full blast. Baker Street was baking in orange with murals by Michael Douglas and printed by Pamela Morton featuring silhouettes of Sherlock Holmes and scenes from the books (1). Bond Street had ribbon-wrapped packages in bright green and cobalt blue (5). June Fraser designed the leafy look of Green Park's tiled walls in flame red (3), while Charing Cross was covered in lime green tiles, framing a scene by David Gentleman of Nelson atop his column (2). All other Charing Cross platforms were redesigned – full platform-length murals on the Northern (monochrome historical figures, 4) and images from the National Gallery on the Bakerloo (6), both lines incorporating the Victoria-/Jubilee-style station-name friezes. Jubilee station-name panels were grey (in keeping with the line colour) with illuminated roundels. Station-name friezes followed the trend started on the Victoria of having the larger lower panel in line colour and a thinner top section carrying directions; the main section was therefore grey with black lettering and white roundels, but the 'WAY OUT' strip was changed from black to yellow with black lettering. From 1979, posters and printed ephemera broadcasted the change from Bakerloo to Jubilee line (7), featuring a stylized 1972 Mk II Stock train.

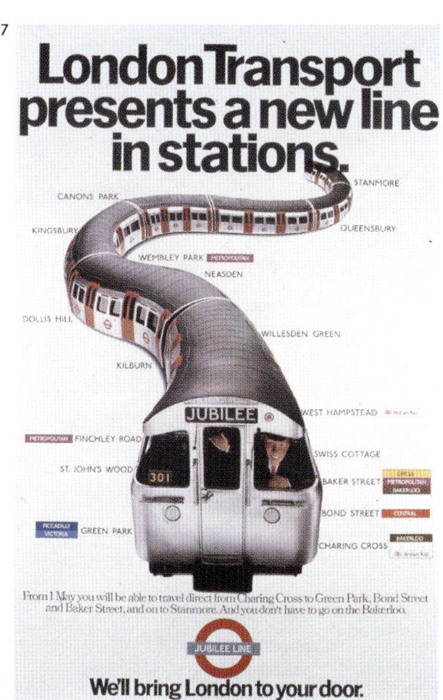

The joy of New Johnston, 1979–97

Though a thinner version of Johnston for illuminated signs had been commissioned in the 1950s (1) and type designer Walter Tracy had tweaked the lower-case letters (1974, 2), it was still not standardized or suitable for photo-typesetting. In 1979 design agency Banks & Miles took on the task to revise it with some quirky ideas (4, not adopted). Their new prodigy Eiichi Kono (p. 236) spent eighteen months painstakingly measuring and delicately hand-inking to produce the first major revision of Johnston's classic letterform (1979–81, sketch of medium weight, 2). He also produced a condensed version (numerals, 3). Kono's increased range of Light, Medium and Bold (with properly proportioned italics, 4) allowed more flexibility for designers. Converted for photo-typesetting in America, it was used pretty much immediately from early 1981 (first poster made by Kono, 5), then added to the LU guidelines and used for all subsequent signage, maps and publicity. The timing was ideal as so many stations were being renovated during that decade. The 1984 HLS report recommended blanket use of New Johnston for all but the very rarest exceptions (i.e. replica heritage signs). Kono's new version of Johnston was the centrepiece of the London Underground Corporate Identity Manual, covering ten categories, from vehicle design to stationery, issued from 1989. An electronic version for desktop publishing based on the original Johnston was released in 1997 by American typefounders P22. Kono's work was so true to the spirit of the original and executed with such technical perfection that it remains the in-house typeface to this day (some-times called TfL Johnston), after very minor revisions for digitization and was revised by Monotype in 2015.

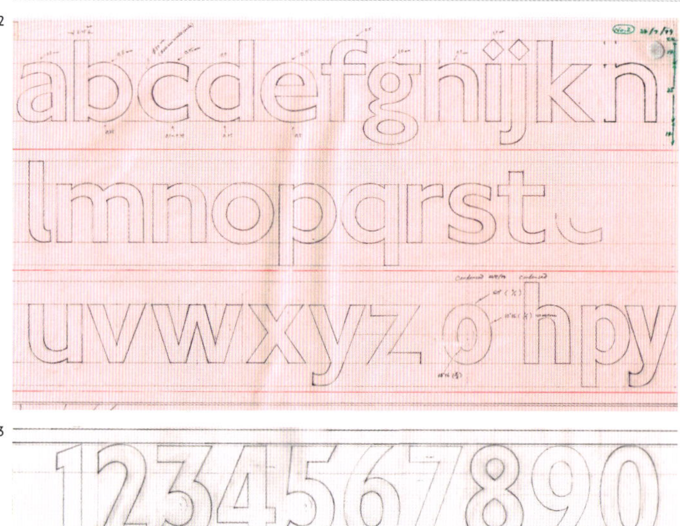

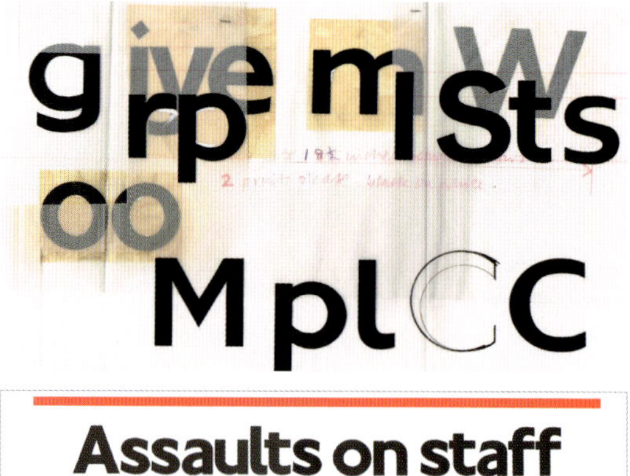

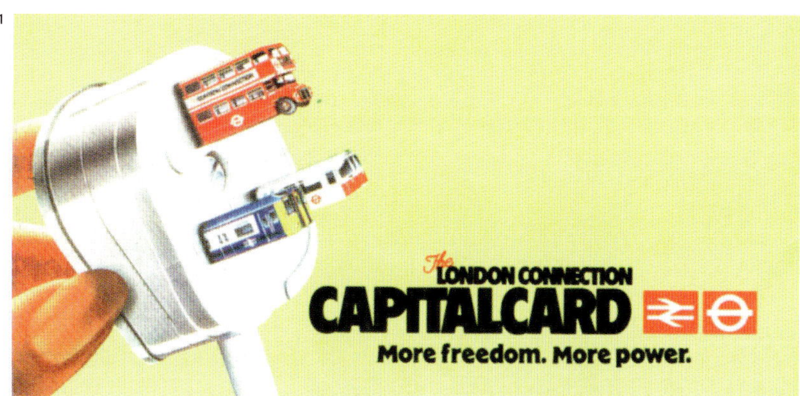

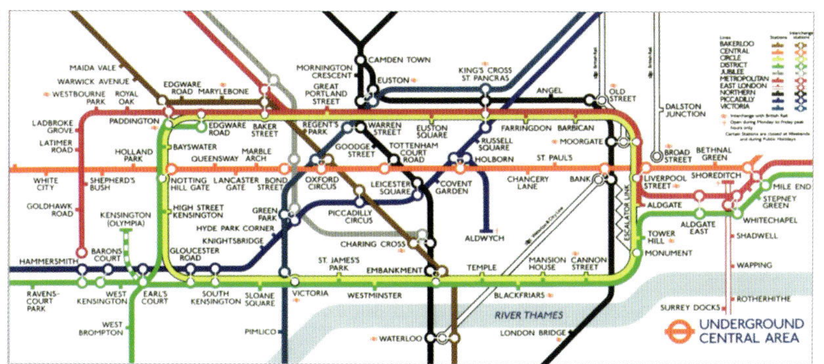

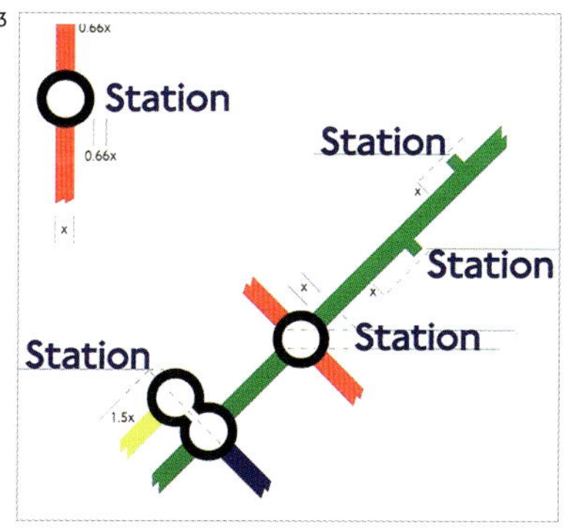

Fare's fair, cool cards and diverse diagrams, 1978–93

Underground publicity officer Tim Demuth (p. 237) made his first map of all London railways in 1973 and produced a new central area diagram in 1979 (2) for inside cars. It was also used as the baseboard for 'The London Game', created to familiarize kids with the map. Demuth expanded his concept for the whole network but only a monochrome version was produced initially (in 1982) and continued working on *London Connections* maps for some years. In 1981 the new Mayor of London, Ken Livingstone, introduced a huge cut in rail and bus fares, dividing the central area into two zones. Zoning of London continued with the introduction of a new ticket which began life in 1985 as the Capitalcard (in-car poster ad with plug image, 1), the same year a new agency, FWT, under Doug Rose, was brought in to redesign the Tube map. The one-day Capitalcard was first issued in 1986 to encourage off-peak travel (Pick would undoubtedly have approved) before being discontinued in 1989 when the Travelcard (a term first coined in 1981) took over, incorporating travel on British Rail. By 1993, HLS guidelines for the Journey Planner (as the Tube map was called from 1987) were included in the *Corporate Identity Manual* and standardization enforced for letter size, spacing and line angles (3).

With a few exceptions, the 1980s station and platform refits were highly regarded – colourful and distinctive. Many incorporated the clever idea of tucking cables into box trunking which doubled as a name frieze (p. 237). Platforms were permitted an individual theme, the first (and perhaps least colourful) was the Bond Street 'wrapping paper' concept (1982, p. 249). More intriguing were the escalator mazes by Nicolas Munro at Oxford Circus (1983, 2). Tiling went from the bland stripes of Piccadilly Circus (Bakerloo line, 1984) to the intricate detail of Eduardo Paolozzi's tessellated mosaic panels at Tottenham Court Road (1984, 1 and p. 232–3). Other examples of murals and platform-long designs include: Annabel Grey's variations on an arch at Marble Arch (1985, 5 and 6) and her hot-air balloon theme at Finsbury Park (1986); David Hamilton's over-printing on vitrified tiles of Brunel's tunnelling-machine drawings at Paddington (Bakerloo line, 1985–7, 3); and Robert Cooper's film-sprocket tiling and enamel neon lights at Leicester Square (Piccadilly line, 1985, 4). Most of these station refits also benefited from the HLS report's insistence on New Johnston lettering. The 1983 reinstatement of Baker Street's original look was the impetus for other sub-surface strip-backs. Most 1980s designs were influenced by the '1980 Design Strategy' and summed up later in *Changing Stations* (Bibliography) – though not all were implemented.

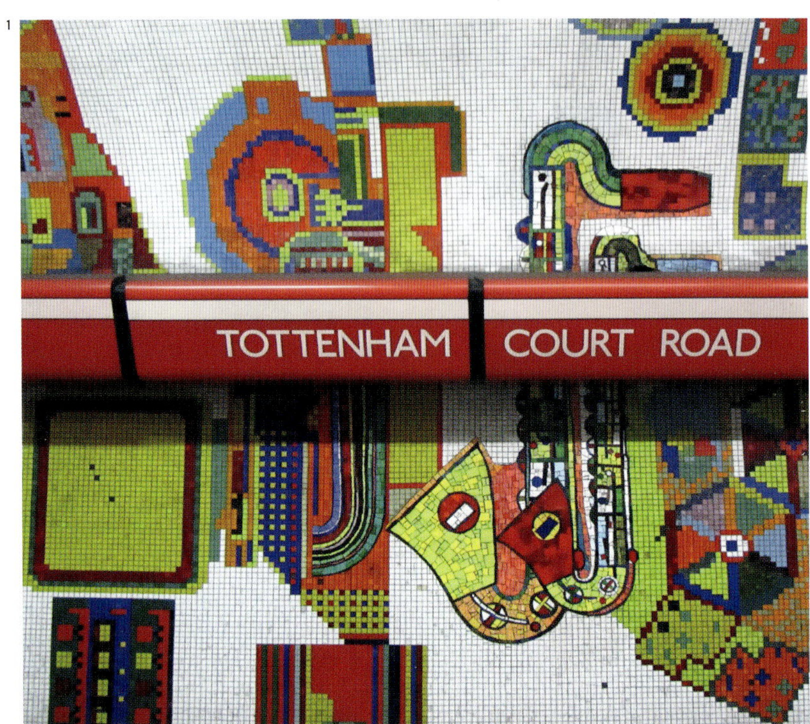

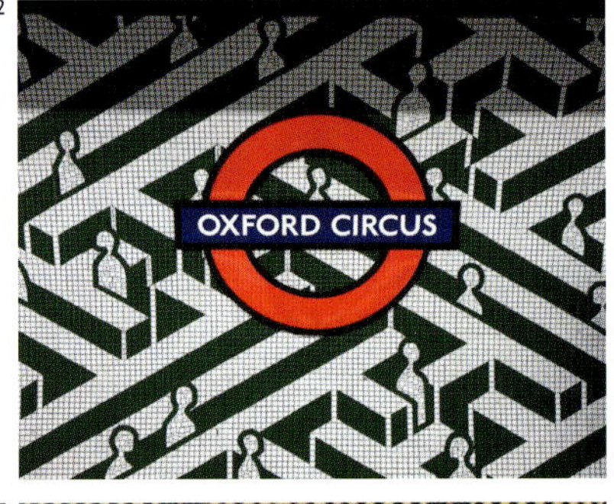

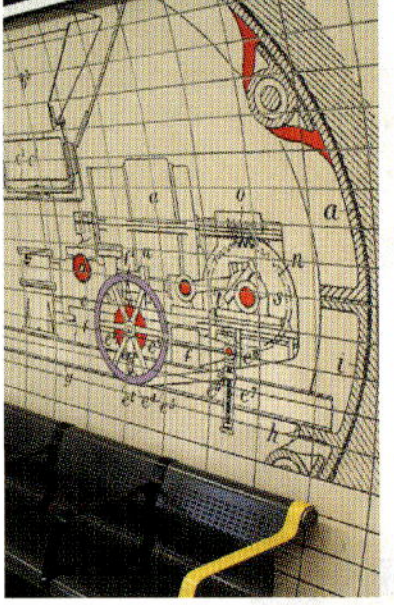

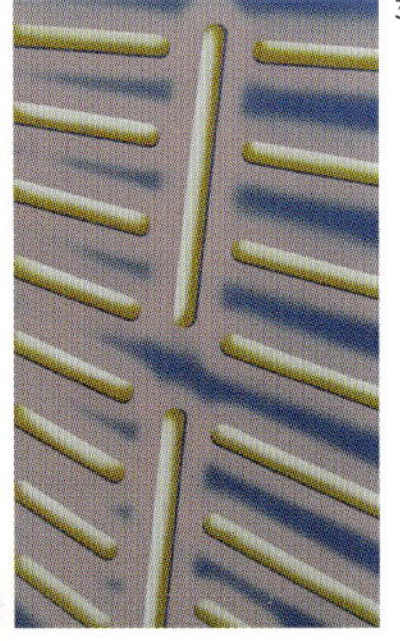

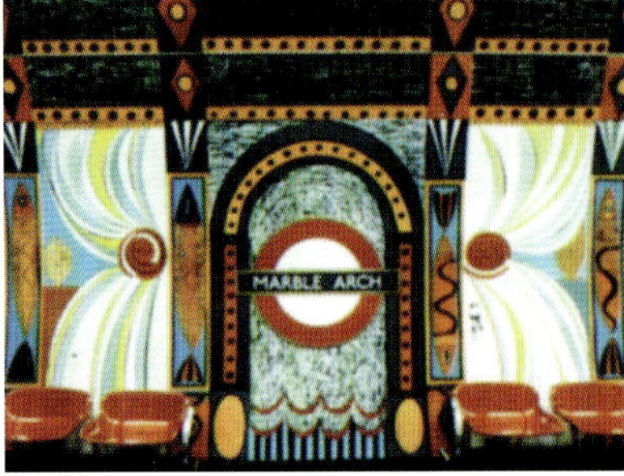

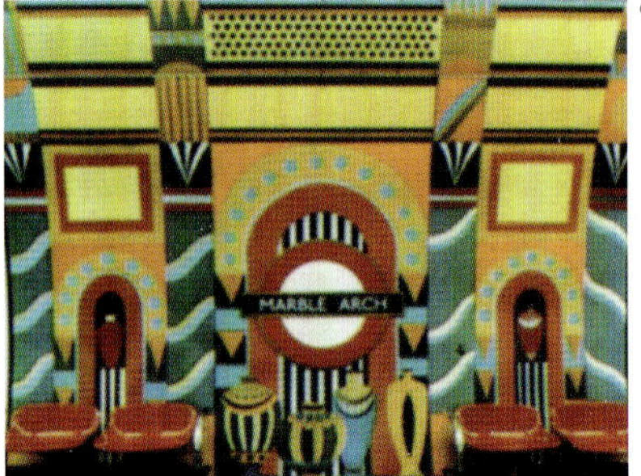

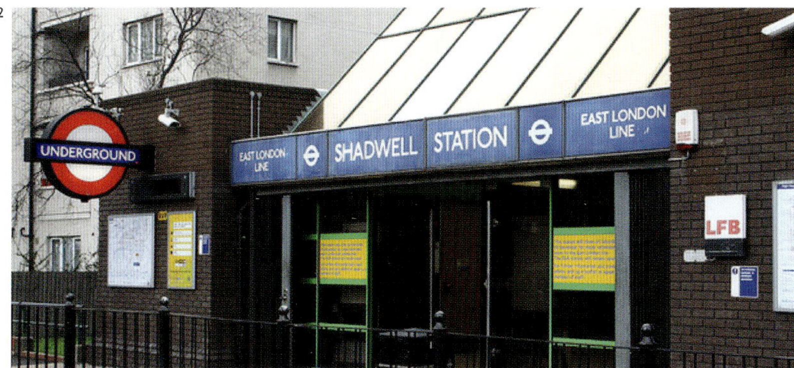

1

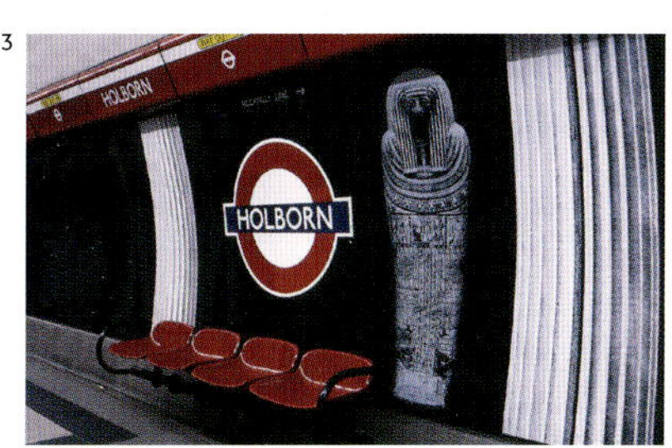

2

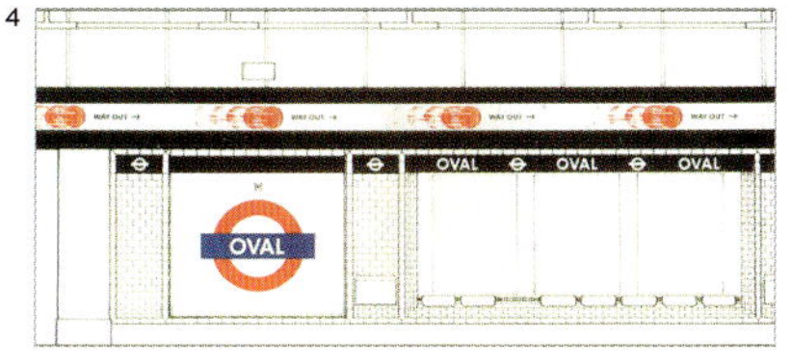

3

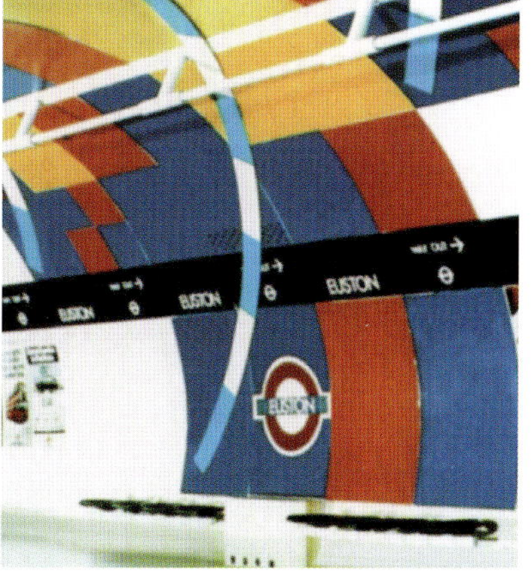

5

4

Henrion Ludlow Schmidt sets new standards, 1984–90

Two ELL station rebuilds – Shadwell (2) with raked glass pavilion roof and Surrey Docks (1) with its five brick wings (both 1983) – while not particularly remarkable, embodied Holden-esque simplicity. Commissioned by Roger Hughes, a report by HLS (1984) recommended complete re-signing throughout the system (p. 238). In came echoes of the diagram on direction signs; out went illuminated black glass boxes with their muddled messages, replaced by 'modular' white enamel signs where each piece of information was displayed separately. Grey mounting trims surrounded most 'tray'-shaped signs from then until the present day, while black backgrounds were reserved for illuminated yellow 'way out' signs. Robert Cooper and David Hamilton's abstract enamel panels at Euston (Northern line, 1987, 5) and Robyn Denny's striking coloured stripes on white enamels at Embankment (Bakerloo line, 1988) hid the cabling. More white enamel sheets and HLS-specified signage were implemented at the Upton Park refit (1989), one of the first surface stations to have them. Further colourful refitting of central London stations led to Allan Drummond's impressive trompe l'oeil enamel friezes of British Museum artefacts at Holborn (3). Although not completed until 1990, it had the red box trunking – contrasting well against Drummond's black backgrounds. Implementation of HLS standards led to some clever ideas being rejected (e.g. Oval, 1980s concept, 4).

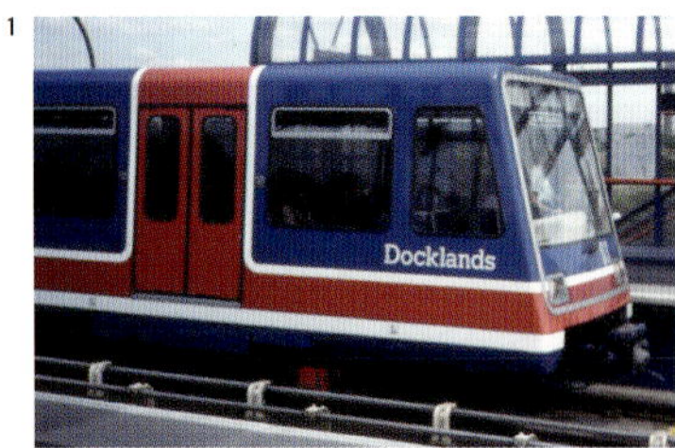

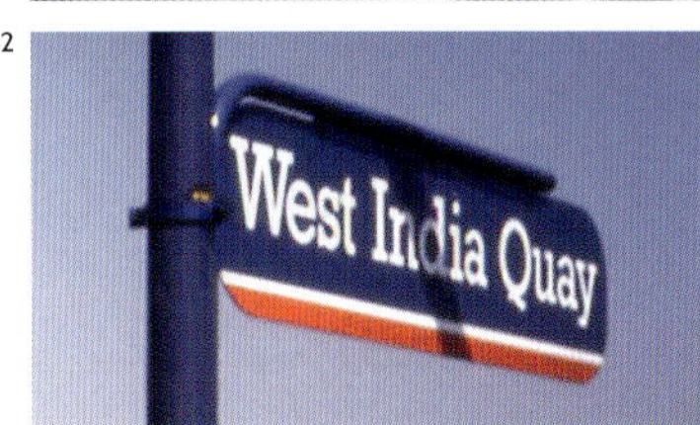

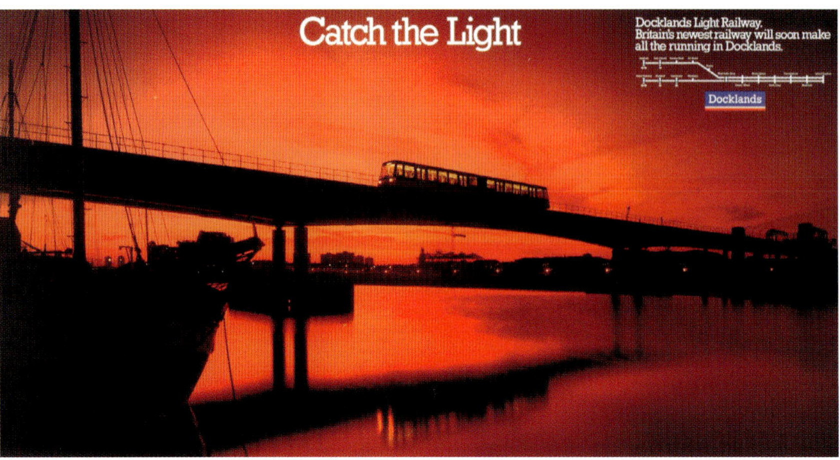

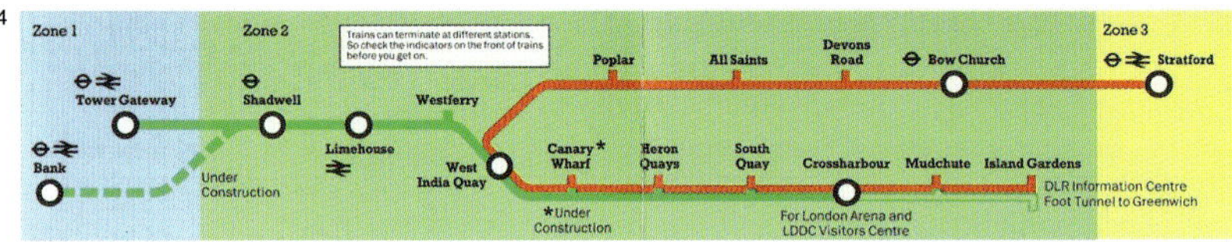

Docklands dabbles with different design, 1987–99

London's newest transport system had its own look (pp. 239–40 and 1). Instead of going for the obvious choice of Johnston lettering, a serif called Rockwell was used for all signage on the DLR when it opened in 1987 (all images except 5). Stephen Jolly (former DLR manager, p. 240) recalls how the chairman Tony Ridley (ex Tyne & Wear Metro) 'wanted to see if things could be done differently … The two principal officers Ben Harding and Bob Bayman and I were keen to try something new with fonts and branding and Bill Clarke (p. 236) gave us the scope to do that. Even so, we all had great respect for the Johnston typeface.' With the exception of the Tube map and a handful of posters, the majority of Underground signage was still all in capital letters. The DLR, however, had embraced lower case as the style of the day, as Jolly again recalls: 'Upper case only was hardly used for anything at the time', and it set the trend for future signage. With the opening of the tunnel to Bank in 1991 (4) and the forthcoming Beckton extension (opened 1994), stations needed elongating so signage was progressively replaced, using a sans-serif (Frutiger, 5). An under-river section to Lewisham opened in 1999, but the DLR was not graphically integrated with the rest of TfL until the opening of the London City Airport branch in December 2005, when roundels were put up and the Johnston typeface introduced.

London Underground by Design

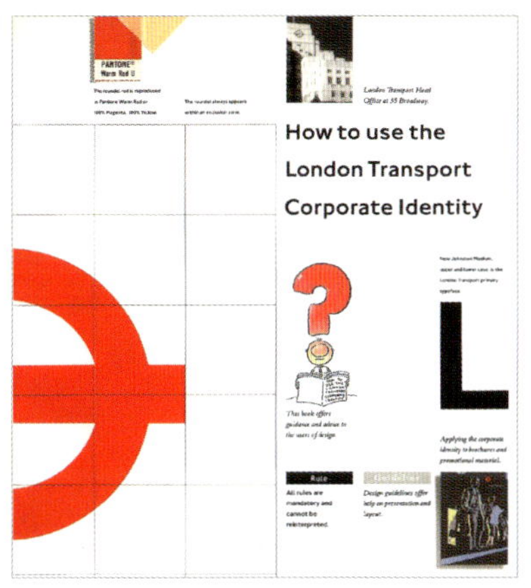

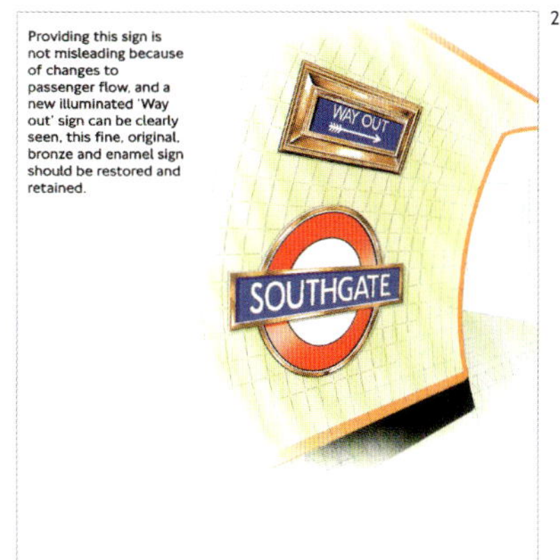

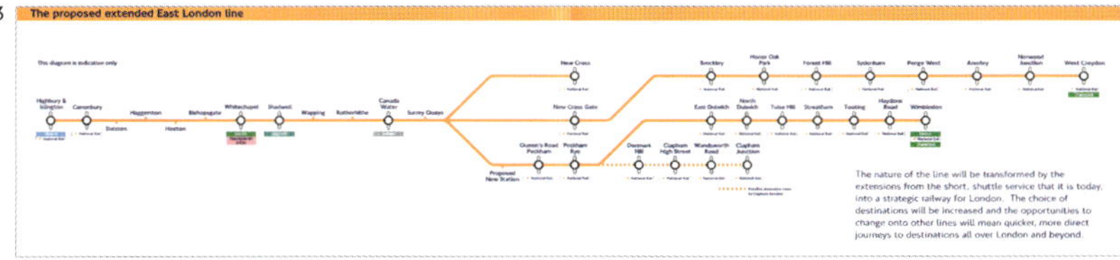

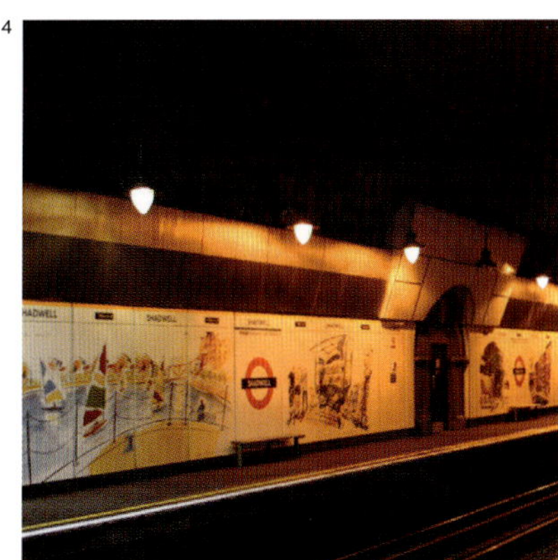

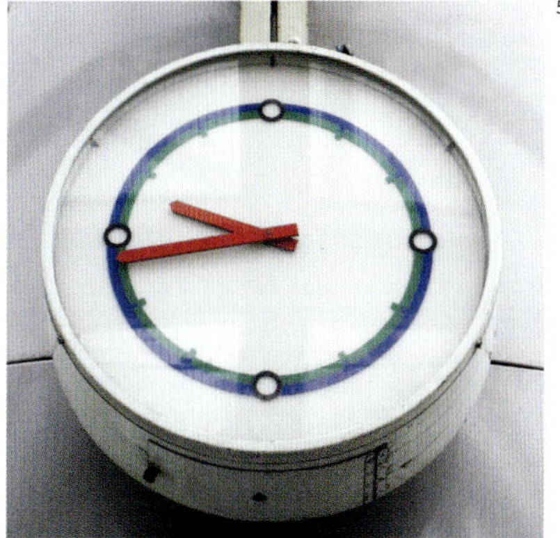

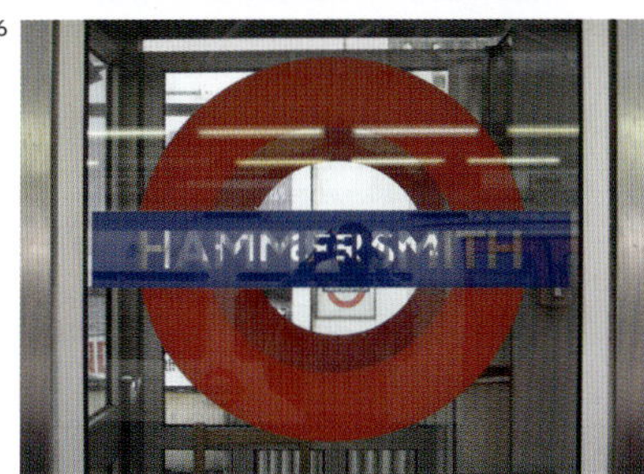

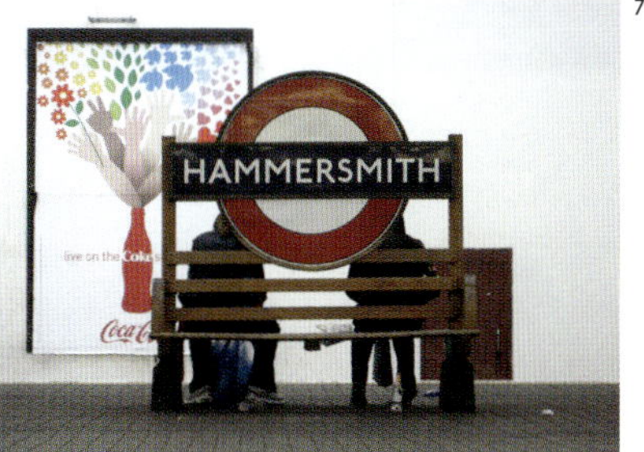

Putting new design strategies into practice, 1991–9

The '1990 Design Strategy' (1) refined the 1980s look. Following its 1992 rebuild, Angel has the Underground's (and Britain's) longest escalator, dropping 27.4m over its 60m length (if not split in half to accommodate access to the proposed Chelsea–Hackney line, it would have been even longer). The 1992–3 station audit (p. 240) recommended urgent repairs with special attention to classic stations – John See's illustrations for the *Heritage Signing Handbook* (1993, 2) are still adhered to. Mike Duffie's architects department produced *Changing Stations*, a summary of refurbishments 1979–93. The ELL was closed for three years from 1995 for a refit in anticipation of its intended extension both north and south (3). Colourful enamelled panels lined the platform walls in tunnelled stations (4) but funding dried up, so when the line re-opened in 1998 there were no extensions to show for the trouble. The only station not to be redecorated was Shoreditch (due to close for the proposed northerly extension) but it hung on until 2006 (after ninety-three years in service). Paul Moss instigated silhouette 'cotton reel' roundels designed by Derek Hodgson, (p. 272) used at Hammersmith, refurbished in 1994 by architects Minale Tattersfield. Original seat-mounted roundels (7) were restored and some clever clock faces put up (5), but the roundel stickers on glass did not really work (6). At the 1996 Bank/Monument refit, an aluminium-framed outline featured in Art Deco-style surroundings.

Revolutionary new train designs, 1992–8

While signage and branding in general was undergoing an overhaul in the 1990s, so was rolling-stock design. For decades train production methods had essentially stayed the same, but the need to replace the entire Central line fleet led to the appointment in 1982 of David Carter's industrial design consultancy DCA, revolutionizing the way vehicles were made. Using a Swiss technology of extruded aluminium for the car bodies, Roger Hughes ordered three prototypes (1, 2 and 3), each encompassing different mechanical and design features. The Red 'A' train (overseen by Hans Peterson), the Blue 'B' one (under Michael Groves) and Green 'C' (Martin Pemberton) were put into passenger service on the Jubilee line between May 1988 and August 1989 to test them. Lighter and more fuel-efficient because of their aluminium bodies, the cars all had externally hung sliding doors, plus varying combinations of large windows, push-button doors, audio-visual passenger information and grab-poles and handrails to replace strap hangers. The production model – 1992 Stock (eighty-five train sets were ordered in 1989) – combined all the best features from the trial (4). They entered service in 1993, the seating upholstered in a reddish moquette called 'London Pride', and they had rubber flooring in dark grey with blue and ivory chips, and grab-poles and hand rails in Central line red. They are also used on the Waterloo & City line (in Network SouthEast livery until 1994).

The 1992 Stock was deemed so successful, in design and safety-wise, that all the remaining older trains on the Underground (some in service since 1938) entered a programme of total refurbishment. The livery of white bodies, red doors and blue skirts became ubiquitous. Flame-resistant materials, grab rails and improved passenger information (including audio announcements) became the norm. Radical new ideas were put forward in a 1990 design competition, though few were adopted (including Seymour Powell's pointed-nose cab, opposite, 1). While refurbishment greatly extended the life of old rolling stock, it was not always cost effective. Refurbishment of the 1983 Stock for operation on the Jubilee line, for instance, was estimated by Warwick

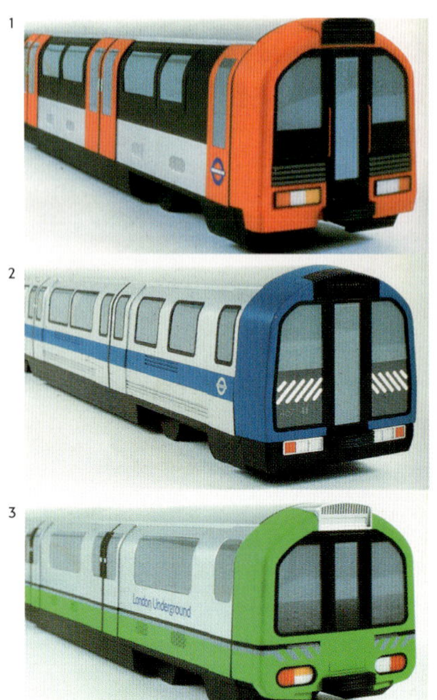

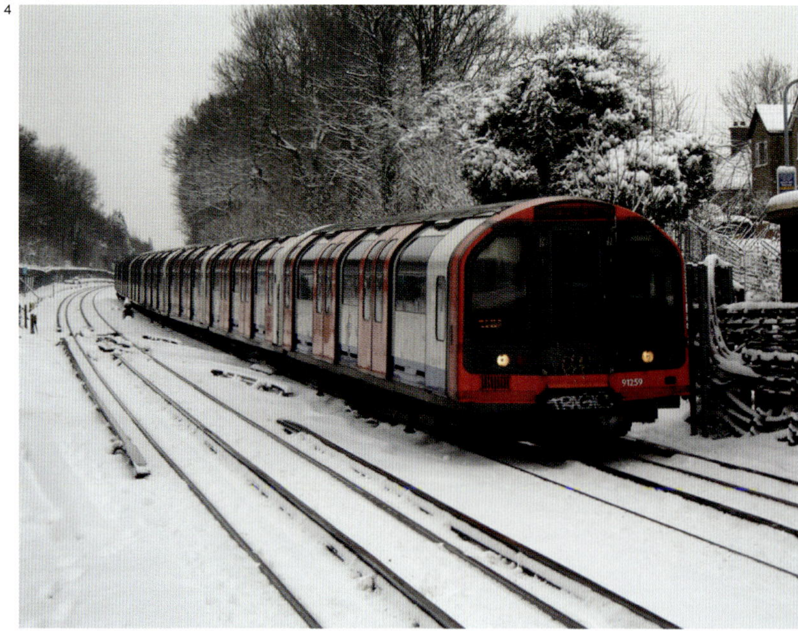

London Underground by Design

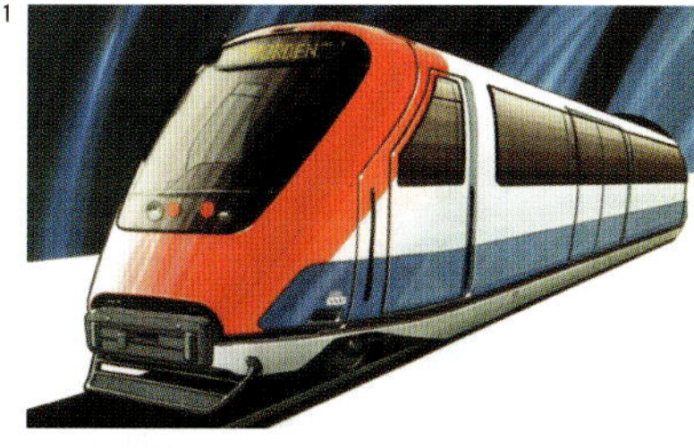

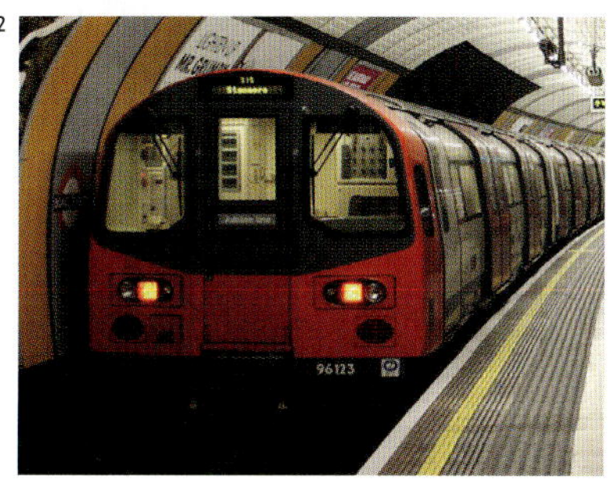

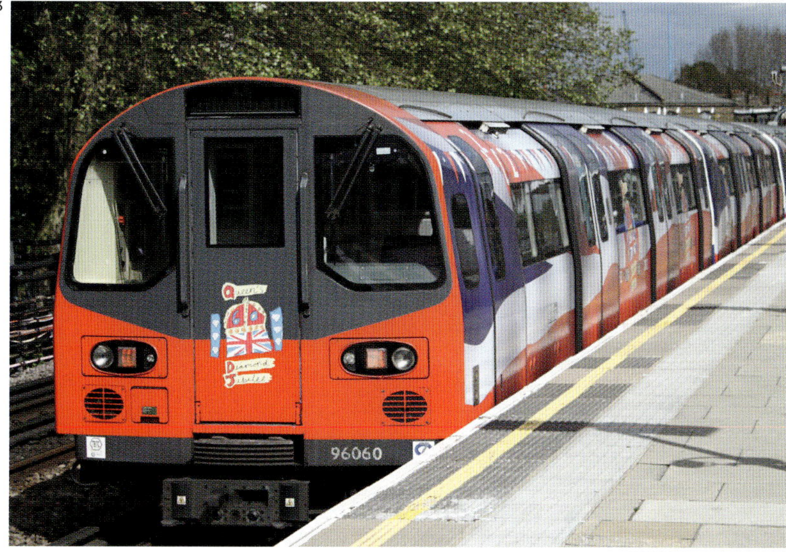

Design consultants to be as expensive as building new trains. Northern line vehicles had to be replaced too and this, combined with the need for the new JLE trains (p. 268), gave rise to the 1995 Stock, the first to be designed with wheelchair access in mind, and 1996 Stock (2). The Northern line was to receive the 1995 Stock, featuring tip-up seats, while the 1996 Stock (in 2012 Queen's Diamond Jubilee livery, 3) was used for the JLE, both lines being equipped with the new trains by the end of 1998. The publicity machine wasted no time advertising the benefits of the new rolling stock: better lit District trains featured on a 1995 poster (4) and a somewhat fanciful bullet-shaped stylization of the 1995 stock adorned a 1996 ad for new Northern line trains (5).

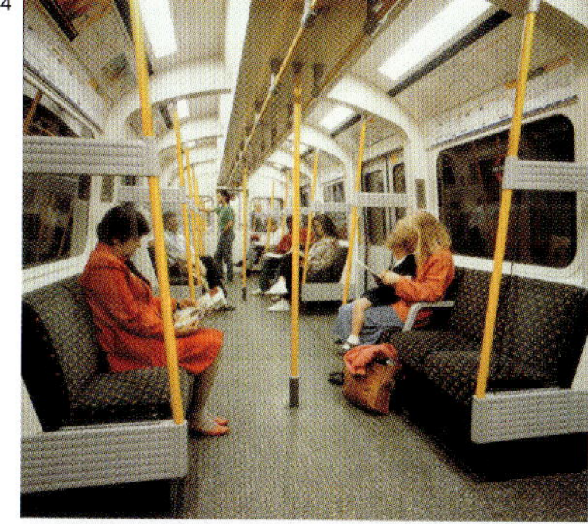

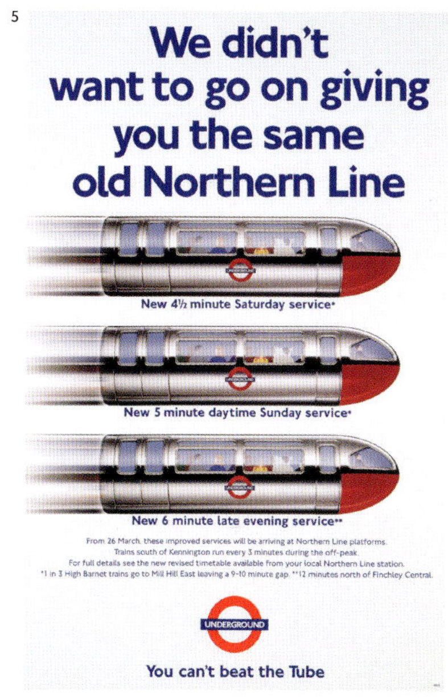

Posters, 1986–90

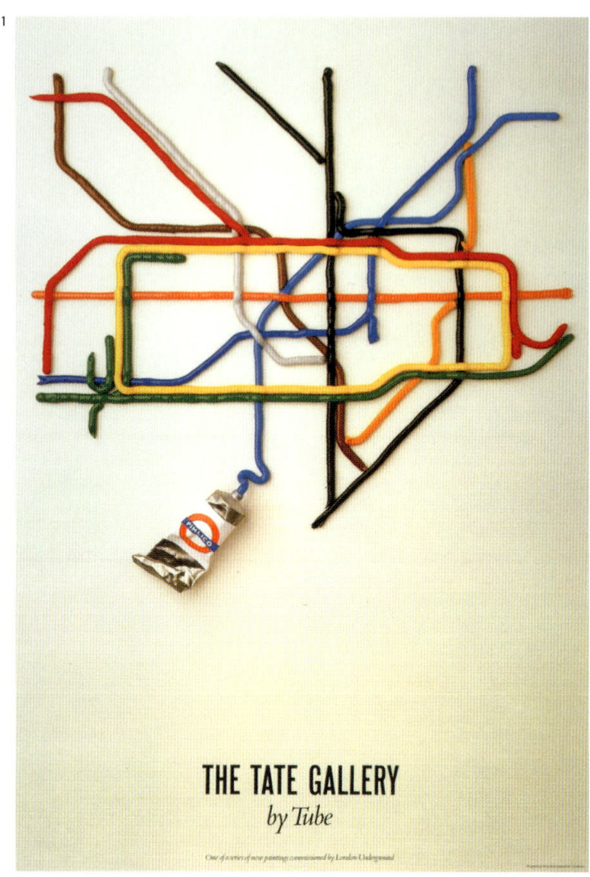

THIS PAGE: Varying in style from wittily functional to purely decorative, posters in the mid 1980s were made more interesting by a revival of the policy of using new or established artists from outside the LU. This gave rise to the (first) 'Art on the Underground' series of posters, commissioned by Henry Fitzhugh in 1986 and including 'Take the Tube to the Park', Peter Lee (1986, 2); 'Criterion Brasserie', Celia Lyttleton (1986, 3); 'The Tate Gallery by Tube', David Booth, Malcolm Fowler and Nancy Fowler/Fine White Line Agency (1986, 1) has become one of the bestselling Tube posters of all time.

OPPOSITE: As well as producing outstanding designs from external sources, the policy arguably improved in-house contributions too, 'Meet your new Waterloo' (4), 'Spruce new Euston' (5), Frank Dickens (all 1986); and 'Keep your personal stereo personal!', Tim Demuth (1987, 6). 'Art on the Underground' works were judged first by artistic merit then by their 'soft-sell' message. Other memorable designs include: 'Fly the Tube to Heathrow', Benoît Jacques (1987, 7); 'Richmond riverside', Spencer Rowell, (1988, 9); 'The new Kew by Tube', Jennie Tuffs (1987, 10); 'The flamingoes by Tube', Kay Gallwey (1987, 11); and Camden Lock, John Bellany (1990, 12). Wilson McLean cleverly folds the pocket map into a paper plane. 'Fly the Tube' (1986, 8) became an outstanding contribution to the series encouraging passengers for Heathrow to take the Underground.

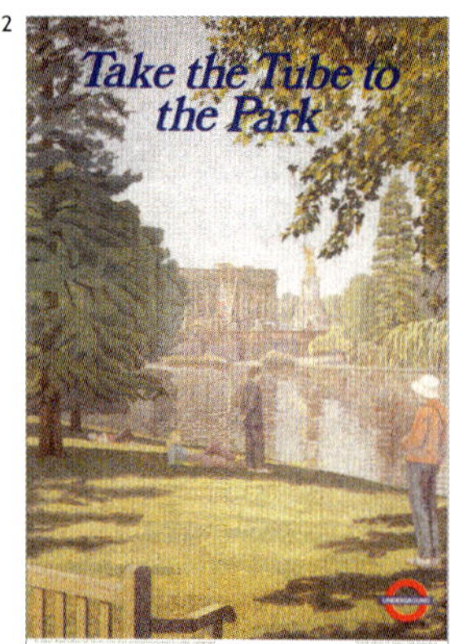

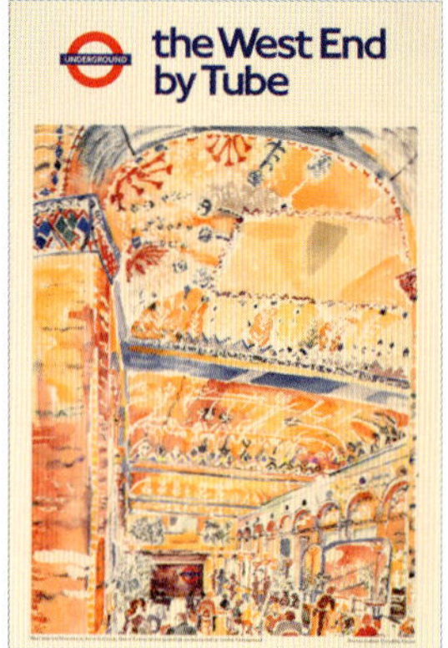

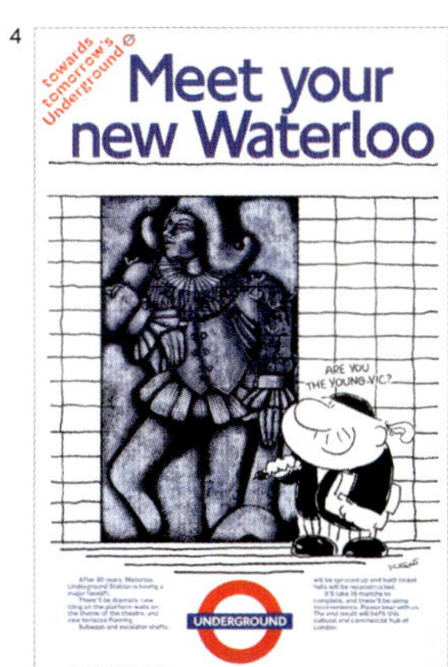

towards tomorrow's Underground
Meet your new Waterloo
ARE YOU THE YOUNG-VIC?
UNDERGROUND

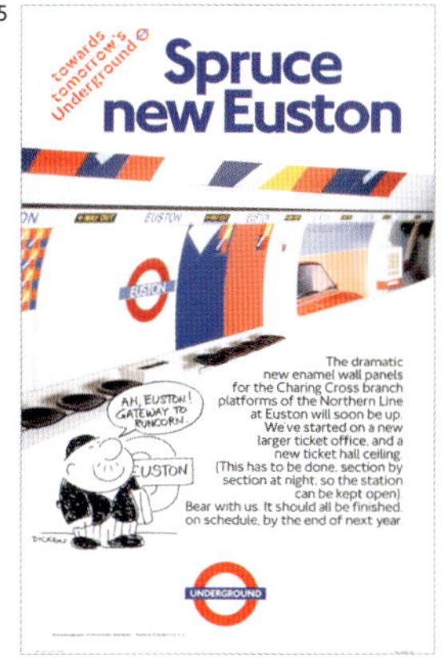

towards tomorrow's Underground
Spruce new Euston
AH, EUSTON! GATEWAY TO RUNCORN.
EUSTON
The dramatic new enamel wall panels for the Charing Cross branch platforms of the Northern Line at Euston will soon be up. We've started on a new larger ticket office, and a new ticket hall ceiling. (This has to be done, section by section at night, so the station can be kept open) Bear with us. It should all be finished, on schedule, by the end of next year
UNDERGROUND

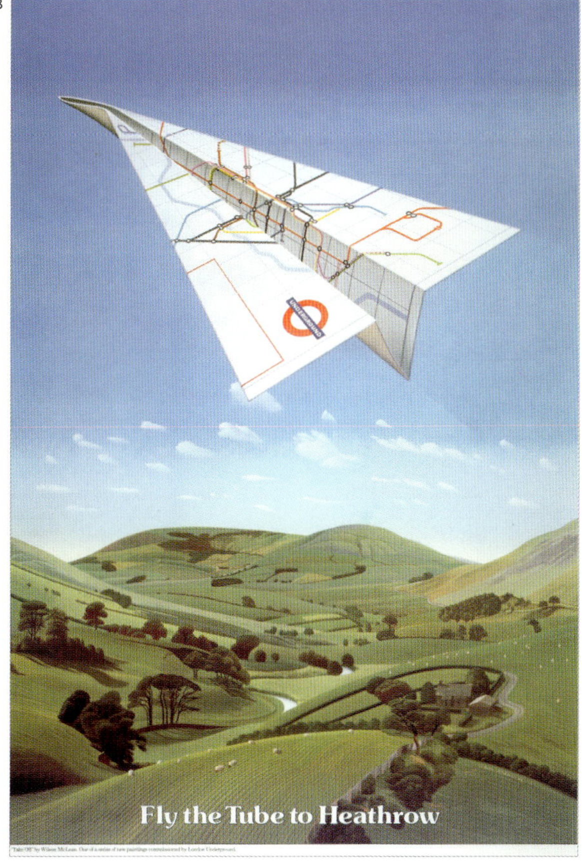

Fly the Tube to Heathrow

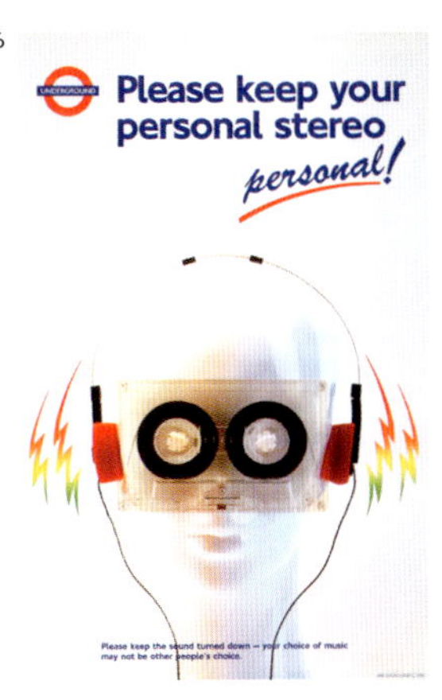

Please keep your personal stereo personal!
Please keep the sound turned down — your choice of music may not be other people's choice.

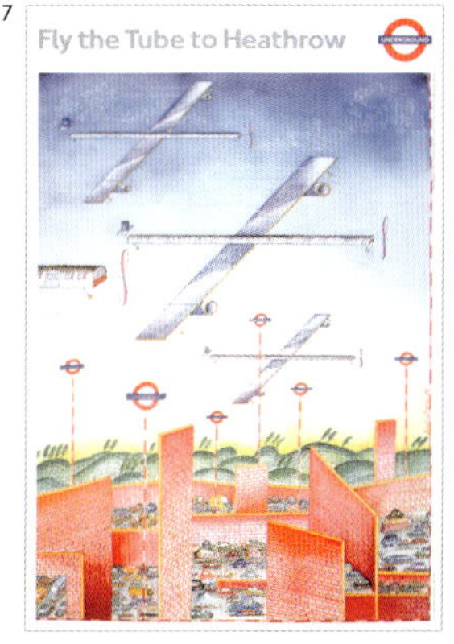

Fly the Tube to Heathrow

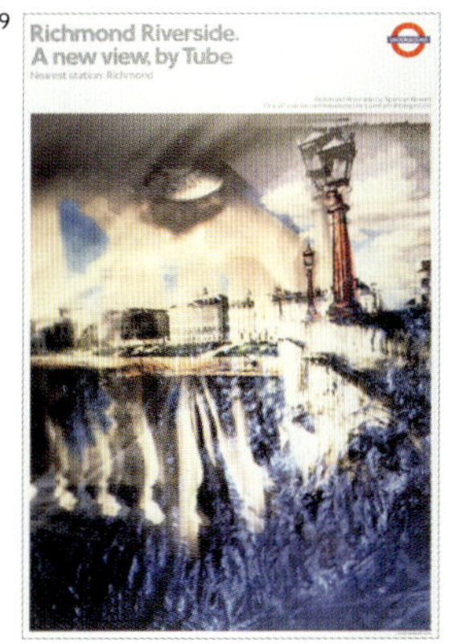

Richmond Riverside. A new view, by Tube
Nearest station: Richmond

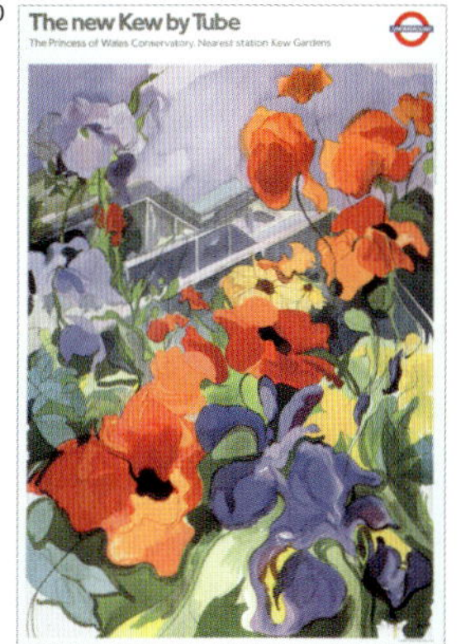

The new Kew by Tube
The Princess of Wales Conservatory. Nearest station: Kew Gardens

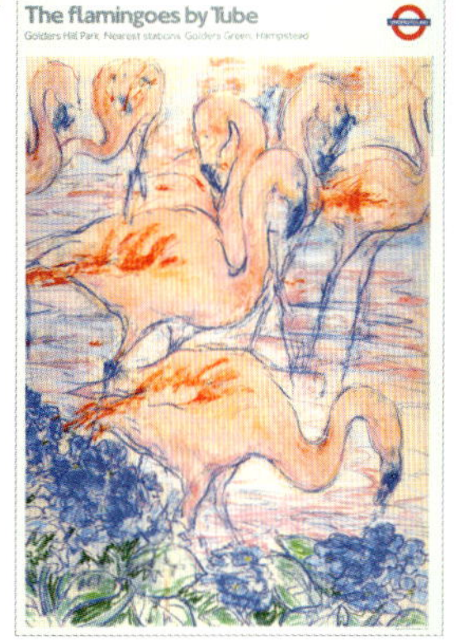

The flamingoes by Tube
Golders Hill Park. Nearest stations: Golders Green, Hampstead

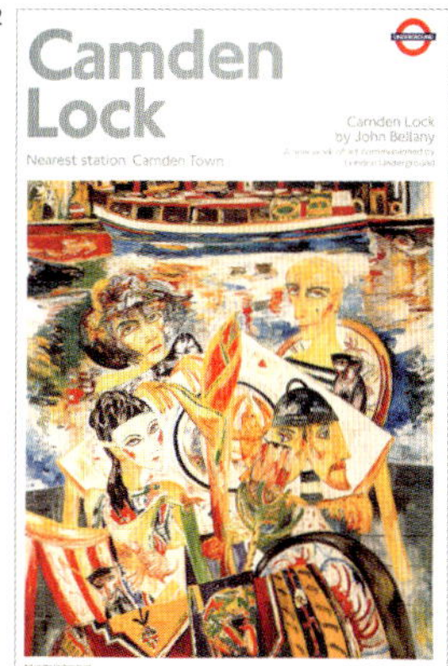

Camden Lock
Nearest station: Camden Town
Camden Lock by John Bellany

Posters from the late 1980s combined inventiveness, as in Nick Hardcastle's taxi 'slugs' of 1987 (2), with a greater emphasis on corporate identity (following implementation of the HLS report, p. 238), as in these extrapolations from bits of the Tube diagram: 'Tube Centenary', Sue Turner/Fine White Line (1990, 1); 'To keep the Underground clean, we're making sweeping changes' (1989, 4); and 'The end of the line for litter', Richard Bird Associates (1988, 5). Promotion of the new Docklands line: 'The Light programme' (1990, 6); 'Architecture in Docklands', Neil Gower (1990, 7) used perennial favourites of mapping and architectural delights along the line. Visual puns returned, for example 'Fly the Tube to Paris', Ian Southwood/Harris Kemp Advertising (1990, 10) and 'Cutting through the traffic', Legend Design (1991, 11). As litter bins were now sealed to prevent bombing, a whole series on personal responsibility was commissioned, such as 'Please take your litter home' (1991, 12); and Richard Spice's colourful and stylish image of riders pocketing trash (1991, 14). Other notable posters include: 'No Entry. No Parking. No Hassle' (1987, 3); 'Going up at Southgate 1930s style' (1989, 9); and 'London's Grandest Corner Shop', for the 55 Broadway refit (1989, 8); 'Monument', Jeffrey Camp (1991, 13); and an optimistic vision of future JLE trains (1995, 15).

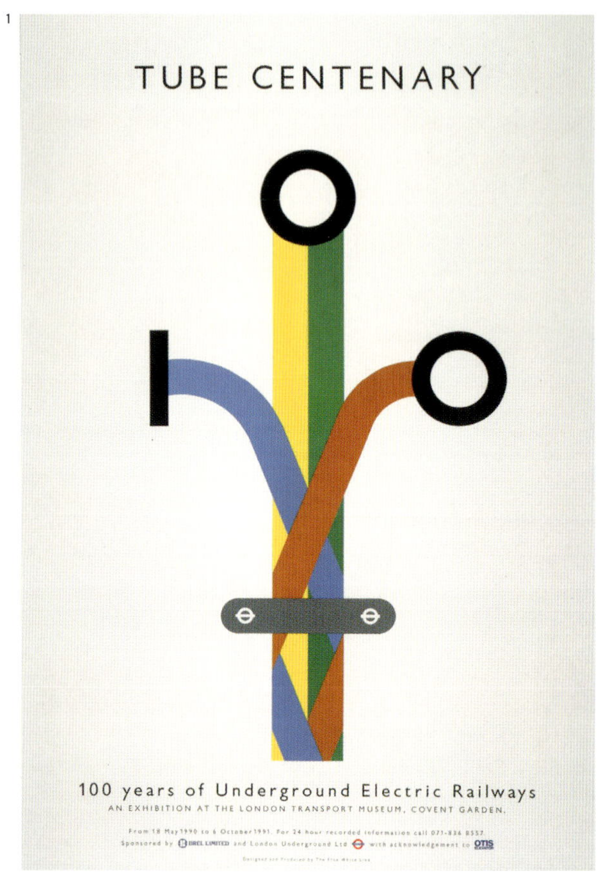

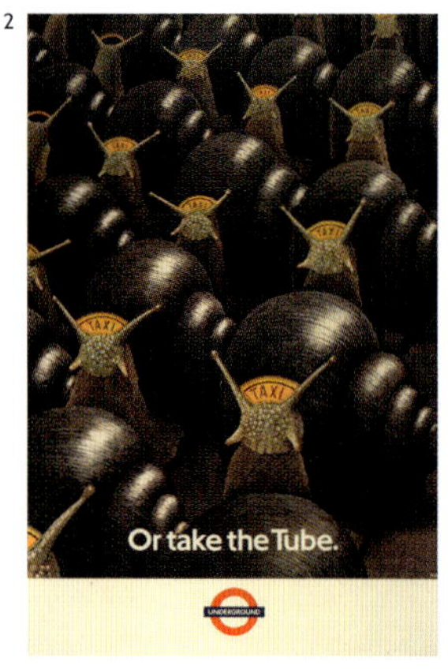

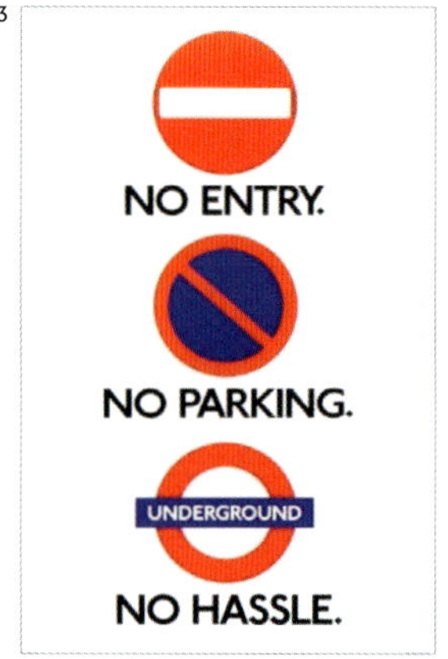

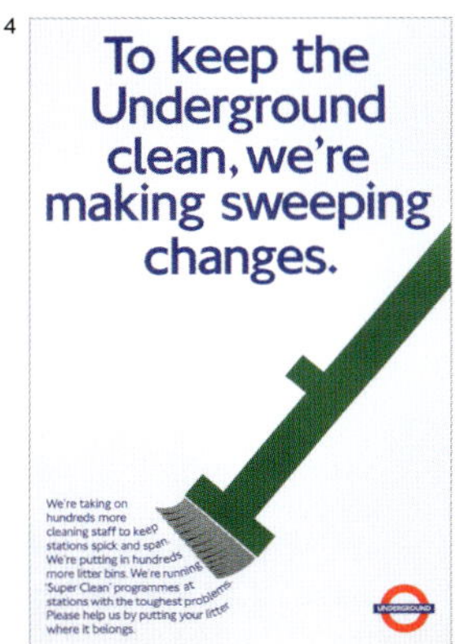

4

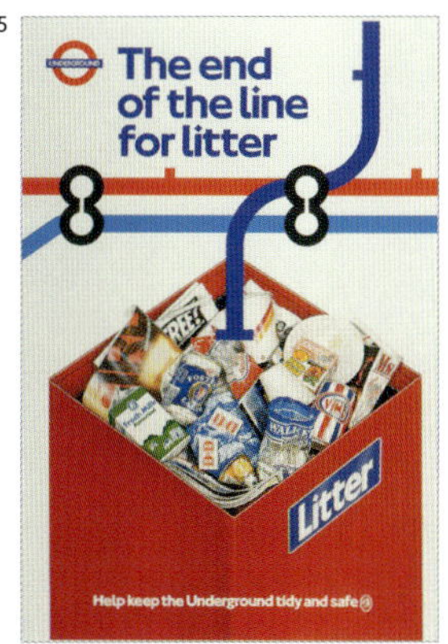

5

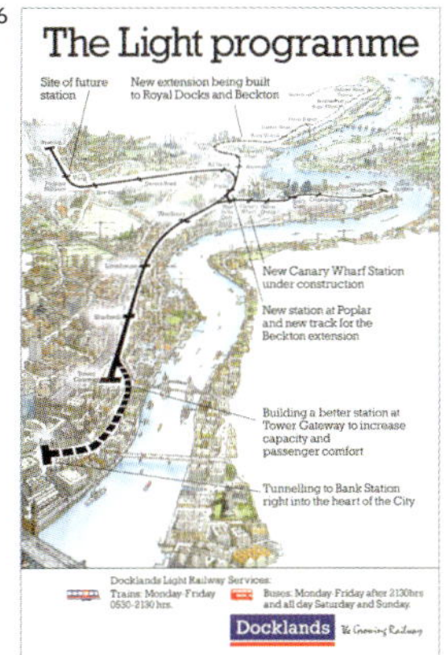

6

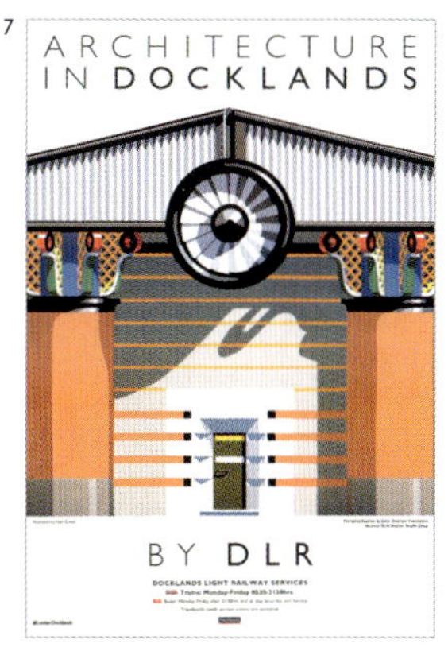

7

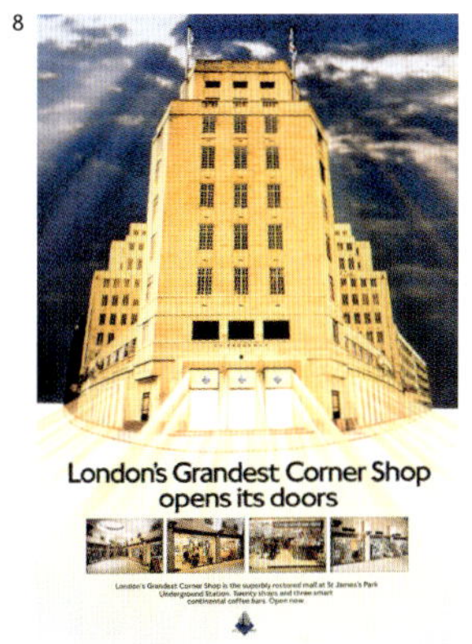

8

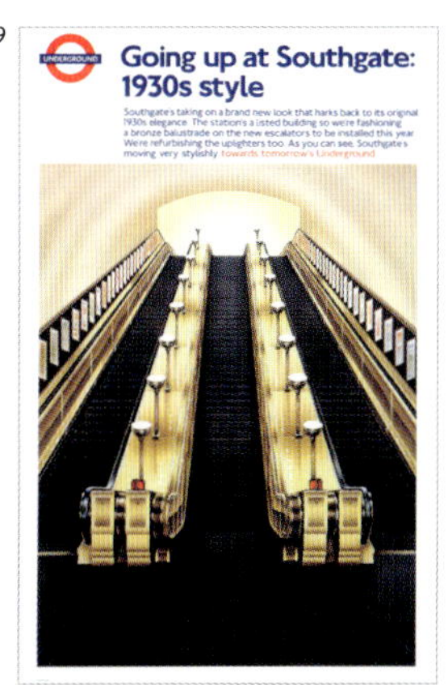

9

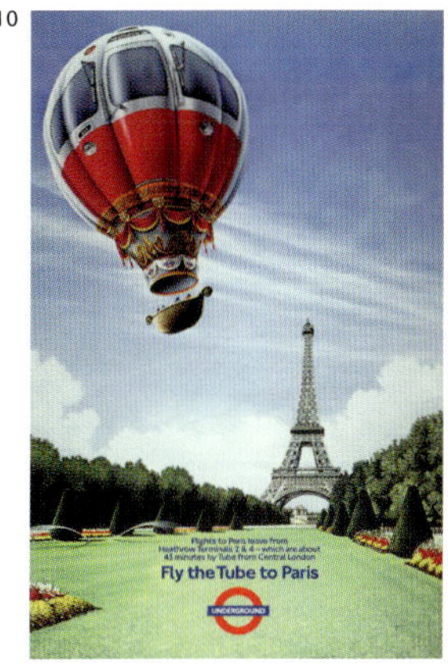

10

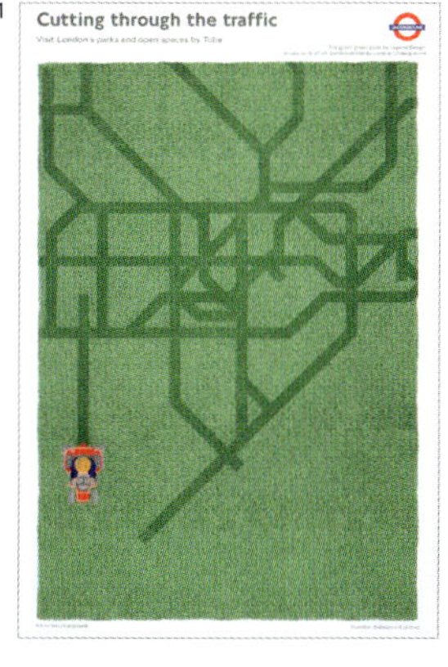

11

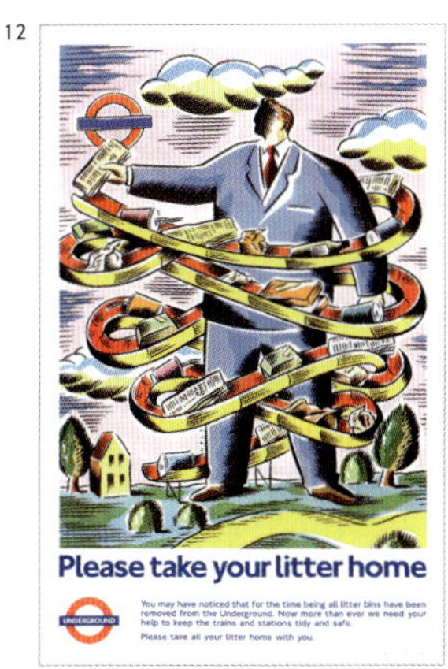

12

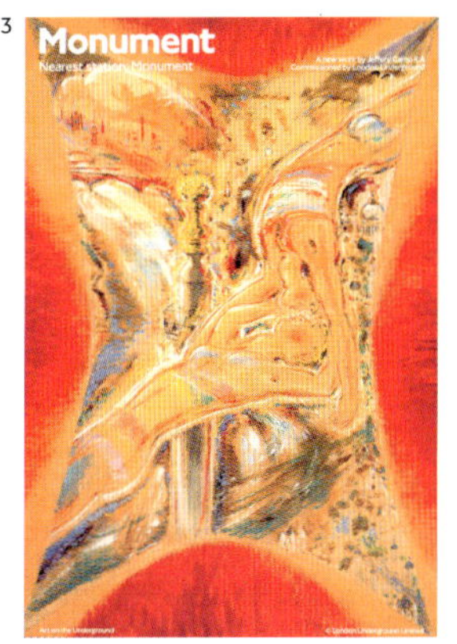

13

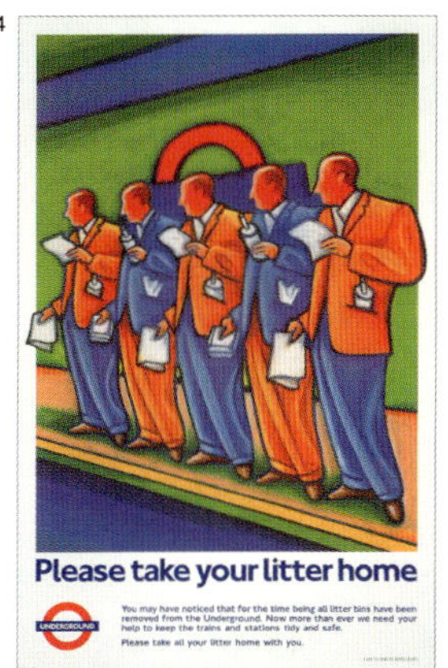

14

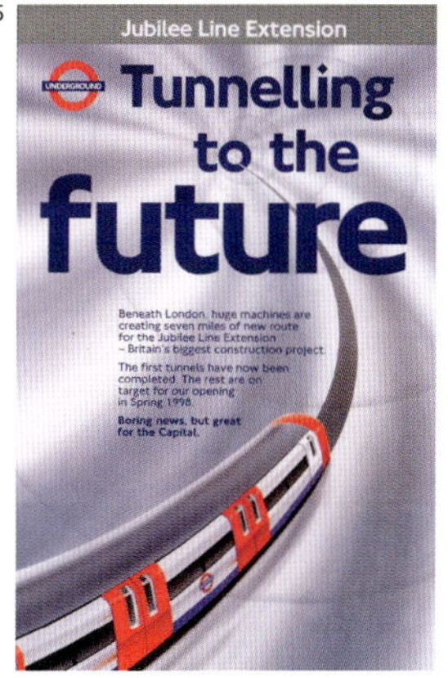

15

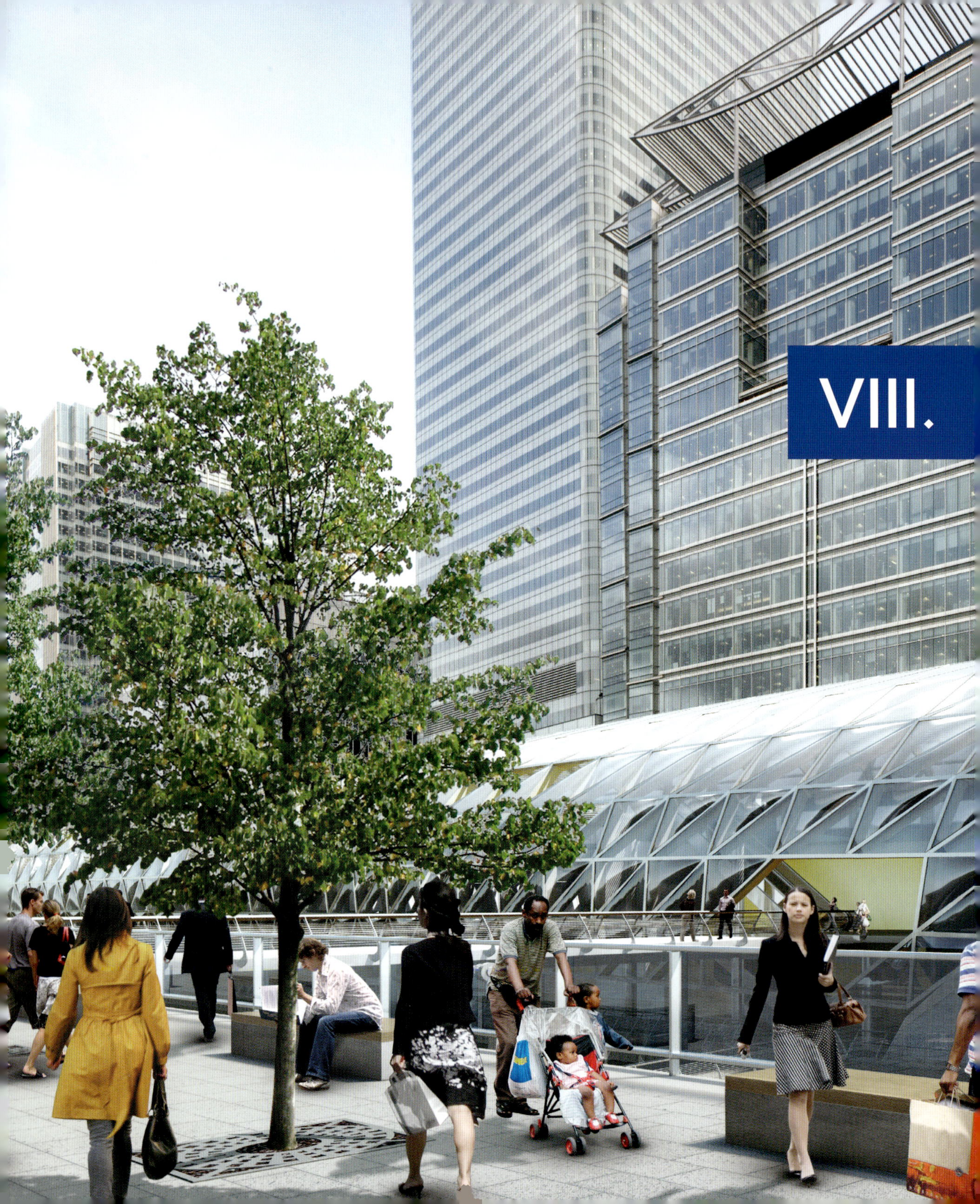
VIII.

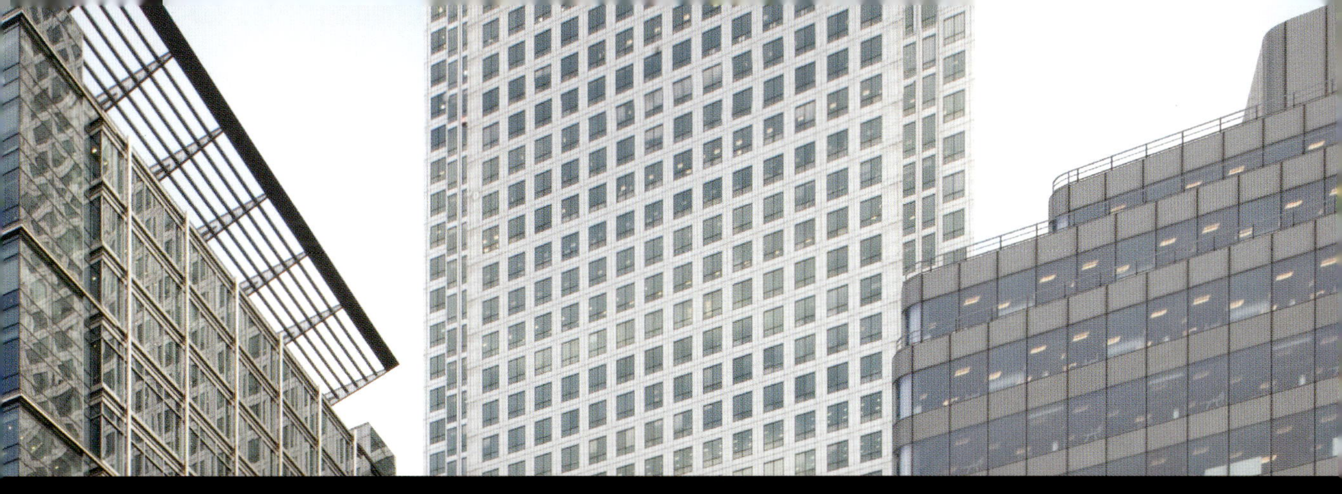

Twenty-first-century Light and Space
2000–13

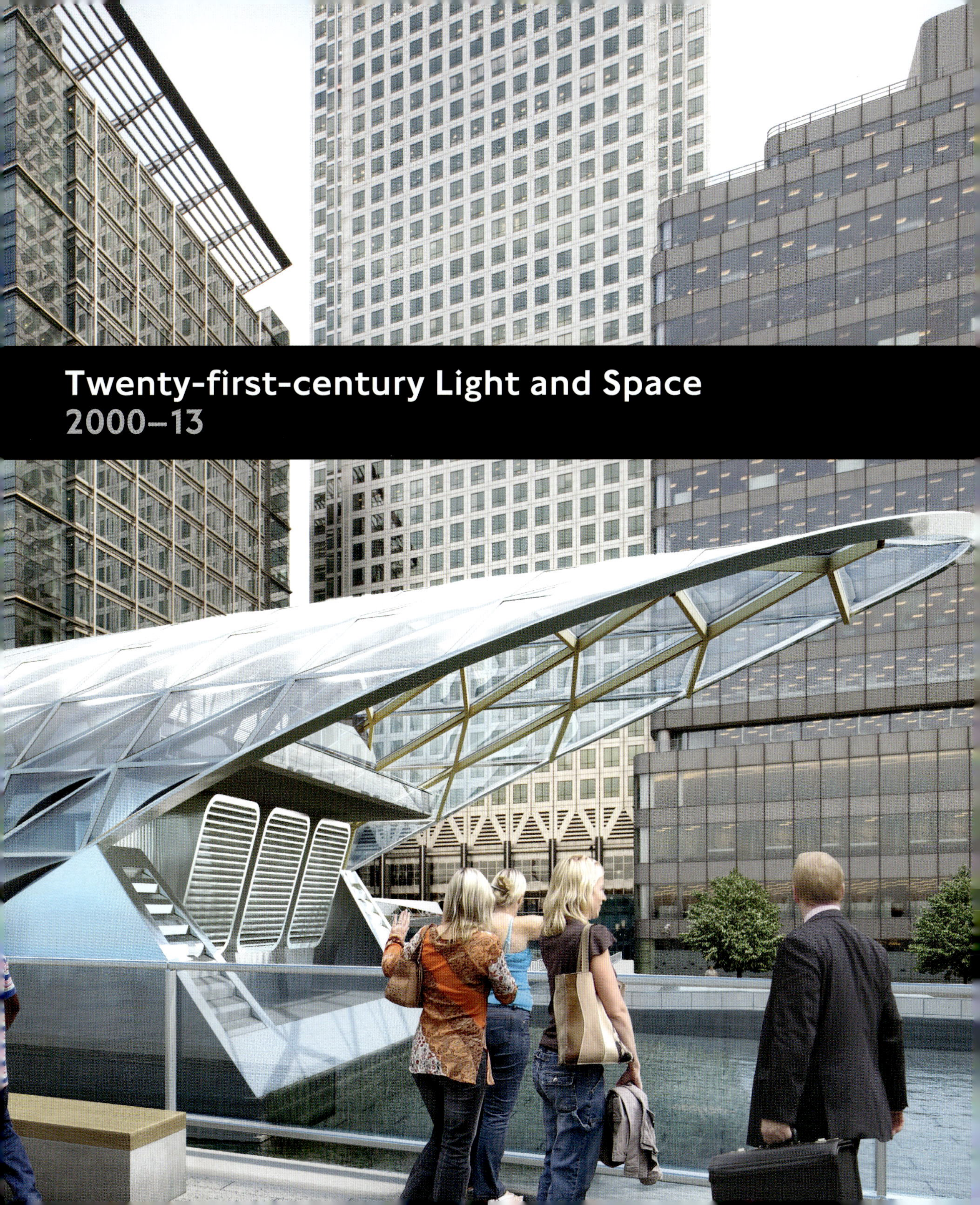

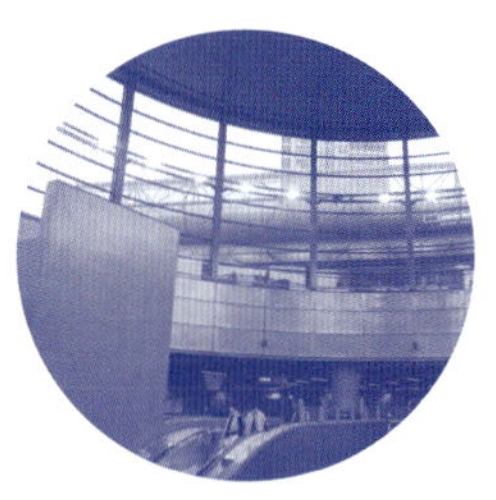

Roland Romano Paoletti, born in London 1932, trained as an architect in Manchester and moved to Hong Kong for construction of the Mass Transit Railway in 1975. He returned to London to take charge of the JLE where he insisted on stations being carved out of the ground (rather than bored in tunnel), Canada Water pictured). He was awarded a CBE in 2000.

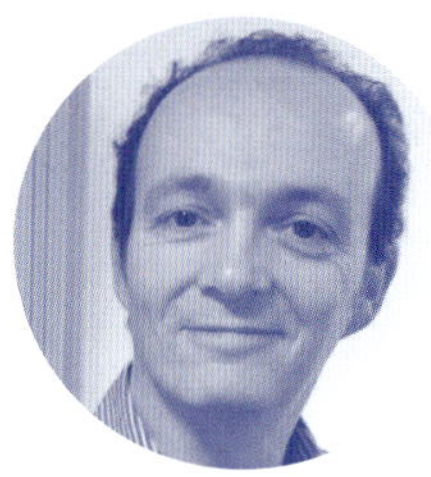

Jerry Hill, born in London 1961, joined the Underground lighting department in 1979. He moved to signage in the mid 1980s, steering through the 1984 HLS recommendations, and is now part of the signage and wayfinding team for TfL.

PREVIOUS PAGES: Canary Wharf Crossrail Station is currently under construction. Surrounded by water and a wharf garden, it was due to open in 2018.

VIII. Twenty-first-century Light and Space, 2000–13

The Jubilee Line Extension was overdue, over budget and over the top; a grandiose vanity project for the new steel heart of British capitalism. And yet it bequeathed to London the most sumptuous, monumental and 'future-proof' Underground stations since Holden's day.

Designing for more light and space

A number of architects were employed to design the stations, with Roland Paoletti at the helm. Each of the eleven sites[1] were treated as individual entities, linked to the rest by materials, colour and signage. From observation of the Washington, DC, Moscow and Munich metros, in addition to Paoletti's own work in Hong Kong, creating a feeling of space was a priority, with extensive use of concrete, glass and metal. New building methods were employed, permitting natural light to enter below, for example at Bermondsey (p. 268), where a lattice of concrete beams allowed daylight to filter onto platforms. There is no doubt too that, as Ian Logan of studiodare (a team of architects working on the project) puts it, 'designers wanted to pay tribute to previous Underground architects' – hence the rotundas at Canada Water and Southwark (pp. 269). The Jubilee line also saw Britain's first deployment of platform-edge doors (PEDs) to reduce draughts and the risk of accident, such as passengers falling under trains. The planned millennium celebrations at the Dome provided the impetus for the JLE to be fully open by New Year's Eve. It was therefore opened in phases: from Stratford to North Greenwich on 14 May 1999, from there to Bermondsey on 17 September, from that station to Waterloo a week later, and finally the all-important section from there to Green Park on 20 November, although Westminster, which did not open until 22 December, was ready only just in time. While the rush to finish caused a £1 billion cost over-run, the station design was so impressive (p. 268–9) that even the normally cynical press were forced to concede it was (almost) worth the investment.

Sign design of the times

The Underground's pioneering work in corporate branding had been summed up in various issues of the graphic standards manual since the 1938 Carr–Edwards report (pp. 206, 218), but then design consultants HLS arrived on the scene, producing a number of exemplary reports (1984–2001, p. 238) on all aspects of signage, plus the Tube diagram, train interiors and internal communications. This led to the complete redrafting and updating of the graphic standards manual in 1989, the 2002 version of which (p. 272) describes itself as 'the culmination of thorough research, design and development', going on to explain how 'By careful and consistent application of the standards documented, [LU] will further enhance the image of the Underground. Stations … are diverse in layout and architecture, and as such, this manual … will establish the set principles to enable effective and consistent solutions to be applied across the network.' Fine aspirations indeed!

PPP or not to be?

The Underground has undergone many management changes since its inception, causing what Christian Wolmar calls a 'stop-go' attitude to investment (2004, Bibliography). By 2003, the scale of the repairs needed was so vast that the government insisted that the newly created Transport for London[2] raise some of the money from outside the Treasury. The resulting Public–Private Partnership (PPP) initiative was forced upon the Underground, giving rise to two companies, Metronet and Tube Lines. They didn't last long. Metronet went into administration in 2007 and TfL took over Tube Lines in 2010, but physical evidence of their brief existence can still be seen on the system. Both companies had been created with a remit to invest in the Underground, but though much was achieved before they disappeared, the project had proved so complex and so costly[3] that London Mayor Boris Johnson branded it a 'colossal waste of money'.

London Overground and a spiraling Circle

Between 2003 and 2006 some south London commuter services were rebranded as the Overground Network ('ON' for short – p. 272–3). This was essentially a marketing exercise with few service improvements, but in November 2007 a different initiative was launched, 'London Overground' – akin to the S-Bahn or suburban rail networks in many German cities – with major infrastructure investment and new rolling stock.[4] Stations and trains were spruced up and rebranded and Oyster card readers installed. On 27 April 2010, the former ELL, rebranded as part of the Overground, was re-opened, with extensions northwards to Dalston Junction and southwards to West Croydon and Crystal Palace.[5] Although in private ownership, the Overground is visually linked with the Underground by bright, clean stations sporting orange roundels in New Johnston (p. 272), while the new rolling stock with orange livery has given the capital a brand 'new train set' (as the 2007 advertising called it). On 13 December 2009, for the first time since its completion in 1884 (p. 16), the Circle line route was altered – 'extended' to Hammersmith [6] – thus becoming a spiral (known to staff as the 'teacup'). This necessitated enamel direction signs to be replaced along the entire Hammersmith & City line, an expensive task, but part of changes that have improved the service overall.

Tube Upgrade Plan

Rising from the ashes of the PPP debacle came the 'Tube Upgrade Plan', a project to renovate stations and buy new rolling stock that is set run into the 2020s (if it survives

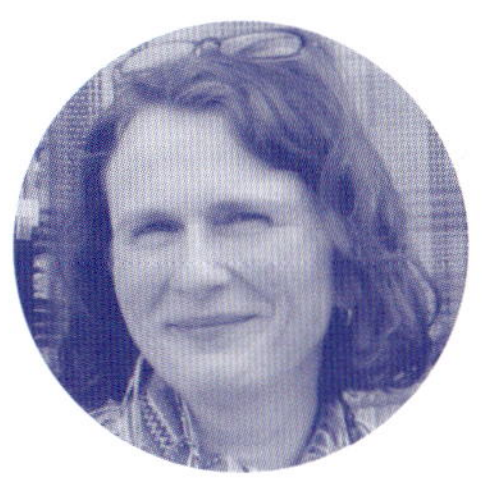

Dorset-based Harriet Wallace-Jones, born 1965, and Emma Sewell (pictured), born in Norwich 1964, are textile designers whose company Wallace Sewell was set up in 1992. Their first moquettes were introduced on the Overground (2008) and Croydon Tramlink (2008). They won the 2010 design competition for a new moquette – named 'Barman' by TfL – which weaves four London landmarks together and is now the standard Tube seat covering.

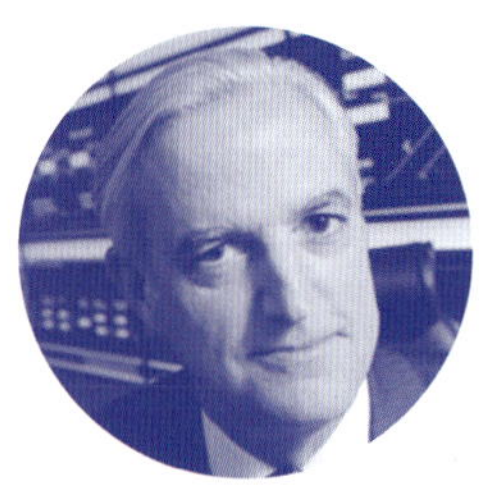

Tim O'Toole, born in America 1955, worked for the US rail industry before transferring to the UK to become managing director of LU 2003–9. He took a keen interest in design and was awarded the CBE for LU's response to the terrorist attacks of 2005.

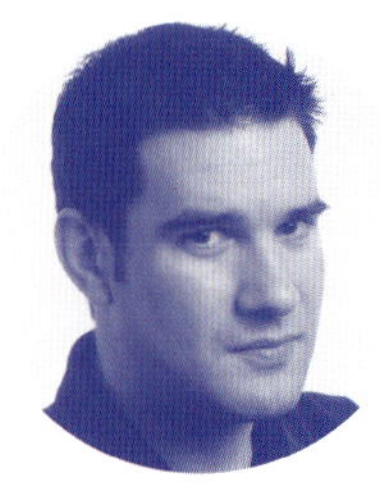

Innes Ferguson, born in Perth, Scotland, 1969, joined LU in 1996 and became head of design at TfL in 2004. As group design manager from 2007, he focused on customer experience for all modes, including congestion charging, Oyster cards, the Overground and the 2012 Olympics. In 2009 he left to work in Sydney, Australia.

public-spending cuts). Engineering works curtailing services have required innumerable images, leaflets and online alerts, including a striking poster of workers rebuilding an Underground diagram from 2007 (p. 274), although later offerings have been less inventive, the most recent series being little more than unimaginatively altered roundels – a heresy against the much-protected corporate identity.[7] By contrast, much of the rebuilding has been carried out sensitively, thanks to the involvement of former Underground boss Tim O'Toole and individuals like Mike Ashworth on the Heritage team in helping to promote the importance of preserving design treasures from the past. One of the most challenging issues has been how to enhance step-free access at stations. Though much of the work has already been completed and the programme is ongoing (including major upgrades at Victoria, Bank and stations being renovated as part of other rail projects), there has been some questioning about these expensive additions. The placement of the wheelchair symbol all over the Tube diagram is contentious on the basis that it has corrupted a design which has taken years to evolve but with little practical benefit.[8]

Olympic Games 2012

Step-free access was crucial for the London 2012 Games, however, where 65 per cent of spectators were expected to arrive by public transport, obliging LU to upgrade all stations close to Olympic venues (including Stratford, West Ham, Green Park and Wimbledon). As part of its commitment to this, TfL opened a DLR extension to Stratford International (where design was neat but relatively spartan, p. 275) and funded a major increase in Overground services, including an order for many new trains. TfL chose magenta for Olympic Games signage so as not to clash with Tube line colours with white New Johnston lettering (p. 275). Appearing at Olympic venues as far afield as Glasgow, Weymouth, Cardiff and Manchester, the London typeface was thus seen extensively outside the capital for the very first time.

Future rail designs for London

A long-held ambition to re-route the Met's Watford branch into the town centre received Department of Transport funding (for 5.5km of track along a former rail alignment) on 14 December 2011. Station design at Ascot Road and Watford Hospital (p. 277), and construction of a new viaduct, is being undertaken by Mike Watkins of Acanthus LW Architects, while the route – known as the Croxley Rail Link – was expected to open in 2016.

A long-mooted project (dating as far back as the 1944 Abercrombie plan)[9] has been the building of mainline-sized rail tunnels under London to link the major termini. The 1974 London Rail Study proposed two such trajectories, coining the term 'Crossrail' in the process, and by 1989 the Central London Rail Study was recommending an east–west scheme. Trials took place in 2003 – an exhibition touring London with maps and a mock-up of full-size trains – but the Act did not receive Royal Assent until July 2008. Construction started the following year for a planned 2018 opening, with an estimated fifty-seven purpose-built electric trains in service each day. As the tunnel – 21km long and running through central London – will link up almost exclusively to Underground stations, forming a super-deep-level express tube (albeit with mainline-sized trains), it is expected that signage will conform to current TfL guidelines and be set in New Johnston (p. 276). It is yet to be seen whether Crossrail forms part of the Overground (despite its newest parts being predominantly in tunnel), and if it keeps the working title or takes another name altogether. (It was re-named the Elizabeth line and delayed until 2019.)

Rumours about extending or possibly splitting the Northern into two separate lines, each with its own name and colour, have also circulated for years. The creation of the Battersea Opportunity Area to regenerate the derelict land around the old power station, not to mention the relocation there of the American Embassy from Grosvenor Square (p. 277), have rekindled plans. The Battersea extension will break out of the Kennington loop (a turnaround facility for Northern line trains currently terminating there) and veer south-west via an intermediate station at Nine Elms[10] to a new terminus alongside the former Battersea Power Station. Public consultation closed in 2011 and tunneling was completed in 2017. Designs were undertaken by Ian Logan and Freddy McBride of studiodare. It will open in 2020.

Another long-proposed route is one running south-west to north-east.[11] Named variously since the 1974 London Rail Study as the 'Chelsea–Hackney', 'Chelney' or 'Hacksea' line, the likeliest chance for success now is as 'Crossrail 2'. The most definite section – a deep-level tube to fit mainline trains – has been safeguarded between Parsons Green and Hackney (Victoria–King's Cross being the absolute priority for some years), although the plan has evolved to include a station, 'Euston–St Pancras', ready for High Speed 2 (from London to the Midlands and northern England) and with links to Eurostar.

Design legacy for London

London will also see new trains (like the EVO, p. 277) and maybe a southern Bakerloo extension (p. 277). Whether any of these or other schemes come to fruition does not detract from the fact that, after 150 years of inspired and innovative design, London has a legacy to be extremely proud of. Thanks to recent and long-overdue investment, the Underground will continue moving every passenger in style well into the twenty-first century. Fit not just for purpose but also for praise.

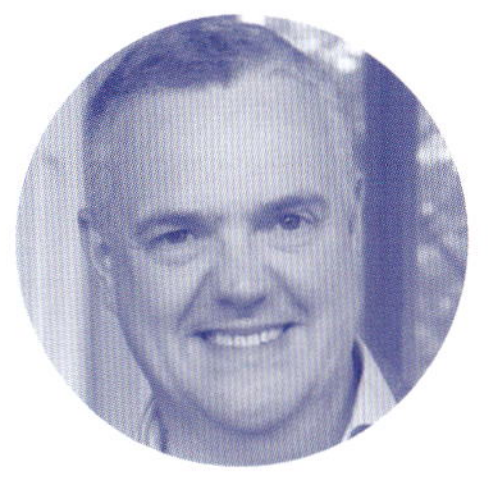

Mike Ashworth, born in Lancashire 1958, is the design and heritage manager at LU. Formerly curator at the London Transport Museum, he was responsible for saving the giant Wood Lane mosaic roundel. He and the Contemporary Customer Environment team have helped to preserve some of the most important pieces of earlier design.

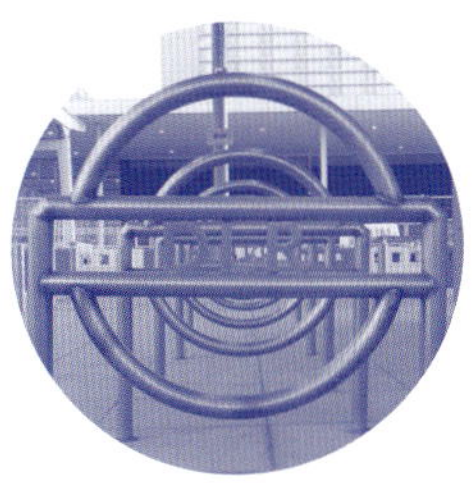

Jon Hunter joined TfL in 2006, becoming group design manager in 2009. He has overseen the organization's design and marketing for the London 2012 Olympics (DLR-branded bike racks at Stratford International, pictured) and the Crossrail project.

Fireproof and future-fit, 2000

Public information was at the heart of JLE construction, which began in 1994 and was expected to take only four years. When the project started there was no Millennium Dome but its North Greenwich siting gave the JLE team an incentive to be ready for the celebrations, and despite having to open in sections (p. 264), the line was completed just in time. In the wake of the 1987 King's Cross fire, and in an attempt to provide what LU managing director Dennis Tunnicliffe has described as 'a timeless quality which will feel as right in 2050 as 1994', all the JLE stations were designed to be much larger than anything previously constructed. Sir Norman Foster's Canary Wharf (1) is so spacious that neighbouring skyscraper One Canada Square could fit horizontally inside. At Westminster (4) a 39m drop from surface to platform level is filled with a mesmeric flight of escalators. Project architect Roland Paoletti (p. 264) wanted to draw light in from above where possible – which Bermondsey, Southwark (2) and Canada Water achieve. Southwark's blue cone wall was inspired by an 1816 stage set for The Magic Flute, while Canada Water's steel-and-glass rotunda (opposite, 2 and 4) harks back to Holden. Though all individual, the stations are linked thematically by Jubilee line grey and signature steel panelling (3), along with copious polished metal and exposed concrete. Flameproof and with step-free access throughout, the JLE was 'fit for the future' in every way – a showcase for quality design and engineering.

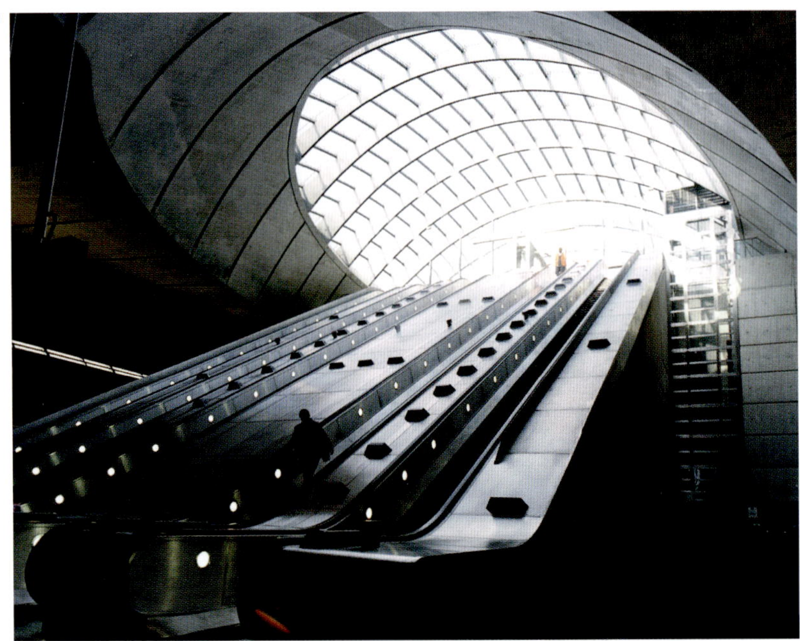

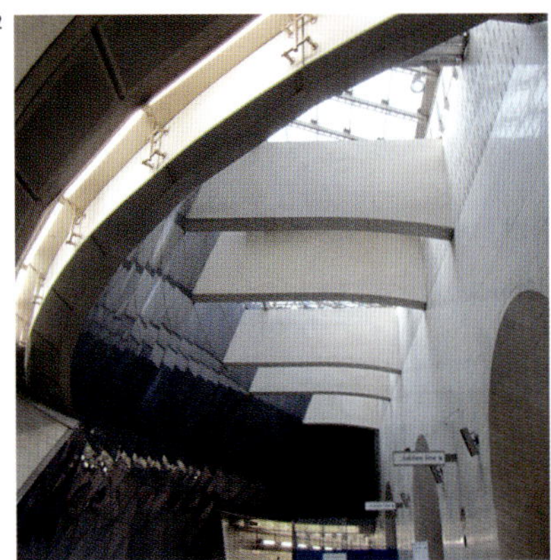

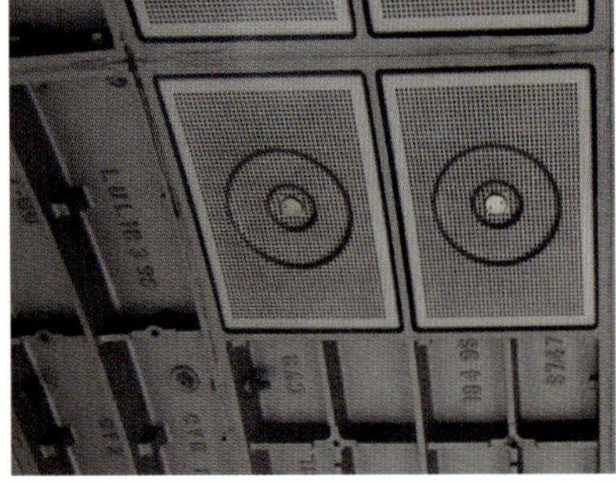

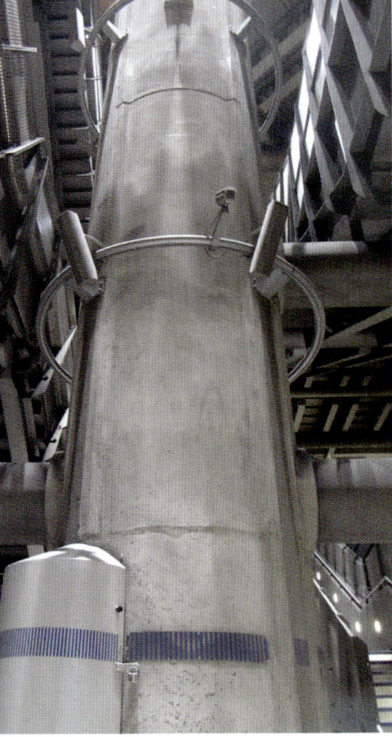

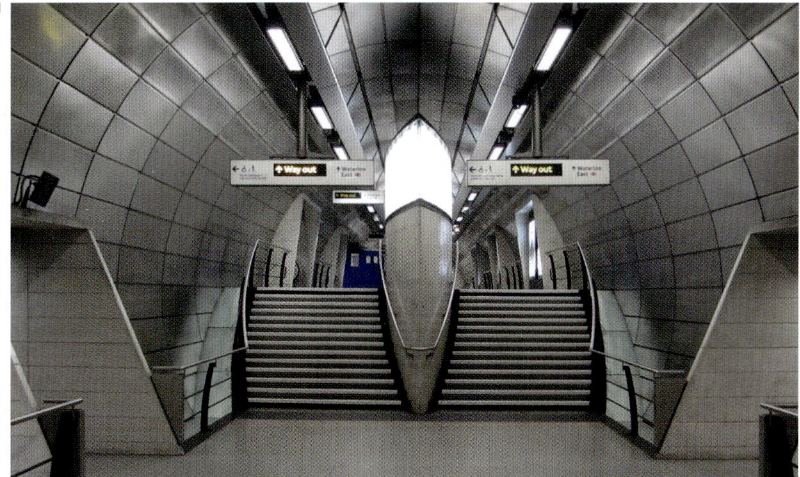

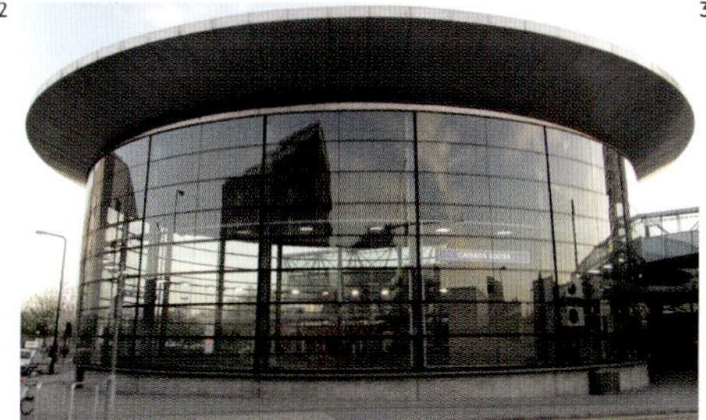

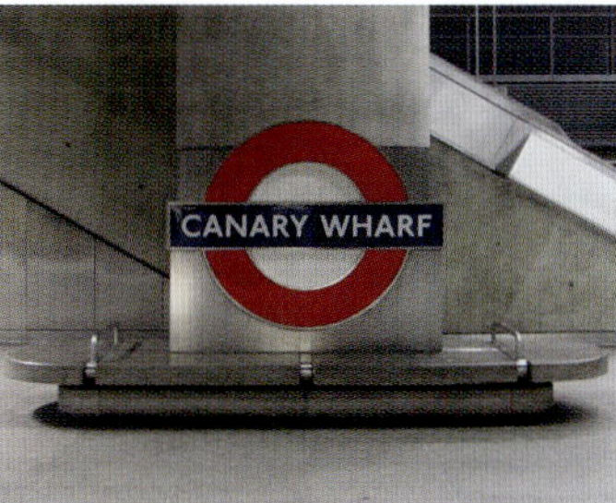

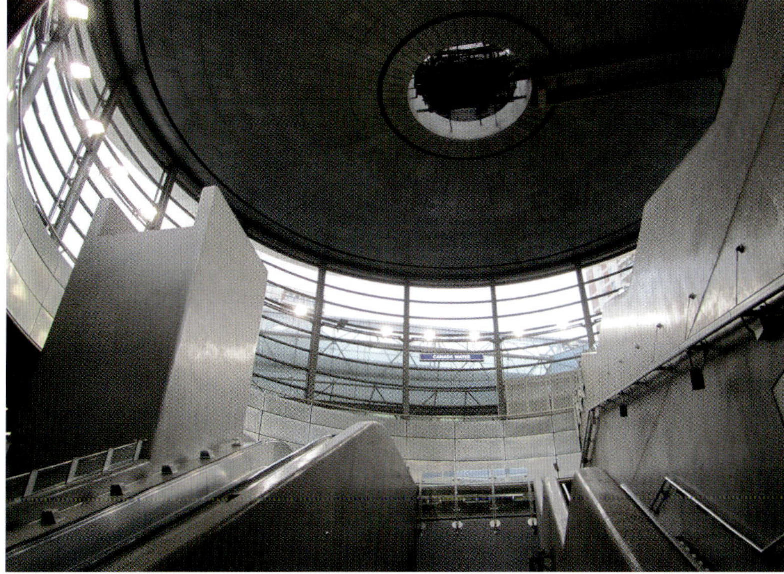

Internal corridors and stairways at the JLE stations are so spacious that they seem like subterranean cities. Take, for example, the magnificent Canada Water (by structural engineers Buro Happold, 2 and 4) or Southwark (by Sir Richard MacCormac, 1), which at street level is also a rotunda — awaiting a twelve-floor office block to be built over it. Passageways are steel clad, resembling a submarine interior. Canary Wharf has the largest platform roundels (3) (though all JLE signage is exemplary): grey cast-aluminium outline roundels, 100cm in diameter and cut away in the middle, are the smartest on the system. Miniature trackside-wall versions (60cm in diameter) are mounted on exposed concrete, steel panelling or blue-painted tunnel linings. The platform friezes are illuminated white frosted glass with blue lettering: station names in capitals and directions to other lines in upper and lower case (which paradoxically at Waterloo is so widely spaced that it looks suspiciously like old not New Johnston). Moquette on the original 1996 Stock was a nested 'J'. The link between the Jubilee and Victoria lines at Green Park was finally opened in 2000 with concealed lighting and speckled mosaic in Piccadilly blue, Jubilee grey and Victoria Cambridge Blue.

Posters, 2000 to present

THIS PAGE: 'Platform for Art' (PFA) (now 'Art on the Underground') was launched in 2000, utilizing a disused platform at Gloucester Road as a display space. The programme has produced hundreds of exciting new works, either exhibited, used as posters or appearing on the pocket map cover. By the noughties, posters were selling fast at London Transport Museum and, with Mike Walton at the fore (p. 241), it became involved in commissioning new works. Among the many excellent PFA posters that emerged were 'Simply River', John Miller (2000, 1); 'Canary Wharf', Trickett & Webb (2003, 2). 'Covers' by Mary Anne Francis (2002, 3) also sprang from the PFA. New York Subway and Underground station names are brought together for 'Fly the Tube', Trickett & Webb (2001, 4). London attractions again inspired scores of wonderful posters, including 'Penguin', Simon Linke (2003, 5); Red-tiled roofs and gardens become a kaleidoscope in 2002 (by muf architecture/art, 6).

OPPOSITE: 'London's garden squares', Andrew Bylo (2004, 7); posters by Lumsden Design Associates from 2004 also look to nature (8, 9 and 10); and a riverside view is offered in 'Exit 11' by Nick Asbury and others (2005, 15). Paul Catherall made a poster for each season in 2006 (11–14). His work was so widely appreciated that another set was commissioned a year later, this time a series of three, 'A new view of London' (16–18).

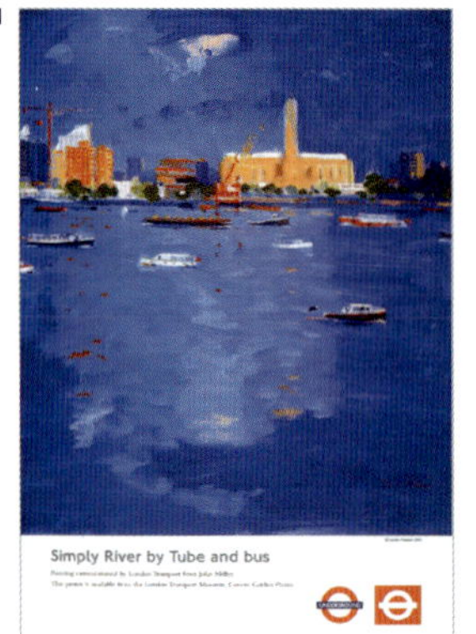

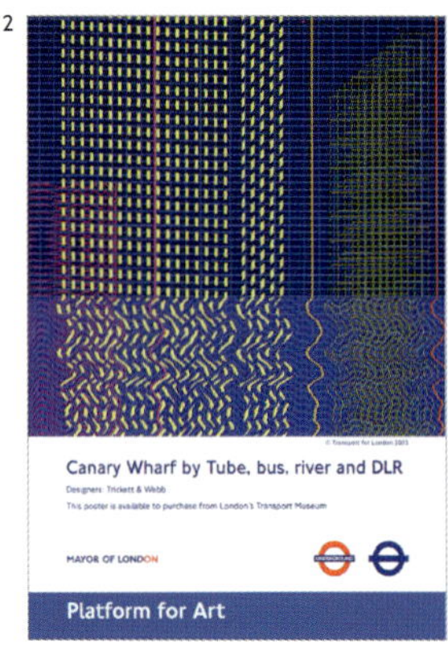

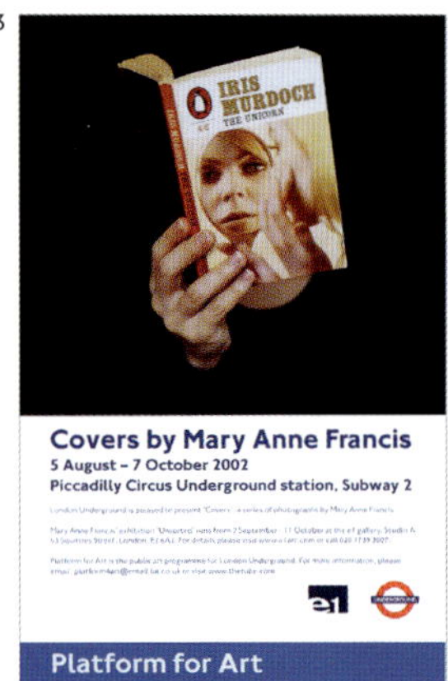

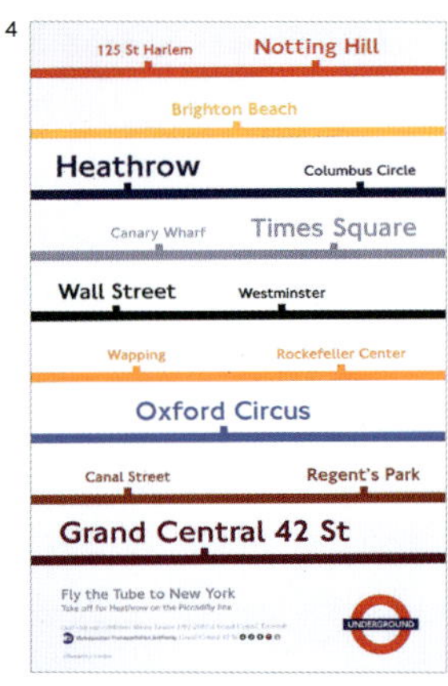

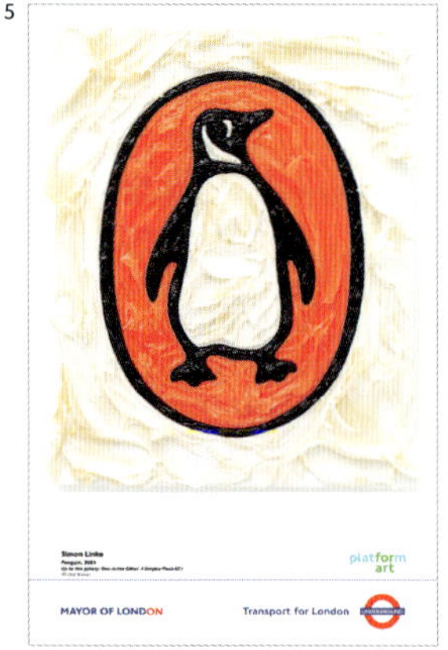

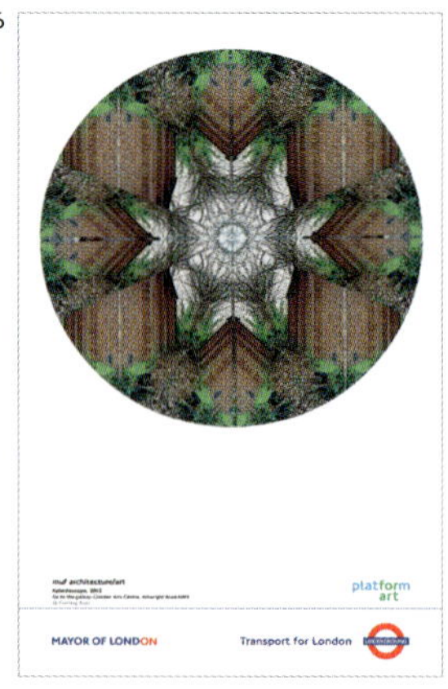

London Underground by Design

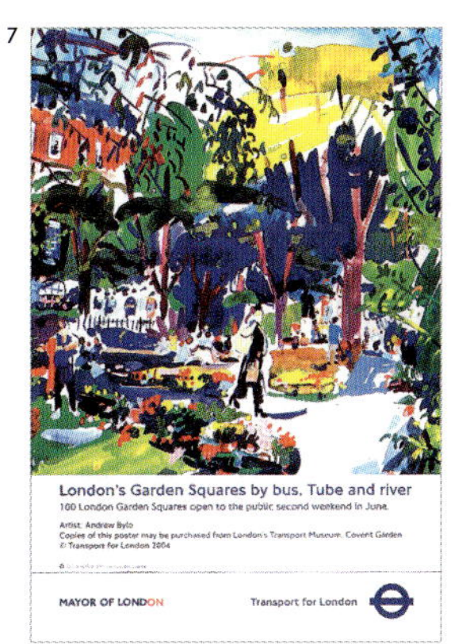

7

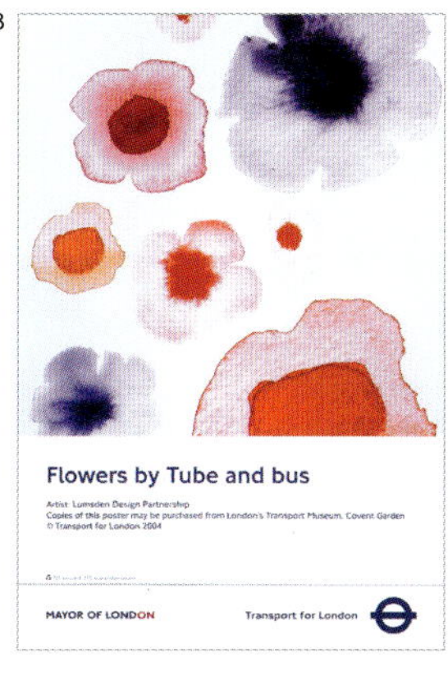

8

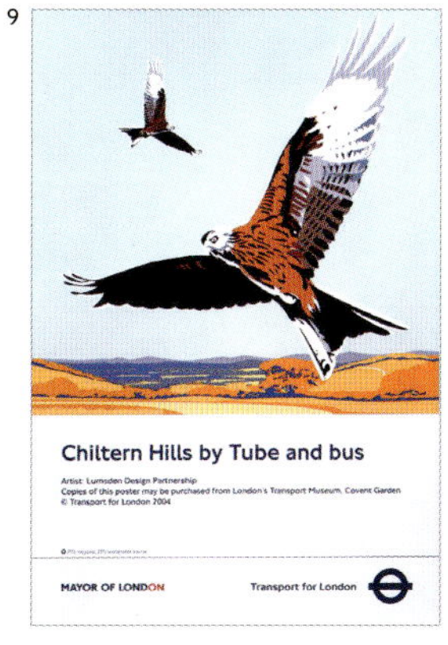

9

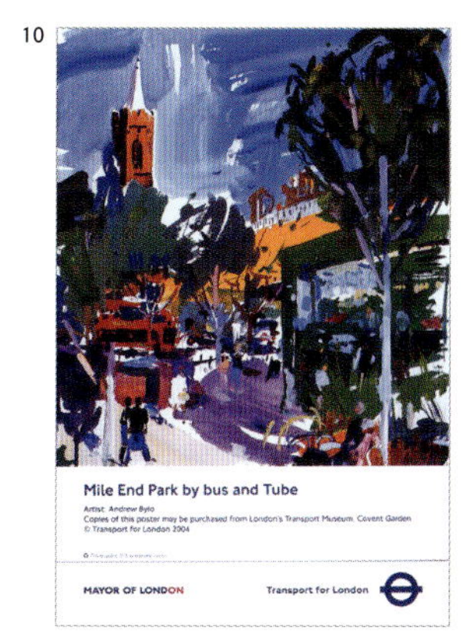

10

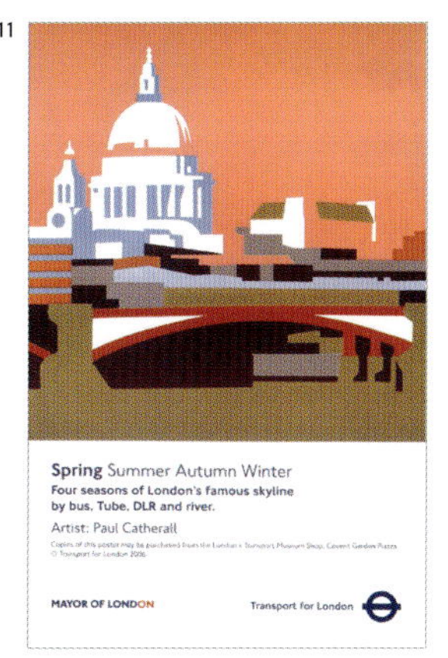

11

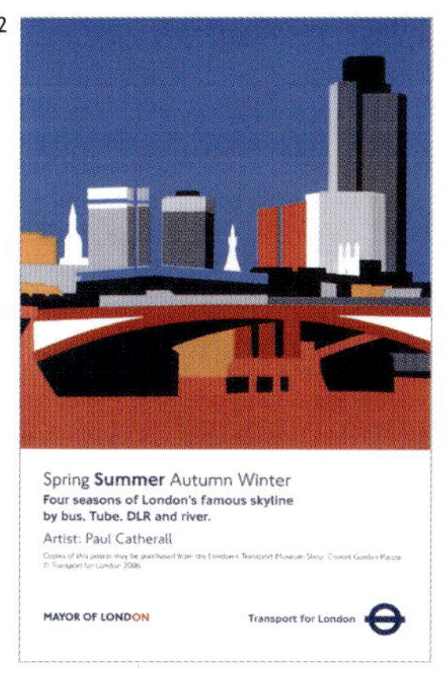

12

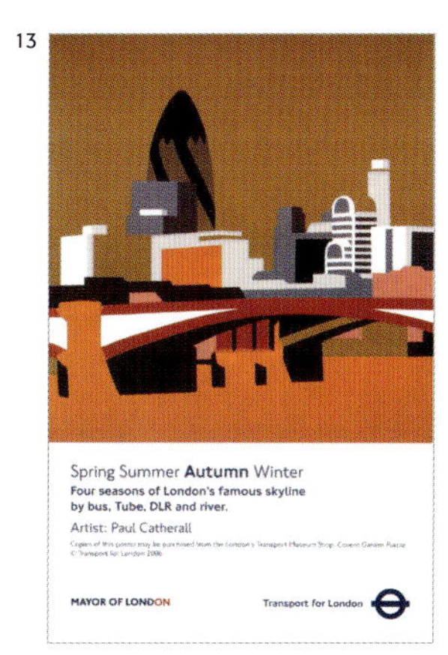

13

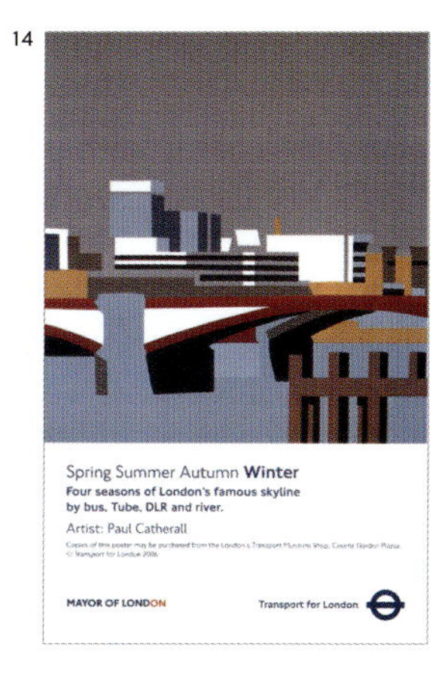

14

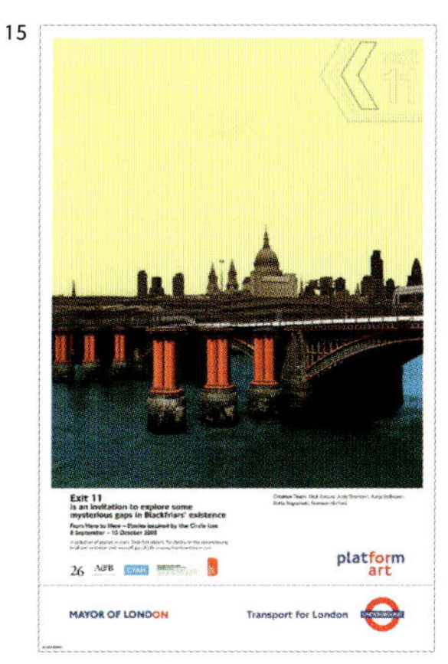

15

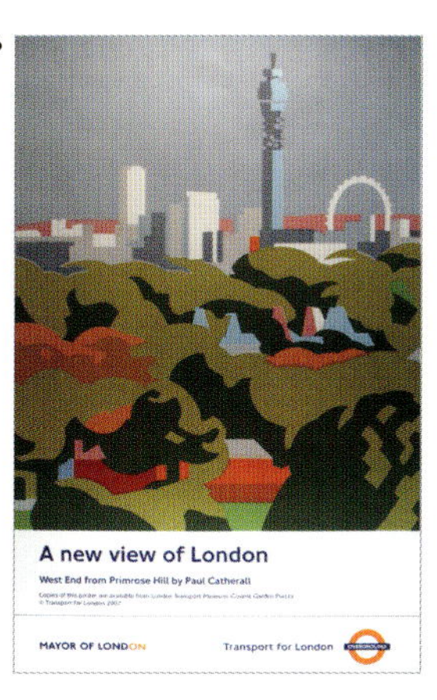

16

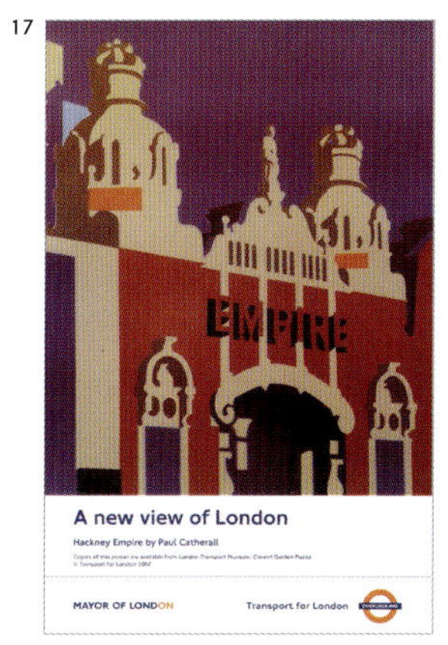

17

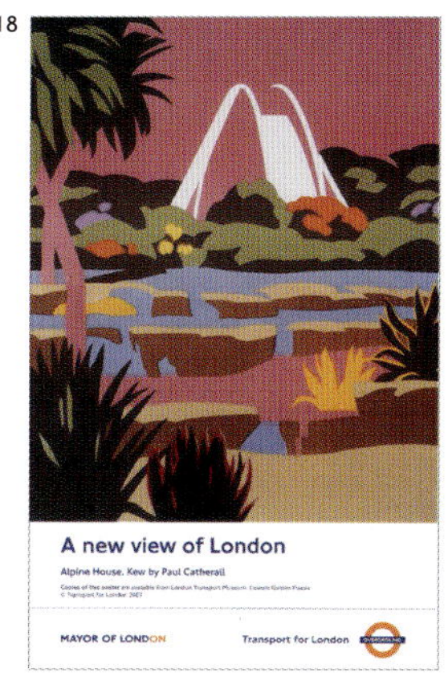

18

Underground/Overground
wandering free, 2007 to present

TfL issued a revised signs manual
in 2002 (p. 264), coinciding with the
official joining of the Docklands line
to the family under the brand name
'DLR'. There was emphasis on uniting
all modes of transport under the TfL
banner by presenting each logo as an
Underground roundel with a different-
coloured ring and bar (2002 set, 2).
The name 'Overground Network' was
applied by the Strategic Rail Authority
and TfL from 2003 to a handful of
south London commuter lines (p. 265),
but by 2007 the 'Overground' brand
was born, also using a roundel, and
signage installed and posters issued
(1). By the time the next section of
former ELL extension was opened
in 2010 via Dalston Junction, with
eighty-three stations, the orange
ring of the Overground had become
well established.

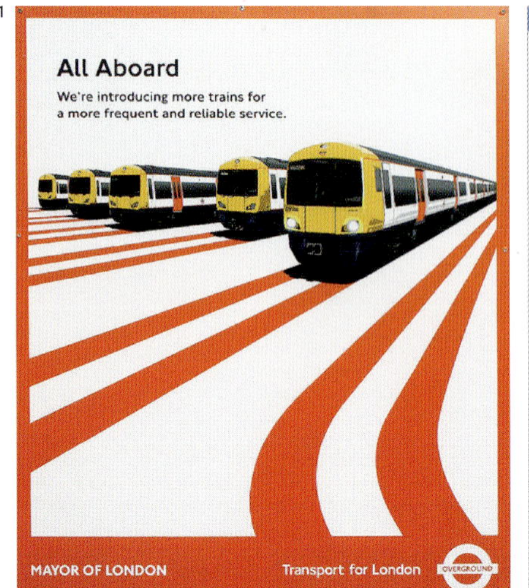

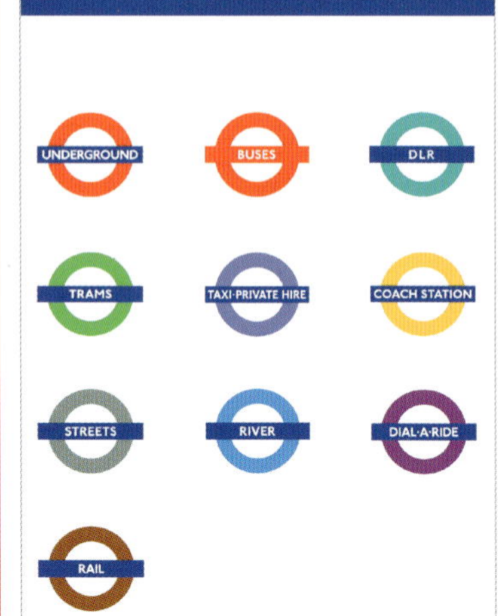

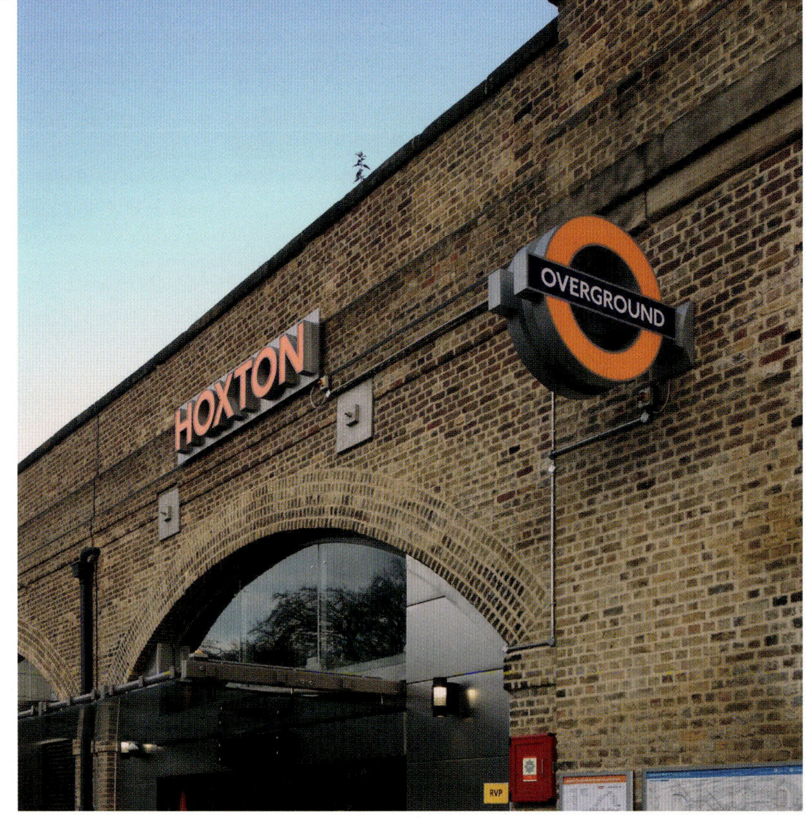

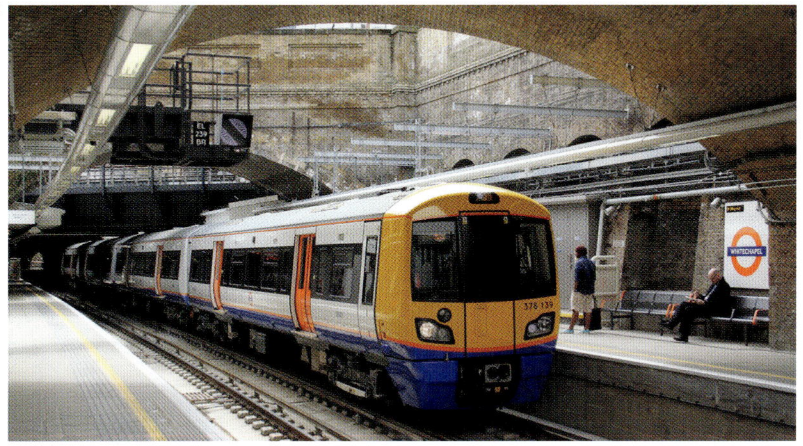

Several former railway alignments were utilized for the extensions in 2010, creating some idiosyncratic features: at Whitechapel, for example, London Overground platforms are *beneath* the London Underground (1), while the 'new' station entrance at Hoxton (opposite, 3) has been cleverly blended into Victorian brick arches to give the impression that it has been there for years and simply modernized. A nice touch are the 3D illuminated letters which spell out station names. Where completely new, Overground stations are sleek and modern, as at Shepherd's Bush (2) and Dalston Junction (3). Trains are Bombardier Class 378 Capitalstars (1) and feature longitudinal seating like those on the Underground. The moquette introduced in 2008 by textile designers Wallace Sewell (p. 265) incorporates the network's orange colour along with echoes of some of LU's most classic seat-cover designs. Totems have to carry multiple mode signs (4).

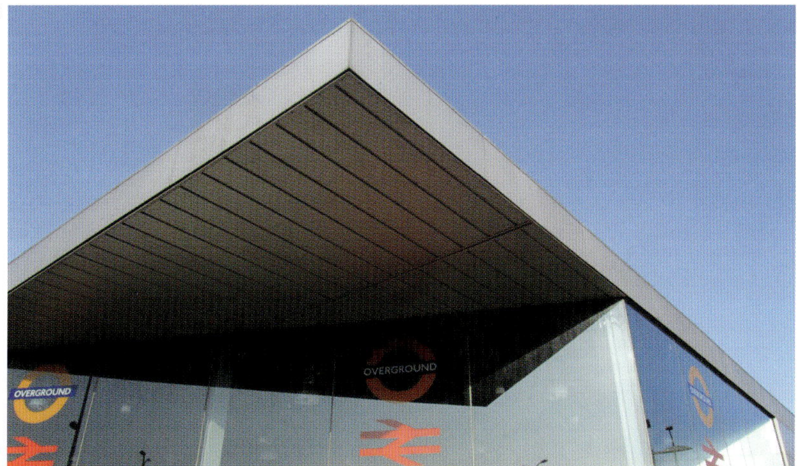

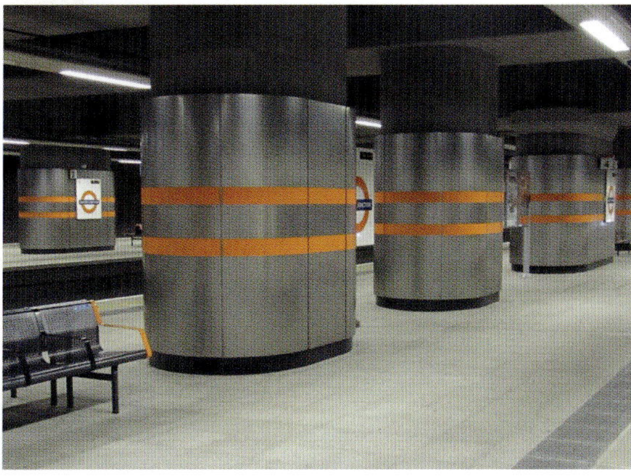

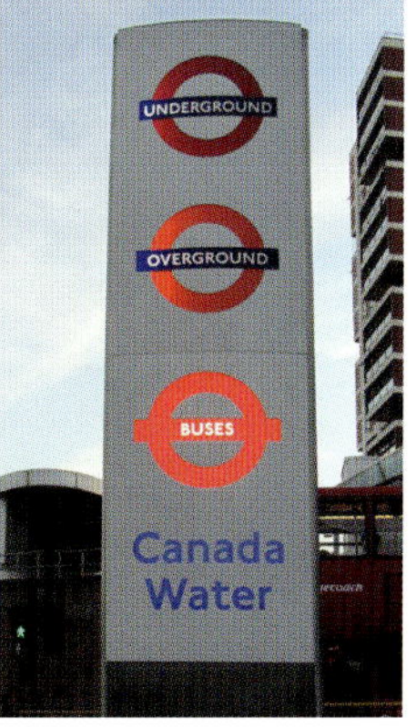

Transforming the Tube, 2002–20

New stations started to make their presence felt: Hounslow East by Acanthus LW Architects (2002, 2) and Elephant & Castle by PGA Design (2003, 1) broke new ground architecturally while echoing some of the classic earlier designs. Walthamstow joint bus garage and Underground station rotunda (2005, 4) was a nod towards Holden as well as the more recent Canada Water (p. 269). Following the end of the PPP (p. 265), TfL revised the 'Tube Upgrade' timetable, publishing user-friendly guides to line changes and a clever new poster appeared from 2007, showing workers balancing on a scaffold of the Tube diagram (3). The opening of a vast new shopping complex (Westfield) necessitated several changes at Shepherd's Bush. Harry Bell Measures's 1900 Central line entrance was demolished and replaced by a new building, joined by a new bus garage and Overground station (p. 273). North of there a 'new' Underground station in shot-peened stainless steel by Ian Ritchie Architects was provided at Wood Lane (2010, 5) on the site of the one closed in 1959. All these new works required a mountain of new signage, much of it produced by A. J. Wells at Newport on the Isle of Wight (coincidentally the only other place where retired Tube trains run in public service – between Sandown and Ryde Pier Head), where the enamelling process involves photo-typesetting, screen-printing and then oven-baking at 800°C!

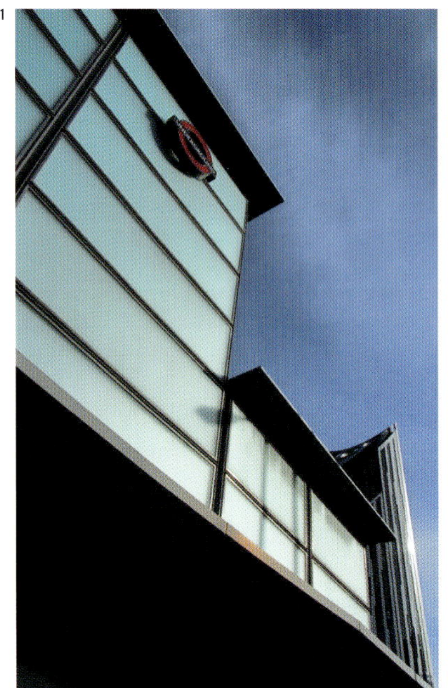

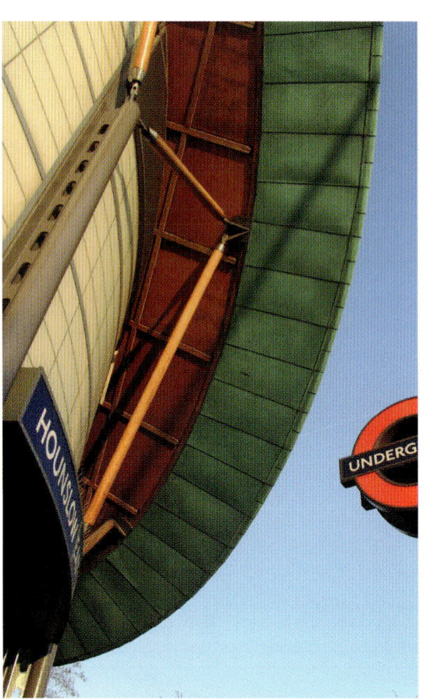

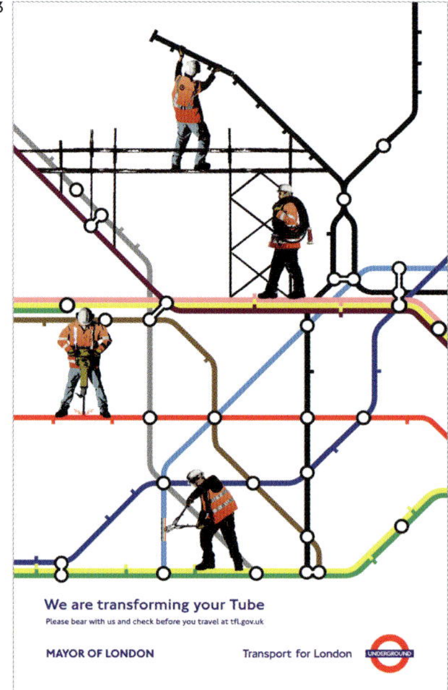

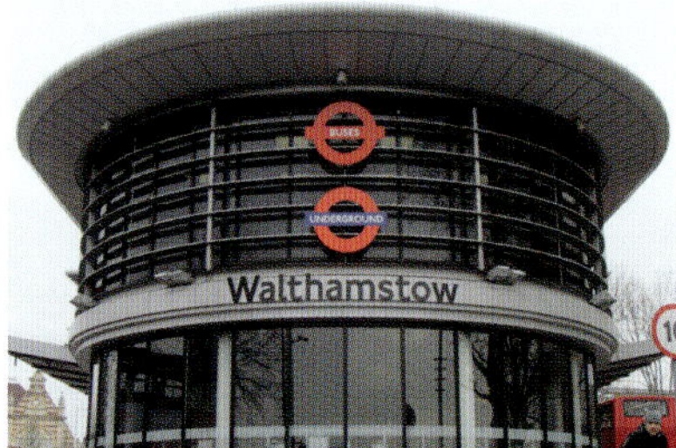

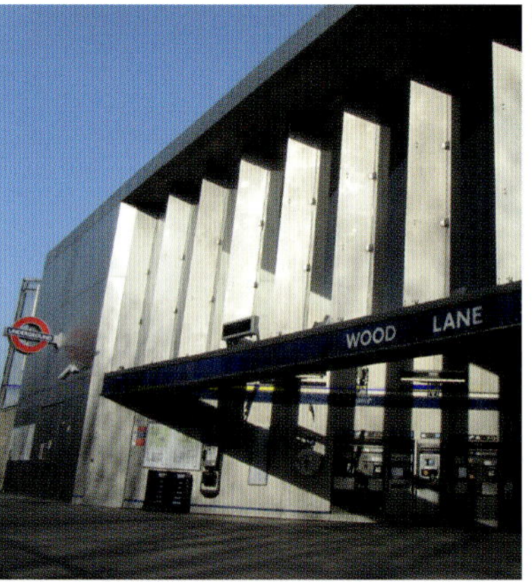

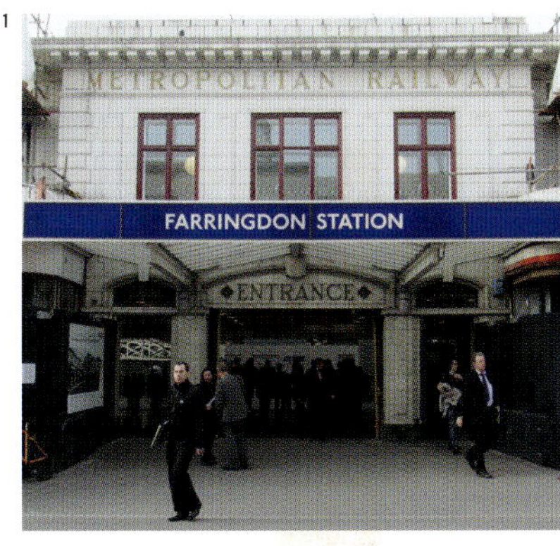

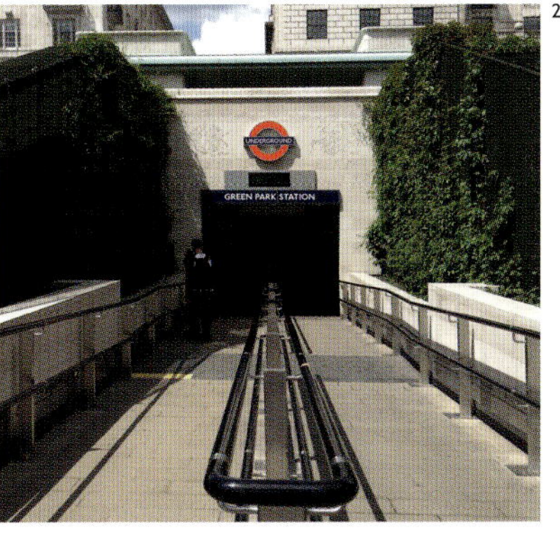

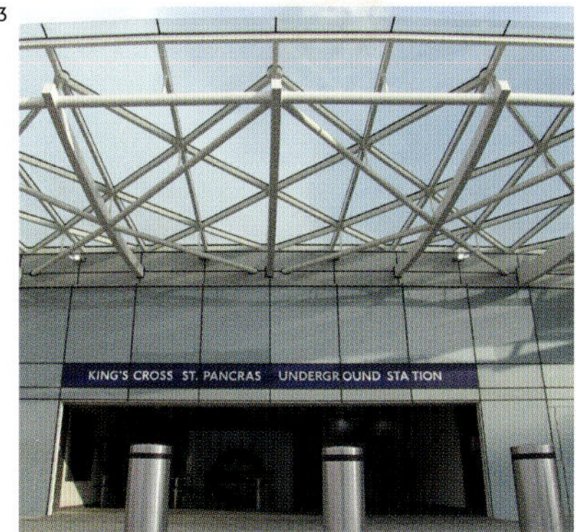

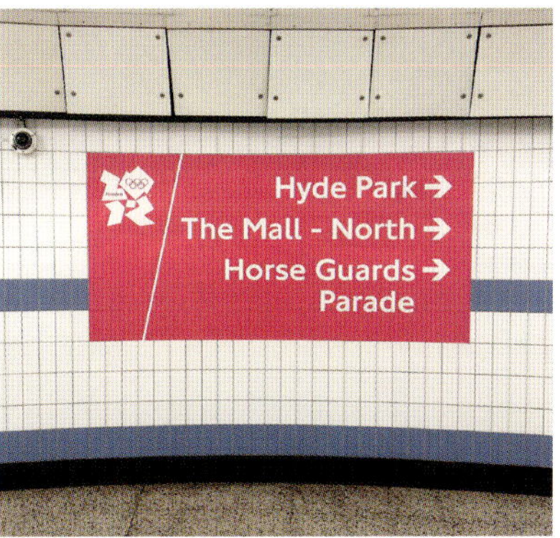

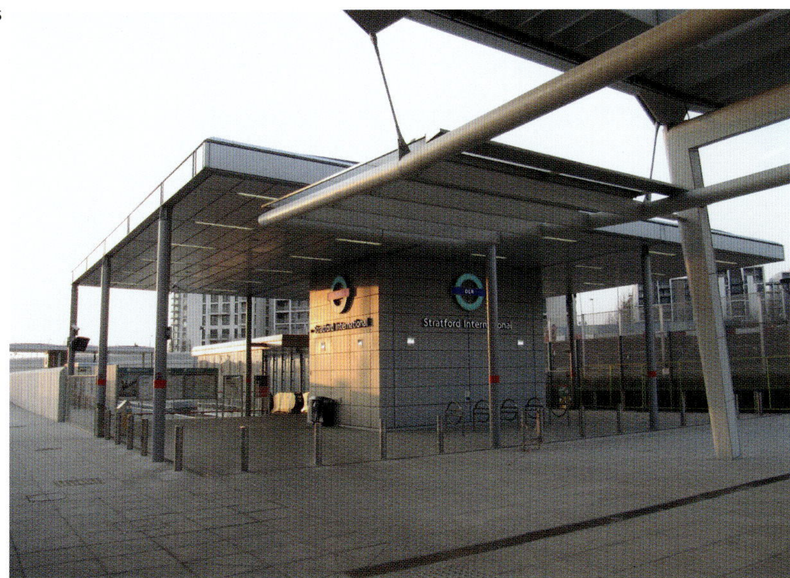

Farringdon has undergone a massive rebuild; the 1923 Clarke facade has been retained and refreshed with a new blue glass canopy (1). It sits opposite a brand new Thameslink/Crossrail ticket hall, and there is a new side entrance in Turnmill Street. King's Cross has several new access points, including to the massive rebuilt western concourse (2012, 3). Blackfriars has been rebuilt in readiness for the improved Thameslink station above, while Green Park has fittingly acquired the greenest central London Tube entrance (2012, 2) – the interior has just been air-conditioned by cold water piped from aquifers into special cooling channels in the tunnels. Stratford International DLR station (2011, 5) opened specifically to serve the Olympic Park and new Westfield shopping centre. Temporary signage to Olympic venues was set in New Johnston (4) and, following successful trials, TfL is now integrating the 'Legible London' surface-level wayfinding signage into 'decision points' within large stations. While the new stations are generally exceptionally well done (if sometimes a little bland), publicity for the upgrades has been less so. It relies on roundel adaptations – a big no-no previously; at some stations where several are displayed next to the name, it can seem confusing too (e.g. p.186).

Elizabeth line, 2009–18

At the time of writing, Crossrail was Europe's biggest construction project, as well as its most expensive, each tunnel-boring machine (1), in operation from March 2012, costing £10 million. The trains (4) cost £1 billion and were among the first recipients of a state-funding guarantee. Although intended to operate as a separate company on mainline rules, it is being designed as a fully integrated part of TfL's rail system – the majority of which in central London will be in tunnel, beneath the Tube, with interlinking passageways (5). Like the RER system of Paris or the Cercanías of major Spanish cities, it will combine an express underground line through the central district with a surface commuter network in the suburbs (diagram, 2). Station architecture is on the grandest scale since the JLE. As on the Jubilee line (p. 264), platforms in central London have been fitted with PEDs and signage will all be in TfL's Johnston100 typeface. At the surface, station entrances (in central London at least) are signed in Johnston as the majority will be joint/rebuilt Underground stations (e.g. Paddington, Bond Street, Tottenham Court Road, Farringdon, Liverpool Street and Whitechapel). The future street signage may be integrated with 'legible London' local area maps and logos topping new totems.

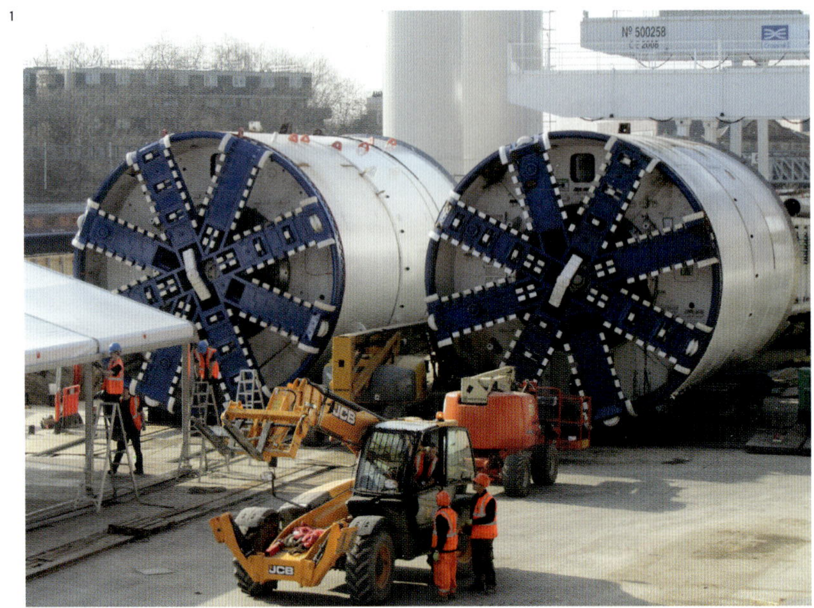

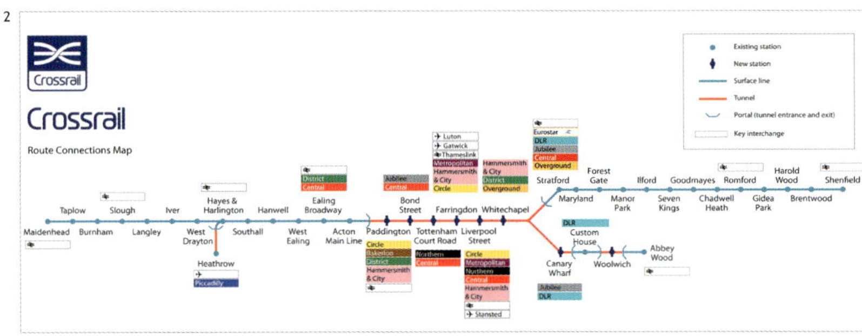

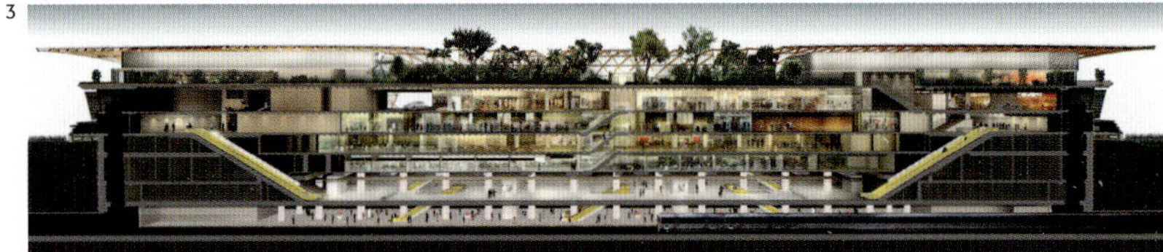

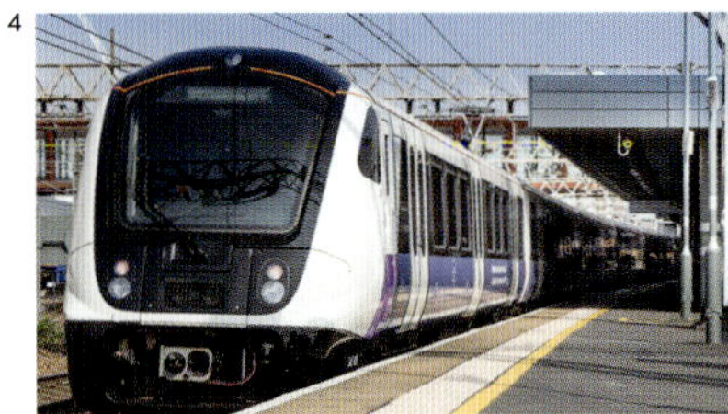

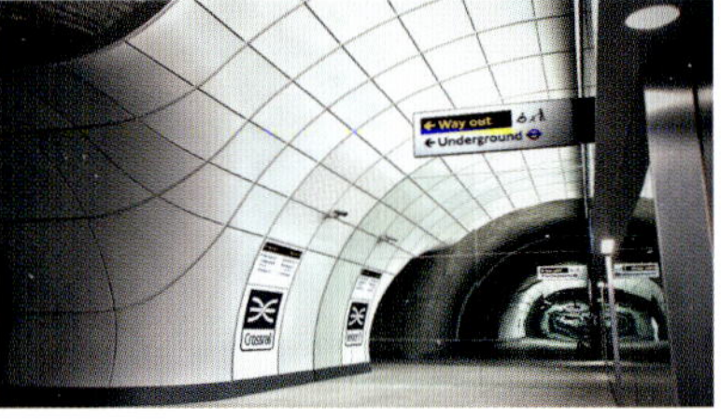

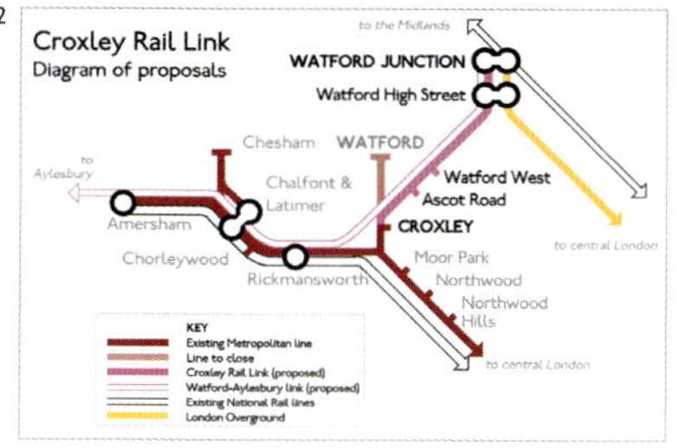

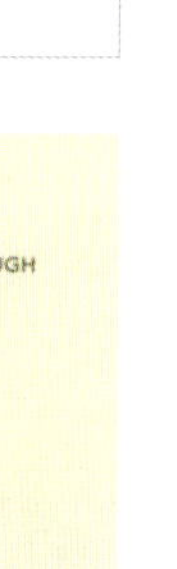

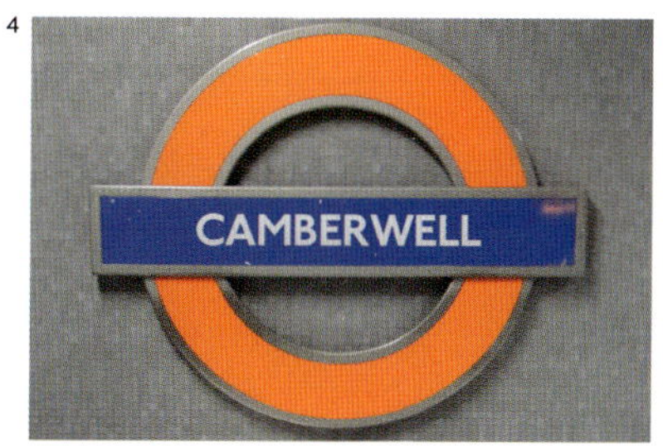

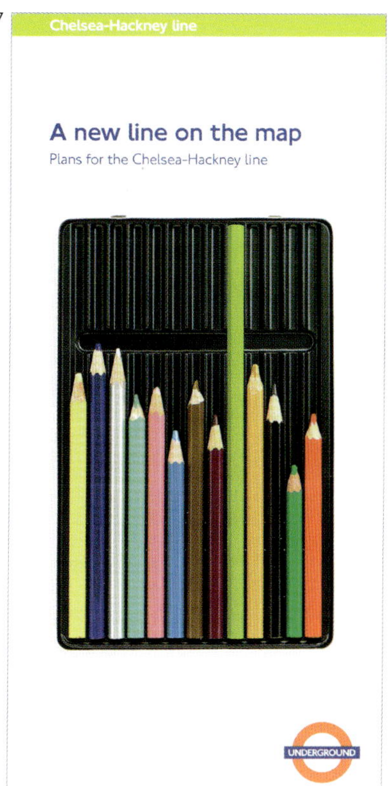

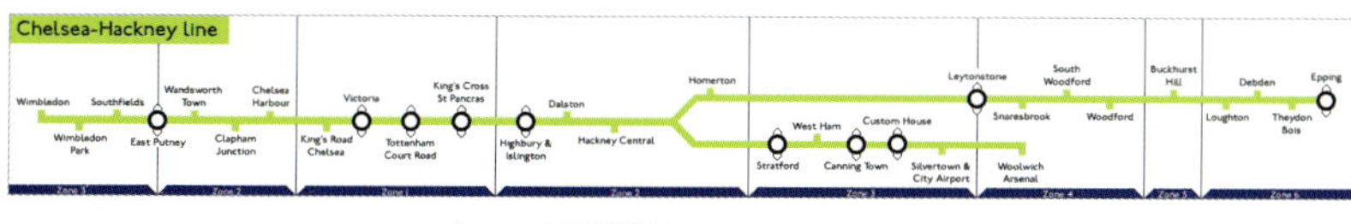

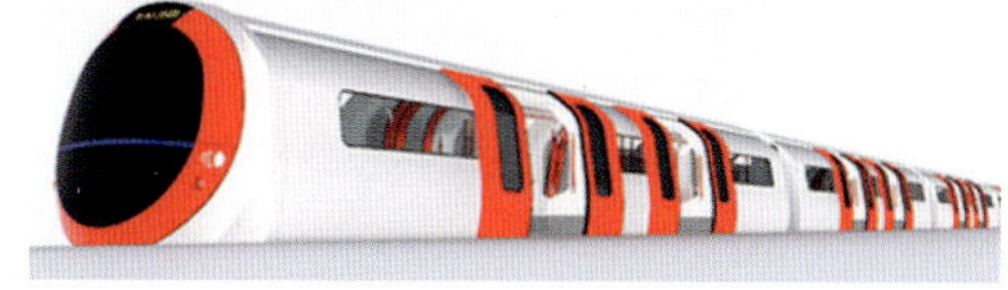

Future developments, 2012 onwards

The Met station at Watford has always been a fair hike from the town centre, so the plan to re-use an abandoned BR line and divert Underground trains along it started in 2012. One day it will serve three intermediate stations between Croxley and Watford Junction (map, 2), including two brand new ones by Acanthus LW Architects – Ascot Road and Watford Hospital (beside the health centre, 1). Consultation on the Battersea extension ended in 2011 (p. 267) and is now under construction. The Chelsea–Hackney scheme (leaflet, 7, and provisional diagram, 5) may finally come to fruition as 'Crossrail 2'. Plans already existed back in 1949 (shown on the map, 3), as part of the NWP, to extend the Bakerloo beyond Elephant & Castle to Camberwell. The idea has been resurrected many times since, most recently in 2010, but it's still possible that an Underground roundel like this (4) may be installed one day; south Londoners live in hope. One thing that passengers will see, however, is the 'EVO train' ('EVO' short for 'evolution'), award-winning designers Priestmangoode working from 2011 to create a brand new type of deep-level Tube train (artist's impression of a proposed Siemens model, 6). At the time of writing, it was unclear whether this would be driverless, but with trials planned from approximately 2017, it looks set to continue the LU tradition of pioneering new design into the 2020s and beyond.

Notes

I. Establishing a New Style of Railway, 1863–89

1. 'Wayfinding', for example, was coined by urban planner Kevin A. Lynch in 1960 (Bibliography) and the concept expanded upon by Romedi Passini in 1984 (Bibliography).

2. The original stations were: 'Paddington (Bishop's Road)', Edgware Road, Baker Street, Portland Road (which became Great Portland Street), Gower Street (which became Euston Square), King's Cross (later King's Cross St Pancras) and Farringdon Street (sometimes referred to as the Victoria Street terminus, it was renamed Farringdon & High Holborn in 1922, then abbreviated to Farringdon in 1936).

3. These models were, for example, used on the GER's Ongar branch (built in 1865); and later they would be serviced by Underground trains.

4. Starting with the more sedate and classical grace of Birmingham Curzon Street (1838), through Brunel's elegant Bristol Temple Meads (1840), Newcastle Central (1850), Nottingham London Road (1857), and the most celebrated of all: George Gilbert Scott's Gothic masterpiece, St Pancras (completed in 1868).

5. Not helped by the decision to use brick in the tunnels (a practice that continued until 1890, p. 34), the walls soon becoming caked in engine soot, thus contributing to the sombre atmosphere.

6. Novels and the theatre played upon fear of the unknown in an age of reason.

7. A contemporary illustration of the opening banquet (where boards were laid over the tracks and platforms at Farringdon Street) showed how the lamps stood out.

8. Parliament agreed the extension as early as 1861, while the first section was still under construction.

9. More than 250 designs for new London lines were lodged with Parliament.

10. The following month a spur opened (now dismantled), branching off from Latimer Road to Kensington (Addison Road, now called Kensington Olympia).

11. Several early stations were reconstructed, however, Hammersmith in grand style between 1907 and 1909 (p. 106).

12. The so-called 'Inner Circle' was to run via the southern parts of the City of London and of Westminster, partially along the Thames, connecting to the new mainline termini at Victoria and Liverpool Street (which opened in 1874).

13. Named after a tavern in the chalet style which opened there in 1804.

14. It had intermediate stops at Bayswater, Notting Hill Gate and Kensington High Street. Gloucester Road was known as Brompton Junction or 'Brompton (Gloucester Road)'. South Kensington was reached by Christmas Eve, 1868.

15. The cut-and-cover method was utilized rarely, for example under Campden Hill between Kensington and Notting Hill Gate.

16. For example, the wall around the Italian Gardens at the north end of the Serpentine in Hyde Park or Osborne House on the Isle of Wight.

17. As there are clearly no colour photos from the period, and with no colour engravings of the signage, archivists can only deduce, from later evidence, that the background must have been blue.

18. At the same time as the District began work on its other contractual obligation, to build a northerly curve to meet the West London Railway (WLR) at Addison Road (though this did not see public service until 1872 when the 'Outer Circle' was started).

19. The style was used again later at Earl's Court and Ealing Broadway in the 1870s – both of which survive, although heavily renovated.

20. Though the effect at Blackfriars of this building-wide signage was a little clumsy, a more delicate fascia would become the norm after Holden's works of the 1920s (p. 132–3).

21. This marked the end of the Met's direct involvement in that side of the Circle, as the cost of going further was deemed prohibitive.

22. The plan of chairman Edward Watkin (p. 15) for stretching the Met all the way to Manchester was beginning to take shape.

23. It inaugurated a distinctly regal-sounding direct service from Mansion House via Ealing Broadway to the royal town of Windsor. Opened in March 1883, it ran for a little over two years.

24. The initial terminus was Hounslow Town until a branch was opened which ran via Heston-Hounslow (now Hounslow Central) to Hounslow Barracks (which later became Hounslow West), rendering the one-stop section to the Town station rather unnecessary; hence it was closed in 1909.

25. From the District's inception there were squabbles with the Met. The appointment in the 1870s of bitter rivals James Staats Forbes (p. 141) and Edward Watkin (p. 151) as chairman respectively of each company greatly exacerbated tension. Watkin planned integrating the Met as a full mainline railway. Forbes, by contrast, wanted the District to host a network of commuter railways to the southern Home Counties.

26. Situated 23m below the river surface, the Thames Tunnel was the first to be built beneath a major navigable waterway. At 11m wide and 6m high, it was constructed 1825–43 under Marc Isambard Brunel and Thomas Cochrane using a 'shield' to protect workers, but following several fatal accidents Marc's son Isambard Kingdom joined the long project, which was eventually completed.

27. Usage declined as it became a haunt for pickpockets and gangs, until the ELR bought the lot in 1865.

28. This closed in 1884, to be replaced by Mark Lane (later renamed Tower Hill) on a different site, slightly to the west. When that closed in 1967, it was replaced by another Tower Hill on the original site of the Tower of London station.

29. Even the Met line was flooded during construction in 1862.

30. A single bored link between Lower Thames Street and Vine Lane, it opened in 1870. Passengers were conveyed under the river by a cable-hauled car, but the rail service closed after just three months, the tunnel converted to pedestrian use, staying open until 1898. (Although damaged in the Second World War, it survives today, carrying telecom cables).

31. The Southwark and City Railway would have been a 2km line linking the southern districts with the City of London but was never funded.

32. The 'St Mary's curve' (no longer in active passenger use) allowed both companies access to the ELR, which they operated jointly. Both spurs opened in the same auspicious month, October 1884.

33. A charge for use of the facility was only lifted in 1908.

34. In 1890 there was a proposal by the South Kensington and Paddington Subway to convert it for rail use, and while this was technically possible, the idea of burrowing under Kensington Gardens was not popular with the public, so it was scrapped.

35. In later years the Met's tentacles would stretch still further, to Brill and to Verney Junction (p. 45), and both lingered on, served by Met (steam) trains until the mid 1930s!

II. The Design of the First Tubes, 1890–1905

1. Electricity had started to be used during the Victorian era, but its potential to power trains had been unproven until then.

2. The City and Southwark Subway Act was passed in 1884. The line was renamed the CSLR just before opening.

3. The change of plan also led to the unfortunate bankruptcy of the cable manufacturer.

4. As did other operators, like Volk's Electric Railway in Brighton, which opened in 1883 and is still running.

5. The first gentlemen's public toilet opened in February 1852 at 95 Fleet Street. Ladies had to hold on a little longer until theirs opened at 51 Bedford Street a few weeks later.

6. The Arts and Crafts movement lasted from the late nineteenth century until at least the 1930s. A backlash against industrialization, it advocated a romantic dedication to traditional skills, influencing textile design, printing and even architectural styles.

7. When the CSLR was combined with the other lines, its design style was so distinctive that, along with the narrow tunnel width, it proved a real headache for designers trying to create a unified look.

8. The CSLR was located entirely underground, with the exception of the maintenance depot at Stockwell.

9. In 1891 the Met took over an existing line between

Aylesbury and Verney Junction, connecting it to their earlier terminal at Amersham in 1894.

10. Watkin's Great Central Railway did make it to Manchester in 1899 via a circuitous route that became Britain's last mainline – and the first major inter city route to close under Beeching, in 1966.

11. The Glasgow Subway used cable traction to pull the trains until 1935; when it was refurbished (1979), it caught the ceramic tile habit in a big way – before this, most platform walls had been painted.

12. The stylish tiling of the Földalatti (more commonly known as Line 1 of the Budapest Metro) has recently been restored to its original glory.

13. Some of the original tiled Boston signs are still visible today, such as at Scollay Square.

14. New York City Subway's first line (IRT) was decorated by Heins & LaFarge with white tiled walls, coloured friezes showing station names, and ceramic images of local and national icons.

15. Compagnie du Chemin de Fer Métropolitain de Paris (CMP) chairman Adrien Bénard led a visit to London in 1899 to look at station design where he was impressed by the decor of the CSLR and soon-to-open Central London Railway. The CMP ordered every Paris interior to be covered in bright white tiles with a bevelled edge.

16. A surface bridge overground extension from Waterloo would have been prohibitively expensive (not to mention undesirable), so LSWR chose a tube with the intention of allowing their customers to make a seamless connection under the Thames to the financial district.

17. The station below Waterloo is not actually under the ground but sited beneath the arches of the platforms above – an 'undercroft', in effect. It is the only line inaccessible from any other. Originally cars were pulled to a siding for maintenance. As the siding was built over by the Eurostar platform, cars now have to be lifted by crane from the street above.

18. It later adopted a third-rail power supply for its 'Southern Electric' overground service.

19. Jackson Sharp of Wilmington, Delaware, made the cars. They were fitted out at Eastleigh with German-built electric motors, and eventually replaced in 1940 by trains designed in the Art Deco style. The line was officially transferred from British Rail to the London Underground in 1994.

20. The steep rise from beneath the Thames, and related problems of electricity supply, restricted its capacity for further development. A costly new tunnel was therefore needed to push the line deeper into the City and to continue north.

21. The section from Borough to King William Street was closed, creating the first abandoned stretch of underground railway – 2.5km of it – after only a decade of use.

22. The South Eastern and Chatham Railway (SECR) and the London, Brighton and South Coast Railway (LBSC) met at London Bridge.

23. On Parisian platforms, the entire tunnel, including the ceiling, was covered in the ubiquitous white tiles.

24. The line was to start at King William Street then run beneath Holborn Circus, High Holborn, New Oxford Street, Oxford Street and Bayswater Road. Following opposition by the Met and District, the CLR resubmitted its proposal with an amended eastern terminus (at Cornhill) and a westerly extension to Shepherd's Bush. It was approved in August 1891, but in November a bill was submitted to extend the eastern end to the GER mainline terminal at Liverpool Street.

25. These included Benjamin Baker, James Henry Greathead and Sir John Fowler.

26. Fundraising caused a delay so the company had to apply for an extension and rather than opening in 1896, as projected, construction of the railway had only just begun.

27. It was such a time-consuming and expensive project that another Parliamentary extension had to be sought.

28. The CLR stations were: Bank, Post Office (now St Paul's), Chancery Lane, British Museum (closed in 1933), Oxford Street (now Tottenham Court Road), Oxford Circus, Bond Street, Marble Arch, Lancaster Gate, Queen's Road (now Queensway), Notting Hill Gate, Holland Park and Shepherd's Bush.

29. A later addition were glass canopies with 'CLR' and 'TUBE STATION' etched on them (p. 96).

30. The public were not admitted until 30 July 1900.

31. The CLR was cheaper and more straightforward in its pricing than the other lines with their complex ticketing arrangements.

32. The CSLR extension to Angel went via Old Street and City Road – the latter now closed.

33. The Whitechapel and Bow was the last constructed using 'cut and cover' until many decades later. It was a joint venture with the London Tilbury and Southend Railway (LTSR) which would allow the District to run its trains right through to Upminster.

34. Including a company the District had previously acquired, the Brompton and Piccadilly Circus Railway (BPCR), which had also been looked upon favourably by Parliament but on which construction had not yet begun.

35. The idea was to head under the Thames to south London, but the GNR became nervous and instead of linking to their services, GNCR was terminated in a stub under Finsbury Park station when it opened (1904), cut back to Drayton Park in 1964. It kept the name Great Northern but the push south never materialized so the odd line stayed unconnected with anything until later re-modelling in 1976.

III. Deep-level Tubes and the Birth of a Logo, 1906–15

1. Stanley Heaps (p. 65) and Israel Walker are known to have been his assistants.

2. Only Waterloo and Great Central were single-storey buildings – both have now gone.

3. In areas with less traffic many of the bays were boarded up or covered with the red faience from relatively early on.

4. While glazed bricks – even of this ravishing hue – were not unique to the UERL (they were seen on many Victorian/Edwardian buildings, especially pubs), running them from floor to roof was fairly unusual.

5. Though Guimard erected no substantial brick-built surface buildings, his intricate Art Nouveau-inspired ironwork 'edicules' (station entrances) with their glazed and enamelled panelling found echoes in Green's work.

6. The initials of the lines also appeared, such as 'GNP&BRy' at Holloway Road (p. 72).

7. At Heath Street (now Hampstead), Gillespie Road (now Arsenal), Euston Road (which became Warren Street) and Great Central, (later renamed Marylebone) at least one old sign, bearing the original name, has been kept.

8. Rome, the original host city, had to fund reconstruction in Naples which had been devastated following the eruption of Vesuvius in 1906.

9. Unofficial names prior to 1908 included: 'Piccadilly Railway' for the GNBR; 'Hampstead Tube' for the CCEHR; 'District' for the MDR; 'Yerkes' Tubes' for the UERL and 'London Electric Railways' (LER) (the latter adopted officially in 1909–10); 'Metro' for the Met'; 'Tuppenny Tube' for the CLR; 'Padded Cell' for the CSLR; and 'the Drain' for the Waterloo & City.

10. The joint committee of bus and rail operators was formed to co-ordinate fare pricing, but competition toppled voluntary agreements. The Met was unhappy with 'Underground', so shamelessly promoted its own name instead.

11. The Bakerloo, Piccadilly and Hampstead tubes were not formally merged until 1909.

12. The *Illustrated London News*, on 2 February 1861, had referred to it as the 'Metropolitan (Underground) railway', and *Harpers Weekly*, on 13 January 1866, as the 'Metropolitan or Underground railroad'.

13. A debate over 'Underground' still lingers: only 40 per cent of it is subterranean, made more ironic after the (mostly underground) East London Line was subsumed into the 'Overground' in 2010 (p. 265).

14. The District stations were photographed first, the Underground sign then inked in on the prints.

15. Shortening long words in the form of abbreviations and acronyms was as common then as today.

16. The Underground logo first used at Wood Lane was unique: it was clipped top and bottom.

17. New Met stations were: Eastcote and Rayners Lane (1906), Preston Road (1908), Dollis Hill & Gladstone Park and Moor Park & Sandy Lodge (both 1909), Ruislip Manor (1912), West Harrow (1913), Goldhawk Road (1914) and North Harrow (1915).

18. The Met's enlarged M and N was first seen from

as early as 1909 but more widespread from 1914 (at the Paddington rebuild for example).

19. Up to ten times per platform on some lines; much more frequently than on the Underground where the name was repeated 3–4 times at most.

20. Similar signage was still in vogue for the Aldgate East 1914 rebuild, but for the Walham Green rebuild (1910) and Ealing Broadway (1911), Ford used sans-serif capitals.

21. Clocks started to appear on later Underground stations, often installed above the glass canopy.

22. The hotel and apartment block at Baker Street was added in the 1920s (p. 140).

23. The problem is trying to date printed items with no date on them nor a photographic record of their having been in use.

24. Another photographic survey of stations was made in 1914, possibly due to Edwardian paranoia about potential bombing by the enemy.

25. Red diamond signage may have been used as early as 1917; it was definitely in use by 1919, continuing until 1933.

26. The ELR signs angered Pick because the UERL had not been consulted. He tried to stop them, but was too late. The designer, W. H. Parsons, defended their 'artistic and effective appearance'.

27. 'The General' had used a winged wheel logo since 1905. It is widely credited as the forerunner of the 'bullseye', though the author of this book suggests a much wider range of influences.

28. London's shortest tubes – LSWR's Waterloo & City and GNR's GNCR – had a chequered ownership history.

29. Sharland's contribution was second only to that of Edward McKnight Kauffer (ninety-six posters), although Kauffer was producing posters over a much longer period (1915–39), twice as long as Sharland (1908–22).

30. The UERL also encouraged migration, to the suburbs, e.g. Alfred France's poster 'Live in a new neighbourhood' and 'Golders Green for Healthy Homes', both from 1910.

31. Starting from about £400, newly constructed houses in Metro-land were good value – even at today's prices (£400 in 1912 = £38,700 in 2012).

32. The first escalators were installed at Earls Court (1911). The CLR extended to Liverpool Street (1912), the Bakerloo made it to Paddington (1913) and Hampstead Tube was extended to a rebuilt Charing Cross (Embankment) in 1914 (p. 102).

IV. Unification by Architecture and Design, 1916–29

1. According to Howes (Bibliography), the first Johnston letters were B, D, E, N, O and U – only the last survives (Pierpoint Morgan Library). The block letters were 'monoline' (with no variations between the thick and thin parts), as requested by Pick – Johnston was still looking into minuscule serifs.

2. There are other sans-serifs which would have been known to Johnston, including the Figgins 1831 'English Two Line Pearl' (p. 221) and its derivative 'Railway Alphabet', already in use on many Met and District stations. Berthold's Akzidenz-Grotesk (created in 1896) and Morris Fuller Benton's Franklin Gothic (1902) and News Gothic (1908) were all in circulation at this time.

3. The looped lower case 'l', a bizarre first attempt at 'g' and linked 'qu' seem anything but sans-serif in style.

4. Arguably influenced by a logo for the American YMCA, which had a bar across an outlined triangle. The white space inside helped draw the viewer's gaze to the bar like the concentric circles on a target, leading to the bullseye.

5. Johnston kept the enlarged U and D but changed the heavy dashes above and below the smaller letters to what he called 'ribbons' – inserting what others have called 'chevrons' or 'pecking' at either end of each dash (p. 127) – to reduce heaviness and create a more decorative effect. These were in use until as late as 1948.

6. Eric Gill was asked to design a full range of weights for Johnston Sans in 1938 but the intervention of war prevented this from happening.

7. The concept was lodged in March 1917 and given the registered design numbers 659,814–25 (the first being the most common seen on station nameboards).

8. Dimensions of registered design 659,814: outermost black outline 12.7mm wide; white outline inside that 12.7mm wide; red ring 15.24cm wide and 106.68cm in diameter (bounded inside and out by a 6.35mm-wide black outline); blue bar 149.86 x 27.94cm; wooden frame around the name (usually painted red) 4cm (width of wooden struts).

9. Circumstantial evidence suggests that one of the earliest may have been West Brompton (p. 128).

10. Watford had three services: the suburban electric LNWR to Euston via a new tunnel from Queen's Park; the North London Railway to Broad Street; and the Bakerloo from Elephant & Castle.

11. Another quirk of this section of the Bakerloo is that none of the stations were permitted to sport Underground bullseye signs north of Queen's Park until Overground services were introduced in 2007.

12. It was the 1921 Trade Facilities Act which helped kick-start pre-war plans. Its aim was to put unemployed people to work on socially useful schemes.

13. The Hampstead Tube extension was shown on maps as 'under construction' from Golders Green via a station called 'Woodstock' (eventually the site of Brent) and Hendon (opened as Hendon Central) from as early as 1913.

14. An agreement had previously been signed with the GNR that no new tubes would be extended north of Finsbury Park.

15. With the possible exception of Burnt Oak, this proved correct. Hendon Central is now on the edge of a major roundabout, for instance, Edgware at a busy bus interchange.

16. Passimeters (wooden booths from which tickets were issued and checked, the first installed at Kilburn Park, 1915) became features of most subsequent stations – only removed when the Universal Ticketing Scheme was introduced in the 1980s.

17. Clark's rebuilds included Willesden Green (p. 138) and St Johns Wood in 1925, Aldgate in 1926, Edgware Road and Notting Hill 1928, Swiss Cottage 1929, Great Portland Street and Northwood Hills and Euston Square 1931.

18. Compare North Harrow with Sudbury Town (p. 164) – though less than 6km apart and completed within just a few months of each other, they could have been from two entirely different eras.

19. The old CSLR tunnels were widened (Clapham Common to Euston), connecting the Highgate and Hampstead tubes via a complex junction south of Camden Town.

20. CSLR surface buildings at Angel, Old Street, Borough, Oval, Stockwell, Clapham North and Clapham Common were all refined later.

21. When the High Barnet branch was opened in 1940, the City section between Morden and East Finchley would form the world's longest rail tunnel until overtaken by a St Petersburg Metro line in 1978.

22. In-house architect Stanley Heaps had made some preliminary drawings for them but these did not please Pick so he called in Holden.

23. Alternate-height nameboards were tried from 1915, starting at Kilburn Park, although the higher ones were later lowered to make way for name friezes (p. 288).

24. It remained the tallest steel-framed building until the completion of another large Holden, the University of London's Senate House, in 1937 (p. 147).

25. At time of writing, summer 2012, the staff are under threat of being moved out of 55 Broadway so it can be refurbished for alternative use.

26. A full-scale mock-up was constructed using wood and scaffolding.

27. Most uplighters were removed (1960s–80s), but a number were restored/remade in the 1990s–2000s.

28. With six District destinations west of Earls Court and two east, sharing Hounslow and South Harrow (eventually to Uxbridge) with the Piccadilly helped redress the balance.

V. New Works, New Board and New Graphics, 1930–45

1. The Piccadilly extension northwards required seven new station buildings on the surface, five of these to have platforms in tunnel (Manor House had a much smaller surface entrance than the others).

2. A movement that flourished in the Netherlands

between about 1910 and 1930. Buildings were generally in brick with curved masonry and decorative features such as miniature towers, stained glass and clerestory windows.

3. It was replaced in the 1960s with individually mounted Johnston capitals but in 2005 these were misguidedly replaced by new letters in a poor-quality sans-serif, so out of character that there were public calls for reverting to Johnston.

4. At Enfield West (car park sign, p. 176), Arnos Grove (direction signs), Manor House (forecourt and illuminated direction signs), Boston Manor (direction signs) and a 'TO THE TRAINS' flared uplighter at Piccadilly Circus. Other instances may have been lost to history.

5. Holden took great care over the bond, mortar and style of brick.

6. Flared uplighters had been installed along the top of the escalators in Piccadilly Circus (p. 165).

7. Some were in open country, others were rebuilds of stations in central London. Holden's firm worked on projects which were not completed until after the Second World War and some schemes that were never realized.

8. Mushroom shelters were erected at Southgate, Turnpike Lane and Enfield West and later at Queensbury and elsewhere.

9. Though designed first, Arnos Grove opened later (19 September 1932) than Chiswick Park; as the temporary terminus of a new line, it was dependent on other stations being ready at the same time.

10. Other examples of 'Streamline Moderne', a style that lasted into the late 1940s, include: the foyer of the Strand Palace Hotel, London (1930), the Midland Hotel, Morecambe (1933), the Daily Express Building, London (1932), Glasgow (1936) and Manchester (1939), many Odeon cinemas, and a number of vehicles (Lockheed Vega, MV *Kalakala* ferry, Hindenburg passenger gondola) and products (Bakelite radios and telephones).

11. For the Cockfosters train shed the concrete was 'tarnished' with the imprint of wooden boards placed in it while still wet.

12. The District had been using strip maps from 1908 and others followed (Piccadilly by 1916, the first to use Johnston Sans); by 1920 both Met and District maps (p. 144) included a fair proportion of the network.

13. Russian railways were shown as straight lines from the 1890s; the Berlin S-Bahn had used a diagram since 1929; LA and Chicago urban rail maps had been simplified in 1911 and 1913 respectively; and gradient diagrams were commonplace in the 1800s.

14. Dow is now acknowledged as having contributed the most to the process of diagrammaticization with his radical LNER maps (1929), which Beck would have seen. It is postulated that Dow's diagrammatic map Great Central Suburban in LNER Gill Sans (1932)

may have spurred Beck to resubmit his own initially rejected design (p. 168).

15. Between the 1931 visual and the first edition (1933), station blobs were replaced with ticks, interchanges became open diamonds, Stanmore and Watford branches were added and Cockfosters was 'UNDER CONSTRUCTION'. The Underground bullseye was inserted lower right and Beck hand-drew Johnston lettering (not typeset until the third edition, of 1933).

16. Although there had been pressure on the Met for years for it to be merged with the Underground, Selbie believed his operation was different from the tube lines. Going ahead with the Stanmore branch (opened in December 1932) was therefore an odd decision, but the Met did it anyway.

17. Due to the topography (Stanmore Hill being one of London's high points, at 152m), the area was not well served by rail (the existing station was facing the wrong direction – away from London), but the selling of the Duke of Chandos's estate made land available for housing development.

18. Stanmore and Kingsbury (p. 180) being almost carbon copies of Watford and Croxley (p. 115).

19. LPTB also took over all sixteen tramway operators plus most London bus and coach services.

20. This extended to the 'LT' letters being incorporated into the tiling at Leicester Square (1936), which also gained a new circulating area similar to that at Piccadilly Circus (p. 144).

21. South Ealing had just a 'temporary' entrance, not converted into a permanent structure until 2006.

22. The Warwick Road entrance to Earl's Court had a bizarre, spaceship-shaped glazed second storey added in the early 1960s to house a control room for the District and Piccadilly lines.

23. The start of the Piccadilly extension programme had been carried out under the supervision of the 'New Works Standards Committee'.

24. Proposed works included the Northern Heights Plan (p. 157), extension of the Central line (p. 154), new Bakerloo tunnels north of Baker Street (p. 158), Met electrification (p. 158), new trains, escalators and various technical improvements.

25. The beautiful glass-fronted 'swan-neck' cinema at Rayners Lane (1936) was converted into an Odeon in 1946 and is now a Zoroastrian Centre; both the station and the cinema are listed buildings.

26. Including the LNER, which electrified lines in Essex and tracks to High Barnet and Alexandra Palace, and the GWR, which upgraded lines to Ruislip.

27. At Upminster, Upminster Bridge, Hornchurch, Elm Park, Dagenham East, Heathway, Becontree and Upney.

28. Not until 1948 was the Underground logo exhibited outside stations towards Barking, and name-sign bullseyes were not placed along that section of the line until 1969.

29. The Carr–Edwards report was submitted to the Traffic Committee with 'drawings of the proposed

standard signs' (p. 192) on 6 April 1938, and, after amendments, was adopted in August of that year.

30. Variations on the roundel were added for no functional reason to some 'WAY OUT' signs and tilted bullseyes with arrows to 'TRAINS', none of which were in the manual (p. 192).

31. A list of stations served from each platform had been shown prior to this (opposite entrances from the bottom of the staircase) from at least 1915. During the 1920s the lists were presented alphabetically – quite confusing – and from 1937 (or earlier, i.e. at Holborn) stations were put back in geographical order. Destination lists were also displayed on the GNCR (e.g. at Essex Road).

32. By contrast, the Paris Métro has always used geographic maps at station entrances, succumbing to diagrams (for pocket maps) only in 1982 and 'Beck rules' diagrams as late as 2000. It was not until 2008 that any large diagrammatic maps were displayed on Paris platforms.

33. A streamlined diesel-powered railcar was also trialled on the Chesham branch in 1935.

34. The first Met victim was the 10km line to Brill. In 1936 the section from Aylesbury to Verney Junction was closed to passengers, which left the section from Rickmansworth to Aylesbury as the only steam service. The tracks to Verney saw their last freight 6 September 1947. Electrification finally went beyond Rickmansworth but only to Chesham and Amersham. Underground services from the latter to Aylesbury were completely withdrawn.

35. The large M and N continued for some years, on a few station canopy signs (Praed Street Paddington, for example, p. 181) and some car livery.

36. Re-signing took until the 1950s to accomplish, although some diamond signs survived longer – the last known at Highbury & Islington making it into the early 1970s! Even less have been archived, but London Transport Museum do hold an ELR green diamond sign from Shoreditch (p. 100).

37. Installed from 1904, station names on the New York Subway (in tiling by Heins & LaFarge) were mostly above head height; the names of Paris Métro stations were placed 2m above the platform from 1900 (in blue paper or enamel, later tiled); and tiled friezes appeared above head height on the Berlin U-Bahn in the 1920s. What virtually no other international system does is place the station name within the system logo, however. Aside from the London Underground, the Madrid and Barcelona Metros are the only other systems to have done so, their diamond logos appearing on platform name signs.

38. Following 55 Broadway and completed in 1937, Senate House on Mallet Street, at 64m high and with nineteen floors, became London's tallest steel structure. Used by the Ministry of Information during the Second World War, the building inspired George Orwell's 'Ministry of Truth' in *Nineteen Eighty-Four*.

39. Although Adams, Holden & Pearson did make

drawings for Bushey Heath and Elstree South, the onset of war delayed the scheme and the stations were never built.

40. These totem signs were recommended in the Carr–Edwards report.

41. Some south Londoners have never been keen on the name 'Northern' line: it is especially irritating that the only substantial stretch of the Underground *south* of the Thames is not named after the compass point it serves. The Kennington to Battersea extension (p. 277) inevitably is splitting the line in two, however, and it has even been mooted that the new section might be called the 'Southern' (though that name is now used by another rail operator).

42. More glazed sections were included in the plans for the station but constructed in brick instead, which is the station's loss, in the ticket-hall area at least.

43. The steam-powered route from Finsbury Park to Alexandra Palace was closed to passengers in 1954, having appeared on Underground maps as 'under construction' from 1937 until at least 1950.

44. The new Bakerloo tunnel and stations enabled the Met to stop serving St John's Wood (Lord's), Marlborough Road and Swiss Cottage (all three closed in 1940) so the Met trains could run non-stop from Baker Street to Finchley Road.

45. These were at Baker Street, Aldgate East, St Paul's, Highgate, Kings Cross (Circle line), Bethnal Green, and stations between Leytonstone and Newbury Park.

46. Manufactured between 1923 and 1934.

47. The last 1938 Stock train was withdrawn from public service in 1988, but a fine example survives in the London Transport Museum and is occasionally run round the system for anniversaries and other special occasions.

VI. Austerity, Nationalization and Celebration, 1946–67

1. Redbridge was effectively the very last station ever built to a substantially Holden design.

2. Not without merit in its own right, the exterior was faced in light grey granite aggregate and the single-storey entrance clad in black tiles, but the monochromatic contrast with Holden's more lavish pre-war edifices in warmer red brick was a sign of the times of austerity.

3. Barkingside, Fairlop, Hainault, Grange Hill, Chigwell and Roding Valley.

4. Whether this was due to austerity or because of anticipated low passenger flow is unclear. A few small improvements were made to frontages/passageways at Roding Valley, Hainault, Theydon Bois, Debden, Leytonstone and Leyton. (Grange Hill was completely rebuilt due to bomb damage.)

5. Visible at Bethnal Green, Wanstead, Redbridge and Gants Hill.

6. White City came into its own when the BBC relocated its television studios to a site opposite

in 1960. The station itself was awarded a coveted architectural prize by the Festival of Britain Committee.

7. Hanger Lane was opened 30 June 1947, though not 'topped out' until 2 January 1949.

8. The reason for such poor investment from 1948 onwards is amply covered in Wolmar's excellent work (2004, Bibliography).

9. Northolt had a scruffy corrugated iron entrance from 1948 to 1966. A circular ticket hall was designed for South Ruislip; although construction began in 1940s, it remained unglazed until 1961. Ruislip Gardens fared worse — it finally gained a bleak little entrance by 1966.

10. Land between Epping and Ongar was locked into the 'Green Belt' (1947), doomed to remain sparsely populated. The 10.4km section was eventually electrified in 1957, becoming the first major section of energized Underground track to close, on 30 September 1994. A lively heritage group hopes to restore services between Ongar and North Weald at some point, eventually aiming for Epping.

11. Set up by Clement Attlee's Labour government, the BTC was responsible for almost all public transportation in the UK, including the whole of London Transport, virtually every railway and thirty-two ports, along with British Road Services, British Waterways and British Transport Police.

12. British Railways chose Gill Sans for all signage from 1948. They also used the lozenge emblem as a station name sign. Both design choices were influenced by the success of Johnston Sans and the Underground's bullseye. Similarity between the corporate identities can be seen in the joint signing from 1948 (p. 226).

13. Lighting had been dimmed and cut back during the war to prevent surface stations being seen from above and to save power.

14. These marked key/interchange stations (i.e. blue for Waterloo, green for Victoria, yellow for Paddington). Quite how the passenger was to differentiate between the colour of the mainline station and that of the Underground line was never addressed, however.

15. The Sperry route indicators were a success (it was fun just to push the button and watch the route light up), although eventually phased out in the 1970s (p. 219).

16. Even the pecking above and below the lines was removed — deemed unnecessary by Hutchinson, who decided the station name should replace 'UNDERGROUND' on exterior signs. On pole-mounted totems the line name was removed from the whites of the bullseyes and placed in a blue bar beneath.

17. The authors of the revisions to the 1938 report admitted this failing, suggesting that new passengers might wander into a bus garage expecting to get on a Tube train.

18. Terminal station has always been used for

direction of travel in Paris and other world systems. Tunnel headwalls on the Underground were to show terminals, however (a change since 1938) but this never happened.

19. The idea was taken so seriously that the Festival of Britain Office was granted government departmental status in March 1948.

20. Station Gate was dismantled after the Festival but became the site of a new entrance for the Underground lines (later rebuilt as the Shell Centre entrance).

21. Built in the modernist style, it was designed by upcoming young architects Leslie Martin, Robert Matthew and Peter Moro of the London County Council Architects' Department. In 1988 it became the first Grade I listed post-war building (restored 2005–7).

22. The Skylon was a tensional integrity (or 'tensegrity') steel structure, internally lit and appearing to be suspended in thin air.

23. Beck had become a tad obsessed with trying to remove diagonals and this major rejig also aided his mission of taking out more of them.

24. Beck submitted several map visuals (1961–4) to accommodate the Victoria line in a single straight line, but no further designs were ever commissioned from him.

25. 'Route C' had been discussed as far back as the 1937 LPTB Second Annual Conference.

26. The Victoria line route was amended to encompass Walthamstow by the mid 1950s.

27. The rebuild of Oxford Circus for cross-platform interchange with the Bakerloo began in 1963 and necessitated the construction of a new ticket hall.

VII. Automation and Regeneration, 1968–99

1. An amalgamation of 'Victoria' and 'King's Cross' – 'Viking' – gained no favour; it was staff member David McKenna who coined the 'Victoria' moniker in 1955.

2. In automatic operation, the driver simply opens and closes the doors and presses 'start' when the train is ready to depart — quite radical for the time.

3. Blackhorse Road has not stood the test of time, however, with none of the grace or enduring qualities of, say, Holden's constructions.

4. Only the train depot at Northumberland Park is on the surface (near Seven Sisters), reached by dedicated tube tunnels.

5. Cross-platform interchanges required Herculean efforts aligning/rebuilding/re-routing tunnels at Euston, Stockwell, Highbury & Islington, Finsbury Park and Oxford Circus.

6. These murals were restored during the 2006–9 renovations.

7. At Chiswick Park, Stamford Brook and Ravenscourt Park.

8. The Queen unveiled a plaque on the station concourse at Victoria, symbolically bought a 5p ticket, rode the new line one stop and got off at Green Park.

9. One proposed connection (to the Central line at Woodford) was a missed opportunity for the Victoria line. Southern termination points mooted were Croydon, Herne Hill and Streatham.

10. The new interchange with the Northern line at Stockwell caused the demise of the domed 1890 CSLR building, which was replaced with a brick-and-glass box with about as much allure as a concrete bunker.

11. Beneath the roundel was the word 'Subway', much to the amusement of Americans; in 1973 this was changed to 'UNDERGROUND SUBWAY'.

12. The idea was to replace rail bridges over the Thames with deep tubes wide enough for mainline trains to make north–south London rail connections. An early 'Crossrail'!

13. Laminate satin-finish prototypes were tried at Aldwych (1979), then installed between 1982 and 1989 at: Bond Street (Central), Charing Cross (Northern), Baker Street (Bakerloo), Oxford Circus (Central and Bakerloo), Euston (Northern), Goodge Street, Tottenham Court Road, Marble Arch, Green Park (Piccadilly), Finsbury Park (Piccadilly), King's Cross (Piccadilly and Northern), Holborn, Waterloo, Piccadilly Circus. Most were replaced with enamelled versions after the King's Cross fire in 1987.

14. Thames Cartography took over 1987–9, producing the first computer-aided diagrams.

15. London was first split into different zones during the popular (but quashed) 1981 'Fare's Fair' campaign.

16. Implemented by Dr Henry Fitzhugh (marketing and development director), Jeff Mills, Paul Moss, Jerry Hill (p. 269) and Corynne Bredin.

17. At Bank, signage – in upper- and lower-case individually mounted letters in the same Rockwell face as the initial DLR signage – was not dissimilar to that at Tyne & Wear Metro stations Haymarket and Monument.

18. At the same time older DLR stations were rebuilt for longer trains.

19. The longest line name to date, it requires lengthier signage. Why 'HammerCity' or other shorter variants were not considered has never been made public.

20. The surveying was undertaken within three months from November 1992 by in-house architects Nick Bailey and others and various private practices (AMS John Architects, Davis & Bayne Partnerships, Fry Drew Knight Creamer, J&L Gibbons, Keith Leicester Architects).

VIII. Twenty-first-century Light and Space, 2000–13

1. The eleven JLE stations and their architects: Westminster (Michael Hopkins & Partners), Waterloo, Southwark (McCormac Jamison Pritchard), London Bridge (Weston Williamson), Bermondsey (Ian Ritchie Associates), Canada Water (Heron/Ove Arup), Canary Wharf (Sir Norman Foster & Partners), North Greenwich (Alsop Lyall & Störmer), Canning Town (Troughton McAslan), West Ham (Heyningen & Haward) and Stratford (Troughton McAslan).

2. Formed in 2000, TfL is part of the Greater London Authority.

3. The cost alone of setting up contracts and hiring consultants topped £500 million.

4. TfL took over Silverlink Metro, part of a franchise that ran the former North London line and the DC route to Watford from Euston.

5. The crucial link from Dalston to Highbury & Islington came into operation on 28 February 2011, while the key southern section between Surrey Quays and Clapham Junction was scheduled to open at the end of 2012.

6. An idea was mooted in 2006 to merge the Hammersmith & City with the Circle to form the 'Hammersmith & Circle line' which would have also run to Wimbledon. Draft maps were produced before the idea was revised to its current form during 2009.

7. Prior to this, only the logo or station name was permitted to be displayed on the roundel.

8. Too complex to convey in abbreviated form, step-free facilities have been detailed on a separate map.

9. It may date back even further, to Sir Joseph Paxton's 1855 scheme to link twelve London termini via an elevated railway encased in glass!

10. Nine Elms was the preferred option – though Vauxhall has also been considered.

11. Plans for a trajectory of this kind go back as far as 1901.

Acknowledgements

A book such as this is rarely just the work of one individual but inevitably it is assembled by an author against the backdrop of many loving and supportive hands. The initial inspiration for this project came during discussions with Mike Ashworth, David Ellis, David Lawrence, Christopher Saynor and Mike Walton who have provided encouragement to the author on several published works. He is indebted to Helen Conford for seeing the possibilities of the book and running with it, the artistic guidance of Jim Stoddart, and the help of Rebecca Lee, Patrick Loughran, Richard Marston, Hannah Bradbury and the publicity department at Penguin.

During the research and production period a number of wise souls kept the author from going even more doolally: Emily Colins, Geoff Edwards, Struan Kerr, Darren Tossell, Rob Shepherd, Maggie Turner and Andrew Williams.

Friends, family and experts who generously cast an eye over the initial drafts include: Pat Chessell, Roman Hacklesberger, Brian Hardy, Peter Lloyd, Jane Penston, Max Roberts, Doug Rose, Simon Sadler and Dr Guy Slatcher – without whom this would have been a lot less coherent.

A number of Underground memorabillia private collectors kindly donated their precious images for inclusion, among them many of those above plus those listed under picture credits (p. 4) and to whom the author is grateful.

Staff and those associated with the London Transport Museum were hugely helpful including: David Bownes, Claire Dobbin, Simon Murphy, Oliver Green, Helen Grove and Caroline Warhurst. Staff at TfL Archives unearthed many important contributions; special thanks go to Stephanie Rousseau and also Danielle Bellagamba, Alex Charvat, Beth Mercer, and Tamara Thornhill. In other parts of TfL: Jerry Hill, David Leboff, Steve Lewis, Kate Reston and the receptionists at 55 Broadway, were all very helpful. Thanks to Kevin McCloud and his team – Gina Pelham and Emma Taylor – for the introduction.

The copy-editor, Kate Parker provided an invaluable contribution with her meticulous eye, wholly justified questioning and unfaltering good humour.

Thanks go to all of these people but also to other family and friends who have provided support and encouragement during what proved to be an inordinately protracted period of long hours, hard slog and occasional irritability: Jennie Doble, Fergus Dudley, Arthur Duke, Stephen Field, Hilary and Alan Hadford, Marc and Mike DiFrancia Cooper, Helen Lawson, Tanya McDonald, Adam Mawson, Alistair Meek, Jacqui Mitchel, Fiona Murray, Susie Pearl, Brian Scott Smith, Simona Valukaite, Julian Worricker and last but by no means least as they are omnipresent: Ying & Yang (the cats).

Sources, Bibliography and Webography

Bibliography

Ashworth, Mike, *Hidden Posters on the London Underground* (London: Monograph/Creative Review, 2010).

Badsey-Ellis, Antony, *London's Lost Tube Schemes* (Harrow Weald: Capital Transport, 2005).

Bains, Phil, *Penguin by Design* (London: Allen Lane, 2005).

—, and Catherine Dixon, *Signs: Lettering in the Environment* (London: Laurence King, 2003).

Barker, T. C., and Robbins, Michael, *A History of London Transport, vols. 1 and 2* (London: George Allen & Unwin, 1963, 1974).

Barman, Christian, *The Man Who Built London Transport* (Newton Abbott: David & Charles, 1979).

Beard, Tony, *By Tube Beyond Edgware* (Harrow Weald: Capital Transport, 2002).

Bennett, David, *Architecture of the Jubilee Line Extension* (London: Thomas Telford Publishing, 2004).

—, *Metro* (London: Mitchell Beazley, 2004).

Blackwell, Lewis, *20th-Century Type* (London: Laurence King, 2004).

Brown, Joe, *London Railway Atlas* (Hersham: Ian Allan Publishing, 2007).

Carr, H. T., and Edwards, W. P. N., *Report on the Standardisation of Signs, Notices and Maps – Railways* (London: London Passenger Transport Board, 8 August 1938).

Chief Public Relations Officer, *Carr–Edwards Report 1938 with Amendments to 1948* (London: London Transport Executive, 10 December 1948).

Clarke, Hedley, *Underground Bullseyes 1972–2000* (Colchester: Connor & Butler, 2007).

Conner, J. E., *London's Disused Underground Stations* (Harrow Weald: Capital Transport, 2001).

Croome, Desmond F., *The Circle Line* (Harrow Weald: Capital Transport, 1998).

—, *The Piccadilly Line* (Harrow Weald: Capital Transport, 1998).

—, and Graeme Bruce J., *The Twopenny Tube* (Harrow Weald: Capital Transport, 2003).

Day, John R., *The Story of London's Underground* (London: London Transport Publicity Office, 1972).

Demuth, Tim, *The Spread of London's Underground* (Harrow Weald: Capital Transport, 2004).

Department of the Chief Architect, *Initial Design Strategy for the Rail System* (London: London Transport, 1980).

Department of the Environment, *London Rail Study Part 2* (London: Greater London Council, 1974).

Department of Transport, *Central London Rail Study* (London: HMSO, 1989).

Dobbin, Claire, *London Underground Maps: Art, Design and Cartography* (London: Lund Humphries, 2012).

Dow, Andrew, *Telling the Passenger Where to Get Off* (Harrow Weald: Capital Transport, 2005).

Edwards, Dennis, *London's Underground Suburbs* (Harrow Weald: Capital Transport, 2003).

Emmerson, Andrew, *The London Underground* (Oxford: Shire Library, 2010).

Foxwell, Clive, *The Metropolitan Line* (Stroud: The History Press, 2010).

Foxwell, Simon, *Mapping London: Making Sense of the City* (London: Black Dog Publishing, 2007).

Garbutt, Paul, *World Metro Systems* (Harrow Weald: Capital Transport, 1989).

Garfield, Simon, *Just My Type: A Book About Fonts* (London, Profile Books, 2010).

Garland, Ken, *Mr Beck's Underground Map* (Harrow Weald: Capital Transport, 1994).

Green, Oliver, *Underground Art*, 2nd edn (London: Laurence King, 2001).

—, and Rawse-Davies, Jeremy, *Designed for London* (London: Laurence King, 1995).

—, and Taylor, Sheila, *The Moving Metropolis* (London: Laurence King, 2001).

Hackelsberger, Christoph, *Subway Architecture in Munich* (Munich: Prestel, 1997).

Halliday, Dr Stephen, *Underground to Everywhere* (Stroud: Sutton Publishing, 2001).

—, *Amazing & Extraordinary London Underground Facts* (Cincinnati: David & Charles, 2009).

Hardy, Brian, *Tube Trains on the Isle of Wight* (Harrow Weald: Capital Transport, 2003).

Harris, Cyril M., *What's in a Name? Origins of Station Names on the London Underground* (Harrow Weald: Capital Transport, 2001).

Hartley, Robert F., *Manchester to Marylebone: A Short History of the Great Central Railway* (Leicester: Leicester Museums, 1986).

Henrion Ludlow Schmidt, *London Underground Heritage Signing Handbook* (London: London Underground Limited, 1 March 1993).

Hinkel, Walter J., et al., *Underground Railways from 1863 to 2010: Yesterday-Today-Tomorrow* (Vienna: Schmid Verlag, 2004).

Hollis, Richard, *Graphic Design: A Concise History* (London: Thames & Hudson, 1997).

Horne, Mike, *The Bakerloo Line* (North Finchley: Douglas Rose, 1990).

—, *Going Green* (Harrow Weald: Capital Transport, 1993).

—, *The Jubilee Line* (Harrow Weald: Capital Transport, 2000).

—, *The Metropolitan Line* (Harrow Weald: Capital Transport, 2003).

—, and Bob Bayman, *The First Tube* (Harrow Weald: Capital Transport, 2000).

Howes, Justin, *Johnston's Underground Type* (Harrow Weald: Capital Transport, 2000).

Hutchinson, Harold F., *London Transport Posters* (London: London Passenger Transport Board, 1963).

Ibrahim, Mecca, *One Stop Short of Barking* (Enfield: New Holland, 2004).

Jackson, Alan A., and Croome, Desmond F. *Rails Through the Clay* (London: George Allen & Unwin, 1962).

Laver, James (ed.), *Art for All: London Transport Posters, 1908–1949* (London: Art & Technics/ London Transport Executive, 1949).

Lawrence, David, *Underground Architecture* (Harrow Weald: Capital Transport, 1994).

—, *A Logo for London* (Harrow Weald: Capital Transport, 2000).

—, *Bright Underground Spaces: The Railway Stations of Charles Holden* (Harrow Weald: Capital Transport, 2008).

Leboff, David, and Demuth, Tim, *No Need to Ask: Early Maps of London's Underground Railways* (Harrow Weald: Capital Transport, 1999).

—, *The Underground Stations of Leslie Green* (Harrow Weald: Capital Transport, 2002).

London Transport Executive, *Underground Railway Signing Study for London Transport* (London: LTE, May 1984).

LUL's Architectural Services, *Changing Stations: A Review of Recent London Underground Station Design* (London: London Underground Limited, 1993).

—, *London Underground Station Design Audit* (London: London Underground Limited, March 1993).

LUL's Communications Department, *Corporate Identity Manual* (London: London Underground Limited, 1989 onwards).

Lynch, Kevin A., *Image of the City* (Cambridge, MA: MIT Press, 1960).

MacCarthy, Fiona, *Eric Gill* (London: Faber & Faber, 1989).

Moss, Paul, *Underground Movement* (Harrow Weald: Capital Transport, 2000).

Ovenden, Mark, *Transit Maps of the World* (New York: Penguin Books, 2007).

—, *Paris Underground: The Maps, Stations and Design of the Metro* (New York: Penguin Books, 2009).

—, *Great Railway Maps of the World* (London: Particular Books, 2011).

Passini, Romedi, *Wayfinding in Architecture* (New York: Van Nostrand Reinhold, 1984).

Roberts, Maxwell J., *Underground Maps After Beck* (Harrow Weald: Capital Transport, 2005).

—, *Underground Maps Unravelled* (Colchester: self-published, 2012).

Rose, Douglas, *The London Underground*

"""

Diagrammatic History, 8th edn (Harrow Weald: Capital Transport, 2007).

—, *Tiles of the Unexpected* (Harrow Weald: Capital Transport, 2007).

Schwandl, Robert, *Berlin U-Bahn Album* (Berlin: Robert Schwandl Verlag, 2002).

—, *Hamburg U-Bahn & S-Bahn Album* (Berlin: Robert Schwandl Verlag, 2004).

—, *Metros in Britain* (Berlin: Robert Schwandl Verlag, 2006).

Simmons, Jack and Biddle, Gordon (eds.), *The Oxford Companion to British Railway History* (Oxford: Oxford University Press, 2000).

Taylor, David, *New Architecture for the Underground* (Harrow Weald: Capital Transport, 2001).

Welbourne, Nigel, *Lost Lines of London* (Hersham: Ian Allan Publishing, 1998).

Wigg, Julia, *Bon Voyage! Travel Posters of the Edwardian Era* (London: HMSO, 1996).

Wildbur, Peter, and Burke, Michael, *Information Graphics: Innovative Solutions in Contemporary Design* (London: Thames & Hudson, 1998).

Wolmar, Christian, *Down the Tube* (London: Aurum Press, 2002).

—, *The Subterranean Railway* (London: Atlantic Books, 2004).

—, *Fire & Steam: How the Railways Transformed Britain* (London: Atlantic Books, 2007).

Webography

Archives, museums and other official sites
- Crossrail (official site):
  crossrail.co.uk
- Department for Transport:
  dft.gov.uk/rail
- Design Museum:
  designmuseum.org
- Docklands Light Railway (operator's site):
  serco.com/markets/transport/docklands.asp
- London Metropolitan Archives:
  search.lma.gov.uk/OPAC_LMA/login.html
- London Overground (operator's site):
  lorol.co.uk
- London Transport Museum:
  Museum: ltmuseum.co.uk
  Photos: ltmcollection.org/photos
  Posters: ltmcollection.org/posters/index.html
  Shop: ltmuseumshop.co.uk/home.html
- London Underground Railway Society:
  lurs.demon.co.uk
- Museum of London:
  museumoflondon.org.uk
- National Railway Museum:
  nrm.org.uk
- Railnews:
  railnews.co.uk
- The Railway Archive:
  railwayarchive.org.uk/index.php

- Transport for London:
  DLR: tfl.gov.uk/modalpages/2632.aspx
  Overground: tfl.gov.uk/modalpages/2688.aspx
  Underground: tfl.gov.uk/tube
- Wikipedia:
  en.wikipedia.org/wiki/London_Underground

Personal research sites
- Abandoned stations:
  abandonedstations.org.uk
- Always Touch Out (latest project news):
  alwaystouchout.com
- BowRoadUK (Kim Rennie's photostream):
  flickr.com/photos/24772733@N05
- Clive Feather's Underground site:
  davros.org/rail/culg
- Doug Rose tiling website:
  omicron.sequence.co.uk/nonchksites/dougrose/index.html
- Edward Johnston Foundation:
  ejf.org.uk
- Eric Gill:
  ericgill.com
- History of London Tube maps:
  homepage.ntlworld.com/clivebillson/tube
- London Tube Map Archive:
  clarksbury.com.cdl/maps.html
- Mark Ovenden's website:
  markovenden.com
- Max Roberts map website:
  tubemapcentral.com
- Metrobits.org (comparing world systems):
  mic-ro.com/metro
- Mike Ashworth's photostream:
  flickr.com/photos/36844288@N00

Blogs and discussion boards/forums
- Annie Mole's London Underground blogspot:
  london-underground.blogspot.co.uk
- Author's blog:
  mapmarks.blogspot.co.uk
- District Dave (discussion board):
  districtdave.proboards.com
- SkyscraperCity Forum:
  Underground generally: skyscrapercity.com/showthread.php?t=285084
- The Transport Forum:
  billz1064.proboards.com/index.cgi?board=lrail

Abbreviations

Bakerloo see 'BSWR'
Board see 'LPTB'
BPCR Brompton and Piccadilly Circus Railway
BSWR/Bakerloo Baker Street and Waterloo Railway
CCEHR/Hampstead Charing Cross, Euston and Hampstead Railway
CLR Central London Railway
CMP Compagnie du Chemin de Fer Métropolitain de Paris
CSLR City and South London Railway
DIA Design and Industries Association
District Metropolitan District Railway
DLR Docklands Light Railway
DRU Design Research Unit
ELL East London line
ELR East London Railway
GER Great Eastern Railway
GLC Greater London Council
GNCR Great Northern and City Railway
GNPBR/Piccadilly Great Northern, Piccadilly and Brompton Railway
GNR Great Northern Railway
GWR Great Western Railway
Hampstead see 'CCEHR'
HCR Hammersmith and City Railway
HLS Henrion Ludlow Schmidt
JLE Jubilee Line Extension
LBSC London Brighton and South Coast
LDDC London Docklands Development Corporation
LMS London, Midland and Scottish Railway
LNER London and North Eastern Railway
LNWR London and North Western Railway
LPTB/Board London Passenger Transport Board
LSWR London and South Western Railway
LT London Transport
LTSR London Tilbury and Southend Railway
LU London Underground
LUL London Underground Limited
Met Metropolitan Railway
NER North Eastern Railway
NWP New Works Programme
PEDs platform-edge doors
PFA Platform for Art
Piccadilly see 'GNPBR'
PPP Public–Private Partnership
RIBA Royal Institute of British Architects
SECR South Eastern and Chatham Railway
TfL Transport for London
UERL Underground Electric Railways of London
WLR West London Railway

Index

Maps, diagrams, drawings and photos are given in **bold**.

London Underground by Design